THE ALL-NEW TREASURY OF
FUN, FACTS AND FRIVOLITY FROM
THE PEOPLE WHO GAVE YOU
THE BOOK OF LISTS

It's THE BOOK OF LISTS #2! After the smashing success of THE BOOK OF LISTS, the authors joyously set out to top themselves with LISTS #2. This is it! Funnier, better, more amusing and more informative than ever!

Here are just a few of the facts you will learn from these pages—

• What famous Hollywood actress slept with Gary Cooper, Bela Lugosi, Eddie Cantor, Frederic March—and, allegedly, the entire University of Southern California football team?

• When ill, Ethiopian Emperor Menelik II would eat a few pages of the Bible to restore his health. Unfortunately, he died in 1913 after eating the entire Book of Kings.

• In the 1950 Florida senatorial election, George Smathers accused his opponent Claude Pepper of being "a practicing homo sapiens" and "practicing celibacy" before marriage. Naturally, Pepper was soundly defeated.

• Quick as a wink (1/10th of a second) is faster than you can say Jack Robinson (1/2 second).

And much, much more . . . also featuring cheerful, loving, opinionated, debate-provoking lists prepared exclusively for this book by President Gerald Ford, Lillian Carter, Ronald Reagan, Uri Geller, Wilt Chamberlain, Truman Capote, Andrew Wyeth, Barbara Walters, Jane Fonda, Martina Navratilova, Neil Simon, Princess Grace of Monaco, Ross Macdonald, Mary McCarthy, the late John Wayne . . . Ken Kesey, Willie Shoemaker . . . and dozens of other celebrities.

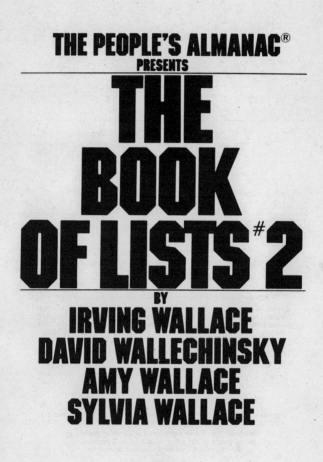

THE PEOPLE'S ALMANAC®
PRESENTS

THE BOOK OF LISTS #2

BY
IRVING WALLACE
DAVID WALLECHINSKY
AMY WALLACE
SYLVIA WALLACE

BANTAM BOOKS
TORONTO · NEW YORK · LONDON

*This low-priced Bantam Book contains the complete
text of the original hard-cover edition.*
NOT ONE WORD HAS BEEN OMITTED.

THE PEOPLE'S ALMANAC ® PRESENTS THE BOOK OF LISTS 2
A Bantam Book

PRINTING HISTORY

William Morrow & Company edition published February 1980
1st printing . . . November 1979
2nd printing . . . January 1980
3rd printing . . . April 1980
A Selection of The Literary Guild August and December 1979

Serialized in PLAYBOY, *August 1979;* COSMOPOLITAN, *August 1979;* GOOD
HOUSEKEEPING, *August 1979;* FAMILY CIRCLE, *August 1979;* BOOK DIGEST,
January 1980; NEW YORK POST, *February 1980;* THE STAR, *February 1980;*
READER'S DIGEST, *February 1980;* EAST/WEST NETWORK, *March 1980;*
GLOBE, *March 1980 and* NATIONAL ENQUIRER, *April 1980.*

Bantam edition / February 1981

ISBN 0-553-13101-X

Published simultaneously in the United States and Canada

*Bantam Books are published by Bantam Books, Inc. Its trade-
mark, consisting of the words "Bantam Books" and the por-
trayal of a bantam, is Registered in U.S. Patent and Trademark
Office and in other countries. Marca Registrada. Bantam
Books, Inc., 666 Fifth Avenue, New York, New York 10103.*

PRINTED IN THE UNITED STATES OF AMERICA

0 9 8 7 6 5 4 3 2 1

To
Carol, Fern,
Judy, Elizebethe

Managing Editor:	CAROL ORSAG
Associate Editors:	ELIZEBETHE KEMPTHORNE
	FERN BRYANT FADNESS
	LAUREL OVERMAN
	LINDA CHASE
	KRISTINE H. JOHNSON
Assistant Editor:	JUDY KNIPE
Staff Researchers:	HELEN GINSBURG
	TORENE SVITIL
	VICKI SCOTT
	ANITA TAYLOR
Editorial Aides:	JOANNE MALONEY
	LINDA LAUCELLA
	LINDA WILCUT
	PATRICIA BEGALLA
	DIANE BROWN SHEPARD
	DANNY BIEDERMAN
Photograph Editor:	ROBERT F. NACEY
Photograph Assistants:	CAROUSEL, INC.
	CLAUDIA PEIRCE
Copy Editor:	WAYNE LAWSON

THEY WROTE THE ORIGINAL MATERIAL

WHEN "THE EDS." IS USED, IT MEANS THE MATERIAL HAS BEEN
CONTRIBUTED BY THE EDITORS OF *The Book of Lists #2.*

A.E.	Ann Elwood	D.W.B.	David W. Barber
A.K.	Aaron Kass	E.C.S.	Edwin C. Stern
A.MC.	Anne McGrath	E.F.	Ed Fishbein
A.T.	Alan Tigay	E.H.C.	Ernest H. Corfine
A.W.	Amy Wallace	F.B.F.	Fern Bryant Fadness
B.D.C.	Bruce D. Clayton	G.D.G.	G. David Goodman
B.F.	Bruce Felton	G.R.S.	Gary R. Shroat
B.H.	Bill Henkin	H.E.A.	Howard Ernest Asaki
B.L.W.	B. L. Williams	I.W.	Irving Wallace
C.M.P.	Carl Maxey Phillips	J.B.	Jeff Berke
C.O.	Carol Orsag	J.Be.	Jeremy Beadle
C.RO.	Christopher Rouse	J.D.	Jim Dawson
D.B.	Danny Biederman	J.Di.	Joseph DiMattia
D.Bi.	Dawn Billmyre	J.E.	John Eastman
D.H.	Doug Huff	J.F.M.	James F. McCloy
D.K.W.	Donald K. Wilson	J.G.	Judi Gumins
D.L.	Don Lessem	J.Hu.	Jannika Hurwitt
D.M.F.	Dillman M. Furey, Jr.	J.L.K.	Jerold L. Kellman
D.M.R.	David M. Ross	J.M.B.E.	John M. B. Edwards
D.P.M.	David P. Monahan	J.M.F.	Judith M. Force
D.S.G.	David S. Goldman	J.N.	James Natal
D.W.	David Wallechinsky	J.R.L.	James R. Longacre

K.A.	Kayti Adkins	R.Fu.	Rupert Furneaux
K.A.M.	Kenneth A. Michaelis	R.H.	Robert Hendrickson
K.C.	Kathleen Campbell	R.J.F.	Rodger J. Fadness
K.D.G.	Kathleen Dunne Gagne	R.K.R.	R. Kent Rasmussen
		R.Ll.	Ralph Llamas
K.H.J.	Kristine H. Johnson	R.S.	Ray Spangenburg
K.V.H.	Karel von Haeften	R.SO.	Roy Sorrels
L.C.	Linda Chase	R.T.	Richard Trubo
L.J.	Larry Jonas	R.W.	Richard Wobbe
L.K.L.	Linda K. Laucella	S.H.	Steve Harvey
L.O.	Laurel Overman	S.L.S.	Sandra L. Scott
L.S.K.	Larry S. Katz	S.R.	Steven Raichlen
M.B.T.	Marguerite B. Thompson	S.W.	Sylvia Wallace
		T.B.	Ted Berkelmann
M.HO.	Michael Horowitz	T.E.	Tony Edwards
M.MC.	Marjorie McCloy	T.K.	Tuli Kupferberg
M.R.A.	Michael R. Aldrich	T.S.	Torene Svitil
M.S.	Mitchell Sommers	V.L.V.	Vicki L. Vickrey
M.S.L.	Michael S. Lasky	V.S.	Vicki Scott
R.A.	Randy Alfred	W.A.D.	William A. De-Gregorio
R.A.S.	Robin Anne Schlossman		
		W.D.	Wendy Dreskin
R.C.B.	Richard C. Brown	W.K.	Walter Kempthorne
R.C.Be.	Robert C. Berlo		

CONTENTS

Most Beautiful Words in the English Language . . . 31 Words Rarely Used in Their Positive Form . . . 7 People Who Ate Their Own Words— or Others' Words . . . 16 Brand Names That Have Become Words . . . 18 Words Worth Reviving . . . 10 Winning Words in the U.S. National Spelling Bee, 1970–1979 . . . Richard Armour Picks 20 of the Worst Puns . . . Charles Hamilton's 10 Most Insulting Letters in History . . . 8 Advertisements That Changed People's Lives . . . 10 Best Censored Stories of Recent Years

9. ARTFUL FACTS

That's Entertainment? 6 Perfectly Wretched Performers . . . 20 Greatest Rock Albums of All Time . . . 12 Artists Who Made *Billboard's* #1—But Never Got into the Top 100 Again . . . Benny Goodman's 7 Best Popular Songs of the 20th Century . . . 13 All-Time Standard Hit Songs by Unlikely Composers . . . Alan Jay Lerner's 10 Best Modern Songwriters . . . Muddy Waters's 10 Greatest Blues Songs of All Time . . . Leonard Feather's All-Time All-Star Jazz Band . . . Productivity of 21 Classical Composers . . . 15 Composers Who Died in Unusual Circumstances . . . Isaac Stern's 10 Best Violinists in History . . . Neil Simon's 11 Funniest Plays in History . . . Helen Hayes's 10 Best Female Stage Roles . . . Shakespeare's 20 Longest Roles . . . Andrew Wyeth's 8 Greatest American Paintings in History . . . Norton Simon's 11 Best Paintings in History . . . 12 Art Riots of the 20th Century

10. SIGHTS AND SOUNDS

17 Movie Stars Who Turned Down Great Roles . . . Jane Fonda's 3 Best Motion Picture Actresses of All Time . . . Grace de Monaco's 5 Best Motion Picture Actresses of All Time . . . John Wayne's 5 Best Motion Picture Actors and Actresses of All Time . . . 19 Movie Stars and How They Were Discovered . . . 10 Popular Film Stars Never Nominated for an Academy Award . . . 10 Special Imprints at Grauman's Chinese Theatre . . . 8 Notable Actors Who Once Appeared in Horror Movies . . . Ring Lardner, Jr.'s 5 Best Screenplay Writers of All Time . . . Robert Wise's 5 Best Motion Picture Directors of All Time . . . 10 Film Scenes Left on the Cutting Room Floor . . . Jane Fonda's 4 Best Motion Pictures of All Time . . . Grace de Monaco's 5 Best Motion Pictures of All Time . . . John Wayne's 5 Best Motion Pictures of All Time . . . The 25 All-Time Box-office Champion Films (Adjusted for Inflation) . . . 10 Movies That Were Part of History . . . 10 Movies Shown Most Often on Television . . . 10 Performers Who Appeared Most Often on Major TV Talk Shows . . . 13 More Outrageous Moments of U.S. TV Censorship . . . The Highest-Rated TV Programs in 11 Countries . . . America's 30 Most Listened-to Radio Stations

11. LITERARY CIRCLES

11 Bestselling Books Rejected by 13 or More Publishers . . . H. L.

sidered or Attempted Suicide . . . 10 People Made Famous by Their
Deaths . . . The 10 Most Attended Funerals of the Last Half-Century
. . . 11 Daring Grave Robberies . . . 27 Celebrated People Who Believed
in Reincarnation

21. LOOSE ENDS 469

The People's Almanac's 13 More Favorite Oddities of All Time . . . 12
Second Places in History . . . 25 Things That Are Not What They
Seem . . . 21 Things and What They Weigh . . . The 13 Most Repressive
Governments in the World . . . 6 Outrageous Plans That Didn't
Happen . . . Henny Youngman's 10 Favorite One-Liners . . . 7 of the
Greatest Cracks of All Time . . . 17 Wonderful Boners . . . 18 More
Unnatural Laws . . . 17 Children Who May Have Lived with Wild
Animals . . . 8 Personal Everyday Lists from Our Readers . . . The
Authors' 7 Thoughts For You, the Reader

FOR LISTOMANIACS ONLY

When we first offered you *The Book of Lists* in 1977, we had no idea what kind of reception you would give our unusual venture. We only knew that we had enormously enjoyed writing the book, and we hoped that you would enjoy it as much. Little did we realize how large a portion of the population was composed of fellow listomaniacs.

Your response was overwhelming. In the United States alone, at least 18 million persons read the book in all editions. In the United States, also, two newspaper syndicates, three book clubs, and 18 magazines reprinted our lists and spread the gospel. Editions appeared in 23 countries, ranging from Finland to France and Japan to India. Numerous grade schools adopted the book (and compiled their own versions), readers formed Lists fan clubs, and a torrent of letters poured in, thousands of them, filled with affection, scholarship, challenges, and constructive criticism. Of the reviews, 99% were loving, and a few were gastronomic, to wit: reading the book was "like eating potato chips," said the daily *New York Times*, the *San Diego Union*, and *Sports Illustrated* magazine, whereas the *Pittsburgh Post-Gazette* and the *Birmingham News* suggested it was like eating peanuts. Other reviews, and many readers, compared reading the book to eating popcorn.

Of course, as we stated in the first book, listmaking is a fascinating and honorable pastime; for the listmaker it provides a memory bank, a therapeutic release, a self-education, an amusement. And for the list reader, lists provide entertainment, a stimulus, a learning process. The idea of lists sounds very modern, so much a part of the miniaturizing, capsulizing, condensing that is prevalent in this hustling 20th century. Yet lists are anything but modern. They are as old as written history.

Certainly, as we mentioned the first time we met you, Hammurabi, king of Babylon, made a list of 282 laws before 1750 B.C. Then, around 1200 B.C., Moses brought a list of 10 Commandments down from Mt. Sinai. Other illustrious listmakers followed. In 1601 Shakespeare gave us a list of rules to live by through Polonius in *Hamlet*. In 1885 Gilbert and Sullivan gave us a list via Ko-Ko, the Lord High Executioner, in *The Mikado*. Now, one more celebrated addition. The venerable Geoffrey Chaucer, who wrote *The Canterbury Tales* between 1380 and 1390, deserves to be on the roll call of great listmakers. In one tale he had a character speak of a list he had made of his 20 favorite books. Chaucer let the first book on the list be known, "Aristotle and his philosophye," but then, infuriatingly, he failed to reveal the other 19 favorite books on that list.

Clearly, as listmakers, we knew from the start that we were not unique, that we were only several of millions of list lovers. But as creators of *The Book of Lists*, we did think that we were unique. We thought we were the first authors in publishing history to invent the idea of an entire book of lists. But we were wrong. We were not the first in publishing history to compile such a book. We were, it turned out, the first in 300 years to do so.

A few months after our original volume had been brought out, we were browsing in a Los Angeles rare books store when we stumbled upon an aged, oversized volume entitled *The Wonders of the Little World* by Reverend Nathaniel Wanley, published in London in 1678. To our astonishment, Wanley had actually written a book of lists, and a superb one, in the 17th century. We bought his book at once and enshrined it in our library.

Curious about our predecessor, we investigated him. Nathaniel Wanley was born in 1634 in Leicester, England. He was educated at Cambridge, graduated a divine. He was vicar of Trinity Church in Coventry. He married a coroner's daughter, who bore him five children. He found time to write a half dozen books, and it was the last of these, published two years before his death in 1680, which gave him his celebrity status and perhaps led to his portrait's being hung in the august Bodleian Library at Oxford.

The last of his books was, of course, *The Wonders of the Little World*. The subjects of some of his numbered lists sound comfortably modern—famous people born by cesarean section, persons with strange birthmarks, victories against great odds, people with remarkable memories, unusual causes of wars, memorable cases of stage fright. From Wanley's list entitled, "Of the Majesty and Gravity in the Countenance and Behavior of some Persons," meaning persons who were great beauties, two samples:

—Parthenopaeus, one of the seven Princes of the Argives, was so exceedingly beautiful that when he was in battle, if his helmet was up, no man would offer to hurt him or to strike at him.

—Phryne was a most beautiful woman, but a strumpet; it is said of her that once at Athens, fearing—in a cause of hers—to be condemned, in pleading for herself she bared her breasts and disclosed some parts of her beauties to the eyes of her Judges, who were so enchanted thereby that they pronounced her guiltless, though at the same time they ordained that thenceforth no woman should be permitted to plead her own cause.

So we must credit Reverend Wanley for inventing the list book in the 17th century. For ourselves, suffice it to believe that we reinvented the list book in the 20th century.

Even before we knew how our first version of *The Book of Lists* would be received, we had planned a second one, because we were turned on to creating list ideas, because it was fun writing them, and because we found the research edifying. Once we learned how much the public welcomed our original lists, and how many readers wanted more and more of them, we were fired to plunge on and complete *The Book of Lists 2*.

This, then is *Lists 2*. It is not a revision. It is not an update. The contents are entirely new from the first page to the last. Our fresh lists grew from four basic sources. The first and main source was ourselves. Almost nightly, month after month, the four of us would gather in a room with pads and pencils and we would brainstorm ideas and entries. Out of such sessions came most of the list ideas to be found in this book, such lists as "7 People Who Ate Their

Own Words—or Others' Words," "16 Famous People Who Grew Marijuana—or Ordered It to Be Grown," "18 Men and Women Who Slept with 3 or More Celebrities," "10 Celebrated People Who Read Their Own Obituaries," and "6 Incestuous Couples of the Bible."

Another important source of our lists was the permanent members of our staff and the 150 free-lance writers who contributed regularly to us. They came up with such provocative lists as "8 Generals Who Never Won a Battle (While General)," "6 Cases of Women and Children Last," "14 Double-Sexed Animals," and "10 Well-Known People Who Died in Someone's Arms."

A third excellent source for our lists was a pool of the world's leading celebrities and experts in every field. They are all in this book, a wonderful and diverse company that includes Henry Ford II, Abbie Hoffman, Lillian Carter, Benny Goodman, Princess Grace of Monaco, Andrew Wyeth, Isaac Stern, Floyd Patterson, President Gerald Ford, C. P. Snow, Uri Geller, Ronald Reagan, Wilt Chamberlain, Julia Child, General William Westmoreland, John Wayne, Truman Capote, Abba Eban, Rebecca West, Marcel Marceau, Ilie Nastase, Jane Fonda, Helen Hayes, Dr. Seuss, and Red Grange.

These celebrity lists offer amusement, surprises, fuel for controversy. To cite a handful of examples: Lillian Carter's list tells us that she believes her son Jimmy Carter has been a greater president than George Washington. Barbara Walters's list tells us that she would liked to have witnessed a Roman orgy. President Gerald Ford's list tells us that he would like to have lived the life of baseball star Lou Gehrig. John Wayne's list of the five best movie actors and actresses of all time includes Elizabeth Taylor, while Princess Grace of Monaco's list of five best movie actresses includes Mae West. Truman Capote's list of the 10 historical figures he would like to have been in another incarnation names J. Edgar Hoover and his great and good friend Clyde Tolson.

However, the most exciting source of our lists proved to be our readers. We had invited readers to send us their list ideas or items, promising to pay for each one we used. A tidal wave of contributions swamped us from every state of the United States, from every part of Great Britain, and from countries as far afield as Tonga, Kenya, and Kuwait. We considered every reader's list with care. Among the ones in this book that originated with readers are "The 8 Most Awful Warships in History," "7 Persons Who Have Gone over Niagara Falls in Barrels," "11 Authors Who Had Books Published by Age 10," "11 Moon Mysteries Uncovered by the Apollo Missions," "21 Famous Women Who Breast-Fed Their Babies," and "10 Unusual Objects Offered at Auction."

What has given this book its infinite variety is the informal collaboration between you, the readers, and us, the authors. You've proved that you have read, heard, seen things we did not read, hear, see. We need your knowledge.

We want the next all-new edition of this book, *The Book of Lists #3*, to be more comprehensive, more entertaining, than the first two editions. To achieve our goal, we need your help. Tell us what you like most about this book. Tell us what we omitted, and what we could do to improve the book. And once again, tell us what you know that we don't know. Ideas, unusual information, clippings—pass them on. Don't be listless. Join in the fun. Our address is:

The Book of Lists
P.O. Box 49699
Los Angeles, Calif. 90049

Now turn the page and step right in—and welcome to the land of listomania.

Irving Wallace
David Wallechinsky
Amy Wallace
Sylvia Wallace

THE
BOOK
OF LISTS #2

1
MEET THE PEOPLE

AGES OF 15 PEOPLE
IF THEY HAD LIVED UNTIL 1981

1.	Clark Gable (1901–1960), U.S. film actor	80
2.	Jean Harlow (1911–1937), U.S. film actress	70
3.	Eva Braun (1912–1945), German wife of Adolf Hitler	69
4.	Billie Holiday (1915–1959), U.S. blues and jazz singer	66
5.	John F. Kennedy (1917–1963), U.S. president	64
6.	Eva Perón (1919–1952), Argentine first lady	62
7.	Judy Garland (1922–1969), U.S. singer and actress	59
8.	Lenny Bruce (1925–1966), U.S. comedian	56
9.	Marilyn Monroe (1926–1962), U.S. actress	55
10.	Ernesto "Che" Guevara (1928–1967), Latin American revolutionary leader	53
11.	Anne Frank (1929–1945), Jewish diarist	52
12.	Martin Luther King, Jr. (1929–1968), U.S. clergyman and civil rights leader	52
13.	James Dean (1931–1955), U.S. actor	50
14.	Janis Joplin (1943–1970), U.S. singer	38
15.	Sharon Tate (1943–1969), U.S. actress	38

Marilyn Monroe at age 55.

12 MOST LIKED NAMES
FOR BOYS AND GIRLS

How do names stack up? Dr. Thomas V. Busse of Temple University in Philadelphia, Pa., asked 2,212 American boys and girls in grades 2–6, 8, and 11 what their reactions were to more than 400 names. The names used were the actual first names of the students who were polled. They were rated Like, Dislike, or Neutral. Here are the results.

Boys	Girls
1. David	1. Linda
1. John	2. Carol
3. Michael	3. Barbara
4. Mark	4. Susan
4. Robert	4. Cindy
6. Paul	6. Diane
7. Richard	7. Nancy
8. Scott	8. Karen
9. Peter	9. Lynn
10. Stephen	10. Anne
10. Gary	10. Christine
10. James	12. Diana

13 LEAST LIKED NAMES
FOR BOYS AND GIRLS

Boys	Girls
1. Altair	1. Shobhana
2. Bela	2. Watonah
3. Faber	3. Rosemede
4. Malig	4. Meta
5. Khalig	4. Temperance
6. Ingmar	6. Simone
7. Lyman	7. Lola May
7. Aubrey	8. Hilary
7. Florian	9. Hallie
10. Schuyler	10. Gillian
11. Stockton	11. Alizon
12. Gardner	12. Myra
12. Rajiv	12. Vaughan

12 FAMOUS PEOPLE
WHO CHANGED THEIR BIRTHDAYS

1. JOHN JAMES AUDUBON, U.S. artist and naturalist (April 26, 1785–January 27, 1851)

   John Audubon enjoyed obscuring the facts surrounding his birth out of wedlock. In fact he was born April 26, 1785, in what is now Haiti, although "officially" he was born May 4, 1780, in New Orleans.

2. HUMPHREY BOGART, U.S. actor (January 23, 1899–January 14, 1957)

   Warner Brothers Pictures claimed that Bogart was born on Christmas Day, 1899, in order to romanticize his background.

3. JAMES CAGNEY, U.S. actor (July 17, 1899–   )

   The studio publicity department moved Cagney's birth year up to 1904 in order to capitalize on his baby-faced appearance.

4. GEORGE M. COHAN, U.S. composer and actor (July 3, 1878–November 5, 1942)

   Cohan's father changed his son's birthday to July 4, setting the stage for the famous Yankee Doodle image.

5. MAUD GONNE, Irish patriot (December 20, 1865–April 27, 1953)

   The inspiration for many works of William Butler Yeats, Gonne claimed 1866 as her birth year—out of embarrassment. Her parents had been married one day before she was born in 1865.

6. LAURENCE HARVEY, British actor (October 1, 1928–November 25, 1973)

   Harvey lied about his age, giving the year of his birth as 1927, in order to get into the Royal South African Navy at age 14.

7. ROCK HUDSON, U.S. actor (November 17, 1925–   )

   Early in Hudson's career, an agent added two years onto the actor's age, placing his birth in 1923 in order to land him more mature parts.

8. ANDREW JACKSON, U.S. president (1755–June 8, 1845)

   Jackson was probably born at sea on a ship bound for America from Ireland in 1755 and not in South Carolina in 1767 as many biographers claim. If Jackson had admitted to his "foreign" birth, he would not have been eligible for the presidency.

9. VICTOR McLAGLEN, British actor (December 11, 1886–November 7, 1959)

   Claiming 1882 as his year of birth, McLaglen added four years to his age so that he could enlist in the London Life Guards and serve in the Boer War.

10. LOLA MONTEZ, Irish dancer and mistress of King Ludwig I of Bavaria (1818–January 17, 1861)

Presenting herself as a Spanish dancer, Montez claimed she had been born in 1823 in Seville, although she was really born in 1818 (the actual day is not known) in Limerick, Ireland.

11. PEARL WHITE, U.S. silent screen actress (March 4, 1897– August 4, 1938)

Youthful-looking White added eight years to her age—giving 1889 as the year of her birth—because she didn't want to play the type of child roles then being given to Mary Pickford.

12. OSCAR WILDE, Irish playwright and poet (October 16, 1854–November 30, 1900)

Wilde changed his birth year to 1856. Like his character Dorian Gray, Wilde was vain about his appearance and feared becoming old.

—R.S.

20 EMINENT MEN LISTED UNDER THEIR MOTHERS' NAMES

The new feminism has brought awareness that in our patriarchal society a married woman loses part of her identity through taking her husband's family name. Should her children happen to become famous, her husband's family is immortalized while her own family is consigned to oblivion. (Picasso is one of the few famous men who chose to use his mother's name, partly because it was less common than Ruiz, his father's name.) It seems fitting to turn the spotlight, for once, upon the maternal branch responsible for contributing half the genetic endowment of some of the world's immortals.

1. William Arden
   (*Shakespeare*)
2. Isaac Ayscough
   (*Newton*)
3. Johann Sebastian Lämmerhirt
   (*Bach*)
4. George Ball
   (*Washington*)
5. Thomas Randolph
   (*Jefferson*)

4

6. Johann Wolfgang Textor
   (*von Goethe*)
7. Wolfgang Amadeus Pertl
   (*Mozart*)
8. Napoleon Ramolino
   (*Bonaparte*)
9. Ludwig Keverich
   (*van Beethoven*)
10. Abraham Hanks
    (*Lincoln*)
11. Charles Wedgwood
    (*Darwin*)
12. Charles Barrow
    (*Dickens*)
13. Giuseppe Uttini
    (*Verdi*)
14. Karl Pressburg
    (*Marx*)
15. Thomas Alva Elliot
    (*Edison*)
16. Sigmund Nathanson
    (*Freud*)
17. George Bernard Gurly
    (*Shaw*)
18. Albert Koch
    (*Einstein*)
19. Charlie Hill
    (*Chaplin*)
20. Ernest Hall
    (*Hemingway*)

—M.B.T.

Johann Sebastian Lämmerhirt.

5

SMALL BUT GREAT—
31 RENOWNED PERSONS UNDER
5 FEET 6½ INCHES TALL

		Height
1.	Alexander Pope, English poet	4 ft. 6 in.
2.	Engelbert Dollfuss, Austrian statesman	4 ft. 11 in.
3.	Olga Korbut, Soviet gymnast	4 ft. 11 in.
4.	Dolly Parton, U.S. singer	5 ft.
5.	Victoria, British queen	5 ft.
6.	John Keats, English poet	5 ft. ¾ in.
7.	Debbie Reynolds, U.S. actress	5 ft. 1 in.
8.	St. Francis of Assisi, Italian saint	5 ft. 1 in.
9.	Henri Marie Raymond de Toulouse-Lautrec, French painter	5 ft. 1 in.
10.	Honoré de Balzac, French novelist	5 ft. 2 in.
11.	Yuri Gagarin, Soviet cosmonaut	5 ft. 2 in.
12.	Margaret Mead, U.S. anthropologist	5 ft. 2 in.
13.	Rosemary Casals, U.S. tennis player	5 ft. 2½ in.
14.	Nikita Khrushchev, Soviet leader	5 ft. 3 in.
15.	Marquis de Sade, French soldier and writer	5 ft. 3 in.
16.	Mickey Rooney, U.S. actor	5 ft. 3 in.
17.	François Marie Arouet (Voltaire), French writer	5 ft. 3 in.
18.	Charles I, British king	5 ft. 4 in.
19.	Sawao Kato, Japanese gymnast	5 ft. 4 in.
20.	James Madison, U.S. president	5 ft. 4 in.
21.	Gustav Mahler, Austrian composer	5 ft. 4 in.
22.	Pablo Picasso, Spanish painter	5 ft. 4 in.
23.	Haile Selassie, Ethiopian emperor	5 ft. 4 in.
24.	George "Baby Face" Nelson, U.S. gangster	5 ft. 4¾ in.
25.	Hirohito, Japanese emperor	5 ft. 5 in.
26.	Aristotle Onassis, Greek shipping tycoon	5 ft. 5 in.
27.	T. E. Lawrence (of Arabia), British soldier and writer	5 ft. 5½ in.
28.	Horatio Nelson, British naval hero	5 ft. 5½ in.
29.	Napoleon Bonaparte, French emperor	5 ft. 6 in.
30.	Joseph Stalin, Soviet political leader	5 ft. 6 in.
31.	Tutankhamen, Egyptian king	5 ft. 6 in.

—J.BE. & The Eds.

THE SHOCKING SIDE OF
10 HEROES AND HEROINES

1. MARTIN LUTHER (1483–1546), German religious reformer

Luther's intolerance was legendary. When the German peasants staged an uprising in 1525 to demand basic rights, he lashed out at them in a bitter diatribe entitled "Against the Murdering and Thieving Hordes of Peasants." When his wife complained about the household servants, he responded, "We must govern them Turkish-fashion; so much work, so much food, as Pharaoh dealt with the Israelites in Egypt." The Jews also triggered his wrath when they failed to convert en masse after his church reforms had been instituted. Enraged at their recalcitrance, he published a tract which recommended that they be deported to Palestine or, at the very least, that their synagogues be burned and all their books be confiscated.

2. GEORGE WASHINGTON (1732–1799), U.S. president

The Revolutionary War commander in chief refused the $500 monthly salary offered him, accepting payment only for expenses. He came out almost $400,000 ahead of what his total salary would have been for 1775–1783. At the same time that Congress was willing to foot the costs for the military, social, and diplomatic functions connected with the post of commander in chief, it was unable to provide back pay and pensions for the regular officers of the U.S. Army. Elected as the first president of the U.S. in 1789, Washington again offered to work for expenses, but this time Congress insisted on paying him an annual salary of $25,000. The action was, according to Marvin Kitman, author of *George Washington's Expense Account* (1970), "the country's first economy wave."

3. HENRY DAVID THOREAU (1817–1862), U.S. naturalist and philosopher

Upon his 1837 graduation from Harvard, Thoreau took his first job, as a schoolteacher in Concord, Mass. He ran a relaxed classroom and was liked by the students. Two weeks into the term, however, a supervising deacon admonished the young schoolmaster for not caning his students. No believer in corporal punishment, an enraged Thoreau promptly flogged six students at random and turned in his resignation. Some of those six resented into adulthood Thoreau's use of their hides to make a point.

4. THOMAS EDISON (1847–1931), U.S. inventor

Convinced that ethics had no place in business, Edison's philosophy was to protect his own interests "and let the other fellows whistle." He demanded that his employees work long hours under chaotic and unsafe conditions, yet paid them the lowest possible wages. Virtually living in his laboratory, Edison seemed unaware of the existence of his family. Both of his wives suffered from severe depressions, and his eldest son, Thomas Alva, Jr., became an alcoholic and a hypochondriac who committed suicide.

5. ROBERT EDWIN PEARY (1856–1920), U.S. explorer

The man who geared his whole life toward being the first to plant a flag on the desolate ice desert at the North Pole ruthlessly "rewarded" the people who had helped him. In *Northward over the Great Ice* (1898), a book recording his early Arctic travels, Peary included a nude photo of his comely Eskimo mistress, Allakasignwah, taken while she was bathing. She had given him a son—at the same time that his wife Josephine was dutifully raising his daughters in the U.S. Another victim of Peary's ambition was Matthew A. Henson, whom Peary referred to as "my colored boy." After 22 years of devoted service—which had included carrying his boss part of the way to what probably was not, in reality, the pole—Henson was brusquely dismissed. He worked at menial jobs for the rest of his life and died impoverished in 1955.

6. MARIE CURIE (1867–1934), Polish-French scientist

"A Story of Love, Mme. Curie and Professor Langevin," announced the headlines of *Le Journal* of Paris in November, 1911. Soon newspapers throughout France made reference to letters that strongly suggested that the widowed Marie Curie was carrying on an affair with Paul Langevin, a married scientist with four children. While crowds thronged around her apartment shouting, "Get the foreign woman out!" and "Husband stealer!" Mme. Curie learned that she had won her second Nobel Prize. Many of her colleagues were convinced that it was awarded out of sympathy for her personal plight rather than for her scientific accomplishments.

Mme. Marie Curie in 1912 at the height of the scandal in her life.

7. ALBERT SCHWEITZER (1875–1965), French physician, theologian, and musician

Contrary to his self-sacrificing image, Schweitzer was always rigorously careful about his own health and diet but allowed his patients and staff members to eat protein-deficient meals and to use water from a frequently contaminated well. Many physicians and local Africans visiting his hospital at Lambaréné in the Gabon province of French Equatorial Africa had difficulty dealing with Schweitzer's "benign dictatorship" and racial paternalism. One African commented, "I'd rather die unattended than be humiliated at Dr. Schweitzer's hospital." Schweitzer's conviction that "simple people need simple healing methods" resulted in his refusal to make necessary hospital improvements, despite available funds.

8. T. E. LAWRENCE (1888–1935), British soldier

In 1917, Lawrence "of Arabia" was viciously beaten and sexually assaulted by Turkish soldiers. He shamefully admitted that during the episode he experienced "a delicious warmth . . . swelling through me." By 1923 he had developed a compulsion to be beaten regularly. He paid a young admirer, John Bruce, to administer the beatings with a birch or metal whip applied to Lawrence's bare buttocks.

9. CHARLES AUGUSTUS LINDBERGH (1902–1974), U.S. aviator

In 1927 William P. MacCracken, Jr., a government aeronautics official, came close to grounding the aviator for reckless flying after Lindbergh's fourth bailout and crack-up as a barnstormer and mail pilot. When Lindbergh's employer vowed to restrain such daredeviltry, MacCracken relented—thus enabling Lindbergh's epic solo flight across the Atlantic. Later Lindbergh outraged the American public when he championed the Nazi cause and expressed concern about the "infiltration of inferior blood" into the U.S. He believed that if America were to take the unwise step of entering W.W. II, it should be on the side of the Germans, not the Allies.

10. JOHN F. KENNEDY (1917–1963), U.S. president

During his wife's frequent absences from the White House, Jack Kennedy engaged in a continuous round of "private parties." His female companions ranged from maids, secretaries, and hatcheck girls to movie stars like Marilyn Monroe. One of his conquests commented, "He did not perceive women as human beings, or even as objects of affection. He had a real need to capture and dominate." The steady stream of women who caught the President's eye and shared his bed prompted his longtime friend Sen. George Smathers to reflect, "There's no question about the fact that Jack had the most active libido of any man I've ever known."

—J.E. & F.B.F.

25 PEOPLE BETTER KNOWN
BY THEIR INITIALS
THAN BY THEIR GIVEN NAMES

1. P. T. (Phineas Taylor) Barnum, U.S. showman
2. G. K. (Gilbert Keith) Chesterton, English novelist
3. E. E. (Edward Estlin) Cummings, U.S. poet
4. W. E. B. (William Edward Burghardt) Du Bois, U.S. civil rights leader
5. T. S. (Thomas Stearns) Eliot, U.S. poet
6. W. C. (William Claude) Fields, U.S. actor
7. E. M. (Edward Morgan) Forster, English novelist
8. B. F. (Benjamin Franklin) Goodrich, U.S. tire manufacturer
9. D. W. (David Wark) Griffith, U.S. motion-picture producer
10. H. R. (Harry Robert "Bob") Haldeman, U.S. presidential assistant
11. W. C. (William Christopher) Handy, U.S. blues composer
12. H. L. (Haroldson Lafayette) Hunt, U.S. businessman
13. R. D. (Ronald David) Laing, British psychiatrist
14. D. H. (David Herbert) Lawrence, English writer
15. E. G. (Everybody's Guess) Marshall, U.S. actor
    Marshall doesn't want to divulge his given names, so this is what he tells people who ask.
16. H. L. (Henry Louis) Mencken, U.S. editor and journalist
17. J. P. (John Pierpont) Morgan, U.S. financier
18. J. C. (James Cash) Penney, U.S. entrepreneur
19. R. J. (Richard Joshua) Reynolds, U.S. tobacco businessman
20. J. D. (Jerome David) Salinger, U.S. novelist
21. O. J. (Orenthal James) Simpson, U.S. football player
22. B. F. (Burrhus Frederic) Skinner, U.S. writer and psychologist
23. I. F. (Isidor Feinstein) Stone, U.S. writer and publisher
24. J. R. R. (John Ronald Reuel) Tolkien, British writer
25. H. G. (Herbert George) Wells, English novelist

—H.E.A., R.A.S., & C.M.P.

UNREALIZED PLANS
OF 8 SPECIAL GENIUSES

1. RICHARD WAGNER (1813–1883), German composer

In 1856 Wagner began to sketch out *Die Sieger* ("The Victors"), an opera based on the life of Buddha. The story concerned a maiden in love with a celibate disciple of Buddha, a man she had spurned in her former incarnation as a proud Brahman princess. The Buddha shows her that she must expiate the arrogant actions of her past life by experiencing unsatisfied passion. Despite explicit racism in much of Wagner's writing, this work refuted ideas of race or caste superiority. It said that all must change their identities until perfection is reached by individuals, not species. Wagner was still struggling with *Die Sieger* in his last hours, but its subject resisted operatic treatment. The characters in overcoming temptations of the flesh did not generate the dramatic conflict needed to inspire Wagner's music. His noble tale of tolerance and love remained a literary exercise.

2. THOMAS A. EDISON (1847–1931),
   U.S. inventor

In 1890 writer George Parsons Lathrop—the son-in-law of Nathaniel Hawthorne—proposed that Edison collaborate with him on a science fiction novel whose hero was to resemble the famous inventor. Edison, who had read Jules Verne with enjoyment, agreed to contribute ideas while Lathrop would furnish the plot. A publisher offered to promote their book, which was tentatively entitled *Progress*. Edison's jottings for the novel contain his predictions for the mid-20th century: advances in chemistry, biochemistry, and optics; new plastic materials; aerial transport and warfare; journeys to Mars. Anticipating Boulle's *Planet of the Apes*, Edison's hero bred anthropoid apes which could speak English after 11 generations. Edison's attention was diverted from the novel by the practical problems of designing ore-separation machinery, one of his many projects. Despite Lathrop's pleas, Edison abruptly terminated their joint literary venture.

3. JOSEPH CONRAD (1857–1924),
   British novelist born in Poland

Conrad's biographer and intimate friend Richard Curle records that the author in his last years was obsessed with the opening scene of an unwritten novel set in some eastern European state. So vividly would Conrad describe the scene that his hearers seemed to experience it vicariously. According to Curle: "In the courtyard of a royal palace, brilliantly lighted up as for a festival, soldiers are bivouacked in the snow. And inside the palace a fateful council is taking place and the destiny of a country is being decided. . . . as [Conrad] pictured that opening scene one could almost feel the tension in the air and one seemed to be warming one's hands with the soldiers around their blazing fire." Curle learned nothing more about this idea, or why it remained merely a collection of haunting images.

4. SIR ARTHUR CONAN DOYLE (1859–1930),
   British novelist

Shortly before his death Doyle sketched out and dictated a plot for a Sherlock Holmes story, which was found among his unpublished papers. It dealt with murder committed by a man on stilts, an idea used later successfully by G. K. Chesterton, who conceived the idea independently.

5. CLAUDE ACHILLE DEBUSSY (1862–1918),
   French composer

Debussy's one opera, *Pelléas and Mélisande*, had been described as "exquisite but creepy, a study in glooms." After its success, Debussy made plans for an opera based on Poe's short story "The

Fall of the House of Usher." The hero of Poe's nightmarish work was a hypersensitive neurasthenic much like Debussy himself; it was inevitable that the composer would be attracted to the story. In 1908 he signed a contract with the Metropolitan Opera Company to produce the opera. A libretto was finished, sketches were made, and then, inexplicably, the idea was allowed to lapse. Debussy's languid efforts to complete *Usher* may have reflected his conviction that his genius was not suited to the stage. He abandoned other equally promising operatic projects after *Pelléas*. One was a *Tristan* to rival that of Wagner, which foundered over stage rights to the play. Another was an *As You Like It*, based on Shakespeare's play (for which Debussy had "an old passion"). The latter was scrapped when Toulet, Debussy's librettist, became an opium addict.

6. FRANK LLOYD WRIGHT (1869–1959), U.S. architect

One of Wright's last designs, never executed, was his most daring: the 528-story Mile-High Illinois building, a space-age skyscraper planned at a 26-ft.-long table. If constructed, it would be almost four times as tall as Chicago's Sears Tower (1,454 ft.). The rapierlike structure would be light, with no sway even at the peak. External elevators using atomic-powered tandem cabs would ascend on ratchet-guided tracks. There would be two decks for 150 helicopters and covered parking for 15,000 cars. Wright estimated a cost of $100 million in 1957, half of which would be required to house the building's potential 130,000 workers at conventional sites. He envisioned 10 such buildings meeting the office-space needs of New York City. Green parks and play areas were to replace existing business districts. Although feasible from an engineering viewpoint, Wright's brainchild frightened promoters, conservative architects, maintenance crews, and firemen, who foresaw insoluble problems.

7. WASLAW NIJINSKY (1890–1950), Russian dancer

When Nijinsky broke with Diaghilev's Russian Ballet, he decided to wait out W.W. I in Switzerland before returning to Russia. He had choreographed three ballets for Diaghilev, which had been produced and praised for originality and beauty. In 1917, just before his mental breakdown, Nijinsky conceived ideas for new ballets, doomed to be stillborn because he worked in isolation, with only his wife as confidante. One, based on Debussy's *Chanson de Bilitis*, would have portrayed lesbian love on the stage. Another was the symbolic representation of his own life; in it he was to assume the persona of a youthful Renaissance painter, seeking all the beauty that love and life can offer. His master would be a universal genius, representing Diaghilev, the great impresario who had once been Nijinsky's lover. Finally, he planned a ballet that was set in a house of prostitution, transmitting the whole scale of sex life, its beauty along with its destructive quality.

8. BUCKMINSTER FULLER, JR. (1895–   ), U.S. builder and designer

In 1928 Fuller set out to revolutionize the housing industry with a mass-produced "Dymaxion House" designed for maximum enhancement of human life and conservation of resources. A central mast bore the weight of symmetrical hexagonal floors suspended on tension cables. Walls were glass, utilizing the sun's energy. Independent of utility companies, the house had its own power generator and provision for recycling waste. Other features were a water-conserving "fog-gun" shower, soundless pneumatic floors, automatic dishwasher and laundry systems, car park, and sun deck. It could be erected anywhere in one day and could withstand dirt, flood, fire, cyclone, and gas attack. In 1946 a prototype was assembled in Wichita, Kans. The estimated selling price for the seven-room structure was $6,400. When no industrial giant showed interest in tooling up, Fuller shifted his attention to exteriors and developed the geodesic dome.

—M.B.T.

Frank Lloyd Wright's unrealized plan for the Mile-High Illinois building, 528 stories, with offices for 130,000 workers. If constructed today it would be four times as high as the tallest building on earth.

8 UNNAMED WOMEN OF THE BIBLE

1. NOAH'S WIFE

She is mentioned five times in the book of Genesis, but only in the context of being one of a group who is present. This is surprising

13

considering how talented and efficient she must have been to have been suddenly uprooted from her home and asked to set up house-keeping in a gopher wood ark filled with birds, snakes, insects, and full-grown animals of every species. This woman, who kept everything in order in the ark for 12 months, is known to us today, not by her own name, but only as "Noah's wife." (Gen. 6:18; 7:7 and 13; 8:16 and 18)

2. THE PHARAOH'S DAUGHTER

Her father, probably Ramses II, decreed that it was necessary to kill all male children born to the Hebrews because the Hebrew population in Egypt was growing too quickly. One day the pharaoh's daughter was bathing in the Nile with her attendants when she noticed a basket containing a three-month-old baby boy. She realized that he was a Hebrew child and decided to raise him rather than allow him to be killed by her father. The baby's sister, Miriam, was standing nearby and offered to find a Hebrew woman to suckle the child. The baby's mother, Jochebed, conveniently close at hand, was summoned and hired as a nurse to care for the child. The pharaoh's daughter later named the baby Moshe, or Moses, and he grew up to become the greatest leader and teacher in the history of the Jews. The woman who saved his life and raised and educated him was known in various history books as Thermuthis, Myrrina, or Mercis. However, the authors of the Bible referred to her only as "the pharaoh's daughter." (Exod. 2:5–10)

3. THE WOMAN PATRIOT OF THEBEZ

Abimelech was a tyrant who ruled over Shechem for three years during the 12th century B.C. Having taken power by slaughtering 69 of his 79 brothers, he continued his bloody ways by killing the entire population of the town of Shechem when they revolted against him. Moving on to the neighboring town of Thebez, he was about to set it ablaze when "a certain woman" appeared on the roof of the town tower and dropped a piece of a millstone on Abimelech's head, crushing his skull. Humiliated at the prospect of being killed by a woman, Abimelech ordered one of his followers to run him through with a sword. With Abimelech dead, his supporters dispersed and Thebez was saved. (Judg. 9:50–55)

4. THE WISE WOMAN OF ABEL

When Sheba, the son of Bichri, led a revolt against King David, David sent his commander in chief, Joab, to track down the rebel and kill him. Joab finally found the culprit hiding in the walled city of Abel. Joab and his soldiers began the destruction of the city, but stopped when a wise woman called out to them to discuss the situation. Joab explained that if the people of Abel turned over to him the rebel Sheba, he and his soldiers would leave them alone. The wise woman easily convinced her people that this was a good deal. Sheba was quickly decapitated, his head was thrown over the wall to Joab, and the city of Abel was saved. (II Sam. 20:15–22)

5. BARZILLAI'S DAUGHTER

When this Gileadite woman married, she retained her own name rather than take her husband's. In fact, her husband, a priest,

14

took *her* family's name. Despite this early display of feminism, or perhaps because of it, the Bible authors do not tell us her name, but refer to her merely as "one of the daughters of Barzillai." (Neh. 7:63)

6. THE SHULAMITE SWEETHEART

According to some scholars, the Song of Songs tells the story of a young Shulamite maiden who attracted the attention of King Solomon. He forced her to come to Jerusalem and tried to convince her to marry him, but she resisted him and insisted on remaining faithful to her shepherd lover. Eventually Solomon gave up and allowed her to return home while he was forced to continue living with the 700 women he had already married. (Song of Solomon)

7. HERODIAS'S DAUGHTER

Known to the historian Josephus as Salome, this most famous of all dancers is not given a name in the New Testament. King Herod was so impressed by the dancing of Herodias's daughter that he offered her any gift, including half his kingdom. After consulting her mother, she asked for the head of John the Baptist on a platter. She got it and promptly turned over the grisly prize to her mom. (Matt. 14:6; Mark 6:22)

8. THE ADULTEROUS WOMAN

Caught in the act of adultery, this woman was brought before Jesus by the scribes and Pharisees, who pointed out that the law required that such an offense be punished by stoning. Jesus ignored them at first and then said "He that is without sin among you, let him first cast a stone at her." One by one her accusers slithered away, and she was not punished. (John 8:3–11)

—D.W.

10 NOTABLE WOMEN WHO WERE OR ARE NUNS

1. JEANINE DECKERS (1933–   )

In 1963, while a Dominican nun in Belgium, Jeanine Deckers recorded the song "Dominique." It skyrocketed to the top of the U.S. charts and earned "the Singing Nun" $100,000, which she promptly turned over to the Dominican order. Although Miss Deckers left the convent in 1966 to focus her energies on a singing career, she remains deeply religious and still upholds her vow of celibacy. All of her music is meant to extol God and his works—including such creations as the birth control pill, which she praised in the song "Glory Be to God for the Golden Pill."

2. DOÑA MARÍA DE GAUCÍN

Doña María successfully embarked upon a second career when she left her convent to become a matador. According to Havelock

Ellis in *The Soul of Spain:* "She was distinguished not only for her courage, but also for her beauty and virtue, and after a few years, during which she attained renown throughout Spain, she peacefully returned to the practice of religion in her convent, without, it appears, any reproaches from the sisters, who enjoyed the reflected fame of her exploits in the bullring."

3. JUNE HAVER (1926–)

In February, 1953, actress June Haver abandoned her career and entered St. Mary's Convent in Xavier, Kans. Six months later she became a novitiate of the Sisters of Charity and donned their habit. In September, 1953, Miss Haver left the convent and returned home to Los Angeles. She complained of severe migraine headaches and stated that she was not able to withstand the rigors of convent life. The following year she married her former co-star Fred MacMurray and retired from the screen.

4. ROSE HAWTHORNE LATHROP (1851–1926)

The youngest daughter of Nathaniel Hawthorne, Rose married at age 20 and established a reputation as a leader of fashionable society and an author of some talent. In 1893 she and her husband separated. Anxious to find new meaning in her life, she learned the rudiments of practical nursing, moved into a tenement on New York's East Side, and began ministering to poor and outcast victims of cancer. After the death of her husband in 1898, Rose adopted the name Mother Mary Alphonsa, and a year later she took her first vows as a sister of the Dominican Congregation of Saint Rose of Lima. Until her death she served as director of the Dominican order she had created—the Servants of Relief for Incurable Cancer.

5. MARIO MARTINO (1937–)

Brought up in a conservative midwestern family, Marie Martino was always convinced she was a boy, but hoped to suppress her "unnatural" desires by entering a convent school. She was dismissed after establishing an unorthodox liaison with another student, but several years later she was accepted into the order of St. Francis and

Sister Mary Dominick . . . transformed into Mario Martino.

16

took her novitiate vows as Sister Mary Dominick. Unable to deal with her sexual urges and the restrictive atmosphere, she left the convent during her second year and obtained a job as a nurse's aide. In 1969, after a sex change operation, Marie Josephine legally became Mario Joseph. The following year Mario married his longtime girl friend, Rebecca, whom he had met in nursing school, and they established the Labyrinth Foundation Counseling Service in New York for transsexuals. Mario has gone on to get his B.A. in psychology and a degree in law.

6. ELIZABETH McALISTER (1940–   )

In 1965 Sister Elizabeth McAlister, an art history teacher at Marymount College in Tarrytown, N.Y., became involved in the antiwar movement and met Father Philip Berrigan. When Berrigan was imprisoned in 1970 for his protest activities, McAlister began writing to him. The following year a federal grand jury indicted them on charges of letter smuggling and conspiracy. As partial evidence the government introduced a letter, allegedly written by McAlister, which discussed in detail a plan to kidnap Henry Kissinger. They were tried in 1972, but all charges were eventually dropped. On May 28, 1973, McAlister and Berrigan announced that they had been secretly married in 1969. Their daughter Frida was born in 1974.

7. JANE CAHILL PFEIFFER (1932–   )

Sometimes referred to as Attila the Nun, Pfeiffer has shown a flair for business ever since she joined IBM at age 23. It was her first job upon leaving a Berkeley, Calif., convent where she had spent six months. She rose to vice-president of IBM but quit in 1976 after marrying Ralph Pfeiffer, Jr., a divorced father of 10. Passing up an offer from President Carter to become secretary of commerce, Pfeiffer decided to accept the $225,000-a-year job of chairman of NBC in 1978. Although imbued with a strong sense of morals, she maintains, "I'm not the avenging angel. I'm not Joan of Arc."

8. SOPHIA (1657–1704)

The ambitious older sister of Peter the Great, Sophia became regent in 1682 and, with the assistance of her chief counselor and lover, Prince Golitsyn, tightened control over the military, encouraged the growth of industry, and brought about peace with Poland. By 1689, however, the 17-year-old Peter had sufficient support to lead a successful revolt against Sophia and to imprison her in Moscow's Novodevichy Convent. After her backers made a futile attempt to restore her to power in 1698, she was forced to take religious vows. As Sister Suzanna, she remained at Novodevichy for the rest of her life. There Peter continued to torment her by having mutilated bodies hung outside her window.

9. EDITH STEIN (1891–1942)

The daughter of Orthodox Jews, Edith Stein renounced her religion in 1904. After receiving her doctorate in philosophy, she became a highly respected member of the University of Freiburg's faculty. In 1922 she converted to Catholicism and switched to teaching at a Dominican girls' school. Adopting the religious name of Teresa Benedicta of the Cross, she joined the Carmelite order in 1934 and continued to produce noteworthy philosophical and spiritual writings. Under the auspices of Hitler's 1942 pronouncement against non-Aryan Catholics, she was seized and taken to Auschwitz, where she was put to death in a gas chamber. In 1962 she became the subject of a beatification effort.

10. MOTHER TERESA (1910–   )

Probably the most famous nun alive today, Mother Teresa was born in Skopje in present-day Yugoslavia. She founded the order of the Missionaries of Charity in 1948. Based in Calcutta, the order transformed an abandoned Hindu temple into a home for the destitute dying and is credited with saving over 8,000 lives. In 1964, when Pope Paul VI gave her his limousine, Mother Teresa immediately raffled it off to pay for the construction of a leper colony. In 1971 she was awarded the $25,000 Pope John XXIII Peace Prize for her continuing efforts on behalf of the poor and the sick, and in 1979 she received the $190,000 Nobel Peace Prize.

—F.B.F.

10 WOULD-BE MEN OF THE CLOTH

1. GABRIEL FALLOPIUS (1523–1562), Italian anatomist

The tubes connecting female ovaries to the uterus, known as Fallopian tubes, were named after this distinguished scholar who once studied to become a priest at the cathedral of Modena. He gave up the Church to pursue the study of medicine and subsequently became a professor of surgery and anatomy at the University of Padua. Fallopius was the first to describe the semicircular canals of the ear which maintain body equilibrium. He was also responsible for naming several body parts, including the vagina, placenta, and clitoris.

2. CHRISTOPHER MARLOWE (1564–1593), English dramatist

Author of the plays *Tamburlaine the Great* and *Doctor Faustus*, Marlowe—at 17—was a divinity student at Benet (now Corpus Christi) College, Cambridge. He never took Anglican orders but instead became a writer whose plays were deemed irreverent and atheistic. At 23 he served as a spy for Queen Elizabeth; at 24 he was arrested on blasphemy charges; at 29 he was murdered in a drunken brawl.

3. JOHANNES KEPLER (1571–1630), German astronomer

Even as a young child, Kepler was deeply religious. He prayed daily, and when he committed a sin, he repented by reciting church sermons. At the University of Tübingen, where he studied to be a Lutheran minister, Kepler was greatly admired, even though he was fascinated by Copernican astronomy, which was prohibited by his fellow theologians. His last year of training was interrupted when he accepted a teaching position in Graz. Kepler intended to return to his studies, but his interest in astronomy grew and became his life's work. He is best known for his laws of planetary motion.

4. CHARLES DARWIN (1809–1882), English naturalist

Pressured by his father to become a clergyman, Darwin went to Christ's College, Cambridge, in 1827 to study for holy orders in the Church of England. He left school, however, to accept a position as naturalist in 1831 aboard the H.M.S. *Beagle*—a voyage that was to change his life. In 1859 his *Origin of Species* rocked the foundations of the Church, and it was Darwin, the "reverent agnostic," who said of the New Testament, "The plain language of the text seems to show that the men who do not believe, and this would include my father, brother, and almost all my best friends, will be everlastingly punished. And this is a damnable doctrine."

5. JOSEPH ERNEST RENAN (1823–1892), French philosopher

Renan trained for the priesthood in three Parisian seminaries and was about to receive the first major order in 1845 when he suffered a crisis of faith and left the Roman Catholic Church. Later, his *Life of Jesus*, a book that portrayed Jesus as a human being, infuriated church officials and caused him to lose his professorship at the Collège de France. Nevertheless, when Renan was asked to become a Protestant, he answered, "I may have lost my faith, but not my reason."

6. JOSEPH STALIN (1879–1953), Russian dictator

The man who caused the imprisonment and death of at least 20 million people set out to be a priest at age 14 after obtaining a scholarship at Tiflis Theological Seminary. He was expelled five years later for his political activities and because he was repeatedly (14 times) caught reading forbidden literature, including the books of Karl Marx, Victor Hugo, and Charles Darwin. Many years later a reporter asked him if the Jesuits had any good qualities. Stalin replied, "Yes, they are systematic and persevering to achieve their

Fifteen-year-old seminary student Joseph Stalin.

sordid ends. But their principal method is spying, prying, worming their way into people's souls and outraging their feelings."

7. WILL DURANT (1885–), U.S. author

Durant, noted historian and coauthor of the 11-volume *Story of Civilization*, was educated in parochial schools, which his mother hoped would change him from "a troublesome and conceited brat into a model priest." His passion for books—he read over 2,000 between the ages of 12 and 19—eventually led him to the conclusion that "Christianity was only one of a hundred religions claiming special access to truth and salvation." Despite his doubts, he entered the seminary at Seton Hall, South Orange, N.J., in 1908, but he withdrew in 1910. His affiliation with the Church was completely broken in 1912 as a result of a speech—"The Origins of Religion"— in which Durant told of how the phallus had, in some societies, been worshiped as a symbol of divine power. He promptly received an "episcopal excommunication."

8. CARL R. ROGERS (1902–), U.S. psychologist

Rogers was 22 years old when he entered Union Theological Seminary in New York to become a Protestant minister. While there, he participated in a seminar organized to explore religious doubts. Rogers later said of the group: "The majority of members . . . in thinking their way through questions they had raised, thought themselves right out of religious work. I was one." Rogers is the creator of the nondirective, "client-centered" theory of psychotherapy, a person-to-person, rather than a doctor-to-patient, relationship that gives the patient more control over therapeutic treatment. Rogers is also a respected author, whose works include the best-seller *On Becoming a Person*.

9. EDMUND GERALD "JERRY" BROWN, JR. (1938–), U.S. governor of California

On August 15, 1956, Brown—then 18 years old—and two high school friends threw their pocket change into the streets of Los Gatos, Calif. "We don't need it," they said. The three friends were approaching Sacred Heart Novitiate, where Brown would spend the next three and a half years in preparation for the priesthood. Life in the seminary was severe; fasting, binding, and self-flagellation were common practices. Brown left the Jesuit order because he "couldn't take the complete suppression of the self." Known for his frugality and austerity, Governor Brown usually works 16 hours a day, 6 days a week. According to the former seminarian, "Idleness is the devil's workshop."

10. BEN VEREEN (1946–), U.S. entertainer

The star of many Broadway shows, including *Jesus Christ Superstar* and *Pippin*, and a hit as Chicken George in TV's *Roots*, Vereen was born in Miami, Fla., and by the age of four was singing in the local Baptist church. Unable to find theater jobs after graduation from the High School for the Performing Arts in New York, he enrolled at Manhattan's Pentecostal Theological Seminary. However, he was distressed at the "hypocritical atmosphere" and left after six months.

—C.O.

THE 5 MOST HATED OR
FEARED PERSONS IN HISTORY

Each year from 1970 to 1979, Mme. Tussaud's Waxwork Museum in London handed 3,500 of the international visitors to its exhibition a questionnaire which asked them which persons—past or present, real or fictional—they hated the most. In ten years, 35,000 persons answered the poll question. This is a complete sum-up of a decade of voting.

CONSENSUS 1970–1979

1. Adolf Hitler
2. Idi Amin
3. Richard M. Nixon
4. Dracula
5. Mao Tse-tung

HARRISON SALISBURY'S
10 GREATEST LEADERS OF
THE 20TH CENTURY

Beginning his career in 1928 at age 20, Salisbury worked for the Minneapolis *Journal* and United Press International before becoming *The New York Times*'s Moscow correspondent in 1949. His *Russia Re-Viewed* won him the 1955 Pulitzer Prize for international reporting. An associate editor for the *Times* since 1972, Salisbury has written nearly 20 books on Russia, China, and the U.S.

1. Franklin D. Roosevelt
2. Vladimir I. Lenin
3. Winston Churchill
4. Mao Tse-tung
5. Mohandas K. Gandhi
6. Joseph Stalin
7. Chou En-lai
8. Dwight D. Eisenhower
9. Charles de Gaulle
10. Woodrow Wilson

—Exclusive for *The Book of Lists 2*

ABBIE HOFFMAN'S
10 HEROES WHO GOT AWAY WITH IT

Abbie Hoffman, a U.S. fugitive since 1973, is the author of the forthcoming *Unauthorized Autobiography of Abbie Hoffman* as well as earlier works including *Steal This Book* and *Revolution for the Hell of It*. He is rumored to be currently working as a barber in Bakersfield, Calif.

1. B. TRAVEN (1882?–1969; 1890?–1969; 1894?–1969?; 1901?–1969)

The man who called himself B. Traven was the world's greatest fugitive as well as the best working-class novelist ever to pick up a pen. He authored over 30 books, including the classic novel *The Treasure of the Sierra Madre*, while on the run from at least four governments. He began his career in Germany as an actor and anarchist, using the name Ret Marut. He was put on trial in 1919 for treason in Munich and was sentenced to death, but escaped. He fled to Moscow, fought with Stalin, and in turn fled to France. Next he became a sailor on "death ships" for the American merchant marine that were sunk to collect insurance money. (His 1934 best-seller was *The Death Ship: The Story of an American Sailor*.) In 1923 he made his way to the oil fields of Mexico where, with Wobbly organizers, he agitated for unions. This activity led to his being hunted as "El Rubio," an enemy of the state. Hiding out in Mexico, he began an immensely successful career as the novelist B. Traven. In addition he became a firmly established photographer, working under the name Traven Torsven. He was also a respected archaeologist and was considered a great medicine healer by the Chiapas Indians. *Life* magazine once offered $5,000 to anyone who could find the elusive author. Late in the 1950s, he emerged from hiding, married, settled down in Mexico City, and successfully managed to blur the facts of his early life. Just before he died, he burned most of his personal papers, but his books remain a proud legacy from a noble champion of freedom.

2. KIM PHILBY (1912—   )

Born Harold Adrian Philby, this Britisher was recruited into the British Secret Service in 1939. A brilliant spy, he was quickly promoted to lead the Soviet section during W.W. II. In 1949 he was assigned to be chief liaison between all Anglo-American Intelligence operations. He won praise from Roosevelt, Truman, and Churchill and was often mentioned as a likely candidate to head British Intelligence. What no one knew was that in 1933 Philby had been recruited as a Russian agent. Until 1951 he successfully eluded suspicion. In that year, the British Secret Service learned that two of their agents, Guy Burgess and Donald Maclean, were double agents working for the Russians. Before they could be arrested, the two fled to Moscow. Someone had informed them of impending arrest, and suspicion fell upon Philby. For 10 years the British tried unsuccessfully to prove that Philby was a double agent. Finally in 1961, when Philby was working as a foreign correspondent in Beirut,

Lebanon, a Russian spy named George Blake was arrested and confirmed what the British had suspected all along. On the night of January 23, 1963, Philby slipped away from pursuing agents on his way to a dinner party. Disguised as an Arab, he walked 300 miles through Syria to Turkey, to surface in Moscow six months later. He now lives a quiet life with his Russian-born wife, Nina, somewhere in Russia—history's most successful double agent.

3. GÜNTER WALLRAFF (1942–   )

Born in Cologne, Germany, Wallraff is the world's best undercover reporter. The author of several books and articles, he has championed the working class by exposing—in a variety of inventive ways—Nazis in positions of power, government spying, and illegal business practices. For four years he posed successfully as a migrant worker, a derelict, a mental patient, a Turkish laborer, a steel worker, and a postal clerk. What emerged were two fascinating exposés of squalid conditions. In 1976, posing as an official in the Bonn government, he managed to arrange a secret arms deal with Portuguese archconservative Gen. Antonio Spinola. In 1977 he infiltrated Germany's largest newspaper, the right-wing *Bild Zeitung*. He documented the fabrication of antiworker articles. On other occasions, he posed as the valet to the bishop of Bavaria, as a police informer, and as a napalm manufacturer. He has been in prison several times, and the courts have ordered numerous censorings of his books. A man of a thousand faces, Europe's most popular reporter carries out his missions undetected. Facing serious charges for impersonating government officials, Wallraff probably is living in exile in Sweden, or underground in Germany.

4. HARRY HOUDINI (1874–1926)

Houdini perhaps got away from it more than with it. He literally could not be locked up. He escaped from a water tank manacled upside down by his ankles and from hundreds of jails and bank vaults. He was the world's greatest escape artist. Extraordinarily dexterous, he could tie and untie a knot with the toes of one foot. Fifty years after his death, many of his tricks remain a secret. Believing he could escape even death, he made elaborate plans to communicate with the living. Several close friends are convinced he managed even that. Rumor has it that Houdini is currently a TV repairman living in Paterson, N.J.

5. FRANCISCO VILLA (1877–1923)

"Pancho" Villa, the fabled Mexican revolutionary, led the last army to get away with invading the United States. It happened on March 9, 1916, at Columbus, N.M. President Wilson ordered General Pershing to track the rebel force into Mexico. Leading the pursuit was George Patton. They failed to capture Pancho Villa, who led them on a madcap chase through the mountains. Villa escaped many close calls during the Mexican Revolution. On July 20, 1923, after he had retired to a ranch in Durango, he was ambushed and shot while driving his automobile.

6. HENRI CHARRIERE, "PAPILLON" (1907–1973)

Henri Charrière was one of the few to escape from the dreaded

French penal colony on Devil's Island. Convicted of murder in France in 1931, Henri Charrière, alias Papillon, was sentenced to hard labor for life. He was sent with hundreds of others on a prison ship to St. Laurent, French Guiana, where he began a series of daring escapes and recaptures. He was finally transferred from the mainland prison to the brutal Devil's Island, after having served three years and nine months in solitary confinement. Papillon finally made his escape from Devil's Island riding two sacks of coconuts through a shark-infested sea to the mainland. His story became a best-selling book in 1970, and the French government subsequently pardoned him for his original crime.

7. D. B. COOPER (1926?–)

Little is known about this modern-day legend. In 1971 D. B. Cooper boarded a plane in Los Angeles with a briefcase he claimed was rigged as a bomb and a request for $200,000. Cooper's extortion was the first of its nature; out of it emerged the word *skyjacker*. He ordered the plane to land in Seattle, where he collected the $200,000 and four parachutes and let the passengers go. The crew remained on board and flew him south. FBI agents guarded every airport on the West Coast. The plane was under continued close scrutiny. Bailing out somewhere over Washington, he was able to foil all attempts to follow him. Although low-level officials claim he perished in the woods, no body or other trace of him was ever found. What no one knows is that D. B. Cooper lost all of the money investing in Arizona real estate and is currently collecting unemployment in Phoenix.

8. RONALD BIGGS (1930–)

England's greatest modern rogue, Ronnie Biggs seems to lead a charmed life. On August 8, 1963, he and his cohorts robbed a Royal Mail train and successfully made off with $7.3 million for a new world's record. Later that year Scotland Yard cracked the case, and Biggs and company were arrested and sent to jail. Much of the money, however, remained at large. Biggs engineered a successful prison escape from England's top-security prison and eventually made his way to Brazil. There he got a woman pregnant, and—according to Brazilian law—being a father of a Brazilian citizen, he was not subject to extradition. His English wife allowed him to marry the Brazilian woman. A popular punk-rock group called the Sex Pistols signed up Biggs as lead singer early in 1978. A smash hit and a movie role followed. Good for you, Ronnie Biggs!

9. RICHARD MILHOUS NIXON (1913–)

Nixon was born on January 9, 1913, in Yorba Linda, Calif., and died the following day. He got away with so much for so long I just couldn't resist including him. Our 37th and most interesting president is currently embarking on a political comeback, speaking in various cities in the U.S. and abroad. Because of the events that occurred during his administration, Nixon will be remembered long after all other presidents of this century become names in trivia contests.

10. ANONYMOUS

Obviously the ones who got away with the most are unknown.

They're smiling when they read this, knowing that compared to them, the above nine are amateurs.

—Exclusive for *The Book of Lists 2*

9 DISPARAGING SOBRIQUETS

1. CHARLES THE SIMPLE (879–929), King of the Franks

Son of Louis the Stammerer, Charles III owes his nickname to his policy of making concessions to the Norse invaders to prevent the complete disintegration of his kingdom. In one concession, Charles gave Rollo, the Norse chieftain, his daughter in marriage and the fiefdom of Normandy. This act, among others, was unpopular with his barons, who later deposed and imprisoned him.

2. LOUIS THE SLUGGARD (966?–987), King of the Franks

His short reign (986–987) marked the end of the Carolingian line. Noted for his self-indulgence, Louis V died at an early age due to a hunting accident. He was also known as Louis the Do-Nothing—but historians have noted that since the power of the kingdom was in the hands of the noblemen, there was little that he could do.

3. ETHELRED THE UNREADY (968?–1016), King of England

Ethelred II's sobriquet is a result of his inability to repel the Danish invasion of England. At first he paid tribute to the Danes, but their raids continued and he was forced to abandon England for Normandy in 1013. In a more generous vein, he has also been called Ethelred the Ill-Advised.

4. LOUIS THE FAT (1081–1137), King of France

Like his father Philip I, Louis VI was fat. At the age of 46, because of his extreme corpulence, he was unable to mount his horse. Yet he was a popular Capetian monarch and was also referred to as Louis the Wide-Awake because of the peace and prosperity of his reign.

5. LOUIS THE QUARRELER (1289–1316), King of France

Louis le Hutin can be translated as Louis the Stubborn or Louis the Quarreler. Louis X's brief reign (1314–1316) ended when he died of pleurisy caused by overindulging in cold wine after becoming overheated playing ball.

6. CHARLES THE BAD (1332–1387), King of Navarre

Charles II was "bad" because of his treacherous nature. His notoriety grew during the Hundred Years' War, when he forced John II of France to grant him lands in Normandy, one of several attempts to further his personal ambition to occupy the French throne.

7. FERDINAND, THE INCONSTANT (1345–1383), King of Portugal

Ferdinand I earned his sobriquet by jilting the daughter of the king of Castile for the more beautiful Leonora Telles, a Portuguese noblewoman. He was also inconsistent in his political policies toward England and Castile.

8. CHARLES, THE MAD (1368–1422), King of France

Charles VI assumed the throne at age 12, when he was referred to as Charles the Well-Beloved. In 1392 he took ill, suffering fever and convulsions—the first of 44 attacks he would subsequently endure. The bouts of madness—in which he sometimes tore his clothing and broke furniture—continued to plague him sporadically for the last 30 years of his reign.

9. IVAN, THE TERRIBLE (1530–1584), Czar of Russia

As a young ruler, Ivan IV tortured animals and tossed dogs from rooftops. Torture and executions were common throughout his reign. In 1570 he marched on Novgorod and killed thousands in a five-week binge—some of them children, who were thrown into the icy river. In 1580 he killed his own son in a mad rage.

—D.P.M.

6 INDIVIDUALS YOU DIDN'T KNOW WERE PARTLY BLACK OR ALL BLACK

1. HANNIBAL (247–183 B.C.)

This great Carthaginian general has been described as very dark-skinned with black, kinky hair and beard. During his time, most residents of Carthage were of mixed Semitic and black African blood.

2. JOHN JAMES AUDUBON (1785–1851)

The famed artist and ornithologist was born in Les Cayes, Haiti (formerly Santo Domingo), the son of a French sea captain and a Creole servant girl. His mother died shortly after giving birth, and Audubon was taken to France to be raised by his stepmother.

3. ALEKSANDER SERGEEVICH PUSHKIN (1799–1837)

Considered the greatest of all Russian poets, Pushkin was an octoroon. His great-grandfather, black Russian general Abram Petrovich Hannibal, was kidnapped from Africa at age eight and presented as a gift to Czar Peter the Great.

4. ALEXANDRE DUMAS *PÈRE* (1802–1870)

The author of *The Three Musketeers* and *The Count of Monte Cristo* was a grandson of the Marquis de La Pailleterie and a Santo

Domingan slave named Marie Cessette Dumas. His father, a mulatto, took the name Dumas when he joined the French army.

5. ALEXANDRE DUMAS *FILS* (1824–1895)

The son of Dumas *père* and thus an octoroon, the younger Dumas in 1852 dramatized his novel *La Dame aux Camélias*, the tale of a self-sacrificing courtesan, which inspired Verdi's *La Traviata* the next year and which afforded movie star Greta Garbo one of her most memorable roles in 1937.

6. PETER USTINOV (1921–   )

This versatile actor-producer had a half-Ethiopian grandmother. As Ustinov recounts in his book *Dear Me*: "My grandmother, whose Christian name was Magdalena, was born in a tent during the Battle of Magdala, which opposed Ethiopian forces to British ones under Lord Napier. . . . My grandmother's youngest sister was still, until recently, a lady-in-waiting at the court of Haile Selassie."

—W.A.D.

John James Audubon, whose mother was black.

10 MEETINGS BETWEEN FAMOUS PEOPLE AND PEOPLE NOT YET FAMOUS

1. NEW YORK, N.Y., 1789. GEORGE WASHINGTON IS INTRODUCED TO WASHINGTON IRVING

As the President browsed in a Broadway shop, a servant of the Irving family spotted him from the street and hustled inside with six-year-old Washington Irving in tow. Informed that the lad had been named after him, the Chief Executive stroked the head that later would conjure up Rip Van Winkle and wished the boy well. *Note:* This pat on the head has been passed on through generations of Americans to the present-day recipient. An older Washington Irving bestowed it upon his publisher, George Putnam, who in turn gave it to young Allan Nevins, the future Pulitzer Prize–winning historian. Years later, at an informal gathering at the Irving Wallace home, Nevins conferred the historic pat on 10-year-old Amy Wallace, saying, "Amy, I pat you on behalf of General George Washington." Amy, who refused to wash her hair for a week afterward, intends to pass along the pat to the next generation.

2. BOSTON, MASS., 1860. RALPH WALDO EMERSON PROOFREADS A SCHOOL PAPER FOR OLIVER WENDELL HOLMES, JR.

While a student at Harvard, young Holmes wrote a 15-page critical essay on Plato and took it to Emerson, an old family friend, for review. The great essayist, then 57 years old with his best work behind him, read it and gave the future Supreme Court justice this advice: "When you shoot at a king, you must kill him." Holmes chucked the piece into a trash can.

3. ÉTRETAT, FRANCE, 1868. ALGERNON CHARLES SWINBURNE MEETS GUY DE MAUPASSANT

The 18-year-old Maupassant, later one of France's greatest writers, witnessed the near drowning of a swimmer who turned out to be the eccentric English poet Swinburne. (According to some versions of the incident, including Maupassant's own, he was actually in on the rescue, but this is disputed by more objective accounts.) When Maupassant introduced himself, the poet invited him to dinner at his villa. Swinburne's guest was shocked by the main dish—roast monkey—and the presence of a large ape, which pushed the young Frenchman's head aside whenever he tried to drink.

4. WASHINGTON, D.C., 1887. GROVER CLEVELAND MAKES A WISH FOR FRANKLIN ROOSEVELT

On a visit to the nation's capital with his parents, five-year-old Franklin Roosevelt was taken to the White House to meet the President. According to FDR, Cleveland looked down at his eventual successor and said, "My little man, I am making a strange wish for you. It is that you may never be president of the United States."

5. PALO ALTO, CALIF., 1894. BENJAMIN HARRISON COUGHS UP 25¢ FOR HERBERT HOOVER

While serving as a guest lecturer at Stanford University, former President Benjamin Harrison inadvertently slipped into a college baseball game without paying the 25¢ admission. Unwilling to grant a freebie even to so distinguished a fan, the student manager of the home team, 19-year-old Herbert Hoover, caught up with Harrison and politely asked him to pay up. He did.

6. INDIANAPOLIS, IND., 1895. LEW WALLACE WARNS BOOTH TARKINGTON OF THE DANGERS OF BREAKING INTO PRINT

During a visit to his hometown a decade before his death,

Wallace, the author of *Ben Hur*, met Tarkington, then 26. Tarkington was wallowing in rejection slips and four years away from publishing his first book. "The publication of my first novel was almost enough to ruin my law practice," said the lawyer turned author to the wide-eyed Tarkington. "As soon as the jury of farmers and village merchants heard the word *novel*, they uttered hearty guffaws. . . . I might as well have appeared in court dressed as a circus clown." Despite the warning, Tarkington went on to write many best-sellers, including *The Magnificent Ambersons* and *Seventeen*.

7. WASHINGTON, D.C., 1905. TEDDY ROOSEVELT SENDS FOR EDWIN ARLINGTON ROBINSON

Favorably impressed by Robinson's *Children of the Night*, a collection of poetry, President Roosevelt sent for the young writer, who was nearly destitute, and offered him a clerkship in the New York Custom House with this admonition: "I expect you to think poetry first and customs second." The post provided Robinson with a livelihood for four years while he continued to write.

8. NEW YORK, N.Y., 1910. SARAH BERNHARDT MEETS LILLIAN GISH IN THE WINGS

Before going west to become a star in D. W. Griffith's epic films, Miss Gish landed a dancing role in Sarah Bernhardt's show. As they waited together in the wings for the opening curtain, the Divine Sarah stroked the young girl's delicate curls admiringly and uttered something to her in French, a language Miss Gish had never before heard.

9. AKRON, O., 1921. HARVEY FIRESTONE GIVES WENDELL WILLKIE A PARTING PREDICTION

After serving a couple years as legal counsel to Firestone Tire and Rubber Company, 29-year-old Willkie decided to switch to private practice. In saying good-bye to the young attorney, Firestone, 53, spoke bluntly: "I like you, young man, but I don't think you will ever amount to a great deal." "Why not?" asked Willkie. "Because I understand you are a Democrat, and no Democrat can ever amount to much," Firestone replied. Nineteen years later, Willkie ran for U.S. President—as a Republican.

10. LINCOLN, NEB., c. 1951. JOHNNY CARSON MEETS DICK CAVETT FOR THE FIRST TIME

In his early teens, Cavett slipped backstage where Carson—in his mid-20s and already fairly well known in Nebraska from his radio and TV appearances in Omaha—was setting up magic tricks for the show that night. Upon learning that young Cavett was a fellow magic buff, Carson showed him a trick or two and later that night interrupted his act to introduce his future talk-show rival to the audience. Cavett was thrilled.

—W.A.D.

2
SWEET LAND OF LIBERTY

LILLIAN CARTER'S
7 BEST U.S. PRESIDENTS
IN HISTORY

The outspoken mother of President Carter, "Miss Lillian" has been called by son Jimmy "the most liberal woman in Georgia." Always active, she joined the Peace Corps at age 68 and served as a nurse in India from 1967 to 1969. President Carter credits his mother with instilling in him a love of reading and an unprejudiced acceptance of people.

1. Abraham Lincoln
2. Woodrow Wilson
3. Harry Truman
4. Theodore Roosevelt
5. John F. Kennedy
6. Jimmy Carter
7. George Washington

—Exclusive for *The Book of Lists* 2

SCIENCE DIGEST'S
CHOICE OF 10 HEALTHIEST
PLACES TO LIVE IN THE U.S.

1. Anywhere, Hawaii
2. Eugene, Ore.
3. San Francisco, Calif.
4. St. Cloud, Minn.
5. Austin, Tex.
6. La Junta, Colo.
7. Utica, N.Y.
8. Kanab, U.
9. Ketchikan, Alaska
10. Middletown, Conn.

THE 10 SAFEST AREAS
OF THE U.S. IN
A NUCLEAR ATTACK

The following 10 areas are unlikely to receive serious amounts of fallout even in a full-scale Soviet attack on American military and industrial targets.

1. The Pacific coast from San Francisco to the Canadian border, including most of Oregon
2. The Channel Islands, southwest of Los Angeles
3. Southwest Utah, including adjacent areas in Nevada and Arizona
4. The Durango area of Colorado and New Mexico
5. The Big Bend region of Texas
6. Southern Texas, below San Antonio
7. North-central New York State
8. The northwestern half of North Carolina, including adjacent parts of Virginia, Tennessee, and South Carolina
9. Northern Florida and much of the Gulf coast
10. Southern Florida, between Fort Myers and Fort Lauderdale

SOURCE: Bruce D. Clayton, *Life after Doomsday*. Boulder, Colo.: Paladin Enterprises, Inc., 1979.

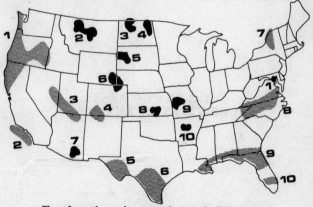

The safest and most dangerous places in the U.S. in case of a nuclear attack. Most dangerous—all black. Safest—striped.

THE 10 MOST DANGEROUS
AREAS OF THE U.S. IN
A NUCLEAR ATTACK

These 10 areas will probably receive over 2,000 incoming warheads during the opening minutes of a nuclear attack on the U.S.

1. Washington, D.C. (military command centers)
2. Central Montana (Minuteman missile silos)
3. The area within 75 mi. of Minot, N.D. (Minuteman missile silos)
4. The area within 80 mi. north, west, or south of Grand Forks, N.D. (Minuteman missile silos)
5. The area within 100 mi. north or east of Rapid City, S.D. (Minuteman missile silos)
6. The area within 120 mi. north or east of Cheyenne, Wyo. (Minuteman missile silos)
7. The area within 50 mi. of Tucson, Ariz. (Titan II missile silos)
8. The area within 50 mi. of Wichita, Kans. (Titan II missile silos)
9. The area within 125 mi. east or south of Kansas City, Mo. (Minuteman missile silos)
10. The area within 50 mi. of Little Rock, Ark. (Titan II missile silos)

SOURCE: Bruce D. Clayton, *Life after Doomsday*. Boulder, Colo.: Paladin Enterprises, Inc., 1979.

THE 20 POOREST
COUNTIES IN THE U.S.

		1975 Per Capita Income	Majority Racial Group
1. Angoon Census Division	Alaska	$ 859	89% Tlingit Indian

Located in the panhandle of southeastern Alaska, Angoon is surrounded by national forestlands. Most of the people are engaged in subsistence fishing and agriculture. The world's largest king salmon caught on sport tackle (87 lb.) was landed at Angoon in 1971. The area was shelled by U.S. gunboats in 1882 during a whaling dispute. Ninety-one years later the U.S. government paid reparations of $90,000 to the residents of Angoon.

		1975 Per Capita Income	Majority Racial Group
2. Tunica County	Mississippi	$1,788	76% Black
3. West Feliciana Parish	Louisiana	1,790	67% Black
4. Mora County	New Mexico	1,822	99.7% Caucasian (primarily Mexican-American)
5. Jefferson County	Mississippi	1,841	75% Black
6. Starr County	Texas	1,849	99.7% Caucasian (primarily Mexican-American)
7. Kemper County	Mississippi	1,859	55% Black
8. Holmes County	Mississippi	1,866	68% Black
9. Quitman County	Georgia	1,910	60% Black
10. Humphreys County	Mississippi	1,917	65% Black
11. Owsley County	Kentucky	1,921	99.6% White
12. Wolfe County	Kentucky	1,923	99.8% White
13. Quitman County	Mississippi	1,938	57% Black
14. Hancock County	Georgia	2,026	74% Black
15. East Carroll Parish	Louisiana	2,035	59% Black
16. Fentress County	Tennessee	2,043	99.9% White
17. Apache County	Arizona	2,053	74% Navaho and Apache Indian
18. Jackson County	Kentucky	2,058	99.7% White
19. Washabaugh County	South Dakota	2,062	56% Sioux Indian
20. Wilcox County	Alabama	2,066	68% Black

SOURCE: U.S. Dept. of Commerce, Bureau of the Census.

THE 12 MOST SEGREGATED CITIES IN THE U.S. WITH POPULATIONS OVER 50,000

A study conducted by the University of Wisconsin Institute for Research on Poverty used the 1970 census block-by-block housing data to calculate the proportion of nonwhites who would have to move to be equally distributed throughout a geographic area. If a city has a nonwhite population of 30% and each city block has 30%

nonwhite residents, it has zero segregation. In the census nonwhites are defined as blacks, Asians, and American Indians, but not Spanish-speaking minorities.

	How Many Nonwhites Would Have to Move
1. Shreveport, La.	97.4%
2. Winston-Salem, N.C.	94.0%
3. Augusta, Ga.	93.3%
4. Montgomery, Ala.	93.2%
5. Charlotte, N.C.	92.7%
5. Dallas, Tex.	92.7%
7. Fort Worth, Tex.	92.6%
8. Jacksonville, Fla.	92.5%
9. Memphis, Tenn.	91.8%
9. Roanoke, Va.	91.8%
11. Atlanta, Ga.	91.5%
11. Birmingham, Ala.	91.5%

SOURCE: Annemette Sorensen, Karl E. Taeuber, and Leslie J. Hollingsworth, Jr., "Indexes of Racial Residential Segregation for 109 Cities in the United States, 1940 to 1970," in *Sociological Focus,* April 1975.

THE 12 LEAST SEGREGATED CITIES IN THE U.S. WITH POPULATIONS OVER 50,000

	How Many Nonwhites Would Have to Move
1. Cambridge, Mass.	52.6%
2. San Francisco, Calif.	55.5%
3. Sacramento, Calif.	56.3%
4. East Orange, N.J.	60.8%
5. Berkeley, Calif.	62.9%
6. Oakland, Calif.	63.4%
7. Camden, N.J.	67.4%
8. Minneapolis, Minn.	67.9%
9. Yonkers, N.Y.	68.0%
10. Portland, Ore.	69.0%
11. New Haven, Conn.	69.1%
12. Seattle, Wash.	69.2%

SOURCE: Annemette Sorensen, Karl E. Taeuber, and Leslie J. Hollingsworth, Jr., "Indexes of Racial Residential Segregation for 109 Cities in the United States, 1940 to 1970," in *Sociological Focus,* April, 1975.

10 OF THE DIRTIEST
POLITICAL CAMPAIGNS
IN MODERN
AMERICAN HISTORY

1. GROVER CLEVELAND v. JAMES G. BLAINE, U.S. PRESIDENTIAL ELECTION (1884)

Blaine supporters discovered that Cleveland, who was a bachelor at the time, had fathered a son by Mrs. Maria Crofts Halpin, an attractive widow who had been on friendly terms with several politicians. Subsequently, Republicans tried to pin an immorality tag on Democrat Cleveland by distributing handbills showing an infant labeled "One more vote for Cleveland" and by having paraders chant, "Ma, Ma, where's my pa? Gone to the White House, ha, ha, ha!" The move, however, backfired badly. Rather than deny the story, Cleveland decided to tell the truth and admit the intimacy. This candor helped defuse the issue, and Cleveland was elected president.

2. ROBERT R. REYNOLDS v. CAMERON MORRISON, U.S. SENATORIAL PRIMARY ELECTION (1932)

In an attempt to oust incumbent Senator Morrison, Reynolds stumped the state of North Carolina exploiting the senator's supposed Communist leanings and his self-indulgent ways. While speaking to rural Tarheel voters, Reynolds would flourish a jar of Russian caviar and say: "Cam eats fish eggs, and Red Russian fish eggs at that, and they cost two dollars. Do you want a senator who ain't too high and mighty to eat good old North Carolina hen eggs, or don't you?" Voters preferred hen eggs and Reynolds.

3. THE PENDERGAST MACHINE v. THE FUSIONIST PARTY, KANSAS CITY MUNICIPAL ELECTION (1934)

Kansas City Democratic boss Thomas Pendergast had to fend off a serious challenge in the municipal election from a fusion ticket—a combination of antimachine Democrats and the bulk of Kansas City's moribund GOP. Worried that the 50,000-plus names with which he had padded the registration books would not be enough, Pendergast had hoodlums in black limousines without license plates shoot up the Fusionist party headquarters on election day. Hundreds of poll watchers were beaten with rifle butts; four people died and eleven people were hospitalized, including a reporter for the Kansas City *Star*. When the polls closed, all but two of the ten Pendergast candidates had been swept to victory. With his grip on Kansas City secure, Pendergast was able to deliver large numbers of votes to get his man, Harry Truman, elected to the U.S. Senate.

4. UPTON SINCLAIR v. FRANK MERRIAM, CALIFORNIA GUBERNATORIAL ELECTION (1934)

In the Republicans' all-out effort to discredit Democratic nominee Sinclair, passages taken from his books were quoted out of context to suggest he was an advocate of free love, an opponent of the Boy Scouts, and a menace to organized religion. Some 2,000 billboards proclaimed that he would turn the state over to the unemployed. In addition, Louis B. Mayer, who was both state GOP chairman and president of M-G-M, ordered theaters to show "news-reels" designed to slander Sinclair. In one of them, an interviewer asked voters whom they were for. A grandmotherly-type interviewee, standing before a California bungalow, said that she supported Merriam "because this little home may not be much, but it is all I have in this world." In contrast, a seedy, unkempt man announced his support for Sinclair, commenting that "his system vorked vell in Russia, so vy can't it vork here?" By election day, on which Sinclair was soundly beaten, the Republicans had spent $10 million—a California record not yet broken.

5. EUGENE TALMADGE v. JAMES V. CARMICHAEL, GEORGIA GUBERNATORIAL PRIMARY ELECTION (1946)

Always eager to engage in race-baiting, former Governor Talmadge attempted to identify Carmichael with integration and northern liberals by hiring a Carmichael look-alike to drive around the state in a limousine. In the backseat were two Amos 'n' Andy caricature blacks, whose sole function was to puff cigars lazily while the ersatz Carmichael introduced himself to shocked gas station attendants. Talmadge lost the popular vote, but he won the primary on September 17 due to the unit rule, a system similar to that of the electoral college. Ironically, although Talmadge also won the general election, he was never sworn in. He died in December, 1946, of a liver ailment.

6. LYNDON JOHNSON v. COKE STEVENSON, U.S. SENATORIAL PRIMARY ELECTION (1948)

During a runoff Senate primary fight with former Texas Governor Stevenson, early indications were that Congressman Johnson had lost. Six days later, however, Precinct 13 in the border town of Alice, Tex., showed a very interesting result. Exactly 203 people had voted at the last minute—in the order they were listed on the tax rolls—and 202 of them had voted for Johnson. While Stevenson protested, Supreme Court Justice Hugo Black upheld the result, and Johnson squeaked by with an 87-vote victory. For this feat, columnist Drew Pearson gave Johnson the sobriquet Landslide Lyndon. It was not until July 30, 1977, that Luis Salas, the election judge in Alice, admitted that he and southern Texas political boss George Parr (who had killed himself in 1975) had rigged the election.

7. CLAUDE PEPPER v. GEORGE SMATHERS, U.S. SENATORIAL PRIMARY ELECTION (1950)

At the start of the McCarthy era, Floridian Claude Pepper, one of the Senate's most outspoken liberals, was on the conservatives' "hit list" along with many other senators. George Smathers lashed out with some typical right-wing invective—he called his opponent "the Red Pepper"—and he launched a campaign to expose Pepper's secret "vices." Smathers disclosed that Pepper was "a known ex-travert," his sister was a "thespian," and his brother a "practicing homo sapiens." Also, when Pepper went to college, he actually "matriculated." Worst of all, he "practiced celibacy" before marriage. Naturally, rural voters were horrified, and Pepper lost.

8. MILLARD TYDINGS v. JOHN M. BUTLER, U.S. SENATORIAL ELECTION (1950)

Senator Tydings, a conservative Democrat from Maryland, had been chosen to head a Senate subcommittee to investigate Wisconsin Senator Joseph McCarthy's charges of Communist infiltration in the State Dept. Tydings's findings were negative: McCarthy's charges were not only "a fraud and a hoax" but "perhaps the most nefarious campaign of half-truths and untruths in the history of this Republic." Seeking revenge, the Wisconsin senator and his supporters descended on Maryland to insure that Butler would defeat Tydings in his bid for reelection. A photograph of American Communist leader Earl Browder was superimposed next to a picture of Tydings, who then appeared to be gazing intently at Browder. Over 300,000 copies of this doctored photograph were circulated statewide, and a resultant fear that a Communist sympathizer might be reelected to office spread. This was enough to force the senator of 24 years' standing into retirement.

9. BENJAMIN ADAMOWSKI v. DANIEL P. WARD, ILLINOIS STATE ATTORNEY ELECTION (1960)

Mayor Richard J. Daley was determined to get rid of Republican Adamowski, who, as state's attorney of Cook County, was investigating corruption in the Chicago Police Dept. Daley turned his machine on full force, and Ward managed to beat Adamowski by 25,000 votes. Adamowski called for a recount, and Daley obliged—at the rate of one precinct a day. With 3,148 precincts, the recount would have taken over eight years. Adamowski managed to get the election board to speed things up, and after 900 precincts had been counted, the margin had been narrowed to 15,000. Adamowski ran out of money for the recount, however, and a special election commission—chaired by a Daley-machine judge—dismissed contempt charges against 600 people charged with vote fraud and seated Ward.

10. CREEP v. THE DEMOCRATIC PARTY CANDIDATES, U.S. PRESIDENTIAL PRIMARY ELECTION (1972)

To ensure President Richard M. Nixon's reelection, White House aides used funds from the Committee for the Re-election of the President (CREEP) to hire Nixon aide Donald Segretti to recruit and organize teams of saboteurs. For openers, the "Dirty Tricks" teams planted the so-called "Canuck Letter" (*Canuck* is a derogatory term for French Canadians). This was designed to hurt Democratic front-runner Edmund S. Muskie among American voters of French-Canadian descent in the crucial New Hampshire primary. In the Florida primary, Segretti's people exploited local anti-busing sentiment by arranging for the distribution of hundreds of posters that said, "Help Muskie in Busing More Children Now." Another Segretti effort in Florida was the dissemination of spurious Muskie literature which accused one candidate—Sen. Henry M. Jackson—of fathering a child out of wedlock in 1929 and of being arrested as a homosexual in 1955 and 1957. It also accused Sen. Hubert Humphrey of having "a well-known call girl" in his car when he was picked up on drunken driving charges in 1967. All of the charges were totally false, but these unscrupulous tactics helped knock Muskie out of the running and ruin the other candidates' chances.

—M.S.

12 GREAT SLIPS OF THE TONGUE IN AMERICAN POLITICS

1. "The United States has much to offer the third world war." (Ronald Reagan, speaking in 1975 on third-world countries; he repeated the error nine times.)

2. "Thank you, Governor Evidence." (President Richard Nixon, referring to Washington Governor Dan Evans in a speech during the Watergate scandal in 1974.)

3. "That is a discredited president." (President Richard Nixon, meaning "discredited precedent," in a speech during the Watergate scandal in 1974.)

4. "I hope that Spiro Agnew will be completely exonerated and found guilty of the charges against him." (John Connally, attempting to defend the scandal-plagued Vice-President in a speech in 1973.)

5. "My heart is as black as yours." (Mario Procaccino, Democratic candidate for mayor of New York, addressing a group of black voters in 1969.)

6. "Frank O'Connor grows on you, like a cancer." (Mario Procaccino, Democratic candidate for mayor of New York, offering an endorsement to a fellow Democrat and political ally in 1965.)

7. "Get this thing straight once and for all. The policeman isn't there to create disorder. The policeman is there to preserve disorder." (Mayor Richard J. Daley of Chicago, defending the actions of his policemen during the Democratic convention in 1968.)

8. "They have vilified me, they have crucified me. Yes, they have even criticized me." (Mayor Richard J. Daley, attacking his opponents.)

9. "Many Americans don't like the simple things. That's what they have against we conservatives." (Republican presidential candidate Barry Goldwater, speaking during the 1964 campaign.)

10. "Why thresh old straw, or beat an old bag of bones?" (Sen. Everett Dirksen of Illinois, defending Clare Boothe Luce during the debate over her nomination as ambassador to Brazil in 1959.)

11. "The right to suffer is one of the joys of a free economy." (Howard Pyle, adviser to President Eisenhower, philosophizing during the 1956 presidential campaign.)

12. "The police are fully able to meet and compete with the criminals." (John F. Hylan, mayor of New York, commenting on a crime wave in 1922.)

—E.F.

DONALD LAMBRO'S 8 LEAST NEEDED U.S. GOVERNMENT PROGRAMS AND AGENCIES

A Washington-based reporter for United Press International, Donald Lambro has spent many years delving into the federal government's waste of the taxpayer's dollar. In his book *The Federal Rathole*, Lambro names over 1,000 areas of federal activity—including programs, agencies, commissions, and bureaus—that should be abandoned. Wasteful government spending costs the American taxpayers over $25 billion each year.

1. THE SMALL BUSINESS ADMINISTRATION

Despite the outlay of tens of billions of tax dollars in loans and loan guarantees at subsidized rates, less than 1% of America's eligible businesses have been helped by the SBA. Its history—scarred by several major congressional investigations—is littered with corruption, widespread mismanagement, and political favoritism. Contrary to the belief that SBA helps low- and middle-income business people, its aid has gone increasingly to upper-income entrepreneurs, many with six-figure incomes. Of 2,400 firms receiving aid for minority-run businesses, only about 30 are known to still exist. Cost: $1.7 billion per year.

2. THE INTERSTATE COMMERCE COMMISSION

This rate-fixing agency is adding billions of dollars in additional costs to virtually everything consumers buy. The oldest of the regulatory agencies, the ICC has become a captive of the trucking industry it is charged with regulating. Under its anachronistic and costly regulations, trucks are required to make uneconomical semifilled hauls and empty backhauls, often on roundabout routes that waste energy and capital. Far worse, the ICC's cartel-protecting decrees have frozen out independent truckers who could offer, through competition, cheaper and more efficient service. Cost: $66.3 million per year.

3. FEDERAL REVENUE SHARING

Begun in 1972, this program is giving over $6.8 billion a year to the nation's states and localities with no strings attached. The money has been spent on everything from municipal golf courses to city hall salaries. But the fact remains that the government has no money to share. Because Washington is operating at an annual deficit, the funds for this program, like many others, must be borrowed at enormous cost to taxpayers. Federal borrowing costs in the fiscal year 1979 were nearly $53 billion. By 1980 interest payments were over $57 billion for the year. Even worse, revenue sharing is going to many states and cities that do not need it. At the end of fiscal 1978, the states enjoyed an aggregate budget surplus of $9 billion, while the federal debt that year was nearly $49 billion. Without revenue sharing, the government's assistance to the states and localities is still impressive: an estimated $83 billion in fiscal 1980.

4. THE OVERSEAS PRIVATE INVESTMENT CORPORATION

OPIC has been selling billions of dollars worth of insurance abroad, providing policies to protect America's biggest multinational corporations against the risks of war, expropriation of property, and currency inconvertibility. Created in 1969 to provide insurance, loans, and loan guarantees for U.S. investors abroad, OPIC has customers that come primarily from *Fortune*'s list of 500 biggest companies and 50 richest banks. An example of an OPIC loan: $414,000 that went to a pleasure-dome resort in Haiti where for $150 a day vacationers enjoy the "elegant, exotic, and erotic," according to the advertising. Cost: little in actual appropriations, but there are millions of dollars outstanding in unsettled claims and guarantees, and potentially billions in future losses to the U.S. Treasury.

5. FEDERAL MOVIEMAKING

No one knows exactly how many films are being produced each year and at what cost, but since W.W. I the government has made an estimated 100,000 films on everything from toothbrushes to soybeans. There have been 585 dental films, including at least 12 films on how to brush your teeth. Four of the 10 major agencies within the Health, Education, and Welfare Dept. have their own filmmaking facilities and equipment. One congressional study found 45 major agencies making films, with at least 1,461 employees supervising the activity. Cost: $150 million per year.

6. MILITARY SERVANTS

Pentagon regulations allow 500 generals and admirals to use enlisted servicemen as servants—valets, social secretaries, cooks, waiters, errand boys, grocery shoppers, chauffeurs, lawn keepers, bartenders at parties, even butlers. Under present pay scales, with housing and other allowances and benefits, our top brass are financially able to hire their own servants, or as one veteran House committee chairman once growled, "They can mow their own lawn." Current estimated cost: $5 million per year.

7. THE NATIONAL INSTITUTE OF EDUCATION

A Senate subcommittee, after examining the research projects funded by this agency, told Congress that "the dismantling of NIE and a return of research activities to their appropriate bureau in the Office of Education . . . may well be the wisest possible course of action." NIE was created to find ways to improve teaching concepts and methods. An examination of NIE's ongoing projects reveals studies on such topics as the political attitudes of college professors and a "Legal History of American Colleges and Universities." The senators were correct when they said the NIE's research was "extrinsic to the real needs of our nation's education system." But the program goes on. Cost: $80 million per year.

8. THE ECONOMIC RESEARCH SERVICE

The ERS is the Agriculture Dept.'s research and analysis arm. It employs 534 economists among a total staff of over 1,000 persons. Many of its studies are prepared expressly for commodity and trade associations, which gladly accept them free of charge. Thus, the wool industry is provided with a study on wool exports. The Potato Chip Institute gets a study on growing vegetable oil markets. The milk producers receive a report on the dairy industry. The ERS is unnecessary because, in the opinion of one top Agriculture Dept. official, the nation's agricultural industries could provide most if not all of this data research and market analysis for themselves. Cost: $28 million per year.

—Exclusive for *The Book of Lists* 2

15 TOP LEISURE-TIME ACTIVITIES OF AMERICAN MEN AND WOMEN

Between June 15 and July 7, 1978, the ABC News–Harris Survey polled a cross section of 1,442 adults nationwide as follows: "I'm going to read you a list of things other people say they do with their leisure time. As I read each one, tell me whether you do it frequently, occasionally, seldom, or not at all." Here are the things men and women say they do most frequently.

MEN

Rank	Activity	
1	Eating	54%
2	Watching television	41%
2	Fixing things around the house	41%
4	Listening to the radio	39%
5	Listening to music at home	35%
6	Reading books	30%
6	Outdoor activities such as hiking, fishing, hunting, or boating	30%
8	Having sex	29%
9	Social activities such as dining out, going dancing, giving or attending parties	25%
10	Participating in sports like golf, tennis, swimming	23%

Rank	Activity	
11	Hobbies such as photography, woodwork, etc.	22%
12	Trying to earn extra money	19%
13	Taking naps	17%
13	Participating in church or club activities	17%
13	Just getting away for a change in scenery	17%

WOMEN

Rank	Activity	
1	Eating	54%
2	Reading books	47%
3	Listening to music at home	42%
4	Watching television	40%
4	Listening to the radio	40%
6	Fixing things around the house	31%
7	Participating in church or club activities	28%
8	Social activities such as dining out, going dancing, giving or attending parties	25%
9	Having sex	22%
10	Hobbies such as photography, woodwork, etc.	19%
11	Participating in sports like golf, tennis, swimming	15%
11	Trying to earn extra money	15%
11	Continuing your education	15%
14	Just getting away for a change in scenery	14%
15	Outdoor activities such as hiking, fishing, hunting, or boating	13%

SOURCE: Louis Harris, *The ABC News–Harris Survey*, vol. I, no. 1. New York: Chicago Tribune–New York News Syndicate, January 1, 1979.

30 MOST COMMON STREET NAMES IN THE U.S.

How creative are we in naming our streets? According to Andy Rooney, commentator for CBS's *60 Minutes*, not very. "In most countries, the great streets have memorable names. London, for instance, has a lot of them—Bond Street, Fleet Street, Carnaby Street, Piccadilly. Paris has the Champs Élysées. What do we have? Michigan Boulevard, Sunset Boulevard. In New York, some of the great streets don't even have names; they have numbers—Fifth Avenue. Some of the numbers are even dull—42nd Street. Would you write a song about a street with a name like that?" The following most common street names certainly bear out Mr. Rooney's comments. They were collected by the U.S. Post Office from their *ZIP Code Directory* and are based on the number of cities out of a possible 370 which have a street by that name.

1. Park	11. Pine	21. 5th
2. Washington	12. Cedar	22. Chestnut
3. Maple	13. Sunset	23. 4th
4. Oak	14. Jackson	24. Adams
5. Lincoln	15. Franklin	25. Virginia
6. Walnut	16. Willow	26. Linden
7. Elm	17. 3rd	27. Woodland
8. Jefferson	18. Wilson	28. Cherry
9. Highland	19. 2nd	29. Rose
10. Madison	20. Laurel	30. 1st

If you're wondering where Main Street is, it is no. 32.

13 AMERICAN THOROUGHFARES WITH UNUSUAL NAMES

Thoroughfare	Location	Zip Code
1. CINDERELLA DRIVE	Chattanooga, Tenn.	37409

A reminder of the time a half-century ago when an imaginative real estate developer laid out a subdivision he called Fairyland. Glass Slipper Trail is near Cinderella Drive, and Wendy Lane and Tinkerbell Circle are not far away.

2. FESSENDEN STREET	Portland, Me.	04103

Though William Pitt Fessenden, a 19th-century senator from Maine, may not be well known today, he has left his mark on Portland, where three adjacent streets are named William, Pitt, and Fessenden in his honor.

3. FUSELAGE AVENUE	Baltimore, Md.	21220

The main street of Aero Acres, a development built by the Glenn L. Martin Company to house W.W. II workers employed in making the Martin bomber, components of which furnished the street names. Left and Right Wing Drive bisect Fuselage Avenue. There is also a Cockpit Street, a Propeller Drive, and a Dihedral Drive.

4. HALA DRIVE	Honolulu, Hawaii	96817

A bit of sly pornography, ancient Hawaiian style, *hala* is a euphemism for the dangling part of the male body.

5. HAVETEUR WAY	San Diego, Calif.	92123

Pronounced "have-it-your-way," it was so named by a tract developer with an addiction to puns who saw to it that Unida (you-need-a) Place and Haveteur Way intersected.

6. LAZY Y STREET   Cheyenne, Wyo.   82001

There is a section of Cheyenne where the streets are named for cattle brands, such as the Lazy Y. Others are A Bar A, Rocking R, T Rail T, and Flying H.

7. MONTMORENCY STREET   George, Wash.   98824

George, Washington, is the creation of Charlie Brown, a shoe salesman and pharmacist from nearby Quincy, Wash. He developed it after buying the land from the federal government for $100,000. Brown named the embryonic town and then named the streets after varieties of cherries such as Bing, Lambert, and Montmorency, which is said to have been the species young George chopped down and did not lie about.

8. NAMELESS STREET   Manning, Ia.   51455

After designating the streets running east and west as First, Second, Third, etc., and those running north and south as girls—May, June, Sue, Anne, etc.—whoever named the streets in Manning, Ia., apparently got tired.

9. SHE STREET   Hanover, Ind.   47243

A street lined with sorority houses and other coed residences, She Street is now part of an expanded Hanover College campus.

10. 326TH STREET   Toledo, O.   43611

One would think that this high-number street would be in a larger city than Toledo, but New York's 264th Street, Chicago's 146th Street, and Los Angeles's 142nd Street present no challenge to

44

Toledo's 326th Street for the distinction of being the highest-numbered street in the U.S.

11. 2½ STREET   Austin, Tex.   78702

   Things grow big in Texas, but the state capital has a street with this tiny fractional name.

12. TYMAN PLACE   Faribault, Minn.   55021

   Local legend has it that the name originates from the fact that the construction boss told the crew making the street to report on the next day at the same "time and place."

13. WONG WAY   Riverside, Calif.   92501

   Named for a Mr. Wong, an eccentric recluse who lived in a nearby building.

—R.C.B.

7 LITTLE-KNOWN PEOPLE WHO INSTIGATED IMPORTANT U.S. SUPREME COURT DECISIONS

1. *MARBURY* v. *MADISON* (1803)

A decision that was to rebound on Presidents John Adams and Richard M. Nixon was triggered in the fading hours of the Adams administration when Adams appointed more than 50 judges to newly created jobs. Last-minute pressures prevented confirmation of these "midnight judges," who, Adams hoped, would carry forth the principles of his defeated Federalist party. On his first day in office (1801), incoming President Thomas Jefferson discovered Adams's list of nominees and refused to accept them. In time, Jefferson did reappoint most of Adams's choices, omitting only four men, among them banker and landowner William Marbury, who had been appointed a justice of the peace. Marbury sued James Madison, Jefferson's secretary of state, contending that Jefferson's presidential action defied an action of the legislative branch of government. The resultant decision, reached after the case dragged on for two years, still stands as the most important in United States history. Reached unanimously and delivered by Chief Justice John Marshall, it held that the court has the constitutional right to "judicial review" of acts of the legislature, a right also extended to include the administrative branch of government. Plaintiff Marbury and Chief Justice Marshall died in the same year—1835.

2. *DRED SCOTT* v. *JOHN SANFORD* (1857)

Dred Scott, an illiterate slave born in 1795 on a plantation owned by Henry Blow in Southampton County, Virginia, was 30 years old when he accompanied his master into free territory that was later to become Minnesota. Returning to Missouri, Scott petitioned for his freedom, basing his claim upon his years of residence in a territory that prohibited slavery under the Missouri Compromise. Eight years later, the Missouri Supreme Court ruled against Scott, contending he was still "property." By a circuitous route, ownership of Scott had by then been transferred to a new master, John Sanford. An appeal by Scott to the U.S. Supreme Court brought about the infamous decision that etched Scott's name in history. In 1857, 80-year-old Chief Justice Roger Taney, presiding over a court which in those days met in a tiny basement room in the Capitol, wrote for the majority that a Negro had "no rights which a white man was bound to respect," adding that blacks were "not the people of the United States" and could not be considered citizens. The outrageous Dred Scott decision further fueled heated pro- and antislavery sentiment and contributed to the start of the Civil War. After passing through many hands, ownership of Dred Scott was returned to Henry Blow, who promptly emancipated him and his family. Scott had one year as a free man in which to enjoy his celebrity. He worked as a moderately ambitious porter in Barnum's Hotel in St. Louis. When he died, Henry Blow paid his funeral expenses. The 13th and 14th Amendments to the Constitution eventually nullified Taney's decision.

L to R—Dred Scott and unidentified friend.

3. *BROWN* v. *BOARD OF EDUCATION* (1954)

Oliver Brown, a 35-year-old black welder of boxcars, was tossed up by history to give his name to the momentous Supreme Court decision ending racial discrimination in public schools. A responsible, religious man, Brown resided in his own home in Topeka, Kans., with his wife and three daughters. Disgusted by a state rule that required seven-year-old Linda to leave home at 7:30 A.M., cross dangerous railroad tracks, and frequently endure cold, rain, or snow while waiting for the bus that would deliver her to her depressing segregated school by 9 A.M., Oliver Brown was ripe for protest when the NAACP took up his case. On a clear September morning, Brown took little Linda's hand and led her up the steps of an all-white school situated three and a half blocks from his house. Together father and daughter entered the school principal's office to enroll Linda in the third grade. Not unexpectedly, Oliver Brown's attempt to register Linda failed. Grouped with similar cases from South Carolina, Virginia, and Delaware, the Brown suit came before the court of Chief Justice Earl Warren. The court's epic decision declared that segregated schools deprived black citizens of equal protection of the law under the 14th Amendment to the Constitution. It broke the back of school systems that deliberately separated black children from their white peers and lighted the way to desegregation of hospitals, parks, public facilities, and the voting places. Brown, who believed God approved of his participation in the case, died in 1961. Linda, now the divorced mother of two, still lives in Topeka, where her children attend public school. A onetime data processor in a Goodyear plant, she resigned to become a university student.

4. *MAPP* v. *OHIO* (1961)

In 1957, Dollree Mapp, a beautiful black divorcée in her late 20s and a onetime companion of ex–light heavyweight champion Archie Moore, was spending the afternoon at home in her two-family house in Shaker Heights, O., when a police sergeant rang her doorbell. The sergeant, acting on an anonymous and unspecific telephone tip, and without a search warrant, made a forced entry into the Mapp home. Exploring the premises, the officer uncovered illegally held pornographic literature. Convicted of illegal possession of lewd material under state law, she appealed to the High Court. In a landmark decision, the court ruled that all states must henceforth abide by federal law as spelled out in the Fourth Amendment to the Constitution, which not only forbids "unreasonable searches and seizures," but also denies the use of evidence so obtained. Dollree Mapp was freed. Nine years after her victory, police in Long Island again entered Ms. Mapp's home. This time, armed with a search warrant, they uncovered a cache of illegal drugs and stolen goods. In 1971 Mapp was convicted of criminal possession of heroin and dealt a sentence of 20 years to life. Determined to be free, she studied law in prison and retained a well-respected attorney for her appeal. Unhappily for Mapp, she remains incarcerated.

5. *GIDEON* v. *WAINWRIGHT* (1963)

In 1962 Clarence Earl Gideon, an obscure convicted felon confined to a Florida state prison for an alleged burglary, applied his pencil to lined sheets of paper and carefully printed a petition to the Supreme Court. Declaring he was too poor to employ counsel, Gideon wrote, "I requested the Florida court to appoint me an attorney, and they refused." Gideon, a tall, skinny, gray-haired man in his 50s with three previous felonies on his record, was a loner; his prison file recorded no name on his mailing or visiting lists. Nonetheless, Gideon yearned for freedom. Aware that poverty had prevented him from hiring counsel, Gideon maintained that no indigent should be denied the constitutional right to due process. To its credit, the Supreme Court plucked Gideon's crude petition from the mass of mail it receives daily and saw merit in his cause. Abe Fortas, who was later to sit on the bench himself, was Gideon's court-appointed counsel (Wainwright, as director of the Florida Division of Corrections, was named defendant), and Gideon's conviction was reversed. Attorney General Robert F. Kennedy declared that Gideon's letter changed the course of American history by establishing the rights of indigents to be provided free legal representation (court appointed) in serious criminal cases. Upon his release, Gideon, the father of three by a previous marriage, remarried and went to work in a gas station in Fort Lauderdale, Fla.

6. *MIRANDA* v. *ARIZONA* (1966)

In 1963 Ernesto Miranda, aged 22, unemployed and under-educated, was arrested for stealing eight dollars from a bank employee in Phoenix, Ariz. A year later Miranda was picked out of a police lineup by a young girl who accused him of kidnapping and rape. Despite Miranda's initial denial of guilt, two hours spent with police interrogators persuaded him to write and sign a confession. However, the Arizona police neglected to advise Miranda of his Fifth Amendment right against self-incrimination. The case moved to the Supreme Court to determine whether the Fifth Amendment, ratified in 1791, extended to "custodial interrogation." Chief Justice Earl Warren held for the court that a suspect must be warned *prior* to interrogation of his right to remain silent as any statement made may be used against him, just as he must also be advised of his right to have an attorney at his side if he so requests. The decision, unpopular with the present court of Chief Justice Warren Burger and with outraged citizens who contend it handicaps arresting officers and coddles criminals, is still on wobbly ground. Although Miranda was the victor in the original case, he was retried when his former common-law wife testified he had confessed the disputed rape to her. This time Miranda was convicted and sentenced to a 20-to-30-year term in Arizona State Prison. In 1972 he was paroled. A brief three years later he got into a fight over a card game and was stabbed to death in a Phoenix skid-row bar. The murder suspects were duly advised of their rights under the Miranda ruling.

7. *UNIVERSITY OF CALIFORNIA* v. *BAKKE* (1978)

An unpredictable twist to the *Brown* v. *Board of Education* drama occurred in 1978, when the Supreme Court was confronted with the case of *Regents of the University of California* v. *Bakke*. The university medical school, in its determination to comply with President John F. Kennedy's call for "affirmative action" in the treatment of minorities, allocated 16 places out of 100 in each new class for "disadvantaged students," a category in which the university included blacks, Chicanos, American Indians, and Asian Americans. Blond, blue-eyed Allan Bakke, aged 33, of Norwegian origin, was an engineer, a former Vietnam marine commander, married, father of three, and unmistakably white. Eager to become a doctor, he applied for admission to the medical school at Davis in 1973 and again in 1974 and each time was rejected. Upon learning he had been passed over in favor of applicants of other races—although his grade average exceeded that of certain "disadvantaged students" who were accepted—Bakke sued the university, claiming "reverse discrimination." The case was heard in the California Supreme Court, and Bakke won. The university then carried the suit to the Supreme Court, which in 1978 ruled for Bakke. In 1979, after an initially frosty reception by much of the student body, Bakke, despite his 15-year absence from academic studies, was holding his own among his classmates and was on his way to fulfilling his personal dream of becoming a physician.

—S.W.

3

IT'S A CRIME

12 MASS MURDERERS WHO GOT THEIR START IN THE U.S. ARMED FORCES

1. ELMER "TRIGGER" BURKE (1917–1958)

While in a U.S. Army ranger battalion during W.W. II, "Trigger" Burke served in Italy, where he charged and destroyed a German machine-gun nest. After the war he became a professional assassin, suspected of six murders. Finally convicted of killing a bartender, he was electrocuted at Sing Sing.

2. DEAN ALLEN CORLL (1940—1973)

Stationed at Fort Hood, Tex., Corll served in the army for a year before getting a hardship discharge. A few years later he moved to Houston where he ran a candy store. Between 1970 and 1973, he sexually assaulted and murdered at least 27 young boys. The grisly spree ended when Corll was killed by one of his two teenage accomplices.

3. ALBERT DeSALVO, "THE BOSTON STRANGLER" (1931–1973)

Enlisting in the U.S. Army at the age of 17, Albert DeSalvo rose to the rank of sergeant in the Military Police before his discharge in 1956. From June, 1962, to January, 1964, he murdered 13 women in the Boston area. Sentenced to life imprisonment in 1967, he was stabbed to death in his cell six years later.

Former army sergeant Albert DeSalvo, better known as "The Boston Strangler," captured while disguised as a navy petty officer, following his escape from a Massachusetts state hospital in 1967.

4. JOHN "LEGS" DIAMOND (1896–1931)

Drafted into the U.S. Army during W.W. I, "Legs" Diamond soon went AWOL. In 1919 he was picked up for desertion and sentenced to a year in Leavenworth. After his release, he became a New York City mobster and was arrested for murder five times before he was killed by fellow gangsters.

5. JOHN DILLINGER (1903–1934)

Wanted by the police for auto theft, John Dillinger joined the U.S. Navy in 1923 and was assigned to the battleship U.S.S. *Utah*. After less than a year, Fireman Third Class Dillinger jumped ship in Boston Harbor and deserted. He was responsible for killing 10 men during his subsequent career as Public Enemy No. 1.

6. ERNEST INGENITO (1925–)

Joining the U.S. Army at the outbreak of W.W. II, Ernest Ingenito served until 1946, when he was dishonorably discharged after having served two years in Leavenworth for assaulting two officers. In 1950 he shot his wife and seven of her relatives. His wife survived, but five of the relatives died. Arrested and judged insane, he was committed to an asylum for life.

7. EDWARD J. LEONSKI (1919–1942)

While attached to a U.S. Army base in Australia, Private Leonski strangled three young Melbourne women in May, 1942. The deranged Leonski admitted to being a "Dr. Jekyll and Mr. Hyde" who had murdered the women "to get their voices." He was found guilty by a U.S. military court and hanged.

8. DR. JEFFREY MacDONALD (1944–)

In the early hours of the morning of February 17, 1970, drug-crazed hippies entered the Fort Bragg, N.C., home of Dr. Jeffrey MacDonald, beat him savagely, and stabbed his 26-year-old wife, Colette, and their two daughters to death. That is the story the Green Beret captain told to army investigators who gave him an honorable discharge. But after reading the army transcripts, Colette Mac-Donald's stepfather, Alfred Kassab, a frozen-egg salesman from Cranbury, N.J., became convinced that Jeffrey—a man whom he had once described as an all-American boy who could be "so charming, butter wouldn't melt in his mouth"—was actually the murderer. Nine and a half years after the crime, MacDonald was brought to trial, convicted of the murders, and sentenced to three consecutive life terms in prison.

9. CARL PANZRAN (1891–1930)

In 1907, while drinking in a saloon in Helena, Mont., Panzran was convinced by a recruiting sergeant to enlist in the U.S. Army. A short time later, he was court-martialed for trying to steal government property and sentenced to three years in Leavenworth. After his release, the former juvenile delinquent became a homosexual rapist and murderer who killed 21 people during the 1920s.

10. JACK SLADE (1824–1864)

After serving in the U.S. Army during the Mexican War, Jack Slade became one of the West's most notorious killers, whose reputation obscured his actual number of victims. Mark Twain, who met Slade in 1861, described him as "so friendly and so gentle-spoken . . . in spite of his awful history." In 1864 Slade was hanged by vigilantes in Virginia City, Mont.

11. HOWARD UNRUH (1921–   )

After serving in the U.S. Army as a tank machine gunner in Italy and during the Battle of the Bulge in Belgium, Howard Unruh was given several commendations and honorably discharged after the war. In 1949, it took him only 12 minutes to shoot and kill 13 people in the streets of Camden, N.J.

12. CHARLES WHITMAN (1941–1966)

Enlisting in the U.S. Marine Corps in 1959, Charles Whitman served until December, 1964, during which time he was rated as a sharpshooter. On the night of July 31, 1966, he murdered his wife and mother. The next morning he carried a small arsenal to the top of the observation tower at the University of Texas in Austin. Before police could stop him, he killed 15 people and injured 31 others.

—R.J.F.

COLIN WILSON'S
10 STRANGEST UNSOLVED
MURDERS IN HISTORY

The son of an English factory worker, Wilson was determined to become "the greatest writer European civilization has produced." At age 24 he won literary acclaim with *The Outsider* (1956), an existentialist book. His ensuing interest in violence as an expression of alienation resulted in the *Encyclopedia of Murder* (1961), a compilation of some 300 criminal cases, coauthored with Patricia Pitman.

1. JACK THE RIPPER (1888)

Jack the Ripper is the obvious name to go at the top of the list, as he is probably the murderer whose name is known in some form in almost every country of the world. More books have been devoted to him than to any other single case. [Jack the Ripper is the name given to an unknown killer who brutally stabbed to death at least five prostitutes in the Whitechapel section of East London. The bodies were horribly mutilated and various internal organs were removed, indicating that the murderer was a doctor or a medical student. The Eds.]

2. THE NEW ORLEANS AXE MAN (1918–1919)

He seems to have been a white man with some kind of curious grudge against Italian grocers! He seems to have killed at least eight people, chiseling his way into their houses through a panel in the back door and attacking them with a hatchet. The murders ceased abruptly in October, 1919—probably because of the death of the axe man—and nothing much seems to be known about motive. It was certainly not money.

3. THE MOONLIGHT MURDERER OF TEXARKANA (1946)

My account of this case in the *Encyclopedia of Murder* is based on the assumption that the man was simply a sadistic sex maniac, an impression I derived from the only account of the case I could find, in a *True Detective* magazine. Subsequent study of actual newspaper accounts of the murders at the time makes me doubtful about this. If sex was involved, they seem curiously reticent about it. It certainly remains one of the classic unsolved cases. [In early 1946, three men and two women were murdered in small towns near the Texas-Arkansas border. The murders occurred on nights when the moon was full. A few days after the last attack, a man fitting the description of the killer committed suicide by throwing himself underneath a moving train. The Eds.]

4. THE CLEVELAND TORSO KILLER (1933–1937)

I used the Cleveland torso murders of the mid-1930s as the basis of my novel *The Glass Cage*, transferring the setting to London and using some of the details of our own Thames nude murders of the 1960s. The unknown killer was obviously a sadistic maniac of enormous strength. What seems curious is that he frequently killed two people at a time, chopped up their bodies, and left them in a heap (mixed up together!) and as often as not kept the heads. The murders ceased abruptly, possibly when the murderer voluntarily had himself incarcerated in a mental home. (The famous policeman Eliot Ness was in charge of the case.) One of the oddest features about the murders is that the killer was probably someone with a home in a fairly quiet street, and he must also have possessed a car. It therefore seems highly probable that he was a man of independent means—and a homosexual.

5. LIZZIE BORDEN (1892)

The Lizzie Borden case needs little comment. While it seems fairly certain that Lizzie committed the murders, no one has ever quite explained how she did it, or what her motive was. [Borden, a 32-year-old spinster, was tried for the hatchet murders of her father and stepmother. Although she was found Not Guilty, it was known that she bitterly resented her stepmother and that she had predicted a family disaster a day before the murders. The Eds.]

6. THE BRIGHTON TRUNK MURDER (1934)

The Brighton trunk murder of 1934 is one of those curious mysteries that *should* have been solved and yet never was. On June 17, 1934, the smell coming from a plywood trunk at the Brighton railway station aroused suspicion. It proved to contain the naked torso of a woman; the legs were found in another suitcase at King's Cross Station. The suntanned skin and the sun-bleached hair suggested that she was probably an upper-class girl in her middle 20s who was about three months pregnant. But in spite of exhaustive police work all over England, the girl was never identified. A certain kind of pure olive oil on the corpse, used by surgeons to stop heavy bleeding, suggested that the murderer could have been a medical man. The trunk was brought into Brighton, yet the police found evidence to suggest that the murderer had traveled with it from Dartford, in Kent, by way of London Bridge. Another baffling touch! Years of police investigation failed to reveal the slightest clue to the murderer or to the identity of the murdered girl, although both probably belonged to the "leisured class." This makes the failure to identify the girl even more baffling. It has been called the perfect murder.

7. THE BLACK DAHLIA (1947)

The Black Dahlia case, which took place in Los Angeles in January, 1947, is basically of psychological interest. The murder was exceptionally violent and cruel—the body had been cut in two at the waist, and the girl (Elizabeth Short) had been suspended upside down and tortured while still alive. Again, police investigations turned up almost no clues. But in subsequent years an enormous number of false confessions to the murder were made—curious evidence of how far it exerted a kind of morbid fascination. The murderer actually sent the police the girl's address book and birth certificate and every name of a man mentioned in the address book was followed up—to no effect. Significantly, one page of the address book had been removed.

8. THE WALLACE CASE (1931)

The murder of Julia Wallace is probably the "classic" English domestic murder case as the Lizzie Borden case is America's classic. It reads exactly like a detective story: the mysterious phone call to the Chess Club asking Wallace to visit an address that later turned out to be nonexistent, the murder of his wife while he was out looking for the nonexistent address, the extremely violent nature of the murder, and the complete absence of motive. Wallace himself was, of course, tried and acquitted, and in my opinion he was probably innocent. Some contemporary students of murder are convinced that the killer is, in fact, still alive and living in South London—but the man refuses to be interviewed. Even so, no one seems to know what his motive could have been.

9. THE MELBOURNE MYSTERY (1953)

I include the Melbourne mystery as an Australian equivalent of the Black Dahlia murder. Fourteen-year-old Shirley Collins set out to go to her first grown-up party on September 12, 1953. The boy who had invited her was due to meet her off the train at Richmond, near Melbourne, at eight o'clock that evening. She never arrived, and on Monday morning her naked body was found 40 mi. from Melbourne. She had been battered to death with beer bottles, and then slabs of concrete had been dropped on her head, completely crushing it. Although her clothes were scattered all around, there were no signs of sexual interference. The mystery here is what happened to Shirley between the time she left her mother at the bus stop near her home at seven o'clock and her death a few hours later. Being a shy girl, she would certainly not have gone off with a stranger. On the other hand, before she left her mother, she commented that she had plenty of time because she was going to meet her boyfriend Ron at West Richmond Station. In fact, this is a completely different place from Richmond Station, where Ron was waiting for her. So she may have gone to the wrong station and hung around waiting for him. Even so, it remains puzzling why she didn't simply take a train back home when she realized that he wasn't going to turn up.

10. THE THAMES NUDE MURDERS (1959–1965)

The Thames nude murders—the murderer became known in the newspapers as Jack the Stripper—took place in London between June, 1959, and February, 1965. All victims were prostitutes, and the method of the murders was probably unique; in most cases, the woman had apparently been asked to perform an act of fellatio on the killer, and then was choked by having her head forced down on his penis. There was a persistent rumor at the time that the murderer was the well-known boxer Freddie Mills, who died shortly afterward. The murderer was obviously a man who drove some kind of a van and who drove around a great deal at night. In one case, the police actually managed to locate the place where one of the bodies had been kept—a warehouse on an industrial estate—but even this brought them no closer to finding the murderer. John du Rose, the detective in charge of the case, is convinced that the man committed suicide shortly after the last murder and hints that he knows his identity. But, like the Ripper case, this one remains unsolved.

Wilson adds: "There are many other cases that I have considered including: the Hall-Mills case, the Le Touquet, the Luard mystery, the Esther Pay case, the green bicycle mystery, and others. Among puzzling contemporary cases, there's the unsolved zodiac murders of San Francisco, and our contemporary Jack the Ripper of Yorkshire who is still at large."

—Exclusive for *The Book of Lists* 2

WHAT 16 FAMOUS OR INFAMOUS PEOPLE WERE DOING WHEN ARRESTED

1. HARVEY BAILEY (1889–?)

Bank robber Bailey had stolen $2 million in 1930—the largest robbery then on record. He was teeing off at the Old Mission Golf Course in Kansas City, Kans., when FBI agents arrested him—and the other members of his golf foursome, bank robbers Tommy Holden, Francis Keating, and Frank Nash—in 1932.

2. MENAHEM BEGIN (1913–)

On September 20, 1940, the future prime minister of Israel, then active in the Zionist movement, was playing chess with his wife in their home in Lithuania when Russian police broke in and arrested him. As he was dragged away, he called out that he conceded the game.

3. ELMER "TRIGGER" BURKE (1917–1958)

In 1946, after robbing a New York City liquor store, syndicate killer Elmer Burke was standing outside the store holding a gun and thumbing through a wad of bills when a passing policeman arrested him.

4. ALEXANDER DUBČEK (1921–)

Dubček and other members of the Czech Presidium were meeting in Prague on August 20, 1968, when word came that the Soviets had invaded the country. Shortly after 4:30 the next morning, Russian parachutists entered the building and arrested Dubček while he was trying to answer a telephone call. The phone was torn from his hands and the cord was cut.

5–6. EMILY HARRIS (1947–) and WILLIAM HARRIS (1945–)

On September 18, 1975, SLA urban guerrillas Emily and William Harris were jogging back to their apartment at 288 Precita Avenue in San Francisco when FBI agents and police armed with shotguns and submachine guns arrested them.

7. PATRICIA HEARST (1954–)

On September 18, 1975, Patricia Hearst was standing in the kitchen of a San Francisco apartment, talking with fellow fugitive Wendy Yoshimura, when FBI agent Tom Padden stuck a gun through the back door window and yelled, "Don't move or I'll blast your head off." Hearst was so surprised that she wet her pants. She was allowed to change clothes before being taken into custody.

8. NINA HOUSDEN (1919–)

In Toledo, O., in 1947, Nina Housden was sleeping in the front seat of her car, which was being repaired in a service station, when police arrested her for murder. The attendant had discovered the dismembered corpse of her husband wrapped in Christmas paper in the backseat of the car.

9. JAMES EARL RAY (1928–)

In Chicago in 1952, James Earl Ray—who was convicted of assassinating Dr. Martin Luther King, Jr., 16 years later—robbed a cab driver of $11.09. Pursued by the police, he ran down a blind alley and jumped over a fence. However, Ray subsequently tripped and crashed through the basement window of a house—falling directly into a washtub, where police caught him.

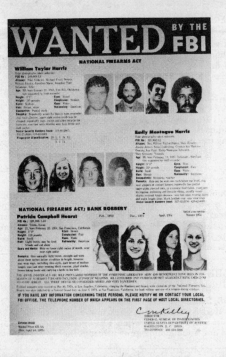

10. MAXIMILIEN ROBESPIERRE (1758–1794)

In 1794 the French dictator Maximilien Robespierre was denouncing and demanding the arrest of his political enemies during a session of the Convention, revolutionary France's legislative assembly, when he was arrested for treason. The day after his arrest, he was guillotined.

11. JULIUS ROSENBERG (1918–1953)

On July 17, 1950, Julius and Ethel Rosenberg were listening to *The Lone Ranger* on the radio when FBI agents arrived and arrested Julius for spying for the Soviet Union. Ethel Rosenberg was arrested less than a month later.

12–13. NICOLA SACCO (1891–1927) and BARTOLOMEO VANZETTI (1888–1927)

On May 5, 1920, in Brockton, Mass., Nicola Sacco and Bartolomeo Vanzetti were riding home in a streetcar, after checking to see whether a friend's car was ready at a repair shop, when police arrested them for robbery and murder.

14. MARQUIS DE SADE (1740–1814)

In 1801, when the police came to arrest him for writing

pornography and committing lewd acts, the Marquis de Sade was consulting with his publisher, Nicolas Massé, who had informed the authorities that De Sade was in his office.

15. JOHN SEADLUND (1910–1938)

After kidnapping and murdering wealthy greeting-card manufacturer Charles Ross in 1937, John Seadlund was placing a $10 bet at the Santa Anita Race Track in California when FBI agents arrested him in 1938.

16. OSCAR WILDE (1854–1900)

In 1895, Oscar Wilde was drinking hock and seltzer and talking to his friend Lord Alfred Douglas at the Cadogan Hotel in London when a Scotland Yard inspector arrested him for sodomy.

—R.J.F.

5 PROMINENT PERSONS PUT ON TRIAL AFTER THEY WERE DEAD

1. FORMOSUS (816?–896), Italian pope

At the instigation of Roman coemperor Lambert, a "cadaveric synod" convened eight months after the pope's death to declare Formosus's five-year pontificate illegal and his acts null and void—chiefly the one that had established Lambert's rival Arnulf as coemperor. Formosus was exhumed and propped in a witness chair while the new pope, Stephen VI, served as prosecutor and a deacon represented the macabre defendant. Found guilty, the corpse was stripped of papal array and tossed into the Tiber River.

2. THOMAS À BECKET (1118?–1170), Archbishop of Canterbury

Becket's influence as a martyr-rebel against the English throne was still so strong 350 years after his death that Henry VIII determined to malign him once and for all—legally. Accordingly, the saint's skeleton was brought before England's Star Chamber, accused of usurping papal authority, and—after a formal trial and defense at public expense—convicted of treason. His bones were publicly burned "to admonish the living of their duty" to the Crown.

3. JOHN WYCLIFFE (1320?–1384), English religious reformer

A constant irritation to the medieval church for his unorthodox views, yet protected by his secular rulers because of his popularity and patriotism, Wycliffe went to the stake 44 years after his death. The Council of Constance in 1415 declared him a heretic and ordered his bones exhumed, burned, and scattered, but sentence was not carried out until 1428.

4. JOAN OF ARC (1412–1431), French heroine

Twenty-four years after Joan died at the stake in Rouen, her case was reopened by Charles VII, the king whom she had crowned and who had then abandoned her to church inquisitors. He appointed three bishops to rehear the case and allowed Joan's family to introduce new evidence. The court annulled the previous verdict, condemning an "atrocious miscarriage of justice." Finally, in 1920, Joan was canonized.

5. MARTIN BORMANN (1900?–1945), German Nazi official

The missing Bormann was tried *in absentia* at the Nuremberg War Crimes Trial in 1946, since there was no proof of his death. His attorney, Dr. Friedrich Bergold, believed his client dead and protested this "quite novel procedure in the legal history of all times." The tribunal convicted Bormann of war crimes and crimes against humanity and sentenced him to hang. Not until 1972 was Bergold's belief confirmed, when workers discovered Bormann's grave on a Berlin construction site.

—J.E.

SIMON WIESENTHAL'S 10 MOST WANTED NAZI FUGITIVES TODAY

Founder and director of the Jewish Documentation Center in Vienna, Wiesenthal is a concentration camp survivor who has spent over 30 years meticulously piecing together evidence that has led to the discovery of almost 1,000 Nazis, including Adolf Eichmann. The task facing him is immense, for the West German government files contain the names of more than 160,000 war criminals still at large. The Laurence Olivier character in the film *The Boys from Brazil* was based on Wiesenthal.

1. HEINRICH MUELLER

Chief of the Gestapo. Fate and whereabouts unknown.

2. RICHARD GLUECKS

Inspector general of all concentration camps. Fate and whereabouts unknown.

3. DR. JOSEF MENGELE

Doctor of concentration camp Auschwitz. Responsible for the deaths of 400,000 people. Lives in Paraguay under the protection of the government.

4. WALTER RAUFF

Head of the branch for gas trucks. Responsible for the deaths of a quarter million people in the gas trucks. He lives in Punta Arenas, Chile. The government refuses extradition.

5. ANTON BURGER

Assistant of Eichmann, deputy commander of Theresienstadt. Escaped from prison in 1948. Whereabouts unknown.

6. ROLF GUENTHER

Eichmann's deputy. Involved in all crimes. Whereabouts unknown.

7. ALOIS BRUNNER

One of Eichmann's deputies. Lives under the name Dr. Fisher in Damascus, Syria. He is responsible for the deaths of thousands of Jews in Czechoslovakia and Greece.

8. JOSEF SCHWAMBERGER

Commander of the ghetto of Przemyśl, Poland. Responsible for the deaths of 15,000 people. Lives somewhere in Argentina.

9. DR. ARIBERT HEIM

Doctor of the concentration camp Mauthausen. Lives somewhere in Europe under a false name.

10. FRIEDRICH WARTZOG

Commander of the concentration camp Lemberg-Janowska, U.S.S.R. He ordered the killing of at least 40,000 people. Whereabouts unknown.

—Exclusive for *The Book of Lists* 2

WANTED: DR. JOSEF MENGELE.
Nazi murderer of 400,000 people.

10 NOTORIOUS CASES
OF TERRIBLE INJUSTICE

1. I. D. COSSON

In August, 1944, 13-year-old I. D. Cosson and his family became the first W.W. II civilian casualties on U.S. soil. Cosson's uncle, father, and two young cousins were killed when an American plane accidentally dropped its bomb load on a small farm just east of Eglin Air Force Base in Florida. Cosson himself barely escaped death; his spine was severed, paralyzing him below the waist. Three years later, the federal government awarded Cosson $3,750 for his injuries, augmented by an additional $15,000 in 1951. However, it was not until June, 1980, that the U.S. Congress voted him an annual allowance of $18,000. Until then, he had been forced to get by on $167 a month Social Security checks.

2. STEPHEN DENNISON

In 1925 at the age of 16, after shoplifting a $5 box of candy from a store in upstate New York, Stephen Dennison was sent to the state reformatory. Two years later he was transferred to the state penitentiary, where, over the years, he broke a number of minor rules. For these infractions, extra time was added to his sentence. Forgotten and ignored by prison bureaucrats, Dennison spent 34 years in prison for originally stealing that box of candy before finally being released in 1959.

3. ALFRED DREYFUS

In 1894 army intelligence officers discovered that a member of the French general staff was giving information to the Germans. Capt. Alfred Dreyfus was promptly arrested for this crime because the treasonous letter was signed with the initial *D*—and because he was the only Jewish officer on the staff. Railroaded through a court-martial in which forged evidence was used against him, Dreyfus was convicted and sent to Devil's Island for life. In 1899 the real traitor, Maj. Marie Charles Esterhazy, confessed, but the French army refused to admit its mistake. However, after four years on Devil's Island, Dreyfus was retried and again convicted. But he was offered clemency and set free. In 1906 the courts reversed his convictions, gave him the Legion of Honor, and promoted him to the rank of major.

4. LEO FRANK

In 1913 in Atlanta, Ga., Leo Frank, a 29-year-old Jewish pencil-factory manager, was arrested for the rape and strangulation-murder of a 13-year-old girl who worked in his factory. The evidence indicated that a janitor named Jim Conley, not Frank, had probably committed the murder. However, mainly because he was a Jew, Frank was convicted and sentenced to hang. In 1915, after Frank's sentence was commuted to life imprisonment, a 40-man mob of middle-class whites stormed the state penitentiary at Milledgeville, seized Frank, took him to the town of Marietta, and lynched him.

60

5. LEONARD HANKINS

In 1933 Leonard Hankins was convicted for robbing a bank and murdering two policemen and a passerby in Minneapolis, Minn. Three years later the FBI arrested Jess Doyle, who confessed to the crimes for which Hankins had been imprisoned. The FBI advised the Minneapolis police of Hankins's innocence, but the local authorities refused to release him because the FBI would not give them its file on Doyle. Even though the FBI had pronounced him guiltless, Hankins spent another 15 years in prison before being pardoned in 1951.

6. JULIUS KRAUSE

In 1931, at the age of 18, Julius Krause and another man were arrested, convicted, and imprisoned for murder and the robbery of a store clerk in Ohio. Four years later, just before he died, the other man told prison officials that Krause was innocent and that his real accomplice in the murder was a man named Curtis Kuermerle. However, the police did nothing about this deathbed confession. Finally, after nine years in prison, Krause escaped, found Kuermerle, persuaded him to confess, and turned himself and Kuermerle in to the authorities. Even though Kuermerle was convicted for the same murder that Krause supposedly had committed, the courts refused to review Krause's case, and he spent another 11 years in prison before being paroled in 1951.

7. SAMUEL A. MUDD

On the night of April 14, 1865, Dr. Samuel Mudd set the broken leg of presidential assassin John Wilkes Booth. Ten days later Mudd was arrested, and on May 10, 1865, he and seven other suspected associates of Booth were led into a military courtroom to face charges of "conspiring . . . to kill and murder . . . Abraham Lincoln." Although the conspiracy charges were never proved, Mudd was found guilty and sentenced to life imprisonment on Garden Key Island—one of the Dry Tortugas Islands off Florida. During the next four years he tirelessly ministered to victims of the yellow fever epidemics that swept through the prison. Mudd was pardoned by President Andrew Johnson in March, 1869, but he returned home to Maryland "frail, weak, and sick . . . never to be strong again."

8. JAMES MONTGOMERY

In 1923 in Waukegan, Ill., a 62-year-old mentally deranged white woman named Mamie Snow claimed that she had been raped by James Montgomery, a 26-year-old black man. After a 20-minute trial Montgomery was convicted because the prosecutor, who was a member of the Ku Klux Klan, suppressed a medical report that showed that Miss Snow was still a virgin. After spending 26 years in prison for a crime that had never occurred, Montgomery was granted a retrial and was acquitted in 1949.

9. GABRIELLE RUSSIER

In 1968 in Marseilles, France, Gabrielle Russier, a 31-year-old teacher, and her pupil Christian Rossi, a 16-year-old Maoist, became lovers. Their affair outraged not only Christian's parents but also the legal authorities, with the result that Christian was sent to a home for juvenile delinquents and later to a mental hospital, where he was forced to take "sleep cures." Harassed by the police, Gabrielle was arrested for corrupting a minor and sent to Les Baumettes penitentiary. Unable to face the loss of her lover, her career, and her physical and mental health because of her imprisonment, Gabrielle committed suicide in 1969.

French schoolteacher
Gabrielle Russier

. . . and her student-lover
Christian Rossi.

10. THE SCOTTSBORO BOYS

In 1931 near Scottsboro, Ala., nine black youths—Haywood Patterson, Clarence Norris, Charley Weems, brothers Andrew and Leroy Wright, Ozie Powell, Willie Roberson, Olen Montgomery, and Eugene Williams—were arrested for raping two white women while traveling in a freight car through northern Alabama. Despite medical reports which showed that neither woman had been raped, all nine were convicted. Eight were sentenced to death, but a 13-year-old defendant was given life imprisonment. After a series of retrials in 1933, 1936, and 1937, only four of them were released, even though one of the women admitted that she had not been raped. In 1943, 1946, and finally in 1950, three more were paroled. The eighth, Haywood Patterson, escaped from prison in 1948, committed a crime in Michigan, and died in prison there in 1952. The ninth, Clarence Norris, was paroled in 1946, but he broke parole and became a fugitive until 1976, when he was given a full pardon by Gov. George Wallace. It had taken 45 years to close the Scottsboro case.

—R.J.F.

4
A STATE OF WAR—
AND DISASTER

10 MEN WHO CONQUERED
THE MOST SQUARE MILES

1. GENGHIS KHAN (1162–1227)

From 1206 to 1227, Mongol chieftain Genghis Khan conquered approximately 4,860,000 sq. mi. Stretching from the Pacific Ocean to the Caspian Sea, his empire included northern China, Mongolia, southern Siberia, and central Asia.

2. ALEXANDER THE GREAT (356–323 B.C.)

From 334 to 326 B.C., the Macedonian king Alexander the Great conquered approximately 2,180,000 sq. mi. His empire included the southern Balkan peninsula, Asia Minor, Egypt, and the entire Near East as far east as the Indus River.

3. TAMERLANE (1336?–1405)

From 1370 to 1402, the Islamic turkicized Mongol chieftain Tamerlane conquered approximately 2,145,000 sq. mi. His empire included most of the Near East, from the Indus River to the Mediterranean Sea and from the Indian Ocean north to the Aral Sea.

4. CYRUS THE GREAT (600?–529 B.C.)

From 559 to 539 B.C., the Persian king Cyrus the Great conquered approximately 2,090,000 sq. mi. He conquered the Median Empire, Babylonia, Assyria, Syria, Palestine, the Indus Valley, and southern Turkestan.

5. ATTILA (406?–453)

From 433 to 453, Attila, king of the Huns and the Scourge of God, conquered approximately 1,450,000 sq. mi. Although he failed in his attempt to conquer Gaul, Attila ruled an empire encompassing central and eastern Europe and the western Russian plain.

6. ADOLF HITLER (1889–1945)

From 1933 to the fall of 1942, Nazi dictator Adolf Hitler conquered 1,370,000 sq. mi., all of which he lost within three years. Hitler's Third Reich included most of continental Europe and extended from the English Channel to the outskirts of Moscow and from North Africa to Norway.

7. NAPOLEON BONAPARTE (1769–1821)

From 1796 to the height of his power in 1810, Napoleon

Bonaparte conquered approximately 720,000 sq. mi. Napoleon's Grand Empire included France, Belgium, Holland, Germany, Poland, Switzerland, and Spain.

8. MAHMUD OF GHAZNI (971?–1030)

From 997 to 1030, Mahmud, the Muslim sultan and Afghan king of Ghazni, conquered 680,000 sq. mi. His Near Eastern empire extended from the Indian Ocean north to the Amu Darya River and from the Tigris River east to the Ganges River in India.

9. FRANCISCO PIZARRO (1470?–1541)

From 1531 to 1541, Spanish adventurer Francisco Pizarro conquered 480,000 sq. mi. Employing treachery and assassination, and taking advantage of internal discord, he subjugated the Inca Empire, which extended from Ecuador south through the Andes to Bolivia.

10. HERNANDO CORTES (1485–1547)

From 1519 to 1526, Hernando Cortes, commanding a small Spanish military expedition, conquered 315,000 sq. mi. Defeating the Aztecs, he seized central and southern Mexico and later subjugated Guatemala and Honduras to Spanish rule.

—R.J.F.

10 MOST DEFEATED NATIONS IN MODERN HISTORY

1. TURKEY

During the 19th century, Turkey lost three wars to Russia—the first in 1812, the second in 1829, and the third in 1878. The Greeks won their independence by defeating the Turks in 1827, while the Egyptians invaded and defeated Turkey in wars fought in 1832, 1839, and 1840. From 1912 to mid-1913, Turkey lost wars to Italy, Greece, Serbia, Bulgaria, and Albania. During W.W. I, Turkey joined the Central Powers and went down to defeat with Germany. Turkey finally won a victory against Greece in 1922.

2. AUSTRIA

Between 1792 and 1814, Austria engaged in—and lost—several disastrous wars with France, and Vienna was twice occupied by French troops. In 1814 Austria won its last victory, entering the war against Napoleon when his eventual defeat had become a certainty. In 1859 Austria lost the Franco-Austrian War after being defeated in two consecutive battles by an allied Franco-Sardinian army. In 1866, in the Austro-Prussian War, the Prussians swiftly defeated the Austrian army. As an ally of Germany during W.W. I, Austria suffered total defeat at the hands of the Allies. As part of Germany during W.W. II, Austria was again defeated by the Allies. Since 1945 Austria has followed a policy of strict neutrality.

3. BOLIVIA

In 1828, three years after winning its independence from Spain, Bolivia was invaded and defeated by Peru. In 1835 Bolivian president Marshal Andrés Santa Cruz successfully united Peru with Bolivia, forming a coalition government known as the Confederation. The alliance lasted until 1839, when Chile took over Bolivia and succeeded in beginning a 50-year exploitation of the country's natural resources. At the outbreak of the War of the Pacific in 1879, Bolivia, once again allied with Peru, suffered a full-scale Chilean invasion and was forced to cede its nitrate-rich Atacama coastal province. From 1932 to 1935, Bolivia fought and lost the brutal, costly Chaco War to Paraguay. Presently ruled by a military junta, Bolivia has lost half its original territory as a result of military defeats since its independence in 1825.

4. EGYPT

Egypt won its independence from Turkey after three wars fought from 1832 to 1840. In 1882 the British defeated the Egyptians and ruled their country until the end of W.W. II. In 1948 Egyptian intervention in the new state of Israel ended in an embarrassing defeat. In 1956 the Israelis, along with British and French expeditionary forces, routed the Egyptian army and seized the Suez Canal in seven days. However, troops were later withdrawn, and the Egyptians kept control of the Suez until 1967, when the Israelis broke their previous record by reaching it in only four days. Although Egypt began the 1973 Yom Kippur War with a successful penetration of Israel's Bar-Lev line along the Suez Canal, the Israeli army quickly recovered and defeated the Egyptians by the end of this 16-day war. Aware that Egypt had lost four wars to the same country in less than 30 years, President Anwar el-Sadat signed a peace treaty with Israel's prime minister Menachem Begin on March 26, 1979.

5. FRANCE

Even though French armies conquered most of Europe during the Napoleonic Wars, France suffered total defeat at Waterloo in 1815. The French imperialistic intervention in Mexico during the 1860s ended in failure, and French troops were forced to withdraw from that country in 1867. During the Franco-Prussian War (1870–1871), the Germans annihilated the French army and occupied northern France. Although France was on the winning side in W.W. I, the victory was so costly in human terms—a whole generation of Frenchmen was virtually wiped out—and achieved so little, that the French themselves later considered it as a defeat. In 1940 the German blitzkrieg swept over France, which was eventually liberated by Anglo-American armies in 1944. In the postwar period, France fought and lost two bloody colonial wars, one in Indochina (1946–1954) and the other in Algeria (1954–1962).

6. BULGARIA

In 1885, seven years after the Russo-Turkish War set up

Bulgaria as an autonomous principality, Bulgaria precipitated a war with Serbia and was defeated. Between 1912 and 1913, during the First Balkan War, Bulgaria—allied with Greece, Serbia, and Montenegro—was victorious over Turkey. However, less than a year later Bulgaria pitted itself against a coalition of Serbia, Greece, Romania, and Turkey during the Second Balkan War and suffered a crushing defeat. During W.W. I, Bulgaria joined the Central Powers and was defeated along with Germany. In W.W. II, Bulgaria again became a German ally and was overrun by the Soviet army in 1944.

7. CHINA

China was defeated by Great Britain in the First Opium War (1839–1842) and by Britain and France in the Second Opium War (1860). Between 1894 and 1895, Japanese armies organized to smash Chinese forces in the Sino-Japanese War. In 1900, British, American, French, Japanese, Russian, and German troops invaded northern China to defeat the armies of the empress during the Boxer Rebellion. In 1931 Japan overran and annexed Manchuria, and in 1937 launched an all-out invasion of China. During W.W. II, Emperor Hirohito's forces occupied large areas of China but were forced to withdraw following Japan's surrender to the U.S.

8. HUNGARY

In 1848 Hungarian patriots raised an army in an attempt to win independence from the Austrian Hapsburgs. A year later, however, the combined Austrian and Russian armies crushed the rebel forces. As a semiautonomous kingdom within the Austrian Empire, Hungary joined the Central Powers against the Allies in W.W. I, only to meet defeat in 1918. In 1919 Hungary lost a short, disastrous war with Romania, Serbia, and Czechoslovakia. During W.W. II, Hungary—now an ally of Nazi Germany—sent troops to the Russian front. The Soviet army invaded Hungary in 1944 and captured Budapest in January, 1945. In 1956 the Hungarians rebelled against continued Soviet domination, but Soviet armored divisions quelled the uprising.

9. FINLAND

As part of the Russian czarist empire, the grand duchy of Finland was defeated by the Germans in W.W. I. Finland was granted independence during the Russian Revolution but was invaded by the Soviet Union in 1939. In the ensuing Russo-Finnish War, only 25,000 Finnish soldiers—compared to 200,000 Soviet troops—were killed. However, Soviet numerical superiority prevailed, and Finland was defeated and forced to cede 10% of its territory to the U.S.S.R. In 1941 Finland became an ally of Nazi Germany and invaded the Soviet Union. The Finns aided the Germans at the siege of Leningrad, but when the tide turned against the Axis powers, Finland was overrun by the Red Army in 1944. Despite the fact that it has lost every war in which it has been involved, Finland has maintained its independence and avoided foreign occupation.

10. GERMANY

Since it was unified as a nation in 1871, Germany has fought two wars and lost both. In the spring of 1918, during W.W. I, Germany appeared to be on the verge of victory after knocking Russia out of the war. However, a few months later the Allies, revitalized by the arrival of the Americans, defeated Germany on the western front. During W.W. II, Germany conquered Poland, France, Denmark, Holland, Belgium, Norway, and the Balkans. But the superior resources and manpower of the U.S. and the Soviet Union resulted in Germany's total defeat in 1945. The cost of its defeats was 1.8 million soldiers killed in W.W. I and 3.5 million in W.W. II, as well as an estimated 10 million civilians who lost their lives in the two wars.

—R.J.F.

8 GENERALS WHO NEVER WON A BATTLE (WHILE GENERAL)

1. REDVERS HENRY BULLER (1839–1908), British

After serving 10 years as a staff officer occupying the posts of British army quartermaster and adjutant general, General Buller was appointed commander in chief of British forces in South Africa at the outbreak of the Boer War. Within several months, Buller lost the battles of Stormberg, Magersfontein, and Colenso, after which he was relieved of his command.

2. JOHN CHARLES FRÉMONT (1813–1890), U.S.

A renowned explorer but an incompetent military commander, John Frémont was given the rank of major general in the Union Army in 1861 and soon after suffered his first defeat at the Battle of Wilson's Creek in Missouri. After a string of defeats to a numerically inferior Confederate army in the Shenandoah Valley, he resigned from the army in 1864.

3. ALEKSEI KUROPATKIN (1848–1921), Russian

As a junior officer, Kuropatkin proved to be a brilliant staff officer and was promoted to the rank of general at the age of 34. Even though he was more of a bureaucrat than a soldier, Kuropatkin was given command of the Russian army in Manchuria at the beginning of the Russo-Japanese War in 1904. During the first year of the war, he lost every battle he fought, including the decisive battles of the Yalu and Mukden. He was relieved of his command in 1905.

4. IRVIN McDOWELL (1818–1885), U.S.

Because of his political connections, Irvin McDowell was promoted from the rank of major to brigadier general at the outbreak of the U.S. Civil War. In 1861, McDowell's Union Army was routed at the First Battle of Bull Run, because of his timidity. At the Second Battle of Bull Run, he was again defeated, after which he was never given another battlefield command.

67

5. PAUL SANFORD METHUEN (1845–1932), British

Following a flamboyant career as a junior officer in Britain's 19th-century colonial wars, Paul Methuen was made a general and given command of the 1st Division of the 1st Army Corps during the Boer War. In 1899, ordering only frontal assaults on the enemy lines, Methuen caused the massacre of his men and lost the battle of Magersfontein. General Buller was his commander and accomplice in the defeat. For almost the next two years, Methuen unsuccessfully chased Boer guerrilla bands until he was captured by them in 1902. Methuen was commander in chief in South Africa (1907–1912) and governor of Malta (1915–1919).

6. HELMUTH VON MOLTKE (1848–1916), German

Even though he had no battlefield experience, General von Moltke was appointed German Army commander in chief in 1906, mainly because he was the nephew and namesake of the Franco-Prussian War hero Count Helmuth von Moltke (1800–1891). In charge of the German invasion of France in 1914, Moltke saw his offensive fail with the German defeat at the Battle of the Marne. Overpowered by a sense of guilt and inferiority after the battle, he had a nervous breakdown and was relieved of his command on November 3, 1914.

7. JAMES WILKINSON (1757–1825), U.S.

A speculator in land and army contracts, Gen. James Wilkinson became the senior officer of the U.S. Army in 1796, even though he was secretly an agent of the Spanish government, which paid him $2,000 a year. During the War of 1812, Wilkinson, commanding an army in battle for the first time, was defeated at Chrysler's Field and at Lacolle Mill, Canada, where 200 British soldiers routed his 4,000-man army. In 1814 he was acquitted by a court-martial and honorably discharged from the army.

8. WILLIAM WINDER (1775–1824), U.S.

During the War of 1812, in his first battle, Gen. William Winder was defeated and captured by the British at the Battle of Stoney Creek, Canada, in 1813. Released by the British, he was appointed inspector general. However, when the British marched on Washington, D.C., in 1814, he was given command of the city's defense. In the subsequent battle he was routed, and the British captured Washington. There was a congressional investigation, but Winder was not blamed for the loss. In 1815 he was honorably discharged.

—R.J.F.

10 COMMANDERS KILLED BY THEIR OWN TROOPS

1. COL. JOHN FINNIS (?–1857), English

On the morning of May 10, 1857, in Meerut, India, Colonel

Finnis, commander of the 11th Native Regiment of the British Indian Army, was informed that his troops had occupied the parade grounds and were in a state of mutiny. He mounted his horse, rode to the parade ground, and began lecturing his troops on insubordination. The inflamed Indian soldiers—known as sepoys—promptly fired a volley at Finnis and killed him. This violent action triggered the Sepoy Mutiny.

2. CAPTAIN GOLIKOV (?–1905), Russian

On June 13, 1905, the crew of the Russian cruiser *Potemkin* mutinied after an unsuccessful protest challenging conditions on the ship. Captain Golikov, the ship's commander, flanked by armed seamen, confronted the mutineers. During the fight that ensued, the mutineers shot Golikov and flung his corpse overboard.

3. KING GUSTAVUS II (1594–1632), Swedish

In 1632, at the Battle of Lützen during the Thirty Years' War, King Gustavus Adolphus was shot in the back while leading his cavalry in a charge against the Catholic armies of the Holy Roman Empire. Who actually killed him remains an unanswered question. However, many historical authorities insist that Gustavus must have been killed by one of his own men, if not accidentally then intentionally by a traitor.

4–5. LT. RICHARD HARLAN and LT. THOMAS DELLWO (?–1971), U.S.

In the early morning hours of March 16, 1971, an enlisted man at the U.S. Army base in Bienhoa, Vietnam, cut a hole through the screen covering a window in the officers' quarters and threw a fragmentation grenade inside. Two lieutenants—Richard Harlan and Thomas Dellwo—were killed. Pvt. Billy Dean Smith was arrested and court-martialed for the crime but later was declared innocent. The real murderer was never found.

6. GEN. THOMAS "STONEWALL" JACKSON (1824–1863), U.S. (Confederate)

On the night of May 2, 1863, at the Battle of Chancellorsville

Confederate Gen. Thomas "Stonewall" Jackson.

during the U.S. Civil War, Confederate general Thomas "Stonewall" Jackson went on a scouting mission ahead of his lines in order to find a way to attack the rear of the Union forces. When he returned, Jackson was fired upon by a North Carolina Confederate regiment which thought he and his staff were Yankee cavalrymen. He died eight days later.

7. CAPTAIN LASHKEVITCH (?–1917), Russian

On March 12, 1917, in Petrograd (now Leningrad), Russian soldiers of the Volynsky Regiment refused to fire on street demonstrators and, instead, beat to death their commanding officer, Captain Lashkevitch. This marked a major turning point in the Russian Revolution, because after killing Lashkevitch, the Volynsky Regiment—the first Russian military unit to mutiny—joined the revolutionary forces.

8. COL. DAVID MARCUS (1901–1948), U.S.

In 1948, U.S. Army colonel David Marcus resigned his post at the Pentagon and enlisted in the newly formed Israeli Army. On the night of June 10, 1948, after overseeing the construction of a relief road from Tel Aviv to besieged Jerusalem during the Israeli war for independence, Marcus was shot and killed while urinating in a field. One of his own sentries had mistaken him for an Arab because he had a bed sheet wrapped around him.

9. NADIR SHAH (1688–1747), Persian

A Turkish tribesman who became a Persian general and then king of the Persian Empire, Nadir Shah was a highly successful conqueror who defeated the Afghans, Mongols, Indians, and Turks. In 1747 Nadir's own military bodyguard murdered him. His death met with widespread approval in Persia because of the harshness and cruelty of his rule.

10. CAPT. PEDRO DE URZÚA (?–1561), Spanish

In 1559 Capt. Pedro de Urzúa led an expedition of Spanish soldiers from coastal Peru across the Andes to the Amazon Basin in search of El Dorado. Two years later, while still searching unsuccessfully for gold, De Urzúa was killed by his own men when they mutinied under the leadership of Lope de Aguirre. De Urzúa's death and the fate of the mutineers was depicted in the 1973 movie *Aguirre, Wrath of God*.

—R.J.F.

12 FAMOUS MEN WHO WERE W.W. I AMBULANCE DRIVERS

1. Louis Bromfield (1896–1956), author
2. Malcolm Cowley (1898–   ), editor and author
3. e e cummings (1894–1962), poet

4. Walt Disney (1901–1966), cartoonist
5. John Dos Passos (1896–1970), author
6. Julian Green (1900–   ), author
7. Dashiell Hammett (1894–1961), author
8. Ernest Hemingway (1899–1961), author
9. Robert Hillyer (1895–1961), poet
10. Sidney Howard (1891–1939), playwright
11. Archibald MacLeish (1892–   ), poet
12. W. Somerset Maugham (1874–1965), author

—F.B.F.

THE 8 MOST AWFUL
WARSHIPS IN HISTORY

1. THE *VASA*, Swedish battleship, 1628

The Swedish Navy felt the need to construct a huge battleship, with 64 guns set in two decks, for its fleet. The *Vasa* was a beautiful ship, but it was top-heavy and did not have adequate ballast. On August 10 it began its maiden voyage from the Stockholm harbor. While the crew waved to the king and the crowds, the ship heeled after a violent gust of wind. The *Vasa* slowly righted itself, but moments later it listed again—so far that water washed into the lower gunport. To the amazement of the people on shore, the *Vasa* sank and an estimated 50 lives were lost. Rediscovered in 1956 and salvaged in 1961, it can be seen today in Stockholm.

The *Vasa* being towed back to port in 1961 after
333 years at the bottom of the sea.

2. *LE PLONGEUR,* French submarine, 1863

This early submarine "monstrosity," built at Rochefort, France, was 140 ft. long and weighed 420 tons. The engine ran on compressed air, and the ship's weapon was a spar torpedo. On the surface it did fairly well. It was not until it submerged that problems started. *Le Plongeur* was impossible to keep steady underwater, especially after diving downwards at a steep angle and then shooting back up toward the surface. The correcting gear was a failure, and sailing on the ship was a frightening experience for the crew. After many unsuccessful tests—including several near tragedies—the French Navy realized the dangers and scrapped the submarine for safety's sake.

3. C.S.S. *HUNLEY,* Confederate submarine, 1864

This craft was originally a boiler, which was made into a submarine. It was 60 ft. in length and looked like a cigar. Eight men turned a crank attached to a propeller to produce movement, and the ship's weapon was an explosive charge on a 15-ft. pole attached to the bow. The *Hunley* was actually a deathtrap. More than a dozen men, including H. L. Hunley, the inventor, drowned or suffocated in test dives before the submarine was ready for battle. On February 17, 1864, off the harbor at Charleston, S.C., the *Hunley* attacked the Union ship *Housatonic,* crippling the enemy ship but going to the bottom with the victim. The *Hunley* proved to be more of a liability to the Confederates than a threat to the Union.

4. H.M.S. *CAPTAIN,* British battleship, 1870

Designed by Capt. Cowper Coles for the British Admiralty, this was an oceangoing turret ship. Its armament consisted of two double 12-in. gun turrets. It was built of iron and had extra armor plate at the waterline, but it proved unstable due to its low freeboard deck. During a storm off Cape Finisterre, Spain, on September 6, 1870, it turned over and sank with its designer aboard. All but 18 of the crew of 500 went down with the ship.

5. U.S.S. *VESUVIUS,* U.S. dynamite cruiser, 1888

Anything but "dynamite," this ship was designed by Edmund Zalinski, who was fascinated by the idea of throwing hundreds of pounds of dynamite at the enemy. The dynamite shells were propelled at their target by compressed air. In theory, this ship's guns would have shaken the world. In reality, the idea fizzled out. The ship's guns could be aimed only by pointing the whole craft, so it was soon apparent that the *Vesuvius* could not defend itself from any enemy vessel. It was eventually scrapped.

6. U.S.S. *KATAHDIN,* U.S. steel-armored ram, 1893

To avoid spending money on expensive shells, the U.S. government decided to ram enemy ships, ostensibly because many naval admirals lived in a dream world in which rams could charge through shot and shell to sink mighty battleships. Developed for a naval tactic that had been obsolete for 20 years, the *Katahdin* had a disappointing career. It was much too slow to be used for ramming, it was unwieldy at sea, and its defensive power was zero. Designated "Ballistic

Experiment Target A," it was mercifully sunk at Rappahannock Spit, Va., by U.S. Navy gunfire 16 years after its completion.

7. H.M.S. *INVINCIBLE*, British battle cruiser, 1907

This ship was certainly not what its name implied. Its design was inspired by Adm. Sir John Fisher (later Lord Fisher), who said that "speed is the best protection." In order to achieve a speed of over 25 knots, the *Invincible* had a reduced armor belt. The thinner protective armor, however, could not withstand a direct attack. Its hull members were weak, there was no side armor aft, and the electrical training gear that drove the turrets was faulty. And, unbelievably, its turrets amidships were arranged *en échelon*—meaning all eight guns could not be brought to bear on the target. The proof of the failure of this design came at the Battle of Jutland in 1916. The *Invincible* received a single hit amidships from the German battle cruiser *Derfflinger*, whereupon it exploded, broke in two, and sank. Twenty-five years later, the British battle cruiser *Hood* was sunk in the same manner by the German battleship *Bismarck*. The British had not changed the battle cruiser's design even after the lesson of Jutland.

8. H.M.S. *FURIOUS*, British light battle cruiser, 1916

Known to the British public as the "H.M.S. *Curious*," this vessel carried two 18-in. guns, which proved to be shattering weapons on this lightly built ship. When the guns were fired, rivets would fly about in the turrets due to the force of the weapons. Needless to say, the *Furious* found it next to impossible to hit an enemy ship with its two-gun battery. Moreover, its armor was pitifully weak. In fact, during a gale at sea, several of its outer plates were dented so badly that they had to be replaced. The addition of the *Furious* to the British fleet served only to lower morale, since it was obvious even to common seamen that it was a floating mistake. After W.W. I, it was converted into an aircraft carrier.

—B.L.W.

10 POPULAR REVOLTS CRUSHED OR BETRAYED BY COMMUNISTS

1. MAKHNOVITE REBELLION (1921)

From 1918 to 1921, during the Russian civil war, an educated Ukrainian peasant named Nestor Makhno led an anarchist peasant uprising in the Ukraine. Makhno's forces fought both the Bolshevik Reds and the counterrevolutionary Whites. In 1920 the Bolsheviks allied themselves with the Makhnovites in order to crush Gen. Peter Wrangel's White army in the Crimea, after which the Bolsheviks turned on Makhno and ruthlessly destroyed his insurgent forces.

2. KRONSTADT MUTINY (1921)

On March 1, 1921, at the Russian naval base at Kronstadt near Leningrad, 15,000 radical and anarchist workers and sailors who were politically to the left of Lenin rebelled against the Communist party's control of the Soviet government. The Communists reacted immediately. Communist leader Leon Trotsky, at the head of a force of elite Communist military units and Cheka secret police, attacked the Kronstadt base, suppressed the rebellion, and jailed some 2,000 mutineers on March 16.

3. BARCELONA UPRISING (1937)

In May, 1937—during the Spanish Civil War—workers from both the anarchist CNT party and the Trotskyite POUM party rose in armed rebellion against the Republican government of Barcelona, Spain. Supplying soldiers and arms, the Spanish Communist party helped the Republican government crush this leftist uprising in order to maintain Communist control of the fight against Franco's Nationalists.

4. SAIGON UPRISING (1945)

In August and September of 1945, Vietnamese workers and peasants in Saigon and Cholon rebelled against the French colonial troops returning to southern Vietnam. Led by the Vietnamese Trotskyite party and various religious sects, this uprising was suppressed not only by French and British troops but by Ho Chi Minh's Communist Viet Minh as well. The Communists viewed the Trotskyites as a greater danger than the European colonial powers.

5. HUNGARIAN REVOLUTION (1956)

Beginning in October, 1956, Hungarian workers, peasants, students, and soldiers drove the occupying Soviet forces from Hungary, and Imre Nagy became the head of a coalition Hungarian government, including noncommunist parties. When Nagy announced Hungary's withdrawal from the Warsaw Pact, the U.S.S.R. sent its tanks back into Hungary and brutally crushed the revolution.

6. PARIS MAY REVOLT (1968)

In May, 1968, the police brutally broke up a small student demonstration at the Sorbonne in Paris, France. This action provoked large-scale student demonstrations throughout Paris and in other major French cities. Within a week, French workers had joined the students in their revolt by going on strike. Fearing loss of control over the workers, the French Communist party publicly denounced the student and worker revolutionaries, announced its support of the government, and called for parliamentary reforms instead of revolution. The French government, with Communist cooperation, suppressed the revolt in late June.

7. PRAGUE SPRING (1968)

In late 1967 and early 1968, the Czechoslovakian Prague Spring revolutionary movement erupted when student and worker demonstrations led to the fall of Czechoslovakia's Stalinist ruler Antonín Novotný, who was replaced by liberal Communist leader

Alexander Dubček. After initiating a series of reforms, Dubček was overthrown when the Soviet Union and its Warsaw Pact allies invaded Czechoslovakia on the night of August 20, 1968. The new regime installed by the Soviet Communists canceled Dubček's reform measures.

8. POLISH UPRISING (1970)

Discontent over Polish premier and Communist party chief Wladyslaw Gomulka's autocratic rule and several years of bad harvests led workers in Poland's Baltic seaports to strike and riot against the Polish government in December, 1970. The Communist Polish United Workers party (PZPR) quickly suppressed the worker demonstrations, but the popular unrest forced Gomulka to resign as premier in favor of the Communist party's first secretary, Edward Gierek.

9. CEYLONESE UPRISING (1971)

In April, 1971, workers, peasants, and students under the leadership of the Maoist Janata Vimukti Peramuna (JVP)—the People's Liberation Front—rebelled against the leftist coalition government of Ceylon (now Sri Lanka). The Ceylonese Communist party and the Trotskyite party, which both belonged to the governing coalition, threw their full support into suppressing the Maoist JVP uprising. The U.S.S.R. sent 24,000 troops to fight against the insurgents. In an unusual display of big-power solidarity, the Ceylonese government also received weapons from Great Britain, the U.S., India, Pakistan, East and West Germany, Egypt, and Yugoslavia.

10. THE TIEN AN MEN INCIDENT (1976)

When Premier Chou En-lai died, a government campaign was begun to discredit his policies. But many still remembered Chou fondly, and thousands of people in Beijing (Peking) began laying wreaths in his honor in front of the Monument of the People's Heroes. The Chinese government responded by removing the wreaths. One hundred thousand people gathered at the monument on April 5, 1976, to protest. By nightfall most of the crowd had gone home, but at 9:30 P.M. the militia and the army moved in, arresting the remaining protesters and beating to death any who resisted. A massive crackdown followed in which local Communist party supporters were urged to turn in to the police anyone who had attended the Tien An Men demonstration.

—R.J.F.

7 SECRET CIA MIND-CONTROL EXPERIMENTS

From 1949 to 1973, the U.S. Central Intelligence Agency (CIA) secretly funded a $25 million program of mind-control experiments at universities, prisons, and hospitals. Within the CIA, the program was variously known as Project Bluebird, Project Artichoke, and MK-

Ultra MK-Delta. At least 39 of the more than 150 separate projects involved human subjects, many of whom did not know that they were acting as guinea pigs, even though the Nuremberg Code of 1947, adopted by the U.S. in 1953, clearly states that medical research should be conducted only with the full consent and knowledge of the subjects. According to data unearthed from CIA archives through the Freedom of Information Act and testimony given at a Senate joint committee hearing in 1977, the program was created in reaction to alarm at the idea that the Soviets and Red Chinese had developed sophisticated brainwashing techniques.

1. EARLY DRUG EXPERIMENTS (Fort Detrick, Md.)

Dr. Frank Olson was an army biochemist working on top-secret germ warfare at Fort Detrick, Md., when he was given LSD as part of a 1953 experiment. During the following two weeks, his personality changed. His wife later reported that "he was very melancholy and talked about a mistake he had made." She did not know of her husband's LSD trip; it is questionable whether he himself knew what had happened to him. Olson went for psychiatric treatment to Dr. Harold Abramson (who later conducted CIA drug experiments at New York's Mount Sinai Hospital), but he remained disturbed. At the end of the two-week period after he took the LSD, Olson—probably unwittingly—ran across his room on the 10th floor of the Statler Hotel in Manhattan and jumped to his death through pulled drapes and a closed window. It was not until June, 1975, that his family found out about the drug experiments by reading the Rockefeller Commission report on CIA activities. His widow and three children sued the government. President Gerald Ford apologized, and the family withdrew the suit. However, a private bill to compensate the family for suffering was introduced into Congress, and in 1976 Olson's widow was awarded $750,000.

2. LSD TESTS ON PRISONERS (U.S. Public Health Service Hospital, Lexington, Ky.)

With money channeled through the Office of Naval Research, LSD and other mind-controlling drugs were tested on prisoners at the U.S. Public Health Service Hospital in Lexington, Ky. The aim of the 11-year project, which took place from 1952 to 1963, was supposedly to find a drug that would substitute for codeine as a painkiller. The question: Why continue to test LSD, which has no painkilling properties? Dr. Harris Isbell, coordinator of the research, carried on a secret correspondence with the CIA, mostly with an operative known as Ray. Isbell once wrote: "I will write you a quick letter as soon as I can get the stuff into a man or two." In addition, Isbell arranged for overseas purchase of drugs for the CIA from European manufacturers, who thought they were sending shipments to public health officials. In 1976 Isbell told the Senate Health Subcommittee that he was still in contact with the CIA; he was not asked for further details.

3. MORE EXPERIMENTS ON PRISONERS (federal penitentiary in Atlanta, Ga., and Bordentown Reformatory in Bordentown, N.J.)

In 1955 Dr. Sidney Gottlieb, who was in charge of the CIA

drug program, approached pharmacologist Dr. Carl Pfeiffer about the possibility of administering LSD to prisoners. With $25,000 paid each year through the Geschikter Foundation, a CIA front, Pfeiffer gave the drug to from 80 to 100 prisoners at the federal penitentiary in Atlanta and the Bordentown Reformatory in New Jersey for the next 11 years. In a 1977 interview, Pfeiffer said that the prisoners had given their consent, but he also stated that he did not believe that consent was always necessary in "wartime conditions."

4. SENSORY DEPRIVATION AND DRUG RESEARCH
   (Allan Memorial Institute of Psychiatry at
   McGill University, Montreal, Canada)

Approximately 25 nurses were placed alone in soundless, dark rooms for a half hour at a time to test the effects of isolation and sensory deprivation on human beings. One experimenter later told a *New York Times* reporter: "That's a long time. One particular nurse, I remember, thought there were snakes coming out from under her chair. She was listed a few months later as a schizophrenic, and she had to go to the hospital." He said that such experiments could have "a profound effect" on some people. Another experimenter, Leonard Rubenstein, had this to say: "It was directly related to brainwashing. They [the CIA] had investigated brainwashing among soldiers who had been in Korea. We in Montreal started to use some [of these] techniques, brainwashing patients instead of using drugs." It was thought that perhaps non-drug techniques could have "beneficial" effects on patients, making them more docile and "positive in attitude." In 1958 Dr. D. Ewen Cameron of the institute received $18,405 to test three drugs—thorazine, LSD, and sernyl—on hospital patients. Sernyl has been withdrawn from the market for human consumption; it is ordinarily used only to temporarily paralyze apes and monkeys. The experiments at McGill, which lasted from 1955 to 1960, were paid for by the Society for the Investigation of Human Ecology, Inc., a CIA front.

5. EXPERIMENTS WITH "CRIMINAL SEXUAL
   PSYCHOPATHS" (Ionia State Hospital, Ionia, Mich.)

The names of criminally insane "sexual psychopaths," some being held without trial, were obtained from the files of Detroit's Recorders Court psychiatric clinic. The project manager for the CIA experiments in which these individuals were tested wrote to the CIA using double envelopes and a fake name. He was evidently Dr. Alex Canty, now dead, then psychiatric associate with the court clinic. Of the three doctors who did the research at the nearby Ionia State Hospital from 1957 to 1960, two are now dead. Approximately 142 subjects were given LSD to see if it would make them confess hidden thoughts. The object: to "explore the research potential that is represented by 142 criminal sexual psychopaths," since they supposedly had the "kind of motivation for withholding certain information that is comparable to operational interrogative situations in the field." So far, no record of prisoner consent has been discovered. After being given the drugs, the prisoners were questioned by doctors using tape recorders and sometimes lie detectors. The project was funded by the Society for the Investigation of Human Ecology, Inc.

6. THE SEARCH FOR THE KNOCKOUT DRUG "K"
(Georgetown University Medical School, Washington, D.C.)

Documents in CIA files unearthed in 1977 revealed that the CIA secretly contributed $375,000 toward construction of an unidentified hospital building at a hospital complex where tests of a knockout drug called "K" were allegedly later conducted on terminally ill cancer patients. A *New York Times* investigative reporter succeeded in verifying that the building was the Gorman Building at Georgetown University Medical School. According to Sen. Richard S. Schweiker, a Republican from Pennsylvania, the knockout drug was actually tested on patients from 1955 to 1961. Dr. Charles Geschikter, founder of the Geschikter Foundation for Medical Research, was professor emeritus of pathology at Georgetown.

7. OPERATION MIDNIGHT CLIMAX (CIA-rented apartments in New York, N.Y., and San Francisco, Calif.)

From 1954 to 1963, these experiments took place in rooms with red drapes, Toulouse-Lautrec posters of cancan girls, and dressing tables trimmed in black velveteen—a stereotype of the brothel. Men were lured from bars, probably by call girls, and without their knowledge were given LSD and marijuana. The subjects were then observed by agents through two-way mirrors in adjoining rooms. The project was carried out in cooperation with the now defunct Federal Bureau of Narcotics and Dangerous Drugs, mostly through senior narcotics agent George White (a.k.a. Morgan Hall). The apartment in New York, called a "field lab" and "safe house," was located at 103 West 13th Street; the address of the apartment in San Francisco has not been revealed. There was no direct proof that moonlighting prostitutes were used, but a former CIA psychologist said that he had interviewed several prostitutes in the New York apartment. Also, several $100 payments for "undercover agents' operating expenses" were listed in CIA documents. During the Senate investigation in 1977, Massachusetts senator Edward Kennedy asked Adm. Stansfield Turner, CIA director, if he could come to any conclusions from these facts. "No, sir," Turner answered as he reached for a glass of water, while those in the hearing room laughed. It was no laughing matter. Some of the "subjects" became violently ill and ended up in the hospital, not knowing what was wrong with them.

—A.E.

17 EXAMPLES OF THE HIGH COST OF BUILDING

Structure	Year Completed/ Opened	Lives Lost during Construction
1. Hoosac Tunnel, Massachusetts	1876	195
2. St. Gotthard Tunnel, Switzerland	1882	310
An additional 877 workers were injured.		

Structure	Year Completed/ Opened	Lives Lost during Construction
3. Brooklyn Bridge, New York	1883	20
4. Firth of Forth Bridge, Scotland	1890	57
5. Simplon Tunnel I, Switzerland-Italy Another 133 were permanently disabled.	1906	39
6. Hudson Tube, New York–New Jersey	1906	20+
7. Madeira-Mamore Railway, western Brazil Work began in 1870; the fourth attempt to complete the railroad succeeded in 1912. Lives lost were mainly due to malaria, yellow fever, beriberi, poison arrows from Indian attacks, snakebites, and attacks by wild animals.	1912	6,000+
8. Panama Canal Most deaths were caused by yellow fever, malaria, and cholera.	1914	25,000+

Workers on the Panama Canal, 1912.

Structure	Year Completed/ Opened	Lives Lost during Construction
9. Gauley Bridge Water Tunnel, West Virginia An additional 1,500 workers were disabled.	1931	476
10. Empire State Building, New York	1931	14
11. Golden Gate Bridge, California	1937	10
12. Mont Blanc Tunnel (rail), France-Italy An additional 800 were injured.	1962	17
13. Phutsholing-to-Thimbu road, Bhutan through the Himalayas	1963	182
14. Mont Blanc Tunnel (road), France-Italy	1965	23
15. Subway in Osaka, Japan Lives lost were due to a gas explosion on April 9.	1970	73+
16. Karakoram Highway from Thakot, Pakistan, to Sinkiang Province, China	1978	400+
17. Monongahela Power Co. water-cooling tower, Willow Island, W.Va. The 170-ft. scaffolding collapsed on April 27.	1978	51

—T.K.

MARK TWAIN'S LIST
OF 27 PEOPLE AND THINGS
TO BE RESCUED FROM
A BOARDINGHOUSE FIRE

1. Fiancées
2. Persons toward whom the rescuer feels a tender sentiment but has not yet declared himself
3. Sisters
4. Stepsisters
5. Nieces
6. First cousins
7. Cripples
8. Second cousins
9. Invalids
10. Young-lady relations by marriage
11. Third cousins and young-lady friends of the family

12. The unclassified
13. Babies
14. Children under 10 years of age
15. Young widows
16. Young married females
17. Elderly married ditto
18. Elderly widows
19. Clergymen
20. Boarders in general
21. Female domestics
22. Male ditto
23. Landlady
24. Landlord
25. Firemen
26. Furniture
27. Mothers-in-law

SOURCE: Bernard De Voto, ed., *Mark Twain: Letters from the Earth.* Copyright © 1962 by The Mark Twain Company. Reprinted by permission of Harper & Row Publishers, Inc.

6 CASES OF
WOMEN AND CHILDREN LAST

1. THE *PHOENIX*, Lake Michigan, 1847

Most of the passengers aboard this steamer, which regularly plied the Great Lakes between Buffalo and Chicago, were Dutch immigrants bound for a new life in America's heartland. A fire that started in the boiler room swept the length and depth of the liner, unimpeded by a hastily formed bucket brigade. The crew crowded into the *Phoenix*'s two lifeboats and only then beckoned for a handful of passengers to fill in the few remaining spaces. As the small twin crafts started for shore, many passengers—including women and children—jumped from the fiery *Phoenix* and tried to latch on to the side of the lifeboats—only to have their hands pried or pounded loose by the crew. Estimates of the number of dead ranged from 190 to 250.

2. THE *ARCTIC*, off the southern coast of Newfoundland, 1854

Capt. James C. Luce did his best to enforce the unwritten law of the sea when his ship, the American liner *Arctic*, began sinking after a collision with another vessel in thick fog. But as the decks filled with seawater, virtually the entire crew ignored the captain's orders and made for the lifeboats. Seeing this, the male passengers scrambled overboard too, leaving the helpless captain alone with the women and children. Of the 435 aboard, only 61 crewmen and 24 male passengers survived.

3. THE *MORNING STAR,* Lake Erie, 1868

Two hours out of Cleveland on its regular run to Detroit, the side-wheeler *Morning Star* rammed at full speed into the stern of the *Courtlandt,* a cargo ship. For a brief time the two vessels remained afloat, tangled in deadly embrace, and then they began to sink as one. A few of the *Morning Star*'s 51 first-class passengers and immigrants, among them women and children, were able to clamber into the two lone lifeboats—but not until most of the all-male crew had secured places. Estimates of the dead ranged from 23 to 32.

4. The *FLORIDA* and The *REPUBLIC,* southwest of Nantucket Island, 1909

Shrouded in fog, the *Florida,* a small Italian emigrant ship bound for New York, rammed into the engine room of the White Star liner *Republic.* It was women and children first, all right, for the passengers on the *Republic* as they rowed from their listing liner to the temporary safety of the *Florida.* But when the *Baltic* arrived to rescue the combined 1,650 passengers and crew from the overloaded and damaged *Florida,* the first-class male survivors of the *Republic* were led to the lifeboats ahead of the Italian women. Although the Italians howled in protest, class privilege prevailed.

5. THE *MORRO CASTLE,* off the New Jersey coast, 1934

Returning from one of its weekly "Forget-the-Depression" cruises to the Caribbean, the flagship of the Ward Line went up in flames in the wee hours of a morning in late summer, possibly as the result of arson. Instead of rousing passengers from their cabins, most crewmen looked out for number one. The first lifeboat launched contained just three passengers; the rest were crew members. Eighty-six of the 318 passengers aboard lost their lives.

6. THE *HELEANA,* Adriatic Sea, 1971

An explosion in the galley rocked the Greek ferry shortly after 6:00 A.M., when most of the 1,100 European tourists were still in pajamas. Survivors later charged that crewmen ignored screams for help from women and children in order to save themselves. An investigation disclosed that the ship had taken aboard 182 more passengers than allowed by law and that this overcrowding had contributed to the death toll of 24.

—W.A.D.

5

MOVING HEAVEN AND EARTH

12 POSSIBLE SITES
FOR THE GARDEN OF EDEN

And the Lord God planted a garden eastward in Eden. . . . And a river went out of Eden to water the garden; and from thence it was parted and became into four heads. The name of the first is Pison: that is it which compasseth the whole land of Havilah, where there is gold; And the gold of that land is good: there is bdellium and the onyx stone. And the name of the second river is Gihon: the same is it that compasseth the whole land of Ethiopia. And the name of the third river is Hiddekel: that is it which goeth toward the east of Assyria. And the fourth river is Euphrates.

—Genesis 2:8–14

1. SOUTHERN IRAQ

Many biblical scholars believe that the Garden of Eden, the original home of Adam and Eve, was located in Sumer, at the confluence of the Euphrates and Tigris (or Hiddekel) rivers in present-day Iraq. They presume that the geographical references in Genesis relate to the situation from the 9th to the 5th centuries B.C. and that the Pison and Gihon were tributaries of the Euphrates and Tigris which have since disappeared. In fact, they may have been ancient canals.

2. EASTERN TURKEY

Other students of the Bible reason that if the four major rivers flowed *out* of the garden, then the garden itself must have been located far north of the Tigris-Euphrates civilization. They place the site in the mysterious northland of Armenia in present-day Turkey. This theory presumes that Gihon and Pison may not have been precise geographical designations, but rather vague descriptions of faraway places.

3. ISRAEL

There are those who say that the garden of God must have been in the Holy Land and that the original river that flowed into the garden *before* it split into four separate rivers must have been the Jordan, which was longer in the days of Genesis. The Gihon would be the Nile, and Havilah would be the Arabian Peninsula. Some supporters of this theory go further, stating that Mt. Moriah in Jerusalem was the heart of the Garden of Eden and that the entire garden included all of Jerusalem, Bethlehem, and Mt. Olivet.

The Garden of Eden—in Mesopotamia, Wisconsin, or Mars?

4. EGYPT

Supporters of Egypt as the site of the Garden of Eden claim that only the Nile region meets the Genesis description of a land watered, not by rain, but by a mist rising from the ground, in that the Nile ran partially underground before surfacing in spring holes below the first cataract. The four world rivers, including the Tigris and Euphrates, are explained away as beginning far, far beyond the actual site of Paradise.

5-6. EAST AFRICA AND JAVA

Since Adam and Eve were the first humans, and since the oldest human remains have been found in East Africa, many people conclude that the Garden of Eden must have been in Africa. Likewise, when archaeologists discovered the remains of *Pithecanthropus* in

Java in 1891, they guessed that Java was the location of the Garden of Eden.

7. SINKIANG, CHINA

Tse Tsan Tai, in his work *The Creation, the Real Situation of Eden, and the Origin of the Chinese* (1914), presents a case for the garden being in Chinese Turkestan in the plateau of eastern Asia. He claims that the river that flowed through the garden was the Tarim, which has four tributaries flowing eastward.

8. LEMURIA

In the mid-19th century a theory developed that a vast continent once occupied much of what is now the Indian Ocean. The name Lemuria was created by British zoologist P. L. Sclater in honor of the lemur family of animals, which has a somewhat unusual range of distribution in Africa, southern India, and Malaya. Other scientists suggested that Lemuria was the cradle of the human race; thus it must have been the site of the Garden of Eden.

9. PRASLIN ISLAND, SEYCHELLES

Gen. Charles "Chinese" Gordon supported the theory that Africa and India used to be part of one massive continent. While on a survey expedition for the British government in the Indian Ocean, he came upon Praslin Island in the Seychelles group. So enchanted was he by this island, and by its Vallée de Mai in particular, that he became convinced that this was the location of the original Garden of Eden. The clincher for Gordon was the existence on Praslin of the coco-de-mer, a rare and exotic tree, which is native to only one other island of the Seychelles and which Gordon concluded was the tree of the knowledge of good and evil.

10. MARS

In his book *The Sky People*, Brinsley LePoer Trench argues that not only Adam and Eve but Noah lived on Mars. He states that the biblical description of a river watering the garden and then parting into four heads is inconsistent with nature. Only canals can be made to flow that way, and Mars, supposedly, had canals. So the Garden of Eden was created on Mars as an experiment by Space People. Eventually the north polar ice cap on Mars melted, and the descendants of Adam and Eve were forced to take refuge on Earth.

11. BRISTOL, FLA., U.S.A.

Elvy E. Calloway, a Baptist minister, claims that the Garden of Eden was on the banks of the Apalachicola River, 1 mi. east of Bristol, Fla. His reasons are that the Apalachicola is the only four-headed river system in the world; that onyx, bdellium, and good gold are found nearby; and that Bristol is the only place where gopher wood (the Torrey tree) grows. And Noah made his ark out of gopher wood.

12. GALESVILLE, WIS., U.S.A.

In 1886 the Rev. D. O. Van Slyke published a small pamphlet which expounded his belief that Eden was the area stretching from the Allegheny Mountains to the Rocky Mountains and that the Garden of Eden was located on the east bank of the Mississippi River between La Crosse, Wis., and Winona, Minn. When the Deluge began, Noah was living in present-day Wisconsin, and the flood carried his ark eastward until it landed on Mt. Ararat.

—D.W.

16 FAMOUS PEOPLE WHO GREW MARIJUANA—OR ORDERED IT TO BE GROWN

1. SHAYKH AZ-ZAWAJI HAYDAR (c. 1150–1221)

Persian founder of the Haydari order of Sufis, he is credited with discovering hashish and cultivating hemp in his monastery in Khurasan. By his order, hemp was planted around his tomb, which is still visited by Sufi pilgrims.

2. JALAL-UD-DIN MUHAMMAD (1483–1530)

First Mogul emperor of India, he loved hashish sweetmeats and planted hemp near Delhi. His grandson Akbar the Great (1542–1605) expanded the empire to include Afghanistan and Bengal and systematized hemp and poppy cultivation throughout northern India.

3. GARCIA DA ORTA (c. 1490–1570)

Portuguese physician in Goa, he grew marijuana and other medicines and discussed their use in his *Colloquies on the Simples and Drugs of India* (1563). The third book printed in India, it was widely consulted by herbalists during the Age of Exploration.

4. FRANÇOIS RABELAIS (1494?–1553)

French author of *Gargantua* and *Pantagruel,* he grew up on a hemp farm which his father had inherited. His intimate knowledge of hemp cultivation is revealed in the chapter on the herb Pantagruelion in book 3 of *Pantagruel.*

5. LEONHARD FUCHS (1501–1566)

German botanist, he grew marijuana and other drug plants and had his artists draw them from life for his book *De Historia Stirpium* (1542). Fuchs gave the plant its present botanical name, *Cannabis sativa.*

6. JAMES I (1566–1625)

Hoping to establish a colonial fiber source, the king of England allowed gardens for hemp and flax cultivation to be given to each

Jamestown colonist in 1611; this was the first private property in Virginia. In 1619 the first representative government in the colonies, the Virginia General Assembly, required all householders having any hemp seed to plant it the next season. This was America's first marijuana law.

7. WILLIAM BYRD II (1674–1744)

In 1737 this Virginia planter, trying to collect bounties for hemp offered by the British government, sowed hemp on his 180,000-acre plantation called Westover. Byrd reported: "It thrives very well in this climate, but labour being much dearer than in Muscovy, as well as the freight, we can make no earnings of it."

8. CAROLUS LINNAEUS (1707–1778)

Swedish father of modern botany and inventor of the binomial classification system for plants and animals, in 1753 he subsumed all varieties of hemp under the name *Cannabis sativa*. Linnaeus raised marijuana on his windowsill while investigating plant sexuality in 1760.

9. GEORGE WASHINGTON (1732–1799)

This U.S. president imported hemp seeds from all over the world and planted them in his vineyard at Mt. Vernon from 1765 to 1796. He hoped to establish an American hemp industry able to compete with those of England, Russia, and Italy.

10. THOMAS JEFFERSON (1743–1826)

One of the most versatile U.S. presidents, he planted an acre of hemp at Monticello in 1811, wrote a pamphlet on hemp cultivation, and invented a power machine for breaking hemp in 1815.

11. HENRY CLAY (1777–1852)

U.S. senator from Kentucky, he got a bill passed in 1810 that required the navy to purchase American hemp products rather than imported ones. This established hemp as the foremost cash crop of Kentucky, a position it held until the Civil War.

12. SIR ROBERT CHRISTISON (1797–1882)

Scottish toxicologist and president of the British Medical Association, Dr. Christison cultivated marijuana in his father's botanical garden at the Edinburgh College of Physicians. His noted works on plant drugs are still consulted by modern pharmacologists.

13. THEODORE ROOSEVELT (1858–1919)

This U.S. president established a federal "poison farm" in Washington, D.C., in 1904, near the site now occupied by the Pentagon. Fields of marijuana, opium, coca, and other drugs were planted so that the U.S. wouldn't have to import them.

14. HENRY FORD (1863–1947)

Pioneer automobile manufacturer, he cultivated a marijuana

crop for "experimental purposes," which he surrounded with a cyclone fence. Supposedly the plot was destroyed after his death, but his family later found the marijuana growing wild.

15. LYNDON BAINES JOHNSON (1908–1973)

While U.S. president, he signed a bill establishing the federal marijuana farm at the University of Mississippi in July, 1968, as a research center for the botany, chemistry, and cultivation of the drug. This farm now supplies most of the marijuana used for official medical research in America.

16. TOMMY RETTIG (1941–   )

Former child star of the TV series *Lassie*, Rettig was arrested in 1972 for growing marijuana on his ranch outside San Luis Obispo, Calif.

—M.R.A.

10 NATIONS WITH THE LEADING OIL RESERVES

		Proven Reserves * (in billions of barrels)
1.	Saudi Arabia	163.4
2.	Union of Soviet Socialist Republics	67.0
3.	Kuwait	65.4
4.	Iran	58.0
5.	Mexico	31.3
6.	Iraq	31.0
7.	Abu Dhabi (of the United Arab Emirates)	28.0
8.	United States	26.5
9.	Libya	23.5
10.	People's Republic of China	20.0

* Estimates of crude oil which geological and engineering data demonstrate with reasonable certainty to be recoverable in future years from known reservoirs under existing and economic operating conditions.

SOURCE: *Oil and Gas Journal*, December 25, 1979. © Petroleum Publishing Co.

25 THINGS THAT
FELL FROM THE SKY

1. HAY

A great cloud of hay drifted over the town of Devizes in England at teatime on July 3, 1977. As soon as the cloud reached the center of town, it all fell to earth in handful-size lumps. The sky was otherwise clear and cloudless with a slight breeze. The temperature was 26°C.

2. GOLDEN RAIN

When yellow-colored globules fell over suburban Sydney, Australia, in late 1971, the minister for health, Mr. Jago, blamed it on the excreta of bees, consisting mostly of undigested pollen. However, there were no reports of vast hordes of bees in the area and no explanation as to why they would choose to excrete en masse over Sydney.

3. BLACK EGGS

On May 5, 1786, after six months of drought, a strong east wind dropped a great quantity of black eggs on the city of Port-au-Prince, Haiti. Some of the eggs were preserved in water and hatched the next day. The beings inside shed several layers of skin and resembled tadpoles.

4. MEAT

The famous Kentucky meat-shower took place in southern Bath County on Friday, March 3, 1876. Mrs. Allen Crouch was in her yard making soap when pieces of fresh meat the size of large snowflakes began to fall from the cloudless sky. Two gentlemen who tasted it said that it was either mutton or venison. Scientists who examined the material found the first samples to be lung tissue from either a human infant or a horse. Other later samples were identified as cartilage and striated muscle fibers. The local explanation was that a flock of buzzards had disgorged as a group while flying overhead.

5. A 3,902-LB. STONE

The largest meteorite fall in recorded history occurred on March 8, 1976, near the Chinese city of Kirin. Many of the 100 stones that were found weighed over 200 lb.; the largest, which landed in the Haupi Commune, weighed over 3,902 lb. It is, by more than 1,000 lb., the largest stony meteorite ever recovered.

6. MONEY

On October 8, 1976, a light plane buzzed the Piazza Venezia in Rome and dropped 500-lire, 1,000-lire, and 10,000-lire bank notes on the startled people below. The mad bomber was not found.

7. SOOT

A fine blanket of soot landed on a Cranford park on the edge of London's Heathrow Airport in 1969, greatly annoying the local park keepers. The official report of the Greater London Council said the "soot" was composed of spores of a black microfungus, *Pithomyces chartarum*, found only in New Zealand.

8. HUMAN WASTE

A 25-lb. chunk of green ice fell from the sky on April 23, 1978, and landed with a roar and a cloud of smoke near an unused school building in Ripley, Tenn. The Federal Aviation Administration claimed the green blob was frozen waste from a leaky airplane toilet. These falling blobs are unfortunately quite common, and Denver, Colo., is the center of such phenomena. At least two Denver families have had ice bombs crash through their roofs. And then there's the story of the unfortunate Kentucky farmer who took a big lick of a flying Popsicle before he discovered what it was.

9. 500 BIRDS

About 500 dead and dying blackbirds and pigeons landed on the streets of San Luis Obispo, Calif., over a period of several hours in late November, 1977. No local spraying had occurred, and no explanation was offered.

10. FIRE

On the evening of May 30, 1869, the horrified citizens of Greiffenberg, Germany, and neighboring villages witnessed a fall of fire, which was followed by a tremendous peal of thunder. People who were outside reported that the fire was different in form and color from common lightning. They said they felt wrapped in fire and deprived of air for some seconds.

11. WHITE FIBROUS BLOBS

Blobs of white material up to 20 ft. in length descended over the San Francisco Bay area in California on October 11, 1977. Pilots in San Jose encountered them as high as 4,000 ft. Migrating spiders were blamed, although no spiders were recovered.

12. LUMINOUS GREEN SNOW

In April, 1953, glowing green snow was encountered near Mt. Shasta, Calif. Mr. and Mrs. Milton Moyer reported that their hands itched after touching it and that "a blistered, itching rash" formed on their hands, arms, and faces. The Atomic Energy Commission denied any connection between the snow and recent A-bomb tests in nearby Nevada.

13. MYSTERIOUS DOCUMENTS

The July 25, 1973, edition of the Albany, N.Y., *Times Union* reported the unusual case of Bob Hill. Hill, the owner of radio station WHRL of North Greenbush, N.Y., was taking out the station garbage at 4:15 P.M. when he noticed "twirling specks" falling from a distance higher than the station's 300-ft. transmitter. He followed two of the white objects until they landed in a hayfield. The objects turned out to be two sets of formulas and accompanying graphs, which apparently explained "normalized extinction" and the "incomplete Davis-Greenstein orientation." No explanation has been made public.

14. BEANS

Rancher Salvador Targino of João Pessoa, Brazil, reported a rain of small beans on his property in Paraíba State in early 1971. Local agricultural authorities speculated that a storm had swept up a pile of beans in West Africa and dropped them in northeastern Brazil. Targino boiled some of the beans, but said they were too tough to eat.

15. SILVER COINS

Several thousand rubles' worth of silver coins fell in the Gorki region of the U.S.S.R. on June 17, 1940. The official explanation was that a landslide had uncovered a hidden treasure, which was picked up by a tornado, which dropped it on Gorki. No explanation was given for the fact that the coins were not accompanied by any debris.

16. MUSHROOM-SHAPED THINGS

Traffic at Mexico City airport was halted temporarily on the morning of July 30, 1963, when thousands of grayish, mushroom-shaped things floated to the ground out of a cloudless sky. Hundreds of witnesses described these objects variously as "giant cobwebs," "balls of cotton," and "foam." They disintegrated rapidly after landing.

17. HUMAN BODY

Mary C. Fuller was sitting in her parked car with her 8-month-old son on Monday morning, September 25, 1978, in San Diego, Calif., when a human body crashed through the windshield. The body had been thrown from a Pacific Southwest Airlines jetliner, which had exploded after being hit by a small plane in one of the worst air disasters in U.S. history. Mother and son suffered minor lacerations.

18. TOADS

Falls of frogs and toads, though not everyday occurrences, are actually quite common, having been reported in almost every part of the world. One of the most famous toad falls happened in the summer of 1794 in the village of Lalain, France. A very hot afternoon was broken suddenly by such an intense downpour of rain that 150 French soldiers (then fighting the Austrians) were forced to abandon the trench in which they were hiding to avoid being submerged. In the middle of the storm, which lasted for 30 minutes, tiny toads, mostly in the tadpole stage, began to land on the ground and jump about in all directions. When the rain let up, the soldiers discovered toads in the folds of their three-cornered hats.

19. OAK LEAVES

In late October of 1889, Mr. Wright of the parish of Penpont, Dumfries, Scotland, was startled by the appearance of what at first seemed to be a flock of birds, which began falling to the ground.

Running toward them, he discovered the objects to be oak leaves, which eventually covered an area 1 mi. wide and 2 mi. long. The nearest clump of oak trees was 8 mi. away, and no other kind of leaf fell.

20. JUDAS TREE SEEDS

Just before sunset in August, 1897, an immense number of small, blood-colored clouds filled the sky in Macerata, Italy. About an hour later, storm clouds burst and small seeds rained from the sky, covering the ground to a depth of ½ in. Many of the seeds had already started to germinate, and all of the seeds were from the Judas tree, which is found predominantly in the Middle East and Asia. There was no accompanying debris—just the Judas tree seeds.

21. FISH

About 150 perchlike silver fish dropped from the sky during a tropical storm near Killarney Station in Australia's Northern Territory in February, 1974. Fishfalls are common enough that an "official" explanation has been developed to cover most of them. It is theorized that whirlwinds create a waterspout effect, sucking up water and fish, carrying them for great distances, and then dropping them somewhere else.

22. ICE CHUNKS

In February of 1965, a 50-lb. mass of ice plunged through the roof of the Phillips Petroleum plant in Woods Cross, U. In his book *Strangest of All*, Frank Edwards reports the case of a carpenter working on a roof in Kempten—near Düsseldorf, Germany—who was struck and killed in 1951 by an icicle 6 ft. long and 6 in. around, which shot down from the sky.

23. PEACHES

On July 12, 1961, unripe peaches were scattered over a small portion of Shreveport, La., from a cloudy sky.

24. DEADLY WHITE POWDER

On Saturday, July 10, 1976, the citizens of Seveso, Italy, were startled by a sudden loud whistling sound coming from the direction of the nearby Icmesa chemical factory. The sound was followed by a thick, gray cloud, which rolled toward the town and dropped a mist of white dust that settled on everything and smelled horrible. It was 10 days before the people of Seveso learned that the white dust contained dioxin, a deadly poison far more dangerous than arsenic or strychnine. By then it was too late. The effects of dioxin poisoning had already begun. The area was evacuated, surrounded by barbed wire, and declared a contaminated zone. All exposed animals were killed, ugly black pustules formed on the skin of young children, babies were born deformed, and older people began to die of liver ailments. The full extent of the tragedy has still not been felt.

25. SPACE JUNK

In September, 1962, a metal object about 6 in. in diameter and weighing 21 lb. crashed into a street intersection in Manitowoc,

Wis., and burrowed several inches into the ground. The object was later identified as part of Sputnik IV, which had been launched by the U.S.S.R. on May 15, 1960. Since 1959 more than 6,000 parts of spacecraft have fallen out of orbit, and many of them have reached the surface of the earth. On July 11, 1979, Skylab, the 77-ton U.S. space station, fell out of orbit over the South Indian Ocean and western Australia. The largest piece of debris to reach land was a one-ton tank.

—D.W.

16 NOTABLE PERSONS STRUCK BY LIGHTNING

If you think that lightning is a danger to be laughed at, bear in mind that it kills more Americans than hurricanes or tornadoes do, and that it causes more than $100 million in property damage annually in the U.S. The chances of being hit by lightning are minuscule, but they are about 30 times as great if you live in Miami as if you live in Los Angeles. The chances are greater still in the humid tropical regions, especially in Africa. Somewhere, at this very moment, about 1,800 thunderstorms are raging. Wherever you happen to be, you'll be safer if you stay indoors when you see the thunderclouds gathering.

1. DIOSCORUS (c. 3rd century A.D.)

A semilegendary ruler in Asia Minor, Dioscorus became so angry when his daughter Barbara converted to Christianity that he condemned her to death and then personally beheaded her. Soon afterwards he was struck dead by lightning. This apparent act of divine retribution later caused his daughter to be venerated as the patron saint of protection against thunder, lightning, and fire.

2. GIROLAMO FRACASTORO (1483–1553)

A noted Italian poet and physician, Fracastoro is credited with coining the term *syphilis*. When he was an infant, he was in his mother's arms when she was struck by lightning. The mother died, but Fracastoro was unhurt.

3–4. HERNÁN PÉREZ DE QUESADA (1503?–1544) and FRANCISCO DE QUESADA (?–1544)

After assisting his famous brother Gonzalo Jiménez de Quesada—who conquered present-day Colombia and founded Bogotá—Hernán Pérez fled the new Spanish colony for political reasons. He was killed by lightning while sailing to Cuba. Colombians attributed his death to divine retribution for his prominent part in the killing of the last of the Chibcha kings; however, another brother, Francisco, who had nothing to do with the Chibcha affair, was killed by the same lightning bolt.

5. GEORG WILHELM RICHMANN (1711–1753)

This Russian physicist attached a device to a lightning rod to measure atmospheric electricity. When he bent over during a thunderstorm to read the instrument, lightning hit the rod. It jumped from the device to his head, killing him instantly.

6. JAMES OTIS (1725–1783)

An American statesman, Otis often said he wanted a bolt of lightning to end his life. His wish was granted as he was talking to family and friends in an interior doorway of a farmhouse. Lightning struck the house's chimney, ran down the frame to the doorway, and jumped to Otis, killing him without leaving a mark. No one else in the house was injured.

7. JESSE BUNKER (1861?–1909)

Lightning kills many farmers, who often find themselves exposed in open flatlands. Perhaps the most notable farmer to die in this manner was Jesse Bunker, the son of Chang Bunker, one of the original Siamese twins.

8. FRANCIS SYDNEY SMYTHE (1900–1949)

This English mountaineer became famous for his pioneering climbs on Mt. Everest, but only after narrowly escaping death in the Alps. Lightning once knocked him unconscious, but his wet clothes drew off most of the electrical charge and thus saved his life.

9. ROY C. SULLIVAN (1912?–   )

A retired park ranger in Virginia, Sullivan is history's most lightning-struck person. Lightning hit him in 1942, 1969, 1970, 1972, 1973, 1976, and 1977. He has lost his eyebrows and a big toenail and has twice had his hair set on fire.

10. JOHN WHITE (1938–1964)

Many sportsmen are hit by lightning because of their exposure on open fields. White, a well-known soccer player in England, received his fatal bolt while playing golf.

11–13. LEE TREVINO (1939–   ), JERRY HEARD (1947–   ), and BOBBY NICHOLS (1936–   )

Spectators laughed when Ben Crenshaw scurried to find shelter from lightning at a golf tournament in June, 1975. The laughter stopped a week later when Trevino, Heard, and Nichols were struck at the Western Open Golf Tournament. All three were hospitalized, but Heard returned to finish the tournament and tied for fourth place. Trevino, one of the top pros, took more than a year to recover fully.

14. RUDY SCHILD (1940–   )

A Harvard astronomer, Schild was working in an Arizona observatory in 1976 when lightning hit his telescope and knocked him unconscious. His heart stopped beating while he was whisked to a hospital, but he recovered quickly and went back to work the same day.

15. NICK NAVARRO (1953?–1978)

This Panamanian jockey was in the midst of a fine season when, after a race on December 28, 1978, he was killed by lightning while walking to his quarters from the track at Calder Race Course in Miami.

16. BECKY GODWIN (1954?–1968)

The daughter of Virginia governor Mills E. Godwin, Jr., Becky stepped out of the ocean surf under a clear sky and was struck by a bolt of lightning from a distant cloud. She received immediate resuscitation treatment but died two days later.

—R.K.R.

Park ranger Roy C. Sullivan
survived being struck by lightning seven times.

10 ECLIPSES THAT
AFFECTED HUMAN LIVES

Can a total or partial blacking out of the sun or moon—a solar or lunar eclipse—have any important consequences on humankind? We know an eclipse can be used effectively in make-believe. Example: a crucial incident in Mark Twain's novel *A Connecticut Yankee at King Arthur's Court,* published in 1889. A factory mechanic of the 1880s is hit on the head during a fight and spun backwards in time. He awakens in 528 A.D. in King Arthur's England. Taken to Camelot, surrounded by the knights of the Round Table, the Connecticut Yankee finds himself condemned to death at the suggestion of the king's magician, Merlin. Remembering that on June 21, the day he is to burn at the stake, there will be an eclipse of the sun, the Yankee warns his captors that if he dies, the sun will darken and die, signaling the end of Camelot. Sure enough, as he is about to burn, an eclipse begins. This saves him. He is released and hailed as a magician greater than Merlin, and ultimately Merlin winds up in prison. Very neat, you may say, but after all, that is fiction. Real life is another thing. Could it happen in real life? Well, it has. Eclipses have played a role in history. If you doubt it, read on.

1. 2640 B.C.—THE CHINESE ASTRONOMERS

The ancient Chinese knew about eclipses. They knew they were caused by a dragon trying to eat the sun. When an eclipse was predicted, noisemakers such as gongs were assembled, and the din they made always drove the dragon away, thus restoring celestial harmony. Emperor Huang Ti or Emperor Chung K'ang had appointed two royal astronomers, Hsi and Ho, to predict an impending eclipse in time for the noisemakers to be assembled. But this particular year the astronomers did not predict the eclipse accurately. The dragon began eating away the sun before the emperor could assemble the noisemakers. All seemed lost until, by a stroke of luck, the dragon had his fill and departed, and the sun shone again. The emperor was not satisfied. It had been too risky. He summoned the royal astronomers and demanded to know why they had failed him. It turned out that the two men had been drunk. They were promptly executed for dereliction of duty.

2. 586 B.C.—THE LYDIANS VERSUS THE MEDES

The Lydians (allies of the Greek Spartans) and the Medes (dominated by Cyrus the Persian) had already been locked in a five-year war in Asia Minor. In 586 B.C.—the sixth year—the two countries clashed again in a crucial daytime battle. On May 28 a solar eclipse occurred, one that had been predicted long before by Thales, a Greek mathematician. "Just as the battle was growing warm," reported the historian Herodotus, "day was on a sudden changed into night. . . . The Medes and Lydians, when they observed the change, ceased fighting, and were alike anxious to have terms agreed on." Thus, because of an eclipse, which was considered a sign of divine displeasure, the long war ended and thousands of lives were saved.

3. 413 B.C.—THE ATHENIAN ERROR

The Athenian army, led by Nicias, was locked in battle with the Spartan army, led by Gylippus, on the island of Sicily. Nicias and his Athenians, who were taking a beating, retreated to Syracuse. There an armada of 73 vessels was waiting to take them to safety. Nicias had agreed to leave, but on the night of August 27 an eclipse of the moon took place. Soothsayers immediately told Nicias and his men that this was a sign that they must not retreat but hold firm. Because of this optimistic advice, Nicias and his troops remained. The Athenians were massacred, their armada destroyed. This was a major turning point in the Peloponnesian War.

4. 840 A.D.—A RULER IS FRIGHTENED TO DEATH

He was the third son of the great Charlemagne, and he was called Louis the Pious because he was truly a religious man and a good man. Crowned emperor of the Holy Roman Empire in 813 A.D., Louis I got rid of his father's mistresses, banished his immoral sisters to nunneries, reformed the Church, and gave aid to the poor. He assigned portions of his kingdom to three of his four sons. When he tried to give a fourth parcel to his remaining son, the first three sons overthrew him and imprisoned him in a monastery for a year. Popular support returned Louis the Pious to the throne. When one son broke an agreement and invaded Saxony, Louis went into battle to defeat him. According to one account, Louis was returning home when—due to exposure—he fell ill on an island in the Rhine near Ingelheim and died. But most sources agree that Louis's life ended when an eclipse, occurring on May 5, literally frightened him to death. After his passing, his empire was weakened by chaos and a series of civil wars.

5. 1032 A.D.—THE HEAVENLY RESCUE

Count Gregory of Tusculum, an independent lord, was one of the most powerful men in Italy. He was determined to control the papacy. When an opening came, Count Gregory used the force of his private army and the wealth of his personal treasury to obtain the election of his 14-year-old grandson, Theophylact, to the chair of St. Peter as Pope Benedict IX. The childish Benedict, arrogant, cruel, a womanizer, was a coward who hid in the Lateran Palace, fearful of a Roman opposition that wanted him out of office. At last came a feast day when he had to celebrate mass in public. His enemies plotted to assassinate him in St. Peter's Basilica. Unable to arm themselves with swords which would betray their intent, the plotters carried pieces of rope. Their plan was to create a disturbance that would divert the pope's guards, then rush the pope, strangle him to death, and escape during the resultant chaos. When the fateful day came, the conspirators pressed through the crowds, ready to strike. Just then, wrote Raoul Glaber in 1824, "about the sixth hour of the day there occurred an eclipse of the sun which lasted until the eighth hour. All faces were as pale as death, and everything that could be seen was suffused with the colors of yellow and saffron." In the confusion of semidarkness, the assassins hesitated, and the pope, now aware of them, fled the basilica to safety. He would rule and abdicate and rule again at least four times in his life before giving up the papacy for good in July, 1048, and retiring to a humble monastery.

6. 1504—COLUMBUS THE MAGICIAN

During his fourth voyage to the New World, Christopher Columbus limped into the West Indies with two damaged ships that were dangerously low on supplies. Anchored off Jamaica for a year, Columbus had to replenish his food stores or suffer starvation and mutiny. After a period of trading, the Jamaican natives decided not to sell any more food to the Europeans. Columbus was desperate. One day, while reading his *Zacuto Almanac*, he learned that shortly, on February 29, there would be an eclipse of the moon. On the day of the predicted eclipse, Columbus summoned the Jamaican chieftains and told them that if they did not give him food, he had the power to blot out the moon. The chieftains ridiculed him. That night, the lunar eclipse began, and the Jamaicans were terrified. At once, Columbus volunteered to bring back the moon if the natives would supply him with food. The natives promised to give him anything he wanted. The eclipse ended, the moon shone once more, and the grateful chieftains heaped food before the explorer, saving Columbus and his crew from starvation.

7. 1764—BIRTH OF A CHAMPION

During the solar eclipse of that year, a chestnut foal was born on the Duke of Cumberland's estate in England. Of course, the colt was named Eclipse. He was destined to become the greatest racehorse in history and to enrich the lives and pockets of all sportsmen who saw him. When the duke dispersed his horses, he had Eclipse auctioned off to a sheep salesman for 75 guineas. Eclipse ran his maiden race at the age of five, winning a 4-mi. heat by over a furlong. So impressed was the renowned gambler Col. Dennis O'Kelly that he bought half interest in the stallion for 650 guineas. By the time Eclipse had won 11 races in a row, O'Kelly bought out his partner's share for 1,000 guineas more. Eclipse proved invincible. Said one observer at the time: "He was never beat, never had a whip flourished over him, never felt the tickling of a spur, nor was he ever for a moment distressed by the speed or rate of a competitor—outfooting, outstriding, and outlasting every horse which started against him." The ugly, bad-tempered colt would not lose. In his two-year career he won 26 consecutive races, and he triumphed in 11 King's Plates at Newmarket. Retired to stud, he sired three English Derby winners. He died on February 27, 1789. One of his hooves, set in gold, was made into a drinking goblet, which stands in the Jockey Club of Newmarket to this day.

8. 1806—THE SHAWNEE PROPHET SPEAKS

He was first known as the great Tecumseh's brother. His original name was Lalawethika ("Loud Voice"), but he was later known as Tenskwatawa ("Open Door"). He claimed to have had a vision and insisted he was a prophet. With his brother, he preached to the Indian tribes east of the Mississippi, exhorting them to unite against white settlers, to give up white customs and to return to Indian traditions. Worried about Tenskwatawa's influence, Gen. William H. Harrison, governor of the Territory of Indiana, challenged him with a message sent to the Indian tribes: "Who is this pretended prophet who dares speak in the name of the Great Creator? If he is really a prophet, ask him to cause the sun to stand still—the moon to alter its course—the rivers to cease to flow—or the dead to arise from their graves." Tenskwatawa took up the challenge. He announced that at noon on June 16, 1806, he would cause the sun to disappear and darkness to fall across the earth. The eclipse came on schedule, and the prophet's supernatural powers were celebrated. However, one of his next major prophecies was wrong. He advised his warriors to attack General Harrison's troops at Tippecanoe, promising them that they would not be harmed by the white men's bullets. The prophet's followers attacked and were crushed, a fourth of the braves slaughtered. In 1840 General Harrison won the contest for the White House with the slogan "Tippecanoe and Tyler Too!" The Shawnee Prophet retired to Canada, lived on a British pension, later died in Kansas.

9. 1879—THE ZULU MASSACRE

Because of a territorial dispute over the Transvaal, as well as a desire to curtail the powers of the Zulu chief Cetewayo, the British went to war against Zululand. Lord Chelmsford led a force of 13,000 against Cetewayo's army of 40,000. On January 22, a large British contingent was encamped on Isandhlwana Hill. The Zulus surrounded the British position and attacked. The British troopers and their allied Natal Kaffirs were struck from all sides. During the height of the battle, at 1:02 P.M., a solar eclipse began. If the British hoped this would play on Zulu superstitions and send them into retreat, they soon learned they were mistaken. "The sun got very dark, like

Cetewayo, king of the Zulus,
whose warriors overcame the British in 1879.

night," said one Zulu, and the Zulus liked to fight by night. The eclipse inspired them to overwhelm the invaders. At the end of three hours the entire British camp was wiped out to a man—1,300 British and Natal Kaffirs dead, beheaded, their stomachs slashed to release the spirits of the dead. Months later the British poured in reinforcements, smashed the Zulus at Ulundi, took control of Zululand, and finally annexed it in 1887.

10. 1905—THE CAPTAIN AND THE SULTAN

In central Africa, elbowing the vastness of the Belgian Congo, stood an independent nation of cannibals called the Mangbettu. This country of 1½ million blacks was ruled by Sultan Yembio. Early on February 18, a Belgian officer, Capt. Albert Paulis, and 20 of his men wandered into the country and were captured by the cannibals. Waiting to be executed, Captain Paulis thumbed through an almanac he carried in his knapsack. He noticed that an eclipse of the moon was due that evening at eight o'clock. Remembering how Columbus had managed to save his crew and his life by using the 1504 eclipse, Captain Paulis decided to try the same trick. A message was sent to Sultan Yembio warning him that if the white men were harmed, their captain had the magical power to kill the moon, and that the death of the moon would also doom the sultan. That night the sultan came to Captain Paulis and dared him to kill the moon. At 8:00 P.M., Paulis pointed to the moon and announced its death. Slowly the moon began to blacken over and disappear. The eclipse was under way. In terror the sultan fell to his knees, promising the Belgian captain anything he wanted if he would save the moon. Paulis demanded that the sultan recognize the authority of the king of Belgium over his domain. The sultan agreed. Captain Paulis waved a hand toward the sky, the eclipse ended, the moon was restored. He and his men were freed, and the 4,000 sq. mi. of the Mangbettu, as well as subsidiary lands, became part of the Belgian Congo.

—I.W., D.P.M., & R.FU.

11 MOON MYSTERIES UNCOVERED BY THE APOLLO MISSIONS

The historic Apollo voyages rank among the greatest technological feats and exploratory missions humanity has as yet undertaken. Between July, 1969, and December, 1972—a three-and-a-half-year period—12 astronauts walked on and explored the surface of this alien lunar world, while another six astronauts orbited the moon, studying with sophisticated equipment vast segments of its surface. The dozen astronauts who landed on the moon spent over 300 hours traversing 60 mi. of the lunar surface. Five nuclear-powered scientific stations were set up, which employed sensitive seismometers, heat-flow probes, and magnetometers. The astronauts also collected and brought back to earth over 837 lb. of carefully selected moon material, mostly rocks and dust. Despite subsequent efforts to study the evidence and data collected—and though much light has been shed on this mystery world—scientists still remain in the dark as to the origin and nature of the planetoid. In fact, the more the experts probe, the more mysteries they uncover.

1. THE PUZZLE OF THE MOON'S ORIGIN

Scientists have offered three major theories to account for the moon's existence in our earth's skies. All three are in trouble, but the least likely emerged from Apollo as the foremost candidate. Some scientists thought that the moon might have been born alongside the earth out of the same cosmic cloud of gas and dust about 4.6 billion years ago. Others opined that the moon was the earth's child, ripped out of the Pacific area perhaps. Evidence from the Apollo journeys indicates, however, that the moon and the earth differ greatly in composition. Scientists at the last lunar conferences—annual rock festivals, NASA scientist Gerald Wasserburg has dubbed them—favored the so-called "capture" theory. This holds that the moon was accidentally captured in the earth's gravitational field and locked into orbit eons ago. Challengers of this theory point out the immensely difficult celestial mechanics involved in such a capture. Thus all three theories are in serious hot water. NASA scientist Dr. Robin Brett sums it up: "It seems much easier to explain the nonexistence of the moon than its existence."

2. THE PUZZLE OF THE MOON'S AGE

Amazingly, over 99% of the moon rocks brought back turned out upon analysis to be older than 90% of the most ancient rocks found on the earth. The very first rock that Neil Armstrong picked up after landing on the Sea of Tranquillity turned out to be more than 3.6 billion years old, while the oldest earth rocks are approximately 3.7 billion years old. Other lunar rocks have been estimated to be 4.3, 4.5, and even 4.6 billion years old—about the age of the earth and its solar system. At the Lunar Conference of 1973, one lunar rock was alleged to be 5.3 billion years old. The most puzzling aspect is that most of these were taken from areas that scientists thought were the *youngest* surfaces of the moon. Based on such evidence, some lunar scientists have concluded that the moon was formed among the stars long before our sun was born.

3. THE PUZZLE OF HOW MOON SOIL COULD BE OLDER THAN LUNAR ROCKS

The perplexing age of the moon is highlighted by an even more puzzling conundrum. Rocks taken from the Sea of Tranquillity, where the U.S. astronauts first landed, were young compared to the soil on which they rested. Upon analysis, this proved to be at least a billion years older. This would appear to be impossible, since the soil was presumably the powdered remains of the rocks lying alongside it. However, chemical analysis of the rocks revealed that the lunar soil did not come from the rocks but from somewhere else.

4. THE PUZZLE OF WHY THE MOON "RINGS" LIKE A HOLLOW SPHERE WHEN A LARGE OBJECT HITS IT

During the Apollo expeditions, ascent stages of lunar modules and spent third stages of rockets crashed on the hard surface of the moon. Every time, these caused the moon, as NASA documents state, to "ring like a huge gong or bell." On the Apollo 12 flight, reverberations lasted from nearly an hour to as much as four hours. So far no scientist has adequately explained this bizarre lunar behavior.

5. THE PUZZLE OF THE MYSTIFYING MARIA OF THE MOON

The strange dark circular areas of the moon (maria), some of which form the "man in the moon" for viewers standing on the earth, are puzzlingly located almost entirely on one side of the moon. When lunar missions landed on these peculiar dark plainlike areas, astronauts found it extremely difficult to drill into the lunar surface. Soil samples are loaded with rare rough metals like titanium (used in supersonic jets and spaceships), along with such rare metallic elements as zirconium, yttrium, and beryllium. Scientists were dumbfounded, because these elements require tremendous heat— about 4,500°F—to melt and fuse with surrounding rock.

6. THE PUZZLE OF THE RUSTPROOF PURE IRON FOUND ON THE MOON

Lunar samples brought back to the earth by both American and Soviet space probes contain pure iron particles. Scientists have concluded that the iron did not come from meteorites. Soviet remote-controlled lunar probe Zond 20 brought back tiny samples in which such pure iron particles were discovered, and TASS announced recently that they have not oxidized even after several years on earth. Pure iron particles that do not rust are unheard of in the scientific world.

7. THE PUZZLE OF THE MOON'S HIGH RADIOACTIVITY

The upper 8 mi. of the moon's crust are surprisingly radioactive. When Apollo 15 astronauts used thermal equipment, they got unusually high readings, which indicated that the heat flow near the Apennine Mountains was hot indeed. In fact, one lunar expert confessed: "When we saw that we said, 'My God, this place is about to melt! The core must be very hot.'" But that is the puzzle. The core is not "very" hot. However, the amount of radioactive materials on the surface is not only "embarrassingly high" but, considering the relatively cold interior, difficult to account for. Where did all this hot radioactive material (uranium, thorium, and potassium) come from? And if it came from the interior, how did it get to the moon's surface?

8. THE PUZZLE OF THE IMMENSE CLOUDS OF WATER VAPOR ON A DRY MOON

The first few lunar excursions indicated that the moon was an extremely dry world. In fact, one lunar expert concluded that it was "a million times as dry as the Gobi Desert." The early Apollo expeditions did not find even the slightest trace of water. But after Apollo 15, the lunar experts were rocked back on their collective heels when a cloud of water vapor more than 100 sq. mi. in size was detected on the moon's surface. Red-faced scientists suggested that two tiny tanks, abandoned on the moon by U.S. astronauts, had somehow ruptured. But the tanks could not have produced a cloud of such magnitude. Nor would the astronauts' urine, which had been dumped into the lunar skies, be an answer. The water vapor appears to have come from the moon's interior.

9. THE PUZZLE OF THE GLASSY SURFACE ON THE MOON

Lunar explorations have revealed that much of the moon's surface is covered with a glassy glaze, which indicates that the moon's hide has been scorched by an unknown source of intense heat. As one scientist put it, the moon is "paved with glass." The experts' analysis shows this did not result from massive meteor impactings. Some feel that an intense solar outburst, a kind of mininova, might have been responsible.

10. THE PUZZLE OF THE MOON'S STRANGE MAGNETISM

Early lunar tests and studies indicated that the moon had little or no magnetic field. Then lunar rocks proved upon analysis to be strongly magnetized. This shocked scientists, who had assumed that the moon had always been without a magnetic field. As the late Dr. Paul Gast of NASA observed, these rocks had "some very strange magnetic properties . . . which were not expected." If the moon did actually have a magnetic field at one time, then it must have possessed a big iron core, but equally valid data and evidence show that such a huge hot core could not have existed inside the moon. Neither could the moon very well have picked up the magnetism from the magnetic field of another body like the earth. In order to do so, the moon would have had to approach so close that it would have been torn apart by the gravitational pull.

11. THE PUZZLE OF THE MYSTERIOUS "MASCONS" INSIDE THE MOON

In 1968, tracking data of the lunar orbiters first indicated that massive concentrations (mascons) existed under the surface of the circular maria. In fact, the gravitational pull caused by them was so pronounced that the spacecraft passing overhead dipped slightly and accelerated when flitting by the circular lunar plains, thus revealing the existence of these hidden stuctures. Scientists have calculated that they are enormous concentrations of dense, heavy matter centered like a bull's-eye under the circular maria. As one scientist put it: "No one seems to know quite what to do with them."

—D.K.W.

6
THE ANIMAL KINGDOM

DR. EDWARD O. WILSON'S
10 MOST INTELLIGENT ANIMALS

Edward O. Wilson is a professor of zoology and curator of entomology at Harvard University and the author of many books and articles on the evolution and behavior of animals, including *The Insect Societies* (1971), *Sociobiology: The New Synthesis* (1975), and *On Human Nature* (1978), for which he won the Pulitzer Prize.

1. Chimpanzee (two species)
2. Gorilla
3. Orangutan
4. Baboon (seven species, including drill and mandrill)
5. Gibbon (seven species)
6. Monkey (many species, especially macaques, the patas, and the Celebes black ape)
7. Smaller toothed whale (several species, especially killer whale)
8. Dolphin (many of the approximately 80 species)
9. Elephant (two species)
10. Pig

Dr. Wilson adds: "I defined intelligence as the speed and extent of learning performance over a wide range of tasks. Insofar as possible, the rank ordering was based in part on actual experiments conducted on learning ability. In those cases where such studies have not been made, I relied on the 'encephalization index,' which measures the size of the brain relative to that of the body as a whole and has been shown to be roughly correlated with intelligence. Although I believe that my rank ordering is relatively sound, much more research is needed in this field of zoology, and changes in position can easily occur, especially near the bottom of the list of 10."

—Exclusive for *The Book of Lists* 2

10 CELEBRATED
COMMUNICATING ANIMALS

1. ARLECCHINO (c. 1960)

Elizabeth Mann Borghese, animal trainer and daughter of writer Thomas Mann, taught her setter, Arlecchino, to take dictation on a special typewriter by hitting the keys with his nose. He began his language training on July 10, 1963, and in six months he could type 20 words. He went beyond dictation, however. Once, when asked where he wanted to go, he spelled out c-a-r.

2. BENJY (1965–1978)

Benjy, the remarkable mongrel dog of Mrs. Betsy Marcus of Brookline, Mass., could sing when he was only nine weeks old. He specialized in "Raindrops Keep Fallin' on My Head," which he performed on *The Ed Sullivan Show* and *The Tonight Show*.

3. CHRIS (1949?–1959?)

Chris, a little mongrel dog from Greenwich, R.I., was psychic. His powers of communication were discovered when he started pawing out words, using a number for each letter—one paw for *a*, two paws for *b*, etc. After he predicted the winning horse at a daily double, a team of parapsychologists from Duke University were called in. Chris was given a battery of tests, which proved his extrasensory abilities. He was only one day off in predicting his own death.

4. CLEVER HANS (*KLUGE HANS*) (c. 1890)

One of the celebrated Elberfeld horses, Clever Hans, a Russian stallion, supposedly could answer questions, indicate notes of the musical scale, and do arithmetic. A scientific commission that investigated him in the late 1800s determined that the horse was responding to subtle, unconscious signals from his master, Karl Krall. Popular songs were written about Clever Hans, and children named their toy horses after him.

5. JACO (1827–1854)

An African gray parrot, Jaco lived in Salzburg and could, like many of his kind, speak German. However, unlike most parrots, he seemed to understand what he was saying. When his master left the house alone, Jaco said "God be with you," but if his master was accompanied by others, he said, "God be with you all."

6. LADY WONDER (1926–1957)

Lady Wonder was a psychic horse who communicated by using her nose to spell out letters on a giant typewriter with rubber keys. She predicted the U.S. would enter W.W. II and, against popular opinion, that President Truman would be reelected. In 1951 she made headline news by directing police to the site of the body of a boy who had been missing for two years. Noted parapsychologist Dr. J. B. Rhine studied Lady Wonder in the 1920s and confirmed her telepathic powers.

7. LIZZIE (1950?–1960)

Lizzie, a female dolphin, died on April 16, 1960, in a pool where she was being kept by well-known neurophysiologist Dr. John Lilly, who had been conducting experiments on human-dolphin communication. Lilly feels that dolphins have a higher form of consciousness than we do and that their language and view of life are based on nonhuman, but highly intelligent, logic. In 1968 Lilly freed his other dolphins, commenting, "I felt I had no right to hold dolphins in concentration camps for my convenience." Lizzie left behind a short tape-recorded sentence which has been interpreted as either "It's six o'clock" or "It's a trick."

8. MOROCCO (c. 1600)

Back in the time of Shakespeare, a white horse named Morocco amazed the populace of England and France by totaling dice, answering questions, and giving people's ages—all with a hoof-pawing code. It is said that when his master was condemned to death for witchcraft, Morocco begged for and saved his life by kneeling down before an official.

9. THE TALKING TORTOISE (1978)

In the summer of 1978, Ugandan officials denied that a giant talking tortoise was walking from village to village outside the capital, Kampala. Tens of thousands of Ugandans, however, said the story was true, and local police near the town of Jinja on Lake Victoria reported that the tortoise entered their station and demanded to see the provincial commissioner of police. Just what the tortoise was upset about was not reported, but its actions so disturbed former president Idi Amin that he threatened to shoot anyone found talking about it.

10. WASHOE (1965–)

She calls an enemy "dirty Jack," makes up words (*drink-fruit* for watermelon, *water-bird* for swan), and understands the rudiments of syntax. Her name is Washoe, and she uses sign language to communicate. Psychologists R. Allen and Beatrice Gardner began training this female chimpanzee to use American Sign Language (a language for the deaf) when she was a year old. Now in an Oklahoma chimpanzee colony, she has taught her companions to speak through sign language too.

—A.E. & The Eds.

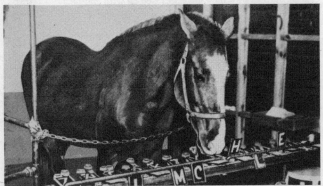

The psychic horse, *Lady Wonder*, who lived to the age of 31, typing out people's thoughts on a large rubber typewriter.

8 UNUSUAL
DOLPHIN INCIDENTS

1. THE DOLPHIN AS NURSE

On October 30, 1954, a group of scientists collecting aquarium specimens off the Gulf Coast of the Florida panhandle exploded dynamite underwater close to a herd of bottle-nosed dolphins. One of the dolphins, stunned by the blast, began swimming with a 45° list. Two of its fellow dolphins swam over and supported it under its flippers to keep it afloat. The entire group of dolphins stayed near the injured one until it recovered; then they all swam away.

2. THE DOLPHIN AS PLAYMATE

In 1955 a one-year-old female bottle-nosed dolphin appeared in Hokianga Harbor at Opononi, New Zealand. For the next year she played with children and adults and was reported to have allowed some children to ride on her back. The townsfolk named her Opo and passed a law that prohibited the molestation of dolphins in the harbor. However, on the day the law went into effect, Opo's dead body was found stranded in a tide pool near Opononi. Apparently fishermen had been using dynamite or gelignite to kill snapper near where Opo was feeding, and she was stunned by the blast. The citizens of Opononi buried the dolphin and covered her grave with flowers.

3. THE DOLPHIN AS LIFEGUARD

Yvonne Vladislavich, a South African woman, was thrown into the Indian Ocean in June, 1971, when the yacht she was on exploded. After a short time, three dolphins approached her. One buoyed her up while the other two circled her, apparently guarding her against possible shark attack. Eventually she drifted toward a marker in the sea and climbed up on it, and the dolphins left her there. Her rescuers determined that she had drifted more than 200 mi., and the dolphins had stayed with her the entire distance.

4. THE DOLPHIN AS GOOD SAMARITAN

According to the Soviet news agency TASS, a Russian fishing boat was approached in the Black Sea in September, 1977, by a small group of dolphins, which circled the boat until the sailors raised anchor and followed the animals. The dolphins led the Russians to a buoy near which a young dolphin was trapped in a fishing net. After the men released the young dolphin, the dolphins guided the boat back to the precise spot at which it had been anchored originally.

5. THE DOLPHIN AS GUIDE

On May 28, 1978, four fishermen—Kobus Stander and his son Barend, from Boston Estate; Wessel Matthee, from Parow; and Mac Macgreggor, from Maitland—were lost in a dense fog off Dassen Island, South Africa. Four dolphins appeared and swam around their boat until they changed course—just in time to avoid running into rocks that protruded above the water but were invisible because of the murk. The dolphins nudged and bumped the boat until it reached calm waters, where they blocked it from going further until the men dropped anchor. Then the dolphins swam away. When the fog lifted, the men found themselves in the very bay from which they had set out earlier.

6. THE DOLPHIN AS PROTECTOR

According to the Soviet news agency TASS, sailors on board the fishing vessel *Nevelskoi*, sailing off the coast of Kamchatka on August 14, 1978, heard a sea lion bellowing for help. The sea lion was surrounded by a number of killer whales. A few minutes later a group of dolphins appeared, and the whales moved off. When the dolphins left, the whales rushed the sea lion. But the dolphins quickly turned around, leaped over the whales' heads, and formed a ring around the sea lion, thus saving its life.

7. THE DOLPHIN AS PILOT

On September 30, 1978, about 50 pilot whales tried to beach themselves at Whangarei Harbor north of Auckland, New Zealand. Government officials attempted to lure the whales back into the sea, and when this failed, they used speedboats to guide a passing group of dolphins into the harbor. Once there, the dolphins took over and led the whales toward open water. At least 30 of the 50 whales survived, and when last seen were 15 mi. out to sea.

8. THE DOLPHIN AS PATIENT

The Soviet news agency TASS reported that during January of 1979 a dolphin tried to jump onto a Russian fishing boat but was unable to do so. After the puzzled sailors had helped the animal aboard, they found that it had a large, bleeding gash on its side. While the ship's doctor sutured the wound, the dolphin lay perfectly still. After surgery, the sailors returned the dolphin to the sea.

—B.H.

8 ANIMALS THAT HAVE EATEN HUMANS

1. BEARS

The North American black bear, although smaller and less aggressive than the grizzly, can be deadly and has been responsible for many harmful attacks on humans. In 1963, when the Alaskan blueberry crop was poor, hungry black bears attacked at least four people, one of whom they killed.

2. CROCODILES

Estuarine crocodiles are the most prolific man-eaters on earth, killing approximately 2,000 people a year. On the night of February

19, 1945, they were responsible for the most devastating animal attack on human beings in recorded history. British troops had trapped 1,000 Japanese infantrymen, many of whom were wounded, in a swampy area in the Bay of Bengal. The noise of gunfire and the smell of blood had attracted hundreds of crocodiles, and by evening the British could hear terrible screams. The following morning, only 20 Japanese were found alive.

3. GIANT SQUID

The giant squid is the most highly developed of the invertebrates. Its eyes are almost exact replicas of human eyes. It has 10 arms, and its body can reach up to 65 ft. in length. Often confused with the octopus, which attacks humans only when threatened, the giant squid is a carnivorous predator. One notable incident occurred on March 25, 1941, when the British ship *Britannia* sank in the Atlantic Ocean. As a dozen survivors clung to their lifeboat, a giant squid reached its arm around the body of a man and pulled him below. Male squid sometimes eat the female after mating.

4. LEOPARDS

Considered one of the most dangerous animals to hunt, the leopard is quick and stealthy and is seldom observed. In the central provinces of India, leopards have been known to invade native huts to find their prey. One, known as the Panawar man-eater, is reputed to have killed 400 people. It was shot in 1910 by Jim Corbett, who also bested the Champawat man-eating tigress the following year.

White hunter Jim Corbett with the Man-Eating Leopard of Rudraprayag, which had killed 125 humans.

5. LIONS

Like tigers, lions do not usually attack humans. Man-eating lions usually hunt in prides, or groups, although occasionally single lions and pairs have become man-eaters. In October, 1943, a lone lion was shot in the Kasama district of what is now Zambia after it had killed 40 people.

6. PIRANHAS

Although there are no confirmed reports of piranha-caused deaths, observers in the river regions of northeastern South America report that many of the natives have lost fingers, toes, or penny-sized chunks of flesh while bathing in piranha-infested waters. There are several species of piranha, the largest of which attains 24 in. in length. They have short, powerful jaws and sharply pointed teeth, and are strongly attracted by the smell of blood. A school of piranhas can strip a wounded alligator of flesh in five minutes, but they are generally sluggish in their movements.

7. SHARKS

Of the 200 to 250 species of shark, only 18 are known to be dangerous to humans. The most notable are the great white, mako, tiger, white-tipped, Ganges River, and hammerhead. The best-known of all individual "rogue" shark attacks occurred on July 12, 1916. Twelve-year-old Lester Stilwell was swimming in Matawan Creek, N.J., 15 to 20 mi. inland, when he was attacked by a great white shark. Both he and his would-be rescuer were killed. In 10 days four persons were killed over a 60-mi. stretch of New Jersey coast. Two days after the last attack, an 8½-ft. great white shark was netted just 4 mi. from the mouth of the creek.

8. TIGERS

A tigress known as the Champawat man-eater killed 438 people in the Himalayas in Nepal between 1903 and 1911. Tigers do not usually hunt humans, unless the animals are old, or injured, or have become accustomed to the taste of human flesh.

Note: AND ONE WHO WOULD NOT. While it is almost certain that wolves have preyed on human beings at some time in history, there are *no* confirmed reports of unprovoked attacks upon humans by North American wolves.

—D.L.

14 DOUBLE-SEXED ANIMALS

1. ATLANTIC SLIPPER SHELL (*Crepidula fornicata*)

Native to North American waters, the male slipper shell wanders around until ready to settle down with—or rather upon—a female. After a while it loses its penis, becomes wholly female, and is in turn settled upon. Thus the mating process creates so-called tower chains of slipper shells in which males are always on the top and females are on the bottom. Wandering males are continually welcomed to the club; only they can fertilize the mature females, who never wander.

2. BARNACLES (*Thoracica*)

Mature barnacles are stationary hermaphrodites—animals having both male and female reproductive organs. They appear to feel safest procreating en masse in one place, but their behavior seems self-defeating. Most of their young, which swim away from the parent colony, settle down together and die from overcrowding. Barnacles pass their population problem on to us by encrusting ships' bottoms. As befits their upside-down way of life, they carry their ovaries in their heads.

3. CLEANER FISH (*Labroides dimidiatus*)

Male chauvinism is carried to extremes by this small blue member of the wrasse family. The cleaner fish is named for its obliging habit of cleaning the mouths and gills of neighboring fishes. The male enjoys a harem of two to five females, whom he terrorizes into remaining with him. The females, however, do not unite against the male; instead, they tend to keep each other in line by forming a hierarchy. It seems that the hierarchy must be preserved at all costs. When the male dies, the top-ranking female immediately takes charge and within a few days begins to develop male organs. After two weeks she is completely transformed into a patriarchal, chauvinist male, and everything proceeds as before.

4. COTTONY-CUSHION SCALE (*Icerya purchasi*)

This scale insect, a pest in California orchards until the citrus industry imported its natural enemy, the Australian ladybird beetle, avoids mating problems by fertilizing itself—a behavior pattern that is unusual even for hermaphrodites. Male specimens are sometimes found, but no females; *Icerya*, it seems, would just rather not bother with an opposite sex.

5. EARTHWORM (*Lumbricus terrestris*)

The problems of making love without arms or legs do not seem to trouble earthworm couples, hermaphrodites who lie head to tail and glue themselves together with their own mucus. Earthworms do it by numbers; their 15th segments emit sperm and their 9th and 10th segments receive and fertilize it, using the clitellum, or saddle, to encase the eggs, which will hatch two to three weeks later. They often remain locked in wormy rapture for several hours.

6. EUROPEAN FLAT OYSTER (*Ostrea edulis*)

This tender bivalve enjoys the best of both sexual worlds. It alternates sex roles, functioning first as a male, then as a female. It can do this because it has both male and female organs, and the process is known as rhythmical consecutive hermaphroditism. In waters around Great Britain, its sex roles change in alternate years, but in warmer Mediterranean waters, it can perform both roles within one season. As an example of hard-shelled romanticism, the European flat oyster is hard to beat. For reasons that have more to do with spring tides than with spring fever, it mates only after a full or new moon.

7. LAND SNAIL (*Helix pomatia*)

This common species of garden snail is a hermaphrodite that copulates with passion and originality. During the winter it burrows underground and seals itself into its shell. When spring comes, it emerges greatly refreshed and seeks a mate. Its female organs include a sac full of "love darts"—bony missiles that it can fire whenever it wants. As two amorous snails embrace, they shoot each other full of these darts, join the soles of their "feet," and quiveringly engage in a mutual exchange of sperm.

8. LIVER FLUKE (*Fasciola hepatica*)

The advantages of being a parasite have never been better demonstrated than by this hermaphrodite flatworm, whose eggs hatch into larvae that reproduce themselves asexually for two generations, so that thousands may descend from one egg. Its most common hosts are domesticated animals such as cattle and sheep. The liver fluke, internalized when cattle swallow infested water, heads unerringly for its host's liver, and there it munches away happily.

9. PARASITIC WASPS (*Habrobracon*)

Small parasitic wasps of the genus *Habrobracon* are often gynandromorphs—that is, crazy-quilt mixtures of male and female chromosomes. Their behavior proves beyond a doubt that the most important sex organ is the mind. For instance, a normal male *Habrobracon* will copulate with a female and sting the moth larva in which the female lays her eggs. A *Habrobracon* gynandromorph with a male head and female body may sting the female and attempt copulation with the moth larva. It may also fuss around the female without attempting copulation, or begin copulation and then suddenly break off, as if remembering an urgent appointment.

10. SEA BASS (*Serranidae*)

Several species of sea bass known as grouper—a fish prized for its delicate taste—undergo a complete sexual transformation, from mature female to mature male. This generally happens during the fish's fifth year. Another Florida species, called the belted sandfish (*Serranus subligarius*), is a hermaphrodite that can fertilize itself.

11. SEA HARE (*Tethys*)

The inability of these marine snails to exchange sperm with a mate—although hermaphroditic—is apparently what drives them to the practice of group sex. A sea hare that mounts another is often mounted by a third, which in turn attracts a fourth, until as many as 12 may be joined in what, to students of human sexual behavior, is traditionally known as a daisy chain. Some excited observers report that there are occasions when the chain becomes a circle. Since the largest sea hares are nearly 30 in. long, their behavior, which takes place in tropical and temperate coastal zones, can justly be called a public scandal.

12. SEA SQUIRT (*Ascidiacea*)

A lopsided bag of organs attached to a voracious mouth, the sea squirt (actually a group of marine animals ranging in length from less than a millimeter to over a foot) begins life as a tadpole but grows up to resemble a plant. It is a hermaphrodite with a difference; besides reproducing itself sexually by the usual egg-and-sperm method, it also puts out shoots like a potato. The latter system, however, tends to create offspring who in turn go the sexual route. The next generation then reverts to shoots. This alternation has ensured sea squirts a worldwide distribution, while keeping them low on the evolutionary scale.

13. SHIPWORM (*Teredo navalis*)

Like the oyster, the shipworm (actually an elongated bivalve, not a worm) lays immense numbers of eggs—up to 5 million a year—and then changes sex roles. It uses its shell to bore through wood, which it eats. In the days of wooden ships and harbor piers, shipworms were the scourge of nations.

14. SPOONWORM (*Bonellia viridis*)

The larva of this marine worm leads a kind of fairy-tale existence. If, while it is still a wriggling juvenile, it comes into contact with the proboscis of an adult female, then—hey, presto!—it becomes a tiny male practically overnight. If not, it establishes itself in or under a rock and grows into a sausage-shaped female some 4 in. long. Since the males remain over 60 times as small, they have to take up residence inside the female in order to fertilize her. The record number of males found in one female is 85. The ones living in her egg sac were doing their duty as procreators—but the rest were merely enjoying a free ride in her intestines.

—J.M.B.E.

12 FAMOUS CAT LOVERS

1. RAYMOND CHANDLER, U.S. author (1888–1959)

During the 1930s Chandler had a black Persian called Taki. He often spoke to her as if she were human. Sometimes he called her his secretary, because she frequently sat on the paper he was about to use or on copy that needed revising.

2. SIR WINSTON CHURCHILL, British statesman (1874–1965)

During Churchill's last years, he acquired a ginger kitten named Jock. Churchill enjoyed having Jock eat with him and would often send the servants to find the cat so that the meal could begin. A great comfort to his aging master, Jock usually slept on Churchill's bed.

Hardboiled detective-story writer
Raymond Chandler and his collaborator Taki.

3. COLETTE, French writer (1873–1954)

There were never less than 10 cats living in Colette's home in southern France, excluding neighborhood cats and cats that were staying with Colette while their owners were on vacation. She wrote several stories that featured cats, including the well-known novel *La Chatte*, and often credited the species of the cat with teaching her self-control and "a particular kind of honorable deceit."

4. SAMUEL JOHNSON, English lexicographer (1709–1784)

Dr. Johnson's biographer James Boswell wrote: "I shall never forget the indulgence with which he [Dr. Johnson] treated Hodge, his cat; for whom he himself used to go out and buy oysters, lest the servants having that trouble should take a dislike to the poor creature."

5. ROBERT E. LEE, U.S. general (1807–1870)

General Lee's letters to his family were often filled with references to cats. While on campaign during the Mexican War, Lee wrote his daughter Mildred and asked her to send him a cat to keep him company.

6. LEO XII, Italian pope (1760–1829)

Micetto was a tabby born in the Vatican and raised by Pope Leo. Micetto was Leo's favorite companion and lived in the folds of the elaborate robes worn by the pope. The French writer and statesman Chateaubriand adopted the cat when the pope died, and it is believed that Micetto's stuffed skin is preserved in a château in France.

7. MOHAMMED, Arabian religious leader (570–632)

The founder of the Muslim faith believed that dogs were unclean. However, cats found favor in his eyes. In order to go to prayers, he once cut off the sleeve of his robe so as not to disturb his sleeping cat.

8. PETRARCH, Italian poet (1304–1374)

Petrarch's chief companion during the last years of his life was his cat. When he died, his cat was put to death and mummified. It lies today in a niche decorated with a marble cat and bearing an inscription said to have been written by the poet. It states that his cat was "second only to Laura," a woman he loved from afar—but a woman historians have never been able to identify.

9. EDGAR ALLAN POE, U.S. author (1809–1849)

The man who penned the classic horror story "The Black Cat" was in reality a great cat lover. He and his wife Virginia took their cat Catarina wherever they went. When Mrs. Poe lay dying of consumption, the cat was by her side, trying her best to keep her mistress warm.

10. ARMAND JEAN DU PLESSIS, CARDINAL RICHELIEU, French statesman and religious leader (1585–1642)

The cardinal made one of his rooms into a cattery, where overseers Abel and Teyssandier fed the cats pâtés of white chicken meat twice daily. When he died, the overseers and the cats were left a pension.

11. ALBERT SCHWEITZER, French medical missionary (1875–1965)

Dr. Schweitzer was passionately fond of animals and was bitterly opposed to their wanton destruction. While in Africa, he had a cat named Sizi. Although left-handed, he often wrote out prescriptions with his right hand because Sizi liked to sleep on his left arm and could not be disturbed.

12. HENRY WRIOTHESLEY, 3RD EARL OF SOUTHAMPTON, English adventurer (1573–1624)

Toward the end of the reign of Elizabeth I, the earl was imprisoned in the Tower of London. Somehow his cat found its way down a chimney to be with him. As a memento, the earl—who was released by James I—had his portrait painted with the black and white cat in the background.

—J.M.F.

10 FAMOUS CAT HATERS

1. JAMES BOSWELL, Scottish author (1740–1795)

Boswell, the well-known biographer of Samuel Johnson, loathed cats. Because he did not wish to offend Dr. Johnson, who was an ardent cat lover, Boswell kept his opinions to himself.

2. JOHANNES BRAHMS, German composer (1833–1897)

Brahms was an avowed cat hater. He spent much time at the window trying to hit neighborhood cats with a bow and arrow—a sport at which he became quite adept.

3. GEORGES LOUIS LECLERC DE BUFFON, French naturalist (1707–1788)

The leading naturalist of his day had high praise for dogs but little use for cats. According to him, cats possess "an innate malice, and perverse disposition, which increases as they grow up." He added that they "easily assume the habits of society, but never acquire its manners."

4. DWIGHT D. EISENHOWER, U.S. president (1890–1969)

During a 1978 lecture at the National Archives in Washington, D.C., David Eisenhower, the president's grandson, told of Ike's terrible temper. The president not only kept a shotgun next to his television to shoot crows at his home in Gettysburg, but also ordered that any cat seen on the grounds should be shot.

5. HENRY III, French king (1551–1589)

A zealous Roman Catholic, Henry was like a lion when persecuting the Protestant minority in France. But the presence of a cat turned the king into a chicken. He fainted if a cat came close to him.

6. NAPOLEON BONAPARTE, French emperor (1769–1821)

During one campaign, an aide-de-camp passed the general's bedroom and was surprised to hear him calling for assistance. Opening the door, the aide saw the emperor, half dressed and sweating profusely, lunging with his sword through the tapestry that lined the walls. His prey? A tiny kitten.

7. FREDERICK SLEIGH ROBERTS, British military leader (1832–1914)

Because of his brilliant successes in Afghanistan and later in the Boer War, Roberts became an earl and the commander in chief of the British army. In his skirmishes with cats, however, he always scored a poor second. When he saw a cat, Roberts got so excited that he had difficulty breathing.

8. PIERRE DE RONSARD, French poet (1524–1585)

Famous for his sonnets, Ronsard was the court poet of Charles IX. For cats, however, he had no beautiful words. He wrote:

There is no man now living anywhere,
Who hates cats with a deeper hate than I;
I hate their eyes, their heads, the way they stare,
And when I see one come, I turn and fly.

9. PERCY BYSSHE SHELLEY, English poet (1792–1822)

Like Benjamin Franklin, Shelley experimented with electricity. On at least one occasion, the poet tied a tomcat to the string of a kite that was flying during a thunderstorm. What happened to the cat is not known.

10. NOAH WEBSTER, American lexicographer (1758–1843)

In his famous dictionary, Webster had very little to say about cats that was good. According to him, the domestic cat is a "deceitful animal and when enraged extremely spiteful."

—J.M.F.

10 MOST PROLIFIC BIRD-WATCHERS

		No. of Species Sighted (*of a Possible 8,600+*)
1.	G. Stuart Keith, New York	5,420
2.	P. Norman Chesterfield, Canada	4,805
3.	Ira Joel Abramson, Florida	4,728
4.	Arnold Small, California	4,467
5.	Peter Alden, Massachusetts	4,400
6.	Ernest S. Booth, Washington	4,388
7.	Michael Gochfeld, New York	3,807
8.	Robert S. Ridgely, Connecticut	3,709
9.	Allan R. Keith, New Jersey	3,636
10.	Bertha H. Massie, Missouri	3,635

SOURCE: American Birding Association, January 1, 1979.

THE DAY OF EXTINCTION FOR 6 BIRDS

1. LABRADOR DUCK, DECEMBER 12, 1872

A small black and white duck indigenous to North America, the Labrador was considered to be a strong and hardy species, and its decline is still mysterious. The duck bred on the east coast of Canada but flew as far south as Philadelphia in the summer. Hunting no doubt contributed to its demise. The last reported Labrador duck was shot down over Long Island in 1872.

2. GUADALUPE ISLAND CARACARA, DECEMBER 1, 1900

A large brown hawk with a black head and gray striped wings, the caracara was last seen alive and collected by R. H. Beck in 1900. One of the few cases where a bird was deliberately exterminated, the caracara was poisoned and shot by goatherds, who thought it was killing the kids in their herds.

3. PASSENGER PIGEON, SEPTEMBER 1, 1914

These brownish-gray pigeons were once so numerous that a passing flock could darken the sky for days. As recently as 1810, an

The last passenger pigeon, Martha, seen here stuffed, died in the Cincinnati Zoo of old age.

118

estimated 2,230,272,000 pigeons were sighted in one flock. But massive hunting by settlers and a century of forest destruction eliminated the passenger pigeon and its native forest habitat. In 1869, 7,500,000 pigeons were captured in a single nesting raid. In 1909, a $1,500 reward was offered for a live nesting pair, but not one could be found. Martha, the last of the passenger pigeons, died of old age in 1914 in the Cincinnati Zoo.

4. CAROLINA PARAKEET, FEBRUARY 21, 1918

The striking green and yellow Carolina parakeet was once common in the forests of the eastern and southern U.S., but because of the widespread crop destruction it caused, farmers hunted the bird to extinction. The last Carolina parakeet, an old male named Incas, died in the Cincinnati Zoo. The zoo's general manager believed it died of grief over the loss of Lady Jane, its mate of 30 years, the previous summer.

5. HEATH HEN, MARCH 11, 1932

An east coast U.S. relative of the prairie chicken, the heath hen was once so common around Boston that servants sometimes stipulated before accepting employment that heath hen not be served to them more than a few times a week. But the bird was hunted to extinction, and the last heath hen, alone since December, 1928, passed away on Martha's Vineyard at age eight, after the harsh winter of 1932.

6. EULER'S FLYCATCHER, SEPTEMBER 26, 1955

Known only from two specimens and one sighting, Euler's flycatcher was an 8½-in. olive and dusky yellow bird. The flycatcher was believed by James Bond (the authority on Caribbean birds, not Ian Fleming's 007) to have perished on Jamaica in 1955 during Hurricane Janet.

—D.L.

7 EXTINCT ANIMALS THAT ARE NO LONGER EXTINCT

1. CAHOW

This ocean-wandering bird nested exclusively on the islets of Bermuda. Also known as the Bermuda petrel, the last of the cahows was believed to have been killed during the famine of 1615, when British colonists built cook fires into which the unwary cahows flew by the thousand. On January 8, 1951, the cahow was rediscovered by Bermuda's conservation officer, David Wingate. Under his protection, the existing 18 birds were encouraged to breed, and now number more than a hundred.

2. DIBBLER

A marsupial mouse, the dibbler was listed as extinct in 1884. In 1967 an Australian naturalist hoping to trap live honey possums caught instead a pair of dibblers. The female of the captured pair soon produced a litter of eight, and they are now being bred in captivity.

3. DWARF LEMUR

The last known dwarf lemur was reported in 1875, and was regarded as extinct. Then in 1966 the small tree-dwelling marsupial was once again seen, near the city of Mananara, Madagascar.

4. MOUNTAIN PYGMY POSSUM

This small marsupial was considered to have been extinct for 20,000 years until Dr. Kenneth Shortman caught one in the kitchen of his skiing lodge, Mount Hothan, in Southeast Australia in 1966. Three more of the tiny possums were discovered in 1970.

5–6. TARPAN and AUROCHS

A primeval forest horse of central Asia and long extinct, the tarpan has been recreated by brothers Lutz and Heinz Heck, curators of the Berlin and Munich zoos, respectively. By selective crossbreeding of russet horses of the Steppes with Iceland ponies and Konik mares, they have created a strain of wild horse identical in appearance to what we know of the mouse-gray tarpan. By the same method, the aurochs, a European wild ox which died out in Poland in 1627, has also been duplicated.

7. WHITE-WINGED GUAN

A flower-eating South American bird, the guan was thought extinct for a century until sighted in September of 1977. An American ornithologist and his Peruvian associate located four of the pheasant-sized birds in remote northwestern Peru.

—D.L.

7
COMING AND GOING—
TRAVEL AND TRANSPORTATION

HENRY FORD II'S
10 MOST INFLUENTIAL
CARS OF ALL TIME

Grandson of the man who put America on wheels with the Model T, Henry Ford II was 28 when he took over the family automobile business in 1945. At the time it was losing $10 million a month. He not only transformed the company into a successful venture but initiated new trends in American automobile manufacturing. He lives in Grosse Pointe Farms, Mich., near the Ford Motor Company in Dearborn. Mr. Ford's list is in chronological order.

1. BENZ (1885)

Otto Benz not only built the first successful internal-combustion engine, but he also built the world's first workable motorcar for public sale.

2. DURYEA (1892–1896)

It was the car that started it all—the first one successfully built in the U.S., and it won America's first auto race in 1895.

3. DeDION BOUTON (1899–1900)

A small but high-speed one-cylinder engine powered this popular car, which was manufactured under license in many countries, including the U.S. Pioneer DeDion began producing cars in the 1880s and built the world's first V-8 engine in 1908.

4. OLDSMOBILE (1900–1905)

This famous curved-dash, one-cylinder car was the first to be produced in volume.

5. FORD MODEL T (1908–1927)

Clearly the most influential car ever built, it changed the way people lived, not only in America, but throughout the world.

6. CADILLAC (1912–1915)

It was the first car with a self-starter and had the first successful V-8 engine produced in volume.

1910 Ford Model-T Runabout sold for $900.

7. PACKARD (1915–1932)

Noted for its high-quality custom bodies, it was, for years, the most wanted and prestigious luxury car.

8. ESSEX COACH (1922)

It was the first successful low-priced closed car and started the industry trend away from open models.

9. VOLKSWAGEN (1936–   )

The Volkswagen won millions of converts the world over to the small car concept. Its dependable air-cooled engine and simplicity of design produced record sales in the postwar period.

10. FORD MUSTANG (1965–1966)

A completely new type of personal car, it won immediate public acceptance and led other manufacturers to follow its design.

Mr. Ford wishes to acknowledge the assistance he received in compiling this list from automotive historians and writers at the Henry Ford Museum in Dearborn, the National Automotive History Collection at the Detroit Public Library, and the Motor Vehicle Manufacturers Association.

—Exclusive for *The Book of Lists 2*

THE TOP 10 VEHICLE RECALLS

	Year of Recall	Number Recalled

1. GENERAL MOTORS   1971   6,682,084

1965–1969 Chevrolets, Chevy IIs, Novas, Camaros; Chevy and GMC trucks. Problem: Possible loss of control should left-front engine mount break.

2. FORD   1972   4,072,000

All 1970–1971 passenger cars except 1970 Mavericks and 1970–1971 convertibles; 1970–1971 Ranchero trucks. Problem: Possible faulty plastic device (a 10¢ part) on front-seat shoulder belts.

3. GENERAL MOTORS   1973   3,707,064

1971 Chevy Biscaynes, Bel Airs; 1972 Chevy Impalas, Caprices; 1971 Pontiac Catalinas, Bonnevilles; 1971 Buick Le Sabres; 1972 Pontiac Granvilles; 1972 Buick Centurions, Electras, Rivieras; 1971–1972 Oldsmobile 88s and 98s. Problem: Danger of steering system jamming.

4. VOLKSWAGEN   1972   3,700,000

Recalled Types 1, 2, and 3 for 1949–1969. Problem: Danger of wiper-arm failure.

5. GENERAL MOTORS   1969   2,966,979

1968–1969 Chevys, Pontiacs, Oldsmobiles, Buicks, Cadillacs, GMC trucks equipped with Quadra-Jet carburetor. Problem: Danger of throttle sticking.

6. HONDA   1977   2,830,000

1969–1977 motorcycles (2,000,000); 1973–1977 Civics, Accords (830,000). Problem: Possible defective exhaust thermo-sensor switch in cars; danger of fuel tank cap opening in motorcycles.

7. GENERAL MOTORS   1969   2,570,914

1965–1969 Biscaynes, Bel Airs, Impalas, Caprices (excluding station wagons). Problem: Exhaust fume hazards.

8. GENERAL MOTORS   1977   2,200,000

1976 Novas, Chevelles, El Caminos, Camaros, full-size Chevy sedans and wagons; Le Mans, Firebirds, Catalinas, Bonnevilles, Venturas, Grand Prix; Cutlass, 88s, 98s, Omegas; Skylarks, Le Sabres, Electras; Cadillac Callases, DeVilles, Broughams (except those with electric fuel injection); GM and Chevy trucks. Problem: Danger of power-brake failure.

9. CHRYSLER   1977–1978   1,670,000

1975–1977 Dodge Darts, Aspens; Plymouth Valiants, Volares, Furies; Dodge Monacos, Coronets, Chargers; Chrysler Cordobas with 318- and 224-cu.-in. engines. Problem: Stalling due to defect in accelerator pump seal.

| 10. FORD | 1978 | 1,500,000 |

1971–1976 Pintos, Mercury Bobcats. Problem: Fuel tanks required modification to reduce danger of fires caused by rear-end collision.

Parts Dept.: All-Time Individual Leader

| FIRESTONE TIRE AND RUBBER CO. 1978 | 10,000,000 tires |

Bubbling and tread separation danger at high speeds.

Dishonorable Mention

| ROLLS-ROYCE | 1978 | 2,000 |

1977 Silver Shadows, Corniche convertibles, Camargues. The recall took place after one owner reported that the brakes had failed. According to Rolls-Royce, their autos never break down; they "fail to proceed."

The hot-line telephone number for auto recall information is 1-800-424-9393.

—S.H.

15 U.S. CITIES IN WHICH YOU ARE MOST LIKELY TO DIE IN A MOTOR VEHICLE ACCIDENT (OVER 100,000 POP.)

		Deaths per 100,000
1.	San Bernardino, Calif.	31.3
2.	Lubbock, Tex.	29.4
3.	Nashville, Tenn.	25.5
4.	Oklahoma City, Okla.	25.4
4.	Fort Worth, Tex.	25.4
6.	Tucson, Ariz.	23.6
7.	Phoenix, Ariz.	23.0
8.	Beaumont, Tex.	22.9
9.	Corpus Christi, Tex.	22.8
10.	Kansas City, Mo.	21.4
11.	Stockton, Calif.	21.1
12.	Kansas City, Kans.	20.7
13.	Fresno, Calif.	20.2
14.	Dallas, Tex.	19.7
14.	Jacksonville, Fla.	19.7

The lowest death rates from motor vehicle accidents in cities over 100,000 population are in Madison, Wis., at 3.6, and Ann Arbor,

Mich., at 3.9. Of cities from 10,000 to 25,000 population, Santa Fe Springs, Calif., has the highest death rate from motor vehicle accidents—64.5 per 100,000.

SOURCE: National Safety Council, *Accident Facts, 1978.*

IN 13 AGE GROUPS—
THE MOST DANGEROUS AND
LEAST DANGEROUS DRIVERS

		Number of Drivers in Fatal Accidents per 100,000 Drivers
1.	20–24	82
2.	Under 20	78
3.	75 and over	62
4.	25–29	51
5.	30–34	46
6.	40–44	37
7.	35–39	33
8.	45–49	32
9.	60–64	31
10.	70–74	30
11.	55–59	27
12.	65–69	27
13.	50–54	25

SOURCE: National Safety Council, *Accident Facts, 1978.*

THE 9 LONGEST NONSTOP
AIRLINE FLIGHTS

Flight	Miles	Time (NB or WB)*	Time (SB or EB)**
1. San Francisco–Hong Kong	6,901	12 hr. 55 min.	13 hr. 10 min.
2. New York–Tokyo	6,751	15 hr. 35 min.	15 hr. 15 min.
3. New York–Bahrain	6,605	15 hr. 30 min.	19 hr. 15 min.
4. Los Angeles–Auckland	6,517	15 hr. 25 min.	17 hr. 30 min.
5. Buenos Aires–Madrid	6,259	14 hr. 15 min.	11 hr. 30 min.

6. New York–Tehran	6,121	14 hr. 55 min.	18 hr. 40 min.
7. Los Angeles–Frankfurt	5,794	12 hr. 10 min.	15 hr. 45 min.
8. New York–Amman	5,719	9 hr. 30 min.	14 hr.
9. Rio de Janeiro–Rome	5,707	11 hr. 55 min.	11 hr. 30 min.

* Northbound or westbound.
** Southbound or eastbound.

—D.M.R.

THE 5 SHORTEST AIRLINE FLIGHTS

Flight	Miles	Time
1. Papa Westray Island–Westray Island, Scotland	1.5	0:02
2. Bethel–Napaiskak, Alaska	7	0:10
3. Saipan–Tinian, Mariana Islands	11	0:10
4. San Francisco–Oakland, Calif.	15	0:23
5. Fullerton–Los Angeles, Calif.	15	0:10

—D.M.R.

THE 19 MOST DANGEROUS AIRPORTS IN THE WORLD

Of the world's 650 international airports, 19 have been given black-star ratings by the International Federation of Air Line Pilots Association. The black star means that IFALPA regards the airport as "critically deficient" from a safety standpoint. The deficiencies that resulted in black-star ratings range from a nighttime noise-abatement program that requires downwind takeoffs and landings and head-to-head traffic at Los Angeles International Airport, to a lack of firefighting equipment at a number of airports in Colombia, to the frequent presence of kangaroos on the runways of some Australian airports. In addition to black stars, IFALPA also assigns red stars for "seriously deficient" airports and orange stars for "deficient" airports. The airport at Tenerife, in the Canary Islands—scene of the worst air disaster in history in 1977—had an orange-star rating at the time of the accident.

1. Los Angeles International, U.S.A.
2. Kai Tak Airport, Hong Kong
3. Khwaja Rawash Airport, Kabul, Afghanistan
4. Tezgaon Airport, Dacca, Bangladesh
5. Trivandrum, India
6. Palmaseca Airport, Cali, Colombia
7. Olaya Herrera Airport, Medellín, Colombia
8. Crespo Airport, Cartagena, Colombia
9. Vasquez Cobo Airport, Leticia, Colombia
10. Sesquicentenario Airport, San Andrés Island, Colombia
11. Rimini, Italy
12. Kerkira Airport, Corfu, Greece
13. Harry S Truman Airport, St. Thomas, Virgin Islands
14. Nausori Airport, Suva, Fiji
15. Henderson Airport, Honiara, British Solomon Islands
16. Fua' Amotu Airport, Tongatapu, Tonga
17. Ujung Pandang, Indonesia
18. Learmonth, Australia
19. Meekatharra, Australia

SOURCE: International Federation of Air Line Pilots Association.

ROBERT CARTMELL'S
5 TOP ROLLER COASTERS

Regarded as the foremost authority on roller coasters in the U.S., Robert Cartmell has assembled a major exhibition on the subject for the Smithsonian Institution in Washington, D.C. He is an associate professor in the art department at the State University of New York at Albany.

1. TEXAS CYCLONE at Astroworld, Houston, Tex.

The world's most exciting roller coaster opened June 12, 1976. Modeled after Coney Island's great Cyclone, the Texas Cyclone has squeezed in more thrills, with a devastating 53° first drop of 92 ft. and a rogues' gallery of drops and roundhouse curves.

2. THUNDERBOLT at Kennywood Park, West Mifflin, Pa.

Rebuilt from a 1920 Pippin coaster in 1968, it uses a natural valley to hide the most frightening parts of the ride. The final drops are 80 and 90 ft., making the finish the highest in the world. The Kennywood Thunderbolt was listed as the ultimate roller coaster in *The New York Times* on June 9, 1974.

The first drop on the Texas Cyclone,
the world's most exciting roller coaster.

3. MISTER TWISTER at Elitch's Gardens, Denver, Colo.

Built in 1969, it is one of the all-time great roller coasters. Ninety-six feet high, crammed with treacherous hills and curves, Mister Twister has the best tunnel ride in existence. The maze of hills and lumber after the first hill is unparalleled.

4. CYCLONE at Coney Island, Brooklyn, N.Y.

Probably the most famous coaster in the world, it was a favorite of Charles Lindbergh. Built in 1927, it's still fast and furious. The first hill seems as close to a vertical drop as is offered anywhere. The fate of the Cyclone has been threatened for years by the proposed expansion of a nearby aquarium.

5. BEAST at Kings Island, 20 mi. north of Cincinnati, O.

It opened in April, 1979, and the statistics speak for themselves: 7,400 ft. long, 141 ft. tall at one point (the highest ever built), speeds up to 70 mph. It includes a 560° spiral with 1½ "sickening" turns. It has you counting backwards at the end to check your sanity. It's the best of the new breed of roller coasters of the 1970s.

—Exclusive for *The Book of Lists* 2

LOWELL THOMAS'S
10 BEST OVERLOOKED TRAVEL
SITES IN THE WORLD

Thomas's career began in radio broadcasting in 1925, and over the decades he has gained world renown as a commentator, film producer, and author. His first book to attract international attention was *With Lawrence in Arabia,* an account of the Middle East during W.W. I and the British adventurer T. E. Lawrence. Among his most recent works are *Book of the High Mountains* and *So Long Until Tomorrow.*

1. The Brooks Range country of northern Alaska
2. The Antarctic continent, especially the area known as the Antarctic Peninsula, which includes a mountain range named for me
3. The South Island of New Zealand
4. Arnhem Land, Australia
5. The Inner Range and valleys of New Guinea
6. Sumatra
7. Borneo
8. Volcanoes of Kamchatka, U.S.S.R.
9. Arctic Siberia
10. Ituri Forest, Zaire

—Exclusive for *The Book of Lists 2*

HARRY B. COLEMAN'S
15 TOP ATTRACTIONS
THROUGHOUT THE WORLD

Since 1973, Harry Coleman has traveled 520,000 mi. in 131 different nations and territories, including three around-the-world expeditions. His last journey was the longest motor trip in history, covering 143,715 mi. and reaching into 113 countries over a period of 20 months (August, 1976, to April, 1978).

1. Rock city of Petra, Jordan
2. Pyramids and Sphinx, Egypt
3. Serengeti National Park, Tanzania
4. Sahara Desert, North Africa
5. Great Wall of China, China
6. Grand Canyon, U.S.
7. Bariloche, Argentina
8. Iguaçu Falls, Argentina and Brazil

9. Machu Picchu, Peru
10. Taj Mahal, India
11. Niagara Falls, U.S. and Canada
12. Kremlin and Red Square, U.S.S.R.
13. Mt. Everest, Nepal
14. Roman Colosseum, Italy
15. Acropolis, Greece

Coleman adds: "The incredible man-made pyramids can only be surpassed by the more recently discovered rock city of Petra. This remote city was carved out of solid stone and dates back to the 2nd century A.D. Bariloche is in a class of its own. Located high in the mountains of Argentina, it is the Swiss Alps, High Sierras, and paradise all in one."

—Exclusive for *The Book of Lists* 2

Entrance to the rock city of Petra in Jordan.

HARRY B. COLEMAN'S
10 LEAST LIKED CITIES

1. BUENAVENTURA, COLOMBIA

Every person I have ever met who has visited this city rates it as the world's worst. The reasons: poverty, thieves, bad government, unfriendly people, corrupt officials, filth, bureaucracy, lack of facilities, and it rains every day. I met nine overlanders coming from Buenaventura, and seven of them had been robbed or assaulted. It is known as the Hell Hole of the World. Congratulations, Buenaventura—you are definitely *número uno*.

2. KOTZEBUE, ALASKA, U.S.

Located above the Arctic Circle, Kotzebue is noted for its high rate of alcoholism, unbelievable filth, violence, and mosquitoes—not to mention that it is completely frozen over nine months of the year.

3. LAGOS, NIGERIA

A nightmare of crowded people and automobiles, this city is plagued with filth, poverty, bad government, and bad weather.

4. CALCUTTA, INDIA

Often considered the poorest and most crowded city in the world, Calcutta is very dirty and suffers from bad government and unemployment.

5. ALGIERS, ALGERIA

Bad government and unfriendly people are major problems, along with poor facilities and thieves.

6. BRINDISI, ITALY

Unlike most Italian cities, this port city is poorly administered and full of hustlers.

7. DOHA, QATAR

Unbelievably hot and humid; more expensive than Scandinavia and Switzerland. No attractions and really no reason to go there.

8. WARSAW, POLAND

A blah city by European standards. Uninteresting and lacking in facilities. Crowded and unfriendly at times.

9. BANGUI, CENTRAL AFRICAN REPUBLIC

Major features are corruption and bureaucracy. Poverty, bad weather, poor facilities, and insects also abound.

10. TEHRAN, IRAN

Major governmental problems and civil disorder, overcrowded and corrupt.

Coleman adds: "I have eliminated countries at war, such as Laos, Cambodia, Vietnam, Angola, Ethiopia, Lebanon, etc. Many cities in India are difficult to evaluate because their poverty and bureaucracy are among the worst, but the people and scenic diversification rank very high. Many people love Saudi Arabia. There is no crime, the people are friendly, and there is plenty of money. But if you're a non-Muslim female who likes to drink and can't stand the heat, then stay out of Saudi Arabia. For these reasons, ratings have a different meaning for everyone."

—Exclusive for *The Book of Lists* 2

THE 10 MOST EXOTIC PROPERTIES FOR SALE

1. A HOUSEBOAT IN PARIS

Location: Seine River, Paris, France
Description: A two-bedroom, completely furnished floating home on the Seine in the middle of Paris. This lovely home is one of a privileged few with a permanent berth space leased from the city. It includes a small yard area and private walkway entrance near the Champs-Élysées.
Price: $90,000

2. A VOLCANO

Location: Lanzarote, Canary Islands
Description: An inactive volcanic mountain formed thousands of years ago by an eruption that shot volcanic ash into the air. The interior is a perfectly round inverted cone with a level floor the size of a football field and contains the remains of an abandoned homestead, including a two-room home and fruit trees. Access is only by dirt trail leading up, around, down, and into the center. Great spot for private retreat, fort, swimming pool, nightclub, or tourist attraction.
Price: $195,000

3. AN ABANDONED MISSILE BASE

Location: 100 mi. north of San Francisco, Calif.
Description: An abandoned U.S. Air Force Titan missile site complex located entirely underneath 60 acres of land. All the missile equipment has been removed, leaving an excess of over one acre of underground storage space, including three silos, each 150 ft. deep, and two massive dome structures.
Price: Originally constructed at a cost of $125 million, it's yours for $350,000.

4. A LIGHTHOUSE ISLAND

Location: The Pacific Ocean, 1 mi. west of the state of Oregon
Description: A solid granite rock, 138 ft. high and about 1½ acres in

area. The Army Corps of Engineers built a three-story lighthouse in 1880 by blasting away a level spot. The lighthouse has four bedrooms, a large kitchen, fireplace, bathroom, and storage and engine rooms within its 3-ft.-thick walls. A 77-step spiral staircase leads to the uppermost lantern room. Practically inaccessible because of the high walls and treacherous seas, this private island is a bastion of seclusion.
Price: $275,000

5. A BIG-GAME HUNTING CAMP

Location: Northern interior, British Columbia, Canada
Description: Covering over a million acres of exclusive hunting rights, this established hunting business is known throughout the world among big-game hunters. There are over 2,000 acres of freehold land and trails throughout the valley and mountain wilderness, where Stone sheep, grizzly bear, and moose wander. Two private airfields and a large family-style lodge make this wilderness retreat a favorite among sportsmen and naturalists.
Price: $1.5 million

6. AN ENTIRE TOWN

Location: North central Oregon
Description: Former U.S. Air Force radar-base station built in 1951. Covering 79 acres, the base contains 27 modern homes, paved streets, sidewalks, gutters, a sewage system, and a playground in the residential section. The commercial-industrial section has 20 buildings consisting of 60,000 sq. ft. of floor space, including two hobby shops, bowling lanes, movie theater, post office, officers' club, two dormitories, wood shop, garage, generator room, photo shop, gymnasium, library, bomb shelter, grocery store, restaurant, and kitchen. Mostly in good repair, this facility is a ready-made town for church, school, or light industry.
Price: $1.2 million

7. A SOUTH SEAS ISLAND TRADING POST

Location: Pigeon Island, Solomon Islands, South Pacific Ocean
Description: A whole 5-acre island leasehold estate consisting of an ongoing trading post, private residence, and guest house. A tropical paradise with a pure white sand beach and sheltered lagoon. Islanders from many miles away come to Pigeon Island to trade their wares. An English family has lived and raised its children here for many years. Everything you need is here; move right in!
Price: $275,000

8. A TROPICAL RAIN FOREST

Location: Caribbean coast of Costa Rica
Description: Nearly 200 acres of thick tropical hardwood jungle adjacent to the National Sea Turtle Park at the mouth of a river that flows into the Caribbean Sea. About 300 in. of rain a year keep this jungle lush and wild—a true naturalist's paradise, hardly visited by anyone other than sports fishermen. A native fishing village a few miles away provides basic necessities.
Price: $200,000

9. A NUDIST RESORT

Location: Jamaica, West Indies
Description: This small Caribbean resort, consisting of several thatched-roof cottages overlooking a private beach, is a favorite among sun worshipers the world over. Informality and make-your-own entertainment are the theme here, where the rich, the famous, and the unknown meet and become equal in their respite from the hustle-bustle worlds they leave behind.
Price: $560,000

FOR SALE—NUDIST RESORT IN JAMAICA.

10. A ROMAN ROAD

Location: Peak district of Derbyshire, England
Description: A 14-acre holding crossed by a totally authentic, documented, original Roman road known as Batham Gate, which connected the Roman spa of Aquae Arnemetiae with the military encampment at Navio. Part of a national park, this freehold estate personally belonged to an amazing number of great historical figures—Henry VIII, Charles II, Elizabeth I, Henry V, William the Conqueror, and Richard III, among 22 monarchs. Owner will convey title by having deed engraved onto beautiful antique silver tray by the English Crown jewelers, Garrard and Co. Ltd. of Regent Street in London.
Price: $150,000

—K.V.H.

This list is an excerpt from the forthcoming book *The Rare Earth Catalog*. Anyone wishing more information about these properties, or wishing to list unusual properties for sale, should write to: Rare Earth Real Estate, Inc., P.O. Box 49699, Los Angeles, Calif. 90049.

10 PLACES
WITH UNLIKELY NAMES

1. CAPE OF GOOD HOPE

When the Portuguese explorer Bartholomeu Dias rounded the southern tip of Africa in 1488, he found the seas so rough he called it the Cape of Storms. This epithet was hardly likely to encourage traffic through this new gateway to India, so Portugal's King John II called it the Cape of Good Hope.

2. GHANA

The former British West African colony known as the Gold Coast became the Republic of Ghana when it combined with Togoland and achieved independence in 1957. The name Ghana was chosen to recall the glory of the famous Ghana Empire of a thousand years earlier. Despite politicians' claims, historians have found no direct connection between modern Ghana and old Ghana, which straddled present-day Mauritania and Mali.

3. GREENLAND

Known by a singularly inappropriate epithet, this great, snow-covered island is a 10th-century example of false advertising. Eric the Red hoped to attract settlers from the more clement Iceland.

4. IDAHO

When a name was needed in 1860 for a new territory in the Pike's Peak mining area, lobbyist and eccentric George M. Willing suggested the Indian word *Idaho*, which he said meant "gem of the mountains." Just before Congress made its final consideration, it was discovered that Willing had invented the term as a hoax. The territory was quickly renamed Colorado. However, two years later, when it came time to name another mining territory in the Pacific Northwest, the controversy had been forgotten, and on March 4, 1863, the territory of Idaho was established. The name was retained when statehood was achieved in 1890.

5. NOME

A classic geographical mistake, "Nome" was miscopied from a British map of Alaska on which "? Name" had been written around 1850.

6. PACIFIC OCEAN

Magellan had the remarkable luck of crossing this ocean without encountering a storm, so he called it *Mar Pacifico*—"the calm sea." The Pacific in fact produces some of the roughest storms in the world.

7. PAGO PAGO

The Polynesian name for this port in American Samoa is Pango Pango. The modern form originated in a 19th-century missionary newspaper there. The missionaries were short of the letter *n*, so they printed these two words—and many others—without it.

8. SINGAPORE

This word derives from the Sanskrit for "city of the lion." Its exact origin is a mystery, since lions are not indigenous to the region.

9. USA

In order to overcome American resentment against products labeled "Made in Japan," the Japanese renamed one of their industrial centers USA before W.W. II. The city's exports were then marked "Made in USA."

10. YUCATÁN

When the Spanish explorer Francisco Fernández de Córdoba landed here in 1517, he naturally asked local Mayans what they called the region. They are said to have answered, *"Yukatán,"* meaning "I don't understand you!"

—R.K.R.

GOOD-BYE COLUMBUS DAY!— 16 POSSIBLE EXPLORATIONS OF AMERICA BEFORE COLUMBUS

1. HSI and HO (c. 2640 B.C.), Chinese

Based on evidence derived from the geographical text *Shan Hai Ching T'sang-chu* and the chronicle *Shan Hai Jing,* it is argued that the Chinese imperial astronomers Hsi and Ho were the first explorers of America in the 27th century B.C. Ordered by Emperor Huang Ti to make astronomical observations in the land of Fu Sang— the territories to the east of China—the two men sailed north to the Bering Strait and then south along the North American coastline. They settled for a while with the "Yao people," ancestors of the Pueblo Indians living near the Grand Canyon, but eventually journeyed on to Mexico and Guatemala. Returning to China, they reported their astronomical studies and geographic discoveries to the emperor.

However, a short time later they were both executed for failin[g to] predict a solar eclipse accurately. (See p. 96)

2-5. VOTAN, WIXEPECOCHA, SUME, and BOCHIA
(c. 800-400 B.C.), Indian

According to Hindu legends and to Central American tribal legends, seafaring Hindu missionaries reached the Americas more than 2,000 years before Columbus. Sailing from India to Southeast Asia, they voyaged to the Melanesian and Polynesian islands and then across the Pacific to South and Central America. Votan was a trader from India who lived among the Mayans as a historian and chieftain, while his contemporary, Wixepecocha, was a Hindu priest who settled with the Zapotecs of Mexico. Two more Hindu emigrants were Sume, who reached Brazil and introduced agriculture to the Cabocle Indians, and Bochia, who lived with the Muycas Indians and became the codifier of their laws.

6. HUI SHUN (458 A.D.), Chinese

Using official Chinese imperial documents and maps from the Liang dynasty, scholars have reconstructed the travels of the Chinese explorer and Buddhist priest Hui Shun and proposed that he arrived in North America in the 5th century. Sailing from China to Alaska in 458, Hui—accompanied by four Afghan disciples—continued his journey on foot down the North American Pacific coast. Reaching Mexico, he taught and preached Buddhism to the Indians of central Mexico and to the Mayans of the Yucatán. Allegedly he named Guatemala in honor of Gautama Buddha. After more than 40 years in America, he returned to China, where he reported his adventures to Lord Yu Kie and Emperor Wu in 502.

7. ST. BRENDAN (c. 550), Irish

Two medieval manuscripts, *The Voyage of Saint Brendan the Abbot* and the *Book of Lismore*, tell of an Irish priest who, with 17 other monks, sailed west from Ireland and reached the "Land Promised to the Saints." Employing a curragh—a leather-hulled boat still in use in Ireland—Brendan and his companions made a sea pilgrimage that lasted seven years during the 6th century A.D. They traveled to Iceland, Greenland, and Newfoundland, and one authority asserts that Brendan reached the Caribbean island of Grand Cayman, which he called the Island of Strong Men. Brendan returned safely to his Irish monastery and reported on his travels, but died soon after. In 1977 Timothy Severin, sailing a modern curragh, retraced Brendan's voyage to America.

8. BJARNI HERJULFSON (986), Norse

According to two medieval Icelandic narratives, the *Flateyjarbok* and *Hauk's Book*, a young Norse merchant named Bjarni Herjulfson sailed from Iceland towards Greenland to visit his father, who lived there, but was blown off course by a gale. When the storm ended, Bjarni sighted a hilly, forested land, which is now thought to have been Cape Cod. Wanting to reach the Norse settlements on Greenland before winter, he did not drop anchor and send men ashore to explore. Instead, he sailed northeast along Nova Scotia and Newfoundland and then headed north to Greenland. He was criticized by the Greenlanders for not investigating the new land, and his discoveries stimulated further exploration of North America.

9. LEIF ERICSON (1003), Norse

In 1003, Leif bought Bjarni Herjulfson's ship and, with a 35-man crew, sailed for North America. While most scholars agree that Ericson did land in North America, there is disagreement about where he landed. The only Viking site ever found in the New World is L'Anse aux Meadows in Newfoundland, which was discovered in 1960 and excavated for the next eight years by Helge Ingstad, a Norwegian explorer. According to Ingstad, Ericson's first landing was at Baffin Island, which he named Helluland; his second was at Labrador, which he called Markland; and finally he reached Newfoundland, which he christened Vinland. To Leif and his companions, Vinland was an abundant country, rich in game, wild wheat, and timber, and its climate was mild compared to Iceland and Greenland. The explorers spent the winter in Vinland, where they constructed a village of "big houses." In 1004 Leif returned to Greenland, where he was given the honorary name of Leif the Lucky.

Leif Ericson, one of the many discoverers of America.

10. THORVALD ERICSON (1004), Norse

The Icelandic sagas record that, soon after Leif Ericson returned to Greenland, he gave his ship to his brother Thorvald. In the autumn of 1004, Thorvald sailed to Leif's Vinland settlement and wintered there. The next summer, while exploring the St. Lawrence region, Thorvald and his crew attacked a band of Indians, killing eight of them. In retaliation, the Indians ambushed the Norsemen, and Thorvald was killed in the ensuing battle. In 1007 the expedition's survivors returned to Greenland and took with them Thorvald's body, which was delivered to Leif for burial.

11. THORFINN KARLSEFNI (1010), Norse

The *Greenlanders' Saga* and *Karlsefni's Saga* are the two medieval sources that give accounts of the Icelander Thorfinn Karlsefni's attempt to establish the first permanent European settlement in America. In 1010, with 60 men and 5 women, Thorfinn—who was Leif Ericson's brother-in-law—sailed to Leif's Vinland camp, where he planned to colonize. In Vinland, Thorfinn's wife gave birth to a son—the first European child born in America—who was named Snorri. Thorfinn explored extensively, traveling as far south as Long Island and the Hudson River and, possibly, Chesapeake Bay. Four years later, Thorfinn and the Norse settlers returned to Greenland because of Indian attacks and because of violent internal discord caused by the shortage of women.

12–13. PRINCE MADOG AB OWAIN GWYNEDD (1170, 1190), Welsh

The Atlantic voyages of this Welsh prince were recorded by the medieval historian Gymoric ap Grono Guntyn Owen and by the 17th-century chroniclers Thomas Herbert and Richard Hakluyt. Because of political conflicts with his brothers, Prince Madog sailed from Abergwili, Wales, in 1170. He voyaged westward across the Atlantic and landed somewhere in the Americas, where he built and fortified a settlement. After several years Madog returned to Wales, leaving 120 men behind in the new colony. In 1190 he again crossed the Atlantic to discover that most of his men had been annihilated, presumably by Indians. Madog himself died in the New World a short time later. The actual site of Madog's settlement is disputed. Possible locations are the Florida peninsula; Mobile, Ala.; and the West Indies.

14. KING ABUBAKARI II (1311), Malian

According to medieval Arab historical and geographical documents and Malian oral epics, King Abubakari II of Mali, a black Muslim, sailed from West Africa to northeastern South America. After learning from Arab scholars that there was land on the west side of the Atlantic, King Abubakari became obsessed with the idea of extending his kingdom into these as yet unclaimed lands. He mobilized the resources of his empire to hire Arab shipbuilders from Lake Chad to build a fleet. (Their descendants were employed by Thor Heyerdahl to construct his reed boat, *Ra I*.) In 1311 the king and his crew sailed down the Senegal River and across the Atlantic. It is believed that while he sighted the north coast of South America, he made his first landfall in Panama. Then King Abubakari and his entourage supposedly traveled south from Panama and settled in the Inca Empire.

15. PAUL KNUTSON (1356), Norwegian

In a letter dated 1354, King Magnus of Norway and Sweden ordered the Norwegian sea captain Paul Knutson to journey to Greenland to restore the Christian faith to the Norsemen still living there. Knutson sailed to Greenland in 1355 and, the next year, to

Vinland, where he established a camp on the North American coast. Knutson's camp was probably at Newport, R.I., where a tower believed to have been constructed by his party still stands. One group of Knutson's men, who explored Hudson Bay and the territory to the south of it, are thought to be responsible for the Kensington Stone, a rock with possible Norse runes carved on its surface, which was found in central Minnesota. Most of the members of the expedition, including Knutson, died in America. A few survivors returned to Norway in 1364.

16. JOHANNES SCOLP and JOÃO VAZ CORTE REAL
(1476), Danish and Portuguese

In 1475 King Alfonso of Portugal and King Christian I of Denmark arranged a joint expedition to North America to find a sea route to China. Danish sea captain Johannes Scolp and a Portuguese nobleman named João Vaz Corte Real were appointed as commanders of the combined fleet. Sailing from Denmark across the North Atlantic to the Labrador coast, they explored Hudson Bay, the Gulf of St. Lawrence, and the St. Lawrence River. Failing to find a sea passage to Asia, they returned to Denmark, where their discoveries were largely ignored.

—R.J.F.

7 PERSONS WHO HAVE GONE OVER NIAGARA FALLS IN BARRELS

The six men and one woman who qualify for Niagara's 158-ft. "fall of fame" are listed below. Asterisks indicate survivors.

1. ANNIE EDSON TAYLOR—1901*

A Michigan schoolteacher (1858–1924?) who hoped to exploit her stunt financially, Taylor was not seriously injured. However, a subsequent vaudeville tour that featured Taylor and her 4½-ft.-long wooden keg netted practically nothing.

2. BOBBY LEACH—1911*

This elderly Canadian souvenir stand operator (1842–1920) suffered numerous broken facial and leg bones while being battered about inside a converted steel furnace boiler. He died several years later after slipping on a discarded orange peel.

3. CHARLES STEPHENS—1920

A 58-year-old English barber, Stephens was yanked through the bottom of his wooden barrel and forced into the Niagara River by the weight of a steel anvil tied to his feet. Only his right arm, which he had strapped to the inside of the barrel, was ever found.

4. JEAN LUSSIER—1928*

Toronto circus acrobat Jean Lussier (born 1893), designed a steel and rubber sphere strong enough to guarantee his survival. A crowd of 100,000 thrill seekers saw the canny daredevil crack—but only a smile.

5. GEORGE STATHAKIS—1930

Self-styled mystic and unpublished author (*The Mysterious Veil of Humanity Throughout the Ages*), Stathakis planned to write about his experience. The 46-year-old Buffalo resident suffocated during the 14 hours that he was trapped in his barrel behind the falls. The notebook he took along to record his impressions was found blank.

6. WILLIAM "RED" HILL, JR.—1951

A Canadian game warden (born 1913) who had been arrested for embezzling hunting license fees, Hill hoped that taking the plunge—in the middle of 14 truck inner tubes held together with cotton netting—would repair his shattered reputation. Whether it did or did not, 200,000 onlookers, including Hill's mother, saw him crash to his death.

7. WILLIAM FITZGERALD—1961*

This black American (born 1931) succeeded in his goal to "integrate the falls." Because his "barrel" was identical to that of Lussier, Fitzgerald emerged from his unique freedom ride none the worse for the experience.

—G.R.S.

Annie Edson Taylor, the first person to
go over Niagara Falls in a barrel.

8
LET'S HAVE A WORD—
COMMUNICATIONS

SO TO SPEAK—
THE TRUTH ABOUT
16 COMMON SAYINGS

1. AT A SNAIL'S PACE

The fastest land snail on record is a specimen named Colly, who in 1970 traversed a 2-ft. piece of glass in 3 min. Colly's pace was .00758 mph.

2. JUST A MOMENT

According to an old English time unit, a moment takes 1½ minutes. In medieval times, a moment was either $\frac{1}{40}$ or $\frac{1}{50}$ hr., but by rabbinical reckoning a moment is precisely $\frac{1}{1,080}$ hr.

3. ALL THE TEA IN CHINA

The United Nations Food and Agricultural Organization estimates that all the tea in China in 1978 amounted to 356,000 metric tons.

4. BY A HAIRBREADTH

Although the breadth of a hair varies from head to head, the dictionary definition of hairbreadth is $\frac{1}{48}$ in.

5. ONLY SKIN-DEEP

The depth of the human skin ranges from $\frac{1}{100}$ in. on the eyelid to $\frac{1}{5}$ in. on the back.

6. EATS LIKE A HORSE

A 1,200-lb. horse eats about 15 lb. of hay and 9 lb. of grain each day. This amounts to $\frac{1}{50}$ of its own weight each day, or 7 times its own weight each year. The real gluttons in the animal kingdom are birds, who consume more than 90 times their weight in food each year.

7. A PICTURE IS WORTH A THOUSAND WORDS

The American Society of Magazine Photographers reports that the base rate for a full-page photo is $75 for black and white, $150 for color. However, an illustration is much more expensive. For example, *Playboy* magazine pays $800 for a full-page color illustration, while its article rate is about 40¢ per word. On this scale, a picture would be worth 2,000 words.

8. QUICK AS A WINK

The average wink, or corneal reflex blink, lasts $1/10$ sec.

9. QUICKER THAN YOU CAN SAY "JACK ROBINSON"

When members of *The Book of Lists* staff were asked to say "Jack Robinson," their speed varied from ½ to 1 sec. It is acknowledged that this may not be a representative sample of the U.S. population.

10. SELLING LIKE HOTCAKES

Sales figures for the International House of Pancakes show that their 485 U.S. restaurants sold a total of 63,487,564 pancakes in 1978. On an individual basis, each branch restaurant sold an average of 130,902 pancakes that year.

11. SINCE TIME IMMEMORIAL

Time immemorial is commonly defined as beyond the memory of any living person, or a time extending so far back as to be indefinite. However, for the purposes of English law, a statute passed in 1275 decreed that time immemorial was any point in time prior to 1189—the year when Richard I began his reign.

12. KNEE-HIGH TO A GRASSHOPPER

According to Charles L. Hogue of the Los Angeles County Museum of Natural History, this figure necessarily depends upon the size of the grasshopper. For the average grasshopper, the knee-high measurement would be about ½ in.

13. HIGH AS A KITE

The record for the greatest height attained by a single kite is 28,000 ft. The kite was flown by Philip R. and Jay P. Kunz in Laramie, Wyo., on November 21, 1967.

14. FASTER THAN A SPEEDING BULLET

Ballistics experts at the Los Angeles Police Dept. say that a bullet from a Colt .45 travels at 800 ft. per sec.; from a .44 Magnum at 1,500 ft. per sec.; and from a .357 Magnum at 1,500 to 1,900 ft. per sec. But the fastest bullet is fired from a .22 caliber rifle and travels at 4,000 ft. per sec.

15. BLOOD IS THICKER THAN WATER

In chemistry, water is given a specific gravity, or relative density, of 1.00, because it is used as the standard against which all other densities are measured. By comparison, blood has a specific gravity of 1.06—only slightly thicker than water.

16. A KING'S RANSOM

The largest king's ransom in history was raised by Richard the Lion-Hearted to obtain his release from Holy Roman Emperor Henry VI in 1194. The English people were forced to contribute almost 150,000 marks to free their sovereign. Nearly as large a ransom was raised by Atahualpa, king of the Incas, when he offered Pizarro a roomful of gold and two roomfuls of silver for his release in 1532. At today's prices, the ransom would be worth close to $7 million. Unfortunately, it was not sufficient to buy Atahualpa his freedom; he was given a mock trial and executed.

—The Eds.

7 WELL-KNOWN SAYINGS ATTRIBUTED TO THE WRONG PERSONS

Saying	Attributed To	Actually Said By
1. Anybody who hates children and dogs can't be all bad.	W. C. Fields	Leo Rosten (at a dinner, introducing Fields): "Any man who hates dogs and babies can't be all bad."
2. Go west, young man!	Horace Greeley	John Soule (Article, Terre Haute *Express*, 1851)
3. Everybody talks about the weather, but nobody does anything about it!	Mark Twain	Charles Dudley Warner (Editorial, Hartford *Courant*, August 24, 1897)
4. Survival of the fittest.	Charles Darwin	Herbert Spencer (*Principles of Biology* and earlier works)
5. That government is best which governs least.	Thomas Jefferson	Henry David Thoreau (who put it in quotation marks in "Civil Disobedience" and called it a motto)
6. Cleanliness is next to godliness.	The Bible	John Wesley (*Sermons*, no. 93, "On Dress")
7. A journey of a thousand miles must begin with a single step.	Confucius	Lao-tzu (*Tao Tê Ching*)

—K.A.

WILLARD R. ESPY'S
10 MOST BEAUTIFUL WORDS IN
THE ENGLISH LANGUAGE

Author of *The Game of Words* and *An Almanac of Words at Play*, Espy has had a long and varied literary career working as a reporter, editor, and writer. His light verse and poems have appeared in such noted magazines as *The Atlantic Monthly, The Nation,* and *American Heritage.*

1. *Gonorrhea*
2. *Gossamer*
3. *Lullaby*
4. *Meandering*
5. *Mellifluous*
6. *Murmuring*
7. *Onomatopoeia*
8. *Shenandoah*
9. *Summer afternoon*
10. *Wisteria*

—Exclusive for *The Book of Lists 2*

31 WORDS RARELY USED
IN THEIR POSITIVE FORM

Positive Form	*Negative Form*
1. *Advertent* (giving attention; heedful)	*Inadvertent*
2. *Algesia* (sensitiveness to pain)	*Analgesia*
3. *Biotic* (of or relating to life)	*Antibiotic*
4. *Canny* (*Scot.*: free from weird qualities or unnatural powers)	*Uncanny*
5. *Clement* (of weather: mild)	*Inclement*
6. *Conscionable* (conscientious)	*Unconscionable*
7. *Consolate* (consoled, comforted)	*Disconsolate*
8. *Corrigible* (correctable)	*Incorrigible*
9. *Couth* (marked by finesse, polish, etc.; smooth)	*Uncouth*
10. *Delible* (capable of being deleted)	*Indelible*
11. *Descript* (described; inscribed)	*Nondescript*
12. *Domitable* (tamable)	*Indomitable*
13. *Effable* (capable of being uttered or expressed)	*Ineffable*
14. *Evitable* (avoidable)	*Inevitable*

15. *Feckful* (efficient; sturdy; powerful)   *Feckless*
16. *Furl* (to draw in and secure to a staff)   *Unfurl*
17. *Gruntle* (to put in good humor)   *Disgruntle*
18. *Gust* (inclination; liking)   *Disgust*
19. *Histamine* (a crystalline base that is held   *Antihistamine*
    to be responsible for the dilation and
    increased permeability of blood vessels
    which play a major role in allergic
    reactions)
20. *Infectant* (an agent of infection)   *Disinfectant*
21. *Kempt* (neatly kept; trim)   *Unkempt*
22. *Licit* (not forbidden by law; allowable)   *Illicit*
23. *Maculate* (marked with spots; besmirched)   *Immaculate*
24. *Nocuous* (likely to cause injury; harmful)   *Innocuous*
25. *Odorant* (an odorous substance)   *Deodorant*
26. *Peccable* (liable or prone to sin)   *Impeccable*
27. *Pervious* (being of a substance that can be   *Impervious*
    penetrated or permeated)
28. *Placable* (of a tolerant nature; tractable)   *Implacable*
29. *Sipid* (affecting the organs of taste; savory)   *Insipid*
30. *Speakable* (capable of being spoken)   *Unspeakable*
31. *Wieldy* (strong; manageable)   *Unwieldy*

—R.A.

7 PEOPLE WHO ATE THEIR OWN WORDS—OR OTHERS' WORDS

1. EMPEROR MENELIK II

He was one of the greatest rulers in African history and the creator of modern Ethiopia. Born in 1844, he was captured during an enemy raid and held prisoner for 10 years. Escaping, Menelik declared himself head of the province of Shewa. He began conquering neighboring kingdoms and developed them into modern Ethiopia with himself as emperor. When Italy tried to take over Ethiopia, Menelik's army met and crushed the Italians at the Battle of Aduwa. This victory, as well as his efforts to modernize Ethiopia (schools, telephones, railroads), made Menelik world-famous. The emperor had one little-known eccentricity. Whenever he was feeling ill, he would eat a few pages of the Bible, insisting that this always restored his health. One day in December, 1913, recovering from a stroke and feeling extremely ill, he had the entire Book of Kings torn from an Egyptian edition of the Bible, ate every page of it—and died. Too much of the Good Book had proved a bad thing.

2. PHILIPP ANDREAS OLDENBURGER

This celebrated 17th-century German law instructor and political historian wrote a pamphlet that offended the authorities. He was arrested and sentenced to eat his own writings. To make matters worse, "he was also flogged during his repast, with orders that the flogging should not cease until he had swallowed the last crumb." Oldenburger died in 1678.

3–4. TWO PAPAL DELEGATES

In 1370 the pope sent two of his delegates to Bernabò Visconti to serve him with a rolled parchment bearing a leaden seal and wrapped in a silk cord, informing him that he had been excommunicated. So infuriated was Bernabò Visconti that he put the two papal delegates under arrest and released them only after he had made them consume the parchment of excommunication, the leaden seal, and the silken cord.

5. THEODOR REINKING

He was a Danish author at the time when Denmark was suffering oppression under Swedish rule. In 1644 Reinking wrote a book in Latin, *Dania ad exteros de perfidia Suecorum*, which blasted the Swedes for the damage they had done to the Danes. The Swedes wasted no time in throwing Reinking into prison. After he had languished in prison several years, Reinking's jailors were ready to mete out his real punishment. He was given a choice: either eat his words or lose his head. Happily, Reinking kept his head—and ate his words, consuming the pages of his book "boiled in broth."

German author Ernst Toller, forced by the
Nazis to eat one of his own books.

6. ERNST TOLLER

Born in 1893 in Samotschin, Prussia (now Poland), he studied law in France. With the outbreak of W.W. I, Toller fought for Germany, was wounded, and became an active pacifist. He was jailed for treason. Upon his release he became a Communist, helped overthrow the Bavarian monarchy, and established a German soviet. When this fell apart, he was arrested again and sentenced to five years behind bars. In prison, he began to write and became one of Germany's leading playwrights with such dramas as *The Machine Wreckers, Hinkemann,* and *Hoppla! Such Is Life!* He also wrote two autobiographical books, *I Was a German* and *Through the Bars.* Free of prison at 30, he saw the rise of Adolf Hitler and toured Russia and the U.S. making anti-Fascist speeches. In 1933, back in Germany, he was detained by the Nazis. Recalled Toller, "It was terrible and inhuman. The guards forced me to swallow almost a complete volume of one of my latest books." Exiled, Toller wound up in New York. Alone (his wife had left him for another man) and impoverished (he had given all his money to Spanish Civil War refugees), Toller committed suicide in his hotel room on May 22, 1939.

7. ISAAC VOLMAR

Author Volmar wrote several booklets in which he satirized the life and activities of Bernhard, Duke of Saxe-Meiningen. Not amused, the duke invited his writer-antagonist to dinner. At the table, according to Frederic R. Marvin, who recorded the incident in 1910, Volmar "was not allowed the courtesy of the kitchen, but was forced to swallow his literary productions uncooked."

—I.W.

16 BRAND NAMES THAT HAVE BECOME WORDS

1. Aspirin
2. Cellophane
3. Corn flakes
4. Cube steak
5. Dry ice
6. Escalator
7. Kerosene
8. Lanolin
9. Linoleum
10. Mimeograph
11. Nylon
12. Raisin bran
13. Thermos
14. Trampoline
15. Yo-yo
16. Zipper

SOURCE: *Stylebook for Writers and Editors.* Washington, D.C.: U.S. News and World Report, Inc., 1977.

18 WORDS
WORTH REVIVING

Susan Kelz Sperling, author of *Poplollies and Bellibones: A Celebration of Lost Words* (New York: Clarkson N. Potter, Inc., Publishers, 1977), brings back to life over 400 obsolete, rare, and dialectal words too delicious to have disappeared from our language forever and weaves them into original stories, poems, playlets, and rounds.

1. *AIMCRIER* (17th century)

An applauder, encourager, the person who cried, "Aim!" to encourage an archer; the one who stood near the target to report the results of each round.

2. *BEDSWERVER* (16th and 17th centuries)

A person unfaithful to the marriage bed. Synonym: *spouse-break*.

3. *BELLIBONE* (16th century)

A lovely maiden, a pretty lass. A whimsically anatomical word. An anglicization of the French *belle et bonne*, "fair and good."

4. *BELLYTIMBER* (17th through 19th century)

Food, provisions; i.e., the "timber" which you feed to your belly as you would feed timber to a fire.

5. *CHANTPLEURE* (14th and 15th centuries)

To sing and weep at the same time.

6. *FELLOWFEEL* (17th through 19th century)

To crawl into the skin of another person so as to share his feelings, to empathize with.

7. *FLESH-SPADES* (18th century)

Fingernails, the digging tools that protrude from our flesh.

8. *KEAK* (17th through 19th century)

To cackle.

9. *LIP-CLAP* (17th century)

A kiss.

10. *LUBBERWORT* (no date given)

Food or drink that makes one idle and stupid, food of no nutritional value, "junk food."

11. *MERRY-GO-SORRY* (16th and 17th centuries)

A tale that evokes simultaneously feelings of joy and sadness, a story containing both good and bad news.

12. *MUBBLEFUBBLES* (16th and 17th centuries)

Depression of the spirits for no apparent reason, melancholy. Also *blue devils*, *mulligrubs*.

13. *MURFLES* (no date given)

Freckles, pimples.

14. *POPLOLLY* (16th through 19th century)

A little darling, an affectionate term from the French *poupelet* that came to be applied to a mistress.

15. *PRICKMEDAINTY* (16th century)

A fancy dresser, always up on the latest in fashion and very finicky about his or her style of dress, a dandy.

16. *SMELLSMOCK* (16th and 17th centuries)

A licentious man with roving eyes, from a term for an errant priest whose extracurricular activities gave him a smelly smock. A lecherous womanizer who knew how to "smell a smock," to recognize an easy conquest.

17. *SNIRTLE* (18th and 19th centuries)

To snicker, to laugh quietly and mockingly.

18. *WURP* (10th through 13th century)

A stone's throw; a glance of the eye.

10 WINNING WORDS IN THE U.S. NATIONAL SPELLING BEE, 1970–1979

The National Spelling Bee, held every June in Washington, D.C., is sponsored by daily and Sunday newspapers throughout the country. It is estimated that 7½ million children, who must be under 16 years old and not past the 8th grade, participate annually in the bee at the local level. All but approximately 100 children are eliminated before the final contest, which lasts two days. Each finalist is given one word at a time; if a child misses a word, he or she is out of the running. This process of elimination continues until there is a champion. First prize is $1,000.

Year	Winning Word	Winning Contestant
1. 1971	*Shalloon:* a lightweight twilled fabric of wool or worsted used chiefly for the linings of coats and uniforms.	Jonathan Knisely Philadelphia, Pa.
2. 1972	*Macerate:* to cause to waste away by or as if by excessive fasting; to cause to become soft or separated into constituent elements by or as if by steeping in fluid.	Robin Kral Lubbock, Tex.
3. 1973	*Vouchsafe:* to grant or furnish often in a condescending manner; to give by way of reply.	Barrie Trinkle Fort Worth, Tex.
4. 1974	*Hydrophyte:* a perennial vascular aquatic plant having its overwintering buds underwater.	Julie Ann Junkin Birmingham, Ala.
5. 1975	*Incisor:* a tooth adapted for cutting.	Hugh Tosteson San Juan, Puerto Rico
6. 1976	*Narcolepsy:* a condition characterized by brief attacks of deep sleep.	Tim Kneale Syracuse, N.Y.
7. 1977	*Cambist:* one who deals in bills of exchange, or who is skilled in the science and practice of exchange.	John Paola Pittsburgh, Pa.
8. 1978	*Deification:* the act or instance of deifying.	Peg McCarthy Topeka, Kans.
9. 1979	*Maculature:* an impression made from an engraved plate to remove ink from recessed areas.	Katie Kerwin Denver, Colo.
10. 1980	*Elucubrate:* to work out or express by studious effort.	Jacques Bailly Denver, Colo.

SOURCE: Scripps-Howard National Spelling Bee.

RICHARD ARMOUR
PICKS 20 OF THE WORST PUNS

Armour has written dozens of books that spoof history and literature and is best known as a madcap satirist. But he is also a serious scholar. He received his Ph.D. from Harvard in 1928 and continues to lecture in universities throughout the U.S. and Europe. Among his many books are *Going Like Sixty: A Light-Hearted Look at the Later Years*, *It All Started with Columbus*, and *It All Started with Nudes*. His selection of the worst puns was chosen from Bennett Cerf's *Laugh Day* and *A Treasury of Atrocious Puns*.

1. The Eskimo stabbed himself with an icicle. He died of cold cuts.
2. In his dessert list, a San Antonio restaurateur suggests, "Remember the alamode."
3. There was an advice-to-the-lovelorn editor who insisted, "If at first you don't succeed, try a little ardor."
4. The commuter's Volkswagen broke down once too often. So he consigned it to the Old Volks Home.
5. When a fire chief responded to a call from a lingerie shop, he found no trace of a blaze. His official report read, "Falsie alarm."
6. The wise old crow perched himself on a telephone wire. He wanted to make a long-distance caw.
7. A talkative musician couldn't hold a job. Every time he opened his mouth, he put his flute in it.
8. A farmer with relatives in East Germany heard that a food package he had sent had never arrived. Optimistically, he reassured them, "Cheer up! The wurst is yet to come."
9. When the promoter of a big flower show was told that a postponement was necessary because the exhibits could not be installed on time, he explained to his backers, "We were simply caught with our plants down."
10. There was an unscheduled event in a Baghdad harem. The sultan barged in unexpectedly—and his 62 wives let out a terrified sheikh.
11. A critic declared that he always praised the first show of a new theatrical season. "Who am I," he asked, "to stone the first cast?"
12. Egotist: a man who's always me-deep in conversation.
13. She was unanimously voted the most popular girl in school by the male half of the senior class. They weighed her in the balance and found her wanton.
14. A hen stopped right in the middle of the highway. She wanted to lay it on the line.
15. The husband of a talkative wife sighed, "I've given that woman the best ears of my life."
16. "It's raining cats and dogs," one man remarked. "I know," said another. "I just stepped into a poodle."
17. In Peru, a gallant cavalier fished a drowning maiden out of a lake—and married her before the Inca was dry.
18. An eccentric bachelor passed away and left a nephew nothing but 392 clocks. The nephew is now busy winding up the estate.
19. The baseball pitcher with a sore arm was in the throws of agony.
20. A Turkish salesman promoted an audience with an old-time sultan. "I don't recall your name," said the sultan pleasantly, "but your fez is familiar."

—Exclusive for *The Book of Lists 2*

CHARLES HAMILTON'S 10 MOST INSULTING LETTERS IN HISTORY

Charles Hamilton obtained his first autograph (from Rudyard Kipling) when he was only 12 years old. He has been collecting documents handwritten by famous persons since then and has become one of the world's leading appraisers. In 1963 he organized the first American auction house devoted solely to autographs. Mr. Hamilton is also the author of *The Robot That Helped to Make a President, The Book of Autographs,* and *The Signature of America.*

1. MARK TWAIN TO THE PROMOTERS OF ACTOR WILLIAM GILLETTE (1883)

Mark Twain was on one occasion associated with William Gillette, the famous actor, and was irked with the business partners who were under contract to promote Gillette. He accused them of "trying (as usual with you) to sneak out of the performance of [your] contract," adding, "I suggest to you couple of piety-mouthing, hypocritical thieves and liars that you change your customary policy this time."

2. JAMES McNEILL WHISTLER TO THEODORE WATTS-DUNTON (1897)

When Theodore Watts, the British poet and former friend of the American artist James McNeill Whistler, decided at age 65 to give his commonplace moniker a little class by adding his mother's name (Dunton), Whistler, famed for his biting wit, sent the new Watts-Dunton a sarcastic three-word query: "Theodore, Watts Dunton?"

3. GEORGE BERNARD SHAW TO TWO ASPIRING AUTHORS (1895)

George Bernard Shaw, the Irish dramatist, habitually insulted people who sent him manuscripts for publication or criticism. To one author he wrote, "The covers of your book are too far apart." To another, who had pasted two leaves of her manuscript together (a favorite trick of beginning authors), then complained on its return with unseparated leaves that Shaw hadn't read it, the dramatist rejoined, "You don't have to eat a whole egg to know it's rotten."

4. A COUNTRY PARSON TO GEORGE BERNARD SHAW (1935)

A country parson turned the tables on Shaw. After hearing that Shaw was an expert at brewing coffee, the rector wrote the dramatist and asked for the recipe. Shaw sent it, adding, "I hope this is an honest request and not a surreptitious mode of securing my autograph." The parson answered, enclosing Shaw's signature cut from his letter, "Accept my thanks for the recipe. I wrote in good faith so allow me to return what it is obvious you infinitely prize, but which is of no value to me, your autograph."

5. RUDYARD KIPLING TO AN AUTOGRAPH HOUND (1928)

Like most celebrities, Rudyard Kipling, the British author, abhorred autograph seekers and rarely answered their supplications. One disgruntled collector complained to the writer, "I have written to you five times for your autograph without success. I hear you get five dollars a word for every word you write. Enclosed is $5. Send me one word." Kipling pocketed the fiver and wrote one unsigned word at the bottom of his correspondent's letter: "Thanks."

6. SIR RICHARD BURTON TO A SKEPTICAL MEMBER OF THE ROYAL SOCIETY (1860)

Sir Richard Burton, the great African explorer and codiscoverer of the source of the Nile, was once ridiculed by a member of the Royal Society of London, who challenged some of Burton's claims. The explorer sent him a textless letter, the original of which has disappeared, but which I have reconstructed with the addition of Sir Richard's authentic signature:

7. JOHN RUSKIN TO A SUPPLICATING MINISTER (1890)

A minister wrote to John Ruskin, the British essayist and art critic, and asked for a loan to help build a church. Ruskin replied with a blistering refusal, "Starve and go to heaven—but don't borrow. Try first begging. If it's really needful, stealing. . . . Of all manner of debtors, pious people building churches they can't pay for are the most detestable. Can't you preach and pray in a coal hole first?"

8. THE PRESIDENT OF A LARGE RAILROAD COMPANY TO AN UNHAPPY CUSTOMER (1945)

A railroad traveler was savagely bitten by bedbugs in his Pullman compartment and complained to the president of the company. He received in the mail an abject apology, explaining that this was the first time the company had ever had such a complaint and that the president had ordered every car fumigated. Accidentally enclosed was his original letter of complaint with a penciled note at the top in the president's hand: "Send this S.O.B. the bedbug letter."

9. AN AUTOGRAPH HOUND TO PRESIDENT HERBERT HOOVER (1930)

An autograph seeker wrote to Herbert Hoover, then president, requesting three signatures, one for himself and two to trade for a signature of Babe Ruth, explaining to the President, "It takes two of yours to get one of Babe Ruth." P.S. Hoover was greatly amused by the insult and sent the signatures.

10. MARK TWAIN TO AN EDITOR OF *THE NEW YORK TIMES* (1907)

Mark Twain, in a fury over the lack of government price controls, wrote a one-sentence letter to *The New York Times* containing five goddams, noting that the "govment [*sic*] lets a goddam man charge any goddam price he wants for his goddam opera box." He signed the letter with the name of his close friend William Dean Howells, the author, and sent a copy to Howells with the following note: "I sent this complaint to N.Y. *Times* with your name signed because it would have more weight "

—Exclusive for *The Book of Lists* 2

8 ADVERTISEMENTS THAT CHANGED PEOPLE'S LIVES

1. AN AD FOR SECRETARY OF THE U.S. NAVY

Being secretary of the navy was not an important job in 1802. There were only three ships in the entire U.S. Navy. When America's first secretary of the navy, Benjamin Stoddert, who had served from 1798 to 1801, quit his post, President Thomas Jefferson had trouble filling the vacancy. At last, in desperation, Jefferson placed an advertisement in newspapers offering the job to a qualified applicant. A Baltimore city councilman, Robert Smith (1757–1842), saw the ad and responded. He was hired, and from 1802 to 1805 he served as secretary of the navy. After a few months acting as attorney general, Smith resumed as unconfirmed secretary of the navy until 1809, conducting the sea blockade against the Barbary States. He then became U.S. secretary of state, until a disagreement with President Madison forced him to resign.

2. AN AD FOR FOOTWEAR CUSTOMERS

The Battle of Gettysburg, during the U.S. Civil War, took place because of a newspaper advertisement. At the end of June, 1863, Gen. James J. Pettigrew was leading his bedraggled Confederate forces through Pennsylvania. His men were in bad shape. Most of them had worn out their shoes and were marching barefooted. Along the way General Pettigrew happened upon a recent copy of a newspaper, the Gettysburg *Compiler,* and in the paper he saw a shoe store ad announcing fine new boots for sale. Immediately General Pettigrew ordered his men to detour and march the 9 mi. to that shoe store in Gettysburg and confiscate all of the footwear. As his men headed for Gettysburg, they were spotted by Union troops, who set out to intercept them. The two sides clashed, and the bloody Battle of Gettysburg was under way. The three-day fight, the biggest and costliest in American history to that point, ended with a Union victory. Yet, in a sense, both sides lost. The Union suffered 3,070 men killed, 14,497 wounded, 5,434 captured or missing; the Confederates suffered 2,592 men killed, 12,706 wounded, 5,150 captured or missing.

3. AN AD THAT GAVE BIRTH TO A MONSTER

Born in London, his name was William Pratt. His family wanted him to be a diplomat. He thought briefly of becoming an actor. He attended King's College, then migrated to Canada, where he toiled as a farmhand. He was 23 in 1910 when he found his life's vocation. "One day in an old copy of *Billboard,* I came across the advertisement of a theatrical agent in nearby Seattle," he later recollected. "His name was Kelly. I went to see him. . . . Two months later, while chopping trees, I received a brief note: 'Join Jean Russell Stock Company in Kamloops, B.C.—Kelly.' I left my axe sticking in a tree." Pratt started acting and gave himself a stage name—Boris Karloff. He wound up in Hollywood and became world-famous as the monster in *Frankenstein.*

4. THE AD THAT PRODUCED *THE MALTESE FALCON*

Late in 1916, a 22-year-old high school dropout named Samuel Dashiell Hammett read an intriguing newspaper advertisement in Baltimore and decided to answer it. Until then, he had worked as a freight clerk, railroad laborer, and stevedore. The ad changed all that. It had been inserted by the Pinkerton National Police Agency. Hammett was hired to become a Pinkerton private detective and to work in San Francisco, the "most politically corrupt" city in the U.S., Hammett would later say. In his eight years as a private eye, Hammett worked on the Nicky Arnstein swindle case and the Fatty Arbuckle rape case, obtained his first agency promotion by catching a criminal who had stolen a Ferris wheel, and refused $5,000 to kill a Montana labor agitator. With this experience behind him, Hammett turned to writing and pioneered the hard-boiled school of detective fiction. At 31 he published *Red Harvest,* followed by *The Dain Curse, The Maltese Falcon, The Glass Key,* and *The Thin Man.* His fictional Sam Spade became a household name. Hammett joined the Communist cause about 1938 and subsequently served a prison term. He died of emphysema in 1961.

5. THE AD THAT PROVOKED THE GREAT MONKEY TRIAL

The state of Tennessee had passed the Butler Act which prohibited the teaching of Darwin's theory of evolution in public schools and colleges. This new law, promoted by the Ku Klux Klan, supported the Fundamentalist view that God had put man on earth and that the first woman had come from Adam's rib. The American Civil Liberties Union (ACLU) of New York found the new law intolerable—one that inhibited academic freedom and made scientific teaching a crime. The ACLU paid for an advertisement in the Chattanooga *News* offering "to pay the expenses of anyone willing to test the constitutionality of the Butler law forbidding the teaching of evolution in any public school." Before answering the ad, a small group of progressives in Dayton, Tenn., summoned a 24-year-old local science teacher named John Thomas Scopes and asked him to admit that he had been teaching evolution in school. Scopes confessed to the crime and was arrested. In July, 1925, the Scopes monkey trial took place, with America's greatest criminal lawyer, Clarence Darrow, defending Scopes and evolution, and America's former secretary of state and three-time presidential candidate, William Jennings Bryan, as prosecutor. The press poured into Dayton and filed two million words in 11 days. Scopes was found guilty and fined $100, but Bryan and the Fundamentalists were made to look like ignorant fools, and the ACLU won a moral victory.

6. AN AD THAT SAVED A PRISONER'S LIFE

On May 2, 1962, a dramatic advertisement appeared in the San Francisco *Examiner*: "I don't want my husband to die in the gas chamber for a crime he did not commit. I will therefore offer my services for 10 years as a cook, maid, or housekeeper to any leading attorney who will defend him and bring about his vindication." One of San Francisco's greatest attorneys, Vincent Hallinan, read or heard about this ad and contacted Gladys Kidd, who had placed it. Her husband, Robert Lee Kidd, was about to be tried for the slaying of an elderly antique dealer. Kidd's fingerprints had been found on a bloodstained ornate sword in the victim's shop. During the trial, Hallinan proved that the antique dealer had not been killed by the sword, and that Kidd's fingerprints and blood on the sword got there because Kidd had once toyed with it while playfully dueling with a friend when they were both out shopping. The jury, after 11 hours, found Kidd to be Not Guilty. Attorney Hallinan refused Gladys Kidd's offer of 10 years' servitude.

7. THE AD THAT STARTED A NAVY MAN ON THE ROAD TO THE WHITE HOUSE

In the 1946 election for representative from the 12th Congressional District of California, Jerry Voorhis, a rich liberal and a good man, decided to run for a sixth term for the Democrats. The Republicans had no one to oppose him. To find a candidate, a "Committee of One Hundred," largely wealthy Republicans, was organized. They prepared an advertisement for a candidate and placed it in 26 newspapers. It read, in part: "Wanted: Congressman candidate with no previous political experience to defeat a man who has represented the district in the House for 10 years. Any young man resident of district, preferably a veteran, fair education, may apply for the job." There were eight applicants. All were voted down. A former president of Whittier College suggested an eager young lawyer and navy man named Richard M. Nixon as a possibility. Herman Perry, a Whittier banker, located 33-year-old Nixon in Baltimore and asked him if he was a Republican. Nixon said he had voted for Thomas Dewey in the 1944 presidential race. The committee brought him back to Whittier. By a vote of 55 to 22, Nixon was selected as the Republican candidate. At the start, Voorhis was considered invincible. He was a New Deal liberal who detested Communists, and almost everyone liked him. Nixon also liked and admired him, but nevertheless set out to destroy him. "For vicious irresponsibility," wrote Theodore White, "there were few campaigns like Nixon's first attack on Voorhis." Nixon smeared Voorhis as a red tool and smashed him, 64,784 votes to 49,431. Nixon was on his way to more triumphs, the presidency, and ultimate disgrace.

8. AN AD FOR A MERCENARY

Daniel Gearhart, a former U.S. Army Green Beret and a veteran of Vietnam, was a 33-year-old unemployed civilian in 1975. He had a wife and four children, and he desperately needed money to pay for their medical bills. Since the only thing he was trained for was fighting, Gearhart decided to advertise his services. He took out an ad in the January, 1976, issue of *Soldier of Fortune* magazine. In the ad he offered himself for hire as a mercenary. Within a few months he was hired by Angola's FNLA movement. He was in Africa only three days as a mercenary before he was captured alive in a Cuban ambush. Tried as a war criminal, he was found guilty and sentenced to death. President Gerald Ford pleaded for his life. No use. Gearhart was executed in July, 1976, leaving behind his bereaved family and $30,000 in debts.

—I.W.

10 BEST CENSORED STORIES OF RECENT YEARS

Project Censored is a nationwide research project begun at Sonoma State University in California in 1976. Significant news stories that have been ignored by the mass media are located, evaluated, and submitted to a panel of prominent judges, who rank them annually. The Sonoma State researchers stress that the suppression of these stories is not so much the result of a "conspiracy" as the media's lack of perception, its drive for profits, its common interest with big business, and a general desire not to rock the boat.

1. CANCER, INC.

Although cancer research has become a billion-dollar industry, results have been minimal. Since President Richard Nixon signed the National Cancer Act in 1971, over $4 billion has been spent. Yet the U.S. still has the highest cancer rate in the world—50% above the world average—and the chance for an American to survive cancer has increased only 1% since the late 1940s.

2. AMERICA'S SECRET POLICE NETWORK

While most Americans are familiar with the FBI and the CIA, few have heard of the LEIU—the Law Enforcement Intelligence Unit. The LEIU links the intelligence squads of almost every major police force in the U.S. and Canada. Although its members are sworn police officers who work for state and city governments, the LEIU is a private organization and thus is not subject to freedom-of-information laws. Consequently, its files are even more secret than those of the CIA and the FBI.

3. BANNED IN THE U.S.—SAFE FOR THE THIRD WORLD

According to a conservative estimate by the World Health Organization, 500,000 people are poisoned each year by drugs and pesticides that continue to be sold to foreign countries by American drug manufacturers despite having been banned in the U.S. American asbestos manufacturers have also been endangering the people of third-world countries in their search for greater profits. In the late 1960s, after research showed that workers in asbestos plants ran a high risk of contracting lung cancer, the U.S. government issued stronger regulations for the industry. However, asbestos manufacturers responded, not by improving working conditions, but by moving their factories to such nations as Mexico, Taiwan, South Korea, India, and Brazil, where manufacturing regulations are less strict.

4. CORPORATE CONTROL OF DNA

Artificially created life has been a scientific reality since 1963, when scientists began creating new life forms from the gene-carrying DNA of other organisms. A number of prominent scientists have expressed the fear that unregulated DNA research leads to dangerous tampering with evolutionary balance, which could result in the release of undetected hordes of lethal new viruses.

5. THE MYTH OF BLACK PROGRESS

In an article in the *Progressive*, author Joel Dreyfuss wrote that most of the indices of poverty, unemployment, and drug abuse in the black population—conditions which were considered a scandal in the 1960s—have actually become worse. For example, only 3% of all professional jobs are held by blacks, a statistic that has not changed since 1969. In addition, the number of black youths under 16 who are arrested today is almost 10 times what it was in 1950. Dreyfuss, who warns that the 1980s could be a decade of racial unrest, says that his article was rejected by major publications because the subject was not considered "exciting" enough.

6. WAR ON SCIENTISTS

Dr. Thomas Mancuso, commissioned by the Atomic Energy Commission in 1964 to measure the safety of nuclear power plants for people who work in them, discovered that low levels of radiation, previously thought to be safe, can be quite deadly. His contract with the government was canceled, and his research funds were cut off— a punishment that is becoming increasingly common among scientists who come up with the "wrong" results.

7. THE REAL IRANIAN STORY

As late as the summer of 1978, prestigious U.S. newspapers like *The New York Times* were informing Americans that the Shah Pahlavi had a "broad base of popular support" and were portraying him as a modernizing, reform-oriented leader. But in the same year, there was an unprecedented general strike and other protests in which an estimated 10,000 Iranians were gunned down by the Shah's security forces. The response of the U.S. government was to send riot-control equipment, advisers, trainers, and more than $2.5 billion in weapons. The mass media failed to report both the inhumanity of the Shah's regime and the official U.S. support of that regime resulting from the Shah's strong ties to the U.S. through Henry Kissinger and David Rockefeller.

8. U.S. GUILTY OF HUMAN RIGHTS VIOLATIONS

In 1979, a panel of seven international jurists came to the U.S. to conduct a nationwide investigation of prison conditions and the judicial system. They found the U.S. guilty of systematic violations of human rights. Their findings were submitted to the U.N. but not reported by the mass media. When U.S. media representatives were asked why the story was not covered, they said, "The big black story now is Andy Young and the fallout from his resignation." There was only room for one sizeable "black story" at a time, the media people explained.

9. WORST NUCLEAR SPILL

While the nation and the world became aware of the disaster at Three Mile Island, the worst nuclear spill in U.S. history was virtually ignored by the media. It occurred at 5 A.M. on July 16, 1979, when 100 million gallons of radioactive water containing uranium tailings breached from a pond into the north arm of the Rio Puerco, near the small town of Church Rock, N.M. Samples of the river water indicated radioactivity 6,600 times the maximum standards for drinking water.

10. THE TRAGEDY IN EAST TIMOR

Human rights violations rivaling those in Cambodia have happened in East Timor with the help of the U.S. but without the American public's knowledge. Since December, 1975, when Indonesian military forces invaded East Timor following a short-lived civil war there, neutral observers have estimated the number of people slaughtered at from 50,000 to 100,000—almost 10% of the population. While the U.N. has repeatedly condemned the Indonesian government for its role in East Timor, the American press has given little coverage to the possible massacre of 100,000 Timorese at the hands of a U.S. ally using U.S. arms.

—D.W.

9
ARTFUL FACTS

THAT'S ENTERTAINMENT?
6 PERFECTLY
WRETCHED PERFORMERS

1. HADJI ALI

Billed as the Amazing Regurgitator, Hadji Ali enjoyed an improbably widespread popularity at the turn of the century as a vaudeville drawing card. His act consisted of swallowing a series of unlikely objects—watermelon seeds, imitation jewels, coins, peach pits—and then regurgitating specific items as requested by his audience. It was impressive, if tasteless, stuff—but his grand finale brought down the house every night. His assistant would set up a tiny metal castle on stage while Ali drank a gallon of water, chased down by a pint of kerosene. To the accompaniment of a protracted drumroll, he would eject the kerosene across the stage in a 6-ft. arc and set the castle afire. Then, as flames shot high into the air, he would upchuck the gallon of water and extinguish the blaze in a trice.

2. THE CHERRY SISTERS

When impresario Oscar Hammerstein found himself in a financial hole, he decided to try a new approach. "I've been putting on the best talent and it hasn't gone over," he told reporters. "I'm going to try the worst." On November 16, 1896, he introduced Elizabeth, Effie, Jessie, and Addie Cherry to New York audiences at his Olympia Theatre. A sister act that had been treading the vaudeville boards in the Midwest for a few years, the girls strutted out onto the Olympia's stage garbed in flaming red dresses, hats, and woolen mittens. Jessie kept time on a bass drum, while her three partners did their opening number:

> Cherries ripe Boom-de-ay!
> Cherries red Boom-de-ay!
> The Cherry Sisters
> Have come to stay!

New York audiences sat transfixed, staring goggle-eyed in disbelief, but they proved more merciful than audiences in the Midwest. They refrained from pelting the girls with garbage and overripe tomatoes at first. Eventually, the Cherry sisters had to put up a wire screen to protect themselves from the inevitable hail of missiles showered on them by their outraged audiences. In later years they denied that anything had ever been thrown at them. Said a writer in *The New York Times:* "It is sincerely hoped that nothing like them will ever be seen again." Another critic wrote, "A locksmith with a strong, rasping file could earn ready wages taking the kinks out of Lizzie's voice." Despite their reputation as the world's worst act, they played consistently to SRO crowds, wowing their fans with such numbers as "The Modern Young Man" (a recitation), "I'm Out upon the Mash, Boys," "Curfew Must Not Ring Tonight," and "Don't You Remember Sweet Alice, Ben Bolt?"

3. RONALD COATES

This 19th-century British eccentric may well have been the worst actor in the history of the legitimate theater. A Shakespearean by inclination, Coates saw no objection to rewriting the Bard's great tragedies to suit his own tastes. In one unforgettable reworking of *Romeo and Juliet*, in which he played the male lead, he tried to jimmy open his bride's casket with a crowbar. Costumed in a feathered hat, spangled cloak, and billowing pantaloons—an outfit he wore in public as well—he looked singularly absurd. Coates, who proclaimed himself a second Garrick, was frequently hooted and jeered offstage for his inept, overblown performances. Quite often he had to bribe theater managers to get a role in their productions, and his fellow thespians, fearing violence from the audience, demanded that he provide police protection before they would consent to appear onstage with him. He was slandered and laughed at throughout the British Isles and often threatened with lynching, but he persisted in his efforts to act. During one dramatic performance, several members of the audience were so violently convulsed by laughter that they had to be treated by a physician. Coates was struck and killed by a carriage—but not until 1848, when he was 74.

4. SADAKICHI HARTMANN

It seemed like a good idea at the time. Billing himself as a Japanese-German inventor, Hartmann was, briefly, a fixture in the New York theater in the early 1900s as he offered soon-to-be-jaded audiences what he called "perfume concerts." Using a battery of electric fans, Hartmann blew great billowing clouds of scented smoke towards his audience, meanwhile explaining in Katzenjammer Kids English that each aroma represented a different nation. Hartmann, who frequently had trouble with hecklers, rarely made it beyond England (roses) or Germany (violets) before being hooted from the stage.

5. FLORENCE FOSTER JENKINS

A taxi collision in 1943 left would-be diva Florence Foster Jenkins capable of warbling a higher F than she'd ever managed before. So delighted was she that she waived legal action against the taxi company, presenting the driver with a box of imported cigars instead—an appropriately grand gesture for the woman universally hailed as the world's worst opera singer. The remarkable career of this Pennsylvania heiress was for many years an in joke among cognoscenti and music critics—the latter writing intentionally ambiguous reviews of the performances she gave regularly in salons from Philadelphia to Newport. "Her singing at its finest suggests the untrammeled swoop of some great bird," Robert Lawrence wrote in the *Saturday Review*. Edward Tatnall Canby spoke of a "subtle ghastliness that defies description." But *Newsweek* was the most graphic, noting: "In high notes, Mrs. Jenkins sounds as if she was afflicted with low, nagging backache." On October 25, 1944, Mrs. Jenkins engineered the most daring coup of her career—a recital before a packed Carnegie Hall. That concert, like her others, saw the well-padded matron, then in her 70s, change costume numerous times. She appeared variously as the tinsel-winged "Angel of Inspiration"; the Queen of the Night from Mozart's *Magic Flute;* and a Spanish coquette, draped in a colorful shawl, with a jeweled comb and a red rose in her hair. Inevitably she seasoned her "coquette" rendition by tossing rose petals plucked from a wicker basket to the audience. On at least one occasion she inadvertently tossed the basket as well. But always she made certain to retrieve the petals for the next performance.

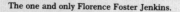

The one and only Florence Foster Jenkins.

6. MRS. ELVA MILLER

While growing up in Kansas, Elva figured that with practice and training she might have a shot at a career in singing. Her friends and family thought otherwise. However, she made the high school glee club and the church choir and even studied voice at Pomona College in Claremont, Calif. But with it all, her voice was reminiscent of cockroaches rustling at dawn in a garbage can. In the 1960s, still convinced she could sing, Mrs. Miller—by now a 50-ish California housewife—recorded on her own a few favorite melodies "just for the ducks of it." She persuaded a local disc jockey to give her an airing and finally cut a nightmarish 45 single of the hit song "Downtown." It sold 250,000 copies in barely three weeks and made "the Kansas Rocking Bird," as she was dubbed, the darling of TV variety shows. "Her tempos, to put it charitably, are free form," said *Time* magazine. "She has an uncanny knack for landing squarely between the beat, producing a new ricochet effect that, if nothing else, defies imitation. . . . [She] also tosses in a few choruses of whistling for a change of pace."

—B.F.

20 GREATEST ROCK ALBUMS OF ALL TIME

Music journalist Paul Gambaccini polled rock critics from major music periodicals and radio stations both in Europe and the U.S. and asked them to list the greatest rock albums of all time in order of preference. The votes were then weighed on a point system, with the following 20 albums clearly in the lead. The complete results of the poll can be found in *Rock Critics' Choice: The Top 200 Albums* by Paul Gambaccini with Susan Ready (New York: Quick Fox, Inc., 1978).

1. *Sgt. Pepper's Lonely Hearts Club Band*. The Beatles, 1967.
2. *Blonde on Blonde*. Bob Dylan, 1966.
3. *Highway 61 Revisited*. Bob Dylan, 1965.
4. *Astral Weeks*. Van Morrison, 1968.
5. *Rubber Soul*. The Beatles, 1965.
6. *Revolver*. The Beatles, 1966.
7. *Exile on Main Street*. The Rolling Stones, 1972.
8. *Let It Bleed*. The Rolling Stones, 1969.
9. *Abbey Road*. The Beatles, 1969.
10. *Born to Run*. Bruce Springsteen, 1975.
11. *The Sun Collection*. Elvis Presley, 1975.
12. *Pet Sounds*. The Beach Boys, 1966.
13. *The Band*. The Band, 1969.
14. *The Velvet Underground and Nico*. The Velvet Underground, 1967.

15. *Layla and Other Assorted Love Songs*. Derek and the Dominoes, 1965.
16. *Forever Changes*. Love, 1967.
17. *Are You Experienced*. Jimi Hendrix Experience, 1967.
18. *The Beatles*. The Beatles, 1968.
19. *Who's Next*. The Who, 1971.
20. *Legend*. Buddy Holly, 1974.

12 ARTISTS WHO MADE *BILLBOARD'S* #1— BUT NEVER GOT INTO THE TOP 100 AGAIN

The Silhouettes 1958 hit *Get a Job* sold over
2 million copies. The jobs they finally got were:
(standing, L to R) Richard Lewis—lamp assembler;
Ray Edwards—contractor; Earl Beal—clothes
presser; (bottom) Billy Horton—truck driver.

Year	Artist	Title
1. 1943	Al Dexter	Pistol-Packin' Mama
2. 1950	Anton Karas	The Third Man Theme
3. 1952	Johnny Standley	It's in the Book
4. 1952	Jimmy Boyd	I Saw Mommy Kissing Santa Claus
5. 1955	Joan Weber	Let Me Go, Lover
6. 1958	Elegants	**Little Star
7. 1958	Silhouettes	**Get a Job
8. 1960	Hollywood Argyles	**Alley-Oop
9. 1963	Singing Nun (Soeur Sourire)	**Dominique
10. 1969	Zager and Evans	**In The Year 2525
11. 1972	Looking Glass	*Brandy
12. 1974	MFSB	*T.S.O.P. (The Sound of Philadelphia)

 * Million seller.
** Two-million seller.

—K.C.

BENNY GOODMAN'S
7 BEST POPULAR SONGS
OF THE 20TH CENTURY

World-renowned as the "king of swing," Goodman popularized jazz in the 1930s and 1940s and initiated the big band era. An orchestra conductor and clarinetist, Goodman has played with such jazz greats as Gene Krupa, Lionel Hampton, and Harry James. In 1962 he and his band made the first jazz tour of Russia and played on opening night to Nikita Khrushchev. He lives in New York City, where he makes occasional appearances in nightclubs.

1. "Stardust" (1929) by Hoagy Carmichael and Mitchell Parish
2. "Sing, Sing, Sing" (1936) by Louis Prima
3. "Body and Soul" (1930) by Johnny Green, Ed Heyman, Robert Sauer, and Frank Eyton
4. "Send in the Clowns" (1973) by Stephen Sondheim
5. "Begin the Beguine" (1935) by Cole Porter
6. "You Are the Sunshine of My Life" (1973) by Stevie Wonder
7. "Alexander's Ragtime Band" (1911) by Irving Berlin

—Exclusive for *The Book of Lists 2*

13 ALL-TIME STANDARD HIT SONGS BY UNLIKELY COMPOSERS

1. HOME, SWEET HOME (1823)

The lyricist John Howard Payne never had a permanent residence. A traveling actor, he was once quoted as saying, "How often I've been to Paris, Berlin, London, or some other city and heard people singing, or a hand organ playing, 'Home, Sweet Home,' and there I was without a shilling or a place to lay my head."

2. OLD FOLKS AT HOME (1851)

When Stephen Foster first wrote this song, often called "Swanee River," he had never heard of a Swanee River. After he had rejected Yazoo and Pee Dee as uneuphonious, he asked his brother for the names of some Southern rivers. His brother picked up an atlas and came across the Suwannee River in Florida. Foster accepted the name but shortened it to Swanee.

3. DIXIE (1860)

"Dixie" was the number-one song of the Confederate soldiers, and some Southern generals insisted on its being played and sung to sustain the morale of their troops. It was written by a citizen of the *North*, minstrel man Dan D. Emmett, who was born in Mount Vernon, O., and who wrote the song in a New York City boarding-house.

4. BATTLE HYMN OF THE REPUBLIC (1862)

This was by far the most popular patriotic song played and sung by the Union troops during the Civil War. The music for this marching song of the North was by William Steffe, a *Southern* composer of camp-meeting hymns. The lyrics were by Julia Ward Howe.

5. SILVER THREADS AMONG THE GOLD (1873)

This 2 million–copy seller was by Hart P. Danks, who was inspired to set to music a poem he had read in a Wisconsin farm journal. Danks, who composed the music for this tale of a couple happily spending their later years together, separated from his wife one year after the song was published.

6. HOW DRY I AM (1891)

A perennial favorite of inebriates, this song was written by two very proper and temperate gentlemen, Dr. Edward Rimbault and Philip Dodridge, the former a noted English scholar. Originally, they wrote it as a religious hymn entitled "Happy Day." But it wasn't long before bar patrons, retaining the original tune, substituted some coarse lyrics, and the number finally became known as "How Dry I Am."

7. MY OLD NEW HAMPSHIRE HOME (1898)

This song extolling the cheerfulness, blissful seclusion, and comforts of a rural abode sold over 1 million copies. It was scribbled down by the songwriting team of Harry von Tilzer and Andrew B. Sterling on an overdue-rent notice slipped under their door in a squalid rooming house on East 14th Street, New York City.

8. HELLO, MA BABY (1899)

"Hello, Ma Baby" is typical of the love songs turned out by veteran songwriter Joe E. Howard. The ones that didn't make it quite as big include "Love's Dreamy Tune," "Just Love Me," and "Let Me Be Your Last Sweetheart." Howard, whose songs seem to stress the permanent nature and enduring qualities of love, was married nine times.

9. TAKE ME OUT TO THE BALL GAME (1908)

There's hardly anyone, child or adult, in the U.S. who doesn't know the words to this song. Called the unofficial theme song of the national pastime, it is included in almost every sing-a-long. But composer Albert von Tilzer, who introduced it in vaudeville, didn't see his first baseball game until 20 years after he wrote the song. Lyrics for the song were written by Jack Norworth.

10. PACK UP YOUR TROUBLES IN YOUR OLD KIT BAG AND SMILE, SMILE, SMILE (1915)

This song won first prize for British staff sergeant Felix Powell in a W.W. I competition for the best morale-building song for the armed forces. Powell, who wrote the music for the song that popular-music authority Sigmund Spaeth called "perhaps the most optimistic song ever written," committed suicide in 1942. Lyricist for the song was George Asaf.

11. CAROLINA IN THE MORNING (1922)

"Carolina in the Morning" was an instantaneous hit, and its popularity has never diminished. It was interpolated into at least three big movie musicals and sung by top-rated entertainers. Yet this tune that presents such a picturesque image of two southern states was composed by Walter Donaldson, who, at the time he wrote the song, had never set foot in either North or South Carolina. Gus Kahn wrote the words to the song.

12. MY BLUE HEAVEN (1927)

Various recordings of this song by just one singer, Gene Austin, reputedly sold over 12 million copies. The melody for this song, so laudatory of marital bliss, was written by Walter Donaldson, a bachelor. The lyricist was George Whiting.

13. IT'S ALL IN THE GAME (1958)

This rock 'n' roll hit, recorded by Tommy Edwards for MGM, was actually written 46 years earlier by a vice-president of the U.S.— Charles G. Dawes, who served under Calvin Coolidge. Originally entitled "Melody in A Major," Dawes's semiclassical tune became a popular ballad in 1951, then resurfaced in 1958 as a rock number and soared to number one on the charts for six weeks. By the early 1960s it had sold over a million copies.

—T.B.

ALAN JAY LERNER'S 10 BEST MODERN SONGWRITERS

The son of the founder of the Lerner Stores never had an interest in the family business and, after writing advertising copy and radio scripts, he turned to song lyrics. His first big success was the musical play *Brigadoon*, which won him the New York Drama Critics' Circle Award. A string of hits followed, including *My Fair Lady, Camelot*, and *Gigi*. Lerner won an Oscar for best screenplay in 1951 for *An American in Paris*. His selection, in alphabetical order:

1. Burt Bacharach
2. Leonard Bernstein
3-4. John Kander and Fred Ebb
5. Burton Lane
6. Richard Rodgers
7. Paul Simon
8. Stephen Sondheim
9. Jule Styne
10. Jimmy Webb

—Exclusive for *The Book of Lists 2*

MUDDY WATERS'S 10 GREATEST BLUES SONGS OF ALL TIME

Born McKinley Morganfield, Muddy Waters was raised in the delta region of Mississippi, where he began to sing, compose, and play the blues. Moving to Chicago, he made his first recording in 1941. He had over a dozen top-10 hits in the 1950s and 1960s, including "I'm Your Hoochie-Coochie Man," "Just Make Love to Me," and "Got My Mojo Workin'." Since then his songs have been sung by the Rolling Stones and other rock groups. He now lives in La Grange, Ill.

1. "Crossroads" by Robert Johnson
2. "Walking Blues" by Robert Johnson
3. "Worried Life" by Big Maceo
4. "How Long, How Long" by Leroy Carr
5. "Feel Like Going Home" by McKinley Morganfield (Muddy Waters)
6. "Long-Distance Call" by McKinley Morganfield (Muddy Waters)
7. "When Things Go Wrong with You" by Tampa Red
8. "Bumble Bee" by Memphis Minnie
9. "Preachin' Blues" by Son House
10. "Prison-Bound Blues" by Leroy Carr

—Exclusive for *The Book of Lists 2*

LEONARD FEATHER'S
ALL-TIME ALL-STAR JAZZ BAND

One of the nation's foremost authorities on jazz, Feather is an accomplished composer who has arranged music for Count Basie and various popular singers in the U.S. and Europe. He is the author of several books, including *From Satchmo to Miles* and *The Encyclopedia of Jazz in the '70s*. He is currently jazz editor for *The Los Angeles Times*.

Leader, composer: DUKE ELLINGTON
Trumpets: LOUIS ARMSTRONG, BIX BEIDERBECKE, ROY ELDRIDGE, DIZZY GILLESPIE, MILES DAVIS
Trombones: JACK TEAGARDEN, J. C. HIGGINBOTHAM, J. J. JOHNSON, BILL WATROUS
Alto saxophones: BENNY CARTER or JOHNNY HODGES, CHARLIE PARKER
Tenor saxophones: COLEMAN HAWKINS or LESTER YOUNG, JOHN COLTRANE
Baritone saxophone: HARRY CARNEY
Piano: ART TATUM
Guitar: CHARLIE CHRISTIAN
Bass: CHARLES MINGUS
Drums: SID CATLETT
Singer: BILLIE HOLIDAY
Guest soloists: BENNY GOODMAN, clarinet
JOE VENUTI, violin
LIONEL HAMPTON or MILT JACKSON, vibraphone
HUBERT LAWS, flute
COUNT BASIE, organ, piano

Leonard Feather adds: "Although Ellington was selected in his capacities as leader and composer, he would also share the piano chores with Tatum. Armstrong and Teagarden, similarly, would relieve Billie Holiday of some of the vocal obligations.

"I find it impossible to choose between such incomparable

talents as Benny Carter and Johnny Hodges, or Coleman Hawkins and Lester Young, so in these cases, as with the vibraphone choice, two names are listed where only one should play.

"Nitpickers may note that the trumpet section includes Bix Beiderbecke, who actually played cornet. The sound of the two instruments is almost indistinguishable, even to some cornet and trumpet players.

"On looking at the list again and finding that Ella Fitzgerald, Red Norvo, and many other giants were omitted, I must emphasize that this is all a rather foolish game that serves only one purpose: It reminds us how many giants jazz produced in a fairly short time."

—Exclusive for *The Book of Lists* 2

Duke Ellington.

PRODUCTIVITY OF
21 CLASSICAL COMPOSERS

Composer	Estimated Composing Span (Years)	Total Hours of Music Composed*	Hours of Music Composed per Year of Composing
1. Franz Schubert (1797–1828)	18	134	7.4
2. Henry Purcell (1659–1695)	16	116	7.3
3. Wolfgang Mozart (1756–1791)	29	202	7.0
4. Franz Joseph Haydn (1732–1809)	54	340	6.3
5. George Handel (1685–1759)	54	303	5.6
6. Johann Sebastian Bach (1685–1750)	47	175	3.7
7. Ludwig van Beethoven (1770–1827)	35	120	3.4
8. Robert Schumann (1810–1856)	26	72	2.8
9. Pëtr Ilich Tchaikovsky (1840–1893)	30	76	2.5
10. Felix Mendelssohn (1809–1847)	27	57	2.1
11. Anton Dvořák (1841–1904)	45	79	1.8
12. Johannes Brahms (1833–1897)	45	71	1.6
13. Franz Liszt (1811–1886)	51	76	1.5
14. Giuseppe Verdi (1813–1901)	63	87	1.4
15. Richard Wagner (1813–1883)	53	61	1.2
16. Béla Bartók (1881–1945)	45	48	1.1
17. Hugo Wolf (1860–1903)	28	28	1.0
18. Richard Strauss (1864–1949)	68	67	1.0
19. Frédéric Chopin (1810–1849)	26	21	0.8
20. Claude Debussy (1862–1918)	34	25	0.7
21. Maurice Ravel (1875–1937)	42	19	0.5

SOURCE: *Classical Music,* April 29, 1978.

15 COMPOSERS WHO DIED IN UNUSUAL CIRCUMSTANCES

1. JEAN BAPTISTE LULLY (1632–1687)

Creator of French grand opera, Lully was a great favorite of King Louis XIV. It was Lully's custom to conduct ensembles by pounding the floor with a large pointed cane. While conducting a "Te Deum" for the king's benefit, he accidentally struck his foot so violently with the cane that he developed an infection. Gangrene set in, followed by blood poisoning, which led to his death.

2. ALESSANDRO STRADELLA (1645?–1682)

Singer, violinist, and composer of more than 200 chamber cantatas, Stradella led a life of mystery and intrigue that has been glorified in eight operas and at least one novel. In 1677 a Venetian senator hired men to murder Stradella after he eloped with the senator's fiancée. Legend has it that the would-be killers refused to carry out their assignment after hearing one of Stradella's oratorios. Five years later a second assassination attempt proved successful.

3. MICHAEL WISE (1648–1687)

A multitalented Englishman known for his quick temper, Wise once began playing the organ in the middle of a religious service attended by King Charles II, simply to express displeasure with the lengthy sermon. On the night of August 24, 1687, Wise quarreled with his wife. In a rage, he rushed out into the street, where he was accosted by a night watchman. Wise struck him and in return received a blow from the watchman's club, which fatally fractured his skull.

4. JEAN MARIE LECLAIR (1697–1764)

Leclair was composer and ballet master to both the French court and the court of the Netherlands. Early one morning he was found murdered in a Paris street near his home. Although the crime was never officially solved, evidence indicates that he may have been killed by his estranged wife.

5. JOHANN SCHOBERT (1720–1767)

A popular composer of chamber music, Schobert died in his Paris home after eating mushrooms that were in fact toadstools. One of his friends, as well as a servant and all the members of his

173

immediate family, with the exception of one young child, also died from ingesting the poisonous mushrooms.

6. FRANZ KOTZWARA (1750?–1793)

Born in Prague, Kotzwara spent much of his life traveling and finally settled in London. A versatile musician, he is best known for his sonata "The Battle of Prague." He led a dissipated private life, and he was particularly fond of a very unusual sexual practice: being hanged and nearly strangled, a practice known as *jeu de coupe-corde*, or "game of cutting the rope." He usually paid young women to hang him from the ceiling for five minutes and then cut the rope. On February 2, 1793, he was discovered dead in a house of ill repute in Covent Garden. Susannah Hill, his accomplice, had not been able to revive him after cutting the rope. She was arrested, tried for murder, and acquitted.

7. CHARLES VALENTIN MORHANGE-ALKAN (1813–1888)

Alkan was noted for his novel—and often bizarre—piano works, composed in a harmonically daring musical style. He lived reclusively and was crushed to death when he accidentally pulled a bookcase over on himself while reaching for a copy of the Talmud.

8. PĔTR ILICH TCHAIKOVSKY (1840–1893)

On October 28, 1893, the illustrious Russian composer conducted the first performance of his Symphony No. 6 in B Minor in St. Petersburg. Called the "Pathetic Symphony" because of its melancholic air, it was not well received. Four days later Tchaikovsky—already feeling ill—knowingly drank a glass of unboiled water even though a cholera epidemic was raging throughout the city. His death on November 6 set off a flurry of rumors that, despondent over the reaction to his symphony, he had committed suicide by purposely contracting cholera.

9. ERNEST CHAUSSON (1855–1899)

Chausson was a wealthy man who switched from the study of law to the composition of introspective chamber music. His career was cut short when he lost control of his bicycle while riding down a steep slope near his home in Limay, France. He crashed into a wall and died instantly.

10. ENRIQUE GRANADOS CAMPINA (1867–1916)

One of the foremost composers of Spanish nationalist music, Granados overcame his terror of deep water and sailed to New York City to hear an operatic adaptation of his piano compositions. He braved the return journey as a passenger on the S.S. *Sussex* and was drowned in the English Channel when the ship was torpedoed by a German submarine. The tragedy was compounded because, by agreeing to play at a reception given by President Wilson, Granados missed the boat on which he was originally scheduled to return to Spain.

11. ALEXANDER SCRIABIN (1872–1915)

This innovative Russian composer developed a pustule on his lip in the spring of 1915 but elected to ignore it. Soon the pustule developed into a carbuncle, which disfigured much of his face. Bedridden with a fever of 106°, Scriabin allowed surgeons to lance his lip several times, but blood poisoning set in and he was dead within hours. No death mask could be cast because of the hideous scarring caused by the emergency surgery.

12. MIECZYSLAW KARLOWICZ (1876–1909)

Considered the greatest Polish composer of the late Romantic era, Karlowicz blended aspects of nationalist music with the ultra-Romantic tradition of Richard Strauss. He was also one of the first of his countrymen to popularize skiing. On one of his frequent solo skiing expeditions in the Tatra Mountains, he was buried by an avalanche.

13. ANTON VON WEBERN (1883–1945)

A brilliant composer whose unconventional music was banned by the Nazis in 1938, Webern was killed because of a tragic mistake. While staying with his daughter in the small Austrian town of Mittersill, he inadvertently failed to respond to a wartime curfew warning and was shot by an overzealous American soldier. The guilt-ridden soldier spent his last years in an asylum.

14. ALBAN BERG (1885–1935)

An outstanding student of Arnold Schönberg, Berg—like Scriabin—died from blood poisoning caused by a carbuncle. In Berg's case, the abscess was located in the small of his back and was the result of an insect bite.

15. WALLINGFORD RIEGGER (1885–1961)

One of the first American composers to employ Schönberg's system of composition, Riegger met his end when he became entangled in the leashes of two fighting dogs. He fell to the ground and sustained a serious head injury. Emergency brain surgery proved futile, and he died shortly thereafter.

—D.W.B. & C.RO.

ISAAC STERN'S
10 BEST VIOLINISTS
IN HISTORY

This Russian-born—but American-trained—virtuoso violinist made his debut with the San Francisco Symphony Orchestra in 1931 at age 11. By the early 1940s, while still a young man in his 20s, Stern had gained wide acclaim and was playing to enthusiastic audiences throughout the U.S. and Europe. Excitement over his appearances continues to this day. He is a member of the original

National Arts Council and was for many years president of Carnegie Hall in New York City.

1. Niccolò Paganini (1782–1840)
2. Antonio Vivaldi (1675?–1741)
3. Ludwig [Louis] Spohr (1784–1859)
4. Henri Vieuxtemps (1820–1881)
5. Henri Wieniawski (1835–1880)
6. Pablo de Sarasate y Navascués (1844–1908)
7. Joseph Joachim (1831–1907)
8. Eugène Ysaye (1858–1931)
9. Bronislaw Hubermann (1882–1947)
10. Jascha Heifetz (b. 1901)

—Exclusive for *The Book of Lists 2*

Niccolò Paganini, London, 1831.

NEIL SIMON'S
11 FUNNIEST PLAYS
IN HISTORY

After several years of writing for television comedians, Simon wrote his first play, *Come Blow Your Horn*, which debuted on Broadway in 1961. A string of hits followed, including *Barefoot in the Park*, *The Odd Couple*, and *The Sunshine Boys*. Among his many screenplays are *The Heartbreak Kid*, *The Goodbye Girl*, and *California Suite*. He lives in Los Angeles, Calif., with his wife, actress Marsha Mason.

1. *Born Yesterday* (1946) by Garson Kanin
2. *Arsenic and Old Lace* (1941) by Joseph Kesselring
3. *Charley's Aunt* (1892) by Brandon Thomas
4. *The Importance of Being Earnest* (1895) by Oscar Wilde
5. *As You Like It* (1599–1600) by William Shakespeare
6. *Room Service* (1937) by John Murray and Allen Boretz
7. *Three Men on a Horse* (1935) by George Abbott and John Cecil Holm
8. *A Flea in Her Ear* (1907) by Georges Feydeau
9. *The Front Page* (1928) by Ben Hecht and Charles MacArthur
10. *You Can't Take It with You* (1936) by Moss Hart and George S. Kaufman
11. *Volpone* (1605–1606) by Ben Jonson

—Exclusive for *The Book of Lists 2*

HELEN HAYES'S
10 BEST FEMALE STAGE ROLES

One of the leading actresses of modern times, Helen Hayes made her Broadway acting debut at age nine in *Old Dutch*. She has appeared in such renowned plays as *Victoria Regina, Mary of Scotland,* and *The Wisteria Trees* and has won Oscars for her film performances in *The Sin of Madelon Claudet* (1932) and *Airport* (1969). She is the mother of TV actor James MacArthur.

1. Marguerite Gautier, in *Camille*
2. Amanda Wingfield, in *The Glass Menagerie*
3. Rosalind, in *As You Like It*
4. Viola, in *Twelfth Night*
5. Peg, in *Peg o' My Heart*
6. Medea, in *Medea*

7. Joan of Arc, in *Saint Joan*
8. Juliet, in *Romeo and Juliet*
9. Sadie Thompson, in *Rain*
10. Mary Tyrone, in *Long Day's Journey into Night*

—Exclusive for *The Book of Lists 2*

SHAKESPEARE'S
20 LONGEST ROLES

Role	Number of Lines	Play
1. Hamlet	1,422	*Hamlet*
2. Falstaff*	1,178	*Henry IV, Parts 1 and 2*
3. Richard III	1,124	*Richard III*
4. Iago	1,097	*Othello*
5. Henry V	1,025	*Henry V*
6. Othello	860	*Othello*
7. Vincentio	820	*Measure for Measure*
8. Coriolanus	809	*Coriolanus*
9. Timon	795	*Timon of Athens*
10. Antony	766	*Antony and Cleopatra*
11. Richard II	753	*Richard II*
12. Brutus	701	*Julius Caesar*
13. Lear	697	*King Lear*
14. Titus	687	*Titus Andronicus*
15. Macbeth	681	*Macbeth*
16. Rosalind	668	*As You Like It*
17. Leontes	648	*The Winter's Tale*
18. Cleopatra	622	*Antony and Cleopatra*
19. Prospero	603	*The Tempest*
20. Pericles	592	*Pericles*

*The total number of lines for Falstaff would be 1,614 if his lines from *The Merry Wives of Windsor* (436) were added, making his the longest Shakespearean role.

—R.W.

ANDREW WYETH'S
8 GREATEST AMERICAN
PAINTINGS IN HISTORY

When asked to explain his worldwide popularity, Wyeth answered, "It's because I happen to paint things that reflect the basic truths of life: sky, earth, friends, the intimate things." The landscapes and people in Wyeth's tempera and watercolor paintings have brought him renown as one of the most gifted contemporary artists. He lives in his hometown of Chadds Ford, Pa., with his wife, Betsy.

1. *Fox Hunt* (1893) by Winslow Homer
2. *Riverdale* (1863) by Fitz Hugh Lane
3. *Colonel George Washington* (1772) by Charles Willson Peale
4. *Hunting* (1874) by Thomas Eakins
5. *The Race Track* (1910) by Albert Pinkham Ryder
6. *Daughters of Revolution* (1932) by Grant Wood
7. *Noah's Ark* (1846) by Edward Hicks
8. *Fur Traders Descending the Missouri* (1845) by George Caleb Bingham

—Exclusive for *The Book of Lists 2*

NORTON SIMON'S
11 BEST PAINTINGS
IN HISTORY

In addition to being one of the wealthiest men in America, Simon, a retired industrialist, is an art collector with one of the most extraordinary collections in the world. His interest in collecting began in 1954, when he purchased a Gauguin, a Bonnard, and a Pissarro. Today his collection includes many of the world's great masterpieces.

1. *Still Life: Lemons, Oranges, and a Rose* (1633) by Francisco de Zurbarán
2. *Madonna and Child with Book* (c. 1504) by Raphael
3. *Portrait of the Artist's Son, Titus* (1653–1654) by Rembrandt
4. *Portrait of a Peasant* (1888) by Vincent van Gogh
5. *Flight into Egypt* (c. 1540) by Jacopo Bassano
6. *The Branchini Madonna* (1427) by Giovanni di Paolo
7. *Woman with Book* (1932) by Pablo Picasso
8. *Tulips in a Vase* (c. 1890–1892) by Paul Cézanne
9–10. *Saints Benedict and Apollonia* (c. 1483); *Saints Paul and Frediano* (c. 1493); pair of panels by Filippo Lippi
11. *The Ironers* (c. 1884) by Edgar Degas

Adds Simon: "Coincidentally, all of these paintings happen to be in the Norton Simon Museum [Pasadena, Calif., open to the public]."

—Exclusive for *The Book of Lists 2*

12 ART RIOTS
OF THE 20TH CENTURY

1. PREMIERE PERFORMANCE OF THE MARQUISE DE MORNY'S PANTOMIME PLAY *RÊVE D'ÉGYPTE*. MOULIN ROUGE, PARIS, JANUARY 3, 1907.

Set in the pharaohs' Egypt, this pantomime featured the controversial French writer and music hall actress Colette and her friend and inamorata the Marquise de Morny. The women portrayed reunited lovers, with the marquise playing the male role. Colette had said, "I become my parts," and it was so on that night, for when the lovers embraced in a long kiss, Colette, almost nude, displayed uninhibited passion. The marquise's husband, his friends, and the audience were outraged. When the curtain came down, the audience was in an ugly mood, and its outrage boiled over into a riotous affair, with people throwing objects at the performers and beating each other with their umbrellas.

2. PREMIERE PERFORMANCE OF ARNOLD SCHÖNBERG'S *PIERROT LUNAIRE*. BERLIN, 1912.

In 1912 Schönberg had yet to develop his 12-tone system, but his composing had already evolved towards a music severe in style, terse in form, atonal, with melodies that were somber and unadorned. *Pierrot Lunaire* was such a work, and it provoked hostility, riots, and scandal. Blows were traded amidst hysteria and laughter. One critic wrote, "If this is music, then I pray my Creator not let me hear it again." Even years later repercussions were still felt, as a man from the premiere audience brought assault charges against another man. In court, a physician testified that the music had been so jarring as to awaken peculiar neuroses.

3. THE ARMORY SHOW (INTERNATIONAL EXHIBITION OF MODERN ART). HELD AT THE ARMORY OF THE 69TH CAVALRY REGIMENT, NEW YORK, FEBRUARY–MARCH, 1913.

In 1913 Americans viewed a major exhibit of European and American art, and most were not impressed. The 1,600 predominantly modern works assembled at the armory included the art of Picasso, Matisse, and Duchamp. Modern American art was represented by the works of such artists as John Sloan, John Marin, and Maurice Prendergast. But most Americans were not ready for the brave new visual worlds. Demonstrations unprecedented in the U.S. marred the show. Howls of laughter and derision were common, and a frenzied mob threatened to destroy canvases, particularly the Cubist paintings and Duchamp's *Nude Descending a Staircase*. Nevertheless, the exhibition was a great success, stirring up curiosity and gaining a few supporters.

4. PREMIERE PERFORMANCE OF IGOR STRAVINSKY'S *RITE OF SPRING* AND THE ACCOMPANYING BALLET BY NIJINSKY. THÉÂTRE DES CHAMPS ÉLYSÉES, PARIS, MAY 29, 1913.

The music performed that night was so revolutionary in concept that many in the audience perceived it as musical anarchy. Also, Nijinsky's dancing was too sensual for the moral and aesthetic palates of many of the upper-class ballet lovers. Together the music and dance shocked the audience. Whistling and catcalls rocked the theater, and sympathetic patrons tried, without success, to silence the upheaval. Fistfights cropped up in the aisles, and gendarmes arrived to expel the worst of the offenders, but pandemonium soon broke out anew and continued until the end of the performance. Years later, the composer-conductor Pierre Boulez referred to the *Rite* as "the cornerstone of modern music."

5. VIOLIN RECITAL BY FRITZ KREISLER. CORNELL UNIVERSITY, DECEMBER, 1919.

After being wounded in W.W. I and subsequently released from the Austrian army, Kreisler came to the U.S. for a concert tour. With war sentiment running high, many of his concerts were canceled—one by a director of public safety, another by a women's club, and yet another due to protests. In December, 1919, more than a year after the Armistice, he played at Cornell University, even though the mayor of Ithaca exhorted citizens not to attend. During the performance irate American Legionnaires cut the electric wires, but Kreisler played on in the blackout for 40 minutes. Disturbances escalated to riotous proportions, and the police were summoned.

6. DADA PERFORMANCE. SALLE GAVEAU, PARIS, MAY 26, 1920.

Well known for provoking their audiences to riotous protest, the Dadaists (who opposed bourgeois values) went all out at this performance—one which many claim was the climax of the Paris Dada anti-art movement. The performers appeared on stage to present their poems, manifestos, and sketches in outrageous attire. André Breton had a revolver tied to each temple, Paul Éluard was dressed as a ballerina, and the others wore tubes or funnels on their heads. These outfits, together with the content of the program, which attacked art, philosophy, ethics, and just about everything the bourgeoisie held sacred, pushed the audience beyond its endurance. Tomatoes, eggs, and beefsteaks were thrown at the performers amid a tremendous uproar. Naturally, the Dadaists considered the evening a great success.

7. PERFORMANCE OF MUSIC FOR PIANO BY GEORGE ANTHEIL. THE PHILHARMONIE, BUDAPEST, 1923.

A composer of avant-garde music that was considered anti-romantic and antiexpressive, Antheil was often subjected to hostile audiences. As a result, he began carrying a gun hidden in a shoulder holster whenever he performed. His opening concert in Budapest provoked the audience because of its harsh and unfamiliar sounds, and a riot broke out. The following night, determined that his music

181

be heard, Antheil ordered the ushers to lock all the doors. Then, with the audience's full attention on him, he pulled out his gun and placed it on the piano, where it remained for the rest of an uninterrupted performance.

8. 4TH PERFORMANCE OF SEAN O'CASEY'S *PLOUGH AND THE STARS*. ABBEY THEATRE, DUBLIN, FEBRUARY 11, 1926.

In the second act of O'Casey's play, set amidst the 1916 Easter Rebellion against the British, actors portraying Irish heroes brought the national flag onto the stage, set up as a tavern. Many patriots in the audience took this as an insult to the men who had died in the Free Ireland struggle. This emotional issue touched off a riot that included fights between members of the audience and the actors. William Butler Yeats, the esteemed poet and senior director of the theater, called the police and then took to the stage to castigate the audience. Later there was a threat to blow up the theater. During following performances the police were present, as were the stench of stink bombs and occasional outbursts, but no more riots erupted.

9. INITIAL SCREENINGS OF LUIS BUÑUEL AND SALVADOR DALI'S *L'ÂGE D'OR*. PARIS, DECEMBER, 1930.

A film that bombards the viewer with violent and erotic surrealistic imagery, *L'Âge d'Or* is concerned with the malice and hypocrisy of man. It vigorously scorns the conventions and institutions of bourgeois society. As expected, bourgeois society was not delighted with the film. One newspaper called it "obscene, repellent, and paltry," and another commented that "country, family, and religion are dragged through the mud." An article in an extreme rightist paper incited reactionary young Frenchmen, and they launched an attack on the theater that did not stop for six days. By that time 120,000 francs' worth of damage had been done. Due to the violent controversy, the film was not shown again publicly for over 35 years.

Luis Buñuel's 1930 depiction of the Catholic clergy
in his film, *L'Âge d'Or*, caused a right-wing riot.

10. UNVEILING OF MURAL BY DIEGO RIVERA.
   HOTEL DEL PRADO, MEXICO CITY, JUNE, 1948.

Diego Rivera's mural *Sunday in the Alameda,* commissioned for the dining room of the new Hotel del Prado in 1948, showed Mexican historian Ignacio Ramírez holding an open book. The words *Dios no existe* ("God does not exist") were clearly printed on one page. Consequently, Archbishop L. M. Martínez refused to bless the government-owned structure, and a mob of youths stormed into the dining room and scraped away the words with a knife. When Rivera restored the words with a fountain pen, local students threatened to obliterate them as often as Rivera replaced them. The hotel had the mural covered, and while its fate remained in limbo, Rivera was denied entrance to a movie house and his home was vandalized. Eventually a priest who preferred to remain anonymous quietly blessed the hotel.

11. APPEARANCE OF LENNY BRUCE.
   THE ESTABLISHMENT CLUB, LONDON, 1962.

During Lenny's engagement at the "liberal" cabaret, the freewheeling social satirist offered his unorthodox views on pornography, sex, and drugs, among other topics. Each night patrons responded uproariously with shouting, walkouts, and fistfights. Russian poet Yevgeny Yevtushenko left in disgust, as did playwright John Osborne. The manager of the club was punched in the nose by the escort of actress Siobhan McKenna. Soon Lenny was declared an undesirable alien and deported from England. His obscenity trials still lay ahead of him.

12. UNAUTHORIZED EXHIBIT OF MODERN ART.
   MOSCOW, SEPTEMBER 15, 1974.

A group of Russian artists whose paintings were in many styles—except Social Realism; the official art of the U.S.S.R.—was unable to obtain either permission or a building for its exhibit, so it was set up on a muddy field in southeast Moscow. Soviet police met this challenge by driving bulldozers and high-pressure water trucks through the exhibit grounds, sending men, women, and children fleeing in panic. Plainclothesmen trampled many paintings underfoot, and the police burned others. Thirty foreign diplomats watched while artists were beaten up, newsmen were manhandled, and U.S. consul Leonard Willems was shoved around. The police defended these actions, saying that the bulldozers and trucks were building "a park of rest and culture." Two weeks later, to appease the U.S.—its détente partner—and to court world opinion, the Soviet government gave permission for a similar exhibit.

—E.H.C.

10
SIGHTS AND SOUNDS

17 MOVIE STARS
WHO TURNED DOWN GREAT ROLES

1. MARLON BRANDO

Turned down the role of Frankie, the musician-junkie, in *The Man with the Golden Arm* (1955). Frank Sinatra got the part and reestablished his career with an electrifying performance.

2. JAMES CAGNEY

Turned down the role of Alfred P. Doolittle in *My Fair Lady* (1964). The role went to Stanley Holloway. Cagney was offered $1 million but didn't want to come out of retirement.

3. MONTGOMERY CLIFT

Expressed enthusiasm for the role of the young writer in *Sunset Boulevard* (1950) but later turned it down, claiming that his audience would not accept his playing love scenes with a woman who was 35 years older. William Holden starred with Gloria Swanson in the widely acclaimed film.

4. BETTE DAVIS

Turned down the role of Scarlett O'Hara in *Gone with the Wind* (1939). The role went to Vivien Leigh. Davis thought that her co-star was going to be Errol Flynn, with whom she refused to work.

5. KIRK DOUGLAS

Turned down the role of Kid Shelleen in *Cat Ballou* (1965). The role won an Academy Award for Lee Marvin. Douglas's agent convinced him not to accept the comedic role of the drunken gunfighter.

6. W. C. FIELDS

Could have played the title role in *The Wizard of Oz* (1939). The part was written for Fields, who would have played the wizard as a cynical con man. But he turned down the part, purportedly because he wanted $100,000 and MGM offered him $75,000. However, a letter signed by Fields's agent asserts that Fields rejected the offer in order to devote all his time to writing *You Can't Cheat an Honest Man*. Frank Morgan ended up playing the wizard.

7. JANE FONDA

Turned down *Bonnie and Clyde* (1967). The role of Bonnie

Parker went to Faye Dunaway. Fonda, living in France at the time, didn't want to move to the States for the role.

8. CARY GRANT

Turned down the male lead (Jean-Marc Clement) in *Let's Make Love* (1960). The role went to Yves Montand. Grant didn't want to work with the film's other star, Marilyn Monroe (Amanda Dell).

9. WILLIAM HOLDEN

Turned down *The Guns of Navarone* (1961). The leading role of Capt. Keith Mallory went to Gregory Peck. Holden wanted $750,000 and 10% of the gross. His offer was rejected.

10. ALAN LADD

Turned down the role of Jett Rink in *Giant* (1956). The role went to James Dean. Ladd felt he was too old for the part.

11. HEDY LAMARR

Turned down the role of Ilsa in *Casablanca* (1942). Ingrid Bergman took over and, with Bogart, made film history. Lamarr hadn't wanted to work with an unfinished script.

12. BURT LANCASTER

Turned down the lead in *Ben-Hur* (1959). The role of Judah Ben-Hur went to Charlton Heston, who won an Academy Award and added another hit to his career of spectacular blockbusters.

13. MYRNA LOY

Turned down the lead (Ellie Andrews) opposite Clark Gable (Peter Warne) in *It Happened One Night* (1934). The role won an Academy Award for Claudette Colbert. A previous film set on a bus had just failed, and Loy thought the film wouldn't have a chance.

It almost happened this way in *It Happened One Night* —but Myrna Loy turned down the Claudette Colbert role.

185

14. PAUL MUNI

Turned down the role of Roy Earle in *High Sierra* (1941). The role went to Humphrey Bogart, who lifted the part to near mythic quality. Muni was tired of playing gangsters.

15. GEORGE RAFT

Turned down the main roles in *High Sierra* (1941), *The Maltese Falcon* (1941), and *Casablanca* (1942), which became three of Humphrey Bogart's most famous roles. Raft rejected the Sam Spade role in *The Maltese Falcon* because he didn't want to work with director John Huston, an unknown at that time.

16. ROBERT REDFORD

Turned down the role of Ben Braddock in *The Graduate* (1967). The role made an instant star of Dustin Hoffman. Redford thought he couldn't project the right amount of naiveté.

17. EVA MARIE SAINT

Known for her selectivity in choosing roles, she erred when she turned down the central role in *The Three Faces of Eve* (1957) after reading an early version of the script. Joanne Woodward won an Oscar for her performance in the film.

—R.S.

JANE FONDA'S 3 BEST MOTION PICTURE ACTRESSES OF ALL TIME

One of Hollywood's most controversial actresses, Jane Fonda is as well known for her political involvements as for her film accomplishments. Her strong commitment to the antiwar movement led to the film *Coming Home*, for which she won the 1978 Oscar for best actress. This was followed by her antinuclear film *The China Syndrome*. Fonda's other movies include *They Shoot Horses, Don't They?*, *Klute*, and *Julia*.

1. Luise Rainer
2. Bette Davis
3. Vanessa Redgrave

—Exclusive for *The Book of Lists 2*

GRACE DE MONACO'S
5 BEST MOTION PICTURE
ACTRESSES OF ALL TIME

Grace Kelly's first major role was opposite Gary Cooper in *High Noon* in 1952. From this film through *Dial M for Murder, Rear Window, To Catch a Thief,* and *The Country Girl* (for which she won an Oscar for best actress in 1955), Miss Kelly was one of America's most popular stars. While at the height of her career, she married Prince Rainier III of Monaco. Although she retired from acting after her marriage, Princess Grace remains an international celebrity.

1. Marie Dressler
2. Mae West
3. Greta Garbo
4. Ingrid Bergman
5. Elizabeth Taylor

—Exclusive for *The Book of Lists 2*

JOHN WAYNE'S
5 BEST MOTION PICTURE ACTORS
AND ACTRESSES OF ALL TIME

John "Duke" Wayne (1907–1979) played superheroes in movies for over 50 years. After acting in low-budget westerns for 10 years, Wayne received critical acclaim for his performance in *Stagecoach* in 1939. A Hollywood institution, he was featured in dozens of movies, including *Red River, Sands of Iwo Jima,* and *The Green Berets.* Wayne received the 1969 Motion Picture Academy Award for best actor for his performance in *True Grit.*

1. Spencer Tracy
2. Elizabeth Taylor
3. Katharine Hepburn
4. Laurence Olivier
5. Lionel Barrymore

—Exclusive for *The Book of Lists 2*

19 MOVIE STARS AND
HOW THEY WERE DISCOVERED

1. RICHARD ARLEN

He was working as a film lab runner at Paramount Studios in 1922 when he was struck by a company car and hospitalized with a broken leg. Studio executives took notice and offered him a chance to act.

2. MARY ASTOR

She was unexpectedly brought to the attention of Harry Durant of the story department at Famous Players–Lasky Corporation in New York in 1920. Mary's father was applying for a script translator job when Durant eyed some photos of Mary that Mr. Astor had in his possession.

3. CLARA BOW

She was on her way to stardom after winning first prize in the national Fame and Fortune Contest sponsored by Brewster Publications in Brooklyn in 1921. Judges Neysa McMein, Harrison Fisher, and Howard Chandler Christy awarded her a trophy, a gown, and a role in a motion picture.

4. WALTER BRENNAN

He got his start in Hollywood films when he did a voice-over for a donkey. The actor volunteered to help a film director who was having difficulty getting the animal to bray on cue.

5. GARY COOPER

Working as a stunt man, he was noticed by director Henry King on the set of *The Winning of Barbara Worth* at Samuel Goldwyn Studios in 1926.

6. DOLORES DEL RIO

She was discovered by producer Edwin Carewe in 1925 during a dinner party at the home of Dolores's parents in Mexico City.

7. ANDY DEVINE

Clad in a Santa Clara University football sweater, he was walking down Hollywood Boulevard in 1925 when he passed a Universal Studios casting director. Devine was recruited on the spot to play an athlete in a studio serial.

8. FARRAH FAWCETT

She was a freshman at the University of Texas in 1968 when she was voted a winner in the Ten Most Beautiful Contest. Photos of the winners were sent to Hollywood and came to the attention of publicist David Mirisch, who persuaded Fawcett's parents to allow her to come to Hollywood.

9. ERROL FLYNN

He was discovered by Cinesound Studios casting director John Warwick in Sydney, Australia, in 1932. Warwick found some amateur footage of Flynn taken in 1930 by Dr. Herman F. Erben, a filmmaker and tropical-disease specialist who had chartered navigator Flynn's schooner for a tour of New Guinea headhunter territory.

10. ROCK HUDSON

Hudson, whose original name was Roy Fitzgerald, was working as a truck driver for the Budget Pack Company in 1954 when another driver offered to arrange a meeting between Fitzgerald and agent Henry Willson. In spite of Fitzgerald's professed lack of faith in his acting abilities, Willson took the aspiring actor under his wing, changed his name to Rock Hudson, and launched his career.

11. BUSTER KEATON

He was discovered by film comedian Fatty Arbuckle on 46th Street in New York in 1917. While Keaton had had some stage experience, he got his first movie part through Arbuckle.

12. CAROLE LOMBARD

She met director Allan Dwan in Los Angeles in the spring of 1921. Dwan watched 12-year-old Carole—then tomboy Jane Alice Peters—playing baseball outside the home of his friends Al and Rita Kaufman.

13. MYRNA LOY

She was singled out by Rudolph Valentino in 1923, when Henry Waxman at Warner Brothers Studios showed Valentino several photographs of chorus girls.

14. IDA LUPINO

She was introduced to director Allan Dwan in England in 1933, while Dwan was casting a film, *Her First Affair*. Forty-one-year-old Connie Emerald was trying out for a part, but Dwan found Connie's young daughter Ida better suited for the role.

15. RYAN O'NEAL

He was befriended by actor Richard Egan in 1962 at the gymnasium where both Egan and O'Neal worked out. "It was just a matter of Ryan himself being so impressive," said Egan.

16. VALERIE PERRINE

She started on the road to success after meeting Hollywood agent Robert Walker in 1971 at a birthday party thrown by Valerie's roommate.

17. ANN SHERIDAN

She won a five-week contract from Paramount Pictures in 1933 after becoming one of 30 winners in the national Search for Beauty Contest—part of a studio promotional campaign. Ann had been entered secretly in the contest by her sister Kitty.

18. LANA TURNER

She was observed in Currie's Ice Cream Parlor across the street from Hollywood High School in January, 1936. Billy Wilkerson, editor of the *Hollywood Reporter*, approached her while she was drinking a Coke.

Lana Turner was discovered in an ice cream parlor in 1936.

19. JOHN WAYNE

He was spotted by director Raoul Walsh at Hollywood's Fox lot in 1928. Walsh was on his way to the administration building when he noticed Wayne—then Marion Morrison, a studio prop man—loading furniture from a warehouse onto a truck.

—D.B.

10 POPULAR FILM STARS
NEVER NOMINATED
FOR AN ACADEMY AWARD

1. Lauren Bacall
2. Tallulah Bankhead
3. John Barrymore
4. Joseph Cotten
5. W. C. Fields
6. Boris Karloff
7. Peter Lorre
8. Myrna Loy
9. Ida Lupino
10. Marilyn Monroe

—The Eds.

10 SPECIAL
IMPRINTS AT GRAUMAN'S
CHINESE THEATRE

When it opened in the spring of 1927 with *King of Kings,* Grauman's Chinese Theatre was merely one of many architecturally unusual movie houses of the era. To make his theater unique, Sid Grauman decided to preserve in cement the handprints and footprints of movie stars in the expansive forecourt. On May 18, 1927, Norma Talmadge became the first celebrity to preserve her prints and signature. The tradition continues today, even though the theater now belongs to Mann Theatres Corporation. More than 156 celebrities—including Darth Vader, C-3P0, and R2D2 of *Star Wars,* and Mickey Mouse, in celebration of his 50th birthday—have added their imprints and messages. Several stars have been persuaded to leave even more of themselves. These special imprints are:

1. John Barrymore's profile
2. Joe E. Brown's mouth
3. Jimmy Durante's nose
4. Betty Grable's leg
5. Sonja Henie's skates
6. Jean Hersholt's pipe
7. Al Jolson's knee
8. Harold Lloyd's glasses
9. Eleanor Powell's tap shoes
10. Monty Woolley's beard

Note: Also immortalized are the pistols of the following cowboys, along with their horses' hoofprints: Gene Autry and Champ, William S. Hart and Pinto Ben, Tom Mix and Tony, and Roy Rogers and Trigger.

—T.E.

8 NOTABLE ACTORS
WHO ONCE APPEARED IN
HORROR MOVIES

1. JAMES ARNESS (*The Thing*, RKO, 1951)

Arness played the monstrous vegetable creature from outer space—a "carrot with brains"—that preyed on an air force base at the North Pole. Director Howard Hawks used the creature sparingly to heighten the suspense, shocking audiences (and sometimes the crew) with surprise confrontations. In the end, an ingenious solution for disposing of the terrible vegetable is reached. The air force men burn it. From this ignominious beginning, Arness went on to play Matt Dillon in the long-running TV western *Gunsmoke*.

2. HUMPHREY BOGART (*The Return of Dr. X.*, Warner Brothers, 1939)

While under contract to Warner Brothers, Bogart was forced to make his first and only horror film. *The Return of Dr. X.* was a follow-up to a silent film made several years before. Bogie played Dr. Maurice Xavier, a noted physician who is also a child murderer. Sent to the electric chair for his crimes, Dr. X. returns from the dead with an unpleasant habit; he requires constant blood transfusions from living and decidedly unwilling victims. In the end justice triumphs, the pretty girl is rescued, and Dr. X. is sent back to his grave, never to return again.

Humphrey Bogart as the notorious Dr. X.

3. CHARLES BRONSON (*House of Wax*, Warner Brothers, 1953)

Still using his real name—Charles Buchinsky—Bronson played the hulking deaf-mute assistant of wax-museum owner Vincent Price. Horribly burned in a fire that destroys his waxworks, Price goes mad. Unable to use his crippled hands, he recreates his greatest statues by coating fresh corpses with wax. The law moves in on Price and Bronson as they attempt to dispatch Phyllis Kirk. The girl is saved and Price meets his end in Technicolor and 3-D.

4. MICHAEL LANDON (*I Was a Teenage Werewolf*, AIP, 1957)

For his first film, Landon wore buck-toothed fangs and fake eyebrows that resembled giant caterpillars. An innocent teenage victim of a mad doctor's secret serum, he turns into a werewolf wearing a baseball jacket. Landon left the movies shortly after this to become *Bonanza*'s Little Joe Cartwright.

5. STEVE McQUEEN (*The Blob*, Tonylyn/Paramount, 1958)

When McQueen, as a typical small-town teenager, reports seeing a thing that resembles a giant air-breathing jellyfish engulf and devour people, he is dismissed as a kid playing a prank. The jellyfish, unchecked, proceeds to eat everybody in its path. Nothing can stop it until McQueen, despite the way the town previously treated him, comes to the rescue. Cornering the blob in a diner, he and the local fire department spray it with a chemical, freeze it, and ship it to the North Pole.

6. JACK NICHOLSON (*The Raven*, AIP, 1963)

An early Nicholson film was a horror comedy also starring Vincent Price, Boris Karloff, and Peter Lorre. Magicians Dr. Craven and Dr. Bedlow journey to the castle of the evil Dr. Scarabus to seek Craven's unfaithful wife, Leonore. Accompanying them are Craven's daughter and Bedlow's son (Nicholson), who provide the love interest. At Leonore's urging, Scarabus turns Bedlow into a raven and challenges Craven to a duel of magic. Craven wins, but decides Scarabus can keep his unfaithful wife.

7. DONALD SUTHERLAND (*Castle of the Living Dead*, Serena/Francinor, 1964)

A troupe of wandering players staying at the castle of the sinister Count Drago (Christopher Lee) is murdered one by one, and the bodies are mummified. The local police sergeant (Sutherland) wants to arrest a member of the troupe to close the case and be done with it. The players object, a fight starts, and Drago's collection of mummies is revealed in the confusion. The sergeant tries to arrest Drago, but the count accidentally cuts himself on a scalpel covered with preserving fluid and is turned into a living statue.

8. ROBERT VAUGHN (*Teenage Caveman*, alternate title, *Out of the Darkness*, AIP, 1958)

Director Roger Corman made this contribution to the rash of teenage horror films that sprang up in the late fifties. With Vaughn in the title role, it was a typical caveman-versus-monster film until the surprise ending. Defying the wise men of his tribe, Vaughn sets out to explore the world across the river. What he discovers is the awful truth: Thanks to an atomic war, man is at the end of his civilization, not the beginning.

—S.L.S.

RING LARDNER, JR.'S 5 BEST SCREENPLAY WRITERS OF ALL TIME

One of the major screenwriters of the 1940s, Lardner won an Oscar in 1942 for *Woman of the Year*. As one of the "Hollywood Ten" who refused to testify before the House Un-American Activities Committee, Lardner served nine months in jail and was blacklisted by the film industry. Although he continued to write screenplays, it was not until 1965 that his own name appeared in the screen credits of *The Cincinnati Kid*. He went on to win the 1970 Oscar for his screenplay of *M.A.S.H.*

1. Nunnally Johnson
2. Ingmar Bergman
3. Michael Wilson
4. Ben Hecht
5. Charles Chaplin

—Exclusive for *The Book of Lists* 2

ROBERT WISE'S 5 BEST MOTION PICTURE DIRECTORS OF ALL TIME

During his nearly 40-year career, producer-director Wise has created numerous box-office successes. His *West Side Story* won both the New York Film Critics' Award for best picture and the Oscar for best picture and direction. In 1965 he received two more Oscars for *The Sound of Music*. Other highly acclaimed films by this outstanding director include *Run Silent, Run Deep; I Want to Live;* and *The Sand Pebbles*.

1. D. W. Griffith
2. Charles Chaplin
3. John Ford
4. Jean Renoir
5. William Wyler

—Exclusive for *The Book of Lists* 2

10 FILM SCENES LEFT
ON THE CUTTING ROOM FLOOR

1. *FRANKENSTEIN* (1931)

In one scene, the monster (Boris Karloff) walks through a forest and comes upon a little girl, Maria, who is throwing flowers into a pond. The monster joins her in the activity but soon runs out of flowers. At a loss for something to throw into the water, he looks at Maria and moves toward her. In all American prints of the movie, the scene ends here. But as originally filmed, the action continues to show the monster grabbing Maria, hurling her into the lake, then departing in confusion when Maria fails to float as the flowers did. This bit was deleted because Karloff—objecting to the director's interpretation of the scene—felt that the monster should have gently put Maria into the lake. Though Karloff's intentions were good, the scene's omission suggests a crueler death for Maria, since a subsequent scene shows her bloodied corpse being carried through the village by her father.

2. *KING KONG* (1933)

The original *King Kong* was released four times between 1933 and 1952, and each release saw the cutting of additional scenes. Though many of the outtakes—including the censored sequence in which Kong peels off Fay Wray's clothes—were restored in 1971, one cut scene has never been found. It is the clip in which Kong shakes four sailors off a log bridge, causing them to fall into a ravine where they are eaten alive by giant spiders. When the movie—with spider sequence intact—was previewed in San Bernardino, Calif., in late January, 1933, members of the audience screamed and either left the theater or talked about the grisly sequence throughout the remainder of the film. Said the film's producer, Merian C. Cooper, "It stopped the picture cold, so the next day back at the studio, I took it out myself."

The giant man-eating spider that was too scary for *King Kong.*

3. *TARZAN AND HIS MATE* (1934)

Considered by many to be the best of the Tarzan films, *Tarzan and His Mate* included a scene in which Tarzan (Johnny Weissmuller), standing on a tree limb with Jane (Maureen O'Sullivan), pulls at Jane's scanty outfit and persuades her to dive into a lake with him. The two swim for a while and eventually surface. When Jane rises out of the water, one of her breasts is fully exposed. Because various groups, including official censors of the Hays Office, criticized the scene for being too erotic, it was cut by MGM.

4. *THE WIZARD OF OZ* (1939)

The Wizard of Oz originally contained an elaborate production number called "The Jitter Bug," which cost $80,000 and took five weeks to shoot. In the scene, Dorothy, the Scarecrow, the Cowardly Lion, and the Tin Woodsman are on their way to the witch's castle when they are attacked by "jitter bugs"—furry pink and blue mosquitolike "rascals" that give one "the jitters" as they buzz about in the air. When, after its first preview, the movie was judged too long, MGM officials decided to sacrifice the "Jitter Bug" scene. They reasoned that it added little to the plot and, because a dance by the same name had just become popular, they feared it might date the picture. (Another number was also cut for previews because some felt it slowed the pacing, but it was eventually restored. "Over the Rainbow" was its title.)

5. *SUNSET BOULEVARD* (1950)

Billy Wilder's film classic about an aging Hollywood film queen and a down-on-his-luck screenwriter originally incorporated a framing sequence which opened and closed the story at the Los Angeles County Morgue. In a scene described by Wilder as one of the best he'd ever shot, the body of Joe Gillis (William Holden) is rolled into the morgue to join three dozen other corpses, some of whom—in voice-over—tell Gillis how they died. Eventually Gillis tells his story, which takes us to a flashback of his affair with Norma Desmond (Gloria Swanson). The movie was previewed with this opening, in Illinois and Long Island. Because both audiences inappropriately found the morgue scene hilarious, the film's release was delayed six months so that a new beginning could be shot in which police find Gillis's corpse floating in Norma's pool while Gillis's voice narrates the events leading to his death.

6. *LIMELIGHT* (1952)

Charlie Chaplin's film about a vaudeville comic on the decline features a scene in which Chaplin, as the elderly Calvero, makes his comeback in a music hall sketch. The routine, which originally ran 10 minutes, has Calvero performing onstage with an old colleague, played by Buster Keaton. It has been said that while Chaplin was good, Keaton was sensational. Consequently, Chaplin allowed only a small portion of the scene to remain in release prints.

7. *FRIENDLY PERSUASION* (1956)

The question of whether or not to bear arms was the problem facing both Gary Cooper *and* the character he was portraying in the screen version of Jessamyn West's novel *Friendly Persuasion*. In the film, Quaker Jess Birdwell finds himself in a dilemma when his pacifist beliefs are strained by events in the Civil War. Offscreen, Gary Cooper claimed that his fans would feel "let down" if he did *not* fire a gun in the film. Author West, an Indiana Quaker who was working on the production as technical adviser, argued that Cooper's Birdwell must resist the temptation to take violent action. As a compromise, director William Wyler shot a scene in which Birdwell defeats a Confederate brigade by pushing a cannon into the enemy lines, thereby giving Cooper's followers that derring-do they had come to expect, while attempting to appease Miss West. It didn't work. Miss West objected, and the scene was cut.

8. *SPARTACUS* (1960)

Of the 167 days it took Stanley Kubrick to shoot *Spartacus*, six weeks were spent directing an elaborate battle sequence in which 8,500 extras dramatized the clash between Roman troops and Spartacus's slave army. Several scenes in the battle drew the ire of the Legion of Decency and were therefore cut. These included shots of men being dismembered. (Dwarfs with false torsos and an armless man with a phony "break-away" limb were used to give authenticity.) Seven years later, when the Oscar-winning film was reissued, an additional 22 minutes were chopped out, including a scene in which Varinia (Jean Simmons) watches Spartacus (Kirk Douglas) writhe in agony on a cross. Her line "Oh, please die, my darling" was excised, and the scene was cut to make it appear that Spartacus was already dead.

9. *SPLENDOR IN THE GRASS* (1961)

As filmed, *Splendor in the Grass* included a sequence in which Wilma Dean Loomis (Natalie Wood) takes a bath while arguing with her mother (Audrey Christie). The bickering finally becomes so intense that Wilma jumps out of the tub and runs nude down a hallway to her bedroom, where the camera cuts to a close-up of her bare legs kicking hysterically on the mattress. Both the Hollywood censors and the Catholic Legion of Decency objected to the hallway scene, finding Miss Wood's bare backside unsuitable for public display. Consequently, director Elia Kazan dropped the piece, leaving an abrupt jump from tub to bed.

10. *EVERYTHING YOU ALWAYS WANTED TO KNOW ABOUT SEX BUT WERE AFRAID TO ASK* (1972)

"What Makes a Man a Homosexual?" was one of the many vignettes filmed for the Woody Allen movie using the title of Dr. David Reuben's bestselling book. The sequence stars Allen as a common spider anxious to court a black widow (Louise Lasser). After doing a mating dance on Lasser's web, Allen makes love to the widow, only to be devoured by her afterward. The scene was finally cut out of the film because Allen couldn't come up with a suitable way to end the piece.

—D.B.

JANE FONDA'S
4 BEST MOTION PICTURES
OF ALL TIME

1. *Citizen Kane*
2. *Les Enfants du Paradis*
3. *Paths of Glory*
4. *The Grapes of Wrath*

—Exclusive for *The Book of Lists 2*

GRACE DE MONACO'S
5 BEST MOTION PICTURES
OF ALL TIME

1. *The Quiet Man*
2. *The Bicycle Thief*
3. *Gone with the Wind*
4. *La Grande Illusion*
5. *Some Like It Hot*

—Exclusive for *The Book of Lists 2*

JOHN WAYNE'S
5 BEST MOTION PICTURES
OF ALL TIME

1. *A Man for All Seasons*
2. *Gone with the Wind*
3. *The Four Horsemen of the Apocalypse*
4. *The Searchers*
5. *The Quiet Man*

—Exclusive for *The Book of Lists 2*

THE 25 ALL-TIME
BOX-OFFICE CHAMPION FILMS
(Adjusted for Inflation)

Usually when the top money-making films are tabulated, the ravages of inflation over the years are ignored. For example, on a strict dollar basis, *Star Wars* (1977) has already reaped $100 million more than *Gone With the Wind* (1939). But this doesn't take into account the fact that the 1939 dollar was worth nearly five times as much as the 1977 dollar, and the average price of a theater ticket in 1977 was $2.23 as compared to 23¢ 38 years earlier. Here, then, is a ranking of the top box-office champs, compiled by Charles Schreger, incorporating the inflation factor.

	U.S.-Canada Rentals in Millions of Dollars
1. *Gone With the Wind* (1939)	382.7
2. *Star Wars* (1977)	187.8
3. *The Sound of Music* (1965)	173.8
4. *Jaws* (1975)	156.4
5. *The Godfather* (1972)	143.2
6. *Snow White* (1937)	128.9
7. *The Exorcist* (1973)	128.2
8. *The Sting* (1973)	123.1
9. *The Ten Commandments* (1956)	109.7
10. *Doctor Zhivago* (1965)	102.4
11. *The Graduate* (1968)	97.7
12. *Mary Poppins* (1964)	91.4
13. *Love Story* (1970)	89.0
14. *Grease* (1978)	88.1
15. *Close Encounters of the Third Kind* (1977)	87.8
16. *Ben-Hur* (1959)	87.2
17. *American Graffiti* (1973)	87.2
18. *Butch Cassidy and the Sundance Kid* (1969)	87.0
19. *Saturday Night Fever* (1977)	81.5
20. *Airport* (1970)	80.6
21. *One Flew Over the Cuckoo's Nest* (1975)	76.1
22. *The Poseidon Adventure* (1972)	69.7
23. *Rocky* (1976)	65.9
24. *M*A*S*H* (1970)	65.4
25. *Smokey and the Bandit* (1977)	65.3

SOURCE: Reprinted with permission from *Los Angeles Times*. Copyright © 1979 by Los Angeles Times.

10 MOVIES THAT WERE
PART OF HISTORY

1. *MANHATTAN MELODRAMA*

This film starred William Powell and Clark Gable as two street-wise city kids who grew up in opposite directions—one good, the other headed for the electric chair. The plot was old hat, even in 1934, but the film was enough to draw John Dillinger into the theater with the "lady in red." He had just left the theater when the tipped-off G-men sprang their trap and killed him in the ensuing fight.

2. *GRAND ILLUSION*

Directed by pacifist Jean Renoir and starring Erich Von Stroheim, this movie was being shown when the German army marched into Vienna in 1938. Not surprisingly, Nazi storm troopers invaded the theater and confiscated the W.W. I antiwar classic in midreel.

3. *THE GREAT DICTATOR*

Produced, directed, and starred in by Charlie Chaplin in 1940, the movie was a brilliant political satire on Nazi Germany. Hitler ordered all prints of the filmed banned, but when curiosity got the best of him, he had one brought in through Portugal and viewed it himself in complete privacy—not once, but twice. History did not record his views on the film.

4. *ROCK AROUND THE CLOCK*

This was a raucous celebration of rock 'n' roll starring Bill Haley and his Comets. In London its young audience took the message to heart in September of 1954. After seeing the picture, over 3,000 Teddy Boys left the theater to stage one of the biggest riots in recent British history.

5. *FOXFIRE*

Starring Jane Russell and Jeff Chandler, this film—a Universal production dealing with a dedicated mining engineer and his socialite wife—was playing in the tourist-section theater of the *Andrea Doria* on the foggy night in July, 1956, when the liner collided with the *Stockholm*. The film was in its last reel when the collision occurred. Fifty people lost their lives in the tragedy.

6. *CAN-CAN*

A 20th Century–Fox production starring Frank Sinatra, Shirley MacLaine, and Maurice Chevalier, it was just a little too lavish for the taste of Russian Premier Nikita Khrushchev during his 1959 visit to the studio where it was being filmed. The cold war heated up briefly when Khrushchev reacted with shocked indignation at the "perversity" and "decadence" of dancer MacLaine's flamboyantly raised skirts.

Soviet Premier Nikita Khrushchev claimed to be morally
outraged by Shirley MacLaine's performance in *Can-Can*.

7. *WAR IS HELL*

A double bill featuring two B-style war movies was playing at
the Texas Theater in Dallas, where Lee Harvey Oswald was captured
after the assassination of John F. Kennedy in 1963. *War Is Hell*,
starring Tony Russell, had just begun when Oswald called attention
to himself by ducking into the theater without paying the 90¢
admission. He was apprehended by the police amid the sound of on-
screen gunfire.

8. *I AM CURIOUS, YELLOW*

The Swedish film starring Lena Nyman as a sexually active
political sociologist was a shocking sensation in 1969. On October 6,
1969, though, Jackie Onassis was the one making headlines after
she allegedly gave a professional judo flip to a New York news
photographer who took pictures of her leaving the movie house
showing the film.

9. *MOHAMMED, MESSENGER OF GOD*

Directed by Moustapha Akkad, this picture, which purported to be an unbiased, authentic study, evoked the wrath of the Hanafi Muslim sect, which assumed that the film would depict the image of the Prophet, an act they consider blasphemous. Demanding that the film be withdrawn from the Washington, D.C., theater where it was opening, small bands of Hanafi gunmen invaded the local city hall and two other buildings on March 10, 1977, killing one man and holding over 100 hostages for two days before surrendering. Their protest turned out to be much ado about nothing. The Prophet was neither seen nor heard in the film; instead, actors addressed the camera as if it were the Prophet standing before them.

10. *THE DEER*

This Iranian film was being shown in the Cinema Rex theater in Abadan, Iran, on August 20, 1977, when arsonists set fire to the building, killing at least 377 people (an additional 45 bodies were discovered later in the charred ruins, but these were not included in the official government totals). Police arrested 10 members of a Muslim extremist group that opposed the shah's reforms and had been implicated in other theater and restaurant fires. However, another version of this incident was sent to *The People's Almanac* by an eyewitness who claims that police chained shut the theater doors and fended off the crowd outside with clubs and M 16's. The fire department, only 10 minutes from the theater, reportedly did not arrive until the fire had burned itself out. Surprisingly, this witness found most of the people had been burned to death in their seats.

—R.S.

10 MOVIES SHOWN
MOST OFTEN ON TELEVISION

In a straw poll, editors of *TV Guide* asked program directors around the country to name the 10 most popular, most often shown movies in their markets. These are the titles the program directors named most frequently.

1. *Casablanca* (1943, with Humphrey Bogart, Ingrid Bergman)
2. *King Kong* (1933, with Bruce Cabot, Fay Wray)
3. *The Magnificent Seven* (1960, with Yul Brynner)
4. *The Maltese Falcon* (1941, with Humphrey Bogart, Mary Astor)
5. *The Adventures of Robin Hood* (1938, with Errol Flynn)
6. *The African Queen* (1951, with Humphrey Bogart, Katharine Hepburn)
7. *The Birds* (1963, with Rod Taylor, Tippi Hedren)
8. *Citizen Kane* (1941, with Orson Welles)

9. *Miracle on 34th Street* (1947, with Maureen O'Hara, Edmund Gwenn)
10. *Girls! Girls! Girls!* (1962, with Elvis Presley)

SOURCE: Reprinted with permission from *TV Guide®* magazine. Copyright © 1977 by Triangle Publications, Inc., Radnor, Pennsylvania.

10 PERFORMERS WHO APPEARED MOST OFTEN ON MAJOR TV TALK SHOWS (January 1, 1976–July 31, 1979)

	Dinah Shore Show	Mike Douglas Show	Merv Griffin Show	To-night Show	Total
1. David Brenner, comedian and entertainer	5	32	13	54	104
2. John Davidson, singer and entertainer	5	13	2	57	77
3. Stan Kann, gadget collector and comedian	5	24	19	25	73
4. Charles Nelson Reilly, actor, comedian, and director	15	1	15	32	63
5. Anthony Newley, singer, songwriter, and actor	8	23	11	15	57
6. Joan Rivers, comedian and director	10	10	11	25	56
7. Mel Tillis, singer and songwriter	9	14	19	12	54
8. Bob Hope, comedian and entertainer	13	12	9	20	54
9. Robert Klein, comedian and actor	10	16	9	18	53
10. Norm Crosby, comedian and malapropist	14	5	12	21	52

—D.BI.

13 MORE OUTRAGEOUS MOMENTS OF U.S. TV CENSORSHIP

1. *I LOVE LUCY* (1952)

This is perhaps television's most notorious example of censorship. When Lucille Ball became pregnant with Desi Jr., her condition was incorporated into the show. Because of sensitivity to questionable language, CBS consulted a minister, a rabbi, and a priest to find a way to present Lucy's pregnancy in an inoffensive manner. It was decided that Lucy could be "expecting" or *enceinte* (French for "pregnant"), but the word *pregnant* could not be used.

2. *MARTIN LUTHER* (1956)

This biographical film on the German religious reformer was scheduled for its U.S. debut on Chicago's WGN television during Christmas week, 1956, but was abruptly canceled because of angry protests by the city's Roman Catholics. "We object to you showing the film because it makes a hero out of a rat," they asserted. Protestants objected in turn, as did the National Council of Churches, which claimed the decision was "a blow to religious liberty." But the network wouldn't change its mind; WGN officials said they didn't want to be "a party to the development of any misunderstanding or ill will among persons of the Christian faith."

3. *U.S. STEEL HOUR* (1956)

Rod Serling wrote a teleplay about the 1955 kidnap-murder of Emmett Till, a black Mississippi teenager who whistled at a white woman. However, the program's producer wanted to avoid the subject of racism. He directed Serling to change the black victim to a Jew, spare him from being murdered, and move the story north into New England. These changes were made, but otherwise the story that aired was the tragedy of Emmett Till.

4. *PLAYHOUSE 90* (1959)

During the April telecast of Abby Mann's award-winning *Judgement at Nuremberg*, the sponsor, the American Gas Association, succeeded in having references to gas extermination of Jews omitted. In one instance in which the phrase "gas ovens" remained in the script, the words were bleeped during the telecast. The AGA claimed, as justification for these deletions, that the Nazis had used cyanide gas—not cooking gas, as it claimed the words implied—to kill their victims.

5. *THE SMOTHERS BROTHERS COMEDY HOUR* (1967)

Responding to CBS censorship of such terms as *freak out* and *sex* on past shows, Tommy Smothers and Elaine May performed a skit about two censors who painstakingly changed the line "My pulse beats wildly in my breast whenever you're near" to "My pulse beats wildly in my wrist whenever you're near." The spoof contained no profanities, yet CBS censors cut it entirely from the program.

6. *THE SMOTHERS BROTHERS COMEDY HOUR* (1968)

CBS censored the display of a Mother's Day card that read, in part, "War is not healthy for children and other living things. . . . We who have given life must be dedicated to preserving it. Please talk peace." CBS gave as its reason—besides the excuse that it didn't permit "political positions"—the explanation that the Los Angeles mothers' group that distributed the card hadn't been cleared by the House Un-American Activities Committee.

7. *THE MERV GRIFFIN SHOW* (1970)

Radical Abbie Hoffman appeared on *The Merv Griffin Show* in April, 1970, a few months after the trial of "the Chicago 8" ended. The censors did not allow the viewers to see his shirt, which was fashioned after an American flag. Every time the camera showed Hoffman, the torso of his body was masked out by a blue square, revealing only his head and hands. According to Hoffman, the censors had made no complaints on earlier occasions when Ricky Nelson, Raquel Welch, Roy Rogers, and Ryan O'Neal had worn the same type of shirt on TV.

8. *HAPPY DAYS* (1974)

ABC decreed, as the first season was being taped, that Fonzie (Henry Winkler) could not wear a black leather jacket because it made him look like a hoodlum. He was supposed to wear sweaters, unless he was riding his motorcycle, when he would be allowed to wear his leather jacket in the interests of safety. To evade ABC's dictum, the program's producer kept Fonzie on or very near his motorcycle—leaning on it or polishing it—during every scene.

9. *JAMES AT 15* (1977–1978)

In the 1977 pilot, James's request for a "condom" was changed to "be prepared," then later cut altogether because NBC wanted no hint of birth control, despite the resultant suggestion of sexual irresponsibility. Later, in an episode aired in February, 1978, James could not use a condom when he made love to a Swedish exchange student because, NBC reasoned, the fear of pregnancy should erode their relationship and emphasize the point that sex holds serious consequences.

10. *LAUGH IN* (1977)

A skit about modern promiscuity showed a family of four women—each from a different generation—getting ready to go out separately for a night on the town. When the youngest woman told her mother that she might stay out all night if she met a man she liked, NBC changed the mother's warning—"Don't forget your pill"—to "Be careful," because the network objected to the implication that women plan in advance to have sex.

11. *NBC MOVIE—THE SUNSHINE BOYS* (1977)

When Walter Matthau called George Burns a *putz*—a Yiddish word literally meaning penis but used commonly to denote a jerk—NBC dubbed the word with *shmo*—another Yiddish word for jerk or boob. Later, when Burns wrote the word *putz* on a mirror for Matthau, the shot was cut altogether.

12. *SOAP* (1977)

When this controversial show went on the air, ABC made the following script changes: Mention of CIA involvement in Vietnamese opium smuggling was deleted; the character Burt Campbell underwent a name change to avoid association with the Campbell Soup Company; all comments about Sun Myung Moon were excised; and whenever the Mafia was mentioned, the scene had to include a positive Italian-American character to balance the negative stereotype.

13. *WELCOME BACK, KOTTER* (1977)

In one episode, a beautiful young teacher fell in love with the show's hero, Gabe Kotter. Trying to get out of an awkward situation, Kotter told her, "You don't want to marry me. I eat crackers in bed." The woman replied, "That's all right. I'm used to crumbs in bed." The censors objected to the implication of sexual promiscuity and had the scriptwriters change her reply to "I eat crackers, too. I'm used to crumbs in bed."

... AND ONE FROM TURKEY

In August, 1979, the *Muppet Show* was removed from Turkish television during the month-long Ramadan fasting period. It was thought that the character of "Miss Piggy" would be offensive to devout Muslims who consider pigs unclean.

—J.D.

THE HIGHEST-
RATED TV PROGRAMS
IN 11 COUNTRIES

1. AUSTRALIA

An open-air concert by The Seekers, held at Melbourne's Myer Music Bowl in 1967, was attended by 200,000 people—a Guinness record for the largest crowd ever assembled in Australia. The one-hour TV special which resulted from the concert drew the biggest TV audience in the country's history.

2. BELGIUM

Le Couturier de ces Dames ("The Ladies' Dressmaker"), a French feature film starring rubber-faced comedian Fernandel, garnered 72.5% of the Belgian TV audience when it aired on September 9, 1966.

3. CANADA

The second game in the first Canadian-Russian hockey series was broadcast on September 4, 1972, and was viewed by 14 million of Canada's 22 million citizens.

4. GREAT BRITAIN

The Royal Variety Performance of 1972, the first in the Royal Variety series, was watched by a record 30 million viewers.

5. JAPAN

"The 14th NHK Kô-haku Utagassen," a show that airs each New Year's Eve, features a competition of popular singers. On December 31, 1963, it was watched in a record 81.4% of Japanese households.

6. THE NETHERLANDS

Een van de Acht ("One out of Eight"), a musical game–quiz show, was broadcast on March 11, 1972. It was watched by 77% of the Dutch TV audience.

7. NEW ZEALAND

George and Mildred, a British-produced comedy series about an incompatible married couple, received the country's highest ratings ever for its November 6, 1977, episode.

8. SWEDEN

The World Championship ice hockey game between Sweden and the Soviet Union, aired in March, 1970, was seen by 82% of the Swedish population.

9. SWITZERLAND

La Fête des Vignerons, covering a national festival held four times each century, was telecast to the largest Swiss TV audience ever in 1975.

10. UNITED STATES

Roots, an eight-part drama aired on ABC, received the largest audience in TV history for its final two-hour episode, aired January 30, 1977. It was seen in 36.38 million homes accounting for 70% of the viewing audience. ABC announced that 130 million Americans saw at least part of that final episode of *Roots*.

11. WEST GERMANY

Tatort, a once-a-month German detective drama, received the country's highest rating in its January, 1971, telecast.

—R.T.

AMERICA'S 30 MOST LISTENED-TO RADIO STATIONS

Station	Market	Number of People Listening*	Format	Owner
1. WOR	New York	181,300	Talk	RKO
2. WBLS-FM	New York	177,500	Disco/Black	Inner City
3. WKTU-FM	New York	169,100	Disco	SJR
4. WCBS	New York	152,400	News	CBS
5. WGN	Chicago	137,800	Middle of the Road	WGN Continental
6. WABC	New York	130,900	Rock	ABC
7. WRFM-FM	New York	118,500	Beautiful	Bonneville
8. WINS	New York	111,200	News	Westinghouse
9. WLS	Chicago	110,000	Rock	ABC
10. WNBC	New York	102,900	Contemporary	NBC
11. WMAQ	Chicago	98,300	Country	NBC
12. KDKA	Pittsburgh	91,500	Middle of the Road	Westinghouse
13. KMOX	St. Louis	91,300	Talk/News	CBS
14. KMET-FM	Los Angeles	91,000	Album-Oriented Rock	Metromedia
15. KGO	San Francisco	89,400	Talk/News	ABC
16. WJR	Detroit	89,000	Middle of the Road	Capital Cities
17. WCCO	Minneapolis-St. Paul	88,200	Middle of the Road/Talk	Midwest Radio-TV Inc.
18. KBIG-FM	Los Angeles	87,300	Beautiful	Bonneville
19. WLOO-FM	Chicago	85,100	Beautiful	Century
20. WPLJ-FM	New York	82,200	Album-Oriented Rock	ABC
21. WMCA	New York	81,700	Talk	Strauss
22. WBBM	Chicago	81,200	News	CBS
23. KABC	Los Angeles	80,900	Talk	ABC
24. KYW	Philadelphia	79,500	News	Westinghouse
25. WCBS-FM	New York	78,000	Oldies	CBS
26. KFI	Los Angeles	76,100	Contemporary	Cox
27. WHN	New York	75,900	Country	Mutual
28. WPAT	New York	74,500	Beautiful	Capital Cities
29. WPAT-FM	New York	73,200	Beautiful	Capital Cities
30. WNEW-FM	New York	72,600	Album-Oriented Rock	Metromedia

*Based on average number of people during average ¼-hour period.
SOURCE: James Duncan, Jr., *American Radio Report*, February, 1980.

11
LITERARY CIRCLES

11 BESTSELLING BOOKS
REJECTED BY
13 OR MORE PUBLISHERS

1. *AND TO THINK THAT I SAW IT ON
   MULBERRY STREET* by Theodor Geisel, "Dr. Seuss"
   (New York: Vanguard, 1937)

   Geisel was on his way home with the manuscript and illustrations for this book after it had been rejected by the 23rd publisher when he ran into an old college friend walking on Madison Avenue. The friend, who happened to be an editor of children's books for Vanguard Press, was interested in seeing Geisel's work. Twenty minutes later "Dr. Seuss" had a contract for his book, which has since gone into over 20 printings.

2. *DUBLINERS* by James Joyce
   (London: Grant Richards, 1914)

   Joyce would not allow any changes to be made in his book of 15 short stories which depict Dublin in its most sordid light. Consequently, it was rejected by 22 publishers. In a letter to Bennett Cerf, Joyce described what happened after this book was finally published by Grant Richards in 1914: ". . . when at last it was printed some very kind person bought out the entire edition and had it burnt in Dublin—a new and private auto-da-fé [burning of a heretic]." These stories have since been hailed as the work of a genius.

3. *M*A*S*H* by Richard Hooker
   (New York: William Morrow, 1968)

   For seven years Hooker worked over his humorous war novel under the close tutelage of an optimistic literary agent, only to see it shot down by 21 publishers before Morrow bought it. A hugely successful film version helped push the book to runaway best-sellerdom. Several sequels followed, and a long-running TV series based on the *M*A*S*H* characters was launched in 1972.

4. *HEAVEN KNOWS, MR. ALLISON* by Charles Shaw
   (New York: Crown, 1952)

   Shaw's humorous novel about an American marine in the South Pacific was rejected by virtually every Australian publisher and by about 20 British firms over a three-year period. After the Australian found an American agent, he quickly sold the book to Crown. Paperback and foreign editions soon followed, and the book was made into a popular film in 1957.

5. *KON-TIKI* by Thor Heyerdahl
   (Chicago: Rand McNally, 1950)

   Twenty publishers decided Heyerdahl's story of his Pacific crossing on a raft wasn't worth publishing before Rand McNally accepted it. The book made the country's top-10 nonfiction list in 1950 and again in 1951, when Heyerdahl's Oscar-winning documentary film of his trip was released. Total sales have since reached the multimillion mark.

6. *JONATHAN LIVINGSTON SEAGULL* by Richard Bach
   (New York: Macmillan, 1970)

   Bach's 10,000-word story about a fast-flying sea gull seemed so unpromising that 18 publishers turned it down before Macmillan accepted it and quietly issued 7,500 copies. Rapidly mounting sales led to the book's adoption by the Book-of-the-Month Club in 1972, a $1 million paperback sale to Avon, many foreign editions, and a 1973 film version. By 1975 more than 7 million copies of the book had been sold in the U.S. alone.

7. *LORNA DOONE* by Richard Doddridge Blackmore
   (London: Sampson Low, 1869)

   The 18 publishers who rejected Blackmore's novel of 17th-century England appeared vindicated when Sampson Low's three-volume edition flopped in 1869. Two years later, however, a single-volume edition proved a big success. Harper's pirated the book in the U.S., where it became the number-one best-seller in 1874. The book has remained in print ever since, and 3 film versions have been produced.

8. *AUNTIE MAME* by Patrick Dennis
   (New York: Vanguard, 1955)

   Some 17 publishers rejected this novel about a free-spirited older woman before Vanguard accepted it. An immediate hit, the book was soon adapted for the stage. After a successful run on Broadway, the play was made into a popular film starring Rosalind Russell. Ten years later a musical version of the play, now called *Mame*, started a long Broadway run. The film *Mame* was released in 1974. Total book sales have been around 2 million copies.

9. *LUST FOR LIFE* by Irving Stone
   (London and New York: Longmans Green and Co., 1934)

   Seventeen publishers rejected Stone's novel about Vincent van Gogh. Once the book was published, however, sales became spectacular, and Doubleday eventually took over publication. *Lust for Life* has sold more than 24 million copies in 70 different editions. Kirk Douglas starred in a popular film version in 1956.

10. *THE PETER PRINCIPLE* by Laurence Peter
    (New York: William Morrow, 1969)

    Sixteen publishers rejected Peter's now famous book about the rise of individuals to their levels of incompetence. However, after Peter wrote a newspaper article on the subject, these same publishers flocked to his door, contracts in hand, and Morrow bought the much rejected manuscript. The book has sold almost 6 million copies, paving the way for *The Peter Plan, Peter's Quotations,* and *Peter's People.*

11. *DUNE* by Frank Herbert (Radnor, Pa.: Chilton, 1965)

Herbert's massive science-fiction tale was rejected by 13 publishers with comments like "too slow," "confusing and irritating," "too long," and "issues too clear-cut and old-fashioned." But the persistence of Herbert and his agent, Lurton Blassingame, finally paid off. *Dune* won the two highest awards in science-fiction writing and has sold over 10 million copies.

Note: If these examples are not enough to prove that the experts aren't always right, here is a final one that will surely encourage would-be writers. In 1977, free-lance writer Chuck Ross submitted a freshly typed copy of Jerzy Kosinski's 1969 National Book Award winner, *Steps,* to 14 publishers and 13 literary agents as an unsolicited manuscript. All 27 failed to recognize Kosinski's work and all 27 rejected the book.

—R.K.R. & K.H.J.

H. L. MENCKEN'S 10 MOST BORING AUTHORS OF ALL TIME

Fëdor Dostoevski.

One of the great journalists and editors of this century, H. L. Mencken (1880–1956) was America's leading iconoclast during the 1920s and 1930s. Very critical of the popular sentimental literature of the period, Mencken promoted such writers as Theodore Dreiser, Sherwood Anderson, and Sinclair Lewis. His books of essays, criticism, and scholarship include his six-volume *Prejudices*, *Notes on Democracy*, *The American Language*, and many more.

1. Fëdor Dostoevski
2. George Eliot
3. D. H. Lawrence
4. James Fenimore Cooper
5. Eden Phillpotts
6. Robert Browning
7. Selma Lagerlöf
8. Gertrude Stein
9. Björnstjerne Björnson
10. Johann Wolfgang von Goethe

SOURCE: Cleveland Amory, *Vanity Fair*. Copyright ©1923, 1951 by The Conde Nast Publications, Inc.

JOHN UPDIKE'S
10 GREATEST WRITERS
OF ALL TIME

Widely acclaimed for his witty, sophisticated style, Updike won the National Book Award for *The Centaur* and was honored with the O. Henry Prize Story Award in 1967 and 1968. A contributor to the *New Yorker* in the mid-1950s, Updike followed his early successes with other well-received works, including *Rabbit Run*, *Couples*, *A Month of Sundays*, and *The Coup*.

1. Homer (whether man or committee)
2. Aeschylus
3. Dante Alighieri
4. William Shakespeare
5. Jean Racine
6. Johann Wolfgang von Goethe
7. Count Leo Tolstoi
8. Sören Kierkegaard
9. Anton Chekhov
10. Marcel Proust

—Exclusive for *The Book of Lists 2*

6 FAMOUS PEOPLE
WHO EACH WROTE ONE NOVEL

1. SARAH BERNHARDT'S ONLY NOVEL—
IN THE CLOUDS—1878

Background: "The divine Sarah," as Oscar Wilde called her, was not only one of the French theater's most exalted stars and the scandalous, eccentric libertine who shocked Europe; she was also a multitalented artist. In her sparkling lifetime she devoted herself to many creative endeavors: She painted, she sculpted, she wrote her memoirs—and she also wrote a short but charming novel, *In the Clouds*.

Synopsis: Sarah Bernhardt's novel was based on her experience in 1877 of ascending in a hot-air balloon outfitted especially for her use. She was accompanied on her journey by her friend Georges Clarin, a noted French painter, and the balloonist Louis Godard. The story, illustrated by Clarin, is told from the point of view of a little straw chair, one of Bernhardt's favorites, which is taken along for the ride. Bernhardt uses her friends' real names and one of her own real-life nicknames, Doña Sol. The foursome—the chair is the fourth character—have an afternoon of lovely little adventures as they float through the heavens over the French countryside. They hold a philosophical discussion inspired by the sad sight of a prison far below. They worry about the possibilities of bad weather. The chair suffers suspense, wondering if it will become ballast dumped overboard to lighten the load of the balloon, but Doña Sol loves the chair too much to let it go. At one point the party descends to a French village, where they are gawked at by the locals as they enjoy a hearty repast.

From the Book:

The sky was magnificent; the weather had donned its most dazzling finery. The meal was extremely gay. It consisted of two main courses; goose liver sandwiches followed by sandwiches made of goose liver. A succulent dessert of oranges topped off the feast. A toast was proposed to Monsieur Giffard, the future of ballooning, fame, the arts, and all things past, present and future, then the wine bottle was sent waltzing into the Vincennes lake. The swans clapped their wings with fright, the lake gathered its brow in a frown, then as the bottle struck bottom, all grew calm again.

A haunting sadness suddenly filled the air.

—Poor bottle! murmured Doña Sol, it reminds me of an aging actress. In her dazzling prime, she gives us all she has. Instead of gratitude, when we have drained her dry we ungratefully condemn her to oblivion without a second thought.

—Come, come! Let's enjoy life. We'll be dead soon enough, Georges Clarin cried.

—What a gloomy bunch, added Godard.—There's no room for sad thoughts aboard. Look how they're weighing down the balloon. Get rid of some ballast fast! The devil with philosophy!

2. WINSTON CHURCHILL'S ONLY NOVEL— SAVROLA—1900

Background: There were two Winston Churchills writing novels at the turn of the century. The American Winston Churchill wrote a succession of vastly popular best-sellers, but he is all but forgotten today. The English Winston Churchill, though not as widely known at the time, went on to become the prime minister of Great Britain and achieved a worldwide fame that his American namesake could not have imagined. The English Churchill wrote his only novel in 1898, when he was 23 years old and serving as an army officer in India. The first 80 pages of the story came easily to him, but then he ran into problems, which he attempted to solve by loading the novel with numerous new characters and twists of plot. *Savrola* achieved a moderate success and earned Churchill a total of $3,500. However, he found novel-writing to be a bit boring and turned his attentions to being a soldier and war correspondent. After completing the book, he went to Africa and was captured by the Boers, from whom he escaped. He returned to England a hero and won his first election to Parliament in 1900, the same year that *Savrola* was published.

Synopsis: Churchill himself summed up the novel as a story in which he "traced the fortunes of a liberal leader who overthrew an arbitrary government only to be swallowed up by a socialist revolution." The setting is Laurania, a small North African country ruled by a tyrannical dictator named Antonio Molara. Savrola is the young, wealthy, and popular leader of the opposition party. In a rousing speech, he tells the members of his party that the most practical way of eliminating Molara is not a general uprising, but a conspiracy. When Molara learns of the speech, he recruits his beautiful wife, Lucille, to compromise Savrola and discover the details of his plan. Instead, they fall in love. Before too long, revolution breaks out and Molara is assassinated by a foreign communist. Savrola calms the crowd and becomes the acknowledged leader of Laurania. However, the admiral of the Lauranian Navy arrives in port and threatens to bombard the city unless Savrola leaves the country. He does so, with Lucille. Much later, Savrola returns by popular demand to rule a peaceful and prosperous Laurania.

From the Book:

The sound of momentous resolution rose again from the crowded hall. He had held their enthusiasm back for an hour by the clock. The steam had been rising all this time. All were searching in their minds for something to relieve their feelings, to give expression to the individual determination each man had made. There was only one mind throughout the hall. His passions, his emotions, his very soul appeared to be communicated to the seven thousand people who heard his words; and they mutually inspired each other.

Then at last he let them go. For the first time he raised his voice, and in a resonant, powerful, penetrating tone which thrilled the listeners, began the peroration of his speech. The effect of his change of manner was electrical. Each short sentence was followed by wild cheering. The excitement of

214

the audience became indescribable. Everyone was carried away by it. Lucille was borne along, unresisting, by that strong torrent of enthusiasm; her interests, her objects, her ambitions, her husband, all were forgotten. His sentences grew longer, more rolling and sonorous. At length he reached the last of those cumulative periods which pile argument on argument as Pelion on Ossa. All pointed to an inevitable conclusion. The people saw it coming and when the last words fell, they were greeted with thunders of assent.

3. JEAN HARLOW'S ONLY NOVEL— *TODAY IS TONIGHT*—1934

Background: Though she played a series of comic and sexy roles, movie star Jean Harlow longed to be known as more than a sex symbol. Her great ambition was to be a writer. The complete story of *Today Is Tonight* came to her in a dream, and she felt an intense urge to write it as a novel. She turned to her friend Carey Wilson, an MGM producer and writer, for help. They wrote and dictated the basic story together, which he then edited. Harlow threw much of herself into the character of the outspoken and courageous Judy, and proved that there was a clever and observant mind inside the famous platinum-blond head. However the book was not published in her

Novelist Jean Harlow.

lifetime. After Harlow's death, her mother, who needed money, sold it to MGM (which Jean had originally hoped would produce it, with herself in the starring role), but the studio never intended to make a movie of it. It was not until 1965, when the manuscript had passed through several hands, that the book was finally published.

Synopsis: Today Is Tonight is the story of a rich, beautiful, and exquisitely happy couple, Judy and Peter Lansdowne, living the romantic "society" life of the Roaring Twenties. One tragic day, Peter is permanently blinded in a riding accident, and their world comes down around them. Judy desperately attempts to conceal from her husband their complete financial ruin, the result of the stock market crash; and the reemergence of long-buried romantic feelings for his best friend and business partner. Then, in a scheme to earn money, she takes a job in a nightclub, posing as a nude and masked Lady Godiva. In order to convince Peter that she is doing charity work in the daytime instead, she reverses his sense of time, by serving him breakfast at night, etc.—thus the title of the book. He eventually discovers her ruse, and she almost leaves him for the other man, but in the end their marriage remains intact.

From the Book:

"Would you hand me a cigarette?" he asked quietly.

Her hands flew to the smoking stand automatically, and she drew a deep penitent breath. "Peter!" she cried in near anguish. "I'm so sorry—I made sure this box was filled before I left."

"I smoked them all," said Peter.

There—I've failed again! I didn't think! I'm thinking for the old Peter—not the new Peter. Why didn't I have the sense to realize that if he didn't have anything else to do—and wouldn't do anything but sit here all day, he'd smoke twice as many cigarettes as usual? But how was I to know how many cigarettes a blind man would need? Tonight, without his knowing it, I'll change that glass cigarette box for the big silver one that holds hundreds. And tomorrow his fingers will tell him the difference and he'll realize that I'm trying to make everything simpler for him. What else is wrong? What dozens of other things have I forgotten to do for him? Not because I don't want to think of everything, but because I think like myself and not like somebody who hasn't any eyes!

4. H. L. HUNT'S ONLY NOVEL— ALPACA—1960

Background: One of the richest men ever, H. L. Hunt had a weekly income in excess of $1 million for the last 40 years of his life. He fashioned his home in Texas after George Washington's Mount Vernon, only on a much grander scale. Hunt, who believed that Calvin Coolidge was the last successful president of the U.S. ("There was no subversive buildup whatever in Washington during Coolidge's term of office"), spent quite a bit of money spreading his anticommunist philosophy through periodicals, radio broadcasts, and youth groups. *Alpaca* is a thinly disguised forum for his political beliefs, which included allocating votes according to the amount of taxes a citizen pays and banning political discussion from radio, television, and large public meetings.

Synopsis: Young, handsome Juan Achala lives in the little nation of Alpaca, which is currently ruled by a dictator. His elders send him away to Europe to meet with respected, wise men who will help him formulate a new constitution for Alpaca. On the way he meets Mara, a beautiful Alpacan traveling to Paris for her operatic debut. Before very long, Mara becomes an international star and then gives up her career. A constitution is written, and Mara and Juan marry, conceive a child, and return to Alpaca to help implement the new constitution. The end. Actually, almost the entire book is devoted to a detailed study of the model constitution. In case the reader didn't catch the eight articles of the constitution when they came up in the plot, Hunt reprints the entire document in the final chapter.

From the Book:

"You are my very life, and yet I would give you up rather than mar your innate self, run the risk of trimming it to fit my own."

"On the contrary," she took him up quickly, "the realness of your love fulfills my life and self. Remember, I told you I was tired of the tinsel substitute which theater provides. Remember, I have loved you since I met you on the boat, and in my dreams before that time. Loved by you, Achala, my independent career is nothing, for I have everything."

"What you are saying I still can hardly believe," he said wonderingly, and then with swift intensity, "I wonder if you recall what 'everything' for us encompasses. Have you forgot that thrilling night when we drove across Paris and back, in a hired cab—but it transported us to the gates of paradise?"

"And the moon was at the full, the sky cloudless, the city chained in slumber, so as not to interrupt!" she exclaimed, her face again radiant.

"Yes," he said, kissing her upturned face, "the same old moon which now rises above the saw-toothed line of cedars on yonder mountain crest. And we haven't forgot, have we?— the sound of splashing waves against the Riviera beach, that night when the world stood still, and did not move at all?"

"Or the miracle," she rejoined, "of the first sunrise we watched together—that glorious sunrise that painted the sky with all possible colors!"

"I shall never forget," he assured her. "Or the way we pelted each other with hot sand, a few hours later, when the sun burned down on the stroke of noon."

"What happiness we have shared!" she said, entering his mood completely. "And shall continue to share! How can you ever doubt my happiness in the sharing?"

"It troubles me, though"—and a shade of his disquiet returned—"that you have insisted on contributing financially to the travel expense of some of our Team."

5. BENITO MUSSOLINI'S ONLY NOVEL— *THE CARDINAL'S MISTRESS*—1909

Background: It was 1909 and the 25-year-old future dictator of Italy was working for the trade union headquarters in Trentino, an Italian area then ruled by Austria. Part of his duty was to assist in the editing of *L'Avvenire,* a Socialist newspaper. One of his assignments was to write the weekly fiction serial, and Mussolini responded with a potboiler called *Claudia Particella, or The Cardinal's Love.* It was published in English in 1929.

Synopsis: The novel begins in 1648 and tells the story of Carl Emanuel Madruzzo, who is the cardinal and archbishop of Trent and the Prince of Trentino, and of his mistress of 20 years, Claudia Particella, whose father is the cardinal's closest friend and counselor. The peasants and the priests hate Claudia and her father and want them banished. They feel that this would transform the cardinal from a tyrant to a benevolent spiritual leader. In fact, Madruzzo wishes nothing more than to give up his power and marry Claudia, but the Vatican refuses to allow it. Mussolini wanted to have Claudia murdered early on, but his editor objected, claiming that the serial was very popular and was increasing circulation. So Mussolini kept the story going and contented himself with killing off several secondary characters instead. Eventually Claudia is poisoned by her enemies and dies, and Cardinal Madruzzo lives out his life in unhappy seclusion.

From the Book:

"The acrid odour of decomposing human flesh compelled us to draw back a few paces. . . . Then Antonio wished to see the woman whom he had so loved, so desired. The body was recognizable by the golden hair which fell over the pure forehead, and by the eyes not yet contaminated. But from the lips, decomposed into a ferocious grin, oozed a dense, whitish liquid."

. . . Don Benizio was accustomed to the sight of corpses. It gave him pleasure to speak of death. He felt a secret satisfaction in the consoling thought of worms devouring, fibre by fibre, the proud carcass of man.

No one could escape this destiny! Neither prince nor pope! Nor the fair women whom Don Benizio coveted with that lust which is born of forced chastity, flagellated by wanton thoughts and images of bestial unions.

Nor—Claudia Particella, the courtesan of Trent, one more of that band of celebrated concubines whom Don Benizio had not been able to conquer!

6. HARRY REASONER'S ONLY NOVEL— *TELL ME ABOUT WOMEN*—1946

Background: Harry Reasoner, a longtime TV newscaster and currently a well-known member of the CBS-TV *60 Minutes* team, seems an unlikely candidate to have written a novel about young love. But not only did he write one, he wrote a very special one. It is stunningly sophisticated for a 22-year-old—he wrote it while he was in the U.S. Army during W.W. II—and seems to be strikingly candid and autobiographical. Written in the hard-boiled style of the 1940s, it is full of wry, cynical, and witty dialogue; it far transcends the average book of its type. Reasoner achieves a beauty and poignancy which make one truly wish he had not given up what might have been a brilliant career as a novelist.

Synopsis: The story concerns a first love affair, set against the background of W.W. II. Joe Wilson is a slightly cynical young small-town reporter (Reasoner was a reporter himself before being drafted), successful with women, but he has never fallen in love. He meets Maris, a beautiful, intelligent, complicated blond, and they fall in love and marry. Then he finds out that she is pregnant by another man, and despite the fact that she miscarries, their relationship is tainted by the suspicion that she has been using him. When Joe is drafted, their separation, combined with the maturing experience of army training which he is unable to share with her, alienates them further. She writes to tell him that she is having an affair and that she wants a divorce. When he returns home on leave, she breaks down and wants him back, wants to keep trying. But their sweet love has been soured, and he recognizes that any attempt to let the marriage drag on would be useless, so he leaves for good.

From the Book:

"Do you love your wife?" I asked him. He'd been married fifteen years. "Passionately. I guess I mean passionately."

"I'm awfully used to her," he said. "I couldn't get along without her very well. Passion doesn't last."

"It's different from when you're young, then, huh? It changes. Even if you stick together, something dies, something else takes its place. For us middle-sized intellectuals."

"That's right," he said. "You lose something, and in a way it's like losing a burden. You lose a kind of uncomfortable, wonderful energy. Maybe you won't."

"Sure," I said. "I'll lose it." I said so, but I suppose I really thought maybe I wouldn't. "It's a kind of death. Kind of a death of the heart."

Gerald said, "You better hope you lose it easy. There are different ways."

A reporter named Fitzgerald had been listening. "You don't need to lose it," he said. "You can take goat glands."

—A.W. & D.W.

12 WRITERS WHO WROTE STANDING UP

1. Lewis Carroll (1832–1898), English mathematician and writer
2. Sir Kenneth Clark (1903–   ), English art authority and writer
3. Benjamin Disraeli (1804–1881), British prime minister
4. Frederic William Farrar (1831–1903), English clergyman and writer
5. Ernest Hemingway (1899–1961), U.S. journalist, novelist, and short-story writer
6. Thomas Jefferson (1743–1826), U.S. president
7. Malcolm Lowry (1909–1957), English novelist
8. Horace McCoy (1897–1955), U.S. novelist

9. Vladimir Nabokov (1899–1977), U.S. (Russian-born) writer
10. William Saroyan (1908–   ), U.S. playwright and writer
11. Thomas Wolfe (1900–1938), U.S. novelist
12. Virginia Woolf (1882–1941), English writer

—I.W.

6 AUTHORS WHO DID NOT USE
ANY (OR MUCH) PUNCTUATION

1. JERZY ANDRZEJEWSKI (1909–   )

A prolific Polish novelist, Andrzejewski's early writings were influenced by Catholicism. Around 1950 he embraced communism, then after three years rejected it. In 1962 he adopted and undertook a new cause, a literary one that disdained punctuation. In that year he brought out his novel *Gates of Paradise*, 16 years later translated from Polish into English and published in London. This entire novel, dealing with the motives behind the Children's Crusade (Andrzejewski feels its leaders were interested in sensual love, not Christian love), was written as one single sentence. The first 40,000 words of the book contained no punctuation whatsoever.

2. GUILLAUME APOLLINAIRE (1880–1918)

Born out of wedlock in Rome, the son of an Italian army officer, who abandoned him, and an aristocratic Polish mother, who neglected him (because she was a roulette fanatic), Apollinaire was haphazardly raised in a series of Catholic schools on the French Riviera. In Paris he became a tutor, a clerk, a ghostwriter, and an author of pornography. Later he made his living as a critic, short-story writer, and poet. He was a pioneer of Futurism and Cubism. He coined the word *surrealism*. He discovered the primitive painter Henri Rousseau. He counted among his friends Picasso, Braque, Matisse, Vlaminck, and Dufy. Fame came to Apollinaire in 1913 with his book of poetry *Alcools*, which enraged many reviewers because of its lack of punctuation. Explained Apollinaire: "As for punctuation, I have eliminated it only because it seemed to me useless, and it actually is useless; the rhythm itself and the division into lines provide the real punctuation and no other is needed."

3. TIMOTHY DEXTER (1747–1806)

He was a leather dresser turned merchant prince before he was an author. He became wealthy by sending and selling coals to Newcastle, and warming pans, stray cats, Bibles, and woolen mittens to the West Indies. Purchasing a huge Georgian mansion in Newburyport, Mass., he decorated the outdoor premises with 40 life-sized wooden statues of such celebrities as Horatio Nelson, Adam and Eve, George Washington, Louis XIV, and himself. He populated his mansion with a wife (whom he regarded as a ghost), a full-time astrologer, a dim-witted giant court jester, an African princess housekeeper, and a fishmonger who acted as poet laureate. In 1802 Dexter turned author, publishing a 24-page philosophical autobiography entitled *A Pickle for the Knowing Ones*. The book, an egotistical, opinionated, coarse defense of Dexter's life-style, related how he had made his fortune, and contained a reminiscence of his youth, a suggestion for the names of his pallbearers, two funny stories, and a hint that he might make a good emperor of the U.S. The most engaging thing about the book was the fact that it consisted of one long sentence, or rather, no sentence at all. Not a single comma, semicolon, quotation mark, apostrophe, exclamation point, or period marred its half-coherent text. Grammatically, it was without beginning or end. Thought melted into thought without a stop. Like the universe, like time itself, it emerged from infinity and receded into infinity. The reception of this literary gem made Dexter realize that a book without punctuation was hardly a book at all. He sought to correct this lapse. In a second printing now lost, or in a separate pamphlet, Dexter added one more page to his book. This page was bound in all printings after 1838. The page consisted of 13 lines of punctuation—rows and rows of colons, commas, question marks, periods, and other stops— which, Dexter suggested, readers "may peper and solt" throughout his book "as they plese."

[Note to Dexter's Second Edition.]

fourder mister printer the Nowing ones complane of my book the fust editon had no stops I put in A nuf here and thay may peper and solt it as they plese

Timothy Dexter's autobiography was written
without punctuation. To satisfy purists, Dexter
gave them all the punctuation they needed.

4. REV. JOHN DOBSON (1794-1847)

This fairly literate English cleric, known for his mathematical tracts, gained a small notoriety for his dislike of all punctuation except the period. In 1815 he published his magnum opus, a two-volume work entitled *The Elements of Geometry*. What distinguished this book was the omission of punctuation throughout, save for a chaste period at the end of each paragraph. "It is doubtful whether any copies were sold," stated one critic. The only thing to spoil the purity of Dobson's prose without stops was a sabotage effort by his publisher, Cambridge Press, which sneaked one colon, one semicolon, one comma, and one period into the title page. In 1871, Augustus De Morgan, another and more famous mathematician, in a book that contained word sketches of quirky authors, included his own biography of Reverend Dobson—written without punctuation.

5. GERTRUDE STEIN (1874-1946)

The Pennsylvania-born eccentric avant-garde writer became one of the most renowned American expatriates in Paris. Numbering Hemingway and Picasso among her friends, Gertrude Stein's salon and art collection (worth $6 million 15 years after her death) were world-famous. Her far-out books, among them *Three Lives* and *The Autobiography of Alice B. Toklas*, gave her literary stature. Her style—using simplification and repetitions—was innovative, and she felt it was superior to the style of James Joyce. Above all, she ignored punctuation. Most of her writings employed only periods, because they had "a life of their own." Occasionally she slipped in a comma, but basically she detested commas. She found them "servile" and felt they made reading too easy. She wrote: "A comma by helping you along holding your coat for you and putting on your shoes keeps you from living your life as actively as you should lead it and to me the use of them was positively degrading." Question marks and exclamation points she found "positively revolting." Stein's best-known written line was "A rose is a rose is a rose is a rose." Until her death, she enjoyed a lovely and enduring homosexual relationship with her companion, Alice B. Toklas.

6. E. E. CUMMINGS (1894-1962)

The son of a Boston pastor, he was a poet and painter who earned an uneasy reputation as the *enfant terrible* of American letters. His individualistic use (or nonuse) of punctuation, grammar, and typography seemed "eccentric" and "puzzling" to his first reviewers, but he achieved a controversial prominence anyway. He did not like commas, periods, or capital letters, but he was fond of parentheses and hyphens. Some of his poems are remarkable for their lack of a single punctuation mark. His original style spawned numerous imitators, none of whom had his lyrical gifts. Always an innovator with a lively sense of fun, he referred to himself as e e cummings and even entitled the prestigious lectures that he gave at Harvard *i:six nonlectures*.

—I. W.

11 AUTHORS WHO
HAD BOOKS PUBLISHED
BY AGE 10

1. ALLEN WELSH DULLES (1893–1969)

The Boer War: A History. Washington, D.C.: Gordon Press, 1902.

This work is in the rare books division of the Library of Congress. The eight-year-old author is the same Allen Dulles who directed the CIA from 1953 until 1961, when he resigned after being implicated in the Bay of Pigs fiasco.

2. HILDA CONKLING (1910–   )

Poems by a Little Girl. London: G. G. Harrap and Co., Ltd., 1920.

Hilda Conkling is the daughter of Grace Walcott Conkling, a minor American poet. She began to dictate her poems at age four, and her book was published when she was nine.

3. BETTY THORPE (1911?–   )

Fioretta; or O cessate di piagarmi. Honolulu: Advertiser Publishing Co., Ltd., 1922.

This book was written when Betty was nine and published when she was ten.

4. NATHALIA CLARA RUTH CRANE (1913–   )

Janitor's Boy and Other Poems. New York: Seltzer, 1924.

Nathalia Crane is from Brooklyn. Her poetry was praised by reviewers for its exceptional maturity and objectivity of vision. This book was published when Nathalia was 10 years old.

5. DAVID STATLER (1928–   )

Roaring Guns. New York: Simon and Schuster, 1938.

This volume, written when David was nine years old, was submitted to the publisher in a 5¢ composition book.

6. ELIZABETH LULING (1930–   )

Do Not Disturb. New York: Oxford, 1937.

Elizabeth Luling is the daughter of English author Sylvia Thompson. This book traces the adventures of two teddy bears, which belonged to Sylvia and her sister.

7. ERLIN HOGAN (1931–   )

The Four Funny Men. New York: E. P. Dutton and Co., 1939.

This is a children's story about a girl, her pet squirrel, and four funny men who live on a nearby hill. The book was written when Erlin was eight and was illustrated by his aunt, Inez Hogan.

8. MINOU DROUET (1947–)

First Poems. New York: Harper, 1956.

When the poems of eight-year-old adoptee Minou Drouet were published, skeptics said the work was so sophisticated that they questioned the authenticity of the authorship. Minou was tested in France by the Society of Authors, Composers, and Music Publishers. She was given one-half hour in which to write a poem on a subject they assigned her. When the judges saw the results, her talent was not questioned again.

9. DOROTHY STRAIGHT (1958–)

How the World Began. New York: Pantheon Books, 1964.

This book was written when Dorothy was only four and published when she reached the ripe old age of six.

10. KALI DIANA GROSVENOR (1960–)

Poems by Kali. New York: Doubleday, 1970.

Kali Grosvenor lives in the East Village of New York City. Her poems are published exactly as she wrote them, when she was six and seven. The primary subject matter is her experiences as a young urban black.

11. BENJAMIN FRIEDMAN (1968–)

The Ridiculous Book. San Francisco: Pee Wee Press, 1978.

Ben did both the text and illustrations for this children's book, which was written and published when he was nine.

Two Special Cases

In these two instances, the authors had written books by the time they were 10, but the books were not published until they were much older.

1. DAISY ASHFORD (1881–1972)

The Young Visiters [sic]. London: Chatto and Windus, 1919.

To all appearances a normal nine-year-old, in 1890 Daisy Ashford wrote a novel of Victorian society which was to become a classic: *The Young Visiters,* or *Mr. Salteena's Plan.* Keenly observed and expertly plotted, it has been called "a sublime work," one of the funniest ever written. Still in print, it has sold more than half a million copies. The authoress ended her literary career at 13. When a grown woman, she discovered the pencil-scrawled manuscript among her deceased mother's effects. In 1919, 32 years after it was written, it was published with a preface by Sir James Barrie (author of *Peter Pan*), who many wrongly believed was its creator. Daisy Ashford bought a farm with the proceeds, observing, "I like fresh air—and royalties." As Mrs. James Devlin, mother of four, she lived near Norwich, England, until her death at age 90.

Renowned author Daisy Ashford.

2. VIRGINIA CARY HUDSON (1894–   )

O Ye Jigs and Juleps. New York: Macmillan, 1962.

This collection of essays was found in a box in an attic and compiled for publication by Karla Kuskin. The essays were written when Virginia was 10 and are concerned with such diverse subjects as the religions of China, church etiquette, personal appearance, springtime, school, and everlasting life.

—M.M.

ROSS MACDONALD'S 10 GREATEST FICTIONAL DETECTIVES OF ALL TIME

A detective novelist in the literate tradition of Dashiell Hammett and Raymond Chandler, Ross Macdonald (original name Kenneth Millar) received the Silver Dagger Award in 1964 for his Lew Archer novel *The Chill* from the Crime Writers' Association of England, which the following year named *The Far Side of the Dollar* the crime novel of the year. Another Lew Archer story, *The Moving Target,* was made into the movie *Harper.*

1. Wilkie Collins's Sergeant Cuff
2. Edgar Allan Poe's C. Auguste Dupin
3. Arthur Conan Doyle's Sherlock Holmes
4. G. K. Chesterton's Father Brown
5. Ellery Queen's Ellery Queen
6. Dashiell Hammett's Sam Spade
7. Dorothy Sayers's Lord Peter Wimsey
8. Raymond Chandler's Philip Marlowe
9. Ngaio Marsh's Inspector Alleyn
10. P. D. James's Inspector Dalgliesh

—Exclusive for *The Book of Lists* 2

ROBERT BLOCH'S 10 FAVORITE HORROR- FANTASY NOVELS

A protégé of the late great fantasy writer H. P. Lovecraft, Robert Bloch sold his first short story at age 17. Since then he has published nearly 400 short stories and 45 books, including the novel *Strange Eons.* The film *Psycho* was adapted from his published work.

1. *Dracula* by Bram Stoker
2. *Frankenstein* by Mary Shelley
3. *Conjure Wife* by Fritz Leiber
4. *Dr. Jekyll and Mr. Hyde* by Robert Louis Stevenson
5. *Burn, Witch, Burn!* by A. Merritt
6. *The Werewolf of Paris* by Guy Endore
7. *Là-bas* by J. K. Huysmans
8. *To Walk the Night* by William Sloane
9. *The Phantom of the Opera* by Gaston Leroux
10. *A Mirror for Witches* by Esther Forbes

Bloch adds: "This classification excludes, by definition, science fiction, humor, or horror with fantasy element—tricky distinctions!"

—Exclusive for *The Book of Lists* 2

THE ORIGINAL TITLES OF 27 FAMOUS BOOKS

1. Original title: *First Impressions*
   Final title: *Pride and Prejudice* (1813)
   Author: Jane Austen

2. Original title: *Mag's Diversions;* also *The Copperfield Disclosures, The Copperfield Records, The Copperfield Survey of the World As It Rolled,* and *Copperfield Complete*
   Final title: *David Copperfield* (1849)
   Author: Charles Dickens

3. Original title: *Alice's Adventures Underground*
   Final title: *Alice's Adventures in Wonderland* (1865)
   Author: Lewis Carroll

4. Original title: *All's Well That Ends Well*
   Final title: *War and Peace* (1866)
   Author: Leo Tolstoi

5. Original title: *The Sea-Cook*
   Final title: *Treasure Island* (1883)
   Author: Robert Louis Stevenson

6. Original title: *The Chronic Argonauts*
   Final title: *The Time Machine* (1895)
   Author: H. G. Wells

Paul Morel

by D H Lawrence

Chapter I.

Antecedents.

"The Bottoms" succeeded to "Hell Row". It was a natural sequence. Hell Row was a block of some half dozen thatched, bulging cottages which stood back upon the brook-course by Greenhill Lane. The row was burned down in 1870, and shortly afterwards, near its site was erected the camp of miners' dwellings known as "the Bottoms".

Bestwood had scarcely come to consciousness when the notorious Row was destroyed. The parish was strewed with groups of dwellings which scarcely made a village. Since the seventeenth century the people of Bestwood have scratched at the earth for coal, and

First page of the manuscript of Sons and Lovers.

7. Original title: *Paul Morel*
   Final title: *Sons and Lovers* (1913)
   Author: D. H. Lawrence

8. Original title: *Stephen Hero*
   Final title: *A Portrait of the Artist as a Young Man* (1916)
   Author: James Joyce

9. Original title: *The Romantic Egotist*
   Final title: *This Side of Paradise* (1920)
   Author: F. Scott Fitzgerald

10. Original title: *The Village Virus*
    Final title: *Main Street* (1920)
    Author: Sinclair Lewis

11. Original title: *Incident at West Egg; also Among Ash Heaps and Millionaires, Trimalchio in West Egg, On the Road to West Egg, Gold-Hatted Gatsby,* and *The High-Bounding Lover*
    Final title: *The Great Gatsby* (1925)
    Author: F. Scott Fitzgerald

12. Original title: *Fiesta; also The Lost Generation, River to the Sea, Two Lie Together,* and *The Old Leaven*
    Final title: *The Sun Also Rises* (1926)
    Author: Ernest Hemingway

13. Original title: *Tenderness*
    Final title: *Lady Chatterley's Lover* (1928)
    Author: D. H. Lawrence

14. Original title: *Twilight*
    Final title: *The Sound and the Fury* (1929)
    Author: William Faulkner

15. Original title: *O Lost*
    Final title: *Look Homeward, Angel* (1929)
    Author: Thomas Wolfe

16. Original title: *Bar-B-Q*
    Final title: *The Postman Always Rings Twice* (1934)
    Author: James M. Cain

17. Original title: *Tomorrow Is Another Day; also Tote the Weary Load, Milestones, Jettison, Ba! Ba! Black Sheep, None So Blind, Not in Our Stars,* and *Bugles Sang True*
    Final title: *Gone with the Wind* (1936)
    Author: Margaret Mitchell

18. Original title: *The Various Arms; also Return to the Wars*
    Final title: *To Have and Have Not* (1937)
    Author: Ernest Hemingway

19. Original title: *Something That Happened*
    Final title: *Of Mice and Men* (1937)
    Author: John Steinbeck

20. Original title: *Proud Flesh*
    Final title: *All the King's Men* (1946)
    Author: Robert Penn Warren

21. Original title: *Salinas Valley*
    Final title: *East of Eden* (1952)
    Author: John Steinbeck

22. Original title: *The Tree and the Blossom*
    Final title: *Peyton Place* (1956)
    Author: Grace Metalious

23. Original title: *Catch-18*
    Final title: *Catch-22* (1961)
    Author: Joseph Heller

24. Original title: *A Jewish Patient Begins His Analysis*
    Final title: *Portnoy's Complaint* (1969)
    Author: Philip Roth

25. Original title: *Come and Go*
    Final title: *The Happy Hooker* (1972)
    Author: Xaviera Hollander with Robin Moore and Yvonne Dunleavy

26. Original title: *The Summer of the Shark;* also *The Terror of the Monster* and *The Jaws of the Leviathan*
    Final title: *Jaws* (1974)
    Author: Peter Benchley

27. Original title: *Before This Anger*
    Final title: *Roots: The Saga of an American Family* (1976)
    Author: Alex Haley

—R.J.F. & The Eds.

WILLIAM BURROUGHS'S
10 FAVORITE NOVELS

Norman Mailer once termed William Burroughs "the only American novelist living today who may conceivably be possessed by genius." A former private detective, reporter, and exterminator, Burroughs earned a cult following with his novel *Naked Lunch* (1956), a surrealistic account of his experiences as a heroin addict. His other works include *Nova Express* and *Exterminator!*

1. *The Process* by Brion Gysin
2. *The Satyricon* by Petronius
3. *In Youth Is Pleasure* by Denton Welch
4. *Two Serious Ladies* by Jane Bowles

5. *The Sheltering Sky* by Paul Bowles
6. *Under Western Eyes* by Joseph Conrad
7. *Journey to the End of the Night* by Louis Ferdinand Céline
8. *Querelle de Brest* by Jean Genet
9. *The Unfortunate Traveller* by Thomas Nashe
10. *The Great Gatsby* by F. Scott Fitzgerald

Note: Brion Gysin's *The Process* (1969) follows the bizarre adventures of a black American professor traveling across the Sahara Desert. English writer Denton Welch (b. 1915) explores an English schoolboy's sexual fears and fantasies in his second novel, *In Youth Is Pleasure* (1945). Thomas Nashe (1567–1601), English pamphleteer and dramatist, anticipated the English adventure novel with *The Unfortunate Traveller*.

—Exclusive for *The Book of Lists* 2

KEN KESEY'S
10 BEST AMERICAN NOVELS

Kesey appeared on the literary scene in 1962 with *One Flew over the Cuckoo's Nest*, a darkly humorous novel set in a mental ward. The film version starring Jack Nicholson won the Academy Award for best picture in 1975. Kesey's other major work is *Sometimes a Great Notion*, the epic tale of an Oregon logging family. His trips across the U.S. with a group of friends in a converted school bus and his experiments with drugs made him a hero of the 1960s counterculture.

1. *Moby Dick* by Herman Melville
2. *DeFord* by David Shetzline
3. *Huckleberry Finn* by Mark Twain
4. *A Farewell to Arms* by Ernest Hemingway
5. *As I Lay Dying* by William Faulkner
6. *The Grapes of Wrath* by John Steinbeck
7. *The Dune Trilogy* by Frank Herbert
8. *On the Road* by Jack Kerouac
9. *From Here to Eternity* by James Jones
10. The westerns of Zane Grey

Note: Like Kesey, David Shetzline (b. 1936) lives in Oregon, where he worked at a variety of odd jobs while writing *DeFord*, his first novel, the story of an aging carpenter.

—Exclusive for *The Book of Lists* 2

DR. SEUSS'S
10 BEST CARTOON CHARACTERS
OF ALL TIME

Theodor Seuss Geisel—better known as Dr. Seuss—began his career as an illustrator for national magazines, writer for the radical newspaper *PM,* and creator of the advertising slogan "Quick, Henry, the Flit!" His immensely popular children's stories (*The Cat in the Hat, Green Eggs and Ham*), which feature outlandish animals, were inspired by childhood visits to the zoo where his father worked as curator. The television adaptations of *How the Grinch Stole Christmas* and *Horton Hears a Who* were both winners of Peabody Awards.

1. Windsor McKay's Little Nemo
2. George Herriman's Krazy Kat and Ignatz Mouse
3. Percy Crosby's Skippy
4. Bill Mauldin's Willy and Joe
5. Sidney Smith's Andy Gump
6. David Low's Colonel Blimp
7. Claire Briggs's Mr. and Mrs.
8. Milton Caniff's Terry and the Pirates
9. Rollin Kirby's Prohibition
10. Dr. Moose's The Mouse in the Hat

—Exclusive for *The Book of Lists 2*

10 RECENTLY PATENTED
INVENTIONS WHOSE
TIME HAS NOT YET COME

1. TOILET LID LOCK (U.S. Patent 3,477,070)

    To prevent unauthorized access to toilet bowl.

2. WHISPER SEAT (U.S. Patent 3,593,345)

    Toilet seat with acoustical liner to prevent sounds from being heard by other persons.

3. COMBINATION DEER-CARCASS SLED AND CHAISE LONGUE (U.S. Patent 3,580,592)

4. EYEGLASS FRAME WITH ADJUSTABLE REARVIEW MIRRORS (U.S. Patent 3,423,150)

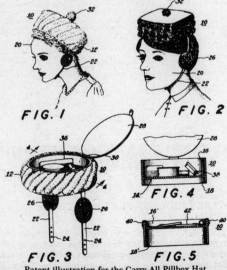

Patent illustration for the Carry-All Pillbox Hat.

5. FLUID-OPERATED ZIPPER (U.S. Patent 3,517,423)

6. POWER-OPERATED POOL CUE STICK (U.S. Patent 3,495,826)

7. CARRY-ALL HAT (U.S. Patent 3,496,575)

A hat with a cavity for carrying cosmetics, jewelry, and the like.

8. SIMULATED FIREARM WITH PIVOTALLY MOUNTED WHISKEY GLASS (U.S. Patent 3,450,403)

Pulling the trigger pivots the glass toward a person's mouth.

9. BABY-PATTING MACHINE (U.S. Patent 3,552,388)

A device for putting a baby to sleep by means of periodic pats upon the rump or hind part of the baby.

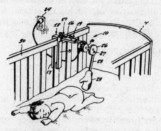

Baby-Patting Machine.

10. ELECTRONIC SNORE DEPRESSOR (U.S. Patent 3,480,010)

Snore is detected and the snorer is electrically shocked.

—J.R.L.

13 LITTLE-KNOWN INVENTORS OF COMMON THINGS

1. MARGARET KNIGHT—FLAT-BOTTOMED PAPER BAG (1869)

A grade school dropout who lived in Springfield, Mass., Margaret Knight loved mechanical devices and machinery. From 1867 to 1869, she devised the heavy machinery necessary to produce the modern flat-bottomed paper bag. The practicality of Knight's paper bag was far superior to the existing paper bag, whose origin is unknown. For the paper bag and dozens of other inventions, she received very little compensation. At her death, her estate was valued at a mere $275.05.

2. JOSEPH GLIDDEN—BARBED WIRE (1874)

A resident of De Kalb, Ill., Joseph Glidden took a rudimentary version of barbed wire—first patented by Henry M. Rose—and changed it into a new type that became a commercial success. Glidden's wire, patented in 1874, featured a new way of holding the barbs securely in place. The improved wire allowed cattle ranchers in the Great Plains area to fence off cheaply and effectively large tracts of land. Glidden, who grew up on a farm in New York, disliked traveling and never visited the West, where his invention was most widely used.

3. WILLIAM PAINTER—CROWN BOTTLE CAP (1892)

A Quaker who lived in Baltimore, Md., William Painter invented the bottle cap, the machinery to manufacture it, and the method to attach it to bottles. Painter, an engineer, formed the Crown Cork and Seal Company to exploit his invention, which eventually made him a millionaire. Painter's bottle cap was the only one used for decades, until the appearance of the twist-off cap in the 1960s.

4. WHITCOMB L. JUDSON—ZIPPER (1893)

On August 29, 1893, Whitcomb Judson of Chicago patented the zipper—two thin metal chains that could be fastened together by pulling a metal slider up between them. Intended for use on shoes and boots, Judson's zipper was marketed in 1896 as the "universal fastener." However, the zipper as we know it today was designed by a Swedish engineer from Hoboken, N.J., Gideon Sundback. In 1913 Sundback patented his "separable fastener," the first zipper with identical units mounted on parallel tapes.

5. JACQUES BRANDENBERGER—CELLOPHANE (1908)

As a hobby, aristocratic Swiss chemist and businessman Jacques Brandenberger spent nearly 10 years experimenting with the machinery needed to mass-produce cellophane, a material he had invented. In 1908 he patented the manufacturing process, and three years later he began to sell his product. At first the transparent sheets were expensive and used only as wrapping paper for luxurious gifts. Today cellophane is produced cheaply and is used primarily by the food industries. The enormous success of cellophane enabled Brandenberger to retire comfortably and collect Louis XV antiques.

6. ROSE CECIL O'NEILL—KEWPIE DOLL (1909)

Born in Pennsylvania, Rose O'Neill was educated in convents in Omaha, Neb., and New York, N.Y. At age 15 she began looking for work as a magazine illustrator and by age 30 she was earning a sizable income. In December, 1909, the *Ladies' Home Journal* printed one of O'Neill's poems with illustrations about a band of Kewpies (Cupid-like imps with tiny wings and curlicues of hair on their foreheads) who stole a wealthy child's Christmas toys. She patented the dolls in 1913 and went on to write and illustrate four successful books that featured Kewpies.

Rose O'Neill (R), inventor of the Kewpie Doll, and her sister.

7. GEORGES CLAUDE—NEON SIGN (1910)

French chemist and physicist Georges Claude invented an electric discharge tube containing neon, which resulted in the first neon sign in 1910. In the late 1920s Claude tried, unsuccessfully, to use seawater to generate electricity. During W.W. II, he believed that Germany would be victorious and collaborated with the Nazis. After the war, Claude was charged with treason, found guilty, and sentenced to life imprisonment.

8. WALLACE HUME CAROTHERS—NYLON (1934)

An extremely emotional, shy, and humorless man, Wallace Hume Carothers worked as a research chemist for E. I. Du Pont de Nemours & Company. At Du Pont, Carothers invented the first nylon thread by squeezing a chemical solution through a hypodermic needle in 1934. Originally known as Polymer 66, nylon was first used for stockings and toothbrushes. Depressed over the death of his sister and feeling himself a failure as a scientist, even though he had been elected to the National Academy of Sciences, Carothers committed suicide in 1937. He never realized the full potential of his creation.

9–10. CARLTON MAGEE and GERALD HALE—
PARKING METER (1935)

In the late 1920s, Carlton Magee, a newspaperman and member of the Oklahoma City Chamber of Commerce, asked mechanical engineering professor Gerald Hale to devise a timing mechanism to regulate parking. Fascinated with the project, Hale invented the parking meter. In 1935, 150 were installed on streets in Oklahoma City. People disliked the new invention, and when similar meters were put on streets in Mobile, Ala., that same year, a group of concerned citizens chopped them down with axes.

11. SYLVAN GOLDMAN—SHOPPING CART (1937)

Oklahoma City supermarket owner Sylvan Goldman looked at a pair of folding chairs in his office and was inspired to invent the shopping cart. On June 4, 1937, he utilized the first shopping carts in his own Standard Supermarkets. Today there are 20 to 25 million shopping carts in the U.S., and 1.25 million new ones are manufactured each year. Goldman became a millionaire.

12. CHESTER CARLSON—XEROGRAPHIC COPIER (1938)

The son of a Swedish immigrant barber, physicist Chester Carlson invented the dry, or xerographic, method of copying in the back room of his mother-in-law's beauty salon in the Queens borough of New York. The patent royalties on the invention, which was bought by the Haloid Company (later Xerox) in 1947, made Carlson a multimillionaire. His first copier is now on display at the Smithsonian Institution in Washington, D.C.

13. ROBERT ABPLANALP—AEROSOL VALVE (1949)

A 27-year-old mechanical engineer and machine shop owner, Robert Abplanalp revolutionized the aerosol spray can industry in 1949 with his seven-part leakproof valve. Abplanalp started the Precision Valve Corporation to manufacture, market, and sell the valve, which has since earned him well over $100 million. Every year Precision Valve manufactures one billion aerosol valves in the U.S. and one-half billion in ten foreign countries. Abplanalp, one of ex-president Richard Nixon's closest friends, commented on his success: "Edison said genius was 99% perspiration and 1% inspiration. I say it's 2% inspiration, 8% work, and 90% luck. I'm a lucky guy." But the world may not be so lucky. Some scientists believe that the fluorocarbons, which were used in spray cans for almost 30 years, are destroying the earth's protective ozone layer.

—R.J.F.

MICHAEL H. HART'S 15 MOST INFLUENTIAL SCIENTISTS IN HISTORY

Michael H. Hart, physicist, astronomer, mathematician, and lawyer, is the author of the book *The 100: A Ranking of the Most Influential Persons in History*. He chose the 100 persons on the basis of the total amount of influence they had on human history and on the everyday lives of human beings. Of the 100 people ranked, scientists and inventors number three out of eight (37). Here are the top 15.

1. ISAAC NEWTON (1642–1727), English mathematician and philosopher

His work in astronomy, optics, mechanics, and physics laid the foundation for modern scientific theories.

2. TS'AI LUN (50?–118? A.D.), Chinese official

    Invented paper.

3. JOHANN GUTENBERG (1400?–1468?), German inventor

    Invented printing from movable type.

4. ALBERT EINSTEIN (1879–1955), German-born
U.S. physicist

    Enunciated the theory of relativity.

5. LOUIS PASTEUR (1822–1895), French chemist

    Founder of the science of bacteriology.

6. GALILEO GALILEI (1564–1642), Italian astronomer
and physicist

    Responsible for the development of the scientific method.

7. CHARLES DARWIN (1809–1882), English naturalist

    Originator of the theory of evolution.

8. EUCLID (c. 300 B.C.), Greek philosopher

    Compiled the basic theories of plane geometry.

9. NICOLAUS COPERNICUS (1473–1543), Polish astronomer

    Regarded as the founder of modern astronomy in establishing
the theory that the earth and the other planets move around the sun.

10. JAMES WATT (1736–1819), Scottish engineer

    Inventor of the steam engine.

11. MICHAEL FARADAY (1791–1867), English chemist
and physicist

    Discovered principles of electromagnetic induction.

12. JAMES CLERK MAXWELL (1831–1879), Scottish
physicist

    Formulated the electromagnetic theory of light.

13. ORVILLE WRIGHT (1871–1948), U.S. inventor

14. WILBUR WRIGHT (1867–1912), U.S. inventor

    Produced the first successful airplane.

15. ANTOINE LAURENT LAVOISIER (1743–1794), French
chemist

    Recognized as the founder of modern chemistry.

SOURCE: Michael H. Hart, *The 100: A Ranking of the Most Influential Persons in History.* © 1978, Hart Publishing Co., Inc.

9 PEOPLE INJURED OR KILLED BY THEIR OWN SCIENTIFIC EXPERIMENTS

1. GALILEO GALILEI (1564–1642), Italian astronomer

Galileo's refinement of the telescope opened up the universe to the eyes of the world, but it also helped to ruin his own already weak eyes. His intensive observations of the sun did irreversible damage to his retinas, possibly contributing to the blindness that afflicted him during the last four years of his life.

2. KARL WILHELM SCHEELE (1742–1786), Swedish chemist

Scheele discovered an incredible number of chemical elements and compounds, but he developed the dangerous habit of sniffing or tasting his discoveries. He had the amazing luck of tasting hydrogen cyanide and living to tell about it, but that luck eventually ran out. He died from symptoms resembling mercury poisoning.

3. JEAN FRANÇOIS PILÂTRE DE ROZIER (1756–1785), French physicist

A physicist and chemist by training, Pilâtre de Rozier ached to be elected to the Académie des Sciences, and he was disappointed when his invention of a respirator (for miners) failed to do the trick. He saw his chance for distinction when the Montgolfiers began experimenting with balloon flights in Paris in September, 1783. Pilâtre de Rozier quickly volunteered to be one of the first humans to ascend in a "captive" balloon, and on November 21 he had the honor of guiding the first free flight. He hoped that later he would be the first person to fly across the English Channel, but J. P. Blanchard and Dr. John Jeffries beat him to it. Nevertheless, he attempted the flight himself on June 15, 1785. He designed his own rig, using a double balloon. One bag contained hydrogen for its lifting powers; the other contained hot air, which could be adjusted easily for ascending and descending. Unfortunately, at about 1,700 ft. the heat used to adjust the air bag ignited the highly volatile hydrogen, and Pilâtre de Rozier and his assistant dropped to their deaths.

4. SIR HUMPHRY DAVY (1778–1829), English chemist

The inventor of the electrolytic technique of chemical analysis seems to have been bent on self-destruction. As a youth he was discharged from his apothecary apprenticeship because he caused too many explosions. When he took up chemistry, he developed the habit of inhaling gases. This practice resulted in the accidental discovery of the anesthetic properties of nitrous oxide, but on other occasions he nearly killed himself, and chemical poisoning left him an invalid the last two decades of his life. His career was further hampered when he permanently damaged his eyes in a nitrogen chloride explosion in 1812.

5. SIR DAVID BREWSTER (1781–1868), Scottish physicist

The inventor of the kaleidoscope did his most important

research on optics and light polarization, a field which naturally required excellent vision. Unfortunately, Brewster almost lost his sight in 1831 when a chemical experiment blew up in his face. He regained the use of his eyes, but vision problems plagued him for the rest of his life.

6. MICHAEL FARADAY (1791–1867), English chemist and physicist

Davy's eye injury in 1812 had one very beneficial result; it enabled Faraday to become Davy's secretary and later his scientific protégé and rival. Faraday went on to refine Davy's electrolysis techniques and to make seminal discoveries in the field of electromagnetics. Faraday also shared some of his mentor's ill fortune. While working with Davy, he not only injured his eyes in a nitrogen chloride explosion but later was affected by chronic chemical poisoning.

7. ROBERT WILHELM BUNSEN (1811–1899), German chemist

Bunsen started his career in organic chemistry but soon found plenty of reason to change fields. He twice nearly died from arsenic poisoning, and in 1843 he lost the use of his right eye in a cacodyl cyanide explosion. He then switched to inorganic chemistry and went on to develop the field of spectroscopy, which led to the discovery of many new elements. He gave his name to a laboratory burner that he had helped to popularize.

8. ELIZABETH FLEISCHMAN ASCHEIM (1859–1905), U.S. X-ray technician

America's second X-ray fatality was also its first female victim. (The first fatality had been Clarence Madison Dally, one of Thomas Edison's assistants, who died in 1904.) Ascheim (*née* Fleischman) took up X-ray work in 1897 to help her brother-in-law's medical practice. For seven years she used the equipment constantly, without taking any precautions whatsoever. She not only exposed herself to radiation in frequent experiments and in routine diagnostic work, she also used it on herself to demonstrate the harmlessness of X-rays to patients. By 1904 she was experiencing severe skin problems. The cancer spread, and one arm was amputated at the shoulder in 1905, but she died later the same year.

9. MARIE SKLODOWSKA CURIE (1867–1934), Polish-born French chemist

The most famous victim of radiation poisoning was undoubtedly Marie Curie, the only person to win two Nobel Prizes in science. Curie and her husband, Pierre (killed in a traffic accident in 1906), discovered radium in 1898, and Marie devoted the rest of her life to radiation research and the therapeutic uses of radiation. She contracted leukemia from overexposure to radioactivity and died painfully in 1934.

—R.K.R.

9 TRAVESTIES OF
MODERN MEDICAL SCIENCE

1. THE INFAMOUS TUSKEGEE SYPHILIS STUDY

In 1932, 400 black males of Macon County, Alabama, suffering from syphilis and 200 uninfected men were entered in a study directed by the U.S. Public Health Service to determine how the syphilitic men would fare over a long period of time if left untreated. Although the men assumed they were receiving medical care (medical personnel visited them often), they did not receive any treatment during the 38 years of the study. Despite acknowledgment that the study was of no medical value after penicillin became available for the treatment of syphilis, the program was not ended until 1971—and only after an estimated 20 to 100 of the infected men had died prematurely. In 1974 a $9 million settlement was negotiated for the survivors and families of the dead.

2. THE CHLOROMYCETIN CONFRONTATIONS

The antibiotic chloramphenicol was discovered in the 1940s and soon hailed as a new wonder drug because of its ability to act against a variety of infectious diseases. In 1952, after three years of record sales around the world, the drug was found to produce a fatal blood disorder in a small but significant group of people. The Parke Davis Company, which controlled the production and distribution of chloramphenicol (trade name Chloromycetin), minimized the dangers of the drug and made a special effort to convince doctors of its safety. Several hundred untimely deaths in the U.S. alone have occurred as a result of this misrepresentation, and yet the drug sales of Chloromycetin continued to be high until 1967, when publicity generated by a congressional hearing slowed down its sales in the U.S. The drug is still sold in large quantities to other countries.

3. THE THALIDOMIDE TRAVESTY

Thalidomide, sold as a sedative, was produced and irresponsibly promoted for human use by a small German pharmaceutical firm (Grünethal) without adequate pretesting in animals. Distributed from 1958 in many countries without marketing controls, it was discovered in 1961 to be the cause of "epidemics" of severely deformed infants. The thalidomide babies were born to mothers who in early stages of pregnancy had taken the drug on the advice of their physicians. Thousands of afflicted infants in West Germany and hundreds in the United Kingdom, the Scandinavian countries, and the U.S. were born before the removal of the drug from the market in 1961.

4. THE PAINFUL UGDP LESSON

In a report released in 1970, the University Group Diabetes Program, a research group involving 12 university medical centers and over 1,000 patients, indicated that tolbutamide, one of the drugs used to treat diabetes, was not only ineffective but dangerous. Patients on the drug ran an increasing risk of cardiovascular disease, including heart attacks. Drug industry spokesmen immediately began discrediting the UGDP with such allegations as faulty trials design, poor management, and unethical procedures in recruiting patients. Despite this attack, the UGDP warnings were confirmed in 1978 and led to the imposition of restrictions on the drug's use. The delaying tactics of the drug industry paid off quite handsomely in their profits, although the Food and Drug Administration (FDA) estimates that hundreds of deaths annually were included in the price.

5. THE 1976 SWINE FLU FIASCO

When a virus with swine flu characteristics appeared among soldiers at Fort Dix in New Jersey in February, 1976, great apprehension was expressed by government health officials that an overdue flu epidemic was brewing. In March, President Ford called for a federal campaign to vaccinate virtually the entire U.S. population, and Congress passed an appropriation bill for $135 million for the project. Vaccinations began the following fall, and although no additional cases of swine flu were discovered, there were a disturbing number of cases of adverse reactions to the vaccine, including heart attacks and paralysis. By the time the program was suspended, 23 people were reported dead. Because of these cases and the government's legal liability for them, the program was ended in December, 1976. Hundreds of claims running into the millions of dollars have been filed against the U.S. government for damages involving the vaccine.

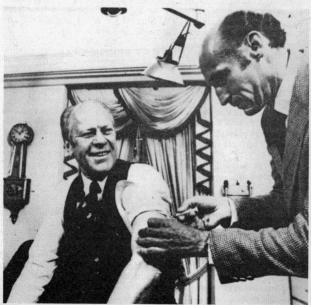

The swine flu fiasco gets under way.

241

6. THE UNSCRUPULOUS DR. STOUGH

Through close working relations with a number of drug companies in the 1950s and 1960s, Dr. Austin Stough developed a lucrative commercial business supplying blood plasma and conducting large-scale testing of drugs in prisons in Alabama, Arkansas, and Oklahoma. His unsanitary procedures for obtaining blood plasma resulted in over 500 cases of hepatitis among prisoners and at least three deaths. Despite knowledge of Stough's dangerous operating conditions, neither the drug companies nor the FDA made any move to regulate testing or disqualify Stough. It was only after public disclosure of his operation that Stough was relieved of *some* of his duties, but Alabama authorities permitted him to continue his drug testing, and Arkansas permitted him to continue his blood plasma program. No criminal charges against Stough were filed.

7. THE SOUTHAM-MANDEL CANCER CELL INOCULATIONS

On July 16, 1963, Dr. Chester Southam, an established cancer researcher, with the approval of Dr. Emanuel Mandel, the hospital medical director, inoculated 22 elderly patients at the Jewish Chronic Disease Hospital in Brooklyn, N.Y., with live cancer cells. The patients were merely asked to consent to a test that would determine their resistance to disease; they were not told that they would receive an injection of live human cancer cells for purposes unrelated to their illnesses. Although none of the patients appeared to develop cancer as a result of the inoculations, the Board of Regents of New York censured Dr. Southam and Dr. Mandel for fraud and deceit and prohibited them from practicing medicine for one year.

8. THE ILLUSORY PRACTICE OF PREFRONTAL LOBOTOMY

From 1940 to 1955, prefrontal lobotomies were performed on some 50,000 mentally ill patients in the U.S. in an attempt to relieve intractable emotional and psychological symptoms. Although apparently alleviating symptoms in some patients, the lobotomies reduced other patients to a near-vegetative condition, or else had little visible effect on their improvement. The operations were curtailed in the late 1950s because of professional and public criticism. However, in 1973 it was revealed that an estimated 100 to 1,000 lobotomies were still being performed annually in the U.S., often in programs receiving federal funding.

9. THE NAZI EXPERIMENTS IN DEATH

The Nuremberg Tribunal in 1946 confirmed that prisoners of the Nazi state had been used as human guinea pigs by German physicians. Healthy prisoners were injected with doses of typhoid, smallpox, diphtheria, and malaria to test even the most unlikely antidotes. Young men were subjected to prolonged exposure to X-rays, and after a period of two to four weeks were castrated so that their organs could be dissected and studied. In experiments dealing with muscle regeneration and bone transplants, healthy legs, arms, shoulder blades, and muscles were removed in operations performed without any anesthesia. Thousands of people died in agony from these and many other experiments. Of 22 defendants at the Nazi

Medical Trial at Nuremberg, 12 were sentenced to hang, 7 were given prison sentences, and 3 were acquitted.

—The Eds.

20 PLACES CONSUMING THE MOST ENERGY

		*Energy Units per Capita per Year**
1.	U.S. Virgin Islands	91,411
2.	Wake Island	24,025
3.	Qatar	23,658
4.	Netherland Antilles	21,311
5.	United Arab Emirates	18,548
6.	Christmas Island	17,537
7.	Luxembourg	14,724
8.	Brunei	13,796
9.	Panama Canal Zone	13,617
10.	United States	11,374
11.	Bahrain	10,302
12.	Canada	9,930
13.	New Caledonia	8,009
14.	Czechoslovakia	7,531
15.	Guam	7,477
16.	Bahamas	7,354
17.	East Germany	7,121
18.	Nauru	7,006
19.	Kuwait	6,771
20.	Australia	6,622

* 1 energy unit equals 10 kilowatt-hours.

SOURCE: *World Energy Supplies,* Statistical Papers, Series J, No. 22. New York: United Nations, 1979.

20 PLACES CONSUMING THE LEAST ENERGY

		Energy Units per Capita per Year
1.	Cambodia (Kampuchea)	4
2.	Nepal	11
3.	Burundi	12

4.	East Timor	15
5.	Rwanda	17
6.	Ethiopia	20
7.	Chad	22
8.	Upper Volta	25
9.	Mali	30
10.	Niger	38
11.	Bangladesh	43
12.	Central African Republic	44
13.	Afghanistan	47
14.	Uganda	48
15.	Comoros	52
15.	Malawi	52
17.	Yemen	53
18.	Benin	56
19.	Haiti	57
20.	Laos	60

Note: The average person in the U.S. Virgin Islands uses more energy in one day than the average person in Cambodia uses in 62 years. One person in Qatar uses as much energy as 2,151 people in Nepal, and one person in the U.S. uses as much energy as 2,843 people in Cambodia.

SOURCE: *World Energy Supplies,* Statistical Papers, Series J, No. 22. New York: United Nations, 1979.

11 RADIOACTIVE WASTE BURIAL SITES

Since the radioactive waste products created by nuclear reactors may remain dangerous for tens, hundreds, or even thousands of years, disposing of them has become a very serious problem. Low-level wastes are interred at the following 11 radioactive waste burial grounds. Six of these sites, marked by asterisks, have been closed by the Nuclear Regulatory Commission because they have accidentally leaked stored radioactive material into the environment.

1. Arco, Ida.
2. Barnwell, S.C.*
3. Beatty, Nev.
4. Hanford, Wash.
5. Los Alamos, N.M.*
6. Morehead, Ky.*
7. Oak Ridge, Tenn.*
8. Richland, Wash.
9. Savannah River, S.C.*

10. Sheffield, Ill.
11. West Valley, N.Y.*

SOURCE: M. L. Wheeler, *Burial Grounds*. Los Alamos, N.M.: Los Alamos Scientific Laboratory, 1976.

—B.D.C.

15 PIECES OF TRASH AND WHEN THEY WILL DISINTEGRATE

Rates of mechanical degradation and biodegradation vary according to temperature, moisture, soil conditions, and size of the object. Photodegradation rates depend on the amount of sunlight received. The following figures are calculated estimates based on average degradation environments.

1. Paper traffic ticket: 2–4 weeks
2. Cotton rag: 1–5 months
3. Degradable polyethylene bag: 2–3 months
4. Piece of rope: 3–14 months
5. Wool stocking: 1 year
6. Bamboo pole: 1–3 years
7. Unpainted wooden stake: 1–4 years
8. Painted wooden stake: 13 years
9. Wooden light pole: 15–36 years
10. Railroad crosstie: 30 years
11–12. Tin or steel can: 100 years
13. Aluminum can: 200–500 years
14. Plastic six-pack cover: 450 years
15. Glass cola bottle: disintegration period unknown

—J.E.

11 INFLUENTIAL COMPUTERS AND/OR THEIR PROGRAMS —PAST TO PRESENT

1. THE ANALYTICAL ENGINE (1835–1869)

Because of lack of government support, English mathematician Charles Babbage (1792–1871) never got to build his invention, whose design presaged the modern electronic computer. Had it seen the light of day, the engine would have used data fed by punched cards, performed arithmetical calculations, and stored information in a memory bank. Lady Lovelace, the mathematically brilliant daughter of Lord Byron, developed some potential problems for the future machine, in effect acting as its first programmer.

2. MARK I (1944)

Conceived by Howard H. Aiken of Harvard University in 1937, the first automatic digital computer was built by International Business Machines in 1944. An automatic sequence controlled calculator, it was used for computing ballistic data. The computer could do three additions per second, working as fast as 20 people on calculators (incredibly slow compared to the speed of today's machines). Mark I took up a lot of space; it was 51 ft. long and 8 ft. high, with 750,000 parts.

3. ENIAC (Electronic Numerical Integrator and Calculator) (1945–1946)

Built only a year or two after Mark I, the first electronic computer was thousands of times faster; it could perform 5,000 additions per second. It, too, was a monster, with 18,000 vacuum tubes, a weight of 30 tons, and a need for 15,000 sq. ft. of floor space. Made at the University of Pennsylvania in Philadelphia, it was designed by physicist John W. Mauchly and electronics engineer J. Presper Eckert, who later started their own computer company. According to legend, when ENIAC was first switched on, lights all over Philadelphia dimmed.

4. UNIVAC I (Universal Automatic Computer) (1951)

Storing its input digitally, the universal automatic computer was delivered to the U.S. government in 1951 to help with the census. It cut the hours of work by humans from 200,000 to 28,000. On October 3, 1963, the computer was retired with full honors after 73,000 hours of operation and is now on display at the Smithsonian Institution.

The original UNIVAC at work.

5. THE "PI" COMPUTER (1961)

In *Mathematics and the Imagination,* published in 1940, Edward Kasner and James Newman stated: "Even today it would require 10 years of calculation to determine pi to 1,000 places." Twenty-one years later, one of the computers at the IBM Data Center calculated pi to 100,265 places in 8 hr. and 43 min. In one slightly long working day it performed 100 times (or more) the amount of work a man could do in 10 years.

6. THE CHECKER-PLAYING COMPUTERS (1962)

Programmed to play checkers, the IBM 704 used by A. L. Samuels in 1955 easily defeated Samuels. In 1962 an IBM Model 7014 electronic computer whipped checkers champion Robert W. Nealey at Yorktown Heights, N.Y. Nealey said, "In the matter of the end game, I have not had such competition from any human being since 1954, when I lost my last game."

7. MACHACK VI (1967)

A computer program devised by MIT student Richard Greenblatt was the first to win a chess match against a human in tournament play. Nicknamed MacHack, the computer's programming was crude compared to later programs, which were able to win against much better players. For example, CHESS 4.5, devised by David Slate and Larry Atkin, won every game at the Paul Masson Tournament in Saratoga, Calif., in 1976. In 1978 a homemade microcomputer—the result of six months' hard work—won the first all-computer tournament, which required that the computers be physically present.

8. THE MOON-LANDING COMPUTER THAT FAILED (1969)

As *Eagle* approached its landing on the moon, the on-board computer, slated to guide the landing, set off an alarm indicating an overload. Astronauts Neil Armstrong and Edwin Aldrin took charge, telemetering measurements to Mission Control in Houston, Tex. Later it was determined that interference from the radar system had scrambled the computer's circuits.

9. THE STORY-WRITING COMPUTER (1973)

Programmed by Sheldon Klein, the computer writes detective stories 2,100 words long. Humans can still do much better, as one may judge from this excerpt: "James invited Lady Buxley. James liked Lady Buxley. Lady Buxley liked James. Lady Buxley was with James in a hotel. Lady Buxley was near James. James caressed Lady Buxley with passion. James was Lady Buxley's lover. Marion following them saw the affair. Marion was jealous."

10. THE IBM 2740s THAT WERE "KILLED" (1976–1977)

Armed terrorists known as Unita Combattenti Communiste planned 10 attacks on computers in Italy, according to E. Drake Lundell, Jr., in an August, 1977, article in *Computerworld.* The first attack occurred in May, 1976, when 15 men burst into a tax office in Rome and destroyed eight IBM 2740 terminals by tossing Molotov cocktails.

11. THE COMPUTER THAT HELPED STEAL
$10.2 MILLION (1978)

In one of the biggest bank thefts in history, computer analyst Mark Rifkin used the services of a computer to transfer $10.2 million from the Security Pacific Bank in Los Angeles to an account in Switzerland. Unable to keep the amazing feat to himself, Rifkin made several revealing remarks to a businessman, who called the FBI. He was arrested on November 5, 1978. While out on bail, Rifkin attempted a second illegal wire-transfer of $50 million and was rearrested. In March, 1979, he was convicted and sentenced to eight years in prison. The computer was not prosecuted.

—A.E.

13
NO PLACE LIKE HOME
—AND FAMILY

THE 10 MOST SERIOUS
GRIEVANCES OF
SOME MARRIED PERSONS

Rank	Husbands' Complaints Regarding Wives	Wives' Complaints Regarding Husbands
1.	Nags me	Selfish and inconsiderate
2.	Not affectionate	Unsuccessful in business
3.	Selfish and inconsiderate	Untruthful
4.	Complains too much	Complains too much
5.	Interferes with my hobbies	Doesn't show his affection
6.	Slovenly in appearance	Doesn't talk things over
7.	Quick-tempered	Harsh with children
8.	Interferes with my discipline	Touchy
9.	Conceited	No interest in children
10.	Insincere	Not interested in home

SOURCE: T. L. Engle and Louis Snellgrove, *Psychology: Its Principles and Applications.* New York: Harcourt Brace Jovanovich, 1969.

RATING THE
10 THINGS THAT MAKE
PEOPLE HAPPIEST

In his book *Happy People* (New York: Harcourt Brace Jovanovich, 1978), Jonathan Freedman presents the results of his research on "what happiness is, who has it, and why." Through magazine surveys, face-to-face interviews, and past research done on the subject, Mr. Freedman estimates that his results are based on the responses of well over 100,000 people. One of the questions in the surveys asked the respondents to rate various aspects of their lives in terms of happiness. Each aspect was rated on a 5-point scale ranging from Not Important to Very Important. Here are the results.

Rank	Single Men	Single Women
1.	Friends and social life	Friends and social life
2.	Job or primary activity	Being in love
3.	Being in love	Job or primary activity
4.	Recognition, success	Recognition, success
5.	Sex life	Personal growth
6.	Personal growth	Sex life
7.	Finances	Health
8.	House or apartment	Body and attractiveness
9.	Body and attractiveness	Finances
10.	Health	House or apartment

Rank	Married Men	Married Women
1.	Personal growth	Being in love
2.	Being in love	Marriage
3.	Marriage	Partner's happiness
4.	Job or primary activity	Sex life
5.	Partner's happiness	Recognition, success
6.	Sex life	Personal growth
7.	Recognition, success	Job or primary activity
8.	Friends and social life	Friends and social life
9.	Being a parent	Health
10.	Finances	Being a parent

SPLIT AFFINITIES—
10 COUPLES WHO MARRIED
EACH OTHER TWICE

1. ELIZABETH TAYLOR and RICHARD BURTON

She had become Mrs. Conrad Nicholson Hilton, Jr., in 1950, Mrs. Michael Wilding in 1952, Mrs. Mike Todd in 1957, and Mrs. Eddie Fisher in 1959. When she and Richard Burton married in 1964, they became the most famous lovers in the world. The marriage lasted until June, 1974, the divorce until October, 1975. The remarriage ended in July of 1976. Her only comment was "Don't ask me about it. He got the divorce." If he hadn't, she wouldn't presently be the wife of the junior senator from Virginia, John Warner, whom she married in 1976.

2. WILLIAM SAROYAN and CAROL MARCUS

In a magazine article entitled "The Funny Business of Marriage," the Pulitzer Prize-winning writer explained his twice failed marriage. He recalled: "In 1942 I met her at last, in 1943 I married her; in 1949 I divorced her. In 1951 I married her again, I divorced her again in 1952, and then I didn't marry her anymore." Actor Walter Matthau did, in 1959.

3. MILTON BERLE and JOYCE MATTHEWS

The first time it lasted six years (1941–1947), the second time less than 10 months (June, 1949, to March, 1950). "It was as if we'd gone straight from the altar on to the rocks," wrote TV's Uncle Miltie in his autobiography. In the book he tells of being consoled at a party by his friend Billy Rose: "If you want a happy new year, Milton, just keep it in mind that blonds like Joyce are a dime a dozen." Milton saved his money and married brunette Ruth Cosgrove. However, Rose forgot his own advice and walked down the aisle twice with Miss Matthews.

Joyce Matthews with four of her husbands.

4. BILLY ROSE and JOYCE MATTHEWS

When supershowman Billy Rose divorced his wife, swimming star Eleanor Holm, in June, 1956, to marry Joyce Matthews, the newspapers announced it as the "New War of the Roses." The skirmishes continued, and the new Mr. and Mrs. Rose were divorced 37 months after the wedding. They were remarried two years later, in December, 1961. As Billy said, "She was living in the house anyway." This marriage lasted two more years.

5. DOROTHY PARKER and ALAN CAMPBELL

At the remarriage of writer Parker and her ex-husband screen-writer Campbell in 1950, someone remarked that most of the guests at the reception hadn't spoken to one another in years. "Including the bride and groom," quipped Parker. Actually the Campbells had been divorced for three years after their first marriage, which lasted 14 years. Although the couple again separated, the second marriage lasted legally until Campbell's death in 1963.

6. NATALIE WOOD and ROBERT WAGNER

It's a love story that reads like a movie script. They were everybody's ideal young couple in love when they married in 1957. And in the tradition of boy-meets-girl, boy must lose girl, so they were divorced in 1962. Ten years passed. They each married someone else and each had a child. These marriages broke up. But Hollywood was not to be denied its happy ending. Bob and Natalie rekindled their love and remarried in 1972—to live happily ever after. Pass the popcorn.

7. JANE WYMAN and FRED KARGER

She'd already been married and divorced once before she married co-star Ronald Reagan. They had two children. She won the Academy Award for *Johnny Belinda* in 1948, and she and Reagan parted company that same year. He went on to Nancy and the governorship of California. Jane met composer Fred Karger on the set of the aptly titled film *Love Song*. They were married in 1952, but the music must have died down, because they divorced in 1954. Jane stated: "I recommend marriage highly for everyone, except me." And as proof of her words she remarried Karger in 1961 and then divorced him in 1963.

8. ELLIOTT GOULD and JENNY BOGART

Murphy's Law, which states that if something can go wrong it will, should have been renamed Gould's Law. He hadn't worked in two years and his sanity was in question when his wife divorced him after only six months of marriage (December, 1973, to June, 1974). It was a problem described as "unchecked eccentricities." He must have checked them, because as of August, 1978, he had four new movies and had remarried his wife. However, Jenny Bogart, daughter of director Paul Bogart, again divorced Gould in 1979. Elliott had been married once before, to Barbra Streisand.

9. WALTER DAVIS and ETHEL DAVIS

After his divorce, Walter listed with a London marriage service to find a new partner. The agency's computer searched through the thousands of names on file and came up with Ethel, his former wife, who had also subscribed to the service. Obviously meant for each other, the two remarried in 1975.

10. LEVI GEER and VINNIE GEER

Sixty years after their first marriage, which lasted four years, Levi and Vinnie remarried in October, 1978. During their long separation, both had had other partners, but one was divorced and the other was widowed. As a result, they found themselves free to marry each other again. Levi advises: "Never give up, never."

—K.C.

10 REALLY DIFFICULT
MOTHERS-IN-LAW

1. SULTANA VĀLIDE NŪR BANŪ (?–1583)

The widow of Selim the Sot, the sultana spent her declining years luring her son, Ottoman emperor Murad III, away from his favorite and powerful Venetian wife, Safieh Baffo. Her bait? A steady stream of voluptuous concubines, delivered on Fridays. Safieh, however, eventually outmaneuvered her mother-in-law. After Murad died in 1595, Safieh used subtle but daring tactics and managed to get her son, Mohammed III, chosen emperor from among Murad's 103 children.

2. MARIE LE VASSEUR (1674–1767)

When the philosopher Jean Jacques Rousseau took as his common-law wife the simple servant girl Thérèse le Vasseur (they met in 1745 and finally married in 1768), he also took on her greedy mother. Marie le Vasseur bled Rousseau for money taken from the small sums he earned by copying music. In a 1764 pamphlet that blackened Rousseau's reputation, Voltaire wrote that Rousseau was a heartless family man and accused him of causing Thérèse's mother's death. Actually, Marie le Vasseur was well treated and lived to be 93.

3. AGNES STERNE (?–1759)

British writer Laurence Sterne was plagued by a demanding and malevolent mother, who asked for money from his wealthy wife. Elizabeth Lumley Sterne, a difficult and quarrelsome woman herself, was miffed by her mother-in-law's brazen requests. Sterne repeatedly said no to his mother, even refusing to bail her out of jail when she was arrested for vagrancy.

4. PRINCESS JULIANE MARIE (1729–1796)

The widowed stepmother of effeminate, half-crazy King Christian VII of Denmark watched as Caroline Matilda, Christian's queen and the sister of George III of England, carried on an affair with Count Johann Struensee, the king's physician. When Caroline Matilda and her lover began to promote democratic reforms, Juliane Marie finally stepped in and engineered a palace revolution in which Caroline Matilda was arrested and Struensee was beheaded. Exiled to Hanover, Germany, Caroline Matilda died in 1775 at the age of 24.

5. TZU HSI (1835–1908)

Few people dared to threaten the power of Tzu Hsi, concubine of Chinese emperor Hsien Fêng. When the emperor died, Tzu Hsi's son, T'ung Chih, ascended the throne, but he soon succumbed to smallpox. T'ung Chih's wife, Alute, an intelligent and tenacious woman, was a possible heir to the throne but overdosed on opium, most likely at her mother-in-law's instigation. Her "convenient" death enabled Tzu Hsi to choose the new emperor.

6. FRANCES CHURCHILL, DUCHESS OF MARLBOROUGH (?–1899)

New York socialite Jennie Churchill, wife of Lord Randolph Churchill and mother of Winston Churchill, did not please her mother-in-law, possibly because Jennie was prettier and more accomplished than the old duchess's daughters. Jennie once summed up their relationship: "We are always studiously polite to each other, but it is rather like a volcano ready to burst out at any moment."

7. SARA DELANO ROOSEVELT (1854–1941)

For three years Sara Delano Roosevelt fought the marriage of her beloved son Franklin (later president of the U.S.) to Eleanor Roosevelt. Once married, Eleanor was a perfect daughter-in-law to the meddling Sara until Franklin was crippled by polio. At that time the two women battled over his future, since Sara wanted him to retire and Eleanor advocated an active political career. Caroline Phillips, a good friend of Eleanor's, wrote: "That old lady with utter charm and distinction and kindliness hides a primitive jealousy of her daughter-in-law, which is sometimes startling in its crudity."

Sara Delano Roosevelt, seen coming between son,
Franklin, and daughter-in-law, Eleanor.

8. MADGE GATES WALLACE (1862–1952)

A cantankerous woman, Madge Gates Wallace lived with Harry S Truman and his wife, her daughter Bess, for 33 years, until she died at the age of 90. She never thought much of Harry, even after he became president, and was heard to remark in his presence that other men would have made better presidents—including that "nice man, Thomas E. Dewey." A proper son-in-law, Harry kept his mouth shut.

9. QUEEN MARY, CONSORT OF KING GEORGE V OF GREAT BRITAIN AND NORTHERN IRELAND (1867–1953)

When King Edward VIII abdicated from the throne to marry "the woman I love," twice-divorced American Wallis Simpson, the royal family refused to recognize his new wife. At the end of W.W. II, Wallis, then Duchess of Windsor, wrote to her mother-in-law, hoping to bring about a rapprochement. Queen Mary's only reply was an icy silence.

10. LILLIAN CARTER (1898–)

After Jimmy Carter's stint in the navy, his wife Rosalynn did not want to return to their home in Plains, Ga., because, as Jimmy wrote, their "married freedom might be cramped or partially dominated by relatives, particularly by her mother or my mother." Lillian Carter has complained that Jimmy pays more attention to Rosalynn than to her and once told a reporter, "I love Rosalynn, but she's kind of . . . reserved."

—A.E.

20 FAMOUS PEOPLE WHO HAD CHILDREN BORN OUT OF WEDLOCK

1. INGRID BERGMAN (1915–)

Ingrid Bergman's relationship with Italian director Roberto Rossellini shocked America. When she left her husband of 12 years to meet Rossellini in Italy, cries of outrage were heard from Hollywood to Washington, D.C., where Sen. Edwin C. Johnson delivered an impassioned speech over an hour long from the Senate floor. He called the actress "a free-love cultist," "a powerful influence of evil," and "Hollywood's apostle of degradation." The birth of their son, Robertino, in February, 1950, brought new outcries of damnation.

2. MARLON BRANDO (1924–)

While filming *Mutiny on the Bounty* in 1961, actor Marlon Brando met a 19-year-old Tahitian restaurant dishwasher named Tarita (full name: Taritatum a Teripaiam). Their romance resulted in the birth in 1962 of a son, who was named Tehotu. Still not married, in 1970 the couple had another child, a daughter named Tarita.

3. BENVENUTO CELLINI (1500–1571)

In 1558 Cellini decided to become a priest, despite the fact that his mistress, Piera, had already borne him three children: Constanza, Jacopo Giovanni, and an unnamed son who had died in infancy. The Italian sculptor was released from his vows in 1560 to marry Piera, but they had three more children—Giovanni, Elisabetta, and Liperata—before they finally legalized their union in 1564.

4. MIGUEL DE CERVANTES (1547–1616)

Shortly before his marriage to Catalina de Salazar y Palacios in 1584, Cervantes's mistress, Ana Franca de Rojas, bore him a daughter, Isabel. The scandal attached to the affair was reignited in 1605, when the author was arrested for alleged involvement in the murder of a Spanish nobleman.

5. PAUL CÉZANNE (1839–1906)

Living on a meager allowance from his father, French painter Paul Cézanne took a beautiful model named Hortense Fiquet as his mistress in the late 1860s. This sexual liaison—the only one in Cézanne's life—produced a son named Paul in 1872.

6. HERNANDO CORTES (1485–1547)

Spanish conquistador Hernando Cortes and his Indian noble-woman counselor, translator, and lover, Doña Marina—who was known as La Malinche—had a son named Don Martín in 1520. Don Martín Cortes inherited 100 slaves and a Mexican estate from his father and was appointed by the Spanish crown as a knight commander of the Order of St. James.

7. CATHERINE DENEUVE (1943–   )

After her divorce from photographer David Bailey in 1970, actress Catherine Deneuve gave birth to her first child, a son named Christian, whose father was film director Roger Vadim. In 1972, she and actor Marcello Mastroianni became the parents of a daughter named Chiara.

8. RENÉ DESCARTES (1596–1650)

Although the French philosopher never married, in 1635 he had a daughter by a young servant named Hélène. When the child, named Francine, died at age five, he was grief-stricken.

9. ALEXANDRE DUMAS, PÈRE (1802–1870)

Dumas's succession of mistresses included dressmaker Marie Labay, by whom he had his son Alexandre in 1824, and actress Belle Krelsamer, who bore him his daughter Marie Alexandrine in 1831. The French author had a prowess undiminished with age and fathered a second son out of wedlock, Henry Bauër, in 1851, and another daughter, Micaëlla Cordier, in 1860.

10. BENJAMIN FRANKLIN (1706–1790)

In 1731, a short time after he married Deborah Read, Benjamin Franklin brought home his newborn son, William. Although Franklin never identified the child's mother, the evidence indicates that she was either a servant girl or a prostitute. Adopted into the Franklin family, William became a lawyer and the colonial governor of New Jersey.

11. GALILEO GALILEI (1564–1642)

Italian astronomer and physicist Galileo Galilei and Marina Gamba, his mistress for 10 years, were the parents of three children: Virginia, born in 1600; Livia, born in 1601; and Vincenzio, born in 1606. The two daughters became nuns, while the son practiced law in Florence, Italy.

12. JOHANN WOLFGANG VON GOETHE (1749–1832)

In 1788 Goethe, noted German author, severed his relationship with the talented Charlotte von Stein, whom he had been involved with for more than a decade, and began living with Christiane Vulpius, an unsophisticated woman 16 years his junior. Christiane subsequently bore him five children, but only their son August, born in 1789, survived to maturity. Goethe finally married Christiane in 1806.

13. WARREN HARDING (1865–1923)

In 1919, while serving in the U.S. Senate, future president Warren Harding and his mistress, Nan Britton, became the parents of a daughter named Elizabeth Ann. Harding's only child, Elizabeth Ann—now Mrs. Henry Blaesig—is a housewife living in southern California.

14. GEORGE HARRISON (1943–)

In 1974 Harrison's wife of eight years, Patti Boyd, left the British musician for his best friend, guitarist Eric Clapton. That same year Harrison became acquainted with Olivia Arias, a Mexican-American secretary who worked for his record company in Los Angeles. In 1978 he and Arias became the parents of a son they named Dhani, a Hindi word meaning "rich person." They married shortly after the birth.

15. ADOLF HITLER (1889–1945)

Although some persons close to Adolf Hitler believed that he died a virgin, West German historian and biographer Werner Maser claimed Adolf Hitler had an 18-month love affair with a French peasant girl while he was stationed as a German army corporal in the village of Wavrin, France, during W.W. I. In 1918, while in a military hospital, Hitler learned that Charlotte had given birth to his son, whom she named Jean Marie. When the Germans occupied France in 1940, Hitler had the Gestapo locate Jean Marie Loret and give him a high-ranking position in the French police administration. Presently, Hitler's son is an unemployed railway worker living in St. Quentin, France.

16. THOMAS JEFFERSON (1743–1826)

From 1790 to 1805, while he was U.S. secretary of state, vice-president, and president, Thomas Jefferson and Sally Hemings, a beautiful slave on his Virginia plantation, had seven children: Tom, Beverly, Eston, Edy, Madison, and two daughters, both named Harriet. The five who lived to maturity—who were legally his slaves—were eventually freed.

17. BERNADETTE DEVLIN McALISKEY (1947–)

While a member of the British Parliament in 1971, the Irish Roman Catholic radical Bernadette Devlin gave birth to a daughter named Roison. Married to Michael McAliskey in 1973, Bernadette has never revealed the identity of Roison's father.

18. NORMAN MAILER (1923–)

The father of eight children by six women, U.S. author Norman Mailer maintains, "I can't make love without making babies." Estranged from his fourth wife, Beverly, Mailer now lives with model Norris Church and their son, John Buffalo, born in 1978.

19. IVAN TURGENEV (1818–1883)

In 1842, while still a literary unknown, Turgenev fathered a daughter, Pelageya, by a seamstress employed in his mother's service. The child was later renamed Paulinette and was brought up by Mme. Pauline Viardot, a French actress with whom Turgenev had long been infatuated.

20. LOPE DE VEGA (1562–1635)

Neither of his two marriages interfered with the Spanish author's love affairs, which resulted in the birth of a son, Fernando, by a woman named Pellicer in 1599, and several children, including daughter Marcela and son Lope Félix, by the famous Spanish actress Micaela de Lujan.

—R.J.F. & F.B.F.

Spanish playwright Lope de Vega, fathered numerous children in and out of wedlock.

11 CURIOUS BIRTHS

1. BORN IN A COFFIN

Gorgias of Epirus was born during the funeral of his mother. The pallbearers were shocked to hear unexpected crying and opened the coffin to discover Gorgias, who had slipped out of the womb and was very much alive.

2. ONE BLACK, ONE WHITE

In 1970, when a hospital nurse in Offenbach, West Germany, first showed Grete Bardaum her twin sons, Grete fainted. The firstborn had white skin, blue eyes, and blond hair, while the second one had brown skin, brown eyes, and black hair. Apparently Grete had made love with a German businessman and a black American soldier in one day; that same day, she had ovulated twice. The baby boys, Berndt and Deiko, are now living with separate foster families. Grete married a third man and has since given birth to a normal set of twins.

3. BORN ON TEXAS SOIL

Deborah Brown and her husband, Robert, fans of the University of Texas Longhorns, were determined to have their second child born on Texas soil despite the fact that they were living in Oklahoma. They solved the problem by arranging to have a sack of Texas dirt brought up from Dallas and placed in a sterile bag under the delivery table at Mercy Hospital in Oklahoma City. So, on October 4, 1978, Deborah Brown gave birth to a son "on Texas soil."

4. SAME TIME, NEXT YEAR

On December 7, 1978, Diane Tuminaro of Lancaster, Calif., gave birth to her second son, exactly one year to the minute after she gave birth to her first son.

5. ALL IN THE FAMILY

Sabrina Leeann Heinrich was born in Houston, Tex., on November 26, 1978, the same birthday as that of her grandmother, her great-grandmother, her aunt, her uncle, and her cousin.

6. 10-YEAR-OLD MOTHER

On July 29, 1969, an unnamed 10-year-old girl in Alexandria, Va., gave birth to a healthy 5-lb. 10-oz. boy.

7. 58-YEAR-OLD MOTHER

On July 16, 1969, 58-year-old Dawie du Plessis of Johannesburg, South Africa, gave birth to a 5-lb. girl. Mrs. Du Plessis, who already had eight children and twelve grandchildren, is believed to be the oldest woman to give birth.

8. DELAYED TWINS

Twins Dougie and Debbie Schee of Delaware, O., were born 48 days apart in 1955.

9. JACK BENNY'S MISPLACED BIRTH

Jack Benny was actually born in Chicago, not in Waukegan, Ill., as his birth certificate states. His mother was in Chicago shopping when she went into labor and was taken to a Cook County hospital. However, she requested that her son's birthplace be recorded as Waukegan because that was where she had carried him for nine months.

10. ALL IN THE FAMILY, PART TWO

Ralph and Carolyn Cummins of Clintwood, Va., have produced five children. Catherine was born on February 20, 1952; Carol on February 20, 1953; Charles on February 20, 1956; Claudia on February 20, 1961; and Cecilia on February 20, 1966.

11. THE MOST UNUSUAL BIRTH OF ALL

The November 7, 1874, issue of the *American Medical Weekly* related a bizarre episode which began during the Battle of Raymond in Mississippi on May 12, 1863. According to Dr. T. G. Capers of Vicksburg, a soldier friend of his was hit in the scrotum by a bullet, which carried away his left testicle. The same bullet apparently penetrated the left side of the abdomen of a 17-year-old girl in a nearby house. Two hundred and seventy-eight days later, the young lady gave birth to a healthy 8-lb. boy "to the surprise of herself and the mortification of her parents and friends." Three weeks later, Dr. Capers operated on the infant and removed a smashed miniball. He concluded that this was the same ball that had carried away the testicle of his young friend; it had then penetrated the ovary of the young lady and—with some spermatozoa upon it—impregnated her. With this conviction he approached the young man and told him the circumstances; the soldier appeared skeptical at first, but consented to visit the young mother; a friendship ensued which soon ripened into a happy marriage. The couple had three more children, none of whom resembled their father as closely as the first.

—D.W.

11 WELL-KNOWN WOMEN WHO HAD CHILDREN AFTER AGE 40

1. SVETLANA ALLILUYEVA (1926–   ), daughter of Joseph Stalin

She married architect William Wesley Peters in April, 1970. Their daughter, Olga, was born in May, 1971, when Svetlana was 45.

2. LUCILLE BALL (1911–   ), U.S. actress and comedian

Her second child, Desi Arnaz, Jr., was born in 1953, when Ball was 42 years old.

3. ELIZABETH BARRETT BROWNING (1806–1861),
   English poet

   Her only son, Robert Wiedemann Barrett Browning, was born
in 1849, when she was 43 years old.

4. YVONNE BRATHWAITE BURKE (1932–   ),
   former congresswoman from California

   Her first child, Autumn Roxanne, was born in 1973, when
Burke was 41 years old.

5. ROSALYNN SMITH CARTER (1927–   ),
   First Lady of the U.S.

   Mrs. Carter's fourth child and only daughter, Amy, was born
October 19, 1967, two months after Mrs. Carter's 40th birthday.

6. AUDREY HEPBURN (1929–   ), U.S. actress

   Her second child, Luca Dotti, was born in 1970, when Hepburn
was 41 years old.

7. ROSE FITZGERALD KENNEDY (1890–   ),
   mother of President John Fitzgerald Kennedy

   Her youngest son, Edward, was born in 1932, when she was
42 years old.

8. ALICE ROOSEVELT LONGWORTH (1884–   ),
   daughter of President Theodore Roosevelt

   After 18 years of marriage to Nicholas Longworth, Alice, aged
41, gave birth to a daughter, Paulina, in 1925. She is said to have
named the child in honor of the Apostle Paul, who preached the
virtues of self-denial.

9. MARTHA MITCHELL (1918–1976), wife of U.S. Attorney
   General John Mitchell

   Her only child by John, a daughter named Martha, was born
in 1961, when Mrs. Mitchell was 43 years old.

10. MARGARETTA FITLER "HAPPY" ROCKEFELLER
    (1926–   ), wife of Vice-President Nelson Rockefeller

    Mark Fitler Rockefeller is the second of two sons born to
Nelson and Happy and is the youngest of six children. He was born
in 1967, when his mother was 41.

11. GLORIA VANDERBILT (1924–   ), U.S. artist

    Her fourth son, Anderson, was born in 1968, when she was 44
years of age.

—V.L.V.

21 FAMOUS WOMEN WHO BREAST-FED THEIR BABIES

1. Karen Black (b. 1942), U.S. actress
2. Lesley Brown (b. 1947), English mother of the first test-tube baby
3. Lillian Carter (b. 1898), mother of U.S. President Jimmy Carter
4. Elizabeth II (b. 1926), Queen of Great Britain
5. Glenda Jackson (b.1936), English actress
6. Cloris Leachman (b. 1926), U.S. actress
7. Pia Lindström (b. 1938), Swedish television news broadcaster, journalist, and daughter of Ingrid Bergman
8. Sophia Loren (b. 1934), Italian actress
9. Margaret Mead (1901–1978), U.S. anthropologist, author, and lecturer
10. Grace Kelly Grimaldi (b. 1929), Princess of Monaco
11. Lynn Redgrave (b. 1943), English actress
12. Vanessa Redgrave (b. 1937), English actress
13. Barbara Rush (b. 1930), U.S. actress
14. Susan St. James (b. 1946), U.S. actress
15. Buffy Sainte-Marie (b. 1941), Native American folksinger and composer
16. Silvia, (b. 1948), Queen of Sweden
17. Carly Simon (b. 1945), U.S. singer and wife of James Taylor
18. Margaret Trudeau (b. 1948), Canadian actress, photographer, and wife of former prime minister Pierre Trudeau
19. Mary Vinton (b. 1944), U.S. owner-president of multimillion-dollar Washington-based Georgetown Leather Design Company
20. Natalie Wood (b. 1938), U.S. actress
21. Joanne Woodward (b. 1930), U.S. actress and wife of Paul Newman

—K.D.G.

10 PRODIGIOUS CHILD PRODIGIES

1. JEAN LOUIS CARDIAC (1719–1726)

Born in France and known as the Wonder Child, Jean could recite the alphabet when he was three months old. At the age of four, he not only read Latin but translated it into English and French. He read Greek and Hebrew and was proficient in such subjects as arithmetic, history, geography, and genealogy at age six. He died in Paris when he was seven.

2. CHRISTIAN FRIEDRICH HEINECKEN (1721–1725)

Christian was known throughout Europe as the Infant of

Lübeck, after his birthplace in Germany. In addition to an astounding faculty for numbers, Christian reportedly knew all the principle events related in the Bible by the time he was one year old. At three he was conversant with world history, geography, Latin, and French. The king of Denmark sent for him in 1724 to confirm stories of the child's extraordinary abilities. Shortly after his stay in Copenhagen, little Christian became ill. He died at age four, soon after predicting his own death.

3. WOLFGANG AMADEUS MOZART (1756–1791)

Most prodigious of all child prodigies, Mozart was born in Salzburg, Austria, where at four he began music lessons with his violinist father. At five he composed minuets, and at six, a virtuoso on violin and harpsichord, he toured with his elder sister, creating a sensation at European courts with his phenomenal ability to sight-read music and improvise. He wrote his first symphony at eight. At 11, forced to compose in solitary confinement for the suspicious Archbishop of Salzburg, he passed the test and was offered the salaried job of concertmaster. At 12, between tours, he wrote two operas and a mass. His reputation grew with the years as operas, concertos, and symphonies of the highest order came from his pen. Today he is regarded as one of the world's supreme geniuses.

4. JOHN STUART MILL (1806–1873)

Called a manufactured genius, Mill was the product of an educational experiment that reads like a record of medieval torture. His irritable father, historian and philosopher James Mill, taught his son Greek at three, history at four, and Latin, geometry, and algebra at eight. By 12 Mill had read Vergil, Horace, Ovid, Terence, Cicero, Homer, Sophocles, Euripides, Aristophanes, Thucydides, and Demosthenes. His father also required him to write English verse and educate his younger siblings. A reaction to this one-sided emphasis on intellect hit Mill in his 20s; questioning life's purpose, he was rescued from depression by Wordsworth's poetry. Instead of becoming a prig or recluse, he developed into a sensitive man of feeling, active in the affairs of the world. An influential thinker and writer in politics, economics, and philosophy, he was devoted to the ideals of justice and the public good.

5. TRUMAN HENRY SAFFORD (1836–1901)

Son of a Vermont farmer, Safford showed precocity at three, when his parents amused themselves with his calculating powers. At seven he studied algebra and geometry, and at nine constructed and published an almanac. At 10 he originated a new rule for obtaining moon risings and settings in one-quarter the time of previous methods. Also at 10, when asked to multiply in his head 365,365,365,365,365,365 by itself, he gave the correct answer in less than a minute: 133,491,850,208,566,925,016,658,299,941,-583,225! Safford's calculating gift was gone by age 16. A man of wide-ranging interests and encyclopedic memory, he graduated from Harvard at 18. He became a professor of astronomy, publishing articles and making important contributions to astronomical calculation.

6. WILLIAM JAMES SIDIS (1898–1944)

"Willie" Sidis, wonder child, was the son of a Harvard psychology professor who used him to prove that children could master the most complex subjects. At six months the infant knew his ABCs; at two years he read adult books. Into advanced mathematics at three, he had mastered French by four. At eight he graduated from high school. After some independent study in Greek, Latin, German, Russian, French, Turkish, and Armenian, Sidis entered Harvard at 11, where he lectured the Harvard Mathematical Society on fourth-dimensional bodies. Sidis became the target of increasing resentment, especially in the press. Bitter against his father, who had treated him as an exhibit, Sidis utterly rejected intellectualism in adulthood. He worked by choice at menial tasks and collected streetcar transfers as a hobby. He died at 46 in a rented room near Boston.

7. JOEL KUPPERMAN (1936–   )

Most famous of the radio Quiz Kids of the 1940s, at five Joel himself sent the show an application letter in which he mentioned his ability to do 98 or 99 times any number in his head. Asked during an audition to multiply 24 by 98, he answered, "Dat would be 2,352." When asked how he got the answer so fast, he replied in his soon-to-be-famous lisp, "Dat is a theequet twick." The "twick," which involved working to the nearest zero, he had discovered himself. His IQ in the 200 range, Joel at five had the highest general mental development of any child tested by the Chicago Public Schools. At 20 he received his M.A. in philosophy from the University of Chicago and at 27 earned his Ph.D. at Cambridge, England. Now on the faculty of the University of Connecticut, he has published scholarly books and articles.

The famous Quiz Kid, Joel Kupperman,
talking to actress Helen Hayes.

8. MICHAEL GROST (1954–   )

Son of a credit union manager from Lansing, Mich., Mike at three astounded his mother by reading aloud to her without previous training. His IQ so high it couldn't be measured, he was underchallenged at school. At four, on his first day in kindergarten, he saw a classmate coloring an apple blue. He remarked with interest, "That's the kind of approach Picasso would use." At 10 Mike moved directly from a fifth grade class to Michigan State University, where he became the youngest U.S. college freshman in nearly a century. Graduating from M.S.U. in three and a half years, he earned his M.A. there at 16 and his Ph.D. at Yale before he was 20. Well adjusted socially, Grost never regretted having been accelerated academically. He is currently on the mathematics faculty of the University of Wisconsin at Milwaukee.

9. KIM UNG-YONG (1963–   )

Many believe this Korean-born prodigy to be the most brilliant person alive today. At birth his body was covered with black fuzz a quarter-inch long, and his father remarked that he looked "like a newborn baby deer." Within three months the hair had fallen off, and he had a mouthful of teeth. He was talking at five months and writing at seven months. Experts estimate his IQ is over 200. When he was four years old, he was fluent in Korean, English, Japanese, and German, and he was solving intricate calculus problems on Japanese television before his fifth birthday. Curiously, his mother and father, both university professors, were born at exactly the same time on the same date—11 A.M., May 23, 1934. He has never received formal schooling, having been educated only by private tutors. In September, 1979, however, his father announced that Kim was about to enter a West German university where he would pursue physics and medical science.

10. JOE HALL (1966–   )

Joe Hall of tiny Plumtree, N.C., son of the high school band director, surprised his mother by copying the alphabet at 14 months. At three he read adult books on space and electronics. At five he was playing the classics on the piano and composing. Then his stunned parents discovered that Joe had leukemia. Having read about it, the child remarked, "I suppose my statistical chances don't look too promising." His intellectual curiosity undimmed, the boy struggled determinedly against his disease. At six a pianist with high school bands, Joe won a countywide contest with his composition "Five Thousand Miles of Universe." Bored with school (his IQ off the scale at 200) and having exhausted the resources of the local library, Joe read—in three weeks—400 lb. of technical material donated by the army. At 10 he corresponded with rocket expert Wernher von Braun and set up his own center for UFO investigation. An 11th grader at age 12 (1978), his leukemia arrested for the fifth year, he studied calculus and did advanced work with computers while continuing his musical pursuits.

—M.B.T. & L.J.

10 PARENTS WHO OBJECTED TO THEIR CHILDREN'S MARRIAGES

1. EDWARD MOULTON BARRETT, father of Elizabeth Barrett Browning

Apparently afflicted with a sexual neurosis, the tyrannical Barrett was violently opposed to having any of his children marry. Elizabeth, addicted to opium because of a chronic spinal ailment, eloped from her London home with poet Robert Browning in 1846. The couple fled to Italy, where they resided until Elizabeth's death.

2. MRS. CAMERON-FALCONET, mother of Lucille Cameron Johnson

Boxer Jack Johnson was at the height of his fame when he began courting 19-year-old Lucille. Outraged at the interracial affair, Lucille's mother charged him with abduction. Although the couple married in 1912, Johnson was brought to trial the following year and convicted on several charges of immorality. Rather than face imprisonment, Johnson fled with his wife to Canada, then Europe. They were divorced in 1924.

3. JEAN FINLEY, mother of Polly Finley Crockett

Polly's mother, wrote frontiersman David Crockett, "looked at me as savage as a meat ax" in 1806, because she wanted Polly to marry another suitor. Although earlier she had laughingly referred to Davy as her future son-in-law, Mrs. Finley nearly threw him out of the house when he proposed to her daughter. When the day arrived, however, she apologized and agreed to host the wedding.

4–5. JESSE ROOT GRANT and HANNAH SIMPSON GRANT, parents of Ulysses S. Grant

Grant's parents were struggling farmers, while the parents of Julia Dent, whom the young soldier met in 1844, were well established and owned a prosperous Missouri plantation. Disturbed that Ulysses was marrying into a slave-owning family, the Grants refused to attend the 1848 wedding but later welcomed Julia into their home. During the early years of their marriage, the young couple were often dependent on the charity of Julia's father.

6. NANCY MOFFETTE LEA, mother of Margaret Lea Houston

The prospect of 46-year-old Sam Houston, the divorced ex-president of Texas, marrying her 20-year-old daughter greatly alarmed the widowed Mrs. Lea. Houston had a definite problem with alcohol, and Margaret was a religious fanatic who hoped to cure him of his affliction and save his soul in the process. Apparently fulfilling mutual needs, they wed with Nancy's reluctant consent in 1840 and produced eight children.

7. LEOPOLD MOZART, father of Wolfgang Amadeus Mozart

The elder Mozart, impresario to his brilliant son, jealously

266

resisted any interest that threatened to distract Wolfgang from music, and thus opposed Wolfgang's betrothal to Constanze Weber in 1782. Reluctant to counter his father but determined to marry, Wolfgang was overjoyed to receive grudging acceptance on the day after the ceremony.

8. EUGENE O'NEILL, father of Oona O'Neill Chaplin

Friends of the playwright speculated that his prejudice against actor Charlie Chaplin stemmed from Chaplin's friendship with an ex-husband of O'Neill's wife, Carlotta. Perhaps more important, Chaplin had already gone through three divorces and was in the midst of a paternity suit brought by the young actress Joan Barry. After her 1943 marriage to Chaplin, Oona never saw her father again, and O'Neill never mentioned her name. Despite the great difference in their ages (Chaplin was 54, Oona 18), they remained married until Chaplin's death 34 years later.

9. SIR TIMOTHY SHELLEY, father of Percy Bysshe Shelley

Sir Timothy had a parliamentary career for his son well planned, and such plans did not include a marriage "out of caste." The father-son relationship was already strained when the rebellious 19-year-old eloped in 1811 with Harriet Westbrook, a merchant's daughter. Sir Timothy reacted by cutting off all communication with his son and severing his allowance. Although the allowance was later reinstated, Shelley and his father never completely reconciled.

10. FRIEDRICH WIECK, father of Clara Wieck Schumann

"The idea of Clara with a perambulator is preposterous," raged Wieck, who feared that marriage would wreck her career as a concert pianist. Despite his furious opposition, Clara's romance with composer Robert Schumann survived six years of enforced separation and Wieck's slanders. Finally wed in 1840, the couple welcomed reconciliation with a chastened Wieck in 1843.

—J.E.

8 PARENTS WHO PREVENTED THEIR CHILDREN'S MARRIAGES

1–2. PARENTS OF VIRGINIA AMBELLA

In 1868, the arrogant young war correspondent Henry Morton Stanley (later famous for tracking down Dr. David Livingstone in Africa) was determined to marry Virginia Ambella, an enchanting Greek girl from Syra, an island near Crete. He enlisted the aid of Egyptian government official Hekekyan Bey in an attempt to pressure the girl's parents. In a letter to Bey, Stanley wrote, "State to them that by refusing me they have lost a most eligible offer." He then added, "If any unhappiness is the result, they have no one to blame but themselves." Despite Bey's support, Stanley was rejected by the parents.

3. QUEEN ANNE (1600–1666), mother of Louis XIV

The regent queen mother of France and prime minister Cardinal Jules Mazarin both opposed the young king's desire to wed Marie Mancini, Mazarin's niece. At issue was Mazarin's insistence on a political alliance with Spain. After an intense war of nerves in the French palace, political reasoning finally overwhelmed the royal heart. Louis wed Maria Theresa, the Spanish princess, but remained indifferent to her throughout their 23-year marriage.

4. NADEZHDA VON MECK, mother of Sonia von Meck

The patroness of Tchaikovsky also took the young French musician Claude Achille Debussy under her wing, employing him to teach piano to her daughters. But "Monsieur Bussykoff," as she called him, aroused her ire in 1882 when he proposed to Sonia. "I don't want a man of Sonia's choice," declared the mother. "I want the one whom I am going to appoint, and Sonia will like him." She dismissed Debussy. Later Sonia married and divorced two of Nadezhda's choices.

5. MRS. NICHOLAS POWER, mother of Sarah Helen Whitman

In 1848, widower Edgar Allan Poe met the attractive Rhode Island widow and began an intense three-month courtship, frowned upon by Mrs. Power because of the poet's dissolute habits. Poe proposed to "Helen" in a Providence graveyard and she accepted, extracting his promise to quit drinking. He didn't, and Mrs. Power, who was a strong influence on Sarah, protested vehemently. Sarah broke the engagement. She later became one of Poe's earliest literary defenders in her book *Poe and His Critics* (1860).

6. REV. EDMUND QUINCY SEWALL, father of Ellen Sewall

In 1839 the 17-year-old Ellen visited Concord, Mass., where she met the Thoreau brothers. John Thoreau proposed a year later and was accepted. But Ellen then realized that she preferred Henry and changed her mind. When the equally smitten Henry proposed by letter, however, Reverend Sewall, who disliked transcendentalists, intervened. Ellen wrote to Henry and refused his offer. She later recalled: "I never felt so badly at sending a letter in my life." Ellen married Unitarian minister Joseph Osgood, and Henry Thoreau occasionally visited the couple. On his deathbed Henry told his sister, "I have always loved her."

7. JOSEPH STALIN, father of Svetlana Alliluyeva

Svetlana was still a schoolgirl in 1942 when she met Alexei Y. Kapler, a Jewish film producer and war correspondent. "Because of him," she wrote, "my relationship with my father was ruined." The enraged, anti-Semitic Stalin tore up Kapler's letters to her, accused him of being a British spy, and had him arrested and exiled for 10 years. The pair met again briefly in 1955, when Kapler was teaching in Moscow's Institute of Cinematography.

8. COUNT WINCENTY WODZINSKI, father of
Maria Wodzinska

Maria's mother approved of her engagement to composer Frédéric Chopin in 1836, but the count saw only Chopin's lowly origins and wretched physique. "If at least he had better health and a little ambition!" he raged. "*No*, a thousand times *no!*" Decidedly nonassertive, Chopin let the romance die with a whimper; he tied Maria's letters together with a ribbon, labeled the bundle *Moja Bieda* ("my sorrow"), and kept it until his death.

—J.E.

15 CELEBRATED PERSONS WHO HAD MISERABLE REPORT CARDS

1. G. K. CHESTERTON (1874–1936), English writer

An obese and unpopular child, Chesterton suffered greatly in school and could not read until he was eight. One of his masters told him, "If we could open your head, we should not find any brain but only a lump of white fat." He stayed at the bottom of his classes until, at 15, a budding friendship with future author E. C. Bentley ended his introversion. His transformation was remarkable, and by the time he was finishing secondary school he was well on his way to a prolific and successful writing career highlighted by the *Father Brown* series.

Future detective-story writer G. K. Chesterton at 15,
when his brain replaced the "lump of white fat" in his head.

2. SIR WINSTON CHURCHILL (1874–1965), British statesman

The man who was to become the most distinguished member of an already illustrious family seemed so dull as a youth that his father thought he might be incapable of earning a living in England.

A hyperactive child, Churchill enjoyed history and literature but refused to study Latin, Greek, or math, and entered Harrow as the rock-bottom student. He improved his standing somewhat over the next four and a half years, but then failed the entrance exams to Sandhurst twice and was taken out of Harrow and placed with a "crammer." He passed the exams on his third try and thereafter encountered few obstacles he could not master.

3. CHARLES DARWIN (1809–1882), English naturalist

The young Darwin did so poorly in a school noted for its classical education that his father once told him, "You care for nothing but shooting, dogs, and rat-catching, and you will be a disgrace to yourself and all your family." After failing dismally in a medical course at Edinburgh University, Darwin languished at Cambridge until his enthusiasm for natural history got him a berth on H.M.S. *Beagle* in 1831. He transformed the voyage into one of history's greatest scientific expeditions, using his findings from the trip to develop his theory of evolution.

4. THOMAS A. EDISON (1847–1931), U.S. inventor

Edison's peculiar inquisitiveness as a young child impressed nobody but his tolerant mother. His first teacher described him as "addled," his father almost convinced him he was a "dunce," and his headmasters warned that he "would never make a success of anything." Under his mother's tutelage, however, Edison became a precocious reader, and he was soon making practical inventions. He eventually patented over a thousand inventions whose worth to humankind is incalculable.

5. PAUL EHRLICH (1854–1915), German bacteriologist

Ehrlich always performed badly at school, and he particularly loathed examinations. He had a flair for microscopic staining work, however, and this carried him through his education despite his ineptness at composition and oral presentations. He eventually used his talent with the microscope to develop the field of chemotherapy, and he was awarded a Nobel Prize in medicine in 1908.

6. ALBERT EINSTEIN (1879–1955), German physicist

Einstein's parents feared their son was retarded because he spoke haltingly until the age of nine and thereafter would respond to questions only after a long period of deliberation. He performed so badly in all high school courses except mathematics that a teacher asked him to drop out, telling him, "You will never amount to anything, Einstein." His enrollment at Zurich's Polytechnic Institute was delayed a year because he failed his entrance exams. Even after graduating from the institute, he had trouble finding and holding a job. Meanwhile, he was formulating his first ideas about the theory of relativity.

7. HENRY FORD (1863–1947), U.S. car manufacturer

Ford made it through school with a minimal grasp of reading and writing, though he did manage to memorize some literary epigrams from McGuffey's *Readers*. However, his ability to fathom the inner workings of machines was evident at an early age. He mended tools on his father's farm and entertained classmates by building waterwheels and steam engines.

8. HEINRICH HEINE (1797–1856), German poet

Despite his mother's counsel to "learn much and be discreet; then no one will be able to take you for a donkey," young Heine performed miserably in his classes at the Franciscan boys' school, particularly in languages. His grasp of German grammar was weak, and he proved equally inept at the tortuous conjugations and declensions of French, Latin, and Greek.

9. GAMAL ABDEL NASSER (1918–1970), Egyptian statesman

Egypt's first president had a dismal school record. From ages 6 to 16, he passed only four grades. He finally managed to graduate from high school, even though his growing obsession with revolutionary politics led to continuous confrontations with his teachers. Dropping out of law school before his first examinations, he then fortuitously enrolled at the Royal Military Academy and graduated as a second lieutenant. In 1952 he led a military coup to oust King Faruk and establish a republic.

10. SIR ISAAC NEWTON (1642–1727), English scientist

The man who now ranks as perhaps the greatest intellect of all time showed little promise as a youth. An idler and mechanical dabbler, Newton was allowed to continue his education only because he proved a complete flop when entrusted with running the family farm. He was then relegated to the lowest form in his school, but he finally snapped out of his mental lethargy when a fight with a bully moved him to better his own standing. His later work in mathematics and physics revolutionized scientific thought.

11. PABLO PICASSO (1881–1973), Spanish painter

Picasso's progress in school was slowed by his refusal to do anything but paint. When his father pulled him out of school at age 10, he could barely read or write. A tutor hired to prepare Picasso for secondary school gave up on the hopeless pupil, who stubbornly refused to learn mathematics. Although he passed his art school examinations with flying colors, he soon quit out of boredom. Afterwards he studied painting on his own in Madrid and Paris, where he struggled several years before making his first impact on the art world.

12. GIACOMO PUCCINI (1858–1924), Italian opera composer

The creator of *Tosca*, *La Bohème*, and *Madame Butterfly* was born into a family of church musicians and was expected to follow the tradition. However, he was utterly unambitious. He did poorly in school and even caused his first music teacher to give up in despair, concluding that he had no talent. Fortunately, the approach of his second music teacher caught his fancy, and from that moment Puccini energetically devoted himself to music.

13. JAMES WATT (1736–1819), Scottish engineer

A lifelong victim of chronic migraine, Watt was a delicate child who was bullied by his classmates and labeled "dull and inept" at his lessons. At 13, however, an interest in geometry launched his rapid intellectual development. He went on to develop the steam engine, thereby helping to start the industrial revolution.

14. ARTHUR WELLESLEY, 1st DUKE OF WELLINGTON (1769–1852), British general and statesman

The frustrated fourth child in a family of high achievers, the young Wellesley did so badly in school that his mother withdrew him from Eton in order to save money for his younger brothers' education. During an additional year of study with a barrister, the only talent he exhibited was for fiddling. Exasperated, his mother pushed him into a military career, believing him to be nothing more than "fit food for [cannon] powder." Unfortunately for Napoleon, Wellesley applied himself so rigorously to his military studies that he eventually rose to the top of the British army.

15. ÉMILE ZOLA (1840–1902), French novelist

Zola passed the Sorbonne's written exams in science and mathematics but failed in the language and literature orals; he forgot the date of Charlemagne's death, he thoroughly botched the German reading test, and he somehow misinterpreted a simple fable. His attempt two months later to enter the University of Marseilles ended even more disastrously; his performance on the written entrance exam was so atrocious that he didn't even take the orals. He lamented in a letter to his friend Paul Cézanne, "I'm a total ignoramus!" Later, be wrote *Nana* and other popular novels, and was the founder of the Naturalist movement in literature.

—R.K.R.

19 PEOPLE WHO WERE EXPELLED OR SUSPENDED FROM SCHOOL

1. GEORGE ARCHER-SHEE (1895–1914)

George was dismissed from the Royal Naval College at Osborne in 1908 for allegedly stealing a five-shilling postal order from a classmate's locker. George's parents took the navy to court. Two years later the boy was cleared of the charge in a celebrated decision. The Archer-Shees were later awarded £4,120 for costs. George was killed in W.W. I while serving in the British Army.

2. JOHN BARRYMORE (1882–1942)

American actor John Barrymore was 16 when he was expelled

from Georgetown Academy in Washington, D.C. A faculty member recognized him, in the company of several other young men, entering a bordello where they had gone to celebrate Washington's Birthday. The next day, when asked to name the other men, Barrymore refused and was expelled.

3. ALEXANDER BERKMAN (1870–1936)

In 1885 Polish-born American anarchist Alexander Berkman was expelled from secondary school in Vilnius, Lithuania, for "precocious godlessness, dangerous tendencies, and insubordination" after he wrote an essay on the nonexistence of God.

4. SARAH BERNHARDT (1844–1923)

At about the age of 16, French actress Sarah Bernhardt was three times suspended from a Catholic convent school in Paris, France. The reasons: making fun of a bishop, throwing rocks at French cavalrymen, and spending an unchaperoned evening with a soldier until well after dark.

Former juvenile delinquent Sarah Bernhardt

5. HUMPHREY BOGART (1899–1957)

The son of a successful physician with inherited wealth, young Bogart was sent to Phillips Academy at Andover, Mass., and after a year was thrown out for "irreverence" and "uncontrollable high spirits." Since attending Yale was suddenly out of the question, Bogie joined the U.S. Navy.

6. RICHARD BOONE (1917–   )

Boone's career at Stanford came to an end in 1937, when he and his Theta Xi fraternity brothers devised an ingenious prank. They fashioned a dummy out of rags and bottles and laid it down in the street. When the next passing car ran over it, Boone cried out, "You've killed my brother!" Unfortunately, the car's driver was Mrs. Herbert Hoover, who sprained her ankle during the resultant confusion. Boone later became an actor, best known for his role as Paladin in the TV series *Have Gun, Will Travel*.

7. GENEVIEVE BUJOLD (1942–   )

At age 15, Bujold was expelled from a convent school when she was caught reading a blacklisted copy of Marcel Pagnol's play *Fanny*. The following year the actress embarked upon her film career by entering Quebec's Conservatory of Drama.

8. SALVADOR DALI (1904–   )

In 1926 Spanish ultramodernist painter Salvador Dali was expelled from the Escuela Nacional de Bellas Artes de San Fernando in Madrid when he refused to allow his professors to critique his paintings.

9. JAMES NEGLEY FARSON (1890–1960)

In 1908 American writer and foreign correspondent James Negley Farson was expelled from Phillips Academy for helping to throw a "tattling" instructor into a duck pond. The instructor had been responsible for the expulsion of Farson's roommate.

10. WILLIAM RANDOLPH HEARST (1863–1951)

In 1885 American newspaper publisher William Randolph Hearst was expelled from Harvard, halfway through his junior year. He had given each of his professors a chamber pot adorned with the professor's name and picture.

11. EDWARD KENNEDY (1932–   )

In 1951, during his freshman year when he was eager to be eligible for the football team, Sen. Edward Kennedy was suspended from Harvard for cheating. It was discovered that a friend had taken a Spanish test for him.

12. BENITO MUSSOLINI (1883–1945)

At age nine, Mussolini was sent 20 mi. from home to a boarding school in Faenza, Italy, run by Salesian priests. The recalcitrant youth was nearly expelled for throwing an inkpot at a teacher who had struck him with a ruler. Finally he went too far—he stabbed a fellow student in the buttocks with a knife. The future dictator was permanently dismissed.

13. EDGAR ALLAN POE (1809–1849)

In 1831 American author and poet Edgar Allan Poe was expelled from West Point when he refused to attend drills and classes for several weeks.

14. JODY POWELL (1943–   )

In 1964, six months before his scheduled graduation from the Air Force Academy in Colorado, Powell—who later became President Jimmy Carter's press secretary—was expelled for cheating on his final exam in the history of military thought. Powell reflected, "You don't know what loneliness is until you drive into your driveway at home, in the Deep South, on Christmas Eve, having just had your ass booted out of a military academy."

15. PERCY BYSSHE SHELLEY (1792–1822)

In 1811, while a student at Oxford, the poet Shelley and his close friend Thomas Jefferson Hogg sent a pamphlet entitled "The Necessity of Atheism," a summary of the arguments of John Locke and David Hume, to the heads of the colleges. When both students refused to answer questions about the pamphlet, they were summarily expelled.

16. PHILIP SHERIDAN (1831–1888)

In 1852, during his senior year at West Point, the future Union Civil War general Philip Sheridan was suspended for a year for assaulting a cadet sergeant.

17. WILLIAM TRAVIS (1809–1836)

At about the age of 16, Col. William Travis, the American commander of Texan forces at the Alamo, was expelled from a South Carolina military academy for inciting the student body to revolt against their instructors and teachers.

18. LEON TROTSKY (1879–1940)

At approximately the age of 10, Russian Communist leader Leon Trotsky was expelled from secondary school in Odessa, Russia, after he incited his classmates to howl at their teacher. Trotsky, however, was the school's best pupil and was readmitted the following year.

19. ORVILLE WRIGHT (1871–1948)

In 1883, during the sixth grade, American inventor and aviator Orville Wright was expelled from his elementary school in Richmond, Ind., for mischievous behavior.

—R.J.F. & The Eds.

14
YOU'RE IN THE MONEY

10 UNUSUAL OBJECTS
OFFERED AT AUCTION

1. GEORGE WASHINGTON'S LAUNDRY BILL

A laundry bill belonging to George Washington, dated 1787, was sold at auction for $1,100. The story goes that Washington hired a lady named Mary Firth to do his laundry—providing, of course, that she purchase her own soap. The document was signed by George Washington and two of his colonels.

2. SWEDENBORG'S SKULL

The skull of Swedish philosopher Emanuel Swedenborg sold at Sotheby Parke Bernet, London, on March 6, 1977, for $2,850. The Swede died in 1772. The skull was purchased by a professor at the Royal Swedish Academy of Science. His reason for purchase: to reunite the skull with its dear departed skeleton in Uppsala, Sweden.

3. PART OF THE LAMB THAT MARY HAD

An autographed manuscript of Sarah Josepha Hale's beloved child's poem "Mary Had a Little Lamb" was offered for sale at Sotheby Parke Bernet, New York, in January, 1975. Also offered were a piece of wool from the lamb that inspired the poem; an autographed manuscript by Mary E. Tyler, for whom the poem was written; a letter from Mrs. Hale's son, Horatio, affirming that his mother wrote the poem; a letter from Mary Tyler authenticating the lamb's wool and how the poem came to be; and a book by Mary E. Tyler and Fannie Dickerson containing the true story of Mary and her lamb. The poem is three pages long, signed, and dated Philadelphia, January 23, 1865. The only known manuscript completed by Mrs. Hale, it was estimated to sell at from $5,000 to $10,000. It didn't sell.

4. LONDON BRIDGE

The London Bridge was put up at auction in 1968 and purchased by McCulloch [oil] Corporation for $2,460,000. It was shipped in 10,000 granite blocks to Lake Havasu City, Ariz., where it was reerected over a channel of Lake Havasu. The new London Bridge was completed in 1973.

5. 180,000 DEAD CATS

In 1890, a firm by the name of Leventon & Co., of Liverpool, England, sold a lot of 180,000 Egyptian mummified cats from a burial ground near Beni Hasaan for 3.15 shillings per ton.

London Bridge . . . spending its retirement in Arizona.

6. PICTURE TAKER

The earliest known photograph of a photographer taking a photograph was sold at auction at Christie's, South Kensington, London, in March, 1977. The quarter-plate daguerreotype shows Jebez Hogg taking a photograph in his studio in 1842 or 1843. The previous record price for a daguerreotype was set in 1973, when a portrait of Edgar Allan Poe sold for $9,000. Jebez Hogg sold for $9,860.

7. OUTHOUSE

A one-seater, 19th-century, oak outhouse sold at auction at a New England sale in 1975. Why would anybody want an old outhouse? The new owner said it would be great for making picture frames. He purchased the outhouse for $140.

8. A STICKY SITUATION

The Americana Mail Auction in November, 1975, offered for sale a Coca-Cola gum wrapper, c. 1908. The wrapper measures 2½ in. in length. It is red with the words "Coca-Cola Gum, Spearmint Flavor" in white. It sold for $90.

9. TWO HEADS ARE BETTER THAN ONE

In 1976 the shrunken head of a South American Jivaro tribesman sold for $9,350 at Christie's. In 1977 Christie's sold the preserved head of a Maori from New Zealand for $20,400. Both heads were from the Hooper collection.

10. JUDY'S FALSE EYELASHES

In 1979 Sid Luft, former husband of the late Judy Garland, held an auction of Miss Garland's personal items in Beverly Hills, Calif. The sale brought in $250,000, including $125 for Miss Garland's false eyelashes.

—J.G.

25 VERY ODD JOBS

1. BELLY BUILDER
Assembles and fits interior parts, or the belly, of pianos.

2. BONE CRUSHER
Tends the machine that crushes animal bones that are used in the manufacture of glue.

3. BOSOM PRESSER
Clothing presser who specializes in pressing bosoms of blouses and shirts.

4. BRAIN PICKER
Places animal head on a table or on hooks in a slaughterhouse, splits the skull, and picks out the brains.

5. BREAST BUFFER
Buffs and smooths the shoe breast, which is the forepart of the heel.

6. CHICK SEXER
Inserts a light to examine the sex organs of chicks, then separates the males from the females. A university degree in chick sexing is offered in Japan.

7. DOPE SPRAYER
Sprays a solution, known as dope, on tanned hides in leather manufacturing.

8. DUKEY RIDER
Couples and uncouples cars being moved in a railroad yard. Rides cars and turns hand brakes to control speed.

9. EGG SMELLER
Smells eggs after they are broken open to check for spoilage.

10. FINGER WAVER
Hairdresser who sets waves in with fingers.

11. FOOT STRAIGHTENER
Straightens and screws into place the feet on watch and clock dials during assembly.

12. HEEL GOUGER
Tends the machine that cuts a cavity to form the seat for a heel in shoe manufacturing.

13. HOG HEAD SINGER

Singes hair from heads of hog carcasses in slaughterhouse with a torch.

14. HOOKER INSPECTOR

Inspects cloth in a textile mill for defects by using a hooking machine which folds the cloth.

15. KISS MIXER

Mixes the ingredients used in processing candy kisses.

16. LEGEND MAKER

Arranges and mounts letters, logos, and numbers on paper backing to make signs and displays.

17. MOTHER REPAIRER

Repairs metal phonograph record "mother" by removing dirt and nickel particles from sound-track grooves. Records are mass-produced by being pressed from the metal mother record.

18. MUCKER

Shovels muck and other debris from work areas and ditches around construction sites and in mines.

19. NECKER

Feeds cardboard and fabric into a machine that wraps them around each other to form the neck of a jewelry box. The neck is the filler between the case and the fabric lining.

20. PANTYHOSE-CROTCH-CLOSING-MACHINE OPERATOR

Operates machine that sews pantyhose crotches closed.

21. SLUBBER DOFFER

Doffs bobbins of yarn from spindles of slubber frames in a textile mill.

22. SQUEEGEE TENDER

Tends a band-building machine that rolls squeegee, or bands of rubber, and gum strips together in tire manufacturing.

23. TOP SCREW

Supervises cowboys—called screws.

24. VAMP CREASER

Tends the machine that creases shoe vamps, the part of the shoe over the instep.

25. WOOD-CLUB-NECK WHIPPER

Uses a machine to wind nylon cord around the neck of a wood golf club during its manufacture.

—J.F.M.

12 HIGHEST-PRESSURE JOBS IN THE U.S.

In a two-year study conducted by NIOSH (National Institute for Occupational Safety and Health) in cooperation with the Tennessee Dept. of Mental Health and Mental Retardation, over 22,000 health records of workers in 130 occupations were analyzed with respect to stress-related diseases. The frequency with which these diseases occurred in the various occupations resulted in the following determination of the highest- and lowest-stress jobs.

1. Manual laborer
2. Secretary
3. Inspector
4. Waitress-waiter
5. Clinical lab technician
6. Farm owner
7. Miner
8. Office manager
9. House painter
10. Manager-administrator
11. Foreman
12. Machine operator

SOURCE: *Occupational Stress*, U.S. Dept. of Health, Education, and Welfare, National Institute for Occupational Safety and Health, 1978.

13 LOWEST-PRESSURE JOBS IN THE U.S.

1. Clothing sewer
2. Checker, examiner of products
3. Stockroom worker
4. Craftsman
5. Maid
6. Heavy-equipment operator
7. Farm laborer
8. Freight handler
9. Child care worker
10. Packer, wrapper in shipping
11. College or university professor
12. Personnel, labor relations
13. Auctioneer-huckster

SOURCE: *Occupational Stress*, U.S. Dept. of Health, Education, and Welfare, National Institute for Occupational Safety and Health, 1978.

PERCENTAGE OF WOMEN
IN 25 JOBS

		Percent Female
1.	Secretaries	99.1
2.	Housekeepers	97.9
3.	Dental assistants	97.8
4.	Prekindergarten and kindergarten teachers	97.4
5.	Cleaners and servants	97.3
6.	Receptionists	97.2
7.	Registered nurses	96.8
8.	Dressmakers	95.4
9.	Keypunch operators	95.3
10.	Telephone operators	91.7
11.	Social workers	64.3
12.	Cooks	56.0
13.	Building managers and superintendents	50.0
14.	Real estate agents and brokers	49.4
15.	Bus drivers	45.5
16.	Editors and reporters	42.3
17.	Dishwashers	33.2
18.	Lawyers	12.8
19.	Dentists	4.6
20.	Electricians	1.3
21.	Automobile mechanics	.6
22.	Fire fighters	.4
23.	Plumbers and pipefitters	.4
24.	Air conditioning, heating and refrigeration mechanics	.0
25.	Roofers and slaters	.0

SOURCE: *Employment and Earnings, 1980.* Bureau of Labor Statistics, U.S. Dept. of Labor.

PERCENTAGE OF
NONWHITES IN 25 JOBS

		Percent Nonwhite*
1.	Cleaners and servants	54.0
2.	Housekeepers	44.3
3.	Clothing ironers and pressers	39.7
4.	Welfare service aides	34.0
5.	Garbage collectors	32.3
6.	Nursing aides, orderlies, and attendants	30.6

		Percent Nonwhite*
7.	Cement and concrete finishers	29.3
8.	Metal furnace tenders, smelters, and pourers	29.0
9.	Taxicab drivers and chauffeurs	28.0
10.	Farm laborers	20.9
11.	Prekindergarten and kindergarten teachers	14.1
12.	Truck drivers	13.3
13.	Chemists	11.2
14.	Physicians	10.7
15.	Clergy	9.2
16.	Sheriffs and bailiffs	8.8
17.	Athletes	4.8
18.	Real estate agents and brokers	2.8
19.	Farmers	2.6
20.	Lawyers	2.5
21.	Surveyors	2.4
22.	Office managers	2.2
23.	Credit and collection managers	1.8
24.	Locomotive engineers	1.8
25.	Airplane pilots	1.4

* Nonwhites are defined as blacks, American Indians, Alaskan natives, Asian and Pacific islanders, and "others." (Hispanics are not included.) They represent 14% of the U.S. population and 11.2% of all employed persons.

SOURCE: *Employment and Earnings, 1980.* Bureau of Labor Statistics, U.S. Dept. of Labor.

17 MAJOR CORPORATIONS THAT PAID NO FEDERAL INCOME TAXES IN THE U.S. IN 1977

Each year Rep. Charles A. Vanik of Ohio releases a corporate tax study that reveals the effective tax rate paid by the nation's largest businesses.

		Worldwide Income	Federal Income Taxes Paid
1.	Commonwealth Edison	$361,589,000	$0
2.	American Electric Power	333,403,000	0
3.	Southern California Edison	317,174,000	0
4.	Rockwell International	266,700,000	0
5.	First Chicago Corp.	152,113,000	0
6.	Esmark	97,999,000	0

	Worldwide Income	Federal Income Taxes Paid
7. Seaboard Coastline Industries	97,263,000	0
8. Inland Steel	88,507,000	0
9. United States Steel	87,200,000	0
10. American Airlines	83,089,000	0
11. National Steel	45,806,000	0
12. Eastern Airlines	34,737,000	0
13. Republic Steel	33,848,000	0
14. Pan American World Airways	33,489,000	0
15. United Brands	17,714,000	0
16. American Motors	5,616,000	0
17. A & P	5,046,000	0

In 1977 Rockwell International received a refund, at taxpayers' expense, of $115,300,000. U.S. Steel received $113,400,000. The big oil companies paid an average tax rate of 11% while the largest banks paid an average rate of 7.1%. Although the legal tax rate for corporations is 48%, in actuality the average corporation pays only 17.2%, the same rate as that for a family of four with an annual income of $26,150.

WASTING THE TAXPAYERS' MONEY—14 WINNERS OF THE GOLDEN FLEECE AWARD

In March, 1975, Sen. William Proxmire of Wisconsin instituted a monthly Golden Fleece Award to be given to "the biggest, most ridiculous, or most ironic example of government spending or waste." Here is a selection of the winners.

1. CONGRESS

In 1975 the House of Representatives allocated $1.3 million to automate 19 elevators but retained operators to run them. Not to be outdone, the Senate, which already had automated elevators with human operators, began construction on a $122 million Senate office building. The building, which is already four years behind schedule with a cost overrun of over 154%, includes a senators-only dining room with a rooftop view. The senators already have two dining rooms.

2. FEDERAL AVIATION ADMINISTRATION

For a $57,800 study of the body measurements of American Airlines stewardess trainees. Seventy-nine separate measurements were made of each woman, including the skinfold of the posterior calf, the length of the buttocks, and the height of the nose. The study was supposedly done to aid in the design of safety equipment, but one wonders why the taxpayers had to foot the bill instead of the airlines or the aircraft manufacturers.

3. DEPARTMENT OF THE NAVY

During the September, 1974, reunion of the Tailhook Association, a private, nongovernmental organization, the Navy Dept. provided 64 aircraft to fly 1,334 officers to the Hilton Hotel in Las Vegas. The flights cost more than $191,000 in tax funds and wasted 347,000 gallons of fuel. The navy also spent $537,000 to repair and refurnish "the official temporary residence of the Vice-President of the United States," who at that time was Nelson Rockefeller. Expenditures included $26,400 for drapes, $21,200 for silverware, and $10,400 for china.

4. FRANK ZARB, ADMINISTRATOR OF THE FEDERAL ENERGY ADMINISTRATION

In 1975 Mr. Zarb spent $25,000 and used almost 19,000 gallons of fuel flying around the country as he gave speeches to business and civic groups about the need to conserve energy. At least half of his trips were made in a plush air force jet that burned enough fuel in one hour to supply the average American driver with gasoline to drive for an entire year.

5. DEPARTMENT OF THE AIR FORCE

The air force maintains a $66 million fleet of 23 ultrafirst-class jets, known as the 89th Military Airlift Wing. The fleet's sole purpose is to transport top government officials at an annual cost to taxpayers of $6 million. The 89th makes 1,000 flights a year, although in almost every case commercial flights are available to the same destination. About 87% of the flights are made for officials of the Dept. of Defense. The air force also gets special notice for its $3,100 study in 1978–1979 to determine whether male airmen should be allowed to use umbrellas while in uniform.

6. NATIONAL AERONAUTICS AND SPACE ADMINISTRATION (NASA)

For requesting $2.8 million to construct a new home for 100 lb. of moon rocks that already inhabit a perfectly adequate $8.7 million concrete structure at the Johnson Space Center in Houston.

7. ARMY CORPS OF ENGINEERS

For the worst record of cost overruns in the entire federal government. Of the 178 major civilian construction projects under way in December, 1976, 83 were over budget by at least 100%. Record setters in the flood-control program were Cooper Lake in Texas—up 325%; Fire Island Inlet in New York—up 325%; and New Orleans to Venice Hurricane Protection in Louisiana—up 1,027%.

8. LAW ENFORCEMENT ASSISTANCE ADMINISTRATION

For spending nearly $27,000 to determine why inmates want to escape from prison. Need we say more? Yes. The LEAA, which is in drastic need of abolition, also spent $2 million to build a police patrol car prototype, complete with wide-angle periscope rearview mirror. Unfortunately, the car is so expensive to produce that local police forces can't afford it.

9. U.S. POSTAL SERVICE

For spending $3.4 million of tax funds on an advertising campaign to encourage Americans to write more letters to one another despite the fact that all classes of mail, including first-class, are operating at a financial loss. The postal service then spent $775,000 to test the results of its ad campaign.

10. FEDERAL DEPOSIT INSURANCE CORPORATION

While Robert E. Barnett was chairman of the FDIC from March, 1976, to May, 1977, agency vehicles and employees were used to transport Mrs. Barnett and her children to the doctor, the museum, and the beach. The FDIC also paid Mr. Barnett's membership fees in a private tennis club in Virginia.

11. NATIONAL INSTITUTE FOR MENTAL HEALTH

For funding a study of behavior and social relationships in a Peruvian brothel. The study was part of a $97,000 grant to a researcher and his assistant. Ironically, the researcher had previously authored a book called *Academic Gamesmanship*. In it he notes that "not all disciplines are in an equally good position to milk the government and foundations." Later he advises, "And, if your research calls for going overseas, you can lead the life of an oriental potentate with an American income in a low-cost-of-living country. Should you remain an expatriate for 18 months or more, you even get a $20,000 tax exemption." The author's stay in Peru, at the taxpayers' expense, lasted 18 months.

12. DEPARTMENT OF DEFENSE

Deep within the budget of the Pentagon is a little-noticed financial category called "Emergencies and Extraordinary Expenses." Included in these "extraordinary" expenses is a $1.2 million annual fund for entertainment and social events. Among the events subsidized by the taxpayers in 1977–1978: a tea party for wives of the Standing Consultative Committee for SALT ($107); a visit from the commander of the Mexican air force, including a trip to Disneyland ($3,284.19); and walnut plaques for the USAF Independence Day Air Attaché Golf Tournament ($2,158.60). Farewell parties are very popular. In one case a retiring official was given a party *by* his colleagues, with full expenses of $176 charged to the taxpayers. Several days later the same official gave a party *for* his friends at a cost of $271.80, charging it, once again, to the taxpayers.

13. NATIONAL HIGHWAY TRAFFIC SAFETY ADMINISTRATION

For spending $120,126 on a dangerously low-slung backward-steering motorcycle that everyone said couldn't work—and didn't. The firm that received the contract tried to cancel it after concluding that the design was useless, but the administration insisted that work

285

continue. When the final product proved a failure, as expected, the NHTSA began work on the equally useless and dangerous low-slung *front*-steering motorcycle.

14. DEPARTMENT OF HOUSING AND URBAN DEVELOPMENT and ECONOMIC DEVELOPMENT ADMINISTRATION

HUD and the EDA spent $279,000 on a community center built in such a remote and isolated spot in the Michigan woods that when it collapsed in February, 1979, no one knew about it for days. HUD had put up $100,000 to construct the center between two small towns in a location with no access road. EDA began building a road but ran out of money. So the center sat, unfinished and unused, for almost three years, until a sharp-eyed woodsman noticed it had fallen down and reported it to the local postmaster.

And an Award of Merit

SMITHSONIAN INSTITUTION

For building its Air and Space Museum on time and under budget. The museum opened four days early, on July 1, 1976, and cost $500,000 *less* than its projected cost when authorized 10 years earlier. In addition, it contained four major features not provided for in the original plans: a large theater, a planetarium, an art gallery, and facilities for handicapped visitors.

—D.W.

10 FAMOUS PEOPLE WHO WERE —OR ARE—DENTISTS

1. GEORGE W. BEERS (1825–1903)

In 1867 he created the official set of rules for lacrosse.

2. EDGAR BUCHANAN (1902–1979)

This American character actor starred in the TV series *Petticoat Junction*, which ran from 1963 to 1969.

3. ZANE GREY (1875–1939)

Before he attended dental school, this U.S. novelist was a "traveling tooth puller" and treated patients in small towns—at the same time that he played baseball for a Baltimore, O., team. In 1892 Grey entered the University of Pennsylvania, graduated in 1896, and opened his first dental office in 1898 in New York. However, he quit dentistry in 1904 to write full time. Grey's most popular western novel was *Riders of the Purple Sage*.

4. DOC HOLLIDAY (1851–1887)

A notorious gunslinger of the Old West, Holliday first practiced dentistry in Atlanta, Ga., then in Griffin, Ga. In 1873 he moved his office to Dallas, Tex., hoping to improve his poor health. A victim of tuberculosis, Holliday suffered from a chronic cough that scared away many patients. He was arrested for the first time in 1875, after which his medical career ended.

5. ALLAN JONES (1907–)

This American singing star appeared in films like *A Night at the Opera* (1935), *Showboat* (1936), and *When Johnny Comes Marching Home* (1943).

6. MAHLON LOOMIS (1826–1886)

A pioneer in wireless telegraphy, Loomis transmitted the first aerial wireless signals a distance of 18 mi. in 1868, thus beating Marconi by 27 years. He patented his discovery in 1872 but was unable to make further refinements due to a lack of money.

7. CARY MIDDLECOFF (1921–)

A professional golfer, Middlecoff won the U.S. Open in 1949 and 1956 and the Masters Tournament in 1955.

8. CHARLES WILLSON PEALE (1741–1827)

Peale was an 18th-century portrait artist who painted George Washington.

9. PAUL REVERE (1735–1818)

He rode from Charlestown to Lexington in 1775 to warn American colonists of the approach of British troops—a feat immortalized in Longfellow's poem "Paul Revere's Ride." In 1768, however, he was a practicing dentist in Boston, who advertised his services in the Boston *Gazette*. He gave up his practice in 1783, after the American Revolution, to engage in the manufacture of silverware.

10. THOMAS WELCH (1825–1903)

He originated unfermented, bottled grape juice and founded the Welch Grape Juice Co.

—R.T.

6 CELEBRATED PEOPLE WHO ONCE WORKED AS TELEPHONE OPERATORS

1. Amanda Blake (1929–), U.S. actress
2. Dorothy Kirsten (1919–), U.S. opera singer
3. Doris Lessing (1919–), British author
4. Patricia Nixon (1912–), U.S. first lady
5. Aristotle Onassis (1906–1975), Greek shipping magnate
6. Margaret Chase Smith (1897–), U.S. politician

—The Eds.

Former telephone operator Patricia Nixon in 1937.

12 RENOWNED PEOPLE WHO WORKED FOR INSURANCE COMPANIES

1. George Eastman (1854–1932), U.S. inventor and industrialist
2. Charles Ives (1874–1954), U.S. composer
3. Wallace Stevens (1879–1955), U.S. poet
4. Franklin Pierce Adams (1881–1960), U.S. journalist
5. Franz Kafka (1883–1924), Austrian novelist
6. Col. Harland Sanders (1890–   ), U.S. franchiser of Kentucky Fried Chicken
7. Warner Baxter (1892–1951), U.S. actor
8. Warren E. Burger (1907–   ), U.S. jurist and chief justice of the Supreme Court
9. Mildred "Babe" Didrikson Zaharias (1914–1956), U.S. athlete
10. Spiro Agnew (1918–   ), U.S. vice-president
11. Medgar Evers (1925–1963), U.S. civil rights leader
12. Jody Powell (1943–   ), U.S. press secretary to President Jimmy Carter

—The Eds.

THE ORIGINAL PROFESSIONS OF 15 NAZI LEADERS

1. MARTIN BORMANN (1900?–1945),
   deputy chief of Nazi party

   Farm estate manager.

2. ADOLF EICHMANN (1906–1962),
   head of the Jewish office of the Gestapo

   Traveling salesman for the Vacuum Oil Company of Austria.

3. HANS FRANK (1900–1946), Nazi commissioner of justice
   and governor-general of occupied Poland

   Industrial lawyer and law professor.

4. WILHELM FRICK (1877–1946), Nazi minister of interior

   Bavarian police officer and informer for Hitler.

5. WALTHER FUNK (1890–1960), Reichsbank president

   Financial newspaper editor.

6. JOSEPH GOEBBELS (1897–1945), Nazi propaganda minister

   Bank clerk, bookkeeper, tutor, floorman on Cologne stock
   exchange, playwright, poet.

7. HERMANN GÖRING (1893–1946), air force minister and
   president of war economy council

   W.W. I fighter ace, Swedish airlines pilot, technical consultant
   for Lufthansa.

8. RUDOLF HESS (1894–   ), deputy chief of Nazi party

   Business wholesaler and exporter, German army officer.

9. REINHARD HEYDRICH (1904–1942),
   deputy chief of Gestapo

   Unemployed German Navy Intelligence officer who had been
   court-martialed and cashiered for having an affair with a teenage
   girl.

10. HEINRICH HIMMLER (1900–1945),
    commander of SS and Gestapo

    Chicken farmer.

11. ADOLF HITLER (1889–1945), Führer of Third Reich

    Architect's draftsman, commercial artist, German army cor-
    poral.

12. RUDOLF HÖSS (1900–1947), commandant of Auschwitz

    German army sergeant, murderer, ex-convict, farm laborer.

13. JOACHIM VON RIBBENTROP (1893–1946), Nazi minister
    of foreign affairs

    Wine and spirits importer, free-lance journalist.

14. ERNST RÖHM (1887–1934),
    Nazi commander of SA (Storm Troopers)

    German army officer.

15. ALFRED ROSENBERG (1893–1946), Nazi commissioner of occupied Eastern Europe

Artist, architect, journalist.

—R.J.F.

15 FAMOUS GURUS AND THEIR FORMER JOBS

1. SRI AUROBINDO (1872–1950), Indian founder of the Vedanta Society

After an extensive education in England, Aurobindo returned to India and became a lecturer in French and a professor of English at Baroda College. During this time he was a noted poet and served as coeditor of the *Bandemataram,* a paper that became the mouthpiece of the Indian nationalist movement. He published two more nationalist papers, the *Karmayogin* and the *Dharma,* before political pressures forced him to flee to Pondicherry, where he established his ashram.

2. YOGI BHAJAN (1929–   ), Sikh religious leader

After working as a bodyguard for the president of India, Bhajan became a captain in the Indian Army. He then served as an intelligence officer in the customs service. Traveling to Canada in 1968, he worked in a factory in Montreal. Before long he had founded 3HO (Healthy, Happy, Holy Organization) and become the best-known exponent of the Sikh religion in America.

3. ELENA PETROVNA BLAVATSKY (1831–1891), Russian cofounder of the Theosophical Society

The high-strung Russian mystic claimed that she reaped a fortune selling ostrich feathers in Africa in the 1850s. Returning to Russia, she supported herself and her lover in the late 1860s by making and selling artificial flowers. In 1873 she sailed to the U.S., where she designed advertising cards for a shirt and collar factory before establishing the Theosophical Society with Henry Steel Olcott in 1875.

4. WERNER ERHARD (1935–   ), U.S. founder of est

Born John Paul Rosenberg, Erhard worked as a construction supervisor after graduating from high school. About 1960 he moved to St. Louis, Mo., and became a used-car dealer operating under the business name of Jack Frost. Another move took him to California, where he established himself as a top-notch door-to-door encyclopedia salesman for Parents Cultural Institute of *Parents' Magazine.* He became a vice-president at the institute in 1967. When it went out of business in 1969, he landed a job as division manager for Grolier Society, Inc., another encyclopedia sales company. He left Grolier in 1971 to found est.

5. GEORGE IVANOVITCH GURDJIEFF (1872–1949), Russian mystic

As a young man, Gurdjieff worked at many jobs, including train stoker, ship's hand, hypnotist, corset merchant, organizer of cattle drives, and trader in carpets and antiques. He made money at whatever he turned his hand to. One of his more ingenious schemes was selling live sparrows, dyed and clipped to look like American canaries. In addition, it is rumored that he spent a decade in Tibet, serving as a Russian spy and tutoring the Dalai Lama.

6. L. RON HUBBARD (1911–   ), U.S. founder of the Church of Scientology

In the 1930s, Hubbard wrote westerns for pulp magazines, using the name Winchester Remington Colt. He switched to the field of science fiction after W.W. II and published nearly 80 stories under the pseudonyms of Kurt Von Rachen and René Lafayette. His best-known SF was published under his own name.

7. JIM JONES (1931–1978), U.S. founder of the Peoples Temple

Jones worked as an orderly at Reid Memorial Hospital in Richmond, Ind., and served briefly as a Methodist pastor before establishing his own church in 1953. He helped finance his church by selling monkeys door to door. After four years as the Indianapolis human relations commissioner, he moved to California, and in 1976 he was appointed chairman of the San Francisco Housing Authority by Mayor George Moscone. The following year Jones left for Guyana.

8. MAHARISHI MAHESH YOGI (1918–   ), Indian founder of Transcendental Meditation

In 1940 the maharishi earned a bachelor's degree in physics from Allahabad University. After graduation he immersed himself in the study of spiritual science, and in 1955 he began the TM movement.

9. MEHER BABA (1894–1969), Indian mystic

While still a young boy in Poona, India, Meher Baba earned

Mystery writer Meher Baba at age 19 in 1913.

a small amount of money writing mystery stories that were published in England's *Union Jack* magazine. He went on to attend Deccan College and at age 19 met Hazrat Babajan, an elderly Muslim woman who became his first spiritual teacher.

10. SUN MYUNG MOON (1920–),
Korean founder of the Unification Church

Educated at Tokyo's Waseda University, Moon worked as an engineer before founding his underground church in North Korea in 1946. After several years in a Communist concentration camp, he fled to South Korea and earned money as a dock worker from 1950 to 1954 while developing his religious philosophy.

11. PETER DEMIANOVITCH OUSPENSKY (1878–1947),
Russian mystic

After studying math at Moscow University, Ouspensky became a noted journalist and author. In 1909 he published *The Fourth Dimension*, a critically acclaimed book dealing with abstract mathematical concepts.

12. SWAMI PRABHUPADA (1896–1977), Indian founder of the International Society for Krishna Consciousness

A graduate of Calcutta University, Prabhupada managed a large pharmaceutical firm in Calcutta, then began his own highly successful chemical factory in Allahabad. Although he became a spiritual leader in the 1930s, he remained in the pharmaceutical business until 1954.

13. BABA RAM DASS (1931–),
U.S. teacher of Hindu mysticism

Born Richard Alpert, he obtained his Ph.D. in psychology and taught at Stanford University, the University of California at Berkeley, and Harvard. In 1963 he was dismissed from Harvard for allegedly involving undergraduates in experiments with the drug psilocybin.

14. SWAMI SATCHIDANANDA (1914–), Indian mystic

Born into a wealthy family, Satchidananda was a prosperous businessman who managed machine shops, worked in the automobile and motion picture industries, and supervised factories. When his wife died, he abandoned his business interests and devoted himself to the attainment of spiritual enlightenment.

15. ALAN WATTS (1915–1973),
British writer and lecturer on Zen Buddhism

In 1945 Watts received a theological degree from Chicago's Northwestern University. He was ordained an Episcopal priest and served at the Northwestern campus until he left the church in 1950. Six months later he affiliated himself with the American Academy of Asian Studies in San Francisco, where he functioned as a teacher and an administrator during the next six years.

—J.HU. & the Eds.

10 SMALL BUSINESSES
MOST LIKELY TO SUCCEED

To determine which businesses are the most likely to succeed—or fail—in today's economy, *Money* magazine polled 26 bankers, business school professors, Small Business Administration officials, members of the Service Corps of Retired Executives, and executives of small business investment companies across the U.S. These people were given a list of the 81 most common small businesses and asked to select candidates for success and failure. (All figures cited represent pretax profits after allowing for salaries.)

1. BUILDING MATERIALS STORES

Due to increased residential construction and do-it-yourself repairs, sales have increased significantly since 1973 and are expected to continue to increase.

2. AUTO TIRE AND ACCESSORIES STORES

Today's car owners are doing more and more repairs themselves, which should help produce a healthy growth rate.

3. LIQUOR STORES

A hardworking retailer can expect something over 3% profit on each dollar of sales.

4. SPORTS AND RECREATION CLUBS

The growing interest in exercise is the key to future profits. A club requires a large initial investment and annual fees of about $1 million to turn about a $26,000 profit.

5. FUNERAL HOMES AND CREMATORIES

Small establishments make roughly $9,200 on every $100,000 they take in. Despite a decreasing death rate, the number of deaths remains around 1.9 million a year and is expected to increase with the senior citizen population.

6. SEED AND GARDEN SUPPLY STORES

The profit ratio is the same as for sports clubs.

7. SPORTING GOODS MANUFACTURERS

Greater participation in outdoor sports is producing estimated growth ranging from 8% a year for bicycle and bicycle parts producers to 19% for the makers of equipment for team sports and snow and water skiing.

8. ENGINEERING, LABORATORY, AND SCIENTIFIC EQUIPMENT

For the period 1980–1983, these industries are expected to grow at an average real growth rate of 5%. Much of this growth is expected to result from increases in aircraft production and the development and operation of the space shuttle.

9. HARDWARE STORES

Hardware stores also benefit from increasing numbers of do-it-yourselfers. High profit margins mean that hardware stores don't need huge sales volume; $650,000 in sales will produce $30,000 in profits.

10. OFFICE SUPPLIES AND EQUIPMENT

This business is remarkably resistant to recession, because a firm always needs office supplies. Profits are substantial; every $1 million in sales can return $40,000.

SOURCE: Research by Ed Henry, *Money* magazine. © 1978, Time Inc. Used by permission of the publisher.

10 SMALL BUSINESSES MOST LIKELY TO FAIL

1. LOCAL LAUNDRIES AND DRY CLEANERS

Since 1972, improved home laundry systems and the increasing use of synthetic fabrics have slowed growth in this business. Older, established cleaners have stayed alive by providing extra services.

2. USED-CAR DEALERSHIPS

Banks have generally soured on making loans to used-car dealers and their customers because of the high risk involved. Current predictions show the business shrinking.

3. GAS STATIONS

Competition and thinning profits have tarnished these once lucrative franchises. To earn $30,000 a year, a station would have to gross about $1.8 million.

4. LOCAL TRUCKING FIRMS

The high cost of unionized labor and governmental regulation make this a risky enterprise. Growth prospects are sluggish.

5. RESTAURANTS

Growth potential in opening a restaurant is good, and profits aren't bad, about 3.5% if you are successful. Still, "for every one that succeeds, probably a dozen fail for lack of management know-how," says Sam Siciliano, a Small Business Administration official.

6. INFANTS' CLOTHING STORES

Babies are not booming, and retail clothing stores, particularly small independent ones, are encountering stiff competition.

7. BAKERIES

Supermarket bakery departments make survival tough for independent stores. Shops that make it do so by offering specialized services.

8. MACHINE SHOPS

Over 5,000 independent shops make this business highly competitive. Each $100,000 in sales yields an average $3,300 in pretax profits.

9. GROCERY AND MEAT STORES

Unless these stores offer special services, like delivery, the going gets rough.

10. CAR WASHES

High turnover, strong competition, and high capital investment make this one of the least attractive businesses for the entrepreneur.

SOURCE: Research by Ed Henry, *Money* magazine. © 1978, Time Inc. Used by permission of the publisher.

THE WORLD'S 7 LARGEST DEPARTMENT STORES

		Sq. ft.
1.	Macy's* (New York, N.Y.)	2,200,000
2.	Hudson's (Detroit, Mich.)	2,150,000
3.	Marshall Field (Chicago, Ill.)	2,100,000
4.	GUM (Moscow, U.S.S.R.)	1,800,000
5.	Harrod's (London, England)	1,500,000
5.	La Samaritaine (Paris, France)	1,500,000
7.	Mitsukoshi (Tokyo, Japan)	(No figures available—but the largest store in the Orient)

*Macy's, with approximately 2,200,000 sq. ft. of selling space, is considered by most experts to be the largest store in the world, but Hudson's and Marshall Field are very close behind and from time to time have claimed the lead.

—R.H.

Rowland H. Macy, about 1872, founder of the
world's largest department store.

25 CONSUMER ITEMS AND
THE BEST TIME TO BUY THEM

1.	Bathing suits	After July 4th, August
2.	Bicycles	January, February, September, October, November
3.	Blankets	January, May, November, December
4.	Books	January
5.	Building materials, lumber	June
6.	Camping equipment	August
7.	Cars (new)	August, September
8.	Cars (used)	February, November, December
9.	Children's clothing	July, September, November, December
10.	Costume jewelry	January
11.	Dishes	January, February, September
12.	Gardening equipment	August, September
13.	Handbags	January, May, July
14.	Hardware	August, September

15. Hosiery	March, October
16. Lamps	February, August, September
17. Linens	January, May
18. Lingerie	January, May, July
19. Luggage	March
20. Paints	August, September
21. Radios, phonographs	January, February, July
22. School supplies	August, October
23. Television sets	May, June
24. Tires	May, end of August
25. Toys	January, February

SOURCE: *Sylvia Porter's Money Book.* Copyright © 1976 by Sylvia Porter. Reprinted by permission of Doubleday and Company, Inc.

16 FAMOUS PEOPLE
WHO WENT BANKRUPT

1. P. T. BARNUM (1810–1891)

Barnum, who made over $2 million hawking freaks and wild animals and allegedly said, "There's a sucker born every minute," often played the fool himself by making embarrassingly bad investments. But the final humiliation came in 1855, when he invested over $500,000 in the Jerome Clock Co., only to find out he'd been swindled again. The loss plunged him into bankruptcy and caused him to contemplate suicide briefly. It also provided a theme for countless moralistic newspaper editorals.

2. ALEISTER CROWLEY (1875–1947)

In 1934 the bisexual author and poet who claimed proficiency in black magic and blood sacrifice was brought into a London court to face his creditors. With Crowley's liabilities set at £5,000, the court receiver declared him bankrupt.

3. DOROTHY DANDRIDGE (1924–1966)

In March, 1963, the black actress filed for bankruptcy in Los Angeles, Calif. Although she had once commanded six-figure movie contracts, she now claimed $5,000 in assets against $128,000 in debts. She blamed her insolvency on bad investments, such as $150,000 worth of dry oil wells, and an ex-husband who had run up his share of the bills.

4. WALT DISNEY (1901–1966)

In 1921 Disney started the Laugh-O-Gram Corp. in Kansas City, Mo., with $15,000 from investors. But he was forced to file for bankruptcy two years later when his backers pulled out because of problems with New York distributors of his animated fairy tales.

Then in July, 1923, Disney left for Hollywood with all his belongings: a pair of pants, a coat, one shirt, two sets of underwear, two pairs of socks, and some salvaged drawing materials.

5. EDWARD III, KING OF ENGLAND (1312–1377)

Not content with the English crown, King Edward itched to rule France too. His ambition led to the Hundred Years' War and to his own financial ruin. Unable to repay a $7 million loan in 1339, he was brought under a petition of bankruptcy. Edward III was the first national ruler to go bankrupt.

6. STEPIN FETCHIT (real name Lincoln Perry, 1902–   )

As the stereotypical shuffling, bug-eyed Negro, Fetchit had a $7 million movie career, $1,000 suits, a fleet of flashy cars, and rambling mansions, complete with a staff of Oriental servants. In 1944 he filed for bankruptcy to escape nearly $5 million in debts.

7. EDDIE FISHER (1928–   )

In 1972, exactly three decades after he began his singing career on Skipper Dawes's radio show in his native Philadelphia, Fisher was declared bankrupt in a federal court in San Juan, Puerto Rico. His debts totaled nearly $1 million.

8. CHARLES GOODYEAR (1800–1860)

During the 1830s, it had almost become a sport for creditors to take poor Goodyear to court, have him declared bankrupt, and toss him into debtors' prisons in Philadelphia, New Haven, and Boston. Still, his wife's unshakable loyalty and his own pluck saw him through the bad times. It was between stays in jail that he discovered how to vulcanize rubber. When he died, he left his family $200,000 in debt.

9. ULYSSES S. GRANT (1822–1885)

Late in life, Grant became a partner in a banking house called Grant and Ward. In 1884 the firm went bankrupt, and the ensuing stock market crash left Grant so buried under in debt that he was forced to hand over all his property, including his swords and trophies. Broke and dying of cancer, he spent his remaining days writing his memoirs to provide an income for his widow. Mark Twain published the book, and 300,000 copies were sold door to door. Twain generously offered the former president 70% of the net profits; after Grant died, his wife received $350,000 in royalties.

10. ISAAC HAYES (1942–   )

This Academy Award-winning singer-composer filed bankruptcy on behalf of his wife and himself in 1976, listing debts of $6 million. Hayes, who won a 1971 Oscar for writing the score for *Shaft*, gave up all his business ventures, including a fast-food endeavor called Hot Buttered Soul Ltd. The largest of Hayes's debts was said to be a $1.7 million loan he had secured at a Memphis bank.

11. ROBERT KRAS (?–   )

Kras's status as a bankrupt was short-lived. Unemployed for

two years and on welfare, with a wife and two children—including an infant suffering from cystic fibrosis—Kras looked to the bankruptcy laws in 1971 to rid himself of debts totaling $6,000. Just one catch— he didn't have the $50 filing fee. A Brooklyn federal court waived the fee and accepted his bankruptcy petition. But in 1973 the U.S. Supreme Court, speaking through Justice Harry Blackmun, invalidated the bankruptcy, saying "equal protection of the law" demands that the $50 fee be paid by rich and poor alike.

12. MICKEY ROONEY (1920–   )

In 1962 the actor filed for bankruptcy in Los Angeles with $1,500 in assets against $346,513.12 in liabilities. Although he had grossed $12 million during his career up to that time, bad investments, multiple alimony payments, a disastrous partnership, and gambling had gobbled it up. His creditors ranged from a grocer clamoring for $385 to a furrier demanding a $1,900 balance due on his wife's leopard coat to a bank calling in $25,000 which Rooney had borrowed to invest in a pay-television operation to a production company that he was obligated to for $168,000.

13. WILLIAM G. STERN (1936–   )

In the early 1970s, Stern had more property in Great Britain under his sole ownership than any other citizen. He said banks competed to lend him money, and he usually borrowed 80% of the purchase price. In 1974 his vast empire crumbled in the British property market crash. He declared bankruptcy in 1979 with what is probably the largest personal debt in history—$208,780,496. A Harvard Law School graduate, Stern is currently working as a consultant with an annual salary of $50,000. He promised to pay off his enormous debt with payments of $12,000 per year. At that rate, the slate will be wiped clean in 17,398 years.

14. FRANCES TROLLOPE (1780–1863)

Although her book *Domestic Manners of the Americans* (1832)—a highly personalized, rather unflattering portrait of the young nation—had brought Trollope £900 the first year, she went through it fast. Her scheme to open a grand emporium in Cincinnati had gone bust, and she considered herself lucky to flee the Queen City with the clothes on her back. Once in England, she tried to keep her creditors at bay but went under in 1834. Bailiffs seized the Trollopes' household goods. To keep her dying husband from debtors' prison, she spirited him to Belgium, where the family began a new life.

15. MARK TWAIN (1835–1910)

Twain lost around half a million dollars on a wide range of inventions that included steam generators and marine telegraphs. But his downfall came when he decided not to invest $5,000 in Alexander Graham Bell's telephone company, because he saw possibilities in the Paige typesetting machine. Ultimately he backed its inventor with more than $250,000. The machine complicated rather than simplified the typesetting process, and in 1894 Twain's losses caused him to declare bankruptcy.

16. JAMES ABBOTT McNEILL WHISTLER (1834–1903)

Whistler often had to borrow money or pawn his pictures to pay his debts. When a bill collector would come and carry off one of his chairs or beds, Whistler didn't get upset. He simply drew a picture of the missing piece of furniture on the floor where it had stood. Once a bailiff who had taken possession of Whistler's house was joshed into dressing up as a butler and serving tea for Whistler and his friends. But such madcap antics couldn't prevent the inevitable, and on May 8, 1879, Whistler became a bankrupt with debts of $10,000.

—W.A.D., A.K., & L.K.L.

THE 12 MOST VALUABLE INTERNATIONAL COINS

	Record Price	Sale Date
1. U.S. 1787 Brasher gold doubloon, Unc. (MS-63)	$725,000	1979

The most valuable non-American coin, a silver decadrachm from Athens, which celebrated the Greek victory over the Persians almost 2,500 years ago.

	Record Price	Sale Date
2. U.S. 1851 Augustus Humbert $50 Proof, (Humbert's personal specimen)	500,000	1980
3. U.S. 1787 Brasher gold doubloon, AU	430,000	1979
4. U.S. 1804 Class III silver $1	400,000	1980
5. U.S. 1852/1 Augustus Humbert $20 gold Proof, (Humbert's personal specimen)	325,000	1980
6. U.S. 1855 Kellogg & Co. $50 Proof, Humbert's personal specimen)	300,000	1980
7. U.S. 1855 Wass, Molitor & Co. $50	275,000	1980
8. Athens, Greece, silver decadrachm, 470 B.C., 42.90 grams, obverse head of Athena, reverse an owl. Found in Sparta, in 1922. Formerly in collection of Professor C. T. Seltman.	272,240	1974
9. U.S. 1849 Cincinnati Mining & Trading Co. $10 gold	270,000	1980
10. U.S. 1854 Kellogg & Co. $50 Proof, (Humbert's personal specimen)	230,000	1980

SOURCE: *Coin World*, 1980.

THE 11 MOST VALUABLE INTERNATIONAL STAMPS

	Value
1. British Guiana 1856 1c magenta	$935,000
2. Hawaii Missionary 2c blue, unused	400,000
3. Sweden 1855 3s orange color error	375,000
4. Mauritius 1847 1p orange "post office" error	200,000
4. Mauritius 1847 2p dark blue "post office" error	200,000
6. Gold Coast 1883 1p on 4p magenta	150,000
6. U.S. Air Mail 1918 24c carmine rose and blue inverted center—the "Inverted Jenny"	150,000
8. Japan 1871 500m blue green denomination inverted	135,000
9. Canada 1851 2p black	125,000
9. U.S. 1867 (z) Grill 1c blue	125,000
11. Spain 1851 2r blue "changed" cliche	115,000

SOURCE: Harmers of San Francisco, Inc., International Stamp Auctioneers. 1980

15
IN A PLAIN BROWN WRAPPER
—LOVE AND SEX

18 MEN AND WOMEN WHO
SLEPT WITH 3 OR
MORE CELEBRITIES

The "It" Girl, Clara Bow . . .
and U.S.C.'s Thundering Herd . . . Were they a couple?

1. CLARA BOW (1905–1965), U.S. actress

Richard Arlen (1901–1976), U.S. actor
Rex Bell (1903–1962), U.S. actor, politician—married 31 years
Eddie Cantor (1892–1964), U.S. actor
Gary Cooper (1901–1961), U.S. actor
Victor Fleming (1883–1949), U.S. director

Bela Lugosi (1882–1956), Hungarian actor
Fredric March (1897–1975), U.S. actor
Gilbert Roland (1905–   ), U.S. actor
"Slapsie" Maxie Rosenbloom (1904–1976), U.S. boxer
There is a persistent but unsubstantiated story that Clara entertained the entire 1927 "Thundering Herd" University of Southern California football team.

2. CHARLIE CHAPLIN (1889–1977),
   English actor, director, producer

   Marion Davies (1897–1961), U.S. actress
   Paulette Goddard (1911–   ), U.S. actress—married 6 years
   Pola Negri (1897–   ), Polish actress
   Edna Purviance (1894–1958), U.S. actress

3. CHARLES II (1630–1685), king of England

   Moll Davies (?–?), English actress
   Nell Gwyn (1650–1687), English actress
   Louise de Kéroualle (1649–1734), Duchess of Portsmouth
   Barbara Villiers (1641–1709), Duchess of Cleveland

4. JOAN CRAWFORD (1904–1977), U.S. actress

   Douglas Fairbanks, Jr. (1909–   ), U.S. actor—married 4 years
   Clark Gable (1901–1960), U.S. actor
   Alfred Steele (1901–1959), U.S. president of Pepsi-Cola—married
      4 years
   Franchot Tone (1905–1968), U.S. actor—married 4 years
   Spencer Tracy (1900–1967), U.S. actor

5. ISADORA DUNCAN (1878–1927), U.S. dancer

   Edward Gordon Craig (1872–1966), English set designer
   Sergei Essenin (1895–1925), Russian poet—married 3 years
   Paris Eugene Singer (1867–1932), son of U.S. founder of Singer
      Sewing Machine Co.

6. MARIE DUPLESSIS (1824–1847), French courtesan

   Alexandre Dumas, *fils* (1824–1895), French playwright
   Antoine Alfred Agénor de Gramont (1819–1880), French foreign
      minister
   Franz Liszt (1811–1886), Hungarian pianist, composer
   Count de Stackelberg (1774?–?), Russian ambassador to Vienna

7. EDWARD VII (1841–1910),
   king of Great Britain and Ireland

   Jennie Jerome Churchill (1854–1921), U.S. socialite, mother of
      Winston Churchill
   Lillie Langtry (1852–1929), English actress
   Margot Tennant (1864–1945), English actress

8. REX HARRISON (1908–), English actor

Kay Kendall (1926–1959), English actress—married 2 years
Lilli Palmer (1914–), German actress—married 14 years
Rachel Roberts (1927–), English actress—married 9 years

9. HOWARD HUGHES (1905–1976),
U.S. industrialist, aviator, film producer

Carole Lombard (1908–1942), U.S. actress
Marilyn Monroe (1926–1962), U.S. actress
Jean Peters (1926–), U.S. actress—married 13 years

10. ALMA MAHLER-WERFEL (1879–1964),
Austrian composer

Walter Gropius (1883–1969), German architect—married 4 years
Oskar Kokoschka (1886–), Austrian playwright and painter
Gustav Mahler (1860–1911), Bohemian composer—married 8 years
Franz Werfel (1890–1945), Czech poet, writer—married 16 years

11. ADAH ISAACS MENKEN (1835?–1868), U.S. actress

Alexandre Dumas, *père* (1802–1870), French novelist
John Carmel Heenan (1835–1873), U.S. boxer—married 3 years
Algernon Charles Swinburne (1837–1909), English poet

12. MARILYN MONROE (1926–1962), U.S. actress

Milton Berle (1908–), U.S. comedian
Harry Cohn (1891–1958), president of Columbia Pictures
Joe DiMaggio (1914–), U.S. baseball player—married 1 year
Howard Hughes (1905–1976), U.S. industrialist, film producer
Arthur Miller (1915–), U.S. playwright—married 5 years
Yves Montand (1921–), French singer, actor
Joe Schenck (1878?–1961), chairman of 20th Century-Fox

13. LOLA MONTEZ (1818?–1861), English dancer, actress

Alexandre Dumas, *père* (1802–1870), French novelist
Franz Liszt (1811–1886), Hungarian pianist, composer
Ludwig I (1786–1868), king of Bavaria

14. ARISTOTLE ONASSIS (1900?–1975), Greek financier

Maria Callas (1923–1977), U.S. opera singer
Jacqueline Kennedy (1929–), U.S. first lady—married 7 years
Eva Perón (1919–1952), Argentinean political figure

15. TYRONE POWER (1913–1958), U.S. actor

Annabella (1909–), French actress—married 7 years
Linda Christian (1924–), U.S. actress—married 6 years
Anita Ekberg (1931–), Swedish actress
Judy Garland (1922–1969), U.S. actress
Lorenz Hart (1895–1943), U.S. lyricist
Sonja Henie (1912–1969), Norwegian skater, actress
Lana Turner (1920–), U.S. actress
Mai Zetterling (1925–), Swedish actress

16. GEORGE SAND (1804–1876), French novelist, playwright

Frédéric Chopin (1810–1949), Polish pianist, composer
Marie Dorval (1798–1849), French actress
Prosper Mérimée (1803–1870), French novelist, lawyer, secretary
    to ministers of commerce and finance
Alfred de Musset (1810–1857), French poet
Jules Sandeau (1811–1883), French writer

17. LEOPOLD STOKOWSKI (1882–1977), Polish conductor

Greta Garbo (1905–   ), U.S. actress
Olga Samaroff (1882–1948), U.S. pianist—married 12 years
Gloria Vanderbilt (1924–   ), U.S. socialite, artist—married 11
    years

18. MICHAEL TODD (1907–1958), U.S. producer

Joan Blondell (1909–   ), U.S. actress—married 2 years
Evelyn Keyes (1919–   ), U.S. actress
Gypsy Rose Lee (1914–1970), U.S. stripper
Elizabeth Taylor (1932–   ), English-U.S. actress—married 1
    year

—J.E. & K.C.

11 PHYSICAL ATTRIBUTES
MEN IMAGINE WOMEN
ADMIRE MOST ABOUT THEM

		Out of 100%
1.	Muscular chest and shoulders	21%
2.	Muscular arms	18
3.	Penis	15
4.	Tallness	13
5.	Flat stomach	9
6.	Slimness	7
7.	Hair (texture, not length)	4
7.	Buttocks	4
7.	Eyes	4
10.	Long legs	3
11.	Neck	2

SOURCE: *The Sunday Times*, London.

11 PHYSICAL ATTRIBUTES
WOMEN *REALLY*
ADMIRE MOST ABOUT MEN

		Out of 100%
1.	Buttocks (usually described by women as "small and sexy")	39%
2.	Slimness	15
3.	Flat stomach	13
4.	Eyes	11
5.	Long legs	6
6.	Tallness	5
6.	Hair	5
8.	Neck	3
9.	Penis	2
10.	Muscular chest and shoulders	1
11.	Muscular arms	0

SOURCE: *The Sunday Times*, London.

12 RELIGIOUS FIGURES
INVOLVED IN SEX SCANDALS

1. A DELPHIC PYTHIA (7th century B.C.), Greek prophetess

During the early years of the Delphic oracle, young beautiful virgins, who were required to take an oath of celibacy, were chosen to act as the Pythia—the high priestess who inhaled Delphi's sacred gases and then prophesied. Around the 7th century B.C., a Thessalian Greek named Echecrates entered the Delphic temple to ask the Pythia a question. Struck by her tremendous beauty, he was overcome with passion, pulled her to the temple floor, and raped her. The scandal that followed outraged the Delphians, who thereafter appointed only unattractive women at least 50 years old as Pythias.

2. JOHN XII (938?–964), Italian pope

The 18-year-old pontiff plundered the church treasury to support his incessant gambling, and he ruled Rome with a gang of hired thugs. It was his insatiable sexual drive, however, that ultimately terminated his pontificate. He had enjoyed the favors of many mistresses, so many in fact that critics accused him of turning the Lateran Palace into a brothel; some even claimed that the Holy Father had raped female pilgrims right in St. Peter's. One day in early May, 964, John was caught in the act by the husband of the current papal paramour. The cuckold, showing little respect for the holder of the keys to heaven, beat John so severely that the pontiff died, without confession or receiving the sacraments, three days later.

3. ALEXANDER VI (1431–1503), Italian pope

Born Rodrigo Borgia in 1431 at Valencia, Spain, he bought his way to the papacy by bribing just enough cardinals to win election on August 11, 1492. At the time that he was crowned, Alexander was the father of at least seven out-of-wedlock children, four by his longtime mistress Vannozza dei Cattanei. At the age of 62 he added 16-year-old Giulia Farnese to his long list of lovers, and their relationship during Alexander's reign as pope was no secret to churchmen or to the rest of the world.

Pope Alexander VI, who bought the papacy in 1492, fathered at least 10 children, including Cesare and Lucrezia Borgia.

4. HULDREICH ZWINGLI (1484–1531), Swiss Protestant reformer

While he was the vicar of Glarus, Switzerland, from 1506 to 1515, Zwingli had what he called a celibacy "slip." Actually, he had a number of affairs with the women in his church. In a limited effort to curb his desires, he vowed not to become involved with virgins, nuns, or married women. After one of his girl friends proudly revealed to the villagers that she had had sexual relations with him, Zwingli was forced to send a written confession to his superiors. After he broke with the Catholic Church, the Vatican published his confession in an effort to discredit him. Zwingli, however, survived the subsequent scandal and became a political and religious leader.

5. JOHN HUMPHREY NOYES (1811–1886), Perfectionist minister

Denied ordination as a preacher in the Congregational Church, John Humphrey Noyes established his own Perfectionist Church, which held that perfect love and sharing was God's will for man. In 1847, when the police learned that love and sharing meant wife-swapping, Noyes and a number of his followers were arrested for adultery. Despite the subsequent scandal, Noyes founded his Oneida Community in Oneida, N.Y., where he and some 300 followers practiced "complex marriage," in which everyone was considered to be married to everyone else. Despite constant scandals over Noyes's doctrine of free love, his community survived for some 30 years.

6. HENRY WARD BEECHER (1813–1887), Congregational minister

In 1874 religious leader and social reformer Henry Ward Beecher, the brother of Harriet Beecher Stowe, author of *Uncle Tom's Cabin*, was charged and tried for adultery in a scandal that rocked Victorian America. Beecher was accused by a member of his Brooklyn Plymouth Church congregation, Theodore Tilton, of having an affair with Tilton's wife, Elizabeth. Later evidence showed that Beecher almost definitely did seduce Mrs. Tilton in his church office by telling her that God willed that they have sex. However, the four-month trial ended in a hung jury after 52 ballots, and Beecher returned to his church with only a slightly tarnished reputation.

7. HORATIO ALGER (1832–1899), Unitarian clergyman and author

In 1864 Horatio Alger became minister of the parish of Brewster, Mass. He was young, energetic, and well liked. He organized games and other kinds of entertainment for the boys of the parish. But after 15 months, church members wondered why he never took an interest in the girls. The elders of the church decided to investigate, and rumors that the reverend was too partial to boys began to circulate. It was discovered that Alger had engaged in homosexual activities with at least two of the parishioners' sons. Alger admitted to pederasty and lost his ministerial position. He fled to New York City, devoted the rest of his life to writing, and became one of America's most successful authors, known for his tales of such characters as Ragged Dick and Phil the Fiddler.

8. FATHER DIVINE (1877?–1965), founder of the Peace Mission Movement

Black religious leader Father Divine, whose real name was recorded by the police as George Baker alias God, ordered the thousands of converts to his Peace Mission Movement to remain celibate even if they were already married. However, Father Divine himself was involved in a number of scandals. In 1931 he was arrested on Long Island, N.Y., for living with a woman other than his wife. Also, it was reported that he seduced a number of his female followers with the line "I am bringing your desire to the surface so that I can eliminate it." In 1946 white Americans were further outraged when 69-year-old Baker married a 22-year-old white Canadian woman.

9. AIMEE SEMPLE McPHERSON (1890–1944), Pentecostal evangelist

A revivalist with a dramatic flair for theatrics who founded the International Church of the Foursquare Gospel, "Sister" Aimee Semple McPherson disappeared from the beach at Santa Monica, Calif., in May, 1926. The police and public were convinced that she had gone for a swim and drowned. However, more than a month later, she reappeared in a Mexican border town, claiming that she had been kidnapped. It was soon learned that she actually had spent 10 days of the time with a married man named Kenneth Ormiston in a honeymoon cottage in Carmel, Calif. Surprisingly, Sister Aimee weathered the scandal, and her popularity as a preacher increased.

10. ELIJAH MUHAMMAD (1897–1975), Nation of Islam prophet

In 1963 Black Muslim minister Malcolm X heard rumors that the leader of his faith, Elijah Muhammad, who claimed to be the prophet of Allah, was involved in a sex scandal. Holding to puritanical Muslim beliefs, Malcolm at first refused to believe these reports, but later he talked to three of Muhammad's former secretaries, who all claimed that they had had sex with the prophet. This led to a complete break between Malcolm X and Muhammad. The scandal became public on July 3, 1963, when two of the former secretaries filed paternity suits against Muhammad on behalf of their four children.

11. BILLY JAMES HARGIS (1925–   ), Christian Crusade founder

Popular right-wing radio evangelist and founder of the American Christian College in Tulsa, Okla., Hargis spoke out against showing sex on TV, claimed that the Communists had invented rock 'n' roll, and sermonized against pornography. But in 1976 *Time* magazine disclosed that he had been having sex with both male and female students from his college. His secret came to light when, on their wedding night, a couple divulged to each other that they both had had sexual relations with Hargis. When confronted by his accusers, the fundamentalist attributed his bisexual activities to "genes and chromosomes." Today Hargis continues to conduct his Christian Crusade.

12. CLAUDIUS VERMILYE, JR. (1929–   ), Episcopal priest

Known as "Bud" Vermilye, he ran Boys Farm, Inc., a home for troubled youths, near Winchester, Tenn. A scandal arose when it was discovered that Vermilye was having sexual relations with several of his charges, some of them no more than 11 years old. He was also inviting wealthy friends to participate in orgies with the boys, sometimes filming the activities and selling the movies to various sponsors and contributors to the home. Some of the "buyers" lived as far away as Saudi Arabia. One 15-year-old finally told the whole story to authorities. The reverend was arrested, tried, and sentenced to prison for 25 to 40 years. He is currently appealing the decision.

—R.J.F., V.S., & J.L.K.

6 INCESTUOUS COUPLES OF THE BIBLE

1-2. LOT and HIS DAUGHTERS

After the destruction of Sodom and Gomorrah, the only survivors, Lot and his two virgin daughters, lived in a cave. One night the daughters plied their father with wine, and the elder daughter seduced Lot in order to "preserve the seed of [their] father." The following night they got him drunk again, and the younger daughter took her turn. Lot apparently had no memory of the events, although nine months later his daughters gave birth to two sons, Moab and Ben-ammi. (Gen. 19:30–38)

3. ABRAHAM and SARAH

Abraham and Sarah had the same father but different mothers. Sarah married her half brother in Ur, and they remained together until she died at the age of 127. (Gen. 20:12)

4. NAHOR and MILCAH

Abraham's brother, Nahor, married his niece, the daughter of his dead brother Haran and the sister of Lot. (Gen. 11:27, 29)

5. AMRAM and JOCHEBED

Amram married his father's sister, and Aunt Jochebed bore him two sons, Aaron and Moses. (Exod. 6:20)

6. AMNON and TAMAR

Amnon raped his half-sister Tamar and was murdered in revenge two years later by Tamar's full brother Absalom. (II Sam. 13:2, 14, 28–29)

SOURCE: *New American Standard Bible.*

—D.W.

8 WOMEN WHO WORE
(OR MAY HAVE WORN)
CHASTITY BELTS

The chastity belt, a device used by men to keep their women faithful, usually consists of a waistband to which are attached front and back straps that go between the legs and hold plates that cover the genitals and anus. The plates are pierced to allow for the passage of body wastes and natural secretions. A padlock secures the chastity belt so that a man can lock his woman into it, take the key, and go off about his business, confident that she will be unable to take lovers—unless they happen to be locksmiths. A modern joke: A Crusader, having entrusted a dear male friend with the key to his wife's chastity belt, gallops off to battle the infidels. He is only a few miles out of town when his friend charges up behind him shouting, "You gave me the wrong key!"

1. CATHERINE-HENRIETTE DE BALZAC D'ENTRAGUES (1579–1633)

Small and graceful, with feline sensitivity, the Marquise de Verneuil was only 20 when she entered into a stormy relationship with Henry IV of France (1553–1610). Though Henry loved her, he did not give her what she wanted most—marriage. (He wed Marie de Médicis instead.) He may have forced young Catherine to wear a chastity belt. The evidence? A 17th-century etching in the Hennin collection at the Bibliothèque Nationale. According to P. G. J. Niel, a French writer of the 1800s, the naked woman wearing the chastity belt is Catherine, and the man to whom she is handing the key is Henry IV. Hidden behind the bed, the woman's lover accepts a duplicate key from a maid in exchange for a bag of money. To underscore the message, the artist included in the etching a jester trying to keep bees from escaping from a basket and a cat watching a mouse. The caption reads: *Du cocu qui porte la clef et sa femme la serrure* ("Of a cuckold who carries the key and his wife the lock").

2. CORPSE OF AN UNKNOWN WOMAN (late 16th or early 17th century)

In 1889 A. M. Pachinger, a Munich collector, was visiting an Austrian provincial town when a 15th-century church was excavated. An old lead coffin was unearthed and opened in a corner of the churchyard. In it were the remains of a woman—probably young when she died (her teeth were good), probably aristocratic (she wore a dress of expensive damask). Her reddish hair was done up in a braided hairdo, and her gloved arms were crossed on her breast. Under the clothing, her pelvis was encased in a chastity belt—a leather-covered iron hoop to which were attached a frontal plate with a saw-toothed slit and an anal plate, which also had a small opening. Pachinger kept the belt, and the woman was reburied. Who was the woman? Why was she buried in a chastity belt? Was her husband so jealous that he feared she would be unfaithful even in death?

3. ANNE OF AUSTRIA (1601–1666)

Item number 6598 in the Cluny Museum in Paris may have been made for Anne of Austria, the wife of Louis XIII and mother of Louis XIV of France. The waistband of this chastity belt is velvet-covered metal, and the curved plate with a toothed slit is ivory. Anne

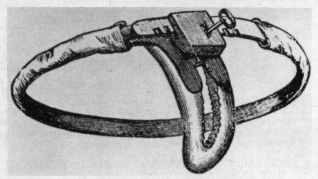

This chastity belt, possibly made for Anne
of Austria, mother of King Louis XIV of France,
may be seen in the Cluny Museum, Paris.

and Louis were married when both were 14 years old. Anne was beautiful and golden-haired, with an exquisite complexion, but nonetheless it was four years before the young Louis slept with her. When he finally got around to sex, however, he became very passionate and jealous—hence the chastity belt.

4. MADAME DE B. (18th century)

At 22, the French writer Voltaire (1694–1778) discovered a chastity belt on his naked mistress, whom he identified only as Mme. de B. His poem *"Le Cadenas"* ("The Padlock") was written to her. It begins: "I triumphed; Love was the master, / And I was nearing these too brief instants / Of my happiness, and yours perhaps. / But a tyrant wants to trouble our good time; / He is your husband: a sexagenary prison-keeper, / He has locked the free sanctuary / Of your charms; and abusing our desires / Retains the key to the sojourn of pleasures." The poem then continues with the story of how Pluto locked the unfaithful Proserpina in a chastity belt forged by the god Vulcan.

5. MARIE LAJON (18th century)

All we know of Marie Lajon and her slick seducer, Pierre Berlhe, comes from a slim book written in 1750 by a lawyer named Freydier. The book consists of Freydier's speech condemning Berlhe at a trial in Nîmes. Supposedly Berlhe seduced the young innocent Marie with promises of marriage. An extremely jealous man, he made her wear a metallic mesh corset with a sharp-pointed genital opening and padlock. To make doubly sure of her chastity, he covered the seams of the apparatus with sealing wax, on which he impressed his seal. When he went away on business trips, he took the key to the chastity belt and the seal with him. Even after the birth of their child, he forced Marie to wear the belt. When it became clear to Marie that he was never going to marry her, she took him to court. At the time of his trial, Berlhe still had the key and seal with him. Freydier's speech, sentimental and maudlin, was a polemic against seducers and a plea against chastity belts. Example: "Having incarcerated the young girl's heart, he next wanted to encase her body in iron and show his tyranny by treating her more cruelly than if she were his slave. What greater examples of barbarism do you want than to put a girl in irons? To enslave her body? To put her in a prison which she must continually carry about with her? To fasten it with a padlock which only the most jealous Florentine could imitate?" The outcome of the case is unknown.

6. ONDINA RANDONE ANCILOTTI (early 20th century)

The Italian sculptor Ancilotti devised a chastity belt—a pair of pants with metal rings, secured by a lock and key—which he persuaded his wife Ondina to wear. To allow her to go to the bathroom, he removed the belt at noon and 8:00 P.M. Once, while pregnant, she was out eating with her friend Adele Gaumier when she felt the urge to relieve herself. She could not do so until she got the key to the belt from Ancilotti. When she heard his whistle in the street, she ran down to get the key from him. Then with the help of Gaumier, she took off the belt, went to the bathroom, put the belt back on, locked it, and returned the key to Ancilotti. For his cruelty to his wife, Ancilotti was arrested and tried. The outcome of the trial is not known.

7. WIFE OF JEAN PARAT (early 20th century)

For years Jean Parat—*le pharmacien tortionnaire* ("the torturing druggist")—was suspected of abusing his wife, but nothing was done about it until 1910, when Paris police investigated and found the woman chained to the bed in the Parat apartment. Under her clothes, she was wearing a chain-mail corset padlocked around her body. Jean was arrested and tried. Jealousy had made him do it, he said, defending his actions, and he pointed out that the chains were long enough so that she could play the piano. Stories with sensational headlines ran in the Paris and London press. On March 5, *Le Rire* ran a cartoon showing Parat dragging his chained wife behind him, with the legend "This is the way to have a faithful wife who is solidly attached to you." Parat was sentenced to prison.

8. HENRI LITTIÈRE'S WIFE (20th century)

No matter how much her husband Henri beat her, Mme. Littière could not stop chasing other men; she had had three affairs in as many months. A baker by trade but medieval scholar by inclination, Henri found the solution to his problem in an old book about the Crusaders, who supposedly locked their wives in chastity belts before going off to battle. He researched the matter further at Paris's Cluny Museum, where he sketched the chastity belts on display. Armed with this information, he had an orthopedist make a contraption of velvet and steel for Mme. Littière. At her chastity-belt fitting, she insisted that she be allowed to wear the belt home and gave the key to Henri with the admonition "Above all, don't lose it."

Not long after, an old lover came to visit Mme. Littière, undressed her, saw the belt, and reported it to the police. Henri thought the first court summons was a joke, but he obeyed the second and appeared before Judge Chaudoye in a Paris court on January 21, 1934. The accusation: cruelty. After Mme. Littière testified that she found it impossible to be faithful, the judge handed down the verdict: a three-month suspended jail sentence and a 50-franc fine.

Note: Readers interested in having a chastity belt made can contact David Renwick of Sheffield, England. Renwick hand-forges iron belts to specification for about $80 each. Most customers order the belts for ornaments or for fun, though Renwick does supply two keys with belts that are to be worn. One man ordered two belts—the first for a woman and the other a male model, which differs only in ornamentation. Some requests are refused. For instance, an order from Italy for 150 belts was far beyond the capacity of Renwick's small operation. Renwick also turned down an Australian man who wanted a belt made for his daughter, who, he claimed, was "misbehaving."

—A.E.

18 MEMORABLE KISSES

1. THE KISS OF LIFE

It was a kiss from God that infused the "spirit of life" into man, according to the account of Genesis (2:7). God is said to have formed Adam from slime and dust and then breathed a rational soul into him. This concept of divine insufflation, which surfaces frequently in religious teachings, is often viewed through the kiss metaphor.

2. THE KISS IN IBERIAN STONE (c. 300–100 B.C.)

One of the earliest depictions of a kiss between a man and a woman is on an Iberian stone relief dating from the 4th to the 2nd century B.C. The piece, featuring the kissers in profile from the shoulders up, was found in Osuna, Spain, and is currently on exhibit in the Madrid National Archaeological Museum.

3. THE BETRAYAL KISS OF JUDAS (c. 29 A.D.)

As told in the New Testament, Judas Iscariot used the kiss as a tool of betrayal around 29 A.D., when he embraced Jesus Christ in the Garden of Gethsemane. Jewish leaders under the high priest Caiaphas had paid Judas 30 pieces of silver to identify Jesus. With a kiss, Judas singled him out. Jesus was arrested, charged with blasphemy, and condemned to death.

4. THE KISS THAT KILLED (14th century)

A young lady in medieval Italy took advantage of her in-laws' tradition of kissing the lips of a marble bust in order to uncover an alleged household treasure. By applying poison to the marble lips, the woman killed two members of the family and proceeded unhampered into a secret room. There she found, not a treasure, but a deformed child. The dying head of the family, her third victim, cursed the woman, promising that her own child as well as the offspring of every seventh generation would be so deformed.

5. THE KISS THAT AWAKENED SLEEPING BEAUTY (17th century)

In the classic fairy tale *Sleeping Beauty*, it is with a kiss that the handsome prince awakens the enchanted princess. This kiss first appeared in Charles Perrault's version of 1697, "La Belle au bois dormant." But in fact, *Sleeping Beauty* dates back to two earlier romances, *Perceforest* and *Pentamerone*. In those stories, the handsome prince finds the sleeping beauty, falls in love with her, rapes her, and leaves.

6. THE KISS THAT COST THOMAS SAVERLAND HIS NOSE (1837)

In 1837, at the dawn of the Victorian Era in Great Britain, Thomas Saverland attempted to kiss Caroline Newton in a lighthearted manner. Rejecting Saverland's pass, Miss Newton not so lightheartedly bit off part of his nose. Saverland took Newton to court, but she was acquitted. "When a man kisses a woman against her will," ruled the judge, "she is fully entitled to bite his nose, if she so pleases." "And eat it up," added a barrister.

7. *THE KISS* BY FRANÇOIS AUGUSTE RODIN (1886)

One of the most renowned pieces of sculpture in the Western world is *The Kiss*, sculpted by French artist François Auguste Rodin in 1886. Inspired by Dante, the figure of two nude lovers kissing brought the era of classical art to an end. Rodin described *The Kiss* as "complete in itself and artificially set apart from the surrounding world."

8. THE FIRST KISS RECORDED ON FILM (1896)

The first kiss ever to be recorded in a motion picture occurred in Thomas Edison's film *The Kiss* between actor John C. Rice and actress May Irwin in April, 1896. Adapted from a short scene in the Broadway comedy *The Widow Jones, The Kiss* was filmed by Raff and Gammon for nickelodeon audiences. Its running time was less than 30 seconds.

9. THE MOST OFTEN KISSED STATUE IN HISTORY (late 1800s)

The figure of Guidarello Guidarelli, a fearless 16th-century Italian soldier, was sculpted in marble by Tullio Lombardo (c. 1455–1532) and put on display at the Academy of Fine Arts in Ravenna, Italy. During the late 1800s, a rumor started that any woman who kissed the reclining, armor-clad statue would marry a wonderful gentleman and settle down with him. Some four to five million superstitious women have since kissed Guidarelli's cold marble lips. Consequently, the soldier's mouth has acquired a faint reddish glow.

10. THE MOVIE WITH 191 KISSES (1926)

In 1926 Warner Brothers Studios starred John Barrymore in *Don Juan*. During the course of the film (2 hr. 47 min.), the amorous adventurer bestows a total of 191 kisses on a number of beautiful senoritas—an average of one every 53 seconds.

John Barrymore, in *Don Juan,* about to implant one of his 191 kisses in the film, a record for a single movie.

11. THE LONGEST KISS ON FILM (1941)

The longest kiss in motion picture history is between Jane Wyman and Regis Toomey in the 1941 production of *You're in the Army Now.* The Lewis Seiler comedy about two vacuum cleaner salesmen features a scene in which Toomey and Wyman hold a single kiss for 3 min. and 5 sec. (or 4% of the film's running time).

12. THE MAJORCA, SPAIN, KISS-IN (1969)

In 1969 an effort was made to crack down on young lovers who were smooching in public in the town of Inca on the island of Majorca. When the police chief began handing out citations that cost offenders 500 pesetas (around $7) per kiss, a group of 30 couples protested by staging a kiss-in at the harbor at Cala Figuera. Following a massive roundup by police, the amorous rebels were fined 45,000 pesetas for their defiant smooching and then released.

13. THE HOMOSEXUAL KISS IN *SUNDAY BLOODY SUNDAY* (1971)

One cinema kiss that turned heads among the moviegoing public was between two male actors, Peter Finch and Murray Head, in the 1971 film *Sunday Bloody Sunday.* The British tale of a bisexual love triangle included a medium close-up shot of this kiss in a scene originally planned to have featured only an embrace from afar. Director John Schlesinger commented that Finch and Head "were certainly less shocked by the kiss than the technicians on the set were. When Finch was asked about that scene by somebody on TV, he said, 'I did it for England.' "

14. THE KISS OF HUMILITY (1975)

In an unprecedented gesture of humility, Pope Paul VI kissed the feet of Metropolitan Meliton of Chalcedon, envoy of Patriarch Demetrios I, who was head of the Eastern Orthodox Church, during a Mass at the Sistine Chapel in Rome in 1975. The two men were commemorating the 10th anniversary of the lifting of excommunications that the churches of Constantinople and Rome had conferred on each other during the 11th century. Taken aback by the pontiff's dramatic action, Meliton attempted to kiss the pope's feet in return but was kept from doing so by Paul. Meliton instead kissed the pope's hand.

15. THE KISS THAT DIDN'T HAPPEN (1975)

King Faisal of Saudi Arabia was engaged in discussions with the Kuwaiti oil minister when the king's nephew, Prince Faisal ibn Mussad Abdel Aziz, burst into the office unannounced. The king stood and, assuming that the prince wished to offer him holy greetings for Mohammed's birthday, lowered his head and waited for the traditional kiss. It never arrived. Instead the prince fired a bullet into the king's head, and then another into his neck, killing him.

16. THE KISS THAT COST $1,260 (1977)

Ruth van Herpen visited an art museum in Oxford, England, in 1977 and kissed a painting by American artist Jo Baer, leaving red lipstick stains on the $18,000 work. Restoration costs were reported to be as much as $1,260. Appearing in court, Van Herpen explained, "I only kissed it to cheer it up. It looked so cold."

17. THE KISS THAT CAUSED A CENSORSHIP DEBATE (1978)

The first kiss to reach the movie screen in India was between actor Shashi Kapoor and actress Zeenat Aman in the 1978 Indian film *Love Sublime*. This landmark kiss, a product of new film guidelines, triggered a nationwide debate over censorship. Kapoor felt that the increased creative freedom would only add logic to Indian love stories and result in less cinema violence. Chief minister and film actor M. G. Ramachandran called for a mass protest, labeling the kissing scenes "an insult."

18. THE LONGEST KISS ON RECORD (1978)

The longest kiss in a "smoochathon" was held between Bobbi Sherlock and Ray Blazina in Pittsburgh, Pa., between May 1 and 6, 1978. Their record smack lasted 130 hr. 2 min. according to the *Guinness Book of World Records*.

—D.B.

RUDOLPH VALENTINO'S
10 ATTRIBUTES OF THE PERFECT
WOMAN

Idolized as the great lover of the screen in the 1920s, Rudolph Valentino starred in such romantic epics as *The Sheik, Blood and Sand,* and *The Eagle.* His death in 1926 caused worldwide hysteria, several suicides, and riots at his funeral. Each year, on the anniversary of his death, hundreds of the faithful gather at his burial site to pay tribute.

Rudolph Valentino's "Perfect Woman"—
appreciating "good food."

1. Fidelity
2. The recognition of the supreme importance of love
3. Intelligence
4. Beauty
5. A sense of humor
6. Sincerity
7. An appreciation of good food
8. A serious interest in some art, trade, or hobby
9. An old-fashioned and wholehearted acceptance of monogamy
10. Courage

SOURCE: Cleveland Amory, *Vanity Fair.* Copyright © 1926, 1954 by The Conde Nast Publications Inc.

5 REAL WIVES OF
5 CELEBRATED HOMOSEXUALS

1. MME. PAUL VERLAINE (MATHILDE MAUTÉ)

Mathilde Mauté was 16 years old, the poet Paul Verlaine 25 when they met. On their wedding day in Paris in 1870, Mathilde was a childlike 17-year-old to whom marriage meant playing house for real. Her groom anticipated a lifetime of joy. Yet in 1884, when French law was changed to permit divorce, Mathilde Verlaine, long separated from her husband, was among the first in line to apply for freedom. What happened in between? Innocent, bourgeois Mathilde soon learned her husband was given to ugly bouts of drunkenness and violence. He indulged in unexplained absences, which filled her alternately with fear and relief. A week before their only child, Georges, was born, Verlaine dragged Mathilde from bed and flung her to the floor. When Georges was three months old, his father threw him against a wall. Once Verlaine tried unsuccessfully to set fire to Mathilde's hair. He became slovenly, sometimes refusing to bathe or change his clothes for a week. And he fell in love—really in love—for the first time in his life. The object of his passion was the gifted poet Arthur Rimbaud, then a 17-year-old country boy recently arrived in Paris. Enslaved by the youngster who offered him physical ecstasy he had never experienced before, Verlaine invited the sullen, self-important Rimbaud to move in with him and Mathilde. Not satisfied with stealing Mathilde's husband, Rimbaud also pilfered an ivory cross that had been in Mathilde's family for years. In 1872 Verlaine abandoned Mathilde and their baby to run off with Rimbaud. The relationship between the two dirty, disheveled lovers was less than idyllic. Inflamed by absinthe and jealousy when Rimbaud took new lovers, Verlaine took a gun and shot the boy. Rimbaud's injury was minor, but Verlaine spent two years in prison for the offense. Rimbaud, a shining talent at 15, was a burned-out case at 20. He abandoned both poetry and homosexuality, became a traveler-trader, and lived in Ethiopia with a native woman. Returning to France to seek a wife, he suffered an illness that cost him his right leg. He died in Marseilles in 1891, aged 37. Verlaine's pathetic son, Georges, briefly a station-master for the Paris Metro, turned alcoholic and died of drink in 1926. As for Mathilde, at 33 she remarried and had two children by a building contractor, M. Delponte, who then divorced her. Verlaine, somewhat rehabilitated, continued to pour forth his poetry. In 1896, aged 52, he died in the lodgings of a sympathetic friend, an aging prostitute named Eugénie Krantz.

2. MRS. PËTR ILICH TCHAIKOVSKY
(ANTONINA IVANOVNA MILIUKOVA)

Antonina Ivanovna Miliukova was 28 years old, a borderline psychopath and a committed nymphomaniac, when in 1877 she fell in love with her music teacher, Pëtr Ilich Tchaikovsky. The object of her desire was, at age 37, a tormented man who detested his homosexuality (at one time he was passionately in love with his sister's son, "Bob") and dreaded exposure of his sexual preference. Unable to persuade Antonina that his predilection for males made

him an unsuitable husband for any woman, especially a nymphomaniac, Tchaikovsky succumbed to her pleading when she threatened suicide. The unconsummated marriage that ensued was stark
horror for the composer. Unhealthily devoted to the memory of his
mother, who had died when he was 14, Tchaikovsky had barely
survived a brief disastrous affair with Désirée Artôt, an opera singer,
and was, even then, enjoying a celestial relationship with Mme.
Nadezhda von Meck, an admiring widow 10 years his senior who
corresponded with him, provided him with an annuity, and accom-
modatingly chose never to meet him. Unable to endure the demented,
sex-starved creature who was his wife, Tchaikovsky sneaked away
one cold night and stood waist-deep in an icy river praying for
pneumonia and subsequent death. Failing to achieve either, he fled
Antonina, seeking refuge with his brother, Anatol. Loyal Anatol never
revealed the details of the two-day coma that followed Pëtr's escape
from home. Antonina accepted her abandonment with fair grace. She
wrote unreproachful letters to her husband, found solace in a mul-
titude of affairs, bore an unknown number of children, and died in
an insane asylum in 1917, 24 years after the demise of Tchaikovsky,
who carelessly or suicidally drank unboiled water during a cholera
epidemic.

3. MRS. OSCAR WILDE (CONSTANCE LLOYD)

They were electrically attracted to each other when they met
at a party in 1881, and passionately in love when they were wed in
St. James's Church, Paddington, England, two years later. During
their courtship, Oscar Wilde often impulsively interrupted his lecture
engagements to rush from London to Dublin for a treasured few
hours with his beloved. "We telegraph each other twice a day," he
boasted. His letters to her made her mad with joy. "My whole life is
yours to do as you will with it," she wrote. What Oscar eventually did
to the life of Constance Lloyd, the demure and pretty girl from Dublin,
is the stuff of tragedy. In the beginning, all was joy. They honey-
mooned in Paris, where Oscar, on a walk with a friend after his first
sexual encounter with Constance, stopped to send flowers and a
lyrical note to the hotel where his bride lay resting—and then
proceeded to describe to his friend, in rapturous and explicit detail,
their lovemaking of the previous night. In London the Wildes moved
into an exquisite house in Chelsea, where, to please him, Constance
entertained in period costumes that set off the eclectic decor of their
home. She smiled bravely at his cynical aphorisms on marriage
expounded before guests. "In married life three is company and two
is none." "One should always be in love. That is the reason one
should never marry." In 1885 she bore him a son, Cyril. In 1886
another son, Vivyan, was born. Her first intimation that Oscar's eyes
were wandering came when rumor reached her that he was infatuated
with an actress and that he frequented the house of an expensive
prostitute. Bitterly, she tolerated his indiscretions, as she tolerated
his sharp, witty gibes at her religiosity. What she could not tolerate
was his fateful homosexual affair with young Lord Alfred Douglas.
Openly flaunting their love, the pair not unexpectedly incurred the
wrath of Douglas's father, the Marquis of Queensberry, who accused
Wilde of sodomy. Ignoring the advice of friends, mistakenly secure
in his fame, Oscar sued Queensberry for libel. To Wilde's astonishment, evidence was revealed that led to his own arrest and a sentence

of two years at hard labor in Reading Gaol. Seeking anonymity after the scandal, Constance gave herself and her children the new surname (an old family name) of Holland. Cyril and Vivyan were sent to Switzerland to be educated, and Constance left England to travel on the Continent. Despite her hurt, Constance kindheartedly journeyed from Genoa to Reading Gaol to deliver the sad news of Oscar's mother's death. But being deprived of his sons proved to be Oscar's greatest grief. "That the law should . . . decide that I am unfit to be with my own children is something quite horrible to me. The disgrace of prison is as nothing compared to it," he wrote. After his release he had a brief holiday in Italy with Alfred Douglas before they parted forever. In 1898 Constance underwent spinal surgery in Genoa and died soon after in a nursing home. Wilde lived on till 1900 in a rundown Paris hotel on the Rue des Beaux Arts, today a chic, jet-set hostelry called L'Hôtel. A bronze plaque over the door bears his name. He is buried in the city's Père Lachaise Cemetery under a sculpture by Jacob Epstein and in the company of Héloïse and Abelard, Honoré de Balzac, Édith Piaf, Colette, Chopin, and Sarah Bernhardt. Oscar would have liked that.

4. MRS. W. H. AUDEN (ERIKA MANN)

One of the most agreeable unconsummated marriages between two consenting adults was formalized in 1935, when Erika Mann, daughter of Nobel Prize-winning author Thomas Mann, became the bride of the brilliant English poet Wystan Hugh Auden. At 30, Erika Mann was the divorced wife of a German actor. Auden, two years her junior, was a discreet practicing homosexual. The couple met for the first time on their wedding day. It was Christopher Isherwood, Auden's sometime lover and lifelong friend, who proposed this strange union. Erika, a political émigré from Nazi Germany, needed a British passport to continue her work as author-lecturer. With a British husband, the coveted passport would automatically become hers. Auden, a man of chivalry, responded to Isherwood's suggestion with a single-word telegram: "Delighted." Happily, the marriage between Auden and Erika Mann ripened into friendship. However, there is no evidence the couple spent so much as a single platonic night together. Erika, when not serving as her father's indispensable editor, traveled widely. She worked in Cairo as a war correspondent, covered the Nuremberg trials as a reporter, and lectured in the U.S., Europe, and the Near East. Auden continued his writing, which included sensitive love poems, many dedicated to Isherwood, his erstwhile companion in the boy bars of Berlin and later in the exotic, erotic, male-staffed bathhouses of Shanghai. Until her death from a brain tumor in 1969, Erika Mann remained the wife of W. H. Auden. Auden subsequently became an American citizen. Toward the end of his life he dwelt in England. He died in Vienna in 1973.

5. MRS. YUKIO MISHIMA (YOKO SUGIYAMA)

Although over 50% of the women polled at the time of Yoko Sugiyama's marriage to Yukio Mishima declared they would commit suicide before becoming the wife of Japan's leading writer, 19-year-old Yoko was elated to be selected from among the applicants submitted to the would-be groom by friends and acquaintances.

Yukio and Yoko Mishima.

Armed with Mishima's shopping list, matchmakers were instructed to find a woman whose height did not exceed his own (Mishima was 5 ft. 2 in. tall); who wanted to marry *him* and not the celebrity he was; who was round-faced and pretty; who would look after his home and enjoy his parents; and lastly, who would refrain from disturbing him while he worked. On June 1, 1958, only two months after their meeting, the couple wed. Following a traditional honeymoon they returned to Tokyo, where Yoko was to learn the harsher truths of her marriage. Her husband was a homosexual (a fact accepted with little joy but greater equanimity in Japan than in the Western world) as well as a neofascist and leader of an 80-man private army called the Shield Society. Worst of all for the young bride, she had acquired a jealous mother-in-law, Shizue, who was to remain the most important woman in Yukio's life. Yoko was not docile in the face of these obstacles to her happiness. She succeeded in ending the all-male parties Mishima hosted at home, at which his weight-lifter friends stripped to their trunks, oiled their bodies, and posed for a photographer. (In 1963 she was deeply upset when Mishima posed nude for a set of pictures that appeared in a book.) The birth of two grandchildren did nothing to alter Shizue's dislike of her daughter-in-law, whom she always sarcastically referred to as "the bride." In 1970 Mishima, still a militaristic emperor worshipper, called for a military coup. When his call went unheeded, he seized the opportunity to commit the ritual act he had once described as the "ultimate masturbation"—hara-kiri. Standing before his followers, he used both hands to plunge a samurai sword into his left side, then drew the blade across his abdomen to his right side. As he had requested, a henchman stepped forward and decapitated him. Yoko heard the

322

news while riding in a taxi. When her husband's body was brought home, Yoko acceded to the wish expressed in his will that he be dressed in his Shield Society uniform with a sword across his chest. The next day he was cremated. He was 45 years old. He died with one dream unfulfilled. He had hoped to take his children to Disneyland. His mother, true to form, blamed Yoko for the death, saying he would never have killed himself if he had had a better wife. In 1979 a public exhibition of his works in a Tokyo department store drew 20,000 people, 70% of them men. The exhibit, approved by Yoko, included a life-sized bronze statue of Yukio Mishima in the nude.

—S.W.

AVERAGE NUMBER OF SPERM
PER EJACULATION FOR 25 MAMMALS

1.	Swine	45,000,000,000
2.	Jackass	14,500,000,000
3.	Horse	8,000,000,000
4.	Dairy cattle	7,000,000,000
5.	Zebu (humped ox)	5,098,200,000
6.	Beef cattle	4,000,000,000
7.	Eurasian buffalo	3,978,000,000
8.	Sheep	3,000,000,000
9.	Goat	1,755,000,000
10.	Dog	1,500,000,000
11.	Rhesus monkey	1,175,900,000
12.	Chimpanzee	1,157,100,000
13.	Crab-eating macaque monkey	549,600,000
14.	Human	500,000,000
15.	Chinchilla	480,000,000
16.	Red fox, silver fox	330,000,000
17.	Gibbon, (ape)	197,600,000
18.	Capuchin monkey	96,600,000
19.	Rat	82,500,000
20.	Squirrel	82,400,000
21.	Rabbit	64,000,000
22.	Cat	60,000,000
23.	Guinea pig	8,235,000
24.	Mink	260,000
25.	Golden hamster	3,450

—L.S.K.

MEMBERS OF SOCIETY—
5 PRESERVED SEX ORGANS
OF FAMOUS MEN

1. GENERAL KANG PING

In the time of the Ming dynasty, when Emperor Yung Lo ruled China (1402–1424), his best friend and favorite military leader was

Gen. Kang Ping. Forced to leave the capital for a journey to another city, the emperor left Gen. Kang Ping in charge of protecting his palace and the beautiful women of his harem who lived inside. Since Gen. Kang Ping knew that the mercurial emperor might worry about the faithfulness of his harem concubines and the loyalty of his army staff, he decided he must anticipate any future accusations of disloyalty. The emperor went off on his travels, and when he returned to the capital he was as paranoid as ever. He immediately accused Gen. Kang Ping of having seduced several of his concubines. The general denied the accusation and said he could prove his loyalty. He pointed to the saddle horse the emperor had used on the journey, and asked that the emperor look in the hollow of the saddle. The emperor looked, and there he found Gen. Kang Ping's penis. The general had castrated himself, preserved his penis, and secretly sent it off with his ruler so that he would later be able to prove his loyalty. So moved was the emperor by his friend's gesture that he elevated him to chief eunuch, and upon Kang Ping's death had a temple built to him and had him venerated as patron saint of all eunuchs.

2. NAPOLEON BONAPARTE

When the exiled former emperor of France died of stomach cancer on May 5, 1821, on the remote island of St. Helena, a postmortem was held. According to Dr. C. MacLaurin, "his reproductive organs were small and apparently atrophied. He is said to have been impotent for some time before he died." A priest in attendance obtained Napoleon's penis. After a secret odyssey of 150 years, the severed penis turned up at Christie's Fine Art Auctioneers in London around 1971. The one-inch penis, resembling a tiny sea horse, an attendant said, was described by the auction house as "a small dried-up object." It was put on sale for £13,300, then withdrawn from bidding. Shortly afterward, the emperor's sex organ (along with bits of his hair and beard) was offered for sale in Flayderman's Mail Order Catalogue. There were no buyers. In 1977 Napoleon's penis was sold to an American urologist for about $3,800.00. Today Napoleon's body rests in the crypt at the Invalides, Paris—sans penis.

3. GRIGORI RASPUTIN

In 1968, in the St. Denis section of Paris, an elderly White Russian female émigré, a former maid in czarist St. Petersburg and later a follower and lover of the Russian holy man Rasputin, kept a polished wooden box, 18 in. by 6 in. in size, atop her bedroom bureau. Inside the box lay Rasputin's penis. It "looked like a blackened, overripe banana, about a foot long, and resting on a velvet cloth," reported Rasputin biographer Patte Barham. In life this penis, wrote Rasputin's daughter Maria, measured "a good 13 inches when fully erect." According to Maria's account, in 1916, when Prince Felix Yussupov and his fellow assassins attacked Rasputin, Yussupov first raped him, then fired a bullet into his head, wounding him. As Rasputin fell, another young nobleman pulled out a dagger and "castrated Grigori Rasputin, flinging the severed penis across the room." One of Yussupov's servants, a relative of Rasputin's lover, recovered the penis and turned the severed organ over to the maid. She in turn fled to Paris with it.

Grigori Rasputin and admirers.

4. JOHN DILLINGER

One of the controversial legends of the 20th century concerns the disposition of bank robber and badman John Dillinger's private parts. When Dillinger was allegedly shot to death by the FBI in front of a Chicago movie theater in 1934, his corpse was taken to the morgue for dissection by forensic pathologists. That was where the legend began. The gangster's penis—reported as 14 in. flaccid, 20 in. erect—was supposedly amputated by an overenthusiastic pathologist. After that, many persons heard that the penis had been seen (always by someone else) preserved in a showcase at the Smithsonian Institution. Since the publication of *The Book of Lists 1*, the authors have received a great number of letters asking if the story of Dillinger's pickled penis is true. The editors called the Smithsonian to prove the story myth or fact and museum curators denied any knowledge of such an exhibit. If it is not among the 65 million objects on display at the Smithsonian, how did that rumor begin? Tour guides at the museum believe that years ago, many people mistakenly entered the building next door to the Smithsonian thinking it was part of the same complex; it was, however, a different museum altogether—the Medical Museum of the Armed Forces Institute of Pathology—and it housed gruesome displays of diseased and oversized body parts, including penises and testes, as well as pictures of victims of gunshot wounds. It was here some visitors claimed they had seen Dillinger's giant penis. The collection has since been moved to the Walter Reed Army Medical Center, but its operators also deny that Dillinger's organ has ever been one of its displays.

5. ISHIDA KICHIZO

He was a well-known Tokyo gangster, and his mistress was a young Japanese geisha named Abe Sada. They were involved in a long, passionate sadomasochistic love affair. He enjoyed having her try to strangle him with a sash cord as she mounted him. Kichizo could make love to Abe Sada only at intervals, because he was married and had children. She could not stand their separations. He offered to set her up in a teahouse and drop in on her once in a while. She suggested they run away together or commit suicide together.

On the night of May 18, 1936, fearing he was going to leave her forever, she started to play their strangling game with her pajama cord, then really strangled him until he was dead. Now she wouldn't have to share him with anyone. Yet she wanted to possess part of him. Taking a butcher knife, she cut off Kichizo's penis and testicles, wrapped them in his jacket, and placed the bundle in a loincloth she tied around her kimono. Abe Sada fled her geisha house, took hotel rooms, fondled Kichizo's penis, and pressed it against her body constantly. Eventually the police caught her and confiscated the penis she had been preserving. She was tried for her crime, found guilty, and sentenced to jail. She languished in prison eight years, all through W.W. II, until the American army of occupation moved into Tokyo. The Americans released all Japanese political prisoners—including Abe Sada, by mistake. In 1947 an "aging but vivacious" Abe Sada owned a bar near Tokyo's Sumida River. A sensational film, *In the Realm of the Senses,* was made about the affair, which made dear Abe and dead Kichizo—and his penis—legend in Japan.

—I.W.

25 WELL-KNOWN WOMEN WHO HAVE HAD ABORTIONS

1. Simone de Beauvoir, novelist, essayist, philosopher
2. Senta Berger, actress
3. Kay Boyle, novelist, short story writer, essayist
4. Alice May Brock, restaurateur (proprietor, Alice's Restaurant), author
5. Hortense Calisher, novelist
6. Judy Collins, singer
7. Catherine Deneuve, actress
8. Nora Ephron, author
9. Lee Grant, actress
10. Lillian Hellman, dramatist, author
11. Elizabeth Janeway, novelist, essayist, reviewer
12. Evelyn Keyes, actress
13. Billie Jean King, tennis champion
14. Ursula Le Guin, science fiction writer
15. Viveca Lindfors, actress
16. Marya Mannes, journalist, essayist, novelist
17. Eve Merriam, poet, playwright
18. Jeanne Moreau, actress
19. Anaïs Nin, diarist, novelist, short story writer
20. Eleanor Perry, dramatist, novelist
21. Françoise Sagan, novelist, dramatist
22. Romy Schneider, actress
23. Susan Sontag, novelist, essayist
24. Gloria Steinem, writer, publisher, lecturer
25. Barbara Tuchman, historian

—D.S.G.

10 RENOWNED TRANSSEXUALS

1. WENDY CARLOS (b. Walter Carlos, 1939), U.S. musician

Famous for co-designing the Moog synthesizer, Carlos saw his first album, *Switched-on Bach,* become a million-seller in the late 1960s. Although successful professionally, his personal life was a shambles because of his anguish at being trapped in a male body. In May, 1969, he began living predominantly as a woman, and he made his last public appearance as Walter in 1970 on the *Dick Cavett Show.* After working with Stanley Kubrick on the score of *A Clockwork Orange* in 1971, Carlos dropped out of sight and underwent a sex-change operation a year later. She lived in virtual seclusion for the next seven years. Finally, on Valentine's Day, 1979, she officially adopted the name Wendy and revealed her new identity in the May, 1979, issue of *Playboy* magazine.

2. CANARY CONN (b. Danny O'Conner, 1949), U.S. singer and journalist

O'Conner felt as if he were a girl from age two and dressed himself in his sisters' clothing as often as possible. Anxious to convince himself and others of his manhood, he played football, dated frequently, and even attempted to join the Marines. At age 21, a year after becoming a husband and a father, he decided to undergo sex reassignment. While having physical characteristics of both sexes, Conn lived with her boyfriend and held odd jobs to pay for her final operation in 1971. An accomplished singer and lyricist, Conn has also worked as a Hollywood reporter and a talk-show host.

3. PAULA GROSSMAN (b. Paul Grossman, 1919), U.S. schoolteacher

In 1971, after 31 years as a music teacher in elementary schools, Grossman requested permission to return to her job at New Jersey's Cedar Hill School in her new sexual role as a woman. The school board fired her, ruling that her presence in the classroom would have a "negative impact." The court battle continued until 1976, when the U.S. Supreme Court declined to review the case. Two years later, however, the New Jersey Superior Court held that Grossman was to receive disability benefits because she was "obviously incapacitated" as a teacher by the school board's uncompromising stance. Meanwhile, Grossman remains married to her wife and plays an active part in raising their three daughters. She also retains her longtime interests in motorcycles, the Civil War, and guns.

4. DAWN LANGLEY HALL (b. Gordon Langley Hall, 1929), British author

The unofficially adopted son of Dame Margaret Rutherford, Hall moved to Charleston, S.C., in 1962 and soon won local approval for his fine taste in antiques and his burgeoning reputation as an author. Known for such eccentricities as arranging a debutante party for his two pet Chihuahuas, Hall chiefly wrote biographies of women and strongly identified with his subjects. In 1966 he began hormone treatments, and two years later—shortly after the final stage of the sexual transformation—Dawn Hall married a 22-year-old black garage mechanic. Although Dame Margaret apparently was delighted with the turn of events, one of Hall's great-aunts complained, "I do wish that Dawn wasn't marrying a Baptist."

5. DEBORAH HARTIN (b. Austin Hartin, 1933), U.S. lecturer

"In school, the boys were on one side of the room, the girls on the other," recalls Hartin. "My object was to get to the other side of the room." In fact, Hartin had such difficulty adjusting to school that he was expelled in the fifth grade. In 1953 he joined the U.S. Navy, hoping to be sent abroad. His plan was to desert and travel to Denmark for a sex-change operation, but he remained stationed in the States throughout his time in the service. Although married and the father of a daughter, Hartin continued to try to find a doctor in the U.S. who would operate on him. On several occasions he tried to castrate himself. Finally the necessary surgery was performed in Casablanca, Morocco, in 1970. During the past decade, Hartin has made numerous radio and television appearances and has lectured on transsexualism at various colleges.

6. NANCY HUNT (former name undisclosed, b. 1927), U.S. journalist

A twice-married father of three, Hunt did not face the fact that he was a transsexual until age 47. After a stint in the army and a degree in English from Yale, Hunt entered the field of journalism and enjoyed a distinguished career as a feature writer for the Chicago *Tribune*. Miserable in a man's body, he went to Vietnam in 1968 as a combat correspondent, hoping to get killed. He survived, however, and after a transitional period of dressing as a woman, he was operated on at age 49. Hunt continues to work at the *Tribune*, although she is now at the copy desk.

"Austin" Hartin—then.   "Deborah" Hartin—now.

7. CHRISTINE JORGENSEN (b. George Jorgensen, 1926), U.S. entertainer

"Ex-GI Returns Home Blond Beauty" was one of the headlines that greeted Christine Jorgensen on February 13, 1953, when she stepped off the plane at New York's International Airport. Prior to becoming the first well-publicized, successful transsexual, Jorgensen had been plagued with the sense that something was wrong with him. After the 98-lb. private was discharged from the army, he came across medical studies that showed that male and female hormones exist in both sexes. Anxious to learn more, he enrolled in a medical technicians' course and began taking estrogen without prescription. In 1950 he flew to Denmark, where Dr. Christian Hamburger completed two of the three operations necessary for the sex change. Capitalizing on the unexpected storm of publicity when she returned to the U.S., the newly emerged Christine launched a career as a nightclub entertainer and actress.

8. JAN MORRIS (b. James Morris, 1927), British journalist

Called "one of the most dashing figures of the British press," Morris remembers that when he was three years old, sitting under the piano that his mother was playing, he first realized that he should have been born a girl. After several years in the British Army and an Oxford education, Morris began living the life of a wandering journalist. Although he fell deeply in love, married, and had five children, he remained largely uninterested in sex, which he always considered "slightly distasteful." Instead, he experienced a parallel excitement in travel and gained fame at age 26 when he covered the ascent of Mt. Everest. After a 10-year transitional period, during which he lived an androgynous life, he underwent a sex-change operation in Casablanca in 1972. In 1960, as a man, he wrote a brilliant book, *Venice*, praising the Italian city of the doges; as a woman, she has written articles attacking the island-city.

9. JUDE PATTON (b. Judith Patton, 1940), U.S. mailman

One of the few female-to-male transsexuals to go public, Patton encountered little peer pressure as a tomboy until age 16. By then she had worn a crew cut for several years, and school counselors began suggesting that she needed psychological help because of her masculine behavior. Determined to remain in men's clothing, she turned down a four-year college scholarship when she was told that female students were required to wear dresses. Because she refused to wear women's attire, only factory work was available to her in the small midwestern town where she lived. Eventually she heard about Stanford University's transsexual program and underwent four operations for sex reassignment in 1972 and 1973. "The surgery was a miracle," Patton says. "For the first time in my life I feel complete." He now works as a postal clerk while pursuing graduate studies to become a clinical psychologist.

10. RENEE RICHARDS (b. Richard Raskind, 1935), U.S. tennis player

Like most transsexuals, Richards had always identified with the opposite sex. In 1975 the successful New York ophthalmologist and tennis player had a sex-change operation and moved to California. After Richards won her first women's tournament at La Jolla, Calif., an investigative reporter uncovered the 6-ft. 2-in. player's past and went on national television with the news of Richards's operation. When she tried to play her next major match, 25 women dropped out of the tournament, the remaining players were required to take a sex-hormone test for the first time in tennis history, and Richards filed a lawsuit. She won her case in 1977, when the New York State Supreme Court ruled that "overwhelming medical evidence [indicates] this person is now female." No longer practicing medicine, Richards devotes full time to her career as a tennis pro.

—J.HU. & The Eds.

16
TIME OUT FOR SPORTS

THE 5 MOST OFTEN TRADED PROFESSIONAL BASEBALL PLAYERS

1. BOBO NEWSOM (1929–1953), traded 16 times

Colorful character who pitched for some of the worst teams in baseball history. Four times was the biggest loser in the American League. Was traded by the Washington Senators on five different occasions.

2. TOMMY DAVIS (1959–1976), traded 11 times

National League batting champion in 1962 and 1963 while with the Los Angeles Dodgers. In second game of 1963 World Series against the New York Yankees, Davis tied three series records: most triples in one game (2); most putouts in one inning (3); and most putouts by a left fielder in one game (6). Held .294 lifetime batting average.

3. JOHN JOSEPH DOYLE (1889–1905), traded 10 times

Known as Dirty Jack. In 1892 became first player ever to be used as a pinch hitter. Was player-manager with New York Giants (NL) in 1895 and with the Washington Senators (NL) in 1898. Held a career batting average of .301.

4. DEACON McGUIRE (1884–1912), traded 10 times

Had one of the longest recorded baseball careers, spanning 28 years. Was player-manager with the Washington Senators (NL) in 1898, with the Boston Red Sox (AL) in 1907–1908, and with the Cleveland Naps (AL) in 1909–1911.

5. BOB MILLER (1957–1974), traded 10 times

Primarily a relief pitcher, he appeared in 694 games throughout his career for 11 major league clubs. Had the dubious honor of being selected by Casey Stengel to be a member of the original New York Mets, who lost 120 games in 1962. Led National League in appearances with 74 in 1964.

—J.B.

11 PROFESSIONAL BASEBALL PLAYERS WHO HAVE HIT 60 OR MORE HOME RUNS IN A SEASON

1. JOSH GIBSON—84, 72, and 69

During his five-year career with the Pittsburgh Crawfords of the Negro leagues, Gibson is reported to have hit 84 home runs in a single season. Unofficial records show him slugging 69 and 72 homers in other seasons for the Crawfords. Gibson was elected to the Baseball Hall of Fame in Cooperstown, N.Y., in 1972.

Home run king Josh Gibson.

2. JOE BAUMAN—72

Bauman's achievement came in 1954 while playing for Roswell, N.M., in the Class C Longhorn League. Despite his performance, he never made it to the major leagues.

3. JOE HAUSER—69 and 63

A former major leaguer not known for his home-run prowess (only 79 in 2,044 at-bats), Hauser hit 69 homers for Minneapolis of the then Class AA American Association in 1933. This topped his earlier feat of 63 in 1930 for Baltimore of the then Class AA International League.

4. BOB CRUES—69

Another slugger who never reached the major leagues, Crues clouted 69 round-trippers for the Class C Amarillo club of the West Texas–New Mexico League in 1948.

5. DICK STUART—66

The good-hit, no-field first baseman, who later earned the nickname of Dr. Strangeglove in the majors, slammed 66 four-baggers for Lincoln, Neb., of the Class A Western League in 1956. A scant two years later he was playing in the majors, where he would hit a big-league career high of 42 homers for the Red Sox in 1963.

6. BOB LENNON—64

Lennon's 64 homers in 1954 while with Nashville of the Class AA Southern Association earned him a promotion to the New York Giants. He went 0–3 as a pinch hitter in the majors that year; in his 79 career at-bats in the majors, he hit one home run.

7. JOHN "MOOSE" CLABAUGH—62

Clabaugh was playing for Tyler of the Class D East Texas League in 1926 when he hit the 62 homers. On the strength of this performance he rose in one season from Class D, the lowest professional level, all the way to Brooklyn of the National League, where he lasted only 11 games.

8. KEN GUETTLER—62

Here is another long-ball hitter who never made it to the major leagues. Guettler hit the 62 homers while playing for Shreveport in the Class AA Texas League.

9. ROGER MARIS—61

Maris set this record-breaking mark in 1961 while with the New York Yankees. It appeared in the official record book with an asterisk; the fine print below pointed out that it took Maris 162 games to break Babe Ruth's 1927 record, which was set in 154 games. Actually, Maris came to the plate 590 times during the season, and Ruth 540.

10. BABE RUTH—60

The New York Yankee hit a home run every 9 trips to the plate during a remarkable 1927 season. His record of 60 stood for 34 years. Ruth wound up with a lifetime total of 714 home runs, a mark that Henry Aaron finally topped in 1974.

11. TONY LAZZERI—60

A teammate of Ruth's during the New York Yankee dynasty of the late 1920s and early 1930s, Lazzeri was the first professional player to hit 60 home runs. This occurred in 1925, when he was with Salt Lake City of the Triple A Pacific Coast League, and when he also scored 202 runs and drove in 222—records that still stand.

Note: Sadaharu Oh, the Japanese superstar who has hit over 830 lifetime home runs, holds the Japanese record for home runs hit in one season with 55.

SOURCE: Bert Randolph Sugar, *Who Was Harry Steinfeldt & Other Baseball Trivia Questions*. New York: Playboy Press, 1976.

10 MAJOR LEAGUERS WITH THE WORST HOME-RUN RECORDS (MINIMUM 2,900 AT-BATS)

	At-Bats	Home Runs
1. Davy Force (1876–1886), ss-2b	2,950	1
2. Emil Verban (1944–1950), 2b	2,911	1
3. Jimmy Slagle (1899–1908), of	4,994	2
4. Al Bridewell (1905–1915), ss	4,167	2
5. Tommy Thevenow (1924–1938), ss	4,164	2
6. Johnny Cooney (1921–1944), of	3,372	2
7. Mile Tresh (1938–1949), c	3,169	2
8. Bill Bergen (1901–1911), c	3,028	2
9. Tom Jones (1902–1910), 1b	3,847	3
10. Lee Tannehill (1903–1912), 3b-ss	3,778	3

Dishonorable Mention:

Bill Holbert (1876–1888), c-of	2,335	0

—R.C.BE.

10 MAJOR LEAGUE PITCHERS WITH THE WORST WON-LOST RECORDS (MINIMUM 100 DECISIONS)

	W–L	W–L%
1. Jim Hughey (1891–1900)	29–80	.266
2. Happy Townsend (1901–1906)	35–81	.302
3. Bill Bailey (1907–1922)	34–78	.304
4. Buster Brown (1905–1913)	48–105	.314
5. George Smith (1916–1923)	39–81	.325
6. Bob Barr (1883–1891)	49–98	.333
7. Hugh Mulcahy (1935–1947)	45–89	.336
8. Rollie Naylor (1917–1924)	42–83	.336
9. Gus Dorner (1902–1909)	36–70	.340
10. Mal Eason (1900–1906)	37–71	.343

Dishonorable Mention (25–95 decisions)

1. Jack Nabors (1915–1917)	1–24	.040
2. Joe Harris (1905–1907)	4–29	.121
3. Crazy Schmidt (1890–1901)	7–36	.163

	W–L	W–L%
4. Ike Pearson (1939–1948)	13–50	.206
5. John Coleman (1883–1890)	23–72	.242

—R.C.BE.

SATCHEL PAIGE'S
10 GREATEST PITCHERS OF ALL TIME

Leroy "Satchel" Paige was 42 and already a legend when he was signed to a major league contract with Cleveland in 1948. For over 20 years he had pitched brilliantly in the Negro leagues. In 1934 he ran off a string of 21 victories and 62 scoreless innings en route to a 31–4 season. He is also said to have thrown some 300 career shutouts, 55 of them no-hitters. In 1965 the 59-year-old Paige started for the Kansas City A's, the oldest player to pitch in the majors.

1. Bob Feller
2. Sam Streeter
3. Don Newcombe
4. Catfish Hunter
5. Sandy Koufax
6. Hilton Smith
7. Bullet Rogan
8. Bob Lemon
9. Allie Reynolds
10. Willie Foster

Note: Streeter, Smith, and Rogan all pitched for the Kansas City Monarchs of the Negro leagues, as did Paige for several seasons. Smith, who often came in for Paige in the later innings, compiled a 161–22 lifetime record. Foster pitched for the rival Chicago American Giants, winning 26 straight in his rookie year in 1926.

—Exclusive for *The Book of Lists 2*

WILT CHAMBERLAIN'S
TOP 10 PLAYERS IN PRO
BASKETBALL HISTORY

The towering presence of Wilt Chamberlain dominated pro basketball for 14 years, during which the 7-ft. 1-in. center set all-time NBA scoring and rebound records and became the only player

George Mikan, picked by Wilt Chamberlain as the
No. 1 basketball player of all time.

in NBA history to score 100 points in a game. Chamberlain led the
Los Angeles Lakers to the NBA championship in 1972 and left
basketball the following year to play for the International Volleyball
Association.

1. George Mikan
2. Oscar Robertson
3. Elgin Baylor
4. Jerry West
5. Wilt Chamberlain
6. Bob Pettit
7. Chet Walker
8. Guy Rodgers
9. Nate Thurmond
10. Walt Frazier

—Exclusive for *The Book of Lists* 2

BOB COUSY'S
9 GREATEST BASKETBALL
PLAYERS OF ALL TIME

The brilliant play-making and shooting of Bob Cousy, whom Red Auerbach called "the greatest backcourt man who ever lived," helped the Boston Celtics become a basketball dynasty in the 1950s and early 1960s. Cousy led the NBA in assists eight consecutive seasons and made the All-Star team each of his 13 years in the league. He retired in 1963, after helping Boston to its fifth consecutive championship, and went into college coaching.

1. Bill Russell
2. Elgin Baylor
3. Dolph Schayes
4. Bob Pettit
5. Jerry West
6. Oscar Robertson
7. Kareem Abdul-Jabbar
8. Julius Erving
9. George Mikan

—Exclusive for *The Book of Lists 2*

THE 20 GREATEST KNOCKOUT
FIGHTERS* (MINIMUM 25 FIGHTS)

		Bouts	Won-Lost-Draws	Knock-outs	KO%	Years Active
1.	Wilfredo Gomez Junior Featherweight, Puerto Rico	30	29–0–1	29	.967	1974–
2.	Carlos Zarate Bantamweight, Mexico	56	54–2	53	.946	1971–
3.	Thomas Hearns Welterweight, U.S.	29	29–0	27	.931	1976–
4.	George Foreman Heavyweight, U.S.	47	45–2	42	.894	1969–77
5.	Sean O'Grady Lightweight, U.S.	70	69–1	62	.886	1975–
6.	Rocky Marciano Heavyweight, U.S.	49	49–0	43	.878	1947–55

	Bouts	Won-Lost-Draws	Knock-outs	KO%	Years Active
7. Juan "Kid" Mesa Jr. Lightweight, Mexico	31	29–2	27	.871	1977–
8. Salvador Sanchez Featherweight, Mexico	36	34–1–1	31	.861	1975–
8. Jose Luis Ramirez Lightweight, Mexico	36	35–1	31	.861	1975–
8. German Torres Mini-Flyweight, Mexico	36	33–3	31	.861	1975–
8. Pedro Galaviz Mini-Flyweight, Mexico	36	32–4	31	.861	1975–
12. Alfonso Zamora Bantamweight, Mexico	35	31–4	30	.857	1973–
13. Danny Lopez Featherweight, U.S.	46	42–4	39	.848	1971–
13. Jose Luis Castillo Lightweight, Mexico	46	43–3	39	.848	1972–
15. Sergio Lozano Middleweight, Mexico	26	22–4	22	.846	1975–
16. Ernesto Espana Lightweight, Venezuela	30	28–2	25	.833	1976–
17. Earnie Shavers Heavyweight, U.S.	68	58–9–1	56	.824	1969–
18. Andy Ganigan Lightweight, U.S.	32	30–2	26	.813	1976–
19. Steve Aczel Cruiserweight, Australia	26	23–3	21	.808	1975–
19. Duane Bobick Heavyweight, U.S.	52	48–4	42	.808	1973–80

*Records as of June, 1980.

—R.LL.

9 NON-BOXERS WHO TOOK ON THE CHAMPIONS

1. LORD BYRON (1788–1824), English poet

Byron sparred with John "Gentleman" Jackson, the former bareknuckled champion, in the poet's Bond Street rooms. Both men wore "mufflers" (mittenlike gloves used for sparring in the early days). The poet boxed in a dressing gown, Jackson in knee breeches and a shirt. Byron, with his legendary temper, was reputedly a tough customer in the ring.

2. HESSIE DONAHUE (?–?), U.S. housewife

John L. Sullivan, world heavyweight champion from 1882 to 1892, invited Hessie and her husband, a boxing instructor, to join his entourage, which was staging boxing exhibitions in theaters around the country. As part of an act they worked out, Hessie, wearing boxing gloves and dressed in a blouse and bloomers, would climb into the ring after Sullivan had disposed of his male challengers, and the two would go at it. During one of their sparring sessions, Sullivan inadvertently hit Hessie in the face, and she countered with a right to the jaw that sent him to the canvas for a full minute. The audience was so delighted that Hessie and Sullivan decided to make a "knock-out" part of their regular routine.

3. PAUL GALLICO (1897–1976), U.S. author

Gallico, author of *The Poseidon Adventure*, was a cub reporter in 1923, assigned to Jack Dempsey's camp at Saratoga Springs prior to the heavyweight champion's title bout with Luis Firpo. Against his better judgment, Gallico asked Dempsey to spar with him for one round. It was, for Gallico, a vivid and somewhat terrifying experience as he was "stalked and pursued by a relentless, truculent professional destroyer." He never saw the punch that flattened him; he was aware only of an explosion in his head, and the next instant he was sitting on the canvas grinning stupidly. He struggled to his feet and finished the round propped up in a clinch with Dempsey, absorbing those taps to the neck and ribs that as an observer had seemed so innocuous to him.

Hessie Donahue, who decked
heavyweight champion John L. Sullivan.

4. J. PAUL GETTY (1892–1976), U.S. entrepreneur

The billionaire oil magnate met Jack Dempsey in 1916, when Dempsey was an up-and-coming young fighter, and the two became good friends. Getty, who kept fit in the fully equipped basement gym in his parents' mansion, used to spar with Dempsey. Dempsey has claimed that, in an altercation over a girl, Getty knocked him out with a left uppercut—the only time Dempsey was ever KO'd by anyone.

5. ERNEST HEMINGWAY (1899–1961), U.S. author

During visits to Hemingway's Havana home, former heavyweight champion Gene Tunney would occasionally allow himself to be talked into sparring bare-fisted with the writer, especially if the two had just downed a thermos of frozen daiquiris. Once Hemingway, in a rambunctious mood, tagged Tunney with a hard punch. Incensed, Tunney feinted his friend's guard down and then faked a menacing punch to the face, as he issued a stern warning: "Don't you ever do that again!"

6. HUGH LOWTHER (1857–1944), British sportsman

Outraged that John L. Sullivan had never fought Jem Smith, the English heavyweight titleholder, the 5th Earl of Lonsdale challenged Sullivan to a bout. According to the earl, he took considerable punishment from the hard-hitting champion—they fought bare-knuckle in those days—but dropped Sullivan in the sixth round with a solid blow to the solar plexus. Though at least two people verified Lowther's version, Sullivan's memoirs make no mention of the fight.

7. GEORGE MITCHELL (?–?), British university student

Following the 1913 first-round knockout of Bombardier Wells, the British heavyweight champion, by Georges Carpentier, the Orchid Man from France, the National Sporting Club of England decided to recoup the country's diminished prestige. The club sent Carpentier the following challenge: that one of their members, George Mitchell, a student at Cambridge, could stay in the ring with him longer than Wells's 73 seconds. The club also offered the Orchid Man £200 just to appear, with a £100 bet thrown in to sweeten the pot. Carpentier agreed with pleasure. The fight, which took place in Paris, opened with Carpentier's sending Mitchell down for a 9 count with a left to the jaw. Mitchell was decked two more times but managed to get up before the full count. He had lasted the required 73 seconds—plus an additional 15 seconds—when the referee called the fight.

8. GEORGE PLIMPTON (1927–   ), U.S. journalist and author

One of Plimpton's early experiments in "participatory journalism" was taking on Archie Moore, the former light-heavyweight champ, in January, 1959. The fight lasted only three rounds, during which Moore cuffed Plimpton around gently, bloodying his nose. The referee called it a draw. Moore was asked how long it would have taken him to polish off his opponent had time been a factor. Moore told Plimpton, " 'Bout the time it would take a tree to fall on you, or for you to feel the nip of the guillotine."

9. ALBERT PAYSON TERHUNE (1872–1942), U.S. journalist and author

Terhune, author of popular dog stories (*Lad: A Dog; The Heart of a Dog*), was once a reporter for the New York *Evening World*. His editor assigned him to fight six boxing greats—Jim Corbett, Kid McCoy, Gus Ruhlin, Jim Jeffries, Bob Fitzsimmons, and Tom Sharkey—and share his experiences with the readers. An excellent amateur boxer who had already sparred with most of these fighters, Terhune jumped at the opportunity for some good copy, but to his surprise he absorbed considerable punishment in each encounter. He later discovered that his editor, to create an authentic experience, had offered a half-page feature to whichever fighter could knock him out first. Terhune suffered a broken hand and lost two teeth, but none of the six knocked him out.

—L.C.

FLOYD PATTERSON'S 10 BEST HEAVYWEIGHTS IN BOXING HISTORY

A Golden Gloves champion and 1952 Olympic gold medalist, 21-year-old Floyd Patterson knocked out Archie Moore in 1956 to become the youngest boxer to win the world heavyweight title. He lost the crown to Ingemar Johansson of Sweden in 1959 but won it back the following year, becoming the first man ever to regain the title.

1. Joe Louis
2. Rocky Marciano
3. Jack Dempsey
4. Jersey Joe Walcott
5. Joe Frazier
6. Cassius Clay
7. Ingemar Johansson
8. Gene Tunney
9. Jack Johnson
10. Ezzard Charles

Patterson adds: "My idea of a champion is not only the way a man fights inside the ring, but how he carries himself outside the ring."

—Exclusive for *The Book of Lists* 2

HENRY ARMSTRONG'S 10 GREATEST NON-HEAVYWEIGHT BOXERS OF ALL TIME

The only fighter to hold three world titles simultaneously, Henry Armstrong won the featherweight title in 1937 and the welterweight and lightweight crowns in 1938. Considered one of the

Lightweight Joe Gans, picked the No. 1 Non-
Heavyweight fighter of all time by Henry Armstrong.

greatest boxers of modern times, Armstrong was elected to the boxing
Hall of Fame in 1954. He is now an ordained Baptist minister.

1. Joe Gans—lightweight
2. Ad Wolgast—lightweight
3. Battling Nelson—lightweight
4. Joe Walcott—welterweight
5. Young Jack Thompson—welterweight
6. Jackie Fields—welterweight
7. Barney Ross—welterweight
8. Sugar Ray Robinson—middleweight
9. Henry Armstrong—featherweight/welterweight/lightweight
10. Lou Ambers—lightweight

—Exclusive for *The Book of Lists* 2

BOBBY FISCHER'S
10 GREATEST CHESS
PLAYERS IN HISTORY

One of the greatest chess players of all time, Bobby Fischer
was the youngest ever to win the U.S. chess championship, at age

14, and he was the youngest international grandmaster in history, at age 15. Adept at psychological warfare as well as chess strategy, Fischer beat Boris Spassky in Reykjavik, Iceland, in 1972 for the World Chess Championship, making him the first American to win the world title.

1. Paul Morphy (U.S., 1837–1884)
2. Howard Staunton (England, 1810–1874)
3. Wilhelm Steinitz (Bohemia, 1836?–1900)
4. Siegbert Tarrasch (Poland, 1862–1934)
5. Mikhail Tchigorin (Russia, 1850–1908)
6. Alexander Alekhine (Russia, 1892–1946)
7. José Raoul Capablanca (Cuba, 1888–1942)
8. Boris Spassky (Russia, 1937–   )
9. Mikhail Tal (Russia, 1936–   )
10. Samuel Reshevsky (U.S., 1911–   )

SOURCE: © 1964 *Chessworld*, published by Frank Brady.

10 FOOTBALL PLAYERS
WHO BECAME *MORE* FAMOUS
IN OTHER FIELDS

1. JOHNNY MACK BROWN (1904–1974)

An All-American halfback at Alabama (1924–1926), Brown played on the first southern team to compete in the Rose Bowl (1926) and was instrumental in leading the Tide to a 20–19 victory over Washington. His exploits drew the attention of Hollywood talent scouts, who beckoned him to a movie career that began in 1926 with *The Bugle Call* and extended over the next 40 years to include more than 300 pictures. In the 1930s, especially, he became famous as the good-looking cowboy hero who never lost his hat in a fight with the bad guys.

2. ERSKINE CALDWELL (1903–   )

In his autobiography Caldwell noted that as a freshman at Erskine College (1920–1921) he was pressured by upperclassmen to make the football team and found that once he had done so, he really enjoyed the sport. Using the poor whites and blacks of his southern homeland as main characters, Caldwell has produced numerous short stories and novels, including *Tobacco Road* and *God's Little Acre*.

3. DWIGHT DAVID EISENHOWER (1890–1969)

By all accounts, the "Kansas Cyclone" was destined for greatness as a running back for Army, but a knee injury in his second season ended a promising grid career. Ike's future lay elsewhere, as commander in chief of allied forces in western Europe in W.W. II and as 34th president of the U.S. However, he never lost his interest and enthusiasm for football and sports in general. During his second term as president, Eisenhower became the first recipient of the Gold Medal Award of the National Football Foundation.

4. GERALD R. FORD (1913–   )

Turning down pro offers from the Chicago Bears and Detroit Lions after a successful stint as a center at Michigan (1931–1935), Ford coached boxing and football at Yale (1935–1941) while studying law. He then turned to politics after a five-year hitch in the navy. He became a U.S. congressman, then vice-president, and subsequently president of the U.S. when Richard Nixon stepped down in 1974. The former College All-Star received recognition for his athletic achievements when he was named to the *Sports Illustrated* 1959 Silver Anniversary All-American Team. He also won the 1972 Gold Medal Award from the National Football Foundation.

5. KRIS KRISTOFFERSON (1936–   )

Although Kristofferson became an outstanding football star at Pomona College (1954–1957) and later attended Oxford on a Rhodes Scholarship, his heart belonged to songwriting and singing. In the early 1970s he became a successful performer of "progressive" country-western music. At the same time, he turned to acting and became famous in such feature films as *Alice Doesn't Live Here Anymore, A Star Is Born,* and *Semi-Tough,* a movie about professional football.

6. RICHARD MILHOUS NIXON (1913–   )

While in office, Nixon was notorious for his fanatical devotion to football, and on several occasions he called professional players before key games and gave them plays—personally mapped out by the President. Nixon's abilities as a player were, however, limited. At Whittier College (1930–1934), he made the starting football squad in his freshman year, when only 11 men tried out for the team. For the next three years he sat on the bench as a reserve tackle, but his coach praised him as a determined young man who, if nothing else, was "wonderful for morale." A former teammate once recalled that Nixon, in his eagerness to win, was offside on nearly every play.

7. VERNON L. PARRINGTON (1871–1929)

This distinguished American scholar received his first exposure to the "new" game of football as an undergraduate at Harvard in the early 1890s, and a short time later as an English teacher at Emporia College, where he played on the school's very informal football team. In 1897 he became a member of the faculty at the University of Oklahoma, and along with his teaching duties came the position of head football coach. Using techniques he had seen earlier at Harvard, he built a winning team with a three-year record of 9-2-1. Turning solely to academic pursuits in 1900, he wrote *Main Currents in American Thought,* which won the Pulitzer Prize as the best work in history for 1928.

8. FREDERIC REMINGTON (1861–1909)

An excellent all-around athlete at Yale, Remington was especially fond of football. According to one story, before an 1879 game with Princeton, he coated his jersey with blood from a nearby slaughterhouse in order to make the contest "look more businesslike." While in college, he also displayed artistic talent and eventually became world-renowned for his realistic paintings of the American West.

9. PAUL ROBESON (1898–1976)

Robeson was an extremely gifted individual who first gained public attention as an All-American end at Rutgers (1915–1918), where he was a Phi Beta Kappa and only the third black to attend. He played professional football with Hammond (1920), Akron (1921), and Milwaukee (1922). When he finally left the game, he moved on to international acclaim as a singer and actor and to controversy as a Communist sympathizer. Still, his fame and popularity endured, and on his 73rd birthday Robeson was honored in a gala celebration at Carnegie Hall.

10. BYRON WHITE (1917–   )

Among the greatest football players of the first half of this century, "Whizzer" White not only became a consensus All-American running back at Colorado (1937) but also received the first five-figure salary ($15,800) as a pro with the Pittsburgh Pirates (1939–1940) and Detroit Lions (1940–1941). After leaving the pro ranks, he practiced law and worked hard for the Democratic party. For his services, President John Kennedy named him deputy attorney general of the U.S. in 1961, and in 1962 appointed him a justice on the U.S. Supreme Court.

—G.D.G.

RED GRANGE'S
10 GREATEST RUNNING
BACKS OF ALL TIME

Perhaps best known for his explosive five-touchdown performance against Michigan in 1924, Harold "Red" Grange, University of Illinois's All-American halfback, also became a superstar in the pros for the Chicago Bears. Known as the Galloping Ghost, he generated national interest in the sport with his electrifying broken field running. He was also an outstanding defensive back. Grange retired from football in 1935 and went into broadcasting. The following list is in alphabetical order.

1. Jay Berwanger—University of Chicago
2. Jim Brown—Syracuse/Cleveland Browns

3. Earl "Dutch" Clark—Colorado/Detroit Lions
4. Clarke Hinkle—Bucknell/Green Bay Packers
5. Ollie Matson—University of San Francisco/Los Angeles Rams
6. Bronko Nagurski—Minnesota/Chicago Bears
7. Ernie Nevers—Stanford/Chicago Cardinals
8. Gale Sayers—Kansas/Chicago Bears
9. O. J. Simpson—University of Southern California/Buffalo Bills (now with the San Francisco 49ers)
10. Jim Thorpe—Carlisle/Canton Bulldogs

—Exclusive for *The Book of Lists 2*

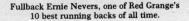

Fullback Ernie Nevers, one of Red Grange's
10 best running backs of all time.

GEORGE BLANDA'S
10 BEST KICKERS
IN FOOTBALL HISTORY

George Blanda's NFL career spanned an astonishing 26 years and made an indelible mark on pro football history. More than 20 years after he broke in with the Chicago Bears in 1949, he was performing game-winning miracles for the Oakland Raiders with last-minute touchdown passes and field goals. Blanda finally retired in 1975 at age 47, having amassed 2,002 points to become the NFL's all-time leading scorer.

1. Lou Groza—Cleveland Browns
2. Gino Cappelletti—Boston Patriots
3. Fred Cox—Minnesota Vikings
4. Jim Turner—Denver Broncos
5. Jan Stenerud—Kansas City Chiefs
6. Jim Bakken—St. Louis Cardinals
7. Mark Moseley—Washington Redskins
8. Tom Dempsey—Buffalo Bills
9. Don Cockroft—Cleveland Browns
10. Lou Michaels—Baltimore Colts

—Exclusive for *The Book of Lists 2*

9 MULTIPLE WINNERS OF
MAJOR GOLF CHAMPIONSHIPS

Golfer	British Open	U.S. Open	P.G.A.	Masters
1. Jack Nicklaus 16 titles	1966-70-78	1962-67-72-80	1963-71-73-75	1963-65-66-72-75
2. Walter Hagen 11 titles	1922-24-28-29	1914-19	1921-24-25-26-27	
3. Ben Hogan 9 titles	1953	1948-50-51-53	1946-48	1951-53
4. Gary Player 9 titles	1959-68-74	1965	1962-72	1961-74-78
5. Harry Vardon 7 titles	1896-98-99; 1903-11-14	1900		
6. Bobby Jones 7 titles	1926-27-30	1923-26-29-30		
7. Gene Sarazen 7 titles	1932	1922-32	1922-23-33	1935
8. Sam Snead 7 titles	1946		1942-49-51	1949-52-54
9. Arnold Palmer 7 titles	1961-62	1960		1958-60-62-64

—E.C.S.

10 BEST PRO HOCKEY PLAYERS OF ALL TIME

The Book of Lists 1 published a list of the 10 greatest pro hockey players of all time compiled by Bill Schroeder, director of the Citizens' Savings Hall of Fame. His selections sparked much controversy among hockey fans, prompting columnist Drew Snider of the Canadian *Sports Journal* to invite readers to submit their choices for the top 10. The 300 respondents unanimously chose Gordie Howe, Bobby Orr, Bobby Hull (the top three on Schroeder's list), and Guy Lafleur.

1. GORDIE HOWE

Played right wing for the Detroit Red Wings, 1946–71; set records for most goals, most assists, most points, and most penalty minutes. Retired in 1980, at age 52, from the New England Whalers.

2. BOBBY ORR

Defenseman for Boston Bruins, 1966–76. MVP in 1970, '71, '72. Won James Norris Trophy for best defenseman 8 years in a row (1968–75).

3. GUY LAFLEUR

Right wing and center for Montreal Canadiens, 1971–present.

4. BOBBY HULL

Left wing for Chicago Black Hawks, 1957–72. NHL scoring leader 7 times; 12 times on All-Star team. Became player-coach with Winnipeg Jets (WHA) in 1972.

5. HOWIE MORENZ

Forward for Montreal Canadiens (1923–34, 1936–37), Chicago Black Hawks (1934–35), New York Rangers (1935–36). Enormously popular player known for his blazing speed. Died at age 35.

6. TERRY SAWCHUK

Goalie for Red Wings (1950–55, 1957–64, 1968–69), Bruins (1955–57), Toronto Maple Leafs (1964–67), Los Angeles Kings (1967–68), and Rangers (1969–70). Was first-team All-Star his rookie year. Holds the record for career shutouts with 103. Died at age 41 of injuries received in a fight with a teammate.

7. MAURICE "ROCKET" RICHARD

Right wing for Canadiens, 1942–60. Part of the famed Canadiens "Punch Line." Only player to score 50 goals in a season (1945). Elected to Hockey Hall of Fame in 1961.

8. DOUG HARVEY

Defenseman for Canadiens (1947–61), Rangers (1961–64), Red Wings (1966–67), St. Louis Blues (1968–69). Coach with Rangers,

Gordie Howe, all-time hockey great.

1961–62. Won James Norris Trophy 7 times. Elected to Hall of Fame in 1973.

9. JEAN BELIVEAU

Center with Canadiens, 1951–71. Only other player besides Howe to exceed 1,000-point mark.

10. FRED "CYCLONE" TAYLOR

Defenseman, rover, and center for Ottawa Senators (1908–09), Renfrew Millionaires (1910–11), Vancouver Millionaires (1913–21). Played one game in 1923. Elected to Hall of Fame in 1945.

—Annotated by the Eds.

JOHNNY LONGDEN'S 10 GREATEST JOCKEYS IN TURF HISTORY

Second only to Willie Shoemaker in career victories, Johnny Longden won over $24 million in his 40 years of racing, highlighted by his Triple Crown victory in 1943 aboard *Count Fleet*. Elected to the Racing Hall of Fame in 1958, Longden retired in 1966 to become a trainer and breeder.

1. Willie Shoemaker
2. George Woolf
3. Eddie Arcaro
4. Sir Gordon Richards
5. Laffit Pincay
6. Jackie Westrope
7. Sandy Hawley
8. Sonny Workman
9. Darrell McHargue
10. Don Meade

—Exclusive for *The Book of Lists 2*

WILLIE SHOEMAKER'S 10 BEST RACEHORSES OF ALL TIME

The winningest jockey in racing history, Willie Shoemaker also holds the record for most stakes wins, and wins in races of over $100,000, including three Kentucky Derbies. Twenty-four percent of his mounts finish first—the best record among name jockeys. The Shoe is still racing, more than 30 years after he rode his first winner in 1949.

1. Swaps
2. Citation
3. Ribot
4. Forego
5. Secretariat
6. Bold Ruler
7. Sea Bird
8. Alleged
9. Exceller
10. Gallant Man

—Exclusive for *The Book of Lists 2*

10 MOST CONTROVERSIAL EVENTS
IN OLYMPIC HISTORY

There have been endless controversies surrounding the modern Olympic Games. Some samples: Paris, 1900—The French refused to hold the finals on Bastille Day, a Saturday, and moved them to Sunday, forcing a half-dozen U.S. competitors and finalists to withdraw since they refused to run on the Lord's Day. Stockholm, 1912—U.S. Indian Jim Thorpe became the world's greatest athlete with his decathlon win, but a year later his gold medal was taken away when it was learned he had once received a few dollars for playing semiprofessional baseball. (His runner-up, Hugo Wieslander of Sweden, refused to accept Thorpe's gold medal.) Antwerp, 1920—The U.S. team revolted against its barracks living quarters and threatened to boycott the Olympics. Berlin, 1936—Adolf Hitler had signs mounted over toilets reading, "Dogs and Jews are not allowed." (Olympic official Comte de Baillet-Latour told Hitler the signs had to be removed. Hitler said, "When you are invited to a friend's home, you don't tell him how to run it, do you?" To which Baillet-Latour replied, "Excuse me, Mr. Chancellor, when the five-circled flag is raised over the stadium, it is no longer Germany. It is Olympia, and we are masters there." The signs were removed.) And Hitler, after personally congratulating the first two medal winners, snubbed Jesse Owens, U.S. non-Aryan, who won four gold medals. Melbourne, 1956—The Dutch refused to compete because of the Soviet Union's repression of Hungarian freedom fighters. Mexico City, 1968—Impoverished students protesting money lavished on the Olympics battled the army, resulting in 260 students killed and 1,200 injured. During the games, after finishing first and third in the 200 meters, U.S. sprinters Tommie Smith and John Carlos, upon the playing of "The Star-Spangled Banner," gave the Black Power salute from the victory podium, and both were dropped from the Olympic team. Munich, 1972—There occurred the single most terrifying happening in Olympic history when eight Black September Arab terrorists took over the headquarters of the Israeli team and caused the deaths of 12 Israelis. At the same Olympics, when 20 countries accused Rhodesia of apartheid and said they would quit the games if Rhodesia participated, Rhodesia was voted out of the games. Montreal, 1976—Canadian Prime Minister Pierre Trudeau banned the athletes from the accredited Republic of China (Taiwan) and eventually forced them out of the games in order to pacify the People's Republic of China (mainland Communists), with whom Canada was involved in big business deals.

Those, and more, have been some of the darker events in modern Olympic history. But they have not involved actual moments of Olympic competition and action. From a long and bitter saga of backbiting, cheating, bad sportsmanship, and officiating politics and prejudices, the author has selected what he considers the 10 most controversial events in actual Olympic competition.

1. MARATHON—ATHENS—1896

The Greeks, hosts to the first modern Olympics, did not have a winner until the last event, the marathon. National hysteria reigned when a 25-year-old Greek postman, Spiridon Louis, won not only the event and the gold medal but 365 free meals and the hand of a Greek millionaire's daughter (which he had to reject because he was already married). Finishing second was another Greek, Harlambos Vassilakos; finishing third, still another Greek, Dimitries Velokas. Fourth came Gyula Kellner, a Hungarian. Kellner protested that he deserved the third-place bronze medal instead of Velokas, because the Greek had cheated. Consternation. A hearing. The Hungarian had seen the Greek ride up toward the stadium in a horse and carriage, get out, and continue on foot. Velokas did not argue. The truth came out. Velokas had hidden a horse and carriage in a park. Tired of running, he rode a back route part of the way and finished on foot in third place. The controversy ended with Velokas disqualified, his singlet with the Greek colors torn from his back, and his bronze medal handed to Kellner (who also received a gold watch for his performance as an informer).

2. MARATHON—PARIS—1900

At the halfway mark, Arthur Newton of the U.S. took the lead and held it. He ran into the stadium assuming he was the winner. To his astonishment, he learned he had come in fifth. There were four other marathoners at the finish line ahead of him. In first place was Michel Teato, a French baker. In second and third place were two other Frenchmen, in fourth place a Swede. Newton protested. None of the four had ever passed him during the race. Unofficial reports drifted in that Teato and his three runners-up had taken a horse and carriage most of the distance or had detoured from the regular route to take a shortcut through Parisian side streets. The judges were indecisive. It took them 12 years to declare Teato the official gold medalist.

3. MARATHON—ST. LOUIS—1904

This was a wild one. Fred Lorz of the U.S. was back in the pack of runners being led by Thomas Hicks, a British-born professional clown who represented the U.S. After 10 mi., Lorz suffered a cramp and dropped out of the race. He hitched a ride from a passing truck headed toward the stadium. Six miles from the finish the truck broke down. Lorz got out, found his cramp had disappeared, and resumed running. He trotted into the stadium in first place. Thousands of spectators came to their feet, cheering him. Alice Roosevelt, the U.S. president's daughter, was about to decorate Lorz with the gold medal when other runners who had just finished converged on them in a rage. They had seen Lorz hitch his truck ride. Angrily, they exposed him. Finally Lorz confessed his hoax. He had meant it as a joke but had got carried away by the adulation. Thomas Hicks was declared the winner. Lorz was disqualified from running for life. A year later this ban was lifted, and he won the U.S. marathon championship.

4. 400 METERS—LONDON—1908

According to Olympic record books, the 400-meter winner is listed as, "W. Halswelle—G.B. (Walkover) 50 s." This bland entry fails to reveal the terrible controversy behind it. In an atmosphere of intense British anti-Americanism, the race got under way. The leading competitors were T. C. Carpenter, W. C. Robbins, John Taylor—all from the U.S.—and a Scotsman and member of His Majesty's Guards, Lt. Wyndham Halswelle, representing Great Britain. When the runners tore into the final stretch, Robbins was ahead, with Carpenter behind him, and the Britisher Halswelle third. As Halswelle moved to the outside to try for the lead, Carpenter edged over from the inside to block him from passing. In the shuffle, one of the Americans elbowed Halswelle. British spectators and officials were infuriated. Seconds later, as Carpenter—in first—tried to break the tape, he found there was none. A vengeful British official had yanked it away. Robbins, in second, also made a tapeless finish. But Halswelle, coming in third, found the tape waiting to be broken. A British judge had already screamed, "Foul!" At last a compromise was reached. The entire 400 meters would be rerun the following day. The Americans refused to run it again. So Lieutenant Halswelle ran it by himself and was given the gold medal, but the controversy over this contest persisted for decades.

5. MARATHON—LONDON—1908

The long-distance runners had started at Windsor Castle, had covered a grueling 26 mi. to the Olympic Stadium in 2 hr. and 50 min., and were approaching the amphitheater, where 80,000 persons, royalty and commoners, waited to see them race the last 385 yd. of cinder track. The leader at this point was the heavy favorite, Charles Hefferon of South Africa, followed by wispy Italian candy-maker Dorando Pietri, with a New York clothing store clerk named Johnny Hayes in third place. As they neared the stadium, Dorando, stimulated by strychnine, sprinted into the lead. The English crowd went wild. The glassy-eyed Dorando smiled weakly, staggered in the wrong direction, and collapsed. Rising, he was pointed in the right direction. He wobbled along, his knees folded once more, and he went down again. Gallant English officials could endure this no longer. The officials, among them A. Conan Doyle, lifted Dorando upright and carried him across the finish line. At that moment the American, Johnny Hayes, having also passed Hefferon, came into the stadium, easily circled the track, and crossed the finish line. His teammates were pounding him with congratulations when the megaphone announcement came: "Marathon winner, Dorando of Italy! Second, Hayes of the United States!" The spectators cheered, the American coach screamed. Hayes had finished on his feet. Dorando had been carried across the finish and had fouled out. As Dorando was rushed to a hospital, hovering between life and death, a bitter four-hour debate ensued over the rightful winner. At last Hayes was declared the victor. Dorando survived to accept a gold cup from the queen as a consolation prize.

6. WOMEN'S 100-METER DASH—BERLIN—1936

Poland was represented by the heavy favorite, the unbeaten and invincible Stella Walsh, whose best time in the dash had been 11.9 sec. in winning the previous Olympics. The U.S. dark horse was a rangy young lady from Missouri named Helen Stephens. The contestants came off their marks fast, and Stephens took the lead and ran Poland's favorite, Walsh, into the dirt. Stephens burst across the finish tape first in 11.5. The Poles were stunned. They shrieked that the American, Helen Stephens, was a male ringer disguised as a woman. Angry words flew, and officials decided there was only one way to end the controversy. Miss Stephens was asked to disrobe and display herself in the nude to women attendants. This she did. It was unanimously agreed she was all woman. That settled it. If possible, the Poles were more embarrassed than Miss Stephens.

7. 400-METER RELAY—LONDON—1948

It was the last event of track and field competition, and the British wanted it. They had not won a single gold medal. But the U.S. relay team was the fastest in the world: Harrison Dillard had already won the 100-meter, Mel Patton had won the 200-meter, Barney Ewell had finished second in both, and Lorenzo Wright was capable of beating any of them. The relay got off at top speed, the Americans—Ewell and Wright—giving the U.S. a slight lead over the British after 200 meters. Then Dillard and Patton opened up, and the U.S. had beaten the British by 8 meters. One problem. Two British judges announced that the U.S. had committed an infraction of the rules and was disqualified, and Great Britain was awarded first place. The infraction had occurred, said the judges, after the first leg of the race, when Ewell passed the baton to Wright. The pass-off had been made outside the legal passing zone. The argument raged for four days, while the British press accused American protesters of bad sportsmanship. Since these were the first Olympic Games officially filmed, the jury of appeals was able to view the movie of the event. The film showed two white lines across the track. One marked the end of the 100-meter leg, the other the end of the 110-meter legal passing zone. The judges had looked at the wrong line. The gold medals were taken back from the British and given to the U.S. relay team.

8. 3,000-METER STEEPLECHASE—MELBOURNE—1956

The three favorites in this rough-and-tumble contest with 35 obstacles to surmount were world record holder Sandor Razsnyoi of Hungary, unbeaten Chris Brasher of Great Britain, and highly rated Ernst Larsen of Norway. The drama unfolded in the final bell lap. The three went into it with Razsnyoi in front, Brasher and Larsen a close second and third. As they came pounding around the last bend, Brasher and Larsen simultaneously decided to go wide to pass the leader in their climactic bids. Doing so, Brasher's left arm struck Larsen in the stomach, making him break stride. Brasher went on, catapulting past Razsnyoi to win the steeplechase by 2.4 seconds in Olympic record time. Brasher was the winner, but there was no gold medal awaiting him. Australian judges declared he had fouled Larsen and was disqualified. Larsen himself had filed no protest. The race was awarded to Razsnyoi. The Hungarians cheered. The British ranted. For three hours the argument raged. Finally the verdict was in. It was decided that Brasher's foul was accidental, not willful, and victory was restored to him.

9. 100-METER FREESTYLE SWIMMING—ROME—1960

It was neck and neck between Lance Larson of the U.S. and John Devitt of Australia. They went into the last 25 meters like thrashing twins. Ten meters from the finish, Devitt was inches ahead. Then, with a last burst of energy, Larson pulled even and touched the end of the pool a hand ahead. Everyone hailed Larson, and even Devitt swam over to congratulate him. The three judges huddled. The automatic timers had Larson finishing in 55.1 sec. and Devitt in 55.2. The judges changed Larson's time to 55.2—and gave first place to the Australian Devitt. The Americans hurled protests and invective, but Devitt remained the unaccountable gold medalist.

10. BASKETBALL—MUNICH—1972

U.S. quintets had won 64 consecutive games and seven Olympic titles in 36 years. This year the U.S. team was pitted against the U.S.S.R. five in the finals. With six seconds to go, the Russians led 49-48 and had the ball. They had started to freeze it when an American, Doug Collins, stole it and dribbled for the basket. Two Russians knocked him down, a foul, and Collins took two free throws and made them both. The horn sounded, and the U.S. jubilantly celebrated a 50-49 victory. But a Bulgarian referee shouted that the game wasn't over. There was still one second to go. He insisted play resume. The Russian in-bounds pass went astray as the horn sounded a second time, with the U.S. the winner. Now a British official intervened. He announced that the clock was wrong. He ordered the clock reset with three more seconds to play. Protesting, the U.S. players took to the court a third time. The Russians got the ball to Aleksandr Belov under the hoop. He fouled two American defenders (uncalled) and easily dumped the ball into the basket, as the horn sounded a third time. The U.S.S.R. had won its dubious title, 51-50. The U.S. team boycotted the award ceremony and rejected its second-place silver medals.

—I.W.

Aleksandr Belov, of the U.S.S.R., scoring the winning
layup against the U.S. in the most controversial
basketball game in Olympic history.

8 SURPRISING
OLYMPIC COMPETITORS

1. JAMES B. CONNOLLY

    Well-known author of sea stories; U.S.; triple jump; Athens, 1896.

2. A. C. GILBERT

    Inventor of the erector set; U.S.; pole vault; London, 1908.

3. NERO

    Emperor of Rome; chariot racing; Greece, 66 A.D.

4. MICHELINE OSTERMEYER

    Concert pianist; France; shot put, discus, high jump; London, 1948.

5. GEORGE PATTON

    W.W. II general; U.S.; pentathlon; Stockholm, 1912.

6. COUNT PAOLO IGNAZIO DI REVEL

    Mussolini's minister of finance; Italy; fencing; Antwerp, 1920.

7. DR. BENJAMIN SPOCK

    Baby doctor, author, political activist; U.S.; rowing; Paris, 1924.

8. VARASDATES

    King of Armenia; boxing; Greece, 390 A.D.

—J.N.

DON BUDGE'S
10 BEST MALE PLAYERS IN
TENNIS HISTORY

A top-ranked player in the 1930s and considered one of the best in tennis history, Budge became the first player ever to achieve a Grand Slam in men's singles by winning the Wimbledon championship, the U.S. championship at Forest Hills, and the French and Australian outdoor championships in 1938. With his famous rolled backhand, Budge is credited with turning a theretofore defensive stroke into a potent offensive weapon.

1. Jack Kramer
2. Ellsworth Vines
3. Lew Hoad
4. Rod Laver
5. Fred Perry
6. Pancho Gonzales

7. Bill Tilden
8. Baron Gottfried von Cramm
9. Pancho Segura
10. Ken Rosewall

—Exclusive for *The Book of Lists 2*

ILIE NASTASE'S
10 BEST MALE PLAYERS IN
TENNIS HISTORY

The *enfant terrible* of tennis, Ilie Nastase is as successful as he is controversial. The Romanian star has to his credit the U.S. indoor championship (1970), the U.S. Open (1972), the Pepsi Grand Slam (1976), and the Challenge Cup (1977 and 1978), to list a handful of his tournament wins. His country honored him as a Master of Sport in 1969.

1. Pancho Gonzales
2. Jimmy Connors
3. Rod Laver
4. Lew Hoad
5. Ken Rosewall
6. Bjorn Borg
7. John Newcombe
8. Manuel Santana
9. Pancho Segura
10. Ilie Nastase's nephew

—Exclusive for *The Book of Lists 2*

MARTINA NAVRATILOVA'S
8 BEST WOMEN TENNIS
PLAYERS OF ALL TIME

Named Rookie of the Year in 1974 by *Tennis World,* Navratilova has enjoyed several brilliant seasons on the Virginia Slims circuit and in 1979 she won her second straight Wimbledon singles title. (She took the women's doubles with Billie Jean King in 1976 and 1979.) The Czech star defected to the U.S. in 1975 in order to play tennis "whenever and wherever" she wishes.

1. Billie Jean King
2. Chris Evert Lloyd
3. Margaret Smith Court
4. Maureen Connolly
5. Maria Bueno
6. Suzanne Lenglen
7. Helen Wills Moody
8. Evonne Goolagong

—Exclusive for *The Book of Lists 2*

THE 20 MAJOR LEAGUE TEAMS WITH THE MOST UNFRIENDLY FANS

Bob McMahon of Ridley Park, Pa., a stockbroker and former college professor, surveyed professional athletes to discover which fans they consider, among other things, the most unfriendly. The 172 respondents included baseball's Pete Rose and Mark Fidrych; Julius Erving and Pete Maravich of the NBA; Fran Tarkenton and O. J. Simpson of the NFL; and Tony Esposito and Gil Perreault of the NHL.

	Points (awarded on 5-4-3-2-1 basis)
Baseball	
1. New York (Yankees)	97
2. Philadelphia	59
3. New York (Mets)	43
4. Chicago (White Sox)	36
5. San Francisco	35
Basketball	
1. San Antonio	48
2. Philadelphia	44
3. New Orleans	30
4. Seattle	29
5. Detroit	24
Football	
1. Oakland	65
2. Philadelphia	61
3. New England	53
4. Baltimore	42
5. Denver	36
Hockey	
1. Philadelphia	88
2. N.Y. Rangers	75
3. Detroit	41
3. N.Y. Islanders	41
5. Boston	34

THE 15 MOST LOPSIDED
SCORES IN U.S. HIGH SCHOOL
SPORTS COMPETITION

Sport	Score	Winner	Loser	Date
1. Football	256–0	Haven High, Haven, Kans.	Sylvia High, Sylvia, Kans.	Nov. 16, 1927
2. Football	233–0	Staunton High, Staunton, Ill.	Gillespie High, Gillespie, Ill.	Nov. 23, 1923
3. Football	216–0	Muskegon High, Muskegon, Mich.	Hastings High, Hastings, Mich.	Sept. 28, 1912
4. Boys' basketball	211–29	Grand Avenue High, De Quincy, La.	Audrey Memorial, Cameron, La.	Jan. 29, 1964
5. Boys' basketball	198–34	W. O. Boston High, Lake Charles, La.	South Cameron High, Creole, La.	1976
6. Boys' basketball	192–31	Resurrection High, Memphis, Tenn.	Christ the King High, Memphis, Tenn.	1945
7. Boys' basketball	182–21	Princeton High, Princeton, La.	C. H. Iron High, Benton, La.	1968
8. Boys' basketball	172–12	Walsh High, Ottumwa, Ia.	Blakesburg High, Blakesburg, Ia.	1969
9. Girls' basketball	162–3	Central High, Lonaconing, Md.	Ursaline Academy, Cumberland, Md.	Feb. 25, 1924
10. Girls' basketball	143–1	Magnolia A&M, Monticello, Ark.	Baptist High, Jonesboro, Ark.	Jan. 10, 1931
11. Girls' basketball	140–2	St. Scholastica Academy, Fort Smith, Ark.	Wesson High, Wesson, Ark.	Mar. 20, 1930
12. Baseball	63–3	Dufur High, Dufur, Ore.	Cascade Locks High, Cascade Locks, Ore.	May 17, 1977

	Sport	Score	Winner	Loser	Date
13.	Baseball	48–0	Lincoln High, Ruston, La.	Hodge High, Jonesboro, La.	1969
14.	Baseball	48–0	Christian High, El Cajon, Calif.	Day High, La Jolla, Calif.	Apr. 14, 1977
15.	Hockey	48–0	Traverse City High, Traverse City, Mich.	Saginaw High, Saginaw, Mich.	Mar. 6, 1979

—D.H.

17
THE BEST OF HEALTH

RATING THE EFFECTS OF
43 PERSONAL CRISES

In the 1920s, Dr. Walter Cannon began recording connections between stressful periods in a person's life and the appearance of physical ailments. A decade later, Dr. Adolf Meyer compiled a "life chart," which specifically correlated health problems with a person's particular life circumstances at the time. This process was refined during the 1950s and 1960s and resulted in the creation of the Social Readjustment Rating Scale (SRRS), which ranks 43 life crises on a scale of Life Change Units (LCUs). The ratings were arrived at by researchers who used in-depth interviewing techniques on an international sample of 5,000 people from Europe, the U.S., Central America, Oceania, and Japan. Because of the consistency with which marriage was rated as one of the most significant life changes, it was given a value of 50 on the scale, and 42 other life crises were judged in relation to it. Some cultural differences surfaced (for example, the Japanese ranked minor law violations near the middle of the list and jail terms second from the top), but on the whole there was a remarkable uniformity of results, cutting across all national and socioeconomic levels. SRRS supporters contend that there is a direct correlation between annual LCUs and stress-related diseases. One of their studies found that with a "mild" stress level (150 to 199 LCUs in a single year), health problems increased 37% above the average; with a moderate level (200 to 299 LCUs), the increase was 51%; and with a major crisis level (300 LCUs and above), 79% more health problems occurred. The researchers noted that what counted was the cumulative total, not whether the life changes in themselves were positive or negative.

Rank	Life Event	LCU Value
1.	Death of a spouse	100
2.	Divorce	73
3.	Marital separation	65
4.	Jail term	63
4.	Death of a close family member	63
6.	Personal injury or illness	53
7.	Marriage	50
8.	Fired from job	47
9.	Marital reconciliation	45
9.	Retirement	45
11.	Change in health of family member	44
12.	Pregnancy	40
13.	Sex difficulties	39

13.	Gain of a new family member	39
13.	Business readjustment	39
16.	Change in financial state	38
17.	Death of a close friend	37
18.	Change to a different line of work	36
19.	Change in number of arguments with spouse	35
20.	Mortgage over $10,000	31
21.	Foreclosure of mortgage or loan	30
22.	Change in responsibilities at work	29
22.	Son or daughter leaving home	29
22.	Trouble with in-laws	29
25.	Outstanding personal achievement	28
26.	Wife begins or stops work	26
26.	Begin or end school	26
28.	Change in living conditions	25
29.	Revision of personal habits	24
30.	Trouble with boss	23
31.	Change in work hours or conditions	20
31.	Change in residence	20
31.	Change in schools	20
34.	Change in recreation	19
34.	Change in church activities	19
36.	Change in social activities	18
37.	Mortgage or loan less than $10,000	17
38.	Change in sleeping habits	16
39.	Change in number of family get-togethers	15
39.	Change in eating habits	15
41.	Vacation	13
42.	Christmas	12
43.	Minor violations of the law	11

SOURCE: T. H. Holmes and R. H. Rahe, "The Social Readjustment Rating Scale," *Journal of Psychosomatic Research*, Vol. 11. Copyright © 1967, Pergamon Press, Ltd.

29 ACTIVITIES AND THE CALORIES THEY CONSUME

Activity	*Calories per Hour*
1. Making mountains out of molehills	500
2. Running around in circles	350
3. Wading through paperwork	300
4. Pushing your luck	250
5. Eating crow	225
6. Flying off the handle	225
7. Jumping on the bandwagon	200
8. Spinning your wheels	175

9.	Adding fuel to the fire	150
10.	Beating your head against the wall	150
11.	Climbing the walls	150
12.	Jogging your memory	125
13.	Beating your own drum	100
14.	Dragging your heels	100
15.	Jumping to conclusions	100
16.	Beating around the bush	75
17.	Bending over backwards	75
18.	Grasping at straws	75
19.	Pulling out the stoppers	75
20.	Turning the other cheek	75
21.	Fishing for compliments	50
22.	Hitting the nail on the head	50
23.	Pouring salt on the wound	50
24.	Swallowing your pride	50
25.	Throwing your weight around (depending on your weight)	50–300
26.	Passing the buck	25
27.	Tooting your own horn	25
28.	Balancing the books	23
29.	Wrapping it up at day's end	12

SOURCE: *Bulletin,* Columbus Industrial Association, July 11, 1977.

10 EMINENT CONSTIPATION SUFFERERS

1. THOMAS JEFFERSON (1743–1826), U.S. president

In 1819 Jefferson found himself in a most embarrassing and traumatic situation. That year his close friend Wilson Cary Nicholas defaulted on a $20,000 bank loan and died shortly afterward. Jefferson, who had cosigned the loan, was held liable for his friend's debts and he was forced to mortgage and sell some of his holdings. Upset by this disaster, Jefferson was stricken with severe indigestion and a stoppage of the bowels that for several days endangered his life.

2. MAXIMILIEN FRANÇOIS MARIE ISIDORE DE ROBESPIERRE (1758–1794), French revolutionist

Between the winter of 1793 and the summer of 1794, Robespierre sentenced more than 6,000 men and women to the guillotine. Some of his associates tried to discourage his use of this inhumane device by describing, in gory detail, the sight of a person being beheaded. The thought of it made Robespierre sick. He vomited regularly, he complained daily of stomach cramps, and he was tormented by constipation. But he still insisted that the machine was a necessary evil. In complete agreement, the Revolutionary Tribunal condemned Robespierre himself to the "maiden" on July 28, 1794—thus ending the Reign of Terror.

3. NAPOLEON BONAPARTE (1769–1821), French emperor

Napoleon was a great believer in hot baths and relied on them to cure every kind of cold and fever. He also thought they could relieve constipation, from which he suffered all his life. He ate very rapidly, usually finishing long before anyone else, which probably didn't help his digestion.

4. WILLIAM HENRY HARRISON (1773–1841), U.S. president

Some of Harrison's presidential portraits show him with tightly compressed lips and a stern expression. He has been praised by moralists and historians as a teetotaler. But there is evidence to indicate that his abstinence was necessary because alcohol irritated his stomach, and that his austere pose was the look of a man who had suffered from a chronic digestive disorder since youth. He seems to have been sensitive to a variety of foods due to a duodenal ulcer, which limited his diet principally to milk, cheese, and meat. His inability to ingest vegetables and other bulk foods led him to resort to strong laxatives for relief from chronic constipation.

5. HENRY JAMES (1843–1916), U.S. novelist

James delighted in being an American expatriate in Europe and spent much of his time traveling across the continent by train. During most of these journeys, he was cursed with constipation. Somewhat of a hypochondriac, James took these attacks so seriously that he likened them to having terminal cancer.

The long-suffering Henry James strolling on the beach at Rye, Sussex, with Mary Hooper Warner, the niece of historian Henry Adams, in 1906.

6. SIGMUND FREUD (1856–1939), Austrian neurologist, founder of psychoanalysis

Due to an extended treatment for cancer of the jaw, upsets of Freud's digestive system became organic rather than psychosomatic, and he suffered from a spastic colon which caused painful abdominal cramps. These were accompanied by alternating constipation and mucous diarrhea.

7. MOHANDAS "MAHATMA" GANDHI (1869–1948), Hindu nationalist and spiritual leader

Although Gandhi experimented widely with meager diets and fasts to relieve his physical complaints and to encourage the restraint of sexual and other passions, during the early 1900s he suffered from constipation, which no diet would cure. He finally tried an "earth treatment" consisting of a poultice of clean earth moistened with cold water and spread on fine linen. Applied to the abdomen at bedtime and removed during the night or in the morning, this proved a radical cure, which he used on himself and his friends.

8. GEORGE GERSHWIN (1898–1937), U.S. composer

Gershwin, who often complained that nobody believed him when he said he was sick, was plagued by chronic constipation, which he referred to as "composer's stomach." Physicians were unable to locate a source of the trouble, so he sought the help of a psychoanalyst, who said the problem was caused by a chronic neurosis. Although psychoanalytic therapy helped him conquer some inhibitions, it did not alleviate his condition. Other efforts to find relief included giving up cigars, taking agar before bedtime, and limiting his diet to cereals, biscuits, and fruits. None of these remedies helped, and he was tortured by constipation until the end of his life.

9. HOWARD HUGHES (1905–1976), U.S. industrialist, aviator, and film producer

Because Howard Hughes suffered from chronic constipation, he kept a supply of books and magazines at hand in the bathroom so that he could scout movie stories while he spent extraordinary lengths of time waiting. He was always seeking remedies for his constipation, which may have been caused by poor nutrition and a longtime use of codeine.

10. JUDY GARLAND (1922–1969), U.S. singer-actress

Judy Garland endured increasingly poor health toward the end of her life. Her liver and kidneys became diseased, and she developed colon and rectal obstructions, which caused excruciating pain. Later she became very weak and painfully thin, but she was unable to eat enough to regain her strength. Solid foods sometimes made her gag, and when she did eat, severe stomach pains accompanied by extreme constipation often followed.

—A.K. & L.K.L.

10 MOST FREQUENTLY PERFORMED OPERATIONS IN THE U.S.

	Operations per Year (1978)
1. DILATION AND CURETTAGE OF UTERUS, DIAGNOSTIC	967,000

Enlargement of the cervix and scraping of the uterus lining to obtain tissue for examination.

2. HYSTERECTOMY	644,000

Removal of the uterus.

3. LIGATION AND DIVISION OF FALLOPIAN TUBES	553,000

Female sterilization.

4. CESAREAN SECTION	510,000

Delivery of a child through an abdominal incision.

4. REPAIR OF INGUINAL HERNIA	510,000

Removal of sac that is protruding through the abdomen and sewing tissue over the defect.

6. EXCISION OF LESION OF SKIN AND SUBCUTANEOUS TISSUE	443,000

Removal of a mole or other skin growth.

7. SALPINGO-OOPHORECTOMY	434,000

Removal of the Fallopian tubes or ovaries.

8. CHOLECYSTECTOMY	432,000

Removal of the gallbladder.

9. REDUCTION OF FRACTURE WITH FIXATION	382,000

Setting of a broken bone

10. OPERATIONS ON MUSCLES, TENDONS, FASCIAE, BURSAS	366,000

Repair of damaged tendons, ligaments, fasciae, and bursas.

SOURCE: *Division of Health Resources Utilization Statistics, National Center for Health Statistics. Unpublished data from the National Hospital Discharge Survey for 1978.*

AMONG THE 8 BIGGEST
HYPOCHONDRIACS IN HISTORY

1. PERCY BYSSHE SHELLEY (1792–1822), English poet

Although Shelley had true illnesses, the poet's friends testified that he exaggerated them greatly. When he grew nervous about the general state of his health, imaginary maladies overcame him. In 1815 he was convinced he had tuberculosis, but later that year the illness vanished as his overall physical condition improved. He was drowned in a boating accident on July 8, 1822, at the age of 29.

2. FLORENCE NIGHTINGALE (1820–1910),
English nurse and hospital reformer

Returning to England in 1856 after performing her good deeds in the Crimea, Nightingale took to her bed the following year, convinced she had terminal heart disease. To friends she confided that her "life hung by a thread" which could "snap at any moment." The Lady of the Lamp remained bedridden until one day, as she had predicted, her heart stopped—in 1910, when she was 90.

3. OSKAR VON REDWITZ (1823–1891),
German poet and dramatist

From the age of 40 to the time of his death at 68, the baron daily went to a physician to speak of a new ailment he was suffering. It was estimated that in 28 years he complained of at least 10,000 different ailments, most of them illnesses never mentioned in medical books and never heard of before by his doctors.

4. THEODORE DREISER (1871–1945), U.S. novelist

Dreiser's hypochondria seems to have stemmed from his preoccupation with death and a feeling of impermanence. He constantly took pills for a variety of imagined ailments. At a dinner party, poet Charles Hanson Towne was astonished when Dreiser's wife, nicknamed Jug, exclaimed, "It's time for your pill, Honeybugs." Dreiser died at age 74 of a heart attack.

5. MARCEL PROUST (1871–1922), French novelist

The author suffered from many real ailments, including bronchial asthma, hay fever, and chronic lung weakness, and his obsession with these afflictions dictated his every move. He showed up at his brother's wedding groaning under three overcoats, several scarves, and chest padding. He was so bulky that he was unable to fit into a pew and had to spend the entire ceremony standing in the aisle. He had the walls of his bedroom lined with cork to reduce dust and noise, and as time went on and his anxiety over the state of his health worsened, he rarely left this room. He died from pneumonia in 1922 at the age of 51.

6. H. L. MENCKEN (1880–1956), U.S. editor and writer

Mencken was a lifelong hypochondriac. He was obsessively

worried about germs and would often wash his hands five or six times while editing a single article. He kept a running list of troublesome symptoms, which were checked out on his regular visits to the hospital. He died in 1956, following an attack of cerebral thrombosis, at age 75.

7. DON HEROLD (1889–1966), U.S. cartoonist and writer

Herold was kept awake nights by a peculiar thumping sensation. Two weeks of X-rays, electrocardiograms, and other tests failed to detect the problem. Little wonder, for the source of Herold's nocturnal throbs turned out to be the thermostat on his electric blanket. He did, however, die of a heart attack at age 77.

8. GOODMAN ACE (1899–), U.S. writer and humorist

As the self-styled founder of Hypochondriacs Anonymous, the gifted comedy writer once claimed that he had an "annual" checkup weekly to ward off a host of terminal illnesses. His frequent symptoms included an accelerated heartbeat, a rapid pulse, and shortness of breath. In 1979 Ace celebrated his 80th birthday.

—W.A.D.

HEARTENING NEWS— 7 PEOPLE WHO SUCCEEDED AFTER SUFFERING STROKES

1. GEORGE FREDERICK HANDEL (1685–1759), German-British composer

Suffered a stroke in 1737, at age 52. Five years later he composed *The Messiah,* and continued to compose until his death.

2. WALT WHITMAN (1819–1892), U.S. poet

Suffered first stroke in 1858 and made a complete recovery. After the stroke he made several revisions and enlargements of *Leaves of Grass,* the poetry volume first published in 1855. A second stroke in 1873 left Whitman partially paralyzed, but he continued revising the book, which did not begin to resemble its final form until 1881. His last revision was published the year of his death.

3. LOUIS PASTEUR (1822–1895), French chemist and microbiologist

Permanently paralyzed on his left side by a stroke in 1868. Pasteur did most of his immunology research after the stroke, developing vaccines for anthrax and chicken cholera in 1881 and for rabies in 1885.

4. WINSTON CHURCHILL (1874–1965), British prime minister and statesman

Suffered first stroke in 1949 and second stroke in 1953. He served as prime minister from 1951 until his resignation in 1955, and he remained active in Parliament until 1959. Among Churchill's accomplishments after his second stroke were supervision of the development of the British hydrogen bomb in 1955 and the publication of his four-volume *History of the English-Speaking Peoples* in 1956–1958.

5. DWIGHT D. EISENHOWER (1890–1969), U.S. president

Made quick and complete recovery from stroke in 1955. The following year Eisenhower was reelected and completed a second presidential term. In retirement, he remained active in Republican party politics and wrote three books. An avid golfer, he scored his only hole in one in 1968, 13 years after his stroke and a year before his death.

6. ELLEN CORBY (1913–   ), U.S. actress

Suffered near-fatal stroke in 1976. Corby, who portrays Grandma Walton on television, was never written out of the script of the popular series; instead, she was referred to as being hospitalized. In 1978, partially paralyzed and with impaired speech, she returned to *The Waltons* show as a regular.

7. PATRICIA NEAL (1926–   ), U.S. actress

Suffered a series of near-fatal strokes in 1965. Though pregnant at the time of the first stroke, she bore a normal child. She resumed acting in 1968 and received an Academy Award nomination for best actress in *The Subject Was Roses*.

—A.T.

7 BODY PARTS YOU DIDN'T KNOW HAD NAMES

1. EPONYCHIUM

Another term for the cuticle of the fingernail, a narrow band of epidermal tissue that extends down over the margin of the nail wall.

2. FRENUM GLANDIS

Found in the male reproductive system, this delicate fold of skin attaches the foreskin to the undersurface of the glans penis.

3. GLABELLA

A flattened area of the frontal bone (forehead area) between the frontal eminences and the superciliary arches (eyebrows) just above the nose.

4. OTOLITHS

Particles of calcium carbonate in the utricles and saccules of the internal ears. The otoliths respond to gravity by sliding in the direction of the ground and causing sensitive hairs to bend, thus generating nervous impulses important in maintaining equilibrium.

5. PHALANX

One of the bones of the fingers or toes. There are two phalanges in each thumb and great toe, while there are three phalanges in all other fingers and toes, making a total of 14 in each hand or foot.

6. PHILTRUM

The vertical groove in the middle portion of the upper lip.

7. PUDENDUM

A collective name for the external genitalia of the female; also known as the vulva. It includes the mons pubis, the labia majora, and the labia minora.

—K.A.M.

5 BODY PARTS
NAMED AFTER ITALIANS

1. ORGAN OF CORTI

The organ of hearing in the internal ear. Named after Alfonso Corti (1822–1878).

2. EUSTACHIAN TUBE

A tube leading from the middle ear to the throat. Its purpose is to equalize pressure in the ear. Named after anatomist Bartolommeo Eustachio (1524?–1574).

3. FALLOPIAN TUBES

The pair of tubes that conduct the egg from the ovary to the uterus in the female. Named after anatomist Gabriel Fallopius (1523–1562).

4. RUFFINI'S CORPUSCLES

Sensory nerve endings which respond to warmth. Named after anatomist Angelo Ruffini (1864–1929).

5. SERTOLI CELLS

Cells of the testis that serve to nourish sperm cells. Named after histologist Enrico Sertoli (1842–1910).

—K.A.M.

Gabriel Fallopius, M.D. who named the vagina,
the placenta, and the clitoris.

HAVE A HEART—7 PRESERVED ONES

1. SHELLEY'S HEART

The most famous of all preserved hearts is that of the poet
Percy Bysshe Shelley. Shelley perished in a storm at sea off Italy in
1822. His body washed ashore, and he was cremated soon after, with
his friends Lord Byron, Edward Trelawny, and Leigh Hunt in an-
guished attendance. After the body had been burned almost to ashes,

Trelawny snatched Shelley's heart out of the fire, burning his hand in the process. He and Hunt squabbled over the heart, and Hunt kept it until Mary Shelley asked for it. Hunt at first refused to give it to her, saying in a letter that she did not deserve it, and that his rights as a loving friend were greater than hers as a failed wife. Eventually, when a third party intervened, Hunt was persuaded to give it up. Mary kept it with her, wrapped in a piece of silk, for the rest of her life. After her death it was found in her desk, dried to dust and enclosed between the pages of *Adonais*, one of her husband's works. Later, the heart was placed in a silver case and finally buried in the grave of Shelley's son Percy in St. Peter's churchyard in Bournemouth. There is a peculiar note of irony to the whole affair: The organ that longest survives a fire is not the heart but the liver—and no one present at Shelley's cremation knew enough about anatomy to tell the difference. This theory would explain the legend that the heart was unusually large.

2. DR. DAVID LIVINGSTONE'S HEART

When Dr. Livingstone died in Africa, natives removed his heart and embalmed the rest of his corpse. They carried the body to Bagamoyo and shipped it to England, where it was interred in Westminster Abbey. But his heart remained in Africa—literally. His devoted followers buried it within the roots of an old African tree, and on the bark of the tree a native carved neatly, "Dr. Livingstone, May 4, 1873."

3. THOMAS HARDY'S HEART

When the great English novelist Thomas Hardy died in 1928, his body became the subject of an unseemly squabble among the townsfolk of Dorchester, where he lived, and the village of nearby Stinsford, his birthplace. Eventually the citizens of Stinsford agreed to his cremation in the other town, so long as they could bury his heart in their village churchyard. "Unfortunately," John Hardy Antell, Hardy's only surviving relative, reported, "Hardy's sister's cat got at the heart when it was on the kitchen table and made off with it in the shrubs." The cat returned a few days later. "But I could never look it in the eye again," said Antell. The burial of a tin, thought by the public to contain the heart, went ahead.

4. ALBERTO SANTOS-DUMONT'S HEART

The great aviation pioneer committed suicide in July, 1932, during a Brazilian revolution. A São Paulo physician embalmed Santos-Dumont's body and kept it in his laboratory for 12 years. After a Brazilian aviation executive discovered the body, he had Santos-Dumont's heart placed in a gold container set inside a crystal casket atop a marble base. This may be seen today in the Air Cadet School of the Ministry of Aeronautics in Rio de Janeiro.

5. JOHN DE BALIOL'S HEART

When Baliol, head of Barnard Castle, Scotland, died in 1269, his grieving widow, Lady Devorguila, retained his heart. She embalmed it and carried it with her in a small ivory casket wherever she went. She called it her "sweet heart and silent companion." Thus the word *sweetheart* was coined. Upon her death, she ordered that her husband's heart be placed on her breast in her grave.

6. PAUL WHITEHEAD'S HEART

Paul Whitehead was the "atheist chaplain" of England's infamous Hell-Fire Club of devil-worshiping debauchees. He married a girl for her money and spent all his time engaged in sex orgies and satanism with fellow club members. When he died in 1774, he willed his heart, and £50 to purchase an urn, to the notorious Sir Francis Dashwood, the club's founder. After a ritual ceremony and the oddly normal music of a fife and drum corps, the heart was placed in a niche in the strange caves Dashwood had built near West Wycombe.

7. JOHANN CARL GOTTFRIED LOEWE'S HEART

This German organist and composer began singing at an early age and was greatly admired for his fine voice. He later became a distinguished composer of lieder. He was personally acquainted with Goethe, whose texts he set to music. In 1821 he was appointed music director and organist at St. Jacobus Church in Stettin, Poland. In 1864 he went into a deep and mysterious trance, from which he recovered six weeks later. Two years after that, he was asked to resign his post, and he retired to Kiel. In Kiel, in 1869, he lapsed into another deep trance, from which he never revived. His embalmed heart is contained within a gold capsule in the left pillar of the church organ of St. Jacobus, where he was music director for so many years.

—A.W.

DR. JUDD MARMOR'S 10 PEOPLE IN HISTORY HE WOULD LIKE TO HAVE ANALYZED

Presently a professor of psychiatry at the University of Southern California, Dr. Marmor received his M.D. from Columbia in 1933. He is former president of the American Psychiatric Association and of the American Academy of Psychoanalysis. In addition to numerous articles, his books include *Modern Psychoanalysis: New Directions and Perspectives* (1968), *Psychiatry in Transition* (1973), *Psychiatrists and Their Patients: A National Survey of Private Practice* (1975), and *Homosexual Behavior: A Modern Reappraisal* (1979).

According to Marmor: Naming 10 people in history whom I would like to have analyzed poses a difficult dilemma for me. My initial impulse is to list 10 preeminent epic figures because it would be such a rewarding privilege to observe the working of their minds—extraordinary persons like Jesus, Einstein, Picasso, Shakespeare, Beethoven, Edison, Paine. However, I have decided against going that route. It would be self-serving. Psychoanalytic treatment is not a luxury to be lightly indulged in either by patient or therapist. It is for people who are in serious need of it because of major mental or emotional conflicts and whose lives might be substantially benefited by it. Accordingly, the 10 historical figures I have chosen are neither the greatest nor the most important figures in their chosen fields, but they were all remarkable individuals of outstanding talent whose lives were either shortened or embittered by their emotional conflicts and difficulties. My omission of blacks and various ethnic groups is not due to prejudice but to an insufficient knowledge of their great historical figures, which makes me unable to make a meaningful choice. I am aware also that my list is dominated by writers and artists and that I have omitted many outstanding personalities from other spheres of accomplishment. This, in part, is a reflection of my personal interests, but it is also due to the necessarily limited size of my list.

1. EMILY BRONTË (1818–1848)

Perhaps the most talented of the Brontë sisters, author of *Wuthering Heights*. A silent, reserved, and stoical woman on the surface, her writings reveal powerful hidden emotions and passions. Died of acute tuberculosis at the early age of 30 without having had the opportunity to fulfill the enormous promise of her single novel and her few remarkable poems.

2. HART CRANE (1899–1932)

American poet of unusual promise who committed suicide at age 32. The child of an unhappy and broken marriage, he drank heavily and was torn by severe conflicts during most of his adult life.

3. EMILY DICKINSON (1830–1886)

Brilliant American poet. The child of distant parents, she became a shy and frightened recluse in her late 30s and wrote little poetry thereafter.

4. VINCENT VAN GOGH (1853–1890)

Dutch artist of matchless luminosity, who suffered from intense feelings of loneliness and inadequacy culminating in a serious mental breakdown in the last years of his life. Shot himself to death at age 37.

5. FRANZ KAFKA (1883–1924)

Remarkably talented Czech writer of fiction dealing with inner despair, fear, and alienation. Caught in a lifelong oedipal struggle with a domineering father, he never resolved his sexual guilts or broke away from his parental ties. Died at 40 of tuberculosis, a disease often precipitated or exacerbated by prolonged emotional stress.

6. YUKIO MISHIMA (1925–1970)

Flamboyant and talented Japanese author. Raised by a semi-psychotic grandmother and a despotic father. His deep feelings of guilt and anger were reflected in an exaggerated militarism and a

Author Franz Kafka on the couch—
"despair, fear, and alienation."

lifelong preoccupation with blood, death, and suicide. Committed seppuku (ritual suicide) at age 45.

7. EDVARD MUNCH (1863–1944)

Extraordinary Norwegian artist and pioneer of 20th-century expressionist painting. Lost his mother at age five and his sister, father, and brother during adolescence. The specter of death and suffering haunted his entire life and colored most of his work.

8. EDGAR ALLAN POE (1809–1849)

Pioneer detective-story writer, romantic poet, and master of the macabre and the phantasmagoric, most of whose adult life was clouded by alcoholic excesses that were responsible for his premature death.

9. AUGUST STRINDBERG (1849–1912)

Sweden's greatest modern writer, whose childhood was marred by poverty and emotional insecurity, and most of whose adult life was clouded by a succession of unhappy marriages that created enormous emotional stress and mental instability.

10. DYLAN THOMAS (1914–1953)

Welsh poetic genius whose magnificent talent was destroyed by emotional turmoil and alcoholism. After a severe depression at age 33, he literally drank himself to death six years later.

—Exclusive for *The Book of Lists* 2

10 PEOPLE WHO WERE 74 PEOPLE

The existence of more than one personality in a single mind is a rare psychological disorder. Only 100 verified cases have been reported. In such cases of multiple personality, the separate selves often have different names and distinct handwriting and electroencephalograms. In other words, the various personalities lodged in the same mind are different people with individual thought and behavior patterns. The following include some of the most notable occurrences of multiple personality.

1. MARY REYNOLDS (1793–1854)

The case of Mary Reynolds, described by Andrew Ellicott in 1815, is believed to be the first published account of multiple personality. Born in England, Mary Reynolds moved to the U.S. at age four, when her family settled in Pennsylvania. She grew up to be a pious, withdrawn, and melancholy young woman. At age 18 she began suffering from "fits," one of which left her blind and deaf for several weeks. After a subsequent attack, she lost her memory completely and underwent a profound personality change. She became an exuberant, gregarious, outdoor person. Five weeks later she fell into an unusually deep sleep. When she woke, she had reverted to her earlier self and had no recollection of the new personality that had emerged. The two personalities alternated at irregular intervals until she was 36, when the second personality took over completely and remained in control for the rest of her life.

2. ANNA WINSOR (?–?)

In the early 1860s, Anna Winsor, emotionally distraught and suffering from paralysis in her right hand, went to Dr. Ira Barrow for treatment. Barrow discovered that Miss Winsor had a distinct second personality, which expressed itself by using her right hand. Because it employed the paralyzed hand, the second personality was nicknamed Old Stump. Independently of the primary personality, Old Stump wrote poetry and sketched; it also protected Miss Winsor when, in a suicidal state, she attempted to injure herself with her left hand. Dr. Barrow observed that Old Stump never slept, even when Anna Winsor did. At night, the right hand would communicate with Dr. Barrow in sign language, write letters, or summon a nurse by rapping on the bedstead.

3. ANSEL BOURNE (1826–?)

In 1857 Ansel Bourne began suffering from excruciating headaches and became deaf, mute, and blind. When he recovered a short time later, he attributed it to divine grace and decided to devote the remainder of his life to spreading God's word. For the next 30 years Bourne divided his time between preaching and working his Rhode Island farm, until he suddenly disappeared on January 17, 1887. When Bourne "came to" on March 14, he found himself living in a small Pennsylvania town, operating a variety store, and using the name Arnold J. Brown. Under hypnosis in 1890, the personality known as Brown reemerged and discussed in detail what had transpired during the "lost" period in 1887. Although Brown stated that he had heard of Bourne, he was unaware of ever having met him. The Brown personality never spontaneously surfaced again. It could be reached only through hypnotic trance, and over the years it was observed to deteriorate gradually.

4. JOHN POULTNEY (1888–?)

In December, 1929, a man wandering aimlessly in the streets of Los Angeles was picked up by the police and taken to see Dr. Shepherd Franz. The man identified himself as C. J. Poulting and gave an account of his life for the past 14 years. However, he had no memory of any event prior to 1915. In March, 1930, C. J. Poulting again became disoriented. When he regained his senses, he identified himself as John C. Poultney, born in Dublin in 1888 (information corroborated by his family in Ireland). He said he was a member of the Irish army and insisted that the present year was 1914. For many months, Poultney continued to slip in and out of "dreamlike" states, during which he would change back and forth from personality 1 (pre-1915) to personality 3 (post-1915). An additional personality, which Franz labeled personality 2, also surfaced occasionally, but its activities remained unknown to personalities 1 and 3. After a year and a half of therapy, Poultney achieved a successful integration of personalities 1 and 3 and returned to his native Ireland.

5. SYBIL DORSETT (pseudonym, 1923–   )

With a tested IQ of 170, Sybil Dorsett graduated from college and led a seemingly normal existence as a schoolteacher. However, in 1954, while working on her master's degree at Columbia University, Sybil sought the help of psychiatrist Cornelia Wilbur because of the anguish caused by progressive periods of amnesia. Dr. Wilbur learned that Sybil as a child had been brutally tortured by her schizophrenic mother. In an attempt to cope psychologically with the situation, Sybil's mind dissociated at an early age and developed three new alternating personalities. Twelve more emerged over the next 20 years. The various selves included a home-loving matron, a religious fanatic, a vivacious seductress, two male personalities, and a central memory personality who called herself Victoria Antoinette Scharleau. After 11 years of therapy, the 16 selves were integrated into a 17th personality. Since leaving therapy, Sybil has become a recognized artist in New York City.

6. CHRIS COSTNER SIZEMORE (1927–   )

In 1952 Chris Sizemore sought psychiatric help because of terrifying blackouts. During therapy, it was discovered that Mrs. Sizemore had two distinct personalities, which her psychiatrist, Dr. Corbett Thigpen, labeled Eve White and Eve Black. Eve White, the personality that had sought help, was very religious, prudish, and soft-spoken, while Eve Black acted out all the anger, aggression, and sensuality that Eve White suppressed. A third personality, Jane, developed during the second year of therapy, but she gave way to an apparently stable and well-integrated fourth personality in 1954. Dr. Thigpen dismissed Mrs. Sizemore as cured and publicized her case history in the highly successful book *The Three Faces of Eve*, which

The final face of the 23 faces of Chris Sizemore.

later became a movie. In 1977, however, Chris Sizemore published her own account of her illness and revealed that during the previous 23 years many new personalities had emerged. In all, she had experienced 22 personalities, nine of which had preceded the basic schism between Eve White and Eve Black. Finally, in 1975, she became aware of her "real self," and she has been well ever since.

7. HENRY DANA HAWKSWORTH (1933–)

Henry Hawksworth's mind has been the home of six separate personalities, four of which developed during his early childhood. His central, usually dominant personality was Dana, a hardworking, intelligent person who became a successful California corporate executive. A second personality was Peter, a young boy who went to amusement parks and wrote poetry. A third was Johnny, a violent, often sadistic character who loved gambling, barroom brawls, and prostitutes. And a fourth was Phil, who emerged only to deal with crises. A transitional fifth personality, Jerry, came into existence later as a result of psychiatric therapy with Dr. Ralph Allison. Since 1976, the five formerly distinct selves have been integrated into a sixth personality—Henry. After the personality fusion, Henry appeared in court to face an old drunk driving charge against Johnny. For the first time in history, multiple personality was used as a defense, and Henry was acquitted because Johnny no longer existed.

8. GINA RINALDI (pseudonym, 1934–)

In December, 1965, Miss Rinaldi, a successful writer, went to see Dr. Robert Jeans because of repeated episodes of amnesia, sleepwalking, and erratic behavior. She revealed herself as a tough, callous woman, full of anger and suspicion and quick to take offense. Within a few months, Gina began referring to the existence of a second personality, Mary Sunshine, who apparently was the original infant personality. A tug-of-war began between Mary and Gina, and in early December, 1966, Gina informed Jeans that Mary Sunshine was planning to strangle her on December 31. No suicide attempt occurred, but when Gina met with Jeans in January, 1967, a third personality, Evelyn, had emerged. Although Evelyn was initially shallow and unfeeling, she developed rapidly through therapy. By May, 1967, the patient was sufficiently well for treatment to be terminated. Now married to a physician, she is leading a normal life and is free from all symptoms of her former illness.

9. CHRISTINA PETERS (1942–)

When she was five years old, as the result of being raped and tortured by her father, Christina splintered into Marie, an altruistic but essentially weak personality, and Linda, the repository of all Christina's rage. The worst of Linda's violent excesses were curbed by a third personality, Charlene. In 1974, after repeated suicide attempts and imprisonment for drug and alcohol addiction, the various personalities became receptive to psychiatric help. A few months into therapy, two new personalities appeared: Babs, a child-like creature with Marie's memory bank, and Michael, a strong figure who helped bring about the eventual personality fusion. In October, 1975, the real Christina was at last able to reemerge. The other personalities lost their separate identities, and Christina began the difficult task of growing into emotional adulthood.

10. WILLIAM MILLIGAN (1955–)

In December, 1978, Billy Milligan was tried for the rape of four Ohio State coeds and found Not Guilty by reason of an unusual form of insanity—multiple personality. The son of a nightclub performer who committed suicide, Milligan fragmented into other personalities by age nine, after a history of alleged sexual abuse and torture by his stepfather. In addition to his core self, Milligan has at least nine other personalities, which include Christene, an affectionate and artistic three-year-old; David, a troubled little boy who bangs his head against the wall; Arthur, a British intellectual; Ragan, an aggressive Slav; and Adelena, a lesbian who is believed to be responsible for causing Milligan to commit the rapes. Doctors predict that during the course of therapy Milligan may reveal yet more personalities—which perhaps have committed undiscovered crimes—but they are optimistic about his eventual recovery.

—F.B.F. & R.J.F.

AMERICA'S TOP 10 JUNK FOODS (BY CATEGORY AND BRAND)

This list is in order of frequency of use as indicated by supermarket sales, volume of consumption, and industry sales.

1. Ice cream/ice milk/sherbet	Kraftco Sealtest®
Top flavor: vanilla	Kraftco Breyers®
2. Breakfast cereals (cold)	Kellogg's Frosted Flakes®
3. Carbonated soft drinks	Coca-Cola®
4. Cookies	Oreos® (Nabisco)
5. Gelatin and instant powder desserts	Jell-O® Gelatin (strawberry), Jell-O® Pudding and Pie Filling (chocolate)
6. Potato chips	Lay's/Lay's Ruffles®
7. Noncarbonated soft drinks	Hi-C® (Coca-Cola® Corp.) various flavors
8. Candy	Snickers® (Mars, Inc.)
9. Chewing gum	Wrigley's® Doublemint
10. Snack pies and cakes	Hostess Twinkies®

Note: Some cold breakfast cereals are considered junk food. Frosted sugar flakes are 44% sugar. This means that almost half of every spoonful is sugar. Some cereals have even more sugar—up to 68%. This constitutes junk food. Hence the inclusion of cereals on the list.

—M.S.L.

14 FOOD ADDITIVES THAT MAY BE HARMFUL TO YOUR HEALTH

1. ARTIFICIAL COLORINGS

Blue No. 1—used in beverages, candy, baked goods, poorly tested; Blue No. 2—used in pet food, candy, beverages, poorly tested; Citrus Red No. 2—skin of some Florida oranges, may cause cancer; Green No. 3—used in candy, beverages, poorly tested; Red No. 3—used in fruit cocktail, candy, baked goods, may cause cancer; Red No. 40—used in soft drinks, pet food, sausage, causes cancer in mice; Yellow No. 5—used in gelatin desserts, pet food, candy, may cause cancer, allergic reaction.

2. BROMINATED VEGETABLE OIL

Emulsifier. Used in soft drinks. Leaves possibly toxic deposits in body tissues.

3. BUTYLATED HYDROXYANISOLE (BHA)*

Antioxidant. Used in dry cereals, shortening, chewing gum, potato chips. Can cause allergic reactions.

4. BUTYLATED HYDROXYTOLUENE (BHT)*

Antioxidant. Used in dry cereals, chewing gum, potato flakes. Can cause allergic reactions and enlarge the liver.

5. CAFFEINE*

Stimulant. Added to soft drinks, occurs naturally in coffee, cacao, tea. Can cause miscarriages, birth defects, insomnia, and nervousness.

6. MONOSODIUM GLUTAMATE (MSG)

Flavor enhancer. Used in soup, sauces, stews. Causes "Chinese restaurant syndrome" (burning sensation in forearms, back of neck; tightness in chest; headache); destroys brain cells in infant mice.

7. PHOSPHORIC ACID, PHOSPHATES

Numerous uses. Added to baked goods, cheese, cured meats, dry cereals, cola drinks, powdered foods. Widespread use has led to a dietary imbalance linked with osteoporosis, a bone disease.

8. PROPYL GALLATE*

Antioxidant. Used in vegetable oils, meat products, chewing gum. Not adequately tested, often unnecessary.

9. QUININE

Flavoring. Used in tonic water, quinine water, bitter lemon. Poorly tested; may be related to birth defects.

10. SODIUM BISULFITE*

Preservative, bleach. Used in sliced fruit, wine, grape juice, dehydrated potatoes. Destroys vitamin B_1.

11. SODIUM CHLORIDE (SALT)

Flavoring, preservative. Used in large quantities in most processed foods. A small amount is necessary, but in excess it can cause high blood pressure and contribute to heart and kidney disease.

12. SODIUM NITRATE, NITRITE

Color fixative. Used in cured meat products. Forms cancer-causing nitrosamines.

13. SUCROSE, DEXTROSE, CORN SYRUP (SUGARS)

Sweeteners. Used in soft drinks, baked goods, and many other foods. No nutritional value, adds empty calories and promotes tooth decay.

14. SULFUR DIOXIDE*

Preservative, bleach. Used in sliced fruit, wine, grape juice, dehydrated potatoes. Highly toxic, destroys vitamin A.

* Generally Regarded As Safe (GRAS) by the Food and Drug Administration.

—Annotated by the Eds.

SOURCE: Adapted from *Chemical Cuisine,* a poster published by the Center for Science in the Public Interest, 1755 S Street NW, Washington, D.C. 20009.

10 FRUITS THAT RIPEN AFTER PICKING

1. Apples
2. Apricots
3. Avocados
4. Bananas
5. Mangoes
6. Muskmelons
7. Papayas
8. Peaches
9. Pears
10. Persimmons

12 FRUITS THAT DO *NOT* RIPEN AFTER PICKING

1. Blackberries
2. Blueberries
3. Cherries
4. Grapefruit
5. Grapes
6. Lemons
7. Oranges
8. Pineapples
9. Plums
10. Raspberries
11. Strawberries
12. Watermelons

8 MAMMOTH CHEESES

1. THE 17½-TON CHEDDAR

Known as the Golden Giant, the largest chunk of cheese in history was 14½ ft. long, 6½ ft. wide, and 6 ft. high. Produced in 1964 by Steve's Cheese of Denmark, Wis., for the Wisconsin Cheese Foundation, it required 183 tons of milk—the daily production of 16,000 cows. After its manufacture, the cheese was shipped via a special tractor-trailor called the Cheese-Mobile to the Wisconsin Pavilion at the New York World's Fair. A refrigerated glass enclosure remained its home until 1965. It was then cut up into 2-lb. pieces which were put on display until 1968, when they were sold for $3 per package. At the 1978 Wisconsin Cheese Makers' Association convention, the two remaining pieces of the cheese were auctioned off for $200 each.

2. THE 6-TON CHEDDAR

This giant was produced by upstate New York cheesemakers under the direction of W. L. Kilsey for the 1937 New York State Fair at Syracuse. Production began on July 12, 1937. It took seven weeks to cure and had to be turned frequently to ensure even ripening. It used the milk of 6,000 cows.

3. THE 4-TON CHEDDAR

Made by Canadian cheesemakers, this 8,000-lb. giant excited

spectators at the 1883 Toronto Fair. Mortician-poet James McIntyre immortalized it in the following cheesy verses:

> We have thee, mammoth cheese,
> Lying quietly at your ease;
> Gently fanned by evening breeze,
> Thy fair form no flies dare seize.

4. THE 1,400-LB. CHEDDAR

Bestowed upon President Andrew Jackson by a New York State cheesemaker, this three-quarter-ton monster ripened in the vestibule of the White House for nearly two years. It was served to the entire city of Washington, D.C., when Jackson threw open the doors of the White House to celebrate Washington's Birthday. According to eyewitnesses, the whole atmosphere for a half-mile around was infected with cheese. The birthday Cheddar was devoured in less than two hours. Only a tiny morsel was saved for the President.

5. THE 1,200-LB. CHESHIRE

In 1801 President Thomas Jefferson received this Cheddar-like tribute from the tiny town of Cheshire in the Berkshire Mountains of Massachusetts. Named the Ultra-Democratic, Anti-Federalist Cheese of Cheshire, it was shipped to Washington, D.C., by sled, boat, and wagon to honor Jefferson's triumph over the Federalists. The originator of the cheese was a preacher named John Leland, who took advantage of all the fuss and publicity to proselytize for his church. Duly impressed, Jefferson donated $200 to Leland's congregation.

6. THE 1,100-LB. CHEDDAR

This half-ton cheese, 9 ft. in diameter, was a wedding gift to Queen Victoria in 1840. Puzzled and somewhat embarrassed by not knowing what to do with it, the queen was relieved when its makers asked if they could borrow it to exhibit it around England. But when they tried to return the grubby, show-worn cheese, Victoria refused to accept it. After lengthy quarrels over its disposition, the Cheddar was finally surrendered to the British Chancery, where it gradually disappeared.

7. THE 1,000-LB. LUNI CHEESE

One of the lesser-known wonders of the ancient world, the 1,000-lb. Luni cheese, named after an ancient town in northern Italy, was reported by Pliny in his *Natural History* about 77 A.D. Manufactured in what is now Tuscany, near the famous Carrara marble quarries in central Italy, the Luni cheese was probably made from a mixture of cow's and goat's milk. It is supposed to have tasted like a cross between Cheddar and Parmesan.

8. THE 1,000-LB. CHEDDAR

The largest cheese to travel halfway around the world, this half-ton Cheddar was taken to London all the way from New Zealand. It was the star attraction at the Wembley Exposition of 1924.

—S.R.

THE 12 HOTTEST CHILIS

How hot is hot? According to scientists, one part in one thousand of the magic ingredient capsaicin can be detected by taste. However, Dr. Roy Nakayama, associate professor at New Mexico State University's agricultural research station, has a taste test scale for the layman. Keeping in mind that drought can increase the fire in any given crop, here is his scale, on which 12 is the hottest rating.

12. Bahamian	6. Sandia
11. Santaca (Japanese)	5. Hot Ancho
10. Tabasco	4. Numex Big Jim
9. Jalapeño	3. Rio Grande
7. Española	1. New Mexico No. 6
7. Cayenne	1. Anaheim

SOURCE: *New Mexico* magazine, May, 1976.

JULIA CHILD'S
10 FAVORITE COOKBOOKS
(BESIDES HER OWN!)
PUBLISHED IN THE U.S.

Star of the Emmy-winning TV show *The French Chef*, Julia Child has delighted millions of viewers with her culinary feats and energetic style. She also has several bestselling cookbooks to her credit, including *Mastering the Art of French Cooking* (2 volumes), coauthored with Simone Beck and Louisette Bertholle, and *From Julia Child's Kitchen*, a compendium of her favorite recipes.

1. *The Classic Italian Cook Book* and its sequel, by Marcella Hazan
2. *The Art of Eating* by M. F. K. Fisher
3. *Larousse Gastronomique*
4. *La Technique* by Jacques Pépin
5. *The Cuisines of Mexico* and its sequel, by Diana Kennedy
6. *American Cooking* and *The Theory and Practice of Good Cooking* by James A. Beard
7. *The Key to Chinese Cooking* by Irene Kuo
8. *The Art of Making Sausages, Patés, and Other Charcuterie* by Jane Grigson
9. *The Joy of Cooking* by Irma Rombauer and Marion Becker
10. *French Provincial Cooking* by Elizabeth David

—Exclusive for *The Book of Lists* 2

25 BEST-LIKED FOODS IN THE U.S. ARMED FORCES

A food preference survey was given to 3,890 members of the army, air force, navy, and marine corps in 1973 and 1974. Out of 378 foods listed, here are the top 25.

1. Milk
2. Grilled steak
3. Eggs to order
4. Corn-on-the-cob
5. Orange juice
6. Strawberry shortcake
7. French fried potatoes
8. Fried chicken
9. Ice cream
10. Milk shake*
11. Bacon
12. Spaghetti with meat sauce
13. Spaghetti with meatballs
14. Beer
15. Bacon, lettuce, tomato sandwich
16. Milk shake*
17. Buttered whole kernel corn
18. Peaches
19. Oranges*
20. French fried shrimp
21. Apples (fresh)
22. Pizza
23. Ham
24. Watermelon
25. Oranges*

* Indicates an item that appeared more than once on the original questionnaire to see if the servicemen would rate it differently when they saw it a second time.

SOURCE: *Chow: A Cook's Tour of Military Food* by Paul Dickson. Copyright © 1978 by Paul Dickson. Reprinted by arrangement with The New American Library, Inc., New York, New York.

25 LEAST-LIKED FOODS IN THE U.S. ARMED FORCES

And here are the 25 foods least-liked, with the foods listed in order of increasing preference; i.e., number 1, buttermilk, is the worst food a serviceperson can imagine.

1. Buttermilk
2. Skimmed milk
3. Fried parsnips
4. Low-calorie soda
5. Mashed rutabagas
6. French fried carrots
7. Prune juice
8. Stewed prunes (canned)
9. French fried cauliflower
10. Creamed onions
11. Kidney bean salad
12. Baked yellow squash
13. Boiled pigs' feet
14. Figs (canned)
15. Carrot, raisin, and celery salad
16. Baked bean sandwich
17. Braised trake*
18. Pickled beet and onion salad
19. Raisin pie
20. Egg drop soup
21. Split pea soup

22. Braised liver with onions
23. Buttered ermal*

24. Chitterlings
25. Sour cream dressing

* These are nonsense foods listed as a control to see what response was given to nonexistent foods. They did considerably better than some "existent" foods. It is interesting to note that a third "nonsense" item—funistrade—finished several places above the bottom 40, between Brussels sprouts and fried okra.

Source: *Chow: A Cook's Tour of Military Food* by Paul Dickson. Copyright © 1978 by Paul Dickson. Reprinted by arrangement with The New American Library, Inc., New York, New York.

16 COMPOUNDS IN TOBACCO THAT ARE DANGEROUS TO NONSMOKERS

The following 16 compounds, found in tobacco smoke and thought to be the most dangerous to nonsmokers, are listed in the order of "risk priority."

1. ACROLEIN

A toxic, colorless liquid with irritating vapors.

2. CARBON MONOXIDE

A highly toxic, flammable gas used in the manufacture of numerous chemical products. Inhalation of carbon monoxide interferes with the transportation of oxygen from the lungs to the tissues in which it is required.

3. NICOTINE

A poisonous alkaloid that is the chief active principle of tobacco. It is also used as an insecticide, and to kill parasitic worms in animals.

4. AMMONIA

A gaseous alkaline compound of nitrogen and hydrogen used as a coolant in refrigerating and air-conditioning equipment, and in explosives, artificial fertilizers, and disinfectants.

5. FORMIC ACID

A pungent liquid acid used in processing textiles and leather. Exposure to the acid irritates the mucous membranes and causes blistering.

6. HYDROGEN CYANIDE

An extremely poisonous liquid used in many chemical processes including fumigation and the case hardening of iron and steel. Hydrogen cyanide gas poisoning is used as a method of capital punishment.

7. NITROUS OXIDES

A group of irritating and sometimes poisonous gases which combine with hydrocarbons to produce smog. Nitrogen dioxide can weaken bodily tissues and increase susceptibility to respiratory ailments.

8. FORMALDEHYDE

A pungent gas used primarily as a disinfectant and preservative. It is extremely irritating to the mucous membranes.

9. PHENOL

A caustic, poisonous acidic compound present in coal and wood tar, which is used as a disinfectant.

10. ACETALDEHYDE

A highly toxic, flammable liquid, which irritates the eyes and mucous membranes and accelerates the action of the heart. Prolonged exposure causes blood pressure to rise and decreases the number of white and red blood cells.

11. HYDROGEN SULFIDE

A poisonous gas produced naturally from putrefying matter and used extensively in chemical laboratories.

12. PYRIDINE

A flammable liquid used in pharmaceuticals, water repellents, bactericides, and herbicides.

13. METHYL CHLORIDE

A toxic gas used in the production of rubber, in paint remover, and as an antiknock agent in gasoline.

14. ACETONITRILE

A toxic compound found in coal tar and molasses residue and used in the production of plastics, rubber, acrylic fiber, insecticide, and perfumery.

15. PROPIONALDEHYDE

A colorless liquid with a suffocating odor used as a chemical disinfectant and preservative, as well as in plastic and rubber production.

16. METHANOL

A poisonous liquid alcohol used in automotive antifreezes, rocket fuels, synthetic dyestuffs, resins, drugs, and perfumes.

—Annotated by the Eds.

SOURCE: *The Journal of Norwegian Medical Associates,* November 10, 1973.

15 PSYCHOACTIVE DRUGS AND PLANTS AND THEIR DISCOVERERS (OR POPULARIZERS)

1. COCA—AMERIGO VESPUCCI (1454–1512), Italian navigator

The first European to describe coca chewing in the New World. In Venezuela in 1499, he asked the natives for drinking water and was offered coca instead. He surmised that "they kept this herb in their mouths to stave off thirst."

2. OPIUM—PARACELSUS (1493?–1541), Swiss physician and alchemist

Introduced opium to Western medical practice when he combined it with gold and pearls in a preparation he called laudanum (Latin for "most highly praised"). He philosophized : "All things are poison, and nothing is without poison. The dose alone makes a thing not poison."

3. LAUDANUM—THOMAS SYDENHAM (1624–1689), British physician

About 1670 perfected tincture of opium (opium dissolved in alcohol), naming it laudanum after Paracelsus's famous concoction. He concluded: "Among the remedies which it has pleased Almighty God to give to man to relieve his sufferings, none is so universal and so efficacious as opium."

4. NITROUS OXIDE (LAUGHING GAS)—HUMPHRY DAVY (1778–1829), British chemist

On December 26, 1799, after months of testing, he was the first to describe the mental effects of the gas. "I existed in a world of new-connected and newly modified ideas. . . . I explained to Dr. Kinglake, 'Nothing exists but thoughts! The universe is composed of impressions, ideas, pleasure, and pain.' "

5. MORPHINE—FRIEDRICH WILHELM ADAM SERTÜRNER (1783–1841), German chemist

Isolated morphine, the active agent in opium, in 1806 (this also marked the discovery of alkaloids). He reported: "In order to subject my previous experiments to a rigorous test, I persuaded three people under the age of 17 to join me in taking morphine. . . . A response occurred quickly in the three young men and . . . I shared the same fate. Lying down, I got into a dreamy state."

6. CANNABIS (MARIJUANA and HASHISH)— W. B. O'SHAUGHNESSY (1809–1890), British surgeon and chemist

Introduced cannabis to Western medicine while working with the substance in India in 1839. He described the following incident:

Humphry Davy—the man who gave us laughing gas.

"The fourth case of trial was an old muscular coolie, a rheumatic malingerer, and to him half a grain of hemp resin was given in a little spirit. The first day's report will suffice for all. In two hours the old gentleman became talkative and musical, told several stories, and sang songs . . . ate the dinners of two persons . . . sought also for other luxuries . . . and finally fell soundly asleep."

7. YAGÉ (AYAHUASCA)—RICHARD SPRUCE (1817–1893), British botanist

In 1851 discovered the widely used hallucinogenic drink of Amazonian tribes, prepared from the bark of giant flowering vines (*Banisteriopsis caapi*). He correctly identified the plant and collected specimens that were still active a century later. Ecuadorean physician Manuel Villavicencio is credited with the first report of the mental effects in 1858. "My head immediately began to swim, and I seemed to take an aerial voyage, wherein I thought I saw the most charming landscapes, great cities, lofty towers, beautiful parks. . . . Then all at once I found myself deserted in a forest and attacked by beasts of prey, against which I tried to defend myself."

8. COCAINE—ALBERT NIEMANN (1840–1921), German chemist

Isolated the alkaloid cocaine, the active agent in the leaves of the coca plant, in 1859, at a laboratory in Göttingen, Germany. Noted a kind of anesthetic effect which made the tongue temporarily insensible to touch, but attached no great importance to this. (Although Friedrich Gaedcke extracted a substance called erythroxylin in 1855 and thus contributed to the isolation of the drug, Niemann's work was more conclusive, and it was he who named the derivative cocaine.)

9. PEYOTE—JOHN RALEIGH BRIGGS (1851–1907), U.S. physician

On June 20, 1886, he ate one third of one peyote button; his description of its effects appeared in print the following year. "It is certainly the most violent and rapid of fruits, or medicines, known to me. . . . I know of nothing like it except opium and cocaine. The most notable point is the rapidity with which it increases the heart's action. Next, the intoxication and subsequent depression. I think it is well worth the trouble to investigate the matter."

10. MESCALINE—ARTHUR HEFFTER (1860–1925), German physician and chemist

Isolated the hallucinatory agent from the many alkaloids in the peyote cactus in 1897. In an experiment on July 23, 1897, he wrote: "While reading, green and violet spots appear on the paper. The same occurs when I look up at the bright sky. . . . I have predominantly images of kaleidoscopic figures, patterned carpets and cloth, luxurious articles of clothing, and architectural scenes."

11. HEROIN—HEINRICH DRESER (1860–1924), German chemist

In 1898, while director of research at the Bayer Company in Darmstadt, Germany, he prepared diacetylmorphine and dubbed this new compound heroin. It was quickly introduced commercially as a safer and quicker pain reliever than morphine. The name was derived from the German *heroisch* ("large, powerful"). Dreser was also responsible for the discovery of aspirin at about the same time.

12. AMPHETAMINE—GORDON ALLES (1901–1963), U.S. chemist

Synthesized amphetamine in 1927 at a laboratory in Los Angeles, Calif. With regard to its medical applications, he noted "its stimulating effect on the central nervous system, and . . . its relative lasting effect on oral administration . . . and as an inhalant." The Benzedrine (amphetamine sulfate) inhaler was introduced in 1932.

13. LSD—ALBERT HOFMANN (1911–   ), Swiss chemist

Synthesized LSD at Sandoz Laboratory in Basel, Switzerland, in 1938 and discovered its mental effect five years later. He wrote: "Last Friday, April 16, 1943, I was forced to stop my work in the laboratory in the middle of the afternoon and to go home, as I was seized by a peculiar restlessness associated with a mild dizziness . . . characterized by extreme activity of imagination. As I lay in a dazed condition with my eyes closed . . . there surged upon me an uninterrupted stream of fantastic images of extraordinary plasticity and vividness and accompanied by an intense, kaleidoscopelike play of colors."

14. PSILOCYBE MUSHROOMS—R. GORDON WASSON
(1898–), U.S. banker and ethnomycologist

On June 29–30, 1955, he and a photographer became the first white men to record their ingestion of the legendary "magic mushrooms." Wasson described it as "a soul-shattering experience. I felt that I was now seeing plain, whereas ordinary vision gives us an imperfect view. I was seeing the archetypes, the Platonic ideals, that underlie the imperfect images of everyday life. The thought crossed my mind: Could the divine mushrooms be the secret that lay behind the ancient Mysteries?"

15. PSILOCYBIN—ALBERT HOFMANN (1911–),
Swiss chemist

In 1958 at Sandoz Laboratory, where he had discovered the effects of LSD 15 years earlier, Hofmann synthesized psilocybin, the main active agent in the psilocybe mushroom. He wrote: "I ate 32 dried specimens. . . . Thirty minutes later the exterior world began to undergo a strange transformation. Everything assumed a Mexican character. . . . When the doctor . . . bent over me to check my blood pressure, he was transformed into an Aztec priest."

—M.HO.

12 NOTABLE EVENTS THAT HAPPENED UNDER THE INFLUENCE OF ALCOHOL

1. THE HANGING OF CAPTAIN KIDD (1701)

Capt. William Kidd was sentenced to death for murder and piracy and led to the gallows at London's Execution Dock on May 23, 1701. The execution itself was a fiasco. As a large group of spectators sang a series of ballads in honor of the pirate, a very drunk public executioner attempted to hang Kidd, who was so smashed that he could hardly stand. Then the rope broke and Kidd fell over into the mud. Though a second attempt at hanging the prisoner succeeded, the sheriff in charge was later harshly criticized in a published editorial for the bungled performance.

2. BOSTON TEA PARTY (1773)

In Boston, Mass., 50 colonials and members of the Committee of Correspondence met at the home of a printer named Benjamin Edes at about 4:00 P.M. on December 16, 1773. Later that evening, they intended to destroy the tea aboard three ships in Boston Harbor as a protest against the British government's taxation of the American colonies. To bolster their resolve, Edes filled a massive punch bowl with a potent rum concoction. Edes's son Peter had the job of keeping the bowl filled, which proved to be an almost impossible task because of the ardor with which the patriots drank. Shortly after 6:00 P.M. the men, most of whom were now in a noisy, festive mood, with a few staggering noticeably, departed and marched to Griffin's Wharf, where the tea ships were anchored. For the next three hours they sobered up—a number becoming violently ill—as they dumped heavy tea chests into the harbor.

3. NAT TURNER REBELLION (1831)

On the night of August 21, 1831, black slave-prophet Nat Turner launched a rebellion in Southampton County, Virginia, which left more than 50 whites and more than 120 blacks dead. Although Turner never touched alcohol, his six followers had feasted on roast pig and apple brandy that night. At the first plantation they attacked, the rebels drank hard cider before massacring the whites living there. Through the night and into the next day, the insurgents raided plantations, killed whites, and confiscated horses, weapons, and brandy. By noon Turner's army had expanded to approximately 60 men, but many of them were so intoxicated that they kept falling off their horses. When Turner caught up with one advance party, they were relaxing in the brandy cellar of a plantation. Learning that a group of whites was approaching, Turner rallied his men and put the whites to flight. But the next day an alarm scattered his new recruits, and he had only 20 men left to fight 3,000 armed white militiamen and volunteers. The rebellion was crushed.

4. VICE-PRESIDENTIAL INAUGURATION OF ANDREW JOHNSON (1865)

As Abraham Lincoln's running mate in the 1864 election, Johnson campaigned incessantly across the country, until he became totally exhausted and contracted malaria. When he awoke on March 4, 1865, the day of his inauguration as vice-president, he could barely get out of bed. To fortify himself, he drank "medicinal" whiskey and quickly became intoxicated because of his weakened condition. When he began to ramble drunkenly through his inauguration address, officials interrupted him and administered the oath of office. Because he slurred his words and repeated his lines incorrectly, this took a considerable amount of time, after which Johnson launched into yet another bout of inebriated oratory. Finally a Supreme Court justice mercifully led him away.

5. LINCOLN'S ASSASSINATION (1865)

On April 14, 1865, actor John Wilkes Booth began drinking at the Kirkwood House bar in Washington, D.C., at three in the afternoon. At 4:00 P.M. he arrived at Deery's saloon and ordered a bottle of brandy. Two hours later he was drinking whiskey at Taltavul's Saloon, next door to Ford's Theater. Having made the final arrangements for his impending crime, Booth returned at 9:30 to Taltavul's, where President Lincoln's valet Charles Forbes, his coachman Francis Burns, and his bodyguard John Parker, an alcoholic policeman, were all drinking. At 10:15, while Parker continued to imbibe—thus leaving the President unprotected—Booth left, went next door to Ford's Theater, and shot Lincoln. Meanwhile, George Atzerodt, Booth's fellow conspirator, who was supposed to assassinate Vice-President Andrew Johnson, had become so intoxicated and frightened that he abandoned the plan.

6. BATTLE OF THE LITTLE BIGHORN (1876)

A controversy still rages over the extent and level of intoxication of the officers and men of the U.S. 7th Cavalry Regiment at the Battle of the Little Bighorn. It is known that Custer's second-in-command, Major Marcus Reno, had a half-gallon keg of whiskey with him on the expedition. When they reached the Rosebud River four days before the battle, the 7th Cavalry troopers may have replenished their supplies of alcohol off a steamboat carrying cases of whiskey. According to Indian veterans of the battle, numerous canteens half full of whiskey were found with the bodies of Custer's men. It is a fact that Reno, who was most likely an alcoholic, was intoxicated when besieged by Indians the night after Custer was defeated.

7. REPUDIATION OF THE CAÑON DE LOS EMBUDOS TREATY (1886)

On March 27, 1886, in the Cañon de los Embudos in Sonora, Mexico, U.S. Army general George Crook and the Chiricahua Apache leader Geronimo negotiated a peace treaty whereby Geronimo and his followers would surrender and be returned to the San Carlos Reservation in Arizona. Unfortunately, the night the treaty was concluded, the Apaches were sold a large quantity of whiskey and mescal by a Swiss-American bootlegger. As the Indian warriors became increasingly intoxicated, they had second thoughts about the agreement. Late in the evening, an inebriated Geronimo declared that he would never surrender to the white man and repudiated the treaty he had just signed. Accompanied by 20 warriors, Geronimo rode away that night to continue the bloody Apache War until he was tracked down five months later.

8. SULLIVAN-KILRAIN FIGHT (1889)

A champagne-loving alcoholic and the current bareknuckle boxing champion, American heavyweight John L. Sullivan met Jake Kilrain—also a heavy drinker—in a title fight on July 8, 1889, in Richburg, Miss. At first Sullivan's manager refused to let his man drink any alcohol. Eventually, to combat exhaustion and the effects of the 112° temperature, Sullivan was allowed to drink cold tea laced with whiskey after the 43rd round. Unfortunately, the whiskey made him violently ill, and he vomited in the center of the ring. After the 36th round, Kilrain, who was taking a terrible beating, was given shots of bourbon between rounds by one of the timekeepers, William "Bat" Masterson. By the time he conceded defeat after the 75th round, Kilrain had consumed an entire bottle of bourbon.

9. THIRD BATTLE OF THE AISNE RIVER (1918)

In May, 1918, during W.W. I, Gen. Erich Ludendorff's German troops reached the Marne River at Château-Thierry only 37 mi. from Paris during the Third Battle of the Aisne River. On the verge of capturing Paris, but after living without any luxuries for years, the German soldiers invaded France's champagne provinces, where well-stocked wine cellars abounded. Drunkenness quickly spread through the ranks; even the German military police joined the revelries. In the village of Fismes on the morning of May 30, the bodies of soldiers who had passed out littered the streets, making it difficult for trucks to drive through the town on their way to the front lines. The intoxication and subsequent hangovers afflicting the Germans slowed their advance and halted it completely in certain sectors. This enabled the French and Americans to establish new defensive lines, counterattack, and end Ludendorff's offensive, which proved to be the Germans' last chance for victory in W.W. I.

10. FOUNDING OF ALCOHOLICS ANONYMOUS (1935)

Alcoholics Anonymous came into existence when a New York stockbroker named Bill W. (an A.A. member uses only his last initial), an alcoholic who had stopped drinking as a result of a spiritual experience, helped a physician named Doctor Bob to quit drinking. During a business trip to Akron, O., Bill W. met Doctor Bob and shared with him his own experiences as an alcoholic and his method of recovering from the disease of alcoholism. Suffering from a severe hangover, the still woozy Doctor Bob had his last drink on June 10, 1935. The next day, with Bill W., he founded what is now called Alcoholics Anonymous. Neither Bill W., who lived until 1971, nor Doctor Bob, who lived until 1950, ever drank again. The fellowship they founded, which is based on the concept of alcoholics helping other alcoholics, now has more than one million members.

11. THE FILMING OF *MY LITTLE CHICKADEE* (1940)

As in almost all of his films, W. C. Fields was intoxicated throughout the production of *My Little Chickadee*. After drinking from two to four martinis with his breakfast each morning, Fields arrived at Universal Studios with a cocktail shaker full of martinis. Apparently at his comic best when drunk, Fields consumed two bottles of gin each day during the filming of *My Little Chickadee*. Fields's inebriated behavior often infuriated his co-star, Mae West,

Slightly under the influence, W. C. Fields, after two bottles of gin, with Mae West in *My Little Chickadee*.

especially once when, in an overly affectionate mood, he prodded and pinched her generous figure and called her "my little brood mare." Although he often required an afternoon nap to diminish the effects of his drinking, Fields was never incapacitated by alcohol during his performance in the movie.

12. THE WRITING OF *A CLOCKWORK ORANGE* (1962)

Even though his work sometimes deals with projected future worlds, English author Anthony Burgess develops his novels from his personal experiences. For example, the brutal rape scene in *A Clockwork Orange* was derived from an assault on his wife during W.W. II, which resulted in the death of their expected child. While writing *A Clockwork Orange,* Burgess became so emotionally involved that he frequently had to calm himself by means of alcohol. As he admitted, "I had to write *A Clockwork Orange* in a state of near drunkenness, in order to deal with material that upset me so much."

—R.J.F.

TRUMAN CAPOTE'S
11 PERSONS IN HISTORY
WHOSE LIVES I WOULD LIKE
TO HAVE LIVED IN
PAST INCARNATIONS

Called "the hope of modern literature" by W. Somerset Maugham, Capote gained literary prominence with his first novel, *Other Voices, Other Rooms* (1948), and widespread popularity with *Breakfast at Tiffany's* (1958). He spent six years researching and writing the controversial best-seller *In Cold Blood* (1966), a "non-fiction novel" about the mass murder of a Kansas farm family.

1. Caligula
2. Catherine the Great
3. Stalin
4. Sigmund Freud
5. Rasputin
6. Cleopatra
7. Henry VIII
8. Madame de Pompadour
9. Alcibiades
10–11. J. Edgar Hoover and Clyde Tolson

Note: Alcibiades (c. 450–404 B.C.) was a brilliant but unscrupulous military commander who alternately led the Athenians and the Spartans to victory. Clyde A. Tolson was Hoover's longtime companion and assistant.

—Exclusive for *The Book of Lists 2*

MARCEL MARCEAU'S
10 PERSONS IN HISTORY
WHOSE LIVES I WOULD LIKE
TO HAVE LIVED IN
PAST INCARNATIONS

The famous French mime first gained recognition in 1947 with his creation of the sad, white-faced clown known as Bip, modeled after the character Pip in Dickens's *Great Expectations*. Marceau formed his own company in 1949 and has toured the world continuously since then, including frequent performances in the U.S. He has made many short films and one full-length movie.

1. Jesus Christ
2. Moses
3. Michelangelo
4. Leonardo da Vinci
5. Siddhartha (Buddha)
6. Mozart
7. Aristotle
8. Shakespeare
9. Einstein
10. Tolstoi

—Exclusive for *The Book of Lists 2*

Siddhartha Gautama, the Buddha.

C. P. SNOW'S
10 PERSONS IN HISTORY
WHOSE LIVES I WOULD LIKE
TO HAVE LIVED IN
PAST INCARNATIONS

Noted as an author, scientist, and civil servant, Snow enjoyed a 20-year career as a molecular physicist at Cambridge prior to serving as a scientific adviser to the British government. Among his many books are the 11-volume *Strangers and Brothers* (1935–1970), *Two Cultures and the Scientific Revolution* (1959), and *The Realists* (1978).

1. Lucretius
2. Sydney Smith
3. Benjamin Franklin
4. Augustus Caesar
5. Lord Melbourne
6. K'ang-hsi
7. Benito Pérez Galdós
8. Goethe
9. Archimedes
10. Veronese

Note: Lucretius (96?–55 B.C.) was a Roman poet and philosopher who wrote *On the Nature of Things*, a long poem which argues that the laws of atomic structure can explain the human mind and soul. Sydney Smith (1771–1845) was an English clergyman and essayist, famous for his wit, political acumen, and anti-Americanism. William Lamb, Lord Melbourne (1779–1848), was a British prime minister and a trusted adviser to Queen Victoria. K'ang-hsi (1654–1722) was a Chinese emperor whose reign was characterized by encouragement of scholarship and the arts. Benito Pérez Galdós (1843–1920) was a Spanish novelist whom many critics rank second only to Cervantes. Paolo Veronese (1528–1588) was an Italian decorative painter, known particularly for his large-scale historical and biblical scenes.

—Exclusive for *The Book of Lists* 2

EMILY HAHN'S
10 PERSONS IN HISTORY
WHOSE LIVES I WOULD LIKE
TO HAVE LIVED IN
PAST INCARNATIONS

The University of Wisconsin's first woman graduate in mining engineering, Hahn also pursued careers as an English teacher, university lecturer, screenwriter, journalist, and author of more than 20 books. Two of her recent volumes are *Once upon a Pedestal* (1974), a history of the American woman's struggle for equality, and *Lorenzo* (1975), a biography of D. H. Lawrence.

1. Herodotus
2. Aphra Behn
3. Ferdinand Magellan
4. Charles II of England
5. Li Ta'i-po
6. Dr. Robert Mearns Yerkes
7. Lady Mary Wortley Montagu
8. Dorothy Osborne
9. Lord Macartney
10. Sir Richard Burton

Note: Aphra Behn (1640–1689) was a novelist, dramatist, and poet, who became the first English woman to earn a living as an author. Li Ta'i-po (?–762), one of "the Eight Immortals of the Wine Cup," is considered by many to be China's greatest poet. Dr. Robert Mearns Yerkes (1876–1956) was a U.S. psychobiologist instrumental in furthering the study of comparative animal psychology. Lady Mary Wortley Montagu (1689–1762) was an English poet and letter writer noted for her wit and defiance of convention. Dorothy Osborne (1627–1695) was the wife of English statesman Sir William Temple. Her letters to him rank among the finest in the English language. Lord George Macartney (1737–1806) was Britain's first diplomatic representative to Peking.

—Exclusive for *The Book of Lists 2*

GERALD R. FORD'S
11 PERSONS IN HISTORY
WHOSE LIVES I WOULD LIKE
TO HAVE LIVED IN
PAST INCARNATIONS

Former star center for the University of Michigan football team, Ford began his congressional winning streak in 1948 with election to the House of Representatives and was chosen by Richard Nixon as vice-president after the resignation of Spiro Agnew in 1973. When Nixon resigned on August 8, 1974, Ford became the 38th president of the U.S. He was defeated by Jimmy Carter in his 1976 presidential bid.

1. George Washington
2. Abraham Lincoln
3. Thomas Jefferson
4. Benjamin Franklin
5. Winston Churchill
6. Alexander Hamilton
7. Douglas MacArthur
8. Mahatma Gandhi
9. Marco Polo
10. Thomas Edison
11. Lou Gehrig

Ford adds: "My selection is based on the understanding that

I would have lived their lives during the period of history in which they lived."

—Exclusive for *The Book of Lists* 2

RONALD REAGAN'S
6 PERSONS IN HISTORY
WHOSE LIVES I WOULD LIKE
TO HAVE LIVED IN
PAST INCARNATIONS

Ex-actor Reagan's six years as president of the Screen Actors Guild whetted his appetite for politics. After doing a political turnabout from liberal to conservative, he easily won the governorship of California in 1966 and was reelected in 1970. Reagan vied for the Republican presidential nomination in 1968 and again in 1976, when he came close to defeating incumbent Gerald Ford.

1. Adam (It would have been wonderful to see the world begin.)
2. Cortes
3. Balboa
4. Lewis and/or Clark
5. Father Junípero Serra
6. And any number of those men who first crossed the plains in the opening of the West. In other words, I'm fascinated by those who saw this new world when it was virtually untouched by man.

—Exclusive for *The Book of Lists* 2

DR. BRUCE MAZLISH'S
10 PERSONS IN HISTORY
WHOSE LIVES I WOULD LIKE
TO HAVE LIVED IN
PAST INCARNATIONS

Professor of history at M.I.T. and associate editor of the *Journal of Interdisciplinary History,* Mazlish stands out as an academic innovator. When his *In Search of Nixon* was published in 1972, the *New York Times Book Review* declared that it held "a pivotal place in the development of the new field of psychohistory." Other recent books include *James and John Stuart Mill* (1975) and *Kissinger* (1976).

1. Buddha	6. Queen Elizabeth I
2. Thucydides	7. Hegel
3. Julius Caesar	8. Abraham Lincoln
4. Machiavelli	9. Verdi
5. Shakespeare	10. Sigmund Freud

Note: Thucydides (471?–400 B.C.) was a Greek historian whose highly acclaimed *History of the Peloponnesian War* laid the foundations for Western historiography. Georg Hegel (1770–1831) was a German philosopher who developed the dialectical method, which greatly influenced the growth of Marxism and existentialism.

Dr. Mazlish adds: "Your invitation gave rise to an interesting two or three days of speculation. I've lived a great many lives vicariously, even if only briefly, in that time."

—Exclusive for *The Book of Lists 2*

MARY McCARTHY'S 10 PERSONS IN HISTORY WHOSE LIVES I WOULD LIKE TO HAVE LIVED IN PAST INCARNATIONS

"Quite possibly the cleverest woman America has ever produced," said one critic about author Mary McCarthy. A graduate of Vassar, she brought notoriety to her alma mater in 1966 with her novel *The Group,* an account of the later lives of seven Vassar women from the class of 1933.

1. Thomas Jefferson	6. St. Augustine
2. Lord Byron	7. Diderot
3. Catullus	8. Thomas Nash
4. Elizabeth I	9. Christine de Pisan
5. Brunelleschi	10. Eleanor of Aquitaine

Lord Byron.

Note: Catullus (84?–54 B.C.) was a Roman lyric poet famous for his autobiographical verses of ill-fated love. Filippo Brunelleschi (1377?–1446) was one of the great Italian architects of the early Renaissance. French author Denis Diderot (1713–1784) edited the *Encyclopedia,* a vast compendium of practical knowledge and 18th-century political thought. Thomas Nash (1567–1601), an Elizabethan author and dramatist, was a onetime collaborator of Christopher Marlowe. Christine de Pisan (1363?–1431) wrote numerous love poems, a biography of Charles V of France, and several works extolling women.

—Exclusive for *The Book of Lists 2*

ANGUS WILSON'S 10 PERSONS IN HISTORY WHOSE LIVES I WOULD LIKE TO HAVE LIVED IN PAST INCARNATIONS

Oxford-educated Angus Wilson was born in England and raised in South Africa. Currently a professor of English literature at East Anglia University in Norwich, England, Wilson has written seven novels, numerous short stories and plays, and several biographies, including *The World of Charles Dickens* (1970) and *The Strange Ride of Rudyard Kipling* (1977).

1. Charles Dickens
2. William Shakespeare
3. Lord Byron
4. Frank Lloyd Wright
5. Michelangelo
6. Felix Mendelssohn
7. Franklin Delano Roosevelt
8. Charles Darwin
9. Sarah Bernhardt
10. Gautama Buddha

—Exclusive for *The Book of Lists 2*

DWIGHT MACDONALD'S 10 PERSONS IN HISTORY WHOSE LIVES I WOULD LIKE TO HAVE LIVED IN PAST INCARNATIONS

Known for his "great erudition, discriminating taste, and acute criticism," Macdonald has been a keen observer of popular culture and politics for the past 50 years. First associated with *Fortune* magazine, he moved on to the *Partisan Review, The New Yorker,* and *Esquire*. In the 1940s he published his own magazine, *Politics*. His books include *Against the American Grain* (1962) and *Dwight Macdonald on Movies* (1969).

1. Thomas Jefferson
2. Max Beerbohm
3. Homer (both of them, the author of the *Iliad* and the authoress—probably Nausicaa—of the *Odyssey*)
4. William Shakespeare
5. Honus Wagner
6. Rosa Luxemburg
7. Sherlock Holmes
8. Jesus
9. The Duke of Wellington
10. Lord Byron

Note: Sir Max Beerbohm (1872–1956) was a British critic, essayist, and caricaturist. Honus Wagner (1874–1955) was one of the best all-around baseball players in history. Rosa Luxemburg (1870–1919) was a German revolutionary who helped form the Polish Socialist party, the Spartacus League, and the German Communist party.

—Exclusive for *The Book of Lists 2*

BRIGID BROPHY'S 10 PERSONS IN HISTORY WHOSE LIVES I WOULD LIKE TO HAVE LIVED IN PAST INCARNATIONS (ON A SYSTEM THAT CONVENIENTLY PERMITS SOME OVERLAPS)

Daughter of an Anglo-Irish novelist, Brigid Brophy is a recognized essayist, critic, novelist, and playwright. Her books include a prize-winning first novel, *Hackenfeller's Ape*; psychoanalytic biographies of Mozart and Aubrey Beardsley; and *Don't Never Forget,* a collection of radio broadcasts.

1. Aristotle
2. Titian
3. Andrew Marvell
4. Thomas Tryon (a fellow vegetarian: "For the lives of all beasts are as sweet to them and they as much desire to continue them as men do and as unwillingly part with them.")
5. George Frederick Handel
6. Balthasar Neumann

7. His Highness's dog at Kew (on the collar of a dog that Alexander Pope gave to Frederick, Prince of Wales: "I am His Highness's dog at Kew;/Pray tell me, sir, whose dog are you?")
8. John Nash
9. [George] Bernard Shaw
10. One of Madame Colette's cats

Note: Andrew Marvell (1621–1678), English author of "The Garden" and "To His Coy Mistress," was one of the best 17th-century poets. Thomas Tryon (1634–1703) was an English ascetic who wrote numerous works on diet and hygiene. Balthasar Neumann (1687–1753) was a multitalented German architect of the baroque period who designed bridges, public buildings, palaces, and more than 100 churches. John Nash (1752–1835) was an English architect and city planner who laid out London's Regent's Park and Regent Street.

—Exclusive for *The Book of Lists* 2

ROBERT PAYNE'S 10 PERSONS IN HISTORY WHOSE LIVES I WOULD LIKE TO HAVE LIVED IN PAST INCARNATIONS

Born in England but now living in New York City, Payne is an inveterate traveler who spent many years in China. His wide-ranging interests have produced books on Asia and the Near East, ancient Greece and Rome, and the Spanish Civil War. He is best known, however, for his memorable biographies of such major figures as Leonardo da Vinci, Gandhi, Hitler, and Stalin.

1. Ananda, the disciple of Gautama Buddha
2. Plato, the disciple of Socrates
3. St. John, the disciple of Jesus
4. [Marcus] Vipsanius Agrippa, the friend of Augustus Caesar
5. Josui Soen, the disciple of Sesshu Toyo
6. Francesco Melzi, the friend of Leonardo da Vinci
7. Tommasco Cavalieri, the friend of Michelangelo
8. John Fletcher, the friend of Shakespeare
9. Joseph Severn, the friend of Keats
10. John Linnell, the disciple of William Blake

Payne adds: "Sesshu Toyo (1419–1506) was the greatest of Japanese painters."

—Exclusive for *The Book of Lists* 2

ABBA EBAN'S
5 EVENTS IN HISTORY I WOULD MOST LIKE TO HAVE SEEN

One of Israel's most respected diplomats, Abba Eban became the first Israeli ambassador to the U.N. in 1949, serving concurrently as ambassador to the U.S. from 1950 to 1959. His skillful diplomacy as foreign minister from 1966 to 1974 saw Israel through the 1967 crisis and won many supporters for the Jewish state. In 1959 he was elected to the Knesset, where he serves today. Published works include *My Country* and *Abba Eban: An Autobiography*.

1. THE RETURN OF THE JEWS FROM BABYLON TO DEDICATE THE SECOND TEMPLE (515 B.C.E.)

   Cyrus, king of Persia, had allowed the return, and it had taken several decades to rebuild the temple. This made possible both the preservation of Judaism and the birth of Christianity.

2. PERICLES' FUNERAL SPEECH ABOUT THE VIRTUES OF ATHENS AFTER THE WAR WITH SPARTA (431 B.C.E.)

3. THE SIGNING OF THE AMERICAN DECLARATION OF INDEPENDENCE IN PHILADELPHIA (July 4, 1776)

4. THE FIRST PERFORMANCE OF BEETHOVEN'S NINTH (CHORAL) SYMPHONY (1824)

   Beethoven had been paid £100 by the London Philharmonic Society to enable a benefit to be organized. He needed the money very badly.

5. WINSTON CHURCHILL'S SPEECH IN THE HOUSE OF COMMONS (May 13, 1940)

   "I have nothing to offer but blood, toil, tears, and sweat."

   —Exclusive for *The Book of Lists* 2

BARBARA WALTERS'S
5 EVENTS IN HISTORY I WOULD MOST LIKE TO HAVE SEEN

Television's most celebrated newswoman made broadcasting history in 1976 when she joined the *ABC Evening News* to become the first female co-anchor of a network news program. As a former panelist and co-host of NBC's *Today Show,* she became famous for her lively, probing interviews of world leaders and celebrities. Now an interviewer with ABC, she is the author of *How to Talk to Practically Anyone about Practically Anything*.

1. MOSES PARTING THE RED SEA (c. 14th century B.C.E.)

2. JESUS PERFORMING THE LOAVES AND FISHES MIRACLE (1st century A.D.)

    (Or any other miracle.)

3. AMELIA EARHART'S LAST HOURS (disappeared July 2, 1937)

    Because I would like to finally uncover the mystery of her disappearance.

4. REAL ROMAN ORGY

    (To watch, *not* to participate.)

5. HITLER'S LAST DAY IN THE BUNKER (April 30, 1945)

—Exclusive for *The Book of Lists 2*

By special request—a Roman orgy in progress.
From the painting by Thomas Couture.

REBECCA WEST'S
5 EVENTS IN HISTORY I WOULD
MOST LIKE TO HAVE SEEN

The astute mind, sharp wit, and psychological insights of Dame Rebecca have won her world renown as one of today's most gifted writers. A journalist best known for her coverage of the war crimes trials in Nuremberg in 1945 and 1946, she is also a novelist and critic of wide acclaim. The author Anthony West is the son of Dame Rebecca and H. G. Wells. Among her best-known books are *Black Lamb and Grey Falcon*, *The Meaning of Treason*, and *A Train of Powder*.

1. THE ARRIVAL OF CORTES AT THE AZTEC TOWN OF TENOCHTITLÁN AND HIS RECEPTION BY THE AZTEC EMPEROR MONTEZUMA (1519)

It must have been so beautiful: more beautiful than any European city, they say. Also, Montezuma and the Aztecs had such beautiful manners. It was a city; they would sacrifice people and that had to be stopped.

2. THE FIRST GLIMPSE CHRISTOPHER WREN GOT OF THE DOME OF ST. PAUL'S (c. 1697)

He had never seen a dome before. He knew what they were and the measurements involved and made one, but he had never set eyes on one. That must have been a moment.

3. THE JAILS IN THE QUARTERS AT SYRACUSE IN SICILY WHEN THE GREEK PRISONERS OF [THE PELOPONNESIAN] WAR WERE TOLD THEY WOULD BE ALLOWED TO GO HOME IF THEY COULD RECITE 10 LINES OUT OF A REALLY GOOD GREEK PLAY (413 B.C.)

That is a tableau expressing real civilization. Think of the experience of repeating good poetry and getting your liberty simultaneously.

4. NAPOLEON GOES ASHORE AT ST. HELENA (October 15, 1815)

I cannot stand the man or anything about him.

5. THE FIRST EASTER MORNING (c. 29 A.D.)

No comment needed, surely.

—Exclusive for *The Book of Lists 2*

JOHN McPHEE'S 5 EVENTS IN HISTORY I WOULD MOST LIKE TO HAVE SEEN

McPhee was a regular contributor to such magazines as *Time* and *The New Yorker* before publishing his first book in 1965. A cult of followers has grown around his successful nonfiction titles, which include *The Curve of Binding Energy, The Survival of the Bark Canoe,* and *Coming into the Country.* He lives in New Jersey, where he lectures in journalism at Princeton University.

1. THE VINDICATION OF COPERNICUS

2. THE CROSS-SECTIONING OF KRAKATOA

3. THE COLLISION THAT PRODUCED THE HIMALAYAS

4. FARINELLI SINGING

Two arias from Hasse's opera *Artasere,* "Pallido è il Sole" and "Per Questo Dolce Amplesso," were sung every night to Philip V, [king] of Spain, for 10 years by Farinelli, the greatest castrato singer of all time.

5. THE ADVANCE OF MAJOR POST-WISCONSIN ICE

By then I'll have lived long enough.

—Exclusive for *The Book of Lists 2*

MARY RENAULT'S
5 EVENTS IN HISTORY I WOULD
MOST LIKE TO HAVE SEEN

Mary Renault is the pseudonym of Mary Challans, who was born in London, England. Her first novel, *The Purposes of Love,* published in 1939, was an immediate success. At the outbreak of W.W. II, she set aside writing to work as a nurse. At the end of the war, she moved to Cape Town, South Africa, where she lives today. Among her most recent books are *Fire from Heaven* and *The Persian Boy.*

1. THE RESURRECTION (c. 29 A.D.)

2. THE FIFTH-CENTURY ACROPOLIS IN ITS PRISTINE STATE, WITH THE SCULPTURE TINTED OF MARBLE, ADORNED WITH GILDING OF BRONZE; AND THE EASEL PAINTINGS OF THE MASTERS STILL ON VIEW

3. ALEXANDER ADDRESSING HIS MEN BEFORE THE BATTLE OF ISSUS (333 B.C.), WHEN HIS ASTONISHING MAGNETISM MUST HAVE BEEN AT FULL POWER

4. A COURT MASQUE OF INIGO JONES

Unsynthetic magnificence.

5. A CHANCE TO READ BYRON'S *MEMOIRS* BEFORE HIS HEIRS DEPLORABLY BURNED THEM (1824)

Note: Inigo Jones (1573–1652) was one of England's first great architects. Masques were allegorical dramas performed by masked actors. They originated at the Medici Court in Florence, Italy, where Jones studied art as a young man. He brought the practice back to England in 1605 and was renowned for the scenery he painted for them as well as the costumes and special effects he designed. The scripts were often written by Ben Jonson.

—Exclusive for *The Book of Lists* 2

The Resurrection of Jesus.
Painting by Benvenuto di Giovanni (1436–c. 1518).

GARRY WILLS'S 5 EVENTS IN HISTORY I WOULD MOST LIKE TO HAVE SEEN

Wills has produced an incisive examination of social change in America in *Nixon Agonistes* and other works. A former contributor to *National Review*, he is now a syndicated columnist and an adjunct professor of humanities at Johns Hopkins University. His latest book,

Inventing America, is a scholarly inquiry into the original meaning of the Declaration of Independence.

1. THE LAST SUPPER (c. 29 A.D.)

2. PAUL CONFRONTING PETER BEFORE THE JERUSALEM CHURCH (1st century A.D.)

3. SHAKESPEARE REHEARSING RICHARD BURBAGE IN THE ROLE OF HAMLET (c. 1600)

4. PATRICK HENRY, IN A RICHMOND CHURCH, URGING HIS FELLOW VIRGINIANS TO FIELD AN ARMY (March 23, 1775)

5. GEORGE WASHINGTON SAYING FAREWELL TO HIS ARMY (1783)

—Exclusive for *The Book of Lists* 2

WILLIAM L. SHIRER'S
5 EVENTS IN HISTORY I WOULD
MOST LIKE TO HAVE SEEN

Shirer is known throughout the world as a distinguished contemporary historian, foreign correspondent, and news commentator. During W.W. II he documented the rise and fall of the Nazis for CBS news and the Universal News Service. Since 1941 he has written such best-sellers as *Berlin Diary, The Rise and Fall of the Third Reich,* and *20th Century Journey.*

1. THE DEATH OF GANDHI (January 30, 1948)

My friends Vincent Sheean and Edgar Snow were at his side at the end, but I, who had known him earlier, missed it. He was the greatest man I ever knew, and the greatest single influence on my life.

2. THE DEATH OF SOCRATES (399 B.C.)

Plato left a memorable account that has always haunted me.

3. THE DEATH OF ADOLF HITLER (April 30, 1945)

Having covered him as a correspondent in Berlin at the height of his barbarous power, I would have liked to see him at the end, when all was lost.

4. AN OLYMPIAD AT OLYMPIA

Preferably the one Socrates walked from Athens to see. I reported the Olympic Games in Europe in 1928 and 1936. The athletes were superb, but there was no philosopher such as Socrates present to impart wisdom.

5. THE SCOPES MONKEY TRIAL AT DAYTON, TENNESSEE (July, 1925)

The day Clarence Darrow cross-examined William Jennings Bryan on the Bible.

—Exclusive for *The Book of Lists* 2

GENERAL WILLIAM WESTMORELAND'S 5 EVENTS IN HISTORY I WOULD MOST LIKE TO HAVE SEEN

After graduating from West Point in 1936, Westmoreland fought during W.W. II in Europe and North Africa, and later in Korea. He attained the rank of general in 1964 and then served as commander of the U.S. armed forces in Vietnam. President Nixon appointed him army chief of staff in 1968, a post he held until his retirement in 1972.

1. THE CRUCIFIXION, RESURRECTION, AND ASCENSION OF JESUS CHRIST (c. 29 A.D.)

A succession of biblical events that have profoundly influenced the civilization of our planet.

2. HANNIBAL CROSSING THE ALPS (218 B.C.)

In 15 days, the Carthaginian military force, with elephants bearing the heaviest loads, crossed the formidable Alps, battling storms, snow, and barbarians—a remarkable example of perseverance over adversity.

3. ROBERT E. LEE'S SURRENDER TO ULYSSES S. GRANT AT APPOMATTOX (April 9, 1865)

Thus, the new nation survived, and constructive endeavors began in earnest to make America an example of unity.

4. SINKING OF THE *TITANIC* (April 14–15, 1912)

Probably the greatest disaster in history caused by human negligence—a reminder that forces of nature can thwart man's ingenuity and self-indulgence.

5. THE FIRST AIRPLANE FLIGHT BY ORVILLE AND WILBUR WRIGHT AT KITTY HAWK, NORTH CAROLINA (December 17, 1903)

An event that was destined to revolutionize transportation and warfare, and began the trail to outer space.

—Exclusive for *The Book of Lists* 2

JACQUETTA HAWKES'S
5 EVENTS IN HISTORY I WOULD
MOST LIKE TO HAVE SEEN

Jacquetta Hawkes is a distinguished English archaeologist and author whose works reflect a poetic view of history. After taking her degree at Cambridge, she worked for UNESCO, then turned to writing full time. In addition to her nonfiction works (*A Land, Man on Earth, Early Britain,* and others), she has written a novel, *Providence Island,* and collaborated with her husband, J. B. Priestley, on a play, *Dragon's Mouth.*

1. THE PAINTING OF THE LEAPING BISON AT ALTAMIRA (c. 30,000 B.C.)

To discover what rites were enacted, and the appearance of the artist and what he wore.

2. THE SIEGE OF TROY (1192–1184 B.C.)

To prove to the unbelievers that it really happened.

3. THE MEETING OF CORTES AND MONTEZUMA (1519)

To witness a unique encounter between two civilizations that had evolved independently over many thousands of years; plus a view of the city of Tenochtitlán.

Cortes meets . . . Montezuma.

. A REHEARSAL OF *HAMLET* (c. 1600)

To observe Shakespeare's face and voice and find out if he did
in fact play the ghost. To settle the argument about the plan of the
Globe Theatre.

. THE OPENING OF THE GREAT EXHIBITION OF 1851

To see the extraordinary wealth of this apotheosis of the British
Empire, with a glimpse of Victoria, Albert, and the mysterious
Chinaman.

—Exclusive for *The Book of Lists* 2

DR. HENRY STEELE COMMAGER'S
5 EVENTS IN HISTORY I WOULD
MOST LIKE TO HAVE SEEN

Dr. Commager, professor of history at Amherst College in
Massachusetts, is one of America's leading historians and educators.
He is a frequent contributor to major magazines and periodicals and
is the author and editor of dozens of books, including *Why the
Confederacy Lost the Civil War, The Struggle for Racial Equality,*
and *The Spirit of Seventy-Six.*

1. ATHENS, 431 B.C.: TO HEAR PERICLES DELIVER
   HIS FUNERAL ORATION

Pericles' funeral oration over the Athenians who died in the
first year of the Peloponnesian War has some claim to being the most
eloquent oration in recorded history. Pericles himself has some claim
to be considered the greatest of Athenian statesmen. The oration
influenced Lincoln's Gettysburg Address.

2. PHILADELPHIA, SEPTEMBER 17, 1787: THE CLOSING
   DAY OF THE CONSTITUTIONAL CONVENTION

After three months of debate, the "fathers" concluded their
debates on a new constitution for the U.S. On this day, most of the
remaining members signed the document that brought the U.S. into
existence (after ratification); this day, Franklin delivered his moving
address: "I have happiness to know that it is a rising and not a setting
sun."

3. PRAGUE, OCTOBER 29, 1787: TO HEAR MOZART
   CONDUCT THE FIRST PERFORMANCE OF
   DON GIOVANNI, IN THE OPINION OF MANY THE
   GREATEST OPERA EVER WRITTEN

What is there to add? The beauty of Prague, the genius of
Mozart . . .

4. NOVEMBER 15, 1805: LEWIS AND CLARK SIGHT THE PACIFIC OCEAN

That day, Clark wrote in his journal, "I landed and formed camp on the highest spot I could find, from this I could plainly see the extent of our journey in full view of the ocean." Thus, the great exploration launched by Columbus in 1492 came to a climax.

5. LONDON, DECEMBER 8, 1941: CHURCHILL ANNOUNCES TO THE HOUSE OF COMMONS THAT THE UNITED STATES HAS ENTERED THE WAR

Let Churchill himself comment: "In the past, we have had a light that flickered; in the present, we have a light which flames, and, in the future, there will be a light which shines over all the land and sea."

—Exclusive for *The Book of Lists 2*

19
THE INEXPLICABLE

WILLIAM H. SPAULDING'S
8 BEST-DOCUMENTED
CASES OF UFOs

One of the leading UFO experts in the world, William Spaulding is a quality control engineer for AiResearch, an aerospace company in Phoenix, Ariz. He has been actively involved in UFOlogy for over 20 years, and since the mid 1960s he has served as western states director for Ground Saucer Watch, Inc., an organization devoted to the serious analysis of UFO data. Much of this classified material was obtained by Spaulding under the FOIA (Freedom of Information Act).

1. McMINNVILLE PHOTOGRAPHS

Paul Trent, a farmer living in McMinnville, Ore., obtained two of the clearest photographs taken in UFO history. In May, 1950, the witness observed a disk-shaped object in the distance. Immediately, Mr. Trent got his camera and took two exposures of the UFO. The photographs were taken in broad daylight and contain both foreground and background information. From the evidence in the photographs, there are two possibilities for the object's true origin. It is either a small model suspended above the electric wires, or it is a large object in the distance. Although one photograph has been reviewed by some of the best photographic experts in the country and it has been stated "that it is one of the best UFO photographs analyzed," it wasn't until the utilization of computer-enhancement processing that the evidence was solidified. After a detailed computer-enhancement process, similar to the analyses being performed by NASA space officials on America's satellite photographs, the picture was judged to be authentic. Absolute measurements and high-resolution pictures verified that the image was large and at an appreciable distance from the camera. Mr. Trent has taken one of the few bona fide photographs of a UFO that met the challenge of science.

2. THE UFOS THAT SHOWED INTELLIGENT CONTROL

On the evening of July 14, 1952, the pilots of a Pan Am airliner approaching Norfolk, Va., noticed a red brilliance east of the city. The glow quickly resolved itself into six bright objects streaking towards the plane at a lower altitude. The UFOs were fiery red. "Their edges were defined, the shape was clearly outlined and evidently circular," Captain Nash related. Within seconds, he said, "We could observe that they were holding a narrow echelon formation—a stepped-up line tilted slightly, with the lead object at the lowest point and each following craft slightly higher." When the line of disks was almost directly underneath the plane, the UFOs flipped up on edge in unison and reversed direction. The exposed edges appeared to the witnesses to be 15 ft. thick, giving the objects an aspect ratio (thickness to diameter) of 1 to 6. As the six objects maneuvered away from the witnesses, two additional UFOs darted from behind and under the airliner and joined up with the now precise formation and sped away at a tremendous speed. The next morning air force investigators questioned the pilots for over two hours. All of the accounts matched, and the investigators told the witnesses that they had seven other reports from ground observers. The pilots calculated the speed of the objects at over 10,000 mph. The performance factor of the UFOs, as well as their precision maneuvering while in formation, prompted the air force to rate this case as an unknown.

3. WASHINGTON, D.C., SIGHTINGS

On two consecutive weekends in July, 1952, UFOs swarmed over Washington, D.C. Highly maneuverable, erratically performing objects were seen visually by pilots exactly where radar showed their location. Three separate radar units showed as many as 12 unidentified targets traveling at speeds of hundreds to thousands of miles per hour, while performing unbelievable maneuvers. Concerned officials in the military sent up interceptors, only to have the UFOs move away at incredible speeds. The radar sets were checked and found to be functioning perfectly. All of the radar blips were solid, strong targets. Later, under pressure, the U.S. Air Force reported that an unusual temperature inversion was causing the targets on the radars and that ground lights were refracted on the layers of air, thus causing the visual stimuli. This was the beginning of the air force foul-up and only the prelude to hundreds of illogical explanations used to pacify the American public.

4. MYSTERY OF THE MAYHER FRAMES

In late July, 1952, in Miami, Fla., a Marine named Ralph Mayher photographed a spectacular unidentified flying object. This was a multiple-witness sighting, and it involved a fiery, oval-shaped object. Mayher managed to obtain close to 50 frames before foreground structures blocked his efforts. The witness reported his sighting to his military supervisors and turned the film over to them for analysis. The cleverest thing that Mayher did was to "clip" the first seven frames from the 16mm film and retain them. As the year went by, the film was never returned to the observer. In late 1957 he received some media coverage on the situation, and soon thereafter the CIA contacted Mr. Mayher about the incident and missing movie footage. Years later GSW (Ground Saucer Watch, Inc.) analyzed the few frames with computer technology and finalized that the UFO was definitely bona fide. If only the *entire* footage could be evaluated. Simultaneously with the photographic analysis, the GSW lawsuit against the CIA was levied. The Mayher incident was one of the prime ingredients of the legal action. Although, to date, the film has not been retrieved, numerous CIA documents supporting the sighting have emerged. It is now only a matter of time before the missing frames will be obtained from the government.

418

5. THE RADAR/VISUAL CASE

An important military case involving fast-moving UFOs occurred on December 6, 1952, aboard a USAF B-29 on a training flight over the Gulf of Mexico. Just prior to dawn a strange radar blip was being recorded on one of the plane's auxiliary scopes. When the sweep made its next revolution, the unknown object had traveled 13 mi.! The astonished crew calculated the speed of the UFO and found it to be over 5,000 mph. Immediately the captain turned on the plane's main radar unit; after a calibration, it too was picking up the unknowns. Then a third set was turned on and began to record the same. The pilot ordered the crew to watch for the UFOs. Astonished, they reported bluish-white blurs of light go flashing by the aircraft. In the next few minutes, groups of UFOs were observed both visually and on all three radars. Nervously the crew watched as the UFOs came even closer to their plane. At those terrific speeds the crew wouldn't have a prayer. Suddenly, a huge UFO appeared on the scopes, over a half-inch spot. Still moving at speeds over 5,000 mph, the smaller objects merged with the larger object. Instantly, the huge blip began to accelerate at an estimated speed of 9,000 mph. Intelligence officers were waiting when the crew landed, and all of the airmen were interrogated. Nothing could shake their story, and nothing was found wrong with the radar sets. The case is still rated as an unknown in the Project Blue Book records.

6. THE B-47 INCIDENT

On September 25, 1957, during a training mission over the Gulf of Mexico and the south-central states, a U.S. Air Force B-47 encountered a UFO "as big as a barn" with a red glow. It paced the aircraft through numerous changes of speed and appeared to jump from one location to another. All of the visual sightings were coordinated with the radar fixes from both the air and the ground. The object was emitting some type of electromagnetic energy with apparent high intensity. After the crew members had been interrogated, governmental pressure was applied, and no records of the incident could be located. The aircraft was equipped for electronic countermeasures missions. The UFO "played" with the plane and literally flew circles around it. Since the plane had sophisticated electronic equipment aboard, it was able to measure the signal pouring from the UFO. The object was emitting large amounts of electromagnetic radiation in a narrow range of the microwave region. It appears that the UFO was using microwave radiation as a propulsion system, and such a system is capable of diminishing or nullifying gravitational forces. It is no wonder that the U.S. government wants to keep stories like this from reaching the public, for it shows beyond a shadow of a doubt that the UFO phenomenon has vast air superiority, and it also indicates the true vulnerability of our military system.

7. A LARGE UFO STARTS THE FLAP OF 1957

The flap of November, 1957, began in earnest a few hours after the second Russian dog-carrying satellite blasted into orbit. The place was the outskirts of Levelland, Tex. One hour before midnight the first witness to a series of mysterious events that evening called the law enforcement office to report a close encounter with a large UFO. The witness reported a strange flash of light in the field. "Then it rose up out of the field and started towards us, picking up speed. When it got nearer, the lights of my truck went out and the motor died. I jumped out and hit the deck as the thing passed directly over the truck with a great sound and a rush of wind. It sounded like thunder, and my truck rocked from the blast. I felt a lot of heat." The object was over 200 ft. in length and glowed an eerie red color as it moved into the distance. Within the next three hours, nine additional sightings were made of what appeared to be the same object. In six of the incidents the witnesses' vehicles suffered severe EME (electromagnetic effects) each time the UFO got close to the witnesses. Although the government's explanation was tenuous at best, this series of low-level UFO encounters offered some "hard" evidence of the existence of the phenomena and changed the attitude of the body politic, which theretofore had scoffed at reports of aerial phenomena.

8. THE IRANIAN ENCOUNTER

In September, 1976, almost six years after the closure of the U.S. Air Force's Project Blue Book UFO investigation, an incident involving two F-4 jets and a UFO occurred over the skies of Tehran, Iran. After a visual sighting of a strange, bright, light object by hundreds of witnesses, Iranian radars started picking up an unidentified target. Two up-to-date jets were vectored towards the UFO to intercept and identify. As the first jet "closed" within 25 nautical mi., the plane lost all communications. Meanwhile the second jet was closing fast. As the pilot watched in amazement, the large UFO dropped a smaller object from beneath its superstructure. Instantaneously the plane lost its communications, and the pilot started to arm his air-to-air missile system as the smaller UFO flew towards the jet aircraft. Surprisingly, the weapon system failed, and the pilot took evasive action (a dive) to miss the object as it "shot over" the top of his canopy, just missing the plane. Then the smaller object flew towards the larger UFO and mated up perfectly, prior to departing from the area. With the U.S. government document on this case available, obtained under the Freedom of Information Act, it was impossible for a government explanation designed to debunk this case to work effectively.

—Exclusive for *The Book of Lists 2*

15 FAMOUS BELIEVERS IN ASTROLOGY

1. SIR FRANCIS BACON (1561–1626), AQUARIUS

Influenced by French royal astrologers, the scientist Bacon became a practicing astrologer and advocated a "purification" of the science of astrology. Later in life, he renounced stargazing.

2. CHARLES DE GAULLE (1890–1970), SAGITTARIUS

One of De Gaulle's earliest horoscopes, done before W.W. II when he was a French army captain, foretold that he was destined to rule France. Throughout his life, he occasionally consulted professional astrologers and palmists.

3. QUEEN ELIZABETH I (1533–1603), VIRGO

Elizabeth had as her personal astrologer the famous seer Dr. John Dee, who utilized a crystal ball. As a reward for his occult services, she installed Dee as the chancellor of St. Paul's in London.

4. IAN FLEMING (1908–1964), GEMINI

James Bond's creator denounced occultism in public, but he had one of his first horoscopes cast during W.W. II while serving in the British Intelligence Service. Fleming was very concerned about the date of his death, which his astrologers never revealed to him.

5. GALILEO GALILEI (1564–1642), AQUARIUS

Galileo practiced astrology but was not always able to ascertain correct information from the stars. In 1609 he prepared the horoscope of the Grand Duke of Tuscany and predicted that he would have a long life. The duke died a few weeks later.

6. CARL JUNG (1875–1961), LEO

Jung found astrology useful in preparing preliminary studies of new psychiatric patients. To test one of his theories, he examined the horoscopes of 483 married couples.

7. JOHANNES KEPLER (1571–1630), CAPRICORN

Kepler's duties as imperial mathematician to Rudolf II included making horoscopes for the Holy Roman emperor. Kepler, seeing no contradiction between this activity and his other, more scientific pursuits, said, "Nature . . . has given astrology as an adjunct and ally to astronomy."

8. MARTIN LUTHER (1483–1546), SCORPIO

In a preface to a book on astrology by Johannes Lichtenberger, Luther wrote that astrology was a warning to the godless. Luther frequently discussed the stars with his theologian friend Philipp Melanchthon. After Luther's death, a papal astrologer cast his horoscope to determine the exact time of his damnation.

9. MARIE ANTOINETTE (1755–1793), SCORPIO

This Austrian-born queen of France retained a court astrologer at Versailles. The horoscope cast at the time of Marie Antoinette's birth foretold such calamity that her natal celebration was canceled.

10. W. SOMERSET MAUGHAM (1874–1965), AQUARIUS

Maugham consulted astrologers and entertained them at his home on the French Riviera. He annoyed several astrologers by paying for their services with only a free dinner.

11. HENRY MILLER (1891–   ), CAPRICORN

Miller's writings contain numerous examples of astrological

symbolism. In the foreword to *Henry Miller: His World of Urania* by Sydney Omarr, Miller wrote that astrology demonstrates that "there is a rhythm to the universe."

12. J. P. MORGAN (1837–1913), ARIES

Morgan consulted his astrologer, Evangeline Adams—said to be a descendant of John Quincy Adams—each month on business matters. Miss Adams's other clients included King Edward VII, Enrico Caruso, and Mary Pickford.

13. PRESIDENT THEODORE ROOSEVELT (1858–1919), SCORPIO

An enthusiastic disciple of astrology, Roosevelt had his natal horoscope mounted on a chessboard, which he studied daily. Well acquainted with astrological jargon, he was most concerned with his Moon opposing Mars.

14. DAME EDITH SITWELL (1887–1964), VIRGO?

Although she sought astrologers to do her horoscope, this English poet always lied concerning her date of birth. She claimed half a dozen signs as her own, so it is doubtful whether she ever had an accurate horoscope cast.

15. SYLVESTER STALLONE (1947–   ), CANCER

Sylvester Stallone's mother was an astrologer, and she predicted he would be a writer. He believes in astrology so strongly that he and his wife planned the birth of their son, Sage, so that he would be a Taurus with Libra Moon and Leo Rising (for intelligence). An astrologer once told Stallone to beware of heavy machinery. Shortly thereafter, while working out in a gym, Stallone severed a muscle when a 300-lb. bench press fell on him.

—R.J.F.

10 INCREDIBLE CLOSE CALLS AND LUCKY BREAKS

1. LAST STAND

Col. Frederick D. Grant, the oldest son of President Ulysses S. Grant and a graduate of West Point, had always been a soldier. In 1874 he married Ida M. Honoré of Chicago. Two years later, Grant was serving in Gen. George A. Custer's 7th Cavalry. General Custer was ordered into the Black Hills to find and destroy the Sioux Indians led by Chief Crazy Horse. On June 25, 1876, in a ravine near the Little Bighorn River in Montana, General Custer and his 266 men were ambushed by Chief Crazy Horse and his 3,500 braves. Custer made his last stand, and in two to three hours he and his troops were massacred. However, the roll of the dead did not include the President's son, Frederick Grant. He had not accompanied Custer to Little Bighorn, because a day or two before the 7th Cavalry marched off on its Indian hunt, Grant had been given "compassionate leave" to be at the bedside of his wife, who was about to give birth to their first child. Grant lived on to become an ambassador to Austria, a police commissioner in Chicago, and a general in the Spanish-American War. He finally died, aged 72, in 1912.

2. FORMAL DRESS

In 1919 a 30-year-old Russian electronics engineer named Vladimir K. Zworykin emigrated to the U.S. He went to work for Westinghouse Electric Company and later for RCA. Along the way, he invented a television transmission tube and a television receiver. He became known, in fact, as the father of modern television. Just after W.W. II began, Zworykin, who was in Beirut, had to stop off in London on business before returning to New York. He started to buy a ticket for an Atlantic crossing on the S.S. *Athenia*. "But I had inadvertently left my tuxedo behind in Lebanon," Zworykin remembered in an interview with author Bruce Felton, "and rather than endure the embarrassment of being improperly dressed in the first-class dining room during the crossing, I decided to shop for dinner dress and take a later ship." The *Athenia* left without Zworykin. Off the coast of Ireland on September 4, 1939, the *Athenia* was torpedoed by a Nazi U-boat. It went to a watery grave with a loss of 128 lives, among them 28 Americans. The 29th American was shopping in London for a new tuxedo.

3. THE VICTIM

On May 21, 1924, two young men in Chicago set out to commit the perfect crime. One was 19-year-old Nathan F. Leopold, Jr., son of a millionaire box manufacturer and a graduate of the University of Chicago. The other was 18-year-old Richard A. Loeb, son of a wealthy vice-president of Sears, Roebuck, and Company and a graduate of the University of Michigan. Four years earlier, Leopold had proposed a homosexual relationship, and Loeb had agreed to it providing his partner would assist him in an effort to get away with murder. The plot included a kidnapping, a killing, and a ransom note. After discussing three possible victims, they settled on a fourth. It was to be young Armand Deutsch, one of the heirs to the Sears, Roebuck fortune. He would be picked up as he left Harvard Preparatory School. Loeb and Leopold parked outside. When Armand Deutsch did not appear, they picked up Loeb's cousin, Robert "Bobby" Franks, instead, took him for a drive, and smashed him on the head four times with a chisel. Franks's body was found in a culvert. Leopold's eyeglasses were discovered nearby. The murderers were caught, and Loeb confessed. As for the intended victim, what had happened to him? On the fateful day designated for his death, Deutsch had been absent from school, kept home because he was ill. Thus reprieved, Deutsch grew up to become a successful Hollywood producer.

4. HAPPY ST. VALENTINE'S DAY

On February 14, 1929, mob leader George "Bugs" Moran had

an appointment to examine a Canadian liquor shipment with seven members of his gang at the S.M.C. Carthage Company warehouse on North Clark Street in Chicago. About to leave for his appointment, Moran was briefly delayed. Meanwhile, his men—Frank and Pete Gusenberg, Adam Heyer, Al Weinshunk, James Clark, John May, Reinhardt Schwimmer—waited in the warehouse for their boss. Suddenly, a Cadillac touring car arrived outside. Four men, two of them wearing police uniforms, got out of the Cadillac and went into the warehouse. Two were holding machine guns, the others carried sawed-off shotguns. They were members of Al Capone's rival gang. They lined Moran's men up against a wall and opened fire, slaughtering all seven of them. Then the killers fled. Five minutes later Bugs Moran arrived at the warehouse. By chance, he had just missed, and thus survived, the St. Valentine's Day Massacre.

5. CELEBRATION IN BOSTON

On the morning of November 28, 1942, someone on the staff of the Boston College Eagles football team made a reservation for the entire squad to hold a victory party at the Cocoanut Grove nightclub that evening. Boston College, led by quarterback Eddie Doherty and fullback Mike Holovak, was the number-one football team in the U.S. Unbeaten in eight contests, scoring 249 points to its opponents' 19 points, Boston College merely had to defeat a pushover, Holy Cross, which had already lost four games and been tied once, to clinch a bid to the Sugar Bowl. That night, in the basement Melody Lounge of the Cocoanut Grove, the satin decorations covering the 900-sq.-ft. ceiling somehow caught fire. (Later, the official report said the fire was of "unknown origin.") The nightclub became an inferno. Within 12 minutes, 490 persons were dead or dying. One room in which everyone was incinerated was the Terrace Room, where the Boston College football team had arranged to have its victory party. The final casualty list included the name of former cowboy film star Buck Jones. But the casualty list did not include the name of even one member of the Boston College team. For that afternoon, the invincible Boston College team had come apart on the gridiron and had been trounced by underdog Holy Cross, 55 to 12, one of the biggest sports upsets of modern times. Defeated and depressed, the Boston team was in no mood for a celebration. At the last minute the players decided to cancel their reservation at the Cocoanut Grove. They went to bed early instead.

6. THE SECONDARY TARGET

Which would be the primary target for the first atom bomb drop in history—Hiroshima or Kokura, Japan? One thing bothered the U.S. Army Air Force about Kokura, an industrial city with a population of 400,000. It was supposed to have a prisoners-of-war camp nearby which held American soldiers. So Hiroshima became the primary target, with Kokura the secondary target. On August 6, 1945, the Superfortress *Enola Gay*, piloted by Col. Paul Tibbets, Jr., hit Hiroshima with a single uranium atom bomb, and 100,000 Japanese were dead or missing and 68,000 injured out of a population of 255,000. Three days later, another drop was scheduled to be made. The primary target, prisoners-of-war camp or no, was designated as Kokura, with Nagasaki the secondary target. Superfortress *Bock's Car*, piloted by Charles Sweeney, headed for Kokura, then learned that the weather was bad around that city. So he turned to Nagasaki, a city of 280,000 persons, and released a more powerful plutonium atom bomb over it. Nagasaki suffered 36,000 people dead, 60,000 injured. By chance, the 400,000 residents of Kokura were spared and lived on to thrive and prosper in the nuclear age. Today Kokura is part of the city of Kitakyushu.

7. "BECAUSE IT'S THERE"

On May 29, 1953, Edmund P. Hillary, a 34-year-old New Zealand beekeeper, and Tenzing Norkay, a Nepalese Sherpa guide, became the first persons in history to reach the summit of 29,000-ft. Mt. Everest, the highest mountain in the world. Hillary survived the rarefied altitude and severe snowstorms to become a legend and earn a knighthood. Seven years later, his luck held and he survived a second time. On December 16, 1960, due back in Nepal in two weeks, Hillary booked a seat on a United Airlines DC-8 jetliner going from Chicago to New York. On that same day a TWA Super-Constellation left Dayton, O., for the same destination. In the rain and fog over New York, the United and TWA jetliners collided. The death toll was 134 passengers and crew members. But Edmund Hillary was not among them. He had arrived late at the Chicago airport and missed his United flight. Fifteen years later his wife was less lucky—losing her life in an air crash near Mt. Everest.

8. DOCTOR'S ORDERS

Elizabeth Taylor was to have accompanied Mike Todd on his trip to New York in 1958 for a Friars Club dinner that was being given in his honor. A couple days before the event, she was stricken with bronchitis; when Todd was ready to leave Los Angeles, she had a fever of 102° and her doctor forbade her to go. The weather was miserable, and Todd had trouble getting anyone else to join him on his private plane. Kirk Douglas, Joe E. Lewis, and Joseph Mankiewicz all made their excuses. But screenwriter Art Cohn went along, hoping to work on a film script en route. The plane crashed in New Mexico, killing all aboard.

9. THE ROCK 'N' ROLL CHARTER

A rock group, the Crickets, had just finished an engagement in Clear Lake, Ia., and had to get to Moorhead, Minn., for their next date. Because they were all tired, their leader, Buddy Holly, chartered a plane in nearby Mason City, Ia. On the plane were to be Holly, Waylon Jennings (a bearded Texan who played country music), and guitarist Tommy Allsup. It was February 3, 1959, and the chartered Beech Bonanza N3749N was ready for takeoff. At the last moment, J. P. "The Big Bopper" Richardson asked Jennings if he could take his place on the plane, because he had the flu. Almost at the same time, Ritchie Valens asked Tommy Allsup if he could take his place on the plane. Both Jennings and Allsup relinquished their seats. The Beech Bonanza took off, then crashed. All hands on board were killed. Because of sheer luck, Waylon Jennings and Tommy Allsup survived.

10. THE SLAUGHTERHOUSE FIVE

Novelist Jerzy Kosinski was flying to Los Angeles to join his friend Voytek Frykowski at a party being given at the Hollywood home of actress Sharon Tate on the evening of August 8, 1969. During the evening some uninvited guests attended the party at Sharon's. Incited by their cult leader, a criminal and vagrant named Charles Manson, his hopped-up followers—Charles "Tex" Watson, Susan Atkins, Patricia Krenwinkel, Leslie Van Houten—shot and stabbed to death the pregnant Sharon Tate, Jay Sebring, Abigail Folger, Steven Parent, and Frykowski. The expected guest, Jerzy Kosinski, was delayed because a French airline clerk had accidentally sent his luggage to New York instead of Los Angeles. Kosinski had just barely missed the party. He later wrote about the close call in a novel entitled *Blind Date*.

—I.W.

10 STUNNING COINCIDENCES

1. HANGING HILL

In 1911 three men were hanged in London for the murder of Sir Edmund Berry at Greenberry Hill. Their names were Green, Berry, and Hill.

2. THE KILLER TAXI

Two brothers in Bermuda were killed by the same taxi and driver, carrying the same passenger, while they were riding the same moped on the same street—but exactly a year apart. Erskine Lawrence Ebbin and his brother Neville were both 17 when they died.

3. TWENTY-THREE

In 1932 bootlegger "Dutch" Schultz (born Arthur Flegenheimer) had 23-year-old Vincent "Mad Dog" Coll murdered on 23rd Street in New York City. Schultz himself was assassinated on October 23, 1935, and his convicted assassin, Charlie Workman, served 23 years of a life sentence before he was paroled.

4. WILD GOOSE

In November, 1974, the family of Noel McCabe was listening to a recording of Frankie Laine singing "The Wild Goose" at their home on Kingston Street in Derby, England, when a Canada goose crashed through a window into the bedroom.

5. FALLING BABIES

In the spring of 1975, a baby in Detroit fell 14 stories and landed on Joseph Figlock, who was walking below. A year later it happened again. Figlock and both babies survived.

6. CODES

In the months before June 6, 1944—the day of the Normandy invasion—the London *Daily Telegraph* crossword puzzle included many top-secret code words for the Allied operations: Omaha, Utah, Mulberry, Neptune, and the code for D-Day itself, Overlord. The puzzle was compiled by a schoolmaster who couldn't have had any knowledge of the codes.

7. A BAD ROAD FOR CLATWORTHYS

Frank Clatworthy was driving home to Washford, Somerset, England, from a party in 1974 when his car overturned. An hour later, his identical twin brother, Jack, crashed on the same road returning from the same party.

8. A DEADLY MOMENT

On January 28, 1975, Charles Davies died at 3:00 A.M. while on vacation at his sister's house in Leicester, England. When his sister called his home in Leeds to relate the bad news, she was told that Charles's wife had also died that day—at 3:00 A.M.

9. SPECIAL THANKS

At age four, Roger Lausier was saved from drowning off a beach at Salem, Mass., by a woman named Alice Blaise. Nine years later, in 1974, on the same beach, Roger paddled his raft into the water and pulled a drowning man from the water. The man was Alice Blaise's husband.

10. IDENTICAL TWINS

James Lews of Lima, O., and James Springer of Dayton, O., are identical twins who were separated shortly after birth. Their adoptive parents—who had no knowledge of each other—named their sons James. Each James married and divorced a woman named Linda. Each named his first son James Alan (Allan). Each likes to vacation on the same Florida beach. Both are 6 ft. tall, weigh 180 lb., have the same hobbies, and have had police training. They met for the first time in 1979, when they were 39 years old.

—T.S.

Identical twins meet for the first time almost 40 years after birth.

7 LIVELY POLTERGEISTS

The German word *Poltergeist* means "a mischievous spirit," or, more simply, "noisy ghost." Poltergeists live up to their name—they knock, rap, and throw things about, usually slowly and sometimes around corners. Ordinarily they remain invisible, content with provoking human consternation by their tricks. The agent for poltergeist activity is often a child or a teenager.

1. "OLD JEFFREY" (1716–1717)

When John Wesley, the founder of Methodism, was 13 years old, a poltergeist visited his home, the Epworth rectory in Lincolnshire, England. It began with groans, which were followed by raps, creaking of machinery, rustling, squeals, and footsteps. The sound of knocking interrupted prayers, especially the prayer for the king, which had been a source of contention between the Wesley parents. The children called the poltergeist "Old Jeffrey," and seven-year-old Kezzy "desired no better diversion than to pursue Old Jeffrey from room to room." Old Jeffrey didn't stop at noise; he also bounced dishes, lifted latches, and pushed people.

2. THE BELL WITCH (1817–1821)

The focus for this Tennessee witch was Betsy Bell, aged 12, blond, blue-eyed, and pretty. The witch hated "Old Jack" Bell, as she called Betsy's father, and harassed him until he died. At his funeral, the witch sang, "Row me up some brandy, O." The Bell witch was a most active poltergeist. She showed up as a doglike creature, then as something that resembled a turkey; made numerous noises; pinched and slapped people; caused Betsy to have fainting fits; prevented Betsy from marrying her sweetheart; cursed and swore; dropped fruit and hazelnuts on the table; gave advice. The witch even stopped Gen. Andrew Jackson's wagon in its tracks when Jackson went to visit the Bells. Jackson's companion fired a silver bullet at the witch. She took the hint and voluntarily disappeared in 1821, promising to return in seven years. She did make a brief reappearance, this time saying she would come back in 107 years. However, 1935 came and went, with no show from the witch.

3. THE ATTIC POLTERGEIST (1835–1847)

A poltergeist lived for 12 years in the house of Joseph Procter, a sober and honest Quaker farmer and mill owner. It knocked, banged, threw things, whistled, and said, "Chuck, chuck" and "Never mind . . . come and get." It lifted beds, rang bells, slammed doors. The night before the Procters finally moved from their house in Willington Mill, England, they heard the sound of boxes being dragged around in the attic, as if the poltergeist were planning to move with them. Luckily it didn't.

4. THE TABLEAU POLTERGEIST (1850–1851)

When Presbyterian minister Eliakin Phelps came home from

church in Stratford, Conn., on March 10, 1850, he and his family found a tableau of 11 figures (10 of them female), dressed in the family's clothes, kneeling in front of Bibles open to passages justifying poltergeists. That was only the beginning. In the 18 months of poltergeist activity, 30 figures mysteriously showed up in the house. In addition, things were thrown slowly, glass broke, messages were written, something grew in the carpet, a turnip fell from the ceiling. The two older children, a boy and girl, suffered through the poltergeist's activities. The boy was once found in a coma in a haystack, and the girl was nearly strangled to death.

5. THE GREAT AMHERST MYSTERY (1879)

The wife of Daniel Teed, an Amherst, Nova Scotia, shoemaker, had two sisters, beautiful 22-year-old Jennie and dark, sullen 19-year-old Esther. Poltergeist activity started after Esther was attacked by their neighbor Bob McNeal. One night a green cardboard box filled with patchwork began rustling under a bed. Put in the middle of the room, it started bouncing on the floor. Esther swelled up like a balloon, then collapsed as if she'd been pricked. Similar events occurred every 28 days. Finally Esther was put in a show to display her talents, but nothing happened when she was onstage. However, when she went to live with a neighbor, lighted matches dropped from a ceiling and burned down his barn. Esther spent four months in jail, guilty or not. U.S. actor Walter Hubbell, who stayed with the Teeds for a while, wrote up the story. His book, *The Great Amherst Mystery*, which came out in 1888, had sold 55,000 copies by 1916.

6. THE SEAFORD POLTERGEIST (1958)

On February 3, 1958, a ceramic figurine and a ship model broke on a dresser in the Herrmann house in Seaford, Long Island, N.Y. This began a two-month-long siege by a bottle-popping poltergeist during which 67 incidents occurred, involving broken bottles containing everything from holy water to bleach. The center of the activity was 12-year-old James. Many eyewitnesses, among them a police officer and two psychic researchers, were present at times when the poltergeist was active. The case was also investigated by engineers and a group of professors from the Science Department at Adelphi University. Ruled out were high-frequency radio waves, vibrations, drafts, peculiar plumbing, hallucination, and hoax. The disturbances ended on March 10.

7. THE BRIDGEPORT POLTERGEIST (1974)

In November, 1974, the Goodin home in Bridgeport, Conn., was visited by pounding noises followed by dishes and cutlery being hurled to the floor and heavy furniture and appliances moving by themselves. The police decided that these bizarre occurrences were a hoax perpetrated by the Goodins' 10-year-old adopted daughter, but a Catholic priest who had been called in by the family wasn't so sure. He could find no trick devices that might have caused the phenomena, and he actually saw furniture move while the daughter was standing next to him. The Goodins wired down their furniture even as they made plans to move. The mystery remains unsolved.

—A.E.

7 MEMORABLE CASES
OF MASS HYSTERIA

1. THE EUROPEAN DANCING MANIA (1374)

It began at Aix-la-Chapelle in 1374 with a procession of
wanderers dancing, twitching, stumbling, lurching, and whirling
their way from one town to the next, all the while shrieking, moaning,
tearing off their clothes, and frothing at the mouth. Their wild
movements exerted a strange but powerful pull on those who watched,
and thousands of villagers along the way joined in. The madness
reached the Netherlands, then Metz and Strasbourg, where musicians accompanied the dancers around the clock in an attempt to
cure them of the sickness. But the attempt backfired; the musicians
only incited the dancers to even wilder revels and drew new hordes
of participants. Pilgrimages were organized to combat the epidemic,
some involving dancing rituals of their own as a combative agent.
The first real improvement came in the early 1500s, when the
physician Paracelsus used cold-water baths to calm the dancers.

2. THE GREAT U.S. RADIO SCARE (1938)

Few of Orson Welles's Mercury Theatre colleagues thought
the radio dramatization of H. G. Wells's *War of the Worlds*—which
Welles had planned for the day before Halloween, 1938—would
garner much of an audience. "Too fantastic," they argued. "It just
isn't believable." Still Welles persisted, pumping Howard Koch's
adaptation of the sci-fi masterpiece about a Martian attack on the
earth full of broadcast-age realism and giving it a northeast U.S.
setting. Rendered jittery by the frequent radio bulletins they had been
hearing that summer and fall about European preparations for war,
over a million listeners across the nation accepted at face value the
program's bogas interviews with alarmed physicists, a reporter's on-
the-spot description of the Martians' landing and his subsequent on-
the-air death by ray gun, and ominous messages from government
officials about the gravity of the situation. Although there were
several messages during the program indicating that it was a work
of fiction, in Hillside, N.J., a man ran into the police station and
demanded a gas mask to protect himself against "the terrible people
spraying liquid gas all over the Jersey Meadows." In Pittsburgh a
man returned home to find his wife about to poison herself. "I'd
rather die this way than like that," she screamed. Fifteen people were
treated for shock in a Newark, N.J., hospital, while reports of a gas-
bomb attack spread through the city. Ten squad cars and an ambu-
lance were dispatched to the Clinton Hill section of Newark. Kansas
City hospitals reported two heart attacks related to the broadcast.
There was panic everywhere. The hysteria had subsided by the
following day, leaving in its wake a nation of embarrassed and
enraged listeners. Welles sensibly went into semiseclusion. The FCC
called the show "regrettable." But columnist Dorothy Thompson
wrote, "Nothing about the broadcast was in the least credible."

3. THE PHANTOM ANESTHETIST OF MATTOON (1944)

" 'Anesthetic Prowler' on the Loose," was the headline of a

front-page story in the Mattoon, Ill., *Daily Journal-Gazette* on September 2, 1944. The next line reported, "Mrs. Corbin and Daughter First Victims." At home with her two young daughters the night before while her husband was working, Mrs. John Corbin (the name is fictitious) had awakened to a nauseatingly sweet odor drifting through her bedroom window and filling the house. Upon trying to rise, she found that her legs and torso were paralyzed. She was able to summon a neighbor, who in turn contacted Mr. Corbin, who immediately returned home. As he pulled into the driveway, he spotted—or so he thought—a prowler wearing dark clothes and a tight-fitting cap. He gave chase, but the stranger escaped. Meanwhile, Mrs. Corbin was beginning to regain the use of her legs. The following evening a second woman phoned police with a similar story. Over the next 12 days, a total of 24 attacks were reported by Mattoon townswomen, who likened the aroma of the incapacitating gas—which left them partially paralyzed, swollen-lipped, and nauseated—to cheap perfume and rotting flowers. Many claimed they'd caught a glimpse of the assailant and that they'd heard the sound of his gas gun. The police spread their nets far and wide to track him down, hypothesizing that he might be a sex fiend, a mad scientist, or an ex-military man trained in chemical warfare. Scouring the area, they turned up nothing and eventually suggested that there was no nocturnal anesthetist at all. A few years later, investigating psychologists diagnosed the affair as a case of mass hysteria aggravated by the wartime separation anxiety so widely felt by housewives whose husbands were being drafted into the armed services.

4. WINDSHIELD PITTING IN SEATTLE (1954)

The Seattle dailies carried news on March 23, 1954, of what appeared to be a strange exercise in vandalism 80 mi. north of the city. There, the papers said, car owners were reporting to police that their windshields had been peppered with tiny "pitting marks," some as large as a fingernail. Additional pittings were reported in that area over the next three weeks. On the morning of April 14, a second city 15 mi. closer to Seattle reported similar damage, and by the afternoon a third town only 45 mi. away followed suit. Seattle itself was struck by early evening. Within 24 hours, city police had received 242 calls about windshield damage to some 3,000 vehicles. That night the mayor called for help from the governor and the President. Car owners were advised to pad their windshields with newspapers. The cause? Some spoke of tiny meteors, others of sand-flea eggs hatching in the glass, but many more were convinced that fallout from the recent hydrogen bomb tests at Eniwetok Atoll was to blame. In all likelihood, however, it was ill-suppressed anxiety over these tests that prompted the hysteria. That June, a University of Washington research team sought in vain for a single case of pitting that could not be attributed to ordinary wear and tear on automobile windshields. Moreover, the tiny, metallic motes many drivers had discovered on the windshields and hoods of their cars turned out to be coal particles, which had been a regular if unobserved part of the Seattle scene for years. Significantly, there were scarcely a dozen pitting-related complaints two days after the 14th of April, and by the 18th there were none. Several newspapers theorized that those who'd seen the pittings had, for the first time, looked *at* their windshields rather than *through* them.

5. THE EAST AFRICAN OUTBREAKS (1962–1963)

A bizarre series of epidemics hit East Africa in 1962–1963, centering mostly around the Lake Victoria area of Uganda and Tanzania. Compulsive laughing overtook the villagers of Bukoba, in what was then Tanganyika. In the department of Kigezi and the town of Mbale in Uganda, 900 victims of an unprecedented "running sickness" were mysteriously driven to run madly about until they fell from exhaustion; generally they clutched chickens as they ran. The mania continued for several weeks and was said by local chieftains to be the work of spirits.

6. HYSTERICAL SYMPTOMS AT A BRITISH GIRLS' SCHOOL (1966)

On a Thursday morning in 1966, the classrooms and corridors of an Anglican girls' school in Blackburn, Lancashire, were abuzz with talk of an unusual incident that had marred a royally sponsored religious ceremony in which the school had participated the previous day. A three-hour holdup had caused 20 girls to step out of the processional line and lie down on the floor to avoid fainting. This Thursday morning, within two hours of the first bell, 10 girls had complained of feeling faint and were told by their teachers to lie down on the floor of the school's main corridor. Here they were fully visible to most of their 540 classmates during the midmorning recess. Soon thereafter, girls were fainting at a steady clip, and by day's end some 141—85 of whom were hospitalized—had suffered dizziness, chills, headaches, and nausea. School was closed until the following Monday, when 79 students suffered like symptoms, with 54 requiring emergency hospital care. Classrooms were scrubbed through Friday, and when classes were resumed the following Monday, there were 58 new complaints—the last of the lot. Medical investigators explained that a recent spate of polio cases in the Blackburn area had created an atmosphere of anxiety, which, inflamed by the church incident, gave rise to the symptoms.

7. THE GREAT MIDWESTERN GAS ATTACK (1972)

The data-processing center of a midwestern university in the U.S. was the scene of a seemingly untraceable "gas attack" in March, 1972, which afflicted 35 female keypunch operators with vomiting attacks and fainting spells. Ten of them required emergency treatment, and the center itself was evacuated and closed for the day. With the employees gone, a team of environmental specialists scoured the building for toxins. Nothing turned up, either in the structure itself or in the urine and blood samples taken from the affected women. Still, when the center reopened the next morning, there were new victims of the mystery gas, which forced a second closing. When it reopened the following day, the women were assured that a simple "atmospheric inversion" had caused the problem. With their anxieties allayed, the women experienced no further attacks. The fictitious "inversion" produced the desired placebo effect. A study later indicated that working conditions in the center had been less than idyllic; the workers did their endlessly repetitive work under the thumb of a strict supervisor, who permitted them to chat among themselves only during lunch and two preassigned coffee breaks. The place was also unbearably noisy due to a construction job, complete with diesel-driven pneumatic jackhammers, just outside the center's windows. According to the investigators, the unfavorable working conditions generated widespread dissatisfaction among the workers, and this ultimately triggered hysterical symptoms.

One Special Case

THE NUNS OF LOUDUN (1633)

History's most famous case of mass hysteria may have been a paid-for performance. When Father Urbain Grandier was named parish priest of St. Pierre du Marché in 1617, he embarked on a career of unabashed wenching and debauchery—with married women, with his own penitents, with the sisters at the local Ursuline convent, and ultimately with Philippa Trincant, daughter of the local public prosecutor. When Philippa became pregnant, her father brought Grandier before the bishop of Poitiers on charges of immorality. Since the bishop was a Richelieu adherent, it did the priest little good to have written satirical broadsides against the powerful cardinal. Grandier was suspended but was reinstated within the year. His political enemies, now including Richelieu, would not rest, however, and they plotted his downfall. A spurned lover of Grandier's, Jeanne des Anges, mother superior of the Ursuline convent, was paid to claim that at his instigation she had become possessed by the demon Asmodeus. She certainly appeared possessed, and so did many of her sisters. At unpredictable moments they would fall to the ground to bare and finger their genitals and to split the air with obscenities. During these seizures their tongues would protrude inhumanly—swollen, blackened, and riddled with warts—and they would subject their bodies to incredible contortions. Grandier was dragged before a kangaroo religious court by his enemies, both lay and clerical, and accused of witchcraft. Scores of "possessed" nuns paraded through the court to point an accusing finger, and in 1633 the priest was imprisoned. By this time the public exorcism of Loudun's nuns had turned the town into a mecca for the morbidly curious, who would thrill to the spectacle of Ursuline sisters thrashing about on the

ÆT. 37.
1627.

Father Urbain Grandier burned at the stake Aug. 18, 1634.

streets. In 1634 Father Grandier was found guilty of "the crime of magic, *maleficia,* and of causing demoniacal possession of several Ursuline nuns . . . as well as of other, secular women." He was sentenced to torture, interrogation, and burning at the stake. But for many years after his death the nuns remained possessed, until Cardinal Richelieu lost interest and stopped paying for their performances; then they were miraculously cured.

—B.F.

8 UNFORGETTABLE
CASES OF AMNESIA

1. LUTHER MAYNARD JONES (1897), U.S. lawyer

Jones was a well-known, wealthy intellectual descended from New Hampshire aristocrats. He was an avowed bachelor with a love for books and antiques, and he had a brilliant law career. But as the years went by, he took less and less of an interest in law and became somewhat detached from society. His partner thought a business trip would be good for him, and in 1897 Jones went to England, where he soon dropped out of sight. Exhaustive attempts to locate Jones turned up nothing. Then, 12 years later, in 1909, an old friend spotted Jones on a London street, but the lawyer said his name was Luther Maynard. Jones was again recognized when he turned up in a London poorhouse. Friends tried to convince the 73-year-old man of his true identity, but he was skeptical and confused. He died shortly after. His last words: "Who am I then, please? Who?"

2. WILLIAM HORATIO BATES (1902), U.S. doctor

Dr. Bates wrote to his wife a few days after he was last seen on August 30, 1902. He said that he had left New York City unexpectedly to perform some difficult eye operations, and that she would hear from him soon. But the next letter did not arrive for six weeks. This time Bates informed his wife that he was in London working at the Charing Cross Hospital. She immediately left for London, but when Dr. Bates saw her, he insisted that he did not know her, and that he was not Dr. Bates. When he vanished from London a short time after, Mrs. Bates gave up and went back to New York, where she died three years later. Suddenly, in 1911, Dr. Bates returned to his New York ophthalmology practice as if nothing had ever happened. He never spoke of the nine missing years. One of his friends commented: "It was as if he had had a chunk of his mind removed, like a slice of watermelon chopped away and eaten by an invisible monster." Bates is best known for his controversial system of "eye relaxation" exercises, now looked upon with disfavor, which he claimed could do away with wearing glasses.

3. SHERWOOD ANDERSON (1912), U.S. writer

Anderson was better known as a paint manufacturer than as

a writer in his home town of Elyria, O. He would daydream to escape the boredom of a routine workday and found relaxation in writing short stories. On November 27, 1912, the 36-year-old Anderson suddenly got up from his desk while dictating a letter to his secretary. He stopped in the middle of a sentence, walked out of the room, and was not seen again until four days later, when he was found in a Cleveland drugstore. Anderson was taken to Huron Road Hospital, where experts agreed that he had succumbed to mental strain and was the victim of amnesia. He reportedly told the story of the missing days for the rest of his life, each time with different details. He simply couldn't remember what really happened. In 1941 Anderson, established as one of America's best writers, died from peritonitis as a result of swallowing a toothpick in an hors d'oeuvre sausage.

4. C. H. PEACHEY (1917), British soldier

In 1917 Peachey, a British soldier wounded on the western front during W.W. I, awakened from a head operation without memory. After his release from the hospital, he wandered about for some time before signing up as a crew member on a steamship bound for Portland, Me. He spent the next 10 years in various mental institutions and sanitariums. In 1927 Peachey had another head operation in New Orleans. But this time when he awakened, he knew his identity. He returned to London on October 2, 1928, and found that he had been listed as a deserter, that his mother had died, and that his wife had remarried and given birth to four children. The only good consequence of the whole ordeal was that his deaf-mute brother was so shocked at seeing him that he partially regained his faculties.

5. BENJAMIN LEVY (1924), U.S. baker

Levy had been missing from his home in Brooklyn, N.Y., for over two years when he was seen on September 25, 1926, in Manhattan. Dressed as a porter, Levy was sweeping the pavement. He insisted he wasn't Ben Levy, or a baker, or a Jew. He claimed to be Frank Lloyd, a Roman Catholic laborer. Both Mrs. Levy and daughter Esther failed to convince Lloyd of his true identity. The local missing persons' bureau matched Lloyd's handwriting with Levy's. They then showed Levy-Lloyd several letters—supposedly written by him—which claimed that he was being holed up in New York Harbor by rumrunners. Lloyd remained cynical, even when he was shown evidence that his fingerprints matched Levy's. But when Levy's 17-year-old nephew walked into the room and said, "Hello, Uncle Benny!" Lloyd began to change his mind. "Well, if even the kid is calling me uncle, maybe there's something to it, but I certainly don't remember ever being Levy." Reluctantly, he went home to Brooklyn.

6. AGATHA CHRISTIE (1926), English mystery novelist

On the evening of December 3, 1926, the 36-year-old writer left her home in Berkshire after learning that her husband had gone off to spend the weekend with his mistress. The next morning a young boy found her abandoned car off the road, and a full-scale search was initiated by the police. Speculation as to her fate ranged from suicide to kidnap, and for the next two weeks one of England's most exhaustive manhunts, complete with scores of track dogs and 15,000 volunteers, failed to turn up a clue. Then, 10 days after her disappearance, Mrs. Christie was identified as a guest in a health spa in Yorkshire. She had registered under another name on December 3 and said she was a visitor from the Cape of Good Hope. Guests at the spa later reported that, despite all the publicity about the missing Mrs. Christie, the writer truly acted like another person and displayed a great deal of interest in the mystery. Her family said later that she had been very upset over the recent death of her mother. However, many believe the famous mystery novelist didn't have amnesia at all, but planned her disappearance to spite her husband.

7. JOHN R. CROSSWHITE (1936), U.S. contractor

In 1973 the elderly John R. Cross, of Joplin, Mo., suffered a stroke. The shock of the experience caused him to remember that his real name was Crosswhite. The longest known case of amnesia on record, Crosswhite had become Cross after an auto accident in 1936 in Cape Girardeau, Mo. Crosswhite was declared legally dead in 1940, and Cross remarried and had another family. Mrs. Crosswhite was still alive in 1973 when the truth was learned, but members of her family feared the 83-year-old woman would not be able to withstand the news. She was never told that her husband was still alive.

8. LAWRENCE JOSEPH BADER (1957), U.S. salesman

On May 15, 1957, 30-year-old Bader left his home in Akron, O., for Cleveland. He told his wife he would spend the afternoon fishing on Lake Erie—despite reports of an expected storm—and would return late. Before he boarded the rented 14-ft. boat, he took care to pay a host of bills, including his life insurance premium. His empty boat was found the following morning, and Bader was believed drowned. Three days later he arrived in Omaha, Neb., as John Francis "Fritz" Johnson. For the next eight years he lived as one of Omaha's most colorful and well-liked citizens, notorious for pranks like sitting on a flagpole for 15 days drinking martinis in order to publicize a polio drive. Then, on February 2, 1965, Johnson, now remarried, was recognized as Bader at a sports exhibition. But Johnson insisted he wasn't Bader and offered to have his fingerprints taken to settle the matter. The next day he learned the prints matched. Mrs. Bader wished he had never been found, and Mrs. Johnson vowed to stay by him. His last two years were unhappy ones. Despite expert opinions that he did have amnesia, the media exploited the bizarre case, claiming he was either a schizophrenic or a clever hoaxer. He died of cancer on September 15, 1966.

—L.O.

URI GELLER'S
10 GREATEST PSYCHICS
OF ALL TIME

Former Israeli paratrooper Uri Geller maintains that his psychic abilities come from the distant planet of Hoova. He began

Russian mystic George Gurdjieff.

his career as a professional psychic in 1969 and since then has appeared in nightclubs and on TV shows throughout the world. His extrasensory powers have been studied at educational and scientific institutes in France, England, and the U.S.

1. George I. Gurdjieff
2. Grigori Rasputin
3. Nikola Tesla
4. Franz Anton Mesmer
5. Nostradamus
6. Elena Petrovna Blavatsky
7. Edgar Cayce
8. Daniel Dunglas Home
9. Nina Kulagina
10. Irene Hughes

George I. Gurdjieff (1872–1949), a Russian mystic, taught followers how to transcend their normal mental and physical limits. Croatian-born Nikola Tesla (1857–1943), a pioneer in electronics, invented the alternating-current motor and the Tesla coil used in radios and TVs. Daniel Dunglas Home (1833–1886), a popular Scottish medium who could levitate and speak languages he didn't know, did readings for Elizabeth Barrett Browning and Napoleon III among others. Nina Kulagina, born in Leningrad in the late 1920s, has been observed by scientists making burn marks appear on her skin and demonstrating other feats of psychokinesis.

—Exclusive for *The Book of Lists 2*

20
REST IN PEACE

10 CELEBRATED PEOPLE WHO READ THEIR OWN OBITUARIES

1. HANNAH SNELL

Her husband walked out on her and joined the British army. To find him, Hannah Snell also enlisted, posing as a man. She fought in several battles and was wounded in the groin. During surgery her true sex was discovered. She became a celebrity, and once out of the army she performed in public houses as the Female Warrior. On December 10, 1779, when she was 56, she opened a copy of the *Gentleman's Magazine* and read her own obituary, which informed her that she had died on a Warwickshire heathland. Perhaps she was superstitious, because reading her death notice snapped something in her mind. Her mental health slowly deteriorated, and in 1789 she was placed in London's Bethlehem Hospital, and she remained there insane until she expired in 1792.

2. DANIEL BOONE

The great American frontiersman had retired and settled down in Missouri. In 1818 an American newspaper in the East trumpeted the news that the renowned hunter had been found dead near a deer lick, kneeling behind a tree stump, his rifle resting on the stump, a fallen deer a hundred yards away. The obituary was picked up across the nation. Daniel Boone read it and laughed. Although he could still trap, he was too old and weak to hunt, and could no longer hit a deer even close up. Two years later, aged 86, Boone finally did die. His best obituary was seven stanzas devoted to him in Lord Byron's *Don Juan*.

3. LADY JANE ELLENBOROUGH

She was one of the most beautiful and sexual women in all history. Her name was Jane Digby. At 17 she married Lord Ellenborough, Great Britain's lord of the privy seal, then left him to run off with an Austrian prince. During her colorful career she was the mistress of novelist Honoré de Balzac, King Ludwig of Bavaria, and Ludwig's son, King Otto of Greece. Her last marriage of 26 years was to Sheikh Medjuel, an erudite Bedouin, head of the Mezrab tribe in the Syrian desert. Returning from a desert trip with Medjuel, the 66-year-old Lady Ellenborough learned that she was dead. Her obituary appeared prominently in *La Revue Britannique*, published in Paris in March, 1873. It began: "A noble lady who had made a great use— or abuse—of marriage has died recently. Lady Ellenborough, some 30 years ago, left her first husband to run off with Count von Schwarzenberg. She retired to Italy, where she married six consecutive times." The obituary, reprinted throughout Europe, called her last husband "a camel driver." The next issue of the publication carried a eulogy of Lady Ellenborough written by her friend Isabel Burton, the pompous and snobbish wife of Burton of Arabia. Mrs. Burton claimed she had been authorized to publish the story of Lady Ellenborough's life, based on dictated notes. Appalled, Lady Ellenborough vehemently wrote the press denying her death—and having dictated an "authorized" book to Mrs. Burton. Lady Ellenborough outlived her obituary by eight full years, dying of dysentery in August, 1881.

4. JAMES BUTLER HICKOK

In March, 1873, "Wild Bill" Hickok, legendary sheriff and city marshal in the Midwest and a constant reader of Missouri's leading newspaper, the *Democrat*, picked up a copy and learned that he was a corpse. Hickok read: "The Texan who corralled the untamed William did so because he lost his brother by Bill's quickness on the trigger." Unsettled by his supposed demise, Wild Bill took pen in hand and wrote a letter to the editor: "Wishing to correct an error in your paper of the 12th, I will state that no Texan has, nor ever will, 'corral William.' I wish to correct your statement on account of my people. Yours as ever, J. B. Hickok." Delighted, the editor of the *Democrat* printed Hickok's letter and added an editorial: "We take much pleasure in laying Mr. Hickok's statement before the readers of the *Democrat,* most of whom will be glad to learn from his pen that he is 'still on the deck.' But in case you should go off suddenly, William, by writing us the particulars we will give you just as fine an obituary notice as we can get up, though we trust that sad pleasure may be deferred for years." Three years later Hickok was murdered while playing poker.

5. ALFRED NOBEL

As the inventor of dynamite, Alfred Nobel, a moody yet idealistic Swede, had become a millionaire. When Nobel's older brother, Ludwig, died of heart trouble on April 12, 1888, a leading French newspaper misread the report and ran an obituary of Alfred Nobel, calling him "a merchant of death." Upon seeing the obituary, Nobel was stunned, not by the premature announcement of his passing but by the realization that in the end he would be considered nothing more than a merchant of death. The printed summary of his life reflected none of his hopes for humanity, his love of his fellow beings, his generosity. The need to repair this false picture was one of several factors that led Alfred Nobel to establish, in his will, the Nobel Prize awards to be given to those who did the most in advancing the causes of peace, literature, and the sciences.

6. P. T. BARNUM

At 80, the great American showman was ailing and knew that death was near. From his sickbed, he told a friend that he would be happier if he had "the chance to see what sort of lines" would be written about him after he was dead. The friend relayed this wish to the editor of the *Evening Sun* in New York City. On March 24, 1891, Barnum opened his copy of the *Evening Sun* and read: "Great and Only Barnum. He Wanted to Read His Obituary; Here It Is." According to the preface, "Mr. Barnum has had almost everything in this life, including the woolly horse and Jenny Lind, and there is no reason why he should not have the last pleasure which he asks for. So here is the great showman's life, briefly and simply told, as it would have appeared in the *Evening Sun* had fate taken our Great and Only from us." There followed four columns of Barnum's obituary, illustrated by woodcuts of him at his present age, of him at 41, of his mother, of his deceased first wife Charity, and of the Swedish singer Jenny Lind. Two weeks later, Barnum was dead.

7. LEOPOLD VON SACHER-MASOCH

This police commissioner's son, born in Galicia, raised in Austria, was fascinated by cruelty and loved pain and degradation. His first mistress, Anna von Kottowitz, birched him regularly and enjoyed lovers that Sacher-Masoch found for her. His second mistress, Fanny Pistor, signed a contract with him agreeing to wear furs when she beat him daily. She fulfilled the contract and treated him as a servant. He had become a famous writer when he met and married a woman named Wanda. She thrashed him with a nail-studded whip every day of their 15-year marriage and made him perform as her slave. After she ran off, Sacher-Masoch married a simple German woman named Hulda Meister. By now he was slipping into insanity, and he tried to strangle her. In 1895 she had him secretly committed to an asylum in Mannheim and announced to the world that he had died. The press published obituaries praising his talent. Undoubtedly, in lucid moments, he read some of his death notices. He finally did die 10 years later in 1905. Because of Sacher-Masoch's life, psychiatrist Richard von Krafft-Ebing coined the word *masochism*.

8. MARK TWAIN

In 1897 the noted American author and humorist was in seclusion, grieving over a death in his immediate family, when he learned that he, too, had been declared dead. A sensational American newspaper had headlined his end, stating that he had died impoverished in London. A national syndicate sent a reporter to Mark Twain's home to confirm the news. Twain, himself, appeared before the bug-eyed reporter and issued an official statement: "James Ross Clemens, a cousin of mine, was seriously ill two or three weeks ago in London, but is well now. The reports of my illness grew out of his illness. The reports of my death are greatly exaggerated." Twain finally lived up to his premature obituaries in 1910.

9. BERTRAND RUSSELL

Once in the 1930s, while the English philosopher was visiting Beijing (Peking), he became very ill. Japanese reporters in the city constantly tried to see Russell, but were always denied access to him. The journalists decided he must be dead, and notified their newspapers of his demise. Word of his death went around the world. Wrote Russell, "It provided me with the pleasure of reading my obituary notices, which I had always desired without expecting my wishes to be fulfilled. One missionary paper had an obituary notice of one sentence: 'Missionaries may be pardoned for heaving a sigh of relief at the news of Mr. Bertrand Russell's death.'" All this inspired Russell to compose his own obituary in 1937 for *The Times* of London.

He wrote of himself: "His life, for all its waywardness, had a certain anachronistic consistency, reminiscent of the aristocratic rebels of the early 19th century. . . . He was the last survivor of a dead epoch." He told *The Times* to run it in 1962, the year in which he expected to die. *The Times* did not need it until 1970.

10. EDWARD V. RICKENBACKER

The former auto-racing driver turned fighter pilot emerged from W.W. I as America's leading ace with 26 confirmed kills. In peacetime he was an executive in the automobile and aviation industries. With the onset of W.W. II, Rickenbacker volunteered to carry out missions for the U.S. War Dept. In October, 1942, on an inspection tour, Rickenbacker's B-17 went down somewhere in the Pacific Ocean. An intensive air search of the area was made. There was no sign of survivors. Newspapers across the U.S. declared Rickenbacker dead. The following month, on Friday the 13th of November, there were new headlines. Rickenbacker and seven others were spotted alive in the Pacific. They had survived on a raft for 23 days. Waiting for Rickenbacker when he returned home was a pile of his obituaries. One, in the New York *Daily News,* was a cartoon showing a black wreath floating on water, with the caption "So Long, Eddie." Another, in the *New York Journal,* bore the headline "End of the Roaring Road?" Grinning, Rickenbacker scrawled across it, "Hell, no! "

Note: Those 10 are the editors' favorite cases, but there have been numerous other celebrated persons who read of their deaths while they were alive, among them U.S. President Thomas Jefferson, magician Harry Houdini, dancer Josephine Baker, singer Jeanette MacDonald, novelist Ernest Hemingway, foreign correspondent Edgar Snow. Also, there have been many famous people who, if they did not read about their deaths, heard rumors or announcements that they had gone to the Great Beyond. The modern living dead have included singer Paul McCartney, vague hints of whose demise were supposedly traced to several Beatles records; actress Bette Davis, whose attorney told her that word of her death was spreading throughout New York, to which Miss Davis replied, "With the newspaper strike on, I wouldn't consider it"; and India's elderly political dissenter J. P. Narayan, who heard Prime Minister Morarji Desai mistakenly deliver a eulogy over his still-warm body in April, 1979.

—I.W.

10 FINAL
CHANGES IN WILLS

1. IVAN THE TERRIBLE (died 1584), Russian czar

His first testament in 1572 bequeathed most of his kingdom to his favorite son, Ivan. The 1560 death of his wife seemed to have unhinged the czar, and his sudden outbursts grew increasingly violent. He not only subjected the Russian people to systematic terror, but struck and killed his heir in 1580 during a fit of rage. A few weeks before his own death, he drew up a new will, naming his second son, Fëdor, as heir and urging him to rule with kindness and to give some thought to tax relief.

2. BENJAMIN FRANKLIN (died 1790), U.S. scientist and statesman

Franklin's codicil, written some nine months before he died, was almost as long as his 1788 will. In it, he set up a philanthropic trust for the cities of Boston and Philadelphia, bequeathing almost $9,000 for them to grant loans at 5% annual interest to young married artisans. He directed that after 100 years the substantial profits should be spent on public works; he granted that he ought to quit his influence after 200 years, and the trust would be terminated with a fund of $18 million. Unfortunately, 19th-century defaults and changing fiscal conditions spoiled the grand plan. In 1979 Boston held only $3.2 million, now loaned to medical students at 2% interest; and Philadelphia had $770,000, invested in mortgages. Final disposition of funds will await 1991.

3. PAUL REVERE (died 1818), U.S. patriot

Revere bequeathed $4,000 to each of his five children in his 1816 will. Two months before he died, he added a codicil that preserved these amounts for his grandchildren instead, specifying that his children could only collect the interest on the amounts during their natural lives. He also willed $500 apiece to all but one grandchild, who had changed his name from Frank to Francis; to him, Revere granted "no part of my estate except one dollar."

4. P. T. BARNUM (died 1891), U.S. impresario

In his 1882 will, Barnum left his daughter Helen a lifelong stipend of $1,500 a year, plus various items that had belonged to her deceased mother. When Helen disgraced the family by leaving her husband to set up housekeeping with a doctor in Chicago, Barnum wrote her out of the will. In an 1889 codicil he stated that, in lieu of the previous bequeathals, Helen had been given a "valuable property" in Colorado. Although Barnum was sure the property was worthless, subsequent explorations revealed mineral deposits that made Helen richer than all of Barnum's other heirs combined.

5. LEO TOLSTOI (died 1910), Russian author

Tolstoi's idea of saintliness worked much hardship on his family. Even as he despised the notion of property inheritance, his own large estate troubled him with paroxysms of guilt. His altruistic intentions to give it all away split his household, and his last days were marred by a violent round of quarrels as his alarmed wife and sons tried to preserve some security for themselves. Hating the very concept of wills, Tolstoi signed several of them in an effort to close every loophole; the last one was signed only four months before his death—on a forest stump in order to avoid family spying. Accordingly, his land and literary estates went "to the people" through his sole family ally, daughter Sasha.

6. J. P. MORGAN (died 1913), U.S. financier

A $250,000 bequest to a "friend," Mary G. McIlvaine, was stipulated in Morgan's will dated January 4, 1913, just before he began a long voyage abroad. Two days later Morgan changed his mind, and the sole clause of his codicil substituted an annual income of $25,000 to Mary. Why did he revise the amount and provision of payment? Had the prospect of sudden fortune corrupted Mary during those two days? Nobody who knew talked about it, and Morgan died in Rome three months later.

7. F. SCOTT FITZGERALD (died 1940), U.S. author

Amid great expectations of success as a Hollywood screen-writer, Fitzgerald drew up his will in 1937. The first thing he specified was "a funeral and burial in keeping with my station in life." His new career fell flat, however, and he began work on a final unfinished novel, *The Last Tycoon.* Shortly before his death, he amended his wishes in pencil to read "cheapest funeral . . . without undue ostentation or unnecessary expense." The actual cost came to $613.25, with $93 in personal cash left over.

8. BILLY ROSE (died 1966), U.S. impresario

Visitors noted that the spectacular showman-protégé of Bernard M. Baruch was still revising his will three days before his lingering death in a Jamaican hospital. During this period, Eleanor Holm, one of his three ex-wives, sent him $40 worth of stone crabs, Rose's favorite delicacy, and found herself bequeathed $10,000 in the late codicil. Rose also included some small legacies to the children of several friends; typically, the friends themselves received nothing. To the distress of two sisters, Rose left most of his $30 million estate to the charitable Billy Rose Foundation, a bequest finally upheld by the courts.

Janis Joplin.

443

9. JANIS JOPLIN (died 1970), U.S. singer

One indication that the heroin overdose she died from may not have been accidental was revealed in her will. Two days before her death, she amended it to include a guest list and $2,500 "so my friends can get blasted after I'm gone." The well-juiced, all-night "farewell party" at a tavern called the Lion's Share in San Anselmo, Calif., a spot where she had often performed, occurred several days after her ashes were scattered from a plane over Marin County.

10. EDWARD V. LONG (died 1972), U.S. senator

Three weeks before his death, the former senator from Missouri changed his will to bequeath most of his estimated $770,000 estate to his five-year-old granddaughter. Long's wife, who had filed for separation, and his daughter were disinherited except for $10 each and some land properties; his secretary of 26 years, Helen Dunlop, was named executrix and was awarded a lifelong stipend of $7,500 a year. Long's widow sued Dunlop for alienation of affections, and the secretary charged that Long had died of poisoning. Exhumation of the remains revealed no foul play, and the various suits and countersuits were settled out of court in 1974.

—J.E.

5 PERSONS
WHO DIED PLAYING CARDS

1. JOHN G. BENNETT (Perfume agent)

Mr. Bennett and his wife Myrtle lived in a fashionable apartment in Kansas City. One unfortunate Sunday afternoon in the autumn of 1929, the Bennetts sat down with their neighbors, the Hoffmans, to play a friendly game of bridge. Mrs. Hoffman later explained, "As the game went on, the Bennetts' criticisms of each other grew more caustic." Finally Bennett dealt and bid one spade on a hand that better deserved a pass. Mr. Hoffman overcalled with two diamonds, and Mrs. Bennett, overeager for a contract, jumped to four spades. In the play of the hand, Bennett was set one. His wife taunted him and they began arguing. John reached across the table and slapped Myrtle, whereupon she told him he was a bum, thus goading him further. John threatened to leave, and Myrtle suggested that the Hoffmans depart as well. But before they could go, Myrtle ran into her mother's bedroom, grabbed the family automatic, dashed back, and shot her husband twice, killing him. Interestingly, if Bennett had established his club suit before drawing trumps, he might have survived the evening.

2. JAMES BUTLER HICKOK (Gunfighter)

When "Wild Bill" entered Deadwood, S.D., in June of 1876, he

444

had a premonition that he would never leave the gulch alive. On August 2 he was playing poker with three friends in a saloon, laughing and having a good time. Normally Hickok sat with his back to the wall, but that afternoon Charlie Rich had taken Bill's seat to tease him and had refused to give it up. Jack McCall, whom Hickok had defeated at poker earlier that day, entered the saloon, drew a .45-caliber Colt and shot Wild Bill Hickok through the back of the head, killing him instantly. Wild Bill, who was 39 years old, was holding two pairs, aces and eights, a hand that has since been known as "the dead man's hand." He died with a smile on his face.

3. AL JOLSON (Entertainer)

Jolson suffered a heart attack while playing gin rummy with friends in his room in San Francisco's St. Francis Hotel on the night of October 23, 1950. He was 64 years old.

4. BUSTER KEATON (Comedian)

Keaton was stricken by a seizure late in the afternoon of January 31, 1966, while playing poker at his home in Hollywood. He expired the following morning at the age of 70.

5. ARNOLD ROTHSTEIN (Gambler)

The man who fixed the 1919 World Series was playing poker in the suite Hump McManus occupied at the Park Central Hotel in New York City when he was shot in the stomach. Rothstein, who owed McManus $320,000 from a previous poker game, stumbled out of the building and was rushed to a hospital, where he refused to name the gunman before he died on November 4, 1928.

—D.W.

7 PEOPLE
WHO DIED LAUGHING

1. CALCHAS (Greek soothsayer; c. 12th century B.C.)

Calchas, the wisest soothsayer of Greece during the Trojan War, advised the construction of the notorious wooden horse. One day he was planting grape vines when a fellow soothsayer wandered by and foretold that Calchas would never drink the wine produced from the grapes. After the grapes ripened, wine was made from them, and Calchas invited the soothsayer to share it with him. As Calchas held a cup of the wine in his hand, the soothsayer repeated the prophecy. This incited such a fit of laughter in Calchas that he choked and died. Another version of Calchas's death states that he died of grief after losing a soothsaying match in which he failed to predict correctly the number of piglets that a pig was about to give birth to.

2. ZEUXIS (Greek painter; 5th century B.C.)

It is said that Zeuxis was laughing at a painting of an old woman that he had just completed when his breathing failed and he choked to death.

3. PHILEMON (Greek poet; 361?–263? B.C.)

This writer of comedies became so engulfed in laughter over a jest he had made that he died laughing.

4. CHRYSIPPUS (Greek philosopher; 3rd century B.C.)

Chrysippus is said to have died from a fit of laughter on seeing a donkey eat some figs.

5. PIETRO ARETINO (Italian author; 1492–1556)

Aretino was laughing at a bawdy story being told to him by his sister when he fell backward in his chair and died of apoplexy.

6. MRS. FITZHERBERT (English widow; ?–1782)

On a Wednesday evening in April, 1782, Mrs. Fitzherbert of Northamptonshire went to Drury Lane Theatre with friends to see *The Beggar's Opera*. When the popular actor Mr. Bannister made his first appearance, dressed outlandishly in the role of "Polly," the entire audience was thrown into uproarious laughter. Unfortunately, Mrs. Fitzherbert was unable to suppress the laugh that seized her, and she was forced to leave the theater before the end of the second act. As the *Gentleman's Magazine* reported in its issue of the following week: "Not being able to banish the figure from her memory, she was thrown into hysterics, which continued without intermission until she expired Friday morning."

7. ALEX MITCHELL (English bricklayer; 1925–1975)

Mr. and Mrs. Mitchell of Brockley Green, Fairstead Estate, King's Lynn, were watching their favorite TV comedy, *The Goodies*. During a scene about a new type of self-defense called "Ecky Thump," Mr. Mitchell was seized by uncontrollable laughter. After a half hour of unrestrained mirth, he suffered a heart attack and died. His wife, Nessie, wrote to *The Goodies* thanking them for making her husband's last moments so happy.

—D.W.

10 WELL-KNOWN PEOPLE WHO DIED IN SOMEONE'S ARMS

1. AUGUSTUS (63 B.C.–14 A.D.), first Roman emperor

The grandson of Gaius Julius Caesar's youngest sister, Julia, and later Caesar's adopted son, he was better known as Octavian. At the age of 77, he became ill en route to his summer villa on the Mediterranean. Unable to complete the trip, he stopped at Nola just outside Naples, at his parental home. Knowing his end was near, he sent for his friends in Rome, and they gathered around him and talked of his life and career. After dismissing them, he sat up in bed, put his arms around the neck of his wife, Livia, kissed her, and then died in her arms. His own father had died in the same room 60 years before.

2. JAUFRÉ RUDEL (fl. 1140–1170), Provençal lyric poet

Only six of his poems survive. What we know of his life comes from his friend and fellow poet Maracabru, who wrote of Rudel's love for the Countess of Tripoli. After writing love poems for several years to this woman he had never seen, he joined a Crusade to be near her. He became ill at sea and was taken ashore at Tripoli. There the countess came to see him, and he died in her arms. It is said that she gave him a lavish funeral and then entered a convent, where she spent the rest of her days.

3. THERESA (1515–1582), Spanish saint and mystic

Theresa is the most revered female saint in the Christian world. Her writings, like those of her great friend St. John of the Cross, depict mystical visions of Christ and the supernatural. In late September, 1582, Theresa fell ill in her native town of Ávila. Her companion, Sister Anna, took her to the convent where she wished to spend the last week of her life alone in silent prayer. A few minutes before she died, she called Anna to her chamber. Holding her crucifix, Theresa embraced Anna and spoke a few words. She then nestled her head in Anna's arms, where she died quietly a few moments later.

4. MICHEL EYQUEM DE MONTAIGNE (1533–1592), French essayist

Montaigne referred to the last day of life as "the master day." One of his fascinations was collecting instances of remarkable demises, and he once said that he hoped he would not demean himself by dying quietly. On September 10, 1592, an attack of gout rendered him totally immobile. He was conscious but could not speak. On September 13, the last day of his life, he forced himself from his bed and got dressed. Fearing his will would not be properly executed, he gave each of his servants cash in the amounts allotted in his will. He then retired and wrote a note asking his wife to send for the priest. In his last moments, he tried in vain to raise himself from his bed. As the priest lifted him, Montaigne clasped his hands, made an unsuccessful effort to speak, and silently died.

5. WILLIAM HAMILTON (1730–1803), British diplomat and archaeologist

Hamilton was 60 years old when he married the beautiful and charming Emma Lyon, aged 30, in 1791. Seven years later, while she and Lord Hamilton were living in Naples, she became Lord Nelson's mistress. Nelson traveled back to England with the Hamiltons, and four months later, in 1792, Emma gave birth to Nelson's daughter, Horatia. The three adults were near-constant companions in the five years that followed. Only in the last year of his life did Hamilton express any discontent with the arrangement. But it was Emma—who had grown fat and loud and had taken to heavy drinking—that he wanted to leave. Out of respect for Nelson, he decided against leaving Emma. Both Emma and Nelson kept a bedside vigil in the last days of Hamilton's life. He died in Emma's arms with Nelson holding his hand.

6. HORATIO NELSON (1758–1805),
British viscount and naval hero

Shortly after Hamilton's death, Nelson returned to sea duty in the war against France. In 1803, during the Battle of Trafalgar off the coast of Spain, Nelson was shot in the spine. In the last hour of his life, he called for his friend Capt. Thomas Hardy, who told him of the impending British victory. Before he died, Nelson told Hardy: "Take care of my dear Lady Hamilton. Take care of poor Lady Hamilton. Kiss me, Hardy." Embracing Nelson, Hardy kissed his forehead as he grew weaker and died. Lady Hamilton's death was more sordid; she recklessly spent the healthy annuities left her by both Hamilton and Nelson, and in 1815 died alone and penniless in France at the age of 54.

7. JOHN KEATS (1795–1821), English poet

After many years of ill health due to tuberculosis, which caused frequent hemorrhages, Keats was advised by his doctors to go to the warmer climate of Italy. He was only 25 years old. His devoted friend, a portrait artist named Joseph Severn, accompanied him on the journey by ship, and the two arrived in Rome in November, 1820. After suffering a violent relapse a month later, Keats tried to commit suicide. Severn remained his constant companion, reading to him from Jeremy Taylor's *Holy Living* and *Holy Dying,* and playing Haydn's sonatas. "When will this posthumous life of mine come to an end?" Keats repeatedly asked his doctor. "I feel the flowers growing over me." He finally gave way the following February and died in Severn's arms. His last words to him were "I shall die easy. Don't be frightened. Thank God it has come."

Portrait of John Keats by his friend Joseph Severn.

8. ELIZABETH BARRETT BROWNING (1806–1861),
English poet

Elizabeth Barrett and Robert Browning wrote letters to each other for nearly a year before they finally met in 1846. Both were gaining wide renown for their poetry. She was 40, an invalid since age 15. He was only 33. They immediately fell in love, but Elizabeth was hesitant about marriage. Not only was she an invalid, but her father had forbidden the union. The two poets were married in secret in 1846 and then left for Italy. Their 14-year marriage was idyllic, even though Elizabeth was frequently ill. She repeatedly sought a reconciliation with her father, but he returned her letters unopened. Shortly after hearing of his death, she suffered a complete physical collapse. Browning never left her bedside, and she spent the entire last day of her life asleep in his arms.

9. CHARLES BAUDELAIRE (1821–1867),
French poet and critic

Baudelaire's life was an unhappy one, plagued with tumultuous love affairs, financial insecurity, fits of depression, and thoughts of suicide. The one constant was his mother. They wrote to each other continuously, even though she was narrow-minded, sometimes spiteful, and often unsupportive. His paralytic death at age 46 was attributed to a combination of syphilis, alcohol, and opium. During his last years, he looked like a man of 60. Few of his friends remained faithful as they watched him stumbling through the streets of Paris drunk, barely able to speak, not even a shadow of the man once famous throughout Europe for his lucidity and eloquence. His mother cared for him during his last bedridden days, after he had been asked to leave a Catholic nursing home in Brussels. He died in her arms, and she reported that he died smiling.

10. MOHANDAS KARAMCHAND GANDHI (1869–1948),
Hindu spiritual leader and nationalist

In the late afternoon of January 30, 1948, Gandhi was shot as he was beginning an evening prayer meeting in the gardens of Birla House in Delhi. One thousand followers who had gathered to pray for Hindu-Muslim unity watched as the assassin approached Gandhi, hands clasped in traditional Hindu greeting, and then fired three shots at near-point-blank range. As Gandhi fell to the ground, his eyes held on his assassin, and he gave a Hindu gesture of forgiveness. He was quickly taken back to Birla House and placed on a couch with his head in the lap of his 16-year-old granddaughter, Mani. He died a half-hour later.

—L.O.

9 TIMELY DEATHS

We read so often in the newspapers about "untimely deaths" that it makes one wonder if anyone ever died a "timely death." Well, people have, and here are some examples.

1. DOMITIAN (51–96 A.D.), Roman emperor

Early astrological predictions had warned that he would be murdered on the fifth hour of September 18, 96 A.D. As the date approached, Domitian had many of his closest attendants executed to be on the safe side. Just before midnight marked the beginning of the critical day, he became so terrified that he jumped out of bed. A few hours later he asked the time and was told by his servants (who were conspiring against him) that it was the sixth hour. Convinced that the danger had passed, Domitian went off to take a bath. On the way he was informed that his niece's steward, Stephanus, was waiting for him in the bedroom with important news. When the emperor arrived, Stephanus handed him a list of conspirators and then suddenly stabbed him in the groin. Domitian put up a good fight, but he was overcome when four more conspirators appeared. He died as predicted, on the fifth hour of September 18, 96 A.D.

2. THOMAS JEFFERSON (1743–1826), U.S. president

The 83-year-old former president was suffering badly from diarrhea, but he had hopes of lasting until July 4, 1826, the 50th anniversary of the signing of the Declaration of Independence. From his sickbed, he asked, "This is the fourth?" When he was informed that it was, he died peacefully.

3. JOHN ADAMS (1735–1826), U.S. president

Adams, like Jefferson, held on until July 4, 1826, before dying at the age of 90. He is reported to have said, "Thomas Jefferson survives. . . . Independence forever," unaware that his old friend had died a few hours earlier.

4. DR. JOSEPH GREEN (1791–1863), English surgeon

While lying on his deathbed, Dr. Green looked up at his own doctor and said, "Congestion." Then he took his own pulse, reported the single word, "Stopped," and died.

5. HENRIK IBSEN (1828–1906), Norwegian poet and dramatist

On May 16, 1906, Ibsen was in a coma in his bedroom, surrounded by friends and relatives. A nurse told the others in the room that the famed playwright seemed to be a little better. Without opening his eyes, Ibsen uttered one word: *"Tvertimod"* ("On the contrary"). He died that afternoon without speaking again.

6. MARK TWAIN (1835–1910), U.S. humorist

Born in 1835, the year of Halley's Comet, Twain often stated that he had come into the world with the comet and would go out of the world with it as well. Halley's comet next returned in 1910, and on April 21 of that year Twain died.

7. ARNOLD SCHÖNBERG (1874–1951), Austrian composer

Schönberg's lifelong fascination with numerology led to his morbid obsession with the number 13. Born in 1874 on September 13, he believed that 13 would also play a role in his death. Because

Arnold Schönberg.

the numerals seven and six add up to 13, Schönberg was convinced that his 76th year would be the decisive one. Checking the calendar for 1951, he saw to his horror that July 13 fell on a Friday. When that day came, he kept to his bed in an effort to reduce the chance of an accident. Shortly before midnight, his wife entered the bedroom to say good night and to reassure him that his fears had been foolish, whereupon Schönberg muttered the word *harmony* and died. The time of his death was 11:47 P.M., 13 minutes before midnight on Friday, July 13, in his 76th year.

8. ELIZABETH RYAN (1892–1979), U.S. tennis player

Elizabeth Ryan won 19 Wimbledon tennis championships between 1914 and 1934—a record that stood for 45 years. On July 6, 1979, the day before Billie Jean King broke her record by winning a 20th Wimbledon title, the 87-year-old Ryan became ill while in the stands at Wimbledon. She collapsed in the clubhouse and died that night.

9. LEONARD WARREN (1911–1960), U.S. opera singer

Warren was performing in Verdi's *La Forza del Destino* on the stage of the Metropolitan Opera in 1960. He had just begun the aria "O fatal urn of my destiny." When he reached the word *fatal,* he suddenly pitched forward, dead of a heart attack.

—D. W.

10 PROMINENT PEOPLE WHO DIED UNDER SUSPICIOUS CIRCUMSTANCES AND NEVER HAD AUTOPSIES

1. MERIWETHER LEWIS (1774–1809), U.S. soldier and explorer

Lewis died of wounds—apparently self-inflicted—while

bunked overnight on the Natchez Trace (now Meriwether Lewis Park in Hohenwald, Tenn.). Reports conflicted as to his mental state, possible motivations, even the weapon used. At least one biographer believed Lewis was murdered. A traveling companion, Maj. James Neelly, quickly buried him, and no official inquest was held.

2. WARREN GAMALIEL HARDING (1865–1923), U.S. president

"The Duchess," Harding's dour wife, refused to allow an autopsy on the President, who died suddenly in San Francisco. Five doctors agreed that death resulted from "an apoplexy," a conclusion challenged by Gaston B. Means in *The Strange Death of President Harding* (1930). According to Means, Harding's wife poisoned her husband to prevent his being disgraced by imminent impeachment. Means was later discredited as a gigantic hoaxer, but enough doubts remained to trouble more reputable scholars.

3. JESS SMITH (1872–1923), U.S. government aide

Smith, who worked for Attorney General Harry M. Daugherty in President Harding's cabinet, liked to show off huge sums of money he mysteriously "earned." When rumors of massive corruption began to spread, Smith was found shot one morning—his head in a waste basket and a pistol in his right hand. The death was labeled suicide, but the bullet had entered his *left* temple. The gun was later "mislaid," and Smith was promptly buried amid whispers that he "knew too much."

4. JACK LONDON (1876–1916), U.S. author

London's doctor testified—21 years after the author's death— that two medical specialists had overruled his own judgment that the ailing London had killed himself with an overdose of morphine and atropine. London's uremia was instead listed as the cause of death, apparently at the behest of Charmain London, his widow, who refused to credit the suicide theory. She also refused to allow an autopsy and had the body quickly cremated.

5. LOUIS RENAULT (1877–1944), French auto manufacturer

Arrested for collaborating with the Nazis, Renault—called "France's Henry Ford"—was healthy when he entered Fresnes Prison in Paris to await trial. A month later, his sudden degeneration and death were attributed to uremia. No autopsy was permitted, but an X-ray taken through the coffin revealed a fractured neck vertebra. When the government finally permitted exhumation 10 years later, the broken bone had been cut out as if with a razor.

6. THOMAS HARPER INCE (1882–1924), U.S. film director

The innovative cinema pioneer died either during or shortly after his birthday cruise aboard William Randolph Hearst's yacht, the *Oneida*. Some of Hollywood's biggest stars accompanied Ince, and accounts of the tragedy ranged from death caused by heart failure to murder in an Agatha Christie-like setting. Hearst himself took enormous pains to cover up or distort the facts. The case still remains an unresolved Hollywood scandal.

7. ELEANOR MEDILL "CISSY" PATTERSON (1884–1948), U.S. newspaper publisher

The coroner's verdict was kidney disease, but her ex-son-in-law, columnist Drew Pearson, questioned the circumstances surrounding the death of the powerful Washington publisher. Of particular interest was the fact that Patterson had announced she was about to make her eighth will and had hinted she might be murdered. Several weeks after the funeral, her financial manager, Charles B. Porter, jumped or fell from a hotel window. The same week, her former social secretary died from a drug overdose. Pearson hinted that all were victims of a sinister corporate plot, with Patterson's *Times-Herald* as the object. But nothing came of his pleas for further investigation.

8. NELSON A. ROCKEFELLER (1908–1979), U.S. vice-president

Official details of Rockefeller's death changed repeatedly in the days following his fatal heart attack on January 26, 1979. The first report indicated Rockefeller was with his 25-year-old aide Megan Marshack when he collapsed in his Manhattan town house at 11:15 P.M. Marshack was said to have immediately placed an emergency medical call. But days later it was announced that the former vice-president had succumbed an hour earlier, at 10:15 P.M., and that Marshack, instead of calling the paramedics, had called her friend, Ponchita Pierce. It was Pierce who called for assistance. The family doctor believed Rockefeller had died instantaneously, but why did two women let an hour pass before calling for help? The Rockefeller family did not wish to pursue the matter and would not consent to an autopsy.

9. ANGELA MARIA "GELI" RAUBAL (1908–1931), Adolf Hitler's niece

Perhaps she was Uncle Adolf's mistress, perhaps not; at any rate, he was insanely jealous and possessive of her. Hours after a prolonged quarrel between them, Raubal was found dead with a bullet from Hitler's revolver in her heart. The official verdict was suicide, though no formal inquest was held. Rumors were rampant: that her corpse showed extensive bruises; that she was murdered by either Hitler or his political ally Heinrich Himmler. A shaken Hitler, still struggling to achieve power in Germany, tried to hush the scandal and laid lavish praise on her memory.

10. JOHN PAUL I (1912–1978), Italian pope

The "smiling pope" died only 33 days after succeeding Paul VI. Revised official accounts of the discovery of his body after an alleged heart attack led Milan's respected newspaper *Corriere della Serra* to hint at foul play. First, the pope's secretary, Father Magee, claimed he found the dead pope in bed shortly after 5:30 A.M. on September 28, saying he appeared to have died while reading *Imitation of Christ* by Thomas a Kempis. Days later, it was learned that a nun actually found John Paul some time earlier, and that he was reading a document written by Pope Paul VI. It was then reported he had taken pills—dubiously prescribed for "aged ailments"—with dinner the last night of his life. Rumors circulated that he was poisoned, and while the demand for an autopsy was widespread, church authorities refused, citing Paul VI's 1975 decree that called autopsies "undignified and unnecessary" in the 20th century.

—J.E.

11 DEATHS FROM STRANGE CAUSES

1. SEWERCIDE

Harald S., 39 years old, was having a little get-together with two of his friends in Nachtigall Square in Wedding, Berlin. They were drinking brandy and soda, and though his friends became more and more cheerful, S. remained silent throughout the evening. Finally he said to his friend Erich N., "Now I'm going to kill myself." His companions did not believe him, and they let him go. He went outside and, just opposite his own house, lifted the cover of a small drainpipe. Then he jumped in headfirst. When the fire brigade came and pulled him out by the legs, S. was dead—a victim of sewer suicide.

2. THE FATEFUL BATH

Pat Burke of St. Louis, Mo., took his first bath in 20 years on August 23, 1903. It killed him. Burke was the second victim of cleanliness in a week at the city hospital, and the third in its history. The first was Billy O'Rourke, who had been bathed on the previous Tuesday. Both men had been scrubbed with a broom.

3. THE FINAL KISS

Li Po (d. 762 A.D.), the great Chinese poet and drunkard, often spouted verses he was too intoxicated to write down. His admirer Emperor Ming Huang served as his secretary and jotted down the poems. Li Po was given a pension that included the right to free drinks whenever he traveled. One well-tanked night he took a boat excursion on a river. Seeing the reflection of the moon on the water, he tried to kiss it, fell overboard, and drowned.

4. THE DEADLY APPOINTMENT

While confined to an insane asylum in 1905, the Italian poet Severino Ferrari was informed that he had been appointed a professor of literature at the University of Bologna. This announcement was such a shock to Ferrari that he dropped dead.

5. THE FATAL SNOOKER SHOT

Mr. Raymond Priestley of Melbourne, Australia, was playing snooker in a garage with a friend when he met his doom. He had climbed onto a crossbeam in the ceiling to attempt a trick shot and was hanging upside down by his legs when he slipped. He crashed down on the concrete floor headfirst and later died from brain damage.

6. THE HIRSUTE ACCIDENT

Hans Steininger was known for having the longest beard in the world. One day in September, 1567, while he was climbing the staircase leading to the council chamber of Brunn in Austria, Steininger stepped on his beard, lost his balance, fell down the stairs, and died.

7–8. DEATH BY HOT TUB

In May, 1979, fifty-eight-year-old Wesley LaRoya, a retired navy lieutenant commander, and his wife, Helen, 53, died from spending too much time in their backyard hot spa in Simi Valley, Calif. The LaRoyas, both of whom suffered from high blood pressure, set the water in their tub at 110°F and fell asleep. They never awoke. An investigation later revealed that the couple had been drinking heavily. Their deaths were due to a combination of hyperthermia, ethylism (alcohol poisoning), and heart disease.

9. LOW BLOW

Harry Houdini, the famed magician whose romance with death was legendary, met his end in an unlikely way, in 1926. In his dressing room in Montreal, Houdini was approached by a student who had heard that the magician could take hard slugs in the stomach without feeling pain. The young man struck two or three unexpected blows, and, according to one account, because his stomach was not held rigid as when he performed, Houdini was "unprepared for them." The man who had cheated death so many times died several days later from peritonitis.

Austrian Hans Steininger,
whose beard caused his downfall in 1567.

10. THE MURDEROUS FLY

After giving a speech in 1159, during which he thundered curses and threatened to excommunicate Emperor Frederick I, Pope Adrian IV went to take a drink from a fountain to cool off. While he was drinking, a fly entered his mouth and stuck in his throat. Physicians were unable to remove it, and Pope Adrian died.

11. THE DEADLY GOAT HAIR

Fabius, a Roman praetor, choked to death because of a single goat hair in the milk he was drinking.

—A.W.

15 WELL-KNOWN PERSONS WHO CONSIDERED OR ATTEMPTED SUICIDE

1. ROBERT CLIVE (1725–1774), British soldier

Rejected by his father (who habitually called him the Booby), a miserable and lonely Robert Clive arrived in India at age 18, his meager funds exhausted, to take a £5-a-year job as clerk for the British East India Company. One day another clerk, Edmund Maskelyne, entered Clive's room to find him holding a pistol. Clive asked Maskelyne to fire the pistol out the window, which he did with a loud report. "Well," remarked Clive, "I must be reserved for something. That pistol I have twice snapped at my own head." Indeed he was reserved for something: to lead 3,200 troops to victory over 50,000 enemy troops; to become governor of Bengal and Baron Clive of Plassey; to establish British dominance in India for more than a century. Clive successfully took his own life at age 49 (because of illness), but not until his destiny had been fulfilled in a most spectacular way.

2. WILLIAM COWPER (1731–1800), English poet

Cowper's depressive tendencies developed into a mania in 1763, when he faced a legal examination for a government post. The day before the scheduled exam, he tried to poison himself, stab himself, and hang himself. His efforts were halfhearted, but they got him out of taking the exam. Afterwards Cowper was obsessed with the notion that he was damned for committing an unpardonable sin. He tried to hang himself again in 1773 and made a final attempt on his life in 1787. He died of natural causes three years later. It is ironic that Cowper's poetry is noted for its cheerfulness.

3. JOHANN WOLFGANG VON GOETHE (1749–1832), German poet

Like a young Hamlet whose times were "out of joint," and

suffering from unrequited love, the 25-year-old Goethe decided upon suicide. In choosing the means, he considered the noble examples of history and decided to emulate the emperor Otto, who had stabbed himself in the heart when defeated in battle. Goethe put a handsome, well-polished dagger next to his bed, and each night before he extinguished his candle, he later recalled, "I tried whether I could succeed in plunging the sharp point a couple of inches deep into my breast." Since he never could, he ultimately threw off his depression and resolved to live. He died a natural death at 82, having become the author of *Faust* and a giant of world literature.

4. MAXIMILIEN DE ROBESPIERRE (1758–1794), French revolutionist

In 1794 the tables were turned on Robespierre, 36, the Jacobin leader largely responsible for the excesses of the Reign of Terror during the French Revolution. Most members of the French National Convention now felt personally threatened by him; they declared him an outlaw and sent troops to capture him and his few remaining followers. Robespierre tried to shoot himself, but succeeded only in shattering his jaw. He was laid on a table, his smashed jaw bound with a crude bandage, while the convention debated his fate for six hours. Later that same day he who had sent so many to the guillotine mounted the steps himself. He shrieked in pain as the executioner ripped the bandage from his jaw. Moments later his head fell into a basket. The worst of the Terror was over; within five days 478 political prisoners were released.

5. MARY WOLLSTONECRAFT GODWIN (1759–1797), English author

When Gilbert Imlay, the father of her daughter, Fanny, rejected her, Mary Wollstonecraft, early feminist and author of *A Vindication of the Rights of Women*, resolved to drown herself at age 36. She walked to the Thames at Battersea Bridge, and finding too many people about, hired a boat and rowed down the river. Heavy rain had begun, and she was thoroughly drenched. At Putney she left the boat and threw herself from the bridge. She did not sink immediately and later recalled the pain of the water entering her lungs. After losing consciousness, she was rescued by an unknown person. Two years later, married to philosopher William Godwin, Mary died after giving birth to her second daughter, who would one day marry the poet Shelley and write *Frankenstein*.

6. ÉLIE METCHNIKOFF (1845–1916), Russian bacteriologist

One of history's luckiest bumblers, Metchnikoff was obsessed with suicide. He made his first serious attempt after his first wife's death in 1873, when he took such a large dose of morphine that he vomited up the poison. As soon as he recovered, he decided to contract fatal pneumonia but soon became distracted and forgot the plan. Seven years later the grave illness of another wife drove him to a second suicide attempt. This time he injected a deadly bacterium into his body but again he survived—claiming to have a new zest for life. Metchnikoff went on to win a Nobel Prize in physiology and medicine in 1908 and spent his last years searching for ways to prolong human life.

7. GUY DE MAUPASSANT (1850–1893),
French novelist and short story writer

With his fame at its height but suffering the last stages of syphilis, the great writer began to deteriorate physically and mentally at 41. He suffered from delusions—that he had seen a ghost, that his body was impregnated with salt, that his brain was running out through his nose. One day at 2:00 A.M. in his house at Cannes, his manservant, awakened by a noise, ran out of his room to find his master covered with blood. De Maupassant exclaimed, "See what I have done. I have cut my throat. It is an absolute case of madness." A doctor was sent for, and with the help of two manservants he stitched up the wound. Afterwards the writer begged everyone's pardon for causing so much trouble. He was transported to a sanitorium in Paris, where he lingered on for more than a year.

8. JOSEPH CONRAD (1857–1924),
English author of Ukrainian birth

In 1878 Conrad, 21, having left his native Poland to become a French seaman, was engaged in smuggling at Marseilles. At first he made a profit, then lost money and plunged heavily into debt. He went to Monte Carlo to try to recoup his losses through gambling with borrowed funds. Returning to Marseilles empty-handed, he invited one of his creditors to tea and, just before the man's arrival, shot himself with a revolver. The bullet went "through and through" near the heart. Upon his recovery he spread the story that he had been wounded in a duel, which was considered more respectable than attempted suicide. The duel story was believed for 60 years and created an aura of romance around him. An uncle set his affairs in order, and Conrad soon returned to sea as a British mariner, about to write some of the world's greatest novels and stories in a language not his own.

9. MAXIM GORKI (1868–1936), Russian writer

Gorki's miserable youth reached a climax in 1887, when the contrast between his intellectual aspirations and the reality of his life as a drudging laborer overwhelmed him. Feeling useless and alienated, he bought a cheap pistol and shot himself in the chest—after writing a suicide note asking that his body be dissected "to find out what sort of devil lived in me for these last months." However, Gorki merely punctured his lung, quickly recovered, and said that he regretted the incident.

10. BELA LUGOSI (1882–1956), U.S. actor of Hungarian birth

The great Hungarian actor, age 70, reached the nadir of his life in 1953 when, unemployed and addicted to drugs and alcohol, divorce separated him from an adored only son. Late one night he telephoned Ed Wood, a producer who had tried unsuccessfully to find him work, and asked him to bring over a bottle of scotch. When Wood arrived, Bela was waving a pistol. With tears streaming down his face, he said, "Eddie, I am going to die tonight." Then he threatened to take Wood with him. Thinking that the slightest sign of panic would trip Bela's trigger finger, Wood suggested a few drinks before any action. Lugosi wept as he told Wood that he had read in the newspaper that people had written to a television station to ask if he were still alive. As Lugosi talked, Wood removed the gun from his hand and slipped it into a drawer. Wood then suggested a personal appearance for the actor, who did not mention suicide again. Lugosi had three more years to live. Ahead lay a fifth marriage and self-commitment to Los Angeles County General Hospital for drug rehabilitation. He died peacefully, holding in his hand the script for a new horror film in which he was to have starred. Soon after his death Lugosi became a national cult hero as his portrayals of Dracula and Ygor (among others), shown frequently to wide audiences on television, achieved enormous popularity and recognition as cinema classics.

11. ARTHUR RUBINSTEIN (1889–   ),
U.S. concert pianist of Polish birth

In Berlin in 1908, 21-year-old Polish pianist Arthur Rubinstein was lonely, hungry, and in debt, his career at an impasse. He felt there was nothing left for him but suicide; the problem was finding a way. He had no gun, no poison, and the idea of jumping out the window was revolting ("I might have to go on living with broken arms and legs"). He chose strangulation with a belt from his robe. He went into the bathroom, stood on a chair, and secured one end of the belt to an overhead hook. Then he tied the other end around his neck and kicked over the chair. The worn-out belt immediately came apart, and Rubinstein fell on the floor with a crash. For a time he lay where he had fallen, weeping. Later, going to the piano, he cried himself out in music. Afterwards, on the street, he saw the world as if reborn. The famed pianist never forgot what the experience taught him: "Love life, for better or for worse, without conditions."

12. R. BUCKMINSTER FULLER (1895–   ),
U.S. builder and designer

Stranded in Chicago in 1927, Buckminster Fuller, 32, reached the depths of despair. His self-confidence shattered over being fired from his job without severance pay, depressed over the death of his little daughter Alexandra, he felt his wife and second daughter, Allegra, would be better off without him. He began drinking heavily and one night walked down to the shore of Lake Michigan with the intention of throwing himself in. But as the chilling wind hit his body and the waves crashed at his feet, he determined to explore the situation logically. He realized for the first time that his intellectual appreciation of the exquisite design of the universe led to belief in a Greater Intelligence, or God. His next insight was that the Greater Intelligence had given him an extraordinary number of experiences for the purpose of sharing them with others. He resolved from that moment to live for others, without worrying about making a living. He reasoned, "If the Intelligence directing the universe really has a use for me, it will not allow us to starve; it will see to it that I am able to carry out my resolve." Not one to carry out his resolve in a small way, "Bucky" is now one of the most famous men in the world, invariably introduced to readers and audiences as poet, prophet, mathematician, philosopher, design scientist, architect, and inventor of the geodesic dome.

13. GAMAL ABDEL NASSER (1918–1970), Egyptian statesman

At age six Nasser studied the Koran and concluded that anyone who committed a single sin would go to hell. He knew that he couldn't possibly get through life without sinning at least once, but he also read in the Koran that a child who died before the age of seven would not go to hell. He therefore reasoned that immediate suicide was his only hope of salvation. Nasser and a friend stole a large lump of sealing wax, which they thought was poisonous. After eating the wax, they lay down to die. For their efforts the boys got stomachaches and a stern lecture on theft and misinterpretation of the Koran.

14. GENE TIERNEY (1920–   ), U.S. actress

Tormented by bouts of severe depression caused in part by a failed marriage and a first child born retarded, the successful Hollywood actress was in and out of mental institutions, over a period of three years, undergoing shock therapy. However, the treatments failed to relieve her anguish, and on a spring day in 1958 she climbed out on the window ledge of her mother's 14th-floor New York apartment. Despondent as she was, the prospect of dying did not frighten her. According to Tierney, she didn't jump because of vanity—the thought of "ending up on the pavement like so much scrambled egg, my face and body broken." When police arrived, she claimed that she had been washing the windows. Following the episode, which she now recalls with "chilling clarity," Tierney spent several months in the Menninger Clinic in Topeka, Kans. Understandably, she still suffers from acrophobia (a fear of heights).

15. MARTIN LUTHER KING, JR. (1929–1968), U.S. civil rights leader

As a youth King often assumed guilt for his own or others' real or imagined sins. In 1941 he mistakenly thought his brother had accidentally killed their grandmother, so 12-year-old Martin threw himself from the upstairs window of his home, but he escaped serious injury. When the grandmother died later that year, King thought he was responsible because he had once sneaked off to a parade on a Sunday. Again the boy leaped from the same window—fortunately with the same harmless results.

—M.B.T. & R.K.R.

10 PEOPLE MADE FAMOUS BY THEIR DEATHS

1. CRISPUS ATTUCKS (March 5, 1770—Boston, Mass.)

Little is known about Attucks except that he was either part black, part Indian, or both. He led the mob that incited a handful of British soldiers to fire in the so-called Boston Massacre. Of the five colonists killed, only Attucks is well remembered, probably because of the irony implicit in his role, i.e., he was a nonwhite martyr to the cause of freedom for *white* settlers in the New World.

2. NATHAN HALE (September 22, 1776—New York, N.Y.)

As a spy for Washington's army, Hale had a competent but brief and unexceptional career working behind British lines in New York. After a relative betrayed him to the enemy, Hale confessed and was quickly hanged. His fame derived solely from his purported last words: "I only regret that I have but one life to lose for my country." Actually, he never spoke those words. What he really said, according to a British officer who heard him, was: "It is the duty of every good officer to obey any orders given him by his commander in chief."

3. CASEY JONES (April 30, 1900—Vaughan, Miss.)

John Luther Jones (nicknamed Casey after his hometown of Cayce, Ky.) was a career railroadman. According to legend, on the night of April 29, 1900, he pulled the Cannonball Express into Memphis and then volunteered to replace an ill engineer on the return run. Early the next morning he rode the train to its collision with a stalled train, after telling his fireman to jump. His body was found with one hand on the whistle cord and the other on the brake. His heroic death saved many lives, causing him ever afterwards to be celebrated in song and legend.

4. HORST WESSEL (February, 1930—Berlin, Germany)

A down-and-out ex-Brownshirt, Wessel was shot to death by

The legendary "Casey" Jones.

a Communist during a period of Nazi-Communist street fighting. However, the killing was motivated, not by politics, but by rivalry over a prostitute. When Nazi propaganda chief Joseph Goebbels learned that Wessel had written a patriotic song, he made Wessel a party martyr and had him honored as an ideal Nazi youth. The "Horst Wessel Song" became the official Nazi anthem.

5. EDWARD SLOVIK (January 31, 1945—near Ste. Marie, France)

Nearly 3,000 Americans were court-martialed for desertion during W.W. II. Of the 49 sentenced to death, only one, Pvt. Eddie Slovik, was shot. In fact, Slovik is the only American serviceman shot for desertion since the Civil War. National interest in the case revived in 1974, when Martin Sheen portrayed Slovik in an NBC-TV movie.

6. JOHN BIRCH (August 25, 1945—near Soochow, China)

Birch went to China as a Baptist missionary in 1940. During W.W. II he worked behind Japanese lines in China as a U.S. Army Intelligence officer. Ten days after the Japanese surrendered, Birch was killed by Chinese Communists while leading an intelligence mission. Robert Welch, Jr., brought Birch's story to light in a biography published in 1953. He described Birch as "the first uniformed casualty of W.W. III," and he named the ultraright-wing John Birch Society after him five years later.

7. J. D. TIPPIT (November 22, 1963—Dallas, Tex.)

Forty-five minutes after the assassination of President Kennedy, Dallas patrolman J. D. Tippit was shot by a man whom the police soon identified as Lee Harvey Oswald, Kennedy's suspected assassin. The alleged link between the two crimes made Tippit's name a household word. Shocked Americans sent hundreds of thousands of dollars to Tippit's widow in a spontaneous outpouring of sympathy.

8. MARY JO KOPECHNE (July 18, 1969—Chappaquiddick, Mass.)

A 28-year-old former secretary of Robert F. Kennedy, Kopechne went to Martha's Vineyard to attend a reunion of fellow RFK staffers. After a party on Chappaquiddick Island, she accepted a ride from Sen. Edward Kennedy and was drowned when his car plunged off a bridge into a pond. Kennedy's unexplained, and apparently bizarre, behavior during the incident made the affair a national scandal whose full impact may not yet have been felt.

9-10. LENO AND ROSEMARY LaBIANCA (August 10, 1969— Los Angeles, Calif.)

The LaBiancas, a prosperous but not at all famous couple, were brutally killed by members of the "Manson Family" the night after Manson followers murdered actress Sharon Tate and her friends. The whole grisly affair has since been known as the Tate-LaBianca murders.

—R.K.R.

THE 10 MOST ATTENDED FUNERALS OF THE LAST HALF-CENTURY

1. JÓZEF PILSUDSKI, Polish statesman (1935)

Marshal Pilsudski's cortege to the Warsaw Cathedral was viewed by at least 500,000 people. Huge crowds numbering in the hundreds of thousands then viewed the body as it lay in state. An estimated 2 million more persons turned out to see the train transporting their leader's body from Warsaw to Krakow, where a procession of 150,000 escorted the marshal's body from the railway station to Wawel Cathedral for the final Mass.

2. GEORGE V, English king (1936)

The line at Westminster Hall, where the king's body lay in state, extended for 3 mi. People were eight abreast, across two bridges and along both banks of the Thames. In all, 568,387 people (306,685 in one day) passed his coffin. Three million thronged into the streets of London to view the procession to Westminster Abbey for the burial.

3. MOHANDAS KARAMCHAND GANDHI, Indian social and religious reformer (1948)

The five-hour procession of Gandhi's body through the streets of Old and New Delhi and the cremation ceremony that followed were witnessed by nearly 1 million people. Another 2 to 3 million were reportedly present when Gandhi's son placed his ashes in the sacred waters of the Ganges and Jumna rivers. More of his ashes were placed in 50 other holy rivers throughout India, bringing to 10 million the number of people who participated in last rites for their martyred idol.

4. JOSEPH STALIN, Soviet dictator (1953)

Millions of Soviet citizens viewed Stalin's body as it lay in state for three days in the Hall of Columns in Moscow. At least 50,000 gathered in nearby Red Square for the burial ceremonies.

5. JOHN F. KENNEDY, U.S. president (1963)

An estimated 300,000 mourners lined Pennsylvania and Constitution avenues to view the passage of the caisson bearing their slain leader from the White House to the Capitol. At the Capitol, an additional 250,000 people filed past the flag-covered coffin in the Great Rotunda. A million people turned out to see the cortege carrying the president from St. Matthew's Cathedral, where Mass was held, to Arlington National Cemetery, where the President was buried; millions more viewed the solemn ceremonies on television.

6. JAWAHARLAL NEHRU, Indian prime minister (1964)

Approximately 1.5 million Indians jammed the streets of New Delhi to view the procession of Nehru's body to Rajghat, the cremation grounds on the banks of the Jumna River. There, more than 100,000 mourners were held back by police lines surrounding the cremation platform, which was only 300 yd. from the place where Gandhi had been cremated in 1948.

7. WINSTON CHURCHILL, British prime minister (1965)

A total of 321,360 persons viewed Sir Winston's body as it lay in state at Westminster Hall for three days. Crowds stood five to ten deep in bitter cold to see the procession to St. Paul's Cathedral for the first state funeral accorded a commoner in 50 years. Television coverage of the five-hour-long ceremonies was viewed by a reported 350 million people worldwide.

8. GAMAL ABDEL NASSER, Egyptian president (1970)

Hundreds of thousands of hysterical mourners crowded around the Kubbeth Palace in Cairo, where the body of the president lay in state. On the day of his burial, millions of Egyptians packed the streets to view the procession. Weeping crowds shouting, "Nasser! Nasser! Nasser!" broke through the lines of soldiers and police along the 6-mi. route, causing hundreds of injuries and nearly overturning the coffin. Three hours later the turmoil ended as Nasser was buried in a white shroud in the garden of a newly completed mosque in the Cairo suburb where he had gathered with fellow revolutionaries to march on King Faruk in 1952.

9. MAO TSE-TUNG, Chinese leader (1976)

An estimated 350,000 people filed past Mao's coffin in Beijing's (Peking's) Great Hall of the People. Approximately 750,000 Chinese from selected groups attended a brief and austere rally in front of the Gate of Heavenly Peace. Coinciding with the rally, China's 800 million citizens were asked to stand for three minutes in silent tribute to Chairman Mao, as sirens and factory whistles sounded all over the land.

10. HOUARI BOUMÉDIENNE, Algerian president (1978)

As the heavily guarded funeral cortege made its way from the Great Mosque of Algiers to the El Alin Cemetery, 2 million mourners went berserk, collapsing with grief and trampling fellow mourners in an attempt to touch the coffin. Many had made the trip to the capital on foot for the burial of their leader, who had ruled Algeria for 13 of its 16 years of independence.

—A.MC.

11 DARING GRAVE ROBBERIES

1. CYRUS THE GREAT (600?–529 B.C.), Persian king

The Mideastern conqueror had lain in his 35-ft.-high limestone tomb for 200 years when officers of Alexander the Great entered it and viewed the golden coffin in 330 B.C. Six years later, when

Alexander himself arrived, he found the tomb vandalized and its treasures gone. He had the tomb guards tortured and one officer executed, restored the skeleton to its chamber, and sealed the entrance with his own signet. Repeated later looting completely emptied the tomb, which still towers stark and white amid the ruins of Pasargadae in southern Iran.

2. WILLIAM I (1027–1087), English king

The elaborate funeral ceremony at St. Stephen's Church in Caen, France, was halted by a bizarre occurrence when the bishops tried to squeeze William the Conqueror's rather ripe corpse into the narrow sarcophagus. The stomach burst, and an overpowering stench quickly drove out the mourners. Vandals broke into the magnificent tomb in 1562 and stole everything except a thighbone, which was reinterred 80 years later in another tomb; but even that fragment did not escape looters during the French Revolution. The empty first tomb still exists in the church.

3. LAURENCE STERNE (1713–1768), British novelist

The author of *Tristram Shandy* was buried in St. George's Fields (now the playground of Hyde Park Nursery School in London), a notorious supply ground for cadavers sold to English medical schools by body snatchers. A horrified friend recognized Sterne's body, stolen only days after burial, on a dissecting table at Cambridge. The body was reburied in the cemetery. In 1969 the Sterne Trust excavated the site, located the dissected skull, and reburied the bones near Sterne's residence in Coxwold, North Yorkshire.

4. BLACK HAWK (1767–1838), Sac chief

Dispossessed of the Sacs' tribal lands and vanquished in the Black Hawk War of 1832, the warrior died as a bitter captive in Iowa and was buried near Burlington in a shallow, canopied grave. Nine months later, James Turner, a local physician, stole the corpse, fled to Illinois, cooked off the flesh in a hog-scalding kettle, and prepared to exhibit the skeleton. The Iowa governor, who had insisted on its return, gave the skeleton to a physician friend, who kept it for 13 years in his office. Black Hawk's wife viewed it there "with the apparent curiosity of a child." A fire destroyed both office and bones in 1853.

5. JOHN SCOTT HARRISON (1804–1878), U.S. congressman

Grave robbery to obtain medical school cadavers was a plague in the American Midwest during the 1800s. The son of one president and the father of another, Harrison was buried in the family plot at North Bend, O. Mourners that day noted that the adjacent grave, which held Augustus Devin, Harrison's recently deceased grandnephew, had been disturbed. Investigation disclosed that Devin's grave was empty, and Harrison's son John joined the impromptu search for the missing corpse. Less than a day later, young John Harrison found, not Devin's body, but his own father's corpse hanging in a shaft at the Ohio Medical College in Cincinnati. It had been stolen during the distraction caused by the Devin theft, apparently moments after burial the day before. Devin's body was also recovered, and the illegal "supplier" was arrested. News of the case resulted in legislation that improved the public image of doctors despite themselves. Harrison was reburied in Spring Grove Cemetery in Cincinnati.

6. SITTING BULL (1834–1890), Sioux chief

The Post Cemetery at Fort Yates, N.D., contained his neglected grave for more than 50 years. Then tourist-oriented businessmen in Mobridge, S.D. (the chief's native area), began a campaign to retrieve the remains. When North Dakota authorities refused to cooperate, several Mobridge boosters crossed the state line one night in 1954, exhumed the bones, and placed them in a shiny new casket. Today at Sitting Bull Park, a marble pedestal and 3-ton granite bust enshrine the tomb. To prevent further resurrection, the coffin was encased in a giant dollop of concrete.

7. HENRI PHILIPPE PÉTAIN (1856–1951), French soldier

A hero in W.W. I but the puppet leader of the Vichy regime during W.W. II, Pétain was serving a life sentence for treason when he died on the Île d'Yeu off the French Atlantic coast and was buried there. A right-wing political group exhumed his coffin in February, 1973, insisting that President Pompidou consent to its reburial among the honored war dead in the Douaumont military cemetery. The same week, police discovered the stolen coffin in a van parked in a courtyard garage near Paris. Pétain was ceremonially reburied, his coffin decorated with a presidential wreath—but, as before, on the Île d'Yeu.

8. FRANCISCO VILLA (1877–1923), Mexican revolutionary leader

Three years after "Pancho" Villa's assassination, a Mexican army captain opened his grave and stole his skull. One popular explanation for the decapitation of the corpse was an alleged reward of $50,000 offered by the U.S. government for evidence that the infamous revolutionary and bandit was really dead. This theory,

Sitting Bull's gravestone at Mobridge, S.D., now protected from grave robbers by barbed wire.

however, has never been proved, and the skull was never found. In 1976 Villa's body was taken from its original burial place in the small town of Parral in northern Mexico to Mexico City, where it was placed in a crypt at the Revolution Monument.

9. CHARLES CHAPLIN (1889–1977),
English film actor, director, producer

"Charlie" Chaplin was buried on December 27 in the Swiss village cemetery of Corsier-sur-Vevey near his home. One morning about two months later, villagers awoke to discover an empty hole at the grave site. The robbers contacted the Chaplin family and demanded $600,000 ransom, which the widow refused to pay. Police traced the calls and finally arrested two East European refugees—one from Poland, one from Bulgaria—who had buried the 300-lb. oak coffin in a cornfield 10 mi. from the village. Chaplin was reburied in a concrete vault at the village cemetery on May 23, 1978. Roman Wardas, mastermind of the crime, was sentenced to from one to four and a half years in prison. His accomplice, Galtcho Ganev, was given an 18-month suspended term.

10. MICHAEL TODD (1909–1958), U.S. film producer

Todd, killed in a plane crash, was buried at Waldheim Cemetery in Forest Park, Ill. In June, 1977, two days after his widow, actress Elizabeth Taylor, had visited the grave, it was vandalized. The bronze coffin was pried open and its contents were removed. A telephone tip three days later led police to a wooded area of the cemetery, where they discovered a rubber bag containing Todd's remains. It was speculated that the robbers, who were never caught, had thought that valuable jewelry was in the coffin, a notion that Todd's son quickly dispelled. The remains were reburied, by family instruction, in a secret location.

11. ALAN WATTS (1915–1973), British philosopher

The popular exponent of Zen and Eastern philosophy was cremated. Most of his ashes were buried at the Zen Center near Mill Valley, Calif., but his widow, Jane, retained three bone fragments in a turquoise-studded brass Tibetan box, enshrined in the Watts home in Sausalito. A burglar stole the box, along with a color television set, in August, 1975. Mrs. Watts issued a warning that the box was protected by a curse that could harm the thief. However, the effectiveness of the curse and the thief's identity remain unknown.

—J.E.

27 CELEBRATED PEOPLE WHO BELIEVED IN REINCARNATION

1. Pythagoras (d. 497? B.C.), Greek mathematician and philosopher
2. Plato (427?–347 B.C.), Greek philosopher
3. Julian (331–363 A.D.), Roman emperor known as Julian the Apostate
4. Leonardo da Vinci (1452–1519), Italian painter and inventor
5. Paracelsus (1493–1541), Swiss physician and alchemist
6. Giordano Bruno (1548?–1600), Italian philosopher and poet
7. Gottfried Wilhelm von Leibniz (1646–1716), German philosopher
8. Benjamin Franklin (1706–1790), U.S. statesman, scientist, and philosopher
9. Johann Wolfgang von Goethe (1749–1832), German poet
10. Percy Bysshe Shelley (1792–1822), English poet
11. Victor Hugo (1802–1885), French novelist and poet
12. Ralph Waldo Emerson (1803–1882), U.S. writer and philosopher
13. Giuseppe Mazzini (1805–1872), Italian patriot
14. Richard Wagner (1813–1883), German composer
15. Henry David Thoreau (1817–1862), U.S. writer and philosopher
16. Walt Whitman (1819–1892), U.S. poet
17. Louisa May Alcott (1832–1888), U.S. novelist
18. Friedrich Nietzsche (1844–1900), German philosopher
19. Thomas Edison (1847–1931), U.S. inventor
20. Paul Gauguin (1848–1903), French painter
21. August Strindberg (1849–1912), Swedish dramatist
22. Luther Burbank (1849–1926), U.S. horticulturist
23. Sir Arthur Conan Doyle (1859–1930), British physician and novelist
24. Henry Ford (1863–1947), U.S. auto manufacturer
25. Piet Mondrian (1872–1944), Dutch painter
26. Carl Gustav Jung (1875–1961), Swiss psychologist and psychiatrist
27. Charles A. Lindbergh (1902–1974), U.S. aviator

—J.DI.

21
LOOSE ENDS

THE PEOPLE'S ALMANAC'S
13 MORE FAVORITE
ODDITIES OF ALL TIME

1. THE FLEA KILLER

Queen Christina of Sweden (1626–1689) abhorred fleas and declared war on them, determined to exterminate personally each one in her household. To this end she had a special miniature cannon built—4 in. in length—and packed it with tiny cannonballs. Whenever she saw a flea, she aimed and fired her Lilliputian cannon at it. This midget cannon is today on exhibit in the Stockholm Arsenal.

2. THE VERSAILLES SKULL

The Versailles Treaty, signed by defeated Germany and the victorious Allies in June of 1919 to seal the end of W.W. I, forced Germany to give up Alsace-Lorraine and all colonies, to allow military occupation of the Rhineland, to pay reparations to the victors—and to give up one human skull. Part VIII, Section II, Article 246 of the Versailles Treaty carried the strangest clause ever inserted in a major international pact: "Within six months of the coming into force of the present treaty . . . Germany will hand over to His Britannic Majesty's Government the skull of the Sultan Mkwawa which was removed from the protectorate of German East Africa and taken to Germany." Sultan Mkwawa had been the leader of the Wahhehe tribe in German-controlled Tanganyika. The sultan led his people in a revolt, which the Germans crushed. The sultan was captured and killed, and his skull was sent to Germany as a souvenir. But the Wahhehe people wanted the skull, which they endowed with magic, returned to them. So they got the British to demand its return in the Versailles Treaty. Years later Germany insisted it had returned the skull to Africa. If so, it has disappeared.

3. SUPER SEX SEGREGATION

During the height of the Victorian Era, the one how-to-do-it-right volume was *Lady Gough's Book of Etiquette*. In this manual of etiquette, the setting up of books by male authors next to books by female authors on any bookshelf was absolutely forbidden—that is, unless the male and female authors happened to be married.

4. THE BIG APPLE

He simply had to be the most prolific father in modern times. He was a Holstein bull named Rag Apple. He did his family-making in Ithaca, N.Y. Through use of artificial insemination, Rag Apple produced 15,000 sons and daughters in three years and four months. Rag Apple met an accidental death in 1948.

5. SKYSCRAPER, U.S.A.

In July, 1941, Franklin D. Roosevelt, President of the U.S., asked Jesse Jones, secretary of commerce, to buy the tallest building in the world, the Empire State Building in New York City. Roosevelt wanted to convert it into a central federal office building. The 102-story structure, constructed of 60,000 tons of steel, large enough to house 15,000 people, would have become the greatest government building in world history. At the time, the Empire State Building was owned largely by the Metropolitan Life Insurance Company and a corporation controlled by John J. Raskob, onetime chairman of the Democratic National Committee. The owners asked $45 million for the property. Jones thought the building was a bad buy and turned it down. Later, Jones confessed that Roosevelt never forgave him for not buying it.

6. THE FEMALE BULLFIGHTER

According to Barnaby Conrad, a leading authority on bullfighting, the story of a certain female matador is one of the oddest in bullring lore. Her name was María Salomé and she came to be known as La Reverte. She was born in Jaén, Spain, in 1880. She made her debut in the bullring in Madrid during 1900. La Reverte was a great crowd pleaser for seven years and received considerable acclaim. Then, in 1908, the Spanish government decreed that it was immoral and illegal for women to fight bulls. About to be banned as a woman, La Reverte publicly took off her wig and removed her falsies and announced that she was not really a woman but a man named Agustín Rodríguez. Therefore, he said, he could not be banned. And, in fact, he tried to continue in the profession as the man he really had been all along. But the crowds, unamused by his fraud, now wanted to lynch rather than olé him. Rodríguez finally left Madrid and died a broken man in Majorca.

7. THE CODETALKERS

In 1918, during a critical period on the western front in W.W. I, the U.S. Army Signal Corps found itself hampered because many of its secret orders, transmitted by field telephone from one battalion to another by various codes, were being intercepted and successfully decoded by the Germans. While trying to solve the problem, a signal corpsman, Capt. E. W. Horner, remembered that one of the least known languages in the world was the American Choctaw Indian language. If he could find any Choctaw Indians in the American Expeditionary Forces, the signals corps would have an unbreakable code. Captain Horner finally found eight Choctaw Indians in uniform. They were assigned to Company D of the 141st Infantry and dispersed to all embattled sectors on the western front. There the Indians sent and received all secret orders in pure Choctaw. The German code decipherers were totally baffled, and in these areas the tide of battle began to turn in favor of the Allies. The idea of Indian codetalkers was used even more effectively in W.W. II. The U.S. Marines in the Pacific combat zone drew speakers from the Navajo tribe of 50,000, knowing that only 28 non-Navajos (anthropologists and missionaries) in the world could understand the language and that none of those were Japanese or German. The number of Navajo codetalkers doing radio transmission was 30 at the beginning of W.W. II and rose to 420 by the time the war ended.

8. LENDING AN EAR

When Wallace J. Murray died in 1978 in Gorham, Me., at the age of 88, there died one of the unheralded geniuses in modern American history. For it was Murray who once made a "silk" purse out of a sow's ear. An M.I.T. graduate, Murray said he made the purse to demonstrate American scientific abilities. His purse is on permanent display at the Smithsonian Institution in Washington, D.C.

A "silk" purse *actually* made out of a sow's ear.

9. THE GREAT DOG SOLDIER

When Juan Ponce de León (1460?–1521), the Spanish conquistador and explorer, repressed native fighters to take control of Puerto Rico and become its governor, one of the leading soldiers in his army was a dog named Bezerillo. Among the natives, this bloodhound, according to the Spanish chronicler Herrera, "knew which of them were in war and which in peace, like a man; for which reason the Indians were more afraid of 10 Spaniards with the dog, than of one hundred without him." Like his master, a foot soldier, the dog was given spoils of victory, "one share and a half of all that was taken, as well as gold, slaves, and other things." Later, when Ponce de León set out to search for the fountain of youth on the Bimini Islands (and found Florida instead, in 1513), he took along the dog Bezerillo, ordering that the bloodhound draw full troop pay and a daily food allowance.

10. THE COW THAT ALMOST FLEW OVER THE MOON

The best all-around flying record for a cow is held by an Iowa guernsey named Fawn. On May 9, 1962, Fawn made her maiden solo flight. Swept up by a tornado, the cow went through the air with the greatest of ease, landed safely a half-mile away in a neighbor's patch, lingered long enough to have an affair with a holstein bull, eventually wandered back to her home pasture, and in due time gave birth to a calf. Five years later, in January, 1967, Fawn was out grazing when another tornado swooped her up. A passing busload of startled tourists saw Fawn flying at a goodly altitude. She went over the tourists' heads for some distance on the opposite side of the road, and landed safely on her four feet once more. After that, she was allowed no more flying time. When a storm warning came, she was always hustled into the shelter of the family barn. This veteran of the wild blue yonder died in prosaic retirement in Scott County, Ia., on July 25, 1978, at the venerable cow age of 25.

11. THE HAREM COMES TO THE AMERICAS

North, Central, and South America have known only one instance of legal polygamy in the 19th century, aside from the Mormon experience in the U.S. Between 1865 and 1870, for five bloody years, Paraguay fought the War of the Triple Alliance with Brazil, Uruguay, and Argentina. For Paraguay the fighting was an utter disaster. Half of Paraguay's population of one million died. Two thirds of the country's young men were killed. At the cessation of hostilities, Paraguay had 190,000 adult women to 29,000 adult men. Because marriage was expensive, half of the nation's children were born out of wedlock. To replenish its population, the government legalized polygamy, allowing all of its males to have multiple wives. Partially as a result of this, Paraguay was soon on the road to its present-day population of almost 3 million persons.

12. THE LOVELY PIG

Many animal specialists believe the pig is among the most mistreated and maligned of barnyard animals. The pig is supposed to be the filthiest of creatures, both fat and lazy. All untrue. The pig is this way because human beings made him this way. Left alone to live according to his nature, the pig would eat less, be far more active, and certainly be among the cleanest of animals. Wild hogs or pigs are, said one expert, "lean, clean, and happy." They are fastidious creatures. They hate slop and swill. Humans have artificially forced pigs to wallow in mud, overeat, oversleep, and become abnormally lazy—in order to fatten them for the marketplace.

13. TOO GOOD TO BE TRUE?

The armies of Turkey's Ottoman Empire occupied Greece in 1821. At one point, the Greeks revolted and attacked, and Turkish soldiers were forced to hole up in the majestic and sacred Acropolis outside Athens. From the height of the Acropolis, the Turks poured rounds of fire down at the Greeks. Suddenly, the Turks ran out of ammunition. They were lost unless they could find more. There was only one hope. They decided to knock down the temple columns of the Acropolis, in order to get at the lead cores and the lead used to secure foundation joints, which could be converted into bullets. When word of this reached the surrounding Greeks, they were horrified to a man. To them, the Acropolis was a holy monument. To let the Turks destroy it for ammunition was unthinkable. So, to prevent this desecration, the Greeks sent their own ammunition to the Turks in order to save the Acropolis, and the battle was resumed. This story was submitted by a reader, Jerry Sankey, who remembered having it related to him by one of his teachers. We have been unable to confirm it—but if true, it is certainly one of the most bizarre facts in history.

—I.W.

12 SECOND PLACES IN HISTORY

1. THE SECOND POPE

After St. Peter, a shadowy figure known as St. Linus the Martyr reigned as the second pope from 67 to 79 A.D. He probably was a Jew, most certainly was born in Tuscany, Italy.

2. THE SECOND CIRCUMNAVIGATION OF THE GLOBE

Almost 60 years after Ferdinand Magellan's voyage, England's Sir Francis Drake sailed around the world in his 75-ft. vessel, *The Golden Hind.* The trip was not uneventful. It included sacking a Spanish treasure ship, going aground on a reef, and suppressing a mutiny in Patagonia. Drake reached his goal, England, in 1580.

3. THE SECOND GROUP TO GO UP IN A BALLOON

The first group to go up in a balloon—a sheep, a duck, and a cock—ascended on September 19, 1783. Viewed by King Louis XVI and Marie Antoinette at Versailles, the three animals were put in the basket of a hot-air balloon. They were in the air for eight minutes and survived the landing without injury. On November 21, 1783, another group, this one comprised of humans, rose in the air from the gardens of the Château La Muette in the Bois de Boulogne. Two Frenchmen, Jean François Pilâtre de Rozier and the Marquis d'Arlandes, were airborne for 25 minutes in free flight.

4. THE SECOND EXPEDITION TO REACH THE SOUTH POLE

A month after Roald Amundsen reached the South Pole in 1911, a doomed party led by Capt. Robert Falcon Scott achieved the same goal. Eleven miles from a food depot when hit by a nine-day blizzard, the last survivors of the party died of cold and starvation. They left behind affecting letters of farewell and diaries documenting their ordeal.

5. THE SECOND WOMAN ELECTED TO THE U.S. CONGRESS

In 1920 Alice Mary Robertson, daughter of missionaries, born in Indian territory, was elected as a Republican representative from the state of Oklahoma. She served in the 67th U.S. Congress, from March 4, 1921 to March 3, 1923. Formerly a teacher and superintendent of schools, Robertson attracted much attention during W.W. I when she organized a canteen service that gave free meals to thousands of soldiers passing through Muskogee, Okla. Pacifist Jeannette Rankin, a Republican from Montana, had been the first to serve in the House, from 1917 to 1919.

6. THE SECOND WOMAN TO SWIM THE ENGLISH CHANNEL

Less than a month after Gertrude Ederle, another American, Mrs. Millie Gade Corson, swam the treacherous English Channel from France to England. The date: August 28, 1926. Her time: 15 hours, 30 minutes, which was 59 minutes longer than Ederle's time.

7. THE SECOND U.S. BILLIONAIRE

First came John D. Rockefeller, then Henry Ford, who started out as an unemployed mechanic with an idea—the plan for an automobile that was to become the Model T. He saw money as "part of the conveyor belt." Ford's assembly conveyor belt, and his paying workers an unprecedented $5 per day, revolutionized the industrial world. When a reporter asked him what it felt like to be a billionaire, his response was "Aw, shit."

8. THE SECOND LEADER OF THE CAPONE GANG

Frank "the Enforcer" Nitti, who started as triggerman and worked his way up to treasurer in Capone's organization, ran the gang along with Capone's brother, Ralph, when Capone went to jail. Nitti served time for tax evasion. When threatened with a second term for labor racketeering, he committed suicide in 1943 by putting a bullet through his head.

9. THE SECOND MAN TO DROP AN A-BOMB

On President Truman's orders, Col. Paul Tibbets, Jr., had dropped an A-bomb on Hiroshima, Japan. Then on August 9, 1945, a 25-year-old major in the U.S. Army Air Force, Charles Sweeney, piloted the B-29 *Bock's Car* to drop Fat Man, a watermelon-shaped plutonium bomb, on Nagasaki, Japan. Result: 36,000 people or more killed. Though his initial response to the mushroom cloud was "What have we done?" Sweeney convinced himself that he was only doing his job.

10. THE SECOND BLACK TO PLAY IN MODERN MAJOR LEAGUE BASEBALL

After Jackie Robinson broke the race barrier, Larry Doby joined the Cleveland Indians in July, 1947, to become the second black to play in the major leagues and the first to play in the American League. Doby's .301 average helped Cleveland win the pennant in 1948, and he made the All-Star team six seasons in a row.

11. THE SECOND TEAM TO CLIMB MT. EVEREST

The second mountaineering team to succeed in climbing Mt. Everest was Swiss. The men were Ernest Reiss and Fritz Luchsinger; they reached the 29,028-ft. summit on May 18, 1956, three years after Sir Edmund P. Hillary and Tenzing Norkay.

12. THE SECOND MAN ON THE MOON

Nineteen minutes after Neil Armstrong set his booted foot on the moon, his companion in the lunar module *Eagle*, Edwin "Buzz" Aldrin, followed. The date: July 21, 1969. Aldrin, a committed athlete, helped Armstrong collect samples, jumped about happily in the moon's lesser gravity, and leaped up the last rung when they reentered the module. He was then 39.

—A.E.

25 THINGS THAT ARE
NOT WHAT THEY SEEM

1. A firefly is not a fly—it's a beetle.
2. A prairie dog is not a dog—it's a rodent.
3. India ink is not from India—it's from China and Egypt.
4. A horned toad is not a toad—it's a lizard.
5. A lead pencil contains no lead—it contains graphite.
6. A Douglas fir tree is not a fir—it's a pine.
7. A silkworm is not a worm—it's a caterpillar.
8. A peanut is not a nut—it's a legume.
9. A panda bear is not a bear—it's a raccoon relative.
10. An English horn is not English and not a horn—it's an alto oboe from France.
11. A guinea pig is not from Guinea and is not a pig—it's from South America and it's a rodent.
12. Shortbread is not a bread—its a thick cookie.
13. Dresden china is not made in Dresden—it's made in Meissen.
14. A shooting star is not a star—it's a meteor.
15. A funny bone is not a bone—it's the spot where the ulnar nerve touches the humerus.
16. Chop suey is not a native Chinese dish—it was invented by Chinese immigrants in California.
17. A bald eagle is not bald—it's got flat white feathers on its head and neck when mature, dark feathers when young.
18. A banana tree is not a tree—it's an herb.
19. A cucumber is not a vegetable—it's a fruit.
20. A jackrabbit is not a rabbit—it's a hare.
21. A piece of catgut is not from a cat—it's usually made from sheep intestines.
22. A Mexican jumping bean is not a bean—it's a seed with a larva inside.
23. A Turkish bath is not Turkish—it's Roman.
24. A koala bear is not a bear—it's a marsupial.
25. A sweetbread is not bread—it's from a calf's or lamb's pancreas or thymus.

—I.W. & W.D.

21 THINGS AND WHAT
THEY WEIGH

1. A hockey puck: 0.38 lb.
2. A hailstone that fell on Coffeyville, Kans: 1.66 lb. (September 3, 1970)
3. Reggie Jackson's bat: 2.25 lb.

4. Average human male brain: 3.1 lb.
5. Chihuahua dog: 5 lb.
6. A brick: 8.75 lb.
7. New York City telephone directory: 14.25 lb.
   (White pages for all five boroughs)
8. A bar of gold at Fort Knox: 27.45 lb.
9. Fred Astaire: 140 lb.
10. A Saint Bernard dog: 190 lb.
    (Large adult)
11. Francis A. Johnson's ball of string: 10,000 lb.
    (In his private museum 50 mi. west of Minneapolis)
12. An *aku* figure on Easter Island: 100,000 lb.
13. The Statue of Liberty: 450,000 lb.
14. A redwood tree: 12,000,000 lb.
    (One of the larger ones)
15. The Eiffel Tower: 14,000,000 lb.
16. R.M.S. *Queen Elizabeth II*: 133,702,000 lb.
17. The Empire State Building: 730,000,000 lb.
18. Great Pyramid of Khufu, Egypt: 11,500,000,000 lb.
19. The concrete in Hoover Dam: 13,200,000,000 lb.
20. The moon: 162,000,000,000,000,000,000,000 lb.
21. Earth: 13,284,000,000,000,000,000,000,000 lb.

(The last two, of course, are theoretical estimates using figures based on the law of gravitation.)

—R.SO.

L to R: The world's largest ball of
string and Francis A. Johnson.

THE 13 MOST REPRESSIVE
GOVERNMENTS IN THE WORLD

1. PARAGUAY

The national motto of Paraguay is "By Reason or by Force." Gen. Alfredo Stroessner, who has ruled the country since 1954, is a classic, old-fashioned South American dictator. Unlike his cohorts in Brazil, Argentina, and Chile, he doesn't bother to present high-sounding "economic" excuses for his tyranny. Smuggling, bribery, and narcotics are big business in Paraguay, and Stroessner stays in power by sharing the profits with military, police, and business leaders. As for the common people, 600,000 of them (out of a population of less than 3 million) have left the country. Most of the rest live in abject poverty with little education. Paraguay's prisons are considered the world's worst, the guards having been well trained by escaped Nazis *and* by CIA "specialists."

2. EQUATORIAL GUINEA

Of all the terrible governments in the world since World War II, one of the worst has been the government of Francisco Macias Nguema Biyogo Negue Ndong, who turned this tiny West African nation into a slave state where the people live in terror and "hopeless

General Alfredo Stroessner of Paraguay—winner of *The People's Almanac*'s Dictator of the Year Award.

resignation." Fortunately, Macias was finally overthrown in August, 1979. Unfortunately, informed sources contacted by *The Book of Lists* in Cameroon report that the military government which has replaced him is best characterized as "same cart, new driver." The population of Equatorial Guinea used to be about 350,000, but since Macias took power in 1968 one out of seven people has been killed and an incredible 45% of the populace are living in exile. Macias systematically exterminated everyone who might oppose him, including two-thirds of the membership of the 1968 National Assembly. Horrible forms of torture are still widespread, and mass public executions have occurred. Whole villages are terrorized by the militia, formerly known as "Youth Marching With Macias," whose members are recruited from the age of seven. In 1976 Macias legalized slavery to provide workers for the cocoa plantations on Macias Nguema Biyogo Island, and over 20,000 people were hauled away from their homes. Anyone wishing to use the beach in Equatorial Guinea must pay a fee of 1500 pesetas (about $22). When his wife fled the country in 1978, Macias made it a punishable offense for a baby to be baptized with her name, and it became illegal to be christened Monica if you lived in Equatorial Guinea. Until the fall of Macias, the nation celebrated five public holidays: Independence Day (March 5), President's Birthday (January 1), Assumption to Power of Life President (September 29), Popular Declaration of Life President (July 14), and Human Rights Day (December 10).

3. BURUNDI

Since 1961 this central African nation of 4 million people has undergone nine violent changes of government as well as the assassination of three prime ministers and one king. In Burundi, as in South Africa, the majority ethnic group is completely subjugated by the minority. The Tutsi, a tall, pastoral people, make up 14% of the population. For over 300 years they have lorded it over the smaller Hutu (85%) and the even smaller Pygmies (1%). Periodically the Hutu rise up, most recently for one week in 1972. On that occasion the Tutsi military government, led by President Michel Micombero, responded by slaughtering one out of every 17 Hutus—ending the lives of 200,000 people in just six weeks. Micombero was overthrown in November, 1976, and the current dictator of Burundi, Tutsi Lt. Col. Jean Baptiste Bagaza, is more restrained in the exercise of his power. However, Bagaza is still at the mercy of the small Tutsi military clique that put him in charge. Consequently, despite Bagaza's attempts to loosen Burundi's feudal caste system, Hutu refugees of the 1972 massacre are not flocking home.

4. URUGUAY

Since the military took over, Uruguay has become, in the words of U.S. Sen. Frank Church, "the biggest torture chamber in Latin America." Uruguay has more political prisoners per capita than any other nation in the world, and it has gained an international reputation for its horribly imaginative methods of torture. Needless to say, the parliament has been abolished, trade unions have been banned, and the press is censored. The country used to have a population of over 3 million, but 400,000 have fled the military dictatorship. Unfortunately, many of these refugees have been rounded up in Argentina and returned to the clutches of the Uruguayan authorities.

5. SOUTH AFRICA

South Africa is a wonderful place to live if you have white skin. Unfortunately, 83% of the population doesn't meet that qualification. The black majority has been herded into tribal homelands called Bantustans and is not allowed free access to the remaining 87% of the country. Extreme racial segregation is rooted in the South African constitution, and it is possible to spend a fairly pleasant vacation in South Africa without being directly exposed to the poverty and restricted life-style of the black majority. Urban Africans who are unemployed for more than one third of the year are defined as "idle Bantus," who may be sent to work camps or detention centers. Freedom of speech is not allowed, and the written word is so censored that *Lady Chatterley's Lover* is still banned in South Africa.

6. GUATEMALA

Since the CIA overthrew Guatemala's last democratically elected president in 1954, the country has been ruled by a succession of corrupt and seemingly cold-blooded generals, the latest being Gen. Romeo Lucas García. Unlike most military dictatorships, the leaders of Guatemala apparently have little interest in jailing their political opponents. Instead, they just murder them. In fact, since 1966 over 20,000 Guatemalans have been tortured, mutilated, and finally executed by death squads with names like the White Hand and Eye for an Eye. Daylight public assassinations—carried out with Mafia-like precision—are commonplace, and the vast majority of Guatemala's 6 million people are forced to live their lives in quiet, impoverished terror.

7. U.S.S.R.

The Soviet government gets credit for being able to repress so many people spread over such a large area for such a long time. Ever since the days of Stalin, when between 8 and 10 million citizens were slaughtered because of their political or personal beliefs (whether real or imagined by Stalin), the people of the Soviet Union have been well aware that expressing oneself is a potentially dangerous undertaking. Alexander Solzhenitsyn has estimated that 66 million dissidents have been imprisoned in forced-labor camps since the camps were established in 1918. The U.S.S.R., like the U.S., moves up several points on the repression scale because of its habit of providing military and financial support to *other* repressive regimes around the world which otherwise would have been overthrown long ago.

8. INDONESIA

The Indonesian political situation is clouded by corruption, severe suppression of individual freedoms, and periodic mass slaughters. Corruption is practically institutionalized, running through society from top to bottom. President Suharto sets the pace with such projects as the $1 million Suharto family mausoleum in Central Java, but the Indonesian champion of corruption is Maj. Gen. Ibnu Sutowo, who while head of the now bankrupt state oil company, Pertamina,

479

managed to secure an illegal loan of $10 billion. Like Sutowo, most of the 55,000 political prisoners in Indonesia have never been brought to trial, despite the fact that most of them were arrested in 1965. Unlike Sutowo, these prisoners have been brutally punished, many of them on the forbidden island of Buru. When pro-Communist elements of the army tried to take power in 1965, they were defeated. General Suharto used the coup as an excuse to set loose Muslim fanatics and his soldiers, who ran amok and killed between 500,000 and 1 million people suspected of being leftists. On the Hindu island of Bali, one out of every 60 people was murdered. In 1975 the U.S.-armed Indonesian army invaded East Timor, killing another 100,000 men, women, and children while annexing the former Portuguese colony.

9. IRAN

It's not easy being an Iranian. No sooner had the Iranian people rid themselves of one of the most evil dictators of this century, Shah Mohammed Reza Pahlavi, and his dreaded secret police, SAVAK, than they acquired a brand-new dictator of equal fanaticism, the Ayatollah Ruhollah Khomeini. Khomeini, attempting to establish his version of a "government of God," banned frozen meat, alcohol, female vocalists, and graven images of the human body. Any book with a woman on the cover was burned, and divorce proceedings initiated by women were canceled. The Khomeini regime has also executed thousands of former supporters of the shah as well as leaders of the Kurdish minority and general nonconformists, charging them with such imaginative crimes as "sowing corruption on earth."

10. CHILE

In 1973 the democratically elected government of Salvador Allende Gossens was overthrown by a military junta led by Gen. Augusto Pinochet Ugarte. Since that time 30,000 people have been killed; there have been 90,000 political arrests; and 1 million Chilean citizens—one tenth of the population—have been forced to leave the country. Pinochet, who believes in "Authoritarian democracy" (with a capital A and small d), claims that the coup was necessary to restore order to the Chilean economy. However, all of his remedies have been at the expense of the poor. Strikes are illegal, and Pinochet has stated that it would be unwise to hold general elections for at least another decade.

11. ARGENTINA

Argentina is a nice place to visit if you want to get away from it all. In fact, since the latest military junta seized power in 1976, over 15,000 people have disappeared. Most of these were last seen being hauled away by the Anti-Communist Alliance, a semilegal torture and death squad composed of members of the police and armed forces. In its campaign to suppress terrorism and subversion, the government of Gen. Jorge Rafael Videla suspended all political and trade union activity, drove 100,000 professionals into exile, arrested 18,000 citizens for political "crimes," and executed at least 4,000 "subversive delinquents." Although one can appreciate the general's desire to protect the people of Argentina from terrorists, it is worth noting his definition of the word *terrorist*. In the words of

General Videla, "A terrorist is not just someone with a gun or a bomb, but also someone who spreads ideas that are contrary to Western and Christian civilization."

12. ETHIOPIA

In the words of novelist Daniachew Worku, "Ethiopia is God's way of putting an end to things." For 58 years, Ethiopia's 28 million people were ruled by the corrupt and brutal King of Kings, Haile Selassie. When he failed to deal with a massive famine that left 400,000 dead, he was overthrown in 1974 and a Marxist military committee, the Dergue, took power. The first chairman of the Dergue, Lt. Col. Atnafu Abate, was tried three years later for the crime of "putting the interests of Ethiopia before ideology." In other words, Atnafu Abate became one of the first people in history to be prosecuted in his own country for being patriotic. Besieged by a wide array of secessionist and revolutionary groups, the Ethiopian government was on the verge of disintegration when it was saved by the U.S.S.R., which sent $1 billion worth of weapons and 17,000 Cuban troops. This allowed military leader Lt. Col. Mengistu Haile Mariam to institute a campaign of Red Revolutionary Terror consisting of the summary killing of political opponents (including children), mass detention, and systematic torture too gruesome to discuss. All this in a country where, even in the best of times, the average family must struggle desperately just to survive.

13. BULGARIA

Of all the Communist governments under the thumb of the U.S.S.R., Bulgaria has shown the least independence, aiding in the 1968 invasion of Czechoslovakia, sending workers to the Soviet Union whenever needed, and generally doing whatever it is told. The Bulgarians themselves have a history of being bright, freedom-loving people, but the Communist party has turned the country into a place of oppressive boredom and dullness. Article 273 of the Bulgarian Penal Code, which forbids "dissemination of untruthful remarks which might incite mistrust of the state power or cause confusion in society," covers just about any problems that might come up.

Note: Awards of Dishonorable Mention go to Korea, where the people have the misfortune of having their country split in half and ruled by two terrible dictatorships which mouth opposite ideologies; Haiti and El Salvador, where murderous regimes keep the population in extreme poverty; all Communist countries in which the people are not free to choose their own profession or to travel outside the country; and Saudi Arabia and the other Arab states of the Persian Gulf where the Koran is law and punishment is meted out by chopping off body parts, including heads.

—D. W.

Fidel Castro—with beard and dignity intact.

6 OUTRAGEOUS PLANS THAT DIDN'T HAPPEN

1. THE PLAN TO HUMILIATE CASTRO

The CIA once developed a plan to make Fidel Castro's beard fall out by dusting his shoes with a hair-removing substance. The attack on Castro's beard was to have taken place during a trip Castro planned to take out of Cuba. However, Castro thwarted the CIA by canceling the trip and saved himself from the embarrassment of exposing his chin in public.

2. THE POISONOUS CROCODILE GALLBLADDER PLAN

In 1962 the CIA explored various means of smuggling a crocodile out of Tanganyika and into the U.S. in order to extract its gallbladder and cook it up as part of a witch doctor's secret recipe. The plan was part of a program to study poisons that could be created from the vital organs of reptiles.

3. THE PLAN TO DISSOLVE THE BERLIN WALL

The CIA seriously investigated the possibility of concocting a chemical mixture which, if applied to the Berlin Wall, would cause it to disintegrate. Unfortunately, a successful formula could not be obtained.

4. THE HUSTON PLAN

On July 23, 1970, President Richard M. Nixon allowed a secret memo to be issued in his name to all U.S. intelligence agencies. The memo, which had been written by 29-year-old White House staffer Tom Huston, called for the creation of an Interagency Committee on Intelligence, which would be run by the White House. The plan authorized opening the mail of private citizens, burglarizing people's homes, and generally increasing domestic spying. The memo was well received by everyone but FBI Director J. Edgar Hoover, who saw it as a threat to his power. Hoover argued that such flagrant illegalities should not be the official, written policy of the U.S. government, and five days later word trickled down from the White House that the plan had been revoked and that each person who had received the memo should return it. In 1973 a copy of the Huston Plan was found in the files of John Dean.

5. THE LIDDY PLAN

The Republican party had planned to hold its 1972 convention in San Diego, but the Nixon White House was quite concerned about the massive antiwar demonstrations that would inevitably occur if the President made a public appearance in California. In January of 1972 the ever inventive White House "plumber" G. Gordon Liddy proposed that radical leaders be kidnapped and detained in Mexico until the convention was over. More practical heads prevailed, and the problem was solved by moving the convention site to Miami Beach.

6. THE WIRED NATION

In his book *The Shadow Presidents,* author Michael Medved relates the extreme disappointment of H. R. Haldeman over his failure to implement his plan to link up all the homes in America by coaxial cable. In Haldeman's words, "There would be two-way communication. Through computer, you could use your television set to order up whatever you wanted. The morning paper, entertainment services, shopping services, coverage of sporting events and public events. . . . Just as Eisenhower linked up the nation's cities by highways so that you could get there, the Nixon legacy would have linked them by cable communications so you wouldn't have to go there." One can almost see the dreamy eyes of Nixon and Haldeman as they sat around discussing a plan that would eliminate the need for newspapers, seemingly oblivious to its Big Brother aspects. Fortunately the Watergate scandal intervened, and Nixon was forced to resign before "the Wired Nation" could be hooked up.

—D.W.

HENNY YOUNGMAN'S
10 FAVORITE ONE-LINERS

The acknowledged king of the one-line joke quips that his career as a comedian was precipitated by the response he got when he played the violin. He debuted on the Kate Smith radio show in the 1930s, later hit the nightclub circuit, and has also appeared on TV and in such films as *A Wave, a Wac, and a Marine* and *Won Ton Ton, the Dog Who Saved Hollywood*.

1. Take my wife—please.
2. My grandson, 22 years old, keeps complaining about headaches. I've told him 1,000 times, "Larry, when you get out of bed, it's feet first."
3. My grandson was so ugly when he was born, the doctor slapped his mother.
4. I once wanted to become an atheist, but I gave up—they have no holidays.
5. A doctor gave a man six months to live . . . he couldn't pay his bill . . . so the doctor gave him another six months.
6. My wife Sadie just had plastic surgery—I cut up her credit cards.
7. I made a killing in the market—I shot my broker.
8. When I go to Israel in Milton Berle's honor, I will have a tree uprooted.
9. My wife is a light eater . . . as soon as it's light, she starts to eat.
10. I said to my wife, "Where do you want to go for your anniversary?" She said, "I want to go to somewhere I've never been before." I said, "Try the kitchen."

—Exclusive for *The Book of Lists* 2

7 OF THE GREATEST
CRACKS OF ALL TIME

1. THE CRACK IN THE LIBERTY BELL

John Marshall was born in Virginia in 1755. Just two years earlier, in June, 1753, a bell was hung in Philadelphia, Pa. It weighed over a ton and had a circumference of 12 ft. at its lip. This bell became the Liberty Bell, and according to popular legend it rang out to celebrate the first public reading of the American Declaration of Independence on July 8, 1776. Marshall was appointed chief justice of the U.S. in 1801. But time eventually caught up with both jurist and chime. A vertical crack appeared in the bell as it dolefully tolled to mourn the death of Justice Marshall in 1835.

2. THE CRACK IN GARRETT'S BARN

It was 2:00 A.M., April 26, 1865, on a farm near Port Royal, Va. A Union Army patrol had trapped a fugitive in a barn on the Richard Garrett property. When the man refused to come out, the barn was set ablaze. Before he could escape the growing flames, the fugitive was shot through a crack in the barn wall by an anxious soldier named Boston Corbett. John Wilkes Booth was then dragged from the burning barn and died soon afterward from a wound in the back of his neck.

3. THE CRACK IN THE SOUTH FORK DAM

In late spring of 1889, heavy rains fell on western Pennsylvania. The deluge swelled the Conemaugh River reservoir, which was formed by the South Fork Dam. Below the dam, in a narrow valley 55 mi. southeast of Pittsburgh, 2,209 inhabitants of a small town were spending the last hours of their lives. On May 31, the dam cracked and then crumbled from the unusual water pressure. Johnstown was inundated to a depth of 30 ft. by 78 million tons of raging water.

4. THE CRACK THAT BISECTS CALIFORNIA

Actually a fracture in the earth's crust, the San Andreas fault extends more than 600 mi. from the northwestern corner of California to the Gulf of California. A sudden movement along 270 mi. of the fault line caused the San Francisco earthquake of April 18, 1906. The horizontal "throw" of the fault ran as high as 21 ft., and the city was devastated by fires that could not be put out, since the water mains had been ruptured.

5. THE CRACK IN ORVILLE WRIGHT'S PROPELLER

While his older brother, Wilbur, was flying his airplane at exhibitions in Europe, Orville Wright was making test flights for the U.S. Army at Fort Myer in Virginia. On September 17, 1908, Orville took off with Lt. Thomas Selfridge as a passenger. One of the plane's two propellers developed a hairline crack, and the craft plunged to earth from an altitude of 75 ft. Orville survived with leg, hip, and rib fractures, but a fractured skull caused Lieutenant Selfridge to become the first human to die in an airplane crash.

6. THE CRACK THAT SANK THE U.S.S. *THRESHER*

On April 10, 1963, the U.S.S. *Thresher,* a nuclear-powered submarine, vanished in 8,400 ft. of water off Cape Cod, Mass. In August of that year, the U.S. Navy's bathyscaphe *Trieste* recovered a piece of copper pipe marked with the *Thresher's* hull number. A naval inquiry concluded that the submarine's saltwater piping had failed. A civilian oceanographer suggested that abnormal currents caused by a storm could have forced the *Thresher* to depths that its hull could not withstand. In either case, piping or hull, a crack initiated the disaster.

7. THE CRACK THAT ALMOST KILLED AN ADMIRAL

Adm. Richard E. Byrd of the U.S. Navy ultimately headed several expeditions to Antarctica without the loss of a man. During his second expedition, commencing on March 28, 1934, Admiral Byrd remained alone at Bolling Advance Weather Base in Antarctica for over four months. The explorer's safety record was almost spoiled when he fell through a roof of snow that covered a long crack in the ice. Fortunately, the admiral fell across the crevasse, which was only 3 ft. wide, and thus was able to save himself. Peering into the frozen chasm afterward, he saw that the emerald-green walls of the fissure widened out and extended to a depth of several hundred feet.

—D.M.F.

17 WONDERFUL BONERS

1. THE TILTED TOWER

When architect Bonanno of Pisa began building the Tower of Pisa in 1174, he made the mistake of using a mere 10-ft. foundation. In the midst of his work, the ground shifted and the tower heeled over, causing the project to be abandoned. It was finally completed in 1350, with three of its eight stories built on a true vertical in an attempt to alter the tower's center of gravity. The effort was unsuccessful, however, and today this boner of a building leans approximately 17 ft. from perpendicular and continues to tilt an additional ¼ in. each year.

2. THE $18.5 MILLION HYPHEN

On July 22, 1962, Mariner I, an American rocket bound for Venus, had to be blasted apart when it began veering off course. A subsequent investigation revealed that the erratic behavior had been caused by the omission of a hyphen from the flight's computer program. The lack of this single piece of punctuation cost U.S. taxpayers $18.5 million.

3. JOSEPH'S COAT WITH SLEEVES

According to the editors of the Cambridge Bible, Joseph's coat of many colors never existed. When the Bible was being translated into English, the scholars made a mistake with the Hebrew phrase, which actually read, "a long garment with sleeves."

4. THE CLOCK THAT STRUCK TOO SOON

In William Shakespeare's *Julius Caesar*, Act II, scene 2, line 114, Caesar asks Brutus, "What is 't o'clock?" Brutus replies, "Caesar, 'tis strucken eight." The Bard had forgotten that striking clocks were not invented until 14 centuries after Caesar's death.

5. LINCOLN'S CONFUSED CORRESPONDENCE

In Abraham Lincoln's famous consolatory letter to Mrs. Lydia Bixby, he wrote, "You are the mother of five sons who have died gloriously on the field of battle." Lincoln was wrong. Sgt. Charles Bixby was killed at the Battle of Fredericksburg in 1863, and Pvt. Oliver Bixby was killed near Petersburg, Va., in 1864. But Corp. Henry Bixby, captured at Gettysburg, was later swapped in an exchange of prisoners; Pvt. George Bixby deserted to join the Confederates; and Pvt. Edward Bixby deserted and fled to Cuba. It should also be noted that Mrs. Bixby was an active pacifist and had attempted to prevent all of her sons from enlisting.

6. *THE NEW YORK TIMES* APOLOGIZES

In 1920 *The New York Times* publicly scoffed at Prof. Robert Goddard, the father of space exploration, for his outrageous claim that rockets could function in a vacuum. "He seems only to lack the knowledge ladled out daily in high schools," the paper stated in the January 13 issue. However, in July, 1969, when Apollo 11 proved all Goddard's assumptions correct, the *Times* published the following statement: "It is now definitely established that a rocket can function in a vacuum. The *Times* regrets [its] error."

7. THE DAM THAT DIDN'T

The Turkish government built a massive reservoir near Konya, with the water held back by the mighty May Dam. Unfortunately, the engineers ignored the topography. Because the reservoir is situated on alluvium overlying karstic limestone, over 30 natural·sinkholes have formed, and all the water that flows into the reservoir drains away underground. The dam is useless.

8. THE LEFT-HANDED PICADOR

Picasso's first copper engraving, made when he was 18, depicted a picador in action. However, Picasso forgot that the actual image would be reversed in the print, and he was taken aback when he saw that the picador held the lance in his left hand. Distressed and disappointed by his blunder, he was about to destroy the plate when an idea occurred to him. He called the engraving *El Zurdo* ("The Left-Hander").

9. THE UNSAFE COMMISSION

As part of their "Think Toy Safety" promotional campaign of the 1970s, the U.S. Consumer Product Safety Commission ordered 80,000 buttons. Unfortunately, the buttons themselves were lethal. Their edges were sharp, their fasteners unsnapped easily, and—worst of all—they were coated with lead paint.

10. CHRISTIAN CHARITY

In 1948, during the Middle East war, U.S. ambassador to the U.N. Warren Austin called upon the Arabs and Jews to settle their differences "like good Christians."

11. DAMN YANKEES

While leading U.S. troops in the Spanish-American War, Gen. Joe Wheeler, a Confederate veteran, became so excited during the storming of Las Guasimas that he roared to his men, "Come on, boys! We've got the damn Yankees on the run!"

12. WATERTIGHT SMITH

During the U.S. Senate inquiries into the sinking of the *Titanic*, the chairman of the committee, Sen. William A. Smith of Michigan, posed the following question: "Why didn't the passengers on the boat go into the watertight compartments and save themselves from drowning?" In the 1912 disaster, the watertight compartments went to the bottom of the Atlantic along with the rest of the ship. Thereafter, the senator, who had shown a singular lack of maritime knowledge during the proceedings, became known popularly as "Watertight Smith."

13. JIM MARSHALL'S REVERSE

One of pro football's most memorable boners occurred on October 28, 1964, when defensive end Jim Marshall of the Minnesota Vikings carried the ball 60 yd. in the wrong direction into the end zone, scoring a safety for the San Francisco 49ers. Nevertheless, Minnesota won 27–22.

14. A CONFUSION OF CONQUISTADORES

In his famous poem "On First Looking into Chapman's Homer," John Keats revealed a lapse in his knowledge of history when he wrote:

> Then felt I like some watcher of the skies
> When a new planet swims into his ken;
> Or like stout Cortez when with eagle eyes
> He star'd at the Pacific . . .

Cortes may have had eagle eyes, but it was Balboa who discovered the Pacific Ocean.

15. THE MOVABLE CHAIR

Although the popular U.S. author Fanny Heaslip Lea maintained that her fiction aspired "to the light touch," the following passage from her novel *Wild Goose Chase* (1929) is definitely heavy-handed: "A deep armchair stood before the fireplace. She took it up between thumb and forefinger, handling it delicately, set it down on the other side, and considered it profoundly."

16. THE WRONG TARGET

On August 7, 1979, a jet in the Spanish Air Force shot itself down when its gunfire ricocheted off a hillside practice target. The pilot ejected to safety.

17. THE EXPLOSIVE RECIPE

A major catastrophe in cookbook history occurred in 1978, when Random House was forced to recall 10,000 copies of *Woman's Day Crockery Cuisine* by Sylvia Vaughn Thompson. In a recipe for silky caramel slices, the crucial ingredient of water had been omitted. The publishing house warned readers: "If the recipe is followed, the condensed milk can could explode and shatter the lid and liner of the crockery cooker."

More readers asked us to include this boner than any other single one. In the opening lines of "The Gift of the Magi," O. Henry wrote: "One dollar and eighty-seven cents. That was all. And 60¢ of it was in pennies." O. Henry never explained how the remaining $1.27 was made up.

Dear readers, in defense of O. Henry, a onetime bank teller and embezzler who knew a good deal about money, there would have been no difficulty in getting together the $1.27 without pennies in 1906, the time the story was written. At that time there were still in circulation 2¢ pieces, which were minted as late as 1872, and 3¢ pieces, which were minted as late as 1889. O. Henry's character would have needed one 2¢ piece or four 3¢ pieces.

—J.BE., W.K., I.W., & F.B.F.

18 MORE UNNATURAL LAWS

Back by popular demand—some more of those nonlegal laws that govern our lives. These are from the book *Murphy's Law, Book Two: More Reasons Why Things Go Wrong* by Arthur Bloch.

1. O'REILLY'S LAW OF THE KITCHEN

Cleanliness is next to impossible.

2. LIEBERMAN'S LAW

Everybody lies; but it doesn't matter, since nobody listens.

3. DENNISTON'S LAW

Virtue is its own punishment.

4. GOLD'S LAW

If the shoe fits, it's ugly.

5. HANDY GUIDE TO MODERN SCIENCE

If it's green or it wriggles, it's biology.
If it stinks, it's chemistry.
If it doesn't work, it's physics.

6. CONWAY'S LAW

In any organization there will always be one person who knows what is going on.
This person must be fired.

7. GREEN'S LAW OF DEBATE

Anything is possible if you don't know what you're talking about.

8. STEWART'S LAW OF RETROACTION

It is easier to get forgiveness than permission.

9. FIRST RULE OF HISTORY

History doesn't repeat itself—historians merely repeat each other.

10. FINSTER'S LAW

A closed mouth gathers no feet.

11. OLIVER'S LAW OF LOCATION

No matter where you go, there you are.

12. LYNCH'S LAW

When the going gets tough, everyone leaves.

13. GLYME'S FORMULA FOR SUCCESS

The secret of success is sincerity. Once you can fake that, you've got it made.

14. MASON'S FIRST LAW OF SYNERGISM

The one day you'd sell your soul for something, souls are a glut.

15. THE SAUSAGE PRINCIPLE

People who love sausage and respect the law should never watch either one being made.

16. HARRISON'S POSTULATE

For every action, there is an equal and opposite criticism.

17. HANLON'S RAZOR

Never attribute to malice that which is adequately explained by stupidity.

18. MUIR'S LAW

When we try to pick out anything by itself, we find it hitched to everything else in the universe.

17 CHILDREN WHO
MAY HAVE LIVED WITH
WILD ANIMALS

1–2. ROMULUS AND REMUS (8th century B.C.)

Twin brothers Romulus and Remus were allegedly raised by a wolf after being abandoned in the countryside by their uncle. A number of years later they were rescued by a shepherd, and they went on to found the city of Rome in 753 B.C. Scholars long considered their childhood adventures to be mythical, but recent studies of children known to have lived with animals have demonstrated that there could well be an element of truth to the Romulus and Remus legend.

3. HESSIAN WOLF-BOY (1344)

In 1344, hunters in the German kingdom of Hesse captured a boy between 7 and 12 years of age who had been living in the wild. Wolves had brought him food and dug holes to shelter him at night. The boy ran on all fours and had an extraordinary ability to leap long distances. Treated as a freak by his human captors, he died shortly after his return to civilization because of an enforced diet of cooked food.

4. LITHUANIAN BEAR-BOY (1661)

In 1661, in a Lithuanian forest, a party of hunters discovered a boy living with a group of bears. The hunters captured him even though he resisted by biting and clawing them. Taken to Warsaw, Poland, and christened Joseph, the boy continued to eat raw meat and graze on grass. Although he never dropped the habit of growling like a bear, Joseph acquired a limited vocabulary and became the servant of a Polish nobleman.

5. IRISH SHEEP-BOY (1672)

In 1672 a 16-year-old boy was found trapped in a hunter's net in the hills of southern Ireland. Since running away from his parents' home as a young child, the boy had lived with a herd of wild sheep. He was healthy and muscular even though he ate only grass and hay. After his capture he was taken to the Netherlands, where he was cared for in Amsterdam by Dr. Nicholas Tulp. The boy never learned human speech but continued to bleat like a sheep throughout his life.

6. FRAUMARK BEAR-GIRL (1767)

In 1767 two hunters captured a girl who attacked them after they shot her bear companion in the mountains near the village of Fraumark, Hungary. The tall, muscular 18-year-old girl had lived with bears since infancy. Later she was locked up in an insane asylum in the town of Karpfen because she refused to wear clothes or eat anything but raw meat and tree bark.

7. WILD BOY OF AVEYRON (1800)

In 1800 hunters captured a 17-year-old boy who had lived alone in the forests of Aveyron, France, since he was an infant. Given the name Victor, the boy was not happy living in civilized society and repeatedly tried to escape. He also growled and gnashed his teeth at first, but later became adjusted to being with humans. When he died at the age of 40, he had learned only three words.

8. DINA SANICHAR (1867)

In 1867 a hunting party found a boy about seven years old living with wolves in a cave near Mynepuri, India. Taken to the Sekandra Orphanage in Agra and given the name Dina Sanichar, the boy refused to wear clothes and sharpened his teeth by gnawing on bones. For 28 years he lived at the orphanage, but he never learned to talk. In 1895 he died of tuberculosis, aggravated by the one human habit he had adopted—smoking tobacco.

9. WILLIAM MILDIN (1883)

An intriguing but not yet fully substantiated case is that of Englishman William Mildin, the 14th Earl of Streatham. (One authority believes the name of this child was actually William Russell.) Shipwrecked on the West African coast at the age of 11 in 1868, Mildin lived with the apes for 15 years before being discovered and returned to England. Mildin may have inspired Edgar Rice Burroughs to create his most famous character—Tarzan of the Apes.

10–11. AMALA AND KAMALA (1920)

In October, 1920, the Reverend J. A. L. Singh captured two girls, one around three years old and the other around five, who had lived with a pack of wolves near the village of Midnapore, India. Named Amala and Kamala by Singh, the girls were mute except for occasional growling sounds, walked on all fours, and loved to eat raw meat. After a year in civilization, Amala died. Kamala eventually acquired a 45-word vocabulary before her death in 1929.

Wolf children Kamala and Amala, Dec. 18, 1920, in Midnapore, India.

12. TARZANCITO (1933)

In December, 1933, a woodcutter captured a boy about five years of age in the jungles of Ahuachapán Province in El Salvador. The boy, nicknamed Tarzancito, had lived alone since infancy, subsisting on a diet of wild fruit and raw fish. Newspaper correspondent Ernie Pyle, who met Tarzancito, reported that when the boy first returned to human society, he communicated by howling and frequently attacked and bit people. Eventually Tarzancito learned to talk and adjusted to human life.

13. CACHARI LEOPARD-BOY (1938)

In 1938 an English sportsman found an eight-year-old boy living with a leopard and her cubs in the North Cachar Hills of India. The boy, who had been carried off by the leopard five years earlier, was returned to his family of peasant farmers. Although nearly blind, he could identify different individuals and objects by his extremely well-developed sense of smell.

14. SYRIAN GAZELLE-BOY (1946)

In 1946 Iraqi soldiers in a jeep chased and captured a 12-year-old boy who had been living with a herd of gazelles in the Syrian desert. Running in leaps and bounds like a gazelle, the boy could outrun all other humans. Because of human mistreatment and lack of understanding, the boy escaped frequently, until he was finally crippled by his captors, who severed his Achilles tendons.

15. SAHARAN GAZELLE-BOY (1960)

In September, 1960, Basque poet Jean Claude Armen discovered and observed a boy who was approximately eight years old living with a herd of gazelles in the desert regions of the Western Sahara. For two months Armen studied the boy, who he speculated was the orphaned child of some nomadic Saharan Moorish family. The boy traveled on all fours, grazed on grass and dug roots, and seemed to be thoroughly accepted by the gazelles as a member of the herd. Since the boy appeared happy, Armen left him with his gazelle family.

16. BURUNDI MONKEY-BOY (1974)

In the spring of 1976, a story appeared in the Johannesburg *Times* about an unusual discovery. In 1974 soldiers in Burundi had reported that they had captured a boy who was traveling with a troop of monkeys. Doctors believed he had been orphaned in the 1972 civil war and subsequently adopted by the monkeys. Despite efforts to civilize him, the boy persisted in his monkeylike behavior, communicating by chattering and grunting, and eating only fruits and vegetables. The story was passed along by behavioral psychologist B. F. Skinner to his protégé Dr. Harlan Lane. With fellow psychologist Dr. Richard Pillard, Lane traveled to Burundi to study the boy. An arduous tracing of his past revealed a history of institutionalization with only a few months unaccounted for. They concluded from this evidence and their own study that the boy's bizarre behavior was due to some type of autism rather than his having lived with monkeys.

17. PASCAL (1974)

This boy was taken to the Catholic mission at Sultanpur, a town in Punjab, India, by a man who allegedly had found him living in a forest with wolves. The boy, an estimated three or four years old at the time, was covered with matted hair and had calluses on his elbows, palms, and knees. According to Father Joseph de Souza, Pascal learned to stand upright in five months, and within two years he was doing chores around the mission. He communicated with sign language. Father Joseph also noted that the boy no longer caught and ate live chickens, but that he was still drawn by the scent of blood. That Pascal actually lived with wolves has not been authenticated.

—R.J.F.

8 PERSONAL EVERYDAY LISTS FROM OUR READERS:

10 BEST REASONS WHY I DON'T HAVE MY HOMEWORK

These reasons have been collected by William R. Jackson of West New York, N.J., who has been teaching for over nine years.

1. My little sister ate it.
2. My dog [or cat] did his duty on it.
3. We ran out of toilet paper.
4. Our furnace broke down and we had to burn my homework to keep from freezing to death.
5. I had to use it to fill a hole in my shoe.
6. I gave it to a friend and his house burnt down.
7. My mother threw it away by mistake.
8. I got hungry and there was no food to eat.
9. I did it, I swear, but I left it next to my poor sick mother who I was helping and caring for all night.
10. Because I didn't feel like it! (Very often the last words ever spoken by a student.)

33 EXCUSES FOR BREAKING THE SPEED LIMIT

Roger W. Betsill, Jr., a Georgia State Trooper for the past nine years, has accumulated the following excuses people gave when caught speeding.

1. I just didn't realize it.
2. I was traveling with the flow of traffic.
3. I was only passing someone.
4. My speedometer must be wrong [or broken].
5. But I had my cruise control set at such and such.
6. Your radar must be wrong.
7. Running late for something.
8. I'm on vacation.
9. I was trying to get to a rest room.
10. Someone else's car.
11. I wasn't paying attention to my driving.
12. Someone sick in vehicle.
13. I didn't know what the speed limit was.
14. I was going downhill.
15. I'm almost out of gas.
16. My accelerator stuck.
17. Someone is dying or just died.
18. I have a fast car and this is a good road.
19. I was just trying to get home.
20. Driver mad at someone.
21. Wife having baby.
22. I was just trying to do someone a favor.
23. I was trying to get away from someone.
24. The kids [or spouse] were fussing.
25. I was trying my car out.
26. I didn't know you were around.
27. I've always driven like this.
28. I was trying to catch someone.
29. I'm just tired and hunting a place to rest.
30. I did not have my CB on [or it was broken].
31. My fuzz buster wasn't on [or it was broken].
32. I just didn't think I'd ever get stopped.
33. I'm allowed to do that where I come from.

DAVID STOVALL'S 10 MOST COMMON QUESTIONS ASKED BY SERVICE STATION CUSTOMERS

David Stovall is a gas station attendant in Fort Worth, Tex.

1. Can I have change for a dollar?
2. Where is the rest room?
3. Is the rest room locked?
4. How do you work this damn pump?
5. Where's the phone?
6. Will you check my oil?
7. Will you check my tires?
8. Are there any motels around here?
9. Wanna buy a watch?
10. Where am I?

13 MOST CLEVER PHONY NAMES GIVEN TO A SUBSTITUTE TEACHER

Students of Chicago public schools gave these names instead of their own when reporting to Irene Kozlowski, a substitute teacher.

1. Anne Chovy
2. Art E. Choke
3. Bud Wiser
4. Frank Furter
5. Chuck Waggon
6. Jim Shoo
7. Sandy Beech
8. Polly Gon
9. Ben Gay
10. Liz Onya
11. Ben Dover
12. Eileen Dover
13. Barb DeWyre

MICHAEL VOGEL'S 10 GREATEST PEOPLE WITH LAST NAMES FROM *T* TO *Z*

Michael Vogel of New York City dedicates this list "to people who go last because of a name."

1. George Washington, U.S. president
2. Jim Thorpe, U.S. athlete
3. Harry Truman, U.S. president
4. Dick Young, U.S. journalist
5. Vincent van Gogh, Dutch painter
6. Barbara Tuchman, U.S. writer
7. H. G. Wells, British writer
8. Zeus, Greek god
9. J. R. R. Tolkien, British writer
10. Leo Tolstoi, Russian writer

11-YEAR-OLD
BRADLEY GOLDSTEIN'S
5 FAVORITE AGES
HE'S ALREADY BEEN

Mr. Goldstein attends school in Denver, Colo.

1. Seven
2. Three
3. Two
4. One
5. Five

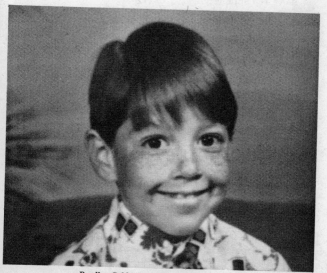

Bradley Goldstein at his favorite age.

497

11-YEAR-OLD BRADLEY GOLDSTEIN'S
5 AGES HE'D MOST LIKE TO BE

1. 21
2. 99
3. 100
4. 117
5. 35

MRS. E. L. STAGER'S
TYPICAL SHOPPING LIST

Mrs. Stager is a housewife in Dayton, O.

1. Apples
2. Chicken legs
3. Milk
4. Ice cream
5. Steaks
6. Stove Top Stuffing
7. Tide
8. Ketchup
9. Aspirin
10. Bread
11. Pastrami
12. Toilet paper (2 packs)
13. Lettuce
14. Pop
15. Twinkies
16. Eggplant
17. Coffee (if enough money is left)
18. Card for Aunt Vera's birthday

Don't forget pop bottles!!!
Remember *coupons!*

THE AUTHORS' 7 THOUGHTS
FOR YOU, THE READER

1. Thank you for having read this far. We hope you will write to us, if you are so moved.
2. Please tell us what you enjoyed most, and least, about this book, and why.
3. If you come across any errors or omissions—or have any suggestions or requests for the next edition—let us know.
4. Send us any clippings or items that you feel we might enjoy or that would help us prepare *The Book of Lists 3*. Please include the sources for any facts or lists you send in, and accompany these with a self-addressed stamped envelope if you want a response.

5. If you send in a *completed* list and we find it acceptable for publication, we will compensate you and give you credit.
6. If you just feel like sounding off about something, feel free to rant and rave in our direction. We read every letter that reaches us.
7. Here is how to get in touch with us. Write to:

The Book of Lists 2
P.O. Box 49699
Los Angeles, Calif. 90049

—D.W., I.W., A.W., & S.W.

INDEX

Douglas, Kirk, 184, 210, 425
Doyle, Arthur Conan, 11, 226, 353, 468
Doyle, John Joseph, 331
Dracula, 21
Drake, Francis, 474
Dreiser, Theodore, 212, 368
Dreser, Heinrich, 392
Dressler, Marie, 187
Dreyfus, Alfred, 60
Drivers, most and least dangerous, 125
Drouet, Minou, 224
Drugs and plants, psychoactive, 390–93
Dubček, Alexander, 55
DuBois, W. E. B., 10
Duck, labrador, 117–18
Dufy, Raoul, 220
Dulles, Allen W., 223
Dumas, Alexandre, fils, 27, 256
Dumas, Alexandre, père, 26–27, 256
Duncan, Isadora, 303
Dunleavy, Yvonne, 229
Dunlop, Helen, 443
Duplessis, Marie, 303
Duran, Roberto, 338
Durant, Will, 20
Duryea (car), 121
Dwarf lemur, 120

E

Earhart, Amelia, 408
Eason, Mal, 334
East Africa, 84
East Orange, N.J., 34
Eastman, George, 288
Eban, Abba, 407
Ebb, Fred, 169
Ebbin, Erskine Lawrence, 426
Ebbin, Neville, 426
Eckert, J. Presper, 246
Eclipses that affected human lives, 96–100
Economic Development Administration (EDA), 286
Economic research service, 41
Ederle, Gertrude, 473
Edes, Benjamin, 393

Edes, Peter, 393–94
Edison, Thomas A., 7, 11, 239, 270, 401, 468
Edward III (king of England), 298
Edward VII (king of Great Britain and Ireland), 303, 422
Edward VIII (king of Great Britain and Ireland), 254
Egypt, 65, 84
Ehrlich, Paul, 270
Eichmann, Adolf, 289
Einstein, Albert, 237, 270, 399
Eisenhower, Dwight David, 21, 116, 343–44, 370
Eleanor of Aquitaine, 403
Elegants, 166
Eliot, George, 212
Eliot, T. S., 10
Elizabeth I (queen of England), 402, 403, 421
Elizabeth II (queen of England), 262
Ellenborough, Jane, 438
Ellenborough, Lord, 438
Ellicott, Andrew, 377
Emerson, Ralph W., 28, 468
Empire State Building, 80
Energy
    places consuming least, 243–44
    places consuming most, 243
English language, most beautiful words in, 145
Ephron, Nora, 236
Epstein, Jacob, 321
Erhard, Werner, 290
Ericson, Leif, 138
Ericson, Thorvald, 138
Erving, Julius, 337
Espy, William R., 145
Essex Coach (car), 122
Ethelred the Unready (king of England), 25
Euclid, 237
Eugene, Ore., 30
Events wished to have been seen, 407–16
Evers, Medgar, 280
Ewell, Barney, 354
Exotic properties for sale, 132–35

F

Fabius, 456
Faisal, (king of Saudi Arabia), 317
Faisal ibn Mussad Abdel Azig (prince), 317
Fallopius, Gabriel, 18, 372
Family, 249–75
Faraday, Michael, 237, 239
Farrar, Frederic W., 219
Farson, James Negley, 274
Faulkner, William, 228, 230
Fawcett, Farrah, 188
Feather, Leonard, 170
Federal Aviation Administration, 283–84
Federal Deposit Insurance Corporation, 285
Federal income taxes, major corporations that paid no, 282–83
Federal moviemaking, 40
Federal revenue sharing, 39–40
Feller, Bob, 335
Felton, Bruce, 423
Ferdinand I, the Inconstant (king of Portugal), 26
Ferrari, Severino, 454
Fetchit, Stepin, 298
Fields, Jackie, 342
Fields, W. C., 10, 184, 191, 396
Figlock, Joseph, 426
Film scenes cut, 195–97
Films, box-office champion, 199
Finch, Peter, 316
Finland, 66
Finley, Jean, 266
Finnis, John, 68–69
Fiquet, Hortense, 256
Firestone, Harvey, 29
Firth of Forth Bridge, 79
Fischer, Bobby, 342
Fisher, Eddie, 298
Fitzgerald, F. Scott, 228, 230, 443
Fitzgerald, William, 141
Fitzherbert, Mrs., 446
Fitzsimmons, Bob, 341
Fleming, Ian, 421
Fletcher, John, 406
Florida, 82

Flycatcher, Euler's, 119
Flynn, Errol, 189
Folger, Abigail, 426
Fonda, Jane, 184, 186, 198
Food additives, maybe harmful, 381–83
Food and Drug Administration (FDA), 241
Foods
    best-liked in armed forces, 387
    junk. See Junk foods, America's top
    least-liked in armed forces, 387–88
Football
    best kickers, 347
    players famous in other fields, 343–45
Forbes, Charles, 394
Force, Davy, 334
Ford, Gerald R., 241, 344, 401
Ford, Henry, 87–88, 270–71, 468, 473
Ford, Henry II, 121
Ford, John, 194
Ford Model T, 122
Ford Mustang, 122
Foreman, George, 337
Formosus (pope), 57
Forster, E. M., 10
Fort Worth, Tex., 34
Foster, Willie, 335
Fracastoro, Girolamo, 93
France, 65
Francis of Assisi, St., 6
Frank, Anne, 1
Frank, Hans, 289
Frank, Leo, 60
Franklin, Benjamin, 256, 400, 401, 415, 442, 468
Franks, Robert, 423
Franz, Shepherd, 378
Frazier, Joe, 341
Frazier, Walt, 336
Frederick I (Roman emperor), 456
Frémont, John C., 67
Freud, Sigmund, 365–66, 398, 402
Freydier, 312
Frick, Wilhelm, 289

Q

Queen, Ellery, 226
Quesada, Francisco de, 93
Quesada, Hernán Pérez de, 93
Questions, gas station customers asked, 495

R

Rabelais, François, 86
Racehorses, best, 350
Rachen, Kurt von, 291
Racine, Jean, 212
Radio stations, most listened to, 208
Radioactive waste burial sites, 244–45
Raft, George, 186
Rainer, Luise, 186
Ramachandran, M. G., 317
Rankin, Jeannette, 473
Raskin, Richard. *See* Richards, Renée
Raskob, John J., 470
Rasputin, Grigori, 324–25, 398, 437
Raubal, Angela M., 453
Rauff, Walter, 58
Ray, James Earl, 55
Razsnyoi, Sandor, 354
Read, Deborah, 256
Readers, lists from, 294–99
Reagan, Ronald, 402
Real, Joao vaz Corte, 140
Reasoner, Harry, 218
Recording artists who faded, 165–66
Redford, Robert, 186
Redgrave, Lynn, 262
Redgrave, Vanessa, 186
Redwitz, Oskar von, 368
Reincarnation, people who believed in, 468
Reinking, Theodor, 147
Reiss, Ernest, 474
Religious figures involved in sex scandals, 306–10
Remington, Frederic, 345
Renan, Joseph E., 19
Renault, Louis, 452

Reno, Marcus, 395
Renoir, Jean, 194
Republic (ocean liner), 82
Reshevsky, Samuel, 343
Rest in peace, 438–68
Rettig, Tommy, 88
Revel, Paolo Ignazio di, 356
Revere, Paul, 287, 442
Revolts crushed or betrayed by communists, 73–75
Reynolds, Allie, 335
Reynolds, Debbie, 6
Reynolds, Mary, 377
Reynolds, R. J., 10
Reynolds, Robert R. v. Cameron Morrison, 35
Ribbentrop, Joachim von, 289
Rice, John C., 315
Rich, Charlie, 445
Richard, Maurice "Rocket", 348
Richards, Gordon, 350
Richards, Grant, 209
Richards, Renée, 329–30
Richardson, J. P., 425
Richelieu, Duc du (cardinal), 115, 433–34
Richmann, Georg Wilhelm, 94
Rickenbacker, Edward V., 440
Ridgely, Robert S., 117
Riegger, Wallingford, 175
Rifkin, Mark, 248
Rinaldi, Gina, 379–80
Rio, Dolores Del, 188
Rivera, Diego, 183
Roanoke, Va., 34
Robbins, W. C., 353
Roberts, Frederick S., 116
Robertson, Alice M., 473
Robertson, Oscar, 336, 337
Robeson, Paul, 345
Robespierre, Maxmilien, 56, 364–65, 457
Robinson, Edwin A., 29
Robinson, Jackie, 474
Robinson, Sugar Ray, 342
Rock albums, greatest, 164–65
Rockefeller, John D., 473
Rockefeller, Margaretta F. "Happy", 261
Rockefeller, Mark F., 261
Rockefeller, Nelson A., 453
Rodgers, Guy, 336

522

524

Z

PHOTO CREDITS

ABOUT THE AUTHORS

IRVING WALLACE is one of the most widely read novelists in the world, with estimated worldwide sales of his twenty-two books, in all editions, at 130 million copies. His first great international success was with *The Chapman Report*, followed by *The Prize*, *The Man*, *The Seven Minutes*, *The Word*, *The Fan Club*, *The People's Almanac* (with his son, David), *The R Document*, and *The Pigeon Project*—all major bestsellers.

DAVID WALLECHINSKY, creator of *The People's Almanac*, coauthored it, as well as *The People's Almanac 2*, with his father, Irving Wallace. They are currently at work on *The Book of Predictions* and *The People's Almanac 3*. David is also coauthor of *Chico's Organic Gardening and Natural Living*, *Laughing Gas*, and *What Really Happened to the Class of '65?* He lives with Flora Chavez in Santa Monica, Calif.

AMY WALLACE, Irving Wallace's daughter, is a graduate of the Berkeley (Calif.) Psychic Institute, and has developed such psychic skills as clairvoyant reading and psychic healing. Besides coauthoring *The Book of Lists* and *The Psychic Healing Book*, she has written with her father, *The Two*, a biography of the original Siamese twins.

SYLVIA WALLACE, a former magazine writer and editor, is married to Irving Wallace. Her first novel, *The Fountains*, was an American bestseller and published in twelve foreign editions. Her second novel, *Empress*, will be published in 1980. In her first collaboration with her family, she helped produce *The Book of Lists #2*. She and her husband live in West Los Angeles, Calif.

Franz Liszt.